张彭春（1892—1957）系中国驻联大代表（1946—1947）、联合国经社理事会代表（1946—1952）、联合国人权委员会委员、副主席（1947—1948）、《世界人权宣言》起草委员会副主席（1947—1948）

张彭春 1948 年 4 月 22 日（56 岁生日）在日内瓦。

公能教育文库

张元龙/总主编　张鉴瀛/总策划

世界合作共赢的中国贡献

张彭春在联合国经济及社会理事会的发言

孙平华 编著

天津社会科学院出版社

图书在版编目（CIP）数据

世界合作共赢的中国贡献 ：张彭春在联合国经济及社会理事会的发言 ：汉文、英文、法文 / 孙平华编著. -- 天津 ：天津社会科学院出版社，2023.1
（公能教育文库 / 张元龙总主编）
ISBN 978-7-5563-0817-0

Ⅰ. ①世… Ⅱ. ①孙… Ⅲ. ①国际合作－经济合作－经济发展－贡献－中国－汉、英、法 Ⅳ. ①F125.4

中国版本图书馆 CIP 数据核字(2022)第 058728 号

世界合作共赢的中国贡献 ：张彭春在联合国经济及社会理事会的发言
SHIJIE HEZUO GONGYING DE ZHONGGUO GONGXIAN ：
ZHANG PENGCHUN ZAI LIANHEGUO JINGJI JI SHEHUI LISHIHUI DE FAYAN
责任编辑：韩　鹏
特约编辑：张雅雯
责任校对：王　丽
装帧设计：高馨月
出版发行：天津社会科学院出版社
地　　址：天津市南开区迎水道 7 号
邮　　编：300191
电　　话：（022）23360165
印　　刷：北京盛通印刷股份有限公司
开　　本：787×1092　　1/16
印　　张：49.75
字　　数：716 千字
版　　次：2023 年 1 月第 1 版　　2023 年 1 月第 1 次印刷
定　　价：130.00 元

该书系2020年教育部哲学社会科学研究后期资助重大项目——“国际人权话语中的中国声音研究”（批准号：20JHQ010）的阶段性研究成果，并得到张伯苓研究会的资助

前　言

在近几年的人权研究过程中，本人系统地研究了中国代表张彭春在联合国参与起草《世界人权宣言》的经过及其所做出的杰出贡献。但由于种种原因，对张彭春在联合国经济及社会理事会（the United Nations Economic and Social Council，or the UNECOSOC，简称"经社理事会"，或在不产生歧义的情况下，简称"理事会"）所做的其他工作却涉及甚少。而作为中国常驻联合国经济及社会理事会首席代表的张彭春，他在该理事会的相关工作是他行使的一项最为重要的外交使命。那么，他又是如何在理事会的各届会议中开展工作、有哪些发言或提案等？这引起了我的研究兴趣。

然而，通过查询国内外文献，却没找到与张彭春在联合国经济及社会理事会工作有关的任何研究和论述，这为学界研究留下了一个重要的空白。究其原因，可能是多方面的，对于国际学者来说，他们的研究兴趣当然不在这里，他们也不愿花费大量时间来探讨当年中国在联合国经社理事会的作用和贡献；而对于国内学术界，虽然不乏对张彭春在人权方面、戏剧方面和教育方面所做贡献的研究，但张彭春当年在联合国所做的其他工作，尤其是在经济及社会理事会的工作，却完全是一项研究的空白。这一方面是联合国档案内容繁多，多年来一直尘封在联合国图书馆和档案馆，只是近年来，联合国文献检索系统的建成和完善，那些原始的档案记录才被人们较为便捷地获取。即便是如此，面对浩如烟海的档案资料，研究头绪很难在短时间内理清，没有浓厚的兴趣和持之以恒的研究精神，很容易半途而废。这也许是为什么至今尚未在国内外学术界发现任何相关研究成果的缘故。但是,张彭春在联合国经社理事会各届会议上的发言内容,对于我们全面了解和把握中国在联合国机构早期所做的贡献,又是十分重要而且是必不可少的,其研究意义和价值不容小觑。

2022 年适逢张彭春先生诞辰 130 周年,由于对张彭春在人权领域贡献的研究,本人去年有幸荣获“伯苓研究贡献奖”,而张伯苓研究会希望将借助张彭春先生诞辰 130 周年之际,举办系列纪念活动,包括出版纪念文集等,尤其是特别重视张彭春在联合国的作用和贡献,为此研究会希望我能够为收集和提供有关张彭春在联合国的言论做些系统的整理工作,得知研究会的目标和需要后,我感到这是一项重要的任务,便欣然应允下来。然而,收集和整理张彭春当年在联合国各种会议发言的档案资料毕竟是一项极为艰辛的工作,首先因为这些资料并不是现成的,需要在海量的联合国档案资料中广泛收集、筛选和甄别,颇有一种“大海捞针”和“沙里淘金”的感觉,因为你并不知道“针”和“金”在哪里,要想避免遗漏,那就只能是认认真真地整体过一遍网、过一遍筛,接着还要进行复核、再验证以确保准确无误等。由于种种原因,通过筛选和收集到的各种相关资料也并不是很健全,特别是一些重要资料的缺失、缺损和归档失误等,为收集和整理造成不少麻烦,也为全面系统研究留下不少遗憾。另外,如何呈现出来,在呈现的过程中如何做到全面完整而且避免疏漏和错误都不是轻描淡写的事情。

幸运的是,由于先前多年的研究积累,以及对联合国档案文献的熟悉,加之 2020 年,我本人申报获批了教育部哲学社会科学研究后期资助重大项目——“国际人权话语中的中国声音研究”(批准号:20JHQ010),在研究的过程中,时常感到张彭春当年在联合国经社理事会各届会议上的发言,应该有重要的研究价值。一方面,联合国经社理事会是联合国人权委员会的领导机构,不仅是各国间协商经济及社会问题的重要机制,也是联合国所搭建的重要国际合作平台,而且在人权委员会的成立及机制建设方面发挥着领导作用;另一方面,张彭春作为中国驻联合国经济及社会理事会首席代表,在理事会有着重要的话语权,为理事会各项工作的顺利开展付出了真诚的努力,并被永远载入联合国历史档案。

基于上述认识,系统整理和研究张彭春在联合国层面代表中国所发出的声音,无疑具有重要的历史价值和重大的现实意义。为此,我倍感这项整理工作是一项十分重要的任务,也是作为学者的一种神圣的使命。正是这种使命感让我责无旁贷,也鞭策和支持我经过几个月的艰辛努力,连续日夜奋战,其间由于眼睛过度疲劳导致视网膜充血一周,但即便如此也一天没有放弃整理工作,可以说是一天一小步,步步维艰,但仍然坚持而没有放弃。虽然,由于各种条件的局限,可能仍有一些不如人意之处,但毕竟,《世界合作共赢的中国贡献:张彭春在联合国经济及社会理事会的发言》已具雏形,通过该书以期能够为建立中国国际话语体系做出自己的不懈努力,同时,也希望这是一个抛砖引玉的机会,以激发更多的相关研究。

回顾历史,人类经历了两次苦不堪言的世界大战,劫后余生的人们在第二次世界大战的废墟上成立了联合国,以期后代不再遭受战祸之灾,并促成国际社会共同合作解决经济、社会、文化或人道主义性质的问题。正如第二任联合国秘书长达格·哈马舍尔德所言:“虽然安理会的存在主要是为了解决冲突……但经济及社会理事会的存在主要是为了消除冲突的根源。”①而张彭春在经济及社会理事会第四届第72次会议上发言指出:“我们这个伟大组织摆在安全理事会面前的主要问题是冲突;摆在经济及社会理事会面前的主要问题是混乱。”②

联合国经济及社会理事会是根据《联合国宪章》设立的一个重要联合国机构,它在处理人口、世界贸易、经济、社会福利、文化、自然资源、工业化、人权、教育科技、妇女地位、卫生及其他有关事项中发挥了重要作用。它是协调联合国内部各专门机构的经济和社会工作的机构。该机构下设有职司委员会(包括麻醉药品委员会、人口与发展委员会、科学和技术促进发展委员会、社会发展委员会、统计委员会和妇女地位委员会、预防犯罪和刑事司法委员会、联合国森林论坛委员会)、区域性委员会(非洲经济委

① 见网址:https://www.un.org/ecosoc/zh/events/2021/ecosoc-75-taking-action-more-sustainable-world(访问时间2022年1月28日)。

② UN Document: E/PV.72, p.2.

员会、欧洲经济委员会、拉丁美洲和加勒比经济委员会、亚洲及太平洋经济社会委员会和西亚经济社会委员会)，并同有关经济、社会、文化方面的联合国专门机构建立工作关系，以及与数百个非政府组织，与各国议会联盟、国际红十字会等，建立咨询关系。该机构的业务活动是联合国系统关于可持续发展三大支柱(包括经济、社会和环境)工作的核心内容。联合国网站上对经济及社会理事会的简要介绍如下①：

> 1946 年 1 月 23 日，经济及社会理事会首次会议在英国伦敦圣公会总部大楼召开。……
>
> 经社理事会下设多个附属机构，其中包括联合国各区域委员会、经社理事会各职司委员会以及专家机构和相关机构，共同组成一个复杂的生态系统。经社理事会负责指导和协调这些附属机构的工作。因此，经社理事会影响着联合国在经济和社会领域以及在可持续发展方面的广泛工作。
>
> 联合国各区域委员会是联合国在各区域的区域前哨。这些区域委员会分布在世界五个地区，其主要目标之一是促进区域实施包括可持续发展目标在内的国际商定发展目标。
>
> 职司委员会(由各国政府组成)和专家机构(以个人身份提供咨询)开展经社理事会的技术工作。职司委员会和专家机构在性别平等和增强妇女权能、统计、人口、社会发展、犯罪和麻醉药品、科学技术、最不发达国家境况、公共管理、税务国际合作以及经济、社会和文化权利等领域提供政策指导。土著问题常设论坛和联合国森林论坛也是经社理事会的附属机构。
>
> 经社理事会敞开大门与民间社会接触。今天，超过 5,100 个非政府组织已签署协议，帮助经社理事会完成任务。非政府组织委员会是经社理事会的一个附属机构，负责审查非政府组织提出的申请书，就

① 见网址：https://www.un.org/ecosoc/zh/events/2021/ecosoc-75-taking-action-more-sustainable-world(访问时间 2022 年 1 月 28 日)

是否给予咨商地位提出建议，供经社理事会作出最后决定。

联合国经济及社会理事会是联合国六大支柱机构之一，其作用是十分重要的。正如号称民国第一外交家的顾维钧在联大第8次全会上发表演讲时，对联合国经济及社会理事会的工作所评价的那样："经济及社会理事会同样是一项创新。其职能范围十分广泛，任务极其重要。在社会、经济、文化或人道主义活动领域，必须开展大量工作，进行研究和规划，制定措施和提出建议，以履行其各项职能。所有这些建设性工作将强化世界和平的基础。"①

纵观张彭春在联合国经济及社会理事会各届会议上的发言，他参加了该理事会前十届会议和第十二届会议，为了更加清楚明了地展现张彭春先生当年在联合国经济及社会理事会所做的努力以及所做出的杰出贡献，这里专门编制了表格（见前言表1）。虽然说这个表格看起来并不复杂，但把这些东西找出来就是一个很花工夫的事情，将所有发言内容全部整理并简要翻译出来也是很不容易的，另外，把所有相关会议纪要做成演示课件作为本书插图，也是一项耗费时间和精力的事情，中间还出现了一次完成全部插图后图像无法显示的情况，继而体验了返工重做的辛酸。若考虑到具体的会议记录及纪要等又涉及许多其他问题，如由于时间久远，有些资料可能已经缺失，而整个理事会也是在不断协商中完善工作机制，且面临的全球性问题又是繁多而复杂的，在建制过程中不免也有这样或那样的问题，没有现成的模式遵循。这些都对收集和甄别带来一定的困难。另外，加之当年的技术设备问题，也为资料的记录、储存等带来很多不便，有的全文记录由于打印质量太差而辨认困难，也有的内容在扫描时漏页或内容缺

① UN Document: A/PV.8, p. 122. (Mr. Koo believed that "The Economic and Social Council is no less an innovation. The scope of its functions is very wide and its task exceedingly important. In the fields of social, economic, cultural or humanitarian activities, a vast amount of work, in study and planning and in devising measures and making recommendations in order to carry out its diverse functions, must be done. All this constructive work will strengthen the foundations of world peace.")

损，等等。另外，文献残缺、误排，甚至命名方面也有一些差错，需要认真辨识和纠正等。

通过现有联合国档案资料整理和研究，发现张彭春在联合国经济及社会理事会历届会议上的发言内容，包括他所参加的共 11 届会议，就目前掌握的资料来看，张彭春在其中至少 164 次会议上进行了不同长短、次数不等的发言。在该书整理与编写过程中，笔者一直与联合国图书馆和档案馆联系，并将所发现的问题不断整理并发给联合国相关部门，虽然期间也有一些收获，如获得经社理事会第三届绝大部分会议全文记录的法语版等，但在寻找其他缺失资料方面却收获不大。这就导致原来的书稿中经社理事会第一届会议的资料只有第 1 次会议的内容，缺乏后面 13 次会议的内容，这无疑对一项全面系统的整理研究是一个重大损失，因为若要了解张彭春先生代表中国在经社理事会所做贡献的全貌，就不能不了解第一届会议的全部内容，哪怕是对其会议纪要的全面把握也无疑将极大地拓展世人对张彭春所做贡献的认识。

由于之前多次与联合国图书馆等联系而未得到令人满意的结果，笔者基本上对能够全面地收入张彭春在第一届会议的发言内容丧失了信心，同时也倍感遗憾。直到开印前的一两天，情况才有了新的转机。在刚刚与其结识恨晚的现任美国纽约大学兼职教授何勇先生[①]的支持下，特别是经何教授转请在联合国工作的得力朋友的鼎力协助下，就在本书即将付印前的一个周末，联合国图书馆找到了原来所缺失的经社理事会第一届会议的绝大部分会议纪要[②]，并将这部分资料扫描上传到联合国文件检索系统！尽

① 何勇先生，1992 年获哥伦比亚大学人类语言学博士学位。毕业后先在纽约新学院大学（New School University）任教，后任纽约中国学院（China Institute，亦称“华美协进社”）教学部主任。2002 年至 2017 年 5 月任联合国中文组组长、现任纽约大学兼职教授。社会工作包括华美人文学会共同主席和大纽约地区中文教师学会执行主任。担任南京大学、南京东南大学、南京理工大学、江苏师范大学和常州大学客座教授、南京师范大学特聘教授、北京语言大学高精尖语言资源创新中心特聘研究员。先后两次获颁“联合国 21 世纪奖”。

② 该部分文件虽然冠以全文记录之名，却实际绝大部分都是会议纪要，而只有前三次会议为全文记录。能否最终找到全文记录，仍然不得而知。

管这些内容的获取、整理、翻译和整合对笔者来说，意味着牺牲了整个周末休息的时间，但能在一个周末时间弥补张彭春在经社理事会第一届会议的其他发言内容，已经是十分幸运的事情了。虽然有些因长期日夜兼程而鞍马劳顿，但还是马不停蹄地继续前行，不敢懈怠，因为笔者深知所补充的这些内容，对世人全面认识张彭春当年代表中国对创立世界卫生组织所做的贡献，无疑提供了更加详实的佐证史料。尤其是全球历经了近三年来的新冠疫情的肆虐，人们更应该体会到当年张彭春先生代表中国向细菌宣战之远见、对创立世界卫生组织所做的贡献之珍贵。另外，这一整理、研究和探索新资料的过程，在某种意义上来说，还客观地促进了联合国档案管理工作的查漏补缺，为完善联合国早期档案资料管理提供了契机。

但是，令人遗憾的是，现有发言内容并不是张彭春在联合国经济及社会理事会发言的全部内容。例如，从会议记录情况的整体来看，第二届、第四届和第五届会议既有全文记录，也有会议纪要，尤其是全文记录的内容真实可信，具有很高的研究价值，但这部分内容仍有部分文件缺乏全文记录，如第四届会议全文记录缺少第 55 次会议、第 68 次会议、第 69 次会议和第 84 次会议，第五届会议全文记录缺少第 113 次会议和第 117 次会议。另外，根据联合国有关文件记录第三届会议也有全文记录，但在联合国文件检索系统却没有提供。① 还有其他各届会议都只有会议纪要，有的会议纪要还因为缺页，而无法看到全貌。

前言表 1：张彭春在联合国经济及社会理事会发言情况表

会议届数	会议次数：本届总次数（会次）	会议时间	会议地点	档案资料	张彭春会议发言情况
第一届	13（1—13）+1②	1946-1-23—1946-2-18	伦敦圣公会总部大楼	全文或纪要	在 8 次会议上发言

① 后经与联合国图书馆多方频繁联络，目前掌握了第三届会议全文记录的法语版，但依然缺少其中的两次会议全文记录。主要鉴于对本书体例的考虑，法语全文记录暂时未收入本书。值得说明的是笔者也将继续追踪相关文件的下落。

② 经社理事会第一届第 14 次会议为闭门会议（Private meeting），因此一般认为，第一届会议共举行了 13 次会议。

续表

会议届数	会议次数：本届总次数（会次）	会议时间	会议地点	档案资料	张彭春会议发言情况
第二届	15(1—15)	1946-5-25—1946-6-21	纽约亨特学院	全文记录+纪要(全)	在7次会议上发言
第三届	22(1—21+1)	1946-9-11—1949-10-2	纽约成功湖+法拉盛草地公园	会议纪要+法语全文记录(缺两次)	在15次会议上发言
第四届	34(51—84)①	1947-2-28—1947-3-29	纽约成功湖	全文记录缺四次②，会议纪要全	在12次会议上发言
第五届	37(85—121)	1947-7-19—1947-8-16	纽约成功湖	全文记录缺两次③，纪要全	在17次会议上发言
第六届	53(122—174)	1948-2-2—1948-3-11	纽约成功湖	仅会议纪要	在20次会议上发言
第七届	51(175—225)	1948-7-19—1948-8-28	日内瓦万国宫	仅会议纪要	在23次会议上发言
第八届	57(226—282)	1949-2-7—1949-3-18	纽约成功湖	仅会议纪要	在20次会议上发言
第九届	61(283—343)	1949-7-5—1949-8-15	日内瓦万国宫	仅会议纪要	在17次会议上发言
第十届	31(344—374)	1950-2-7—1950-3-6	纽约成功湖	仅会议纪要	在16次会议上发言

① 前三届会议编号都是从第1次会议算起，前三届共举行了50次会议，这就造成了相应会议记录命名的混乱；而从第四届会议起，会议编号以总次数计算，也就是第四届的第1次会议，称为第四届第51次会议，依次类推，从而也避免了相关会议记录文件命名的混乱。

② 缺第四届第55次会议、第68次会议、第69次会议和第84次会议全文记录。

③ 缺第五届第113次会议和第117次会议全文记录。

续表

会议届数	会议次数：本届总次数（会次）	会议时间	会议地点	档案资料	张彭春会议发言情况
第十一届	62(375—436)	1950-7-3—1950-8-16	日内瓦万国宫	仅会议纪要	于焌吉、查修、曹保颐等参会
第十二届	44(437—480)	1951-2-20—1952-3-21	智利圣地亚哥	仅会议纪要	在9次会议上发言
合计	480	大约6年	英、美、瑞士日内瓦、智利	纪要/全文	在164次会议上发言

尽管有上述诸多问题存在，通过全面整理和初步研究，我们还是不难发现张彭春将借鉴二战教训作为出发点，明确联合国是人类未来的希望所托。在经济和社会发展方面，他强调世界各国之间的合作与互惠，体现了重要的“合作共赢”的中国价值观；在世界人权保障机制的构建过程中，他以其博大精深的中国智慧，积极建言献策、赢得各国同事的赞赏，为联合国人权机制建设贡献了中国人的聪明才智，也为全球人权治理打下了坚实的基础；在东西文化差异方面，他大力提倡和弘扬中国传统文化，以文化多元的世界观，既肯定了各文化之间存在的差异，也强调了多元文化间彼此可以互相学习借鉴，而且这种“文化互鉴”理念也为各国代表就一系列问题达成共识做出了贡献。虽然这是发生在七十多年前的事情，但是“合作共赢”的价值观、国际人权保障制度建设及全球人权治理的中国智慧以及各国“文化互鉴”的思想，真正契合了当今中国所大力倡导的“人类命运共同体”理念。

首先，张彭春先生作为中国驻联合国经济及社会理事会首席代表，所做的第一件大事就是倡议召开国际卫生会议，促使由中国和巴西代表团在旧金山会议期间所提出建立世界卫生组织的议案，能够具体落实下来，为世界卫生组织的创建立下了汗马功劳。例如，1946年2月7日，联合国经社理事会第一届第5次会议在英国伦敦召开，中国代表张彭春参加了本次会议并在会议上发言,提出了召开国际卫生会议的议案,被会议所接受和采纳。当时张彭春先生呼吁:"主席先生,在提交这项召开国际卫生会议的议案时,我感到我实际上是在提交一份新的宣战书,一场消灭导致世界上的疾病和瘟疫的细菌的战争。这场战争不是针对人类自身,而是针对人类的共同敌人。总之,一场新的战争已经在这里提出,我们将宣战,并用血、汗、泪去进行战斗。"[①] 1946 年 5 月 27 日上午 10 时 30 分,联合国经社理事会第二届第 2 次会议,在美国纽约亨特学院召开,张彭春参加了本次会议,并在会上再次提议召开国际卫生会议,为促进世界卫生组织的建立大声疾呼。[②] 正是由于国际卫生会议的召开,世界卫生组织才最终得以建立,而该组织成为"经济及社会理事会主持下所建立的第一个专门机关"[③]。由此可以看出张彭春对世界卫生组织的创建的远见、热情和重大贡献。他的演讲内容至今读来仍具有鼓舞人心的力量。张彭春先生的呼吁和演讲,对促进世界卫生组织的建立发挥了关键性的作用。

其次,在联合国经济及社会理事会的指导下,建立了联合国人权委员会,张彭春在人权委员会第一届会议上当选为副主席,参与起草《世界人权宣言》和国际人权两公约,为国际人权保障机制的构建倾注了大量心血,成为构建国际人权体系的重要设计师,他当年的努力和付出为全球人权治理打下了坚实的基础。通过对联合国历史档案的研究,本人不仅归纳了张彭春对起草《世界人权宣言》的贡献,也系统归纳提炼出了"张彭春多元主义人权思想",并详细地分析了其理论基础、社会基础、丰富内涵和当代价值。现有参考文献见本人的另外著作:《〈世界人权宣言〉研究》[④](北京大学出版社 2012 年版)、《张彭春:世界人权体系的重要设计师》[⑤](社会

---

① 见本书第一章相关内容。

② UN Document: E/PV. 2, pp. 31-32. (Verbatim record of the Second Meeting of the Second Session of the Economic and Social Council)

③ UN Document: A/PV. 39, p. 40. (顾维钧在联大第 39 次全体会议上的发言中不仅对经济及社会理事会的工作给予高度评价,还对世界卫生组织寄予厚望,并且进一步指出:"健康不良、愚昧与贫穷一日流行,就一日没有而且也不能有真的人权的保障。")

④ 孙平华:《〈世界人权宣言〉研究》,北京大学出版社 2012 年版。

⑤ 孙平华:《张彭春:世界人权体系的重要设计师》,社会科学文献出版社 2017 年版。

科学文献出版社 2017 年版）以及 *Historic Achievement of a Common Standard：Pengchun Chang and the Universal Declaration of Human Rights*①（Springer 2018）和 *Chinese Contributions to International Discourse of Human Rights*②，（Springer 2022）等。至于张彭春在联合国人权委员会、起草委员会、联大第三委员会及联大全会上的发言，内容极为丰富，也极为重要，将收入本人所编著的另一部书中，目前该书暂定名为《全球人权治理的中国智慧：张彭春在联合国人权委员会及联大第三委员会等的发言》，敬请关注和期待，这里不再赘述。

第三，张彭春善于运用儒家经典名言的风格，彰显了中国传统文化思想的光芒，为国际社会全球治理做出了卓越贡献。早在经社理事会第一届第 1 次会议上，张彭春便引用了孟子的“以善服人者，未有能服人者也；以善养人，然后能服天下”③，为经社理事会成员间的精诚合作指明了方向。在经社理事会第二届第 7 次会议上，张彭春引用了包含儒家思想的经典篇章——《礼记·礼运大同篇》。该经典“虽然只有 107 个字，却字字珠玑，句句破的，把以天下为己任，以仁德为核心，以孝悌为宗旨，以人伦为基准的中华民族传统文化的主题揭示得明晰深邃，字显意蕴，折射出了五千年文明的礼仪仁光”④。在经社理事会第四届第 78 次会议上，张彭春引用了孟子的“民为贵，社稷次之，君为轻”⑤和“尽信《书》，则不如无《书》”⑥的思想。在经社理事会第五届第 88 次会议上，张彭春再次引用孟子的名言：“大人者，不失其赤子之心。”⑦而在经社理事会第十届第 346 次会议上，张

① Sun, Pinghua. *Historic Achievement of a Common Standard：Pengchun Chang and the Universal Declaration of Human Rights*. Singapore：Springer，2018.

② Sun, Pinghua. *Chinese Contributions to International Discourse of Human Rights*. Singapore：Springer，2022.

③ 《孟子·离娄章句下》

④ 儒家文化的经典《礼记·礼运大同篇》，每天话资讯（公众号 2019-01-21）。（2022 年 3 月 1 日访问）。网址为：https://www.360kuai.com/pc/98a4cb45396fcf05a?cota=4&kuai_so=1&tj_url=so_rec&sign=360_e39369d1。

⑤ 《孟子·离娄章句下》

⑥ 《孟子·尽心章句下》

⑦ 《孟子·离娄章句下》

彭春也间接引入了体现中华传统思想的“徒善不足以为政,徒法不能以自行”①。张彭春善于运用儒家经典的风格不仅给理事会成员留下深刻的印象,也有力地促进了国际社会就相关问题达成共识,在联合国创建初期的全球治理中发挥了不可替代的作用。这也为当今中国找回文化自信提供了典型案例。

第四,张彭春担任亚洲和远东工作组主席,在积极促成和建立亚洲和远东经济委员会(即亚洲及太平洋经济委员会的前身)方面,起到了重要的主导作用,并做出了杰出贡献。早在 1946 年 6 月 4 日召开的联合国经济及社会理事会第二届第 7 次会议上,张彭春就促进欠发达地区发展发表了长篇演讲,为改善“全世界人民的生存状况”而大声疾呼:“全世界人民都渴望生活水平的提高,对其中一些人来说,生活水平的提高目前意味着他们摆脱饥饿。除非为实现这一目标而采取行动,否则世界的良心就无法得以安宁。”②他还进一步引用了前面提到的《礼记·礼运大同篇》,为理事会的工作指明了努力的方向。1947 年 3 月 18 日,联合国经济及社会理事会第四届第 72 次会议上,张彭春作为亚洲和远东工作组主席,在会议上做亚洲和远东工作组报告,以人道主义情怀,呼吁国际社会善待战争受害国,并给予积极的合作和援助,为达到此目的,他恳请理事会通过他所建议设立亚洲和远东经济委员会的议案。③ 1947 年 3 月 28 日,联合国经济及社会理事会通过决议,设立了亚洲和远东经济委员会,该委员会与欧洲经济委员会为同等重要之区域委员会。另外,张彭春还对拉丁美洲经济委员会的成立发挥了极大的促进作用。

第五,张彭春不仅为审议新闻自由小组委员会的报告、审议麻醉药品委员会的报告、审议理事会关于世界卫生组织的决议草案、审议和讨论国际难民组织决议草案及修正案、审议建立人口委员会议案、审议国际难民组织特别委员会财政报告、审议人权委员会的报告、审议经济委员会报告、

---

① 《孟子·离娄章句上》

② UN Document:E/PV. 7, pp. 25-36.

③ UN Document:E/PV. 72, pp. 57-62.

审议理事会非政府组织报告、审议专门机构的报告、审议欧洲经济委员会的报告、审议国际劳工组织的报告、审议拉丁美洲经济委员会的报告等做出诸多重要贡献，还详细阐述了对世界经济形势的看法和主张，提出了许多建设性意见、为完善联合国工作机制和促进理事会各项工作的顺利开展做出了卓越的贡献。

另外，值得提及的是，张彭春作为联大代表，还参与了联大第三委员会的各届会议以及几次联合国大会的全体会议，在联合国层面有力地发出了中国声音，成为中国驻联合国机构的杰出代言人。他所发出的中国声音，被联合国会议纪要或全文记录所永远铭记，成为我们深入研究和系统挖掘的宝藏。

总之，就目前来看，张彭春先生在联合国经济及社会理事会各届会议上的发言内容，虽仍有缺失和遗憾，但资料已经十分丰富，现收集整理出来，如能为构筑中国话语体系尽一份力也就感到欣慰和满足了。将来如有机会，再做补充和完善。

由于笔者水平有限，加之时间紧迫，书中定有不当之处，敬请学界同批评指正。

中国政法大学教授
中国第一位人权法学博士
英国埃克塞特大学法学院访问学者
《埃斯特角宣言》中国惟一原始签署人
加拿大《政治与法律杂志》特约审稿人
新加坡《国际中国研究杂志》特约审稿人
美国《政治科学与公共事务杂志》特约审稿人
于北京市海淀区昆玉河畔
2022年4月28日

目 录

第一章　联合国经社理事会第一届会议

（全文或纪要）

联合国经济及社会理事会（简称："联合国经社理事会"或"经社理事会"）在成立之初，便召开了第一届会议。1946 年 1 月 23 日，在英国伦敦圣公会总部大楼，召开了第 1 次会议，本届会议共举行了 13 次会议，其他会议分别为：1946 年 1 月 29 日下午 5 时召开的第 2 次会议、2 月 1 日召开的第 3 次会议、2 月 5 日召开的第 4 次会议、2 月 7 日召开的第 5 次会议、2 月 8 日召开的第 6 次会议、2 月 11 日召开的第 7 次会议、2 月 12 日召开的第 8 次会议、2 月 13 日召开的第 9 次会议、2 月 15 日召开的第 10 次会议、2 月 16 日召开的第 11 次会议和第 12 次会议、2 月 18 日召开的第 13 次会议。[①] 另外，2 月 18 日下午还召开了本届第 14 次会议，本次会议为闭门会议。

中国代表张彭春参加了本届会议，并在其中的 8 次会议上发言，包括第 1 次会议、第 5 次会议、第 6 次会议、第 8 次会议、第 10 次会议、第 11 次会议、第 12 次会议和第 14 次会议发言。原来的联合国档案记录仅有第 1 次会议的全文记录[②]，近日刚刚更新的联合国经社理事会记录文件中，本届会议前三次会议（即第 1 次会议、第 2 次会议和第 3 次会议）为全文记录，而后面的均为会议纪要。[③] 鉴于此，在前言表 1 中将本届会议档案资料的情况用"全文或纪要"来概括，可以说，最新的更新是令人兴奋的事

① UN Document: E/PV. 38-50, p. 1.

② UN Document: E_1stsess-_PV-1-14-EN.

③ UN Document: E/1stsess. /PV. 1-14.

情，但文件本身的问题仍给笔者留下遗憾。

另外，在张彭春女儿张新月和女婿郑师拙撰写出版的《张彭春生平及著作》[①]一书中，收入了张彭春1946年2月7日在伦敦第一届经社理事会会议上的发言，本次发言中提议召开国际卫生会议，根据这个发言的时间，应该是经社理事会第一届第5次会议，张彭春的本次发言译文也被崔国良、崔红收入其主编的《张彭春论教育与戏剧艺术》一书[②]。为了尽可能全面的收集相关会议内容，现将这个发言内容作为补充资料一并收入本书。

① Ruth H. C. and Sze-Chuh Cheng (ed.), 1995. *Peng Chun Chang* (1892-1957): *Biography and Collected Works*. Privately Printed. p. 151.

② 崔国良、崔红主编，董秀桦英文编译：《张彭春论教育与戏剧艺术》，南开大学出版社2004年版，第600-601页。

1. 张彭春在经社理事会第一届第 1 次会议上的发言

1946 年 1 月 23 日下午 5 时至晚上 7 时 26 分，在英国伦敦圣公会总部大楼，召开了联合国经社理事会第一届第 1 次会议。这是一次非常重要的大会，本次会议的主要议程为：执行秘书宣布会议开幕、预备委员会报告第三章介绍、通过临时议事规则、选举主席和副主席、主席致辞、经社理事会的组织即各委员会的建立（一般性讨论）、通过会议议程。中国代表张彭春为理事会本届会议提名了副主席人选，并在本次会议上发表了著名演讲，阐述了“忠诚”的思想对国际组织的重要意义。其具体发言内容①如下：

【全文记录】

Mr. CHANG (China): I have the honour to nominate a very prominent and experienced scholar and scientist, Mr. Stampar, the representative of Yugoslavia, to be the first Vice-President of this Council.

Mr. Stampar has had eminent experience, especially in the field of health, in my country, in the days when he was serving in collaboration with the old League of Nations.

Mr. CHANG (China): The Chinese delegation has the honour to congratulate the Council on the eminent and supremely qualified men whom we have elected to be the officers of this first session of the Council. The Chinese delega-

① UN Document: E_1stsess-_PV-1-14-EN, p. 3, 14.

tion is especially gratified with the inauguration of this all-important organ of the United Nations, mainly for two reasons:

First, the United Nations must, as a living institution, attain and nourish a new loyalty on the part of the peoples of the world. It is hoped that, through constructive co-operative activities to be promoted by the Economic and Social Council, this new loyalty may be engendered and fostered. People, by nature, develop devotion to, interest in, and support of an organization only after having experienced positive benefits derived from being members of that organization. The efforts of this Council, designed for human welfare, therefore, are closely and vitally related to a new loyalty which is essential in maintaining the very existence of the United Nations Organization itself.

Secondly, it is through co-operative effort in the solution of common problems that peoples can attain real mutual understanding. A proper perspective and a comparative approach can make us more sympathetic to one another's efforts for the betterment of our estate.

A new loyalty must be cultivated; a deeper mutual understanding must be promoted. Through the activities of the Economic and Social Council, may the United Nations, the hope of humanity, grow, prosper and endure.

A saying from the Chinese thinker, Mencius, may be appropriate. I will first say it in Chinese, which I hope you will understand — after all, Chinese is one of the official languages.

以善服人者,未有能服人者也;以善养人,然后能服天下。[①]

I will now try a lame translation: "Subdue people with goodness" — this

---

① 笔者根据张新月和郑师拙编写的《张彭春生平及著作》一书,补充了该句中文内容,而联合国会议记录中漏掉了这句中文,根据上下文,当时张彭春先讲了这句中文,然后又将该句翻译为英文。《张彭春生平及著作》第 150 页,还为本次发言添加了一个标题:"A New Loyalty"。另外,将本书所收入内容与联合国会议记录相对比,发现两个版本也略有不同,具体体现在发言开头部分。(See:Ruth, H. C. and Sze-chuh Cheng. 1995. *Peng Chun Chang* (1892-1957): *Biography & collected works*. Privately Printed.)

is already one step higher than "subdue people with force." "Subdue people with goodness; people can never be subdued. Nourish people with goodness; the whole world can be subdued."

"Nourish people with goodness" — that is the function of this Council, and the whole world is waiting to be thus subdued.

【全文影像】

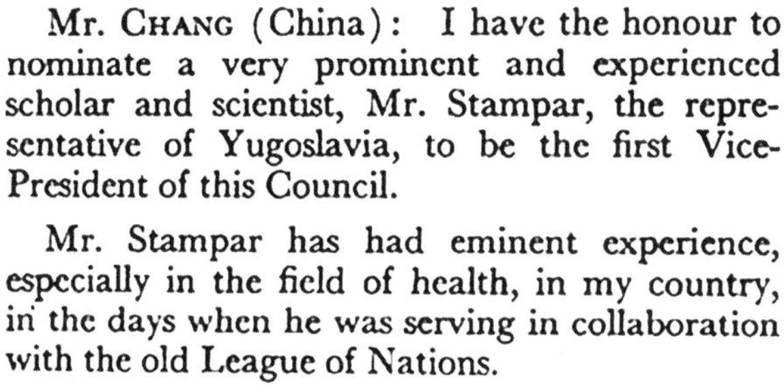

Mr. CHANG (China): I have the honour to nominate a very prominent and experienced scholar and scientist, Mr. Stampar, the representative of Yugoslavia, to be the first Vice-President of this Council.

Mr. Stampar has had eminent experience, especially in the field of health, in my country, in the days when he was serving in collaboration with the old League of Nations.

图片 1.1 张彭春在经社理事会第一届第 1 次会议上的发言①(1)

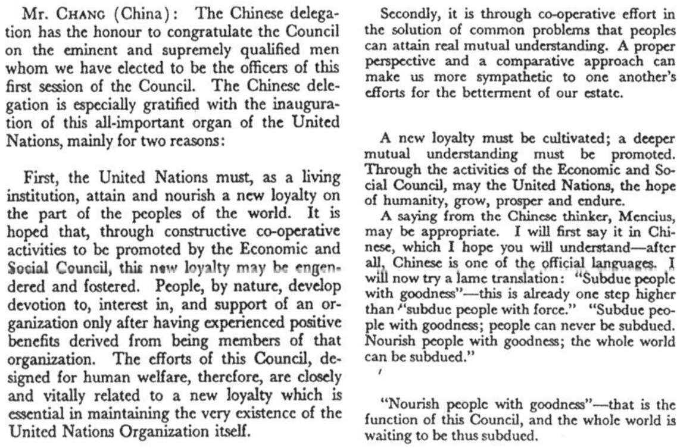

Mr. CHANG (China): The Chinese delegation has the honour to congratulate the Council on the eminent and supremely qualified men whom we have elected to be the officers of this first session of the Council. The Chinese delegation is especially gratified with the inauguration of this all-important organ of the United Nations, mainly for two reasons:

First, the United Nations must, as a living institution, attain and nourish a new loyalty on the part of the peoples of the world. It is hoped that, through constructive co-operative activities to be promoted by the Economic and Social Council, this new loyalty may be engendered and fostered. People, by nature, develop devotion to, interest in, and support of an organization only after having experienced positive benefits derived from being members of that organization. The efforts of this Council, designed for human welfare, therefore, are closely and vitally related to a new loyalty which is essential in maintaining the very existence of the United Nations Organization itself.

Secondly, it is through co-operative effort in the solution of common problems that peoples can attain real mutual understanding. A proper perspective and a comparative approach can make us more sympathetic to one another's efforts for the betterment of our estate.

A new loyalty must be cultivated; a deeper mutual understanding must be promoted. Through the activities of the Economic and Social Council, may the United Nations, the hope of humanity, grow, prosper and endure.

A saying from the Chinese thinker, Mencius, may be appropriate. I will first say it in Chinese, which I hope you will understand—after all, Chinese is one of the official languages. I will now try a lame translation: "Subdue people with goodness"—this is already one step higher than "subdue people with force." "Subdue people with goodness; people can never be subdued. Nourish people with goodness; the whole world can be subdued."

"Nourish people with goodness"—that is the function of this Council, and the whole world is waiting to be thus subdued.

图片 1.2 张彭春在经社理事会第一届第 1 次会议上的发言②(2)

① UN Document: E_1stsess-_PV-1-14-EN, p. 3.

② UN Document: E_1stsess-_PV-1-14-EN, p. 14.

【全文译文】

张先生(中国):我荣幸地提名南斯拉夫代表、一位非常杰出且经验丰富的学者和科学家斯坦珀先生担任理事会第一副主席。

斯坦珀先生在与前国际联盟合作履职期间,在我国有着杰出的经历,特别是在卫生领域中。

张先生(中国):中国代表团荣幸地向理事会祝贺,我们选出的杰出而极为称职的人士,担任理事会第一届会议的官员。中国代表团对联合国这一极其重要的机构的成立,感到特别满意,主要原因有两个:

第一,联合国作为一个有生命力的机构,必须赢得和培养世界各族人民的新的忠诚。希望通过经济及社会理事会推动的建设性合作活动,能够产生和培养这种新的忠诚。从本质上讲,人们只有在经历了作为组织成员所带来的积极利益后,才会对组织做出奉献、产生兴趣并给予支持。因此,本理事会为人类福利而作出的努力,与维持联合国组织本身的生存所必需的新的忠诚密切相关。

第二,只有通过合作性的努力解决共同问题,各国人民才能实现真正的相互理解。正确的观点和比较的方法可以使我们更好地理解彼此为改善我们的状况所作的努力。

必须培养新的忠诚;必须促进彼此加深相互了解。通过经济及社会理事会的活动,愿寄予人类厚望的联合国得以成长、繁荣和持久。

中国思想家孟子的一句话可能是恰当的。我将首先用中文说,我希望各位能听懂——毕竟,中文是官方语言之一。

“以善服人者,未有能服人者也;以善养人,然后能服天下。”

我现在尝试一个蹩脚的翻译:“用善征服人”——这已经比“用武力征服人”高了一步;但“以善征服人;人永远不能被征服。以善去养育人;整个世界都可以被征服”。

“以善养人”——这是本理事会的职能,而整个世界正等待着被这样征服。

2. 张彭春在经社理事会第一届第5次会议上的发言

联合国经社理事会第一届第5次会议,于1946年2月7日下午3时至5时,在英国伦敦圣公会总部大楼召开,该次会议的主要议题是召开国际卫生会议的问题:中国代表团提出的决议草案。① 中国代表张彭春参加了本次会议,并在会议上发言,其具体发言内容②会议纪要、纪要影像和纪要译文如下:

【会议纪要】

Mr. CHANG (China) presented the following draft resolution on the calling of an International Health Conference:[1]

"Whereas there is urgent need for international action in the field of public health;

[1] Document E/2.

---

① 笔者注:在联合国经社理事会第一届第5次会议上,张彭春第一个发言并提出召开国际卫生会议的决议草案,接着南斯拉夫代表、加拿大代表、乌克兰代表、美国代表、秘鲁代表、捷克斯洛伐克代表、英国代表、法国代表、希腊代表纷纷发言表示大力支持中国代表所提出的决议草案。接着,中国代表张彭春对各国代表的大力支持表示感谢。最后,会议主席建议将中国所提出的决议的语言提交给起草委员会,本次会议结束,下次会议接着继续讨论中国的决议草案。(见:UN Document: E/1stsess./PV. 1-14, pp. 54-58.)

② UN Document: E/1stsess./PV. 1-14, pp. 54-55, pp. 57-58.

"Whereas this need was recognized at the United Nations Conference on International Organization in a Declaration, proposed jointly by the delegations of Brazil and China, and unanimously approved, recommending 'That a General Conference be convened within the next few months for the purpose of establishing an international health organization';

"Whereas the Governments of Brazil and China have requested that the United States call a general conference for the aforementioned purpose and have received a sympathetic reply from the Government of the United States; therefore be it

"Resolved, that the Economic and Social Council approves the calling of an international conference of the United Nations to consider the scope of, and the appropriate machinery for, international action in the field of public health and, in this connexion, to give consideration to proposals for establishing a single International Health Organization of the United Nations;

"That the Members of the United Nations be urged to send as representatives to this conference, experts in public health;

"That in order to expedite the preparations for the conference, each member of the Council may, if it so desires; designate an expert to constitute forthwith a technical committee, which would prepare draft documents to be circulated to the Members of the United Nations by the Secretariat for consideration at the conference."

Mr. Chang recalled that, at this San Francisco Conference, the delegations of Brazil and China had proposed jointly the calling of such a conference and Mr. Chang reported that the Brazilian delegation had authorized him to state that the proposed resolution had its whole-hearted support.

It was a truism that nations co-operate better in war than in peace, and the present resolution proposed a declaration of war against the common enemies of mankind. One of the results of war was that often the qualities of the enemy are acquired, and it was to be hoped that in the war against those microbes which recognize no national boundaries, the United Nations might learn not to indulge in national pride and prejudice.

Mr. CHANG (China) expressed deep appreciation for the unanimous support his resolution had received. He pointed out that the last paragraph of the resolution provided for the setting up of a technical committee to prepare draft documents for the Members of the United Nations. He approved of the suggestion that a small nuclear committee be set up immediately, and proposed that this group should consider the date and the agenda. The group might consult with persons concerned in the convening of the conference. The United States had already been requested by China and Brazil to convene the conference.

Referring to the form of the resolution, Mr. Chang said that the original text of the resolution was in Chinese and that the first translation had not been made by any member of his delegation.

【纪要影像】

Mr. CHANG (China) presented the following draft resolution on the calling of an International Health Conference:[1]

"*Whereas* there is urgent need for international action in the field of public health;

"*Whereas* this need was recognized at the United Nations Conference on International Organization in a Declaration, proposed jointly by the delegations of Brazil and China, and unanimously approved, recommending 'That a General Conference be convened within the next few months for the purpose of establishing an international health organization';

"*Whereas* the Governments of Brazil and China have requested that the United States call a general conference for the aforementioned purpose and have received a sympathetic reply from the Government of the United States; therefore be it

"*Resolved,* that the Economic and Social Council approves the calling of an international conference of the United Nations to consider the scope of, and the appropriate machinery for, international action in the field of public health and, in this connexion, to give consideration to proposals for

[1] Document E/2.

图片 1.3　张彭春在经社理事会第一届第 5 次会议发言纪要(1)

establishing a single International Health Organization of the United Nations;

"That the Members of the United Nations be urged to send as representatives to this conference, experts in public health;

"That in order to expedite the preparations for the conference, each member of the Council may, if it so desires, designate an expert to constitute forthwith a technical committee, which would prepare draft documents to be circulated to the Members of the United Nations by the Secretariat for consideration at the conference."

Mr. Chang recalled that, at the San Francisco Conference, the delegations of Brazil and China had proposed jointly the calling of such a conference and Mr. Chang reported that the Brazilian delegation had authorized him to state that the proposed resolution had its whole-hearted support.

It was a truism that nations co-operate better in war than in peace, and the present resolution proposed a declaration of war against the common enemies of mankind. One of the results of war was that often the qualities of the enemy are acquired, and it was to be hoped that in the war against those microbes which recognize no national boundaries, the United Nations might learn not to indulge in national pride and prejudice.

图片 1.4　张彭春在经社理事会第一届第 5 次会议发言纪要(2)

Mr. CHANG (China) expressed deep appreciation for the unanimous support his resolution had received. He pointed out that the last paragraph of the resolution provided for the setting up of a technical committee to prepare draft documents for the Members of the United Nations. He approved of the suggestion that a small nuclear committee be set up immediately, and proposed that this group should consider the date and the agenda. The group might consult with persons concerned in the convening of the conference. The United States had already been requested by China and Brazil to convene the conference.

Referring to the form of the resolution, Mr. Chang said that the original text of the resolution was in Chinese and that the first translation had not been made by any member of his delegation.

图片 1.5　张彭春在经社理事会第一届第 5 次会议发言纪要(3)

【纪要译文】

张先生(中国)提交了关于召开国际卫生会议的如下决议草案[1]：

“鉴于迫切需要在公共卫生领域采取国际行动；

“鉴于这一需要在联合国国际组织会议上由巴西和中国代表团共同提出并一致通过的一项宣言中得到承认，其中建议‘在今后几个月内召开一次大会，以建立一个国际卫生组织’；

“鉴于巴西和中国政府已请求美国为此目的召开一次大会，并已得到美国政府的积极答复；所以让我们

“决定经济及社会理事会批准召开一次联合国国际会议，审议公共卫生领域国际行动的范围和适当机制，并在这方面考虑建立一个单一的联合国国际卫生组织的建议；

1 文件 E/2。

“敦促联合国会员国派公共卫生专家作为代表参加这次会议；

“为了加快会议的筹备工作，理事会每个成员如果愿意，可以：指定一名专家立即组成一个技术委员会，该委员会将编写文件草案，由秘书处分发给联合国会员国，供会议审议。”

张先生回顾说，在这次旧金山会议上，巴西和中国代表团共同提议召开这样一次会议，张先生报告说，巴西代表团授权他声明，巴西代表团全心全意支持拟议的决议。

众所周知，各国在战争中比在和平时期合作得更好，而目前的决议提议对人类的共同敌人宣战。战争的结果之一是，敌人的品质往往是后天获得的，人们希望，在与那些不分国界的微生物的战争中，联合国可以学会不要沉溺于民族傲慢与偏见。

张先生（中国）对他的决议获得一致支持深表感谢。他指出，该决议最后一段规定设立一个技术委员会，为联合国会员国编写文件草案。他赞成立即成立一个小型核心委员会的建议，并建议由该小组考虑日期和议程。该小组可与召集会议的有关人员协商。中国和巴西已经要求美国召开这次会议。

关于决议的形式，张先生说，决议的原文是中文，首次翻译并非由中国代表团的任何成员所为。

补充资料

1946 年 2 月 7 日，在英国伦敦召开了联合国经社理事会第一届第 5 次会议。中国代表张彭春参加了本次会议，并在会议上发言，提出了召开国际卫生会议的议案，严肃地指出应对人类面临的疾病和瘟疫的威胁，国际社会应摒弃偏见和傲慢、向人类的共同敌人宣战，并大力提倡国际合作精神。其所提议案被会议所接受和采纳，而正是在他所提议召开的国际卫生会议上，世界卫生组织才得以正式成立。其具体发言内容①如下：

【会议发言】

WAR AGAINST MICROBES

It is tedious and, as a matter of fact, discourteous to speak on the obvious. But two observations may be appropriate. First, it is sadly realized that nations co-operate much better in war than in peace. We have had in recent months — and, we may say, in recent hours — more than one occasion to remind us of the tragic truth of the observation just made. Therefore, Mr. President, in presenting this resolution for the calling of an International Health Conference, I feel that I am actually proposing the declaration of a new war, namely, a war against microbes that cause and condition disease and pestilence in the world. This war is to be fought not against fellow humans but against common enemies of mankind. Nevertheless, a new war is here proposed and a war, it is hoped, will be declared and fought through with blood, sweat and tears. And, as a product of this war, we seriously hope that the spirit of co-operation that we recently experienced in actual warfare would be continued for the true blessing of man.

My second observation is that in war we often acquire qualities of the enemy against whom we fight. Perhaps — again, it is sad to admit — at this very moment, we are still suffering from some of the qualities that we learned, either consciously or unconsciously, from our recent foes. Some of these qualities are altogether undesirable. These we must try to obliterate from our usage. But in regard to the enemies that I am proposing to fight against, namely, the microbes

---

① 该英文发言内容选自于：Ruth, H. C. and Sze-chuh Cheng. 1995. *Peng Chun Chang* (1892–1957): *Biography & collected works* (*p*. 151). Privately Printed.（值得说明的是：该次会议发言内容使用的是第一人称进行讲述，这可能来自张彭春先生当年演讲的手稿。）

that cause diseases, there is something that we may learn from these enemies that is not undesirable but may even be considered supremely beneficial. I mean to imply that they are quite devoid of any man-made bias of national demarcations. They go from place to place without passports, visas, and custom barriers. And they have no sense of national pride or distinction. We must chase these enemies from place to place without being restricted by national boundaries. From these enemies in this fight, may we learn something of their not giving too much attention to national differentiation?

Sir, I am sure you would agree that the observations I have made are far from being flippant. They are serious — tragically serious. And I hope that, in passing the resolution now proposed by the Chinese Delegation, we shall enhance international co-operation through the declaration of a new war on microbes, and secondly, that we may learn something from these enemies of ours in not indulging over much in national pride and prejudice.

【相关译文】[①]

向细菌宣战

通常,讲一些显而易见的事显得乏味和失礼,然而我要讲的两点意见却是适宜的。首先,我们悲哀地意识到,各国在战争时期的合作要比在和平时期好得多。在近几个月,甚至可以说近几个小时里,不止一个场合提醒着我们这种悲哀的事实。所以,主席先生,在提交这项召开国际卫生会议[②]的议案时,我感到我实际上是在提交一份新的宣战书,一场消灭导致世界上的疾病和瘟疫的细菌的战争。这场战争不是针对人类自身,而是针

① 该译文节选自崔国良、崔红主编,董秀桦英文编译:《张彭春论教育与戏剧艺术》,天津:南开大学出版社,2004 年版,第 600—601 页。

② 这里值得说明的是:董秀桦英译将"an International Health Conference"译为"世界卫生大会"。笔者根据当时媒体报道及联合国对世界卫生组织(The World Health Organization)名称的确定过程,将张彭春所建议召开的会议名称"an International Health Conference"翻译为"国际卫生会议"

对人类的共同敌人。总之,一场新的战争已经在这里提出,我们将宣战,并用血、汗、泪去进行战斗。此外,我们真诚地希望,作为这场战争的成果,我们在近期实际战争中经历过的合作精神能够为真正赐福予人类而继续光大。

我的第二点意见是,在战争中,我们常常学到我们所反对的敌人的品质。在这个特别的时刻,我们不得不再次悲哀地承认,我们现在仍然因为有意无意地从我们的敌人那里学到的一些品质而遭受着痛苦。其中一些品质是完全不能接受的,必须努力消除。至于我提出的与之进行战斗的敌人,即导致疾病的细菌,我们则可以从它们那里学到一些东西。这些东西不仅不是不能接受的,反之甚至对我们很有帮助。我的意思是,细菌完全没有任何人为的国家界限的偏见,它们往来于各处不需要护照、签证,也没有海关的屏障。它们也没有民族自尊和区别的意识。我们只有在没有国界限制的情况下才能把这些敌人从一个地方驱赶①到另一个地方。在这场战斗中,我们是否可以从这些敌人那里学到它们不那么注意国家间区别的优点?

主席先生,我相信您不会认为我提出的意见是轻率无礼的。这些意见是严肃的,非常严肃的。希望在通过中国代表团提出的这项议案的过程中,我们将通过对细菌的宣战增进国际合作。此外,我们也可以在不过多地沉湎于国家的傲慢与偏见方面向我们的敌人学习。

① 一些新闻媒体报道都采用了“追踪”一词,如1946年2月9日《大公报》(上海版)第3版。笔者认为这个报道所使用的“追踪”要比“驱赶”可能更好些。

3. 张彭春在经社理事会第一届第 6 次会议上的发言

联合国经社理事会第一届第 6 次会议，于 1946 年 2 月 8 日下午 5 时至晚上 7 时 30 分，在英国伦敦圣公会总部大楼召开，该次会议的主要议题是继续讨论召开国际卫生会议的问题：中国代表团提出的决议草案。[①] 中国代表张彭春参加了本次会议，并在会议上发言，其具体发言内容[②]会议纪要、纪要影像和纪要译文如下：

【会议纪要】

Decision: *The Council agreed*:

(1) *That the original text of the resolution on the calling of an international health conference be approved in principle.*

(2) *That the report and recommendations of the technical committee will be submitted to the next session of the Economic and Social Council.*

(3) *That a Drafting Committee, consisting of the representatives of China, United States of America, Colombia, United Kingdom, Union of Soviet Socialist Republics, France, Greece and Canada, be appointed.*

Mr. CHANG (China) enquired whether the preparatory committee could

---

① 本次会议继续讨论由中国代表张彭春所提出的召开国际卫生会议的决议草案，比利时代表、苏联代表、挪威代表也都表示大力支持，因此理事会做出决定，并原则上批准了中国代表所提出的召开国际卫生会议的决议草案。历史实践证明，正是由于国际卫生会议的召开，世界卫生组织才得以最后建立。

② UN Document: E/1stsess./PV. 1-14, p. 61.

decide on the programme of the conference or whether it would report to the next session of the Council, thereby making it definite that the conference would not meet until after that session.

Decision: *The Council agreed that the Drafting Committee should prepare a resolution on the lines indicated and that the date of the conference should be discussed when the date of the Council's next session had been fixed.*

【纪要影像】

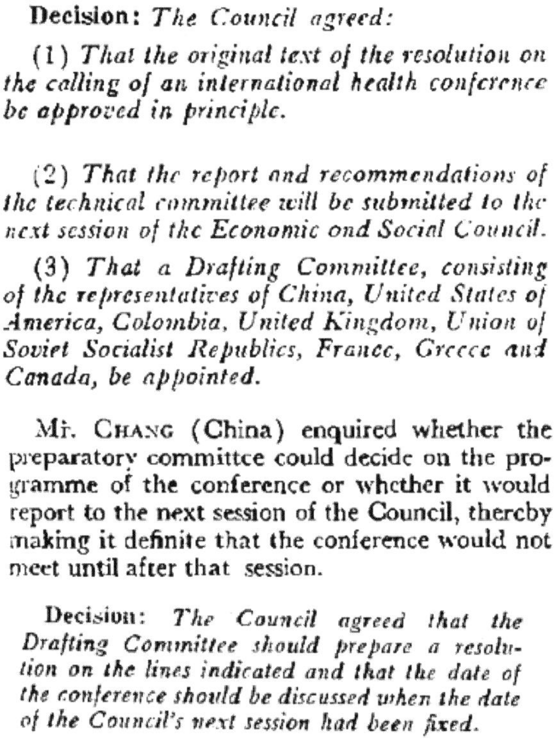

Decision: *The Council agreed:*

(1) *That the original text of the resolution on the calling of an international health conference be approved in principle.*

(2) *That the report and recommendations of the technical committee will be submitted to the next session of the Economic and Social Council.*

(3) *That a Drafting Committee, consisting of the representatives of China, United States of America, Colombia, United Kingdom, Union of Soviet Socialist Republics, France, Greece and Canada, be appointed.*

Mr. CHANG (China) enquired whether the preparatory committee could decide on the programme of the conference or whether it would report to the next session of the Council, thereby making it definite that the conference would not meet until after that session.

Decision: *The Council agreed that the Drafting Committee should prepare a resolution on the lines indicated and that the date of the conference should be discussed when the date of the Council's next session had been fixed.*

图片 1.6　张彭春在经社理事会第一届第 6 次会议发言纪要

【纪要译文】

决定:理事会同意:

(1)原则上批准关于召开国际卫生会议的决议原文。

(2)技术委员会的报告和建议将提交给经济及社会理事会下届会议。

(3)任命一个起草委员会,由中国、美国、哥伦比亚、英国、苏联、法国、希腊和加拿大的代表组成。

张先生(中国)询问,筹备委员会是否可以决定会议的方案,或者是否将向理事会下届会议报告,从而明确会议将在该届会议之后举行。

决定:理事会商定,起草委员会应按照指示的内容编写一份决议,并在理事会下届会议日期确定后讨论会议日期。

4. 张彭春在经社理事会第一届第 8 次会议上的发言

联合国经社理事会第一届第 8 次会议,于 1946 年 2 月 12 日下午 5 时至晚上 7 时 35 分,在英国伦敦圣公会总部大楼召开,该次会议的主要议题是召开国际贸易和就业会议的问题。中国代表张彭春参加了本次会议,并在会议上发言,其具体发言内容[①]会议纪要、纪要影像和纪要译文如下:

【会议纪要】

Mr. CHANG (China) fully appreciated the value of the United States resolution, but suggested that it paid perhaps too much attention to the elimination of restrictive practices and did not sufficiently stress the importance of positive measures for the development of under-industrialized areas. While not suggesting any specific amendment, he asked that this point be borne in mind when the final text was being drafted.

① UN Document: E/1stsess./PV. 1-14, p. 80.

【纪要影像】

Mr. CHANG (China) fully appreciated the value of the United States resolution, but suggested that it paid perhaps too much attention to the elimination of restrictive practices and did not sufficiently stress the importance of positive measures for the development of under-industrialized areas. While not suggesting any specific amendment, he asked that this point be borne in mind when the final text was being drafted.

图片 1.7 张彭春在经社理事会第一届第 8 次会议发言纪要

【纪要译文】

张先生(中国)充分赞赏美国决议的价值,但认为该决议可能过于重视消除限制性惯例,而没有充分强调采取积极措施促进欠工业化地区发展的重要性。虽然没有提出任何具体的修正,但他要求在起草最后案文时牢记这一点。

5. 张彭春在经社理事会第一届第10次会议上的发言

联合国经社理事会第一届第10次会议，于1946年2月15日下午5时至晚上7时15分，在英国伦敦圣公会总部大楼召开，该次会议的主要议题是继续讨论召开国际卫生会议：起草委员会提交的决议草案。① 中国代表张彭春参加了本次会议，并在会议上发言，其具体发言内容②会议纪要、纪要影像和纪要译文如下：

【会议纪要】

Mr. CHANG (China) referred to the declaration proposed jointly by the delegations for Brazil and China at San Francisco, in which it was recommended "that a general conference be convened within the next few months for the purpose of establishing an international health organization". He drew the attention of the Council to the fact that many months had elapsed since this declaration had been unanimously approved in May 1945.

Decision: *The Council decided, by eleven votes to five, that the Secretary-General should call the international health conference not later than 20 June* 1946.

---

① 本届第9次和第10会议仍然围绕召开国际卫生会议的问题继续展开讨论。在第9次会议上主席提交了由起草委员会起草的决议；张彭春在第10次会议上再次发言参与讨论，最后会议根据投票结果，以11票对5票，决定秘书长应在不迟于1946年6月20日召开国际卫生会议。

② UN Document: E/1stsess./PV.1-14, p. 88.

【纪要影像】

Mr. CHANG (China) referred to the declaration proposed jointly by the delegations for Brazil and China at San Francisco, in which it was recommended "that a general conference be convened within the next few months for the purpose of establishing an international health organization". He drew the attention of the Council to the fact that many months had elapsed since this declaration had been unanimously approved in May 1945.

Decision: *The Council decided, by eleven votes to five, that the Secretary-General should call the international health conference not later than 20 June 1946.*

图片 1.8　张彭春在经社理事会第一届第 10 次会议发言纪要

【纪要译文】

张先生(中国)提到巴西代表团和中国代表团在旧金山共同提出的宣言,其中重申"将在今后几个月内召开一次大会,以建立一个世界卫生组织"。他提请理事会注意,自该宣言于 1945 年 5 月获得一致通过以来,已经过去了好几个月。

决定:理事会以 11 票对 5 票决定,秘书长应不迟于 1946 年 6 月 20 日召开世界卫生大会。

6. 张彭春在经社理事会第一届第11次会议上的发言

联合国经社理事会第一届第11次会议，于1946年2月16日上午10时45分至下午1时35分，在英国伦敦圣公会总部大楼召开，该次会议的主要议题是讨论经社理事会核心委员会组成问题。中国代表张彭春参加了本次会议，并在会议上发言，其具体发言内容①会议纪要、纪要影像和纪要译文如下：

【会议纪要】

Mr. CHANG (China) stressed the fact that the composition of the commissions was the responsibility of the Council. It would surely be impossible for a small sub-committee to ascertain the opinions of all fifty-one of the United Nations, more especially now that the General Assembly had adjourned. The Council was not a body of experts and the composition of the full commissions would better be left to experts. He, therefore, proposed that each member of the Council should have the right to nominate an expert for all the nuclear commissions with the exception of the Commission on Narcotic Drugs. No country would be obliged to nominate an expert, but each would have the right to do so.

Mr. CHANG (China) announced that his proposal had been made for purely practical reasons and without the intention of putting the members of the Council in a privileged position. Two considerations should be taken into ac-

① UN Document: E/1stsess./PV.1-14, p. 93, pp. 94-95.

count with regard to his proposal:

(1) That the Council believed that experts should be selected, regardless of the country to which they belong; and

(2) That his proposal must be regarded as a transitional measure.

It would be impossible for the Council to have knowledge of experts representing all parts of the world, but the experts on the nuclear commissions would be in a better position to nominate further experts. Should the United Kingdom representative wish to state that a member of the Council might nominate an expert who was not a national of his country, Mr. Chang had no objection.

【纪要影像】

Mr. CHANG (China) stressed the fact that the composition of the commissions was the responsibility of the Council. It would surely be impossible for a small sub-committee to ascertain the opinions of all fifty-one of the United Nations, more especially now that the General Assembly had adjourned. The Council was not a body of experts and the composition of the full commissions would better be left to experts. He, therefore, proposed that each member of the Council should have the right to nominate an expert for all the nuclear commissions with the exception of the Commission on Narcotic Drugs. No country would be obliged to nominate an expert, but each would have the right to do so.

图片 1.9　张彭春在经社理事会第一届第 11 次会议发言纪要

Mr. CHANG (China) announced that his proposal had been made for purely practical reasons and without the intention of putting the

members of the Council in a privileged position. Two considerations should be taken into account with regard to his proposal:

(1) That the Council believed that experts should be selected, regardless of the country to which they belong; and

(2) That his proposal must be regarded as a transitional measure.

It would be impossible for the Council to have knowledge of experts representing all parts of the world, but the experts on the nuclear commissions would be in a better position to nominate further experts. Should the United Kingdom representative wish to state that a member of the Council might nominate an expert who was not a national of his country, Mr. Chang had no objection.

图片 1.10　张彭春在经社理事会第一届第 11 次会议发言纪要

【纪要译文】

张先生(中国)强调,各委员会的组成是理事会的责任。一个小型的小组委员会肯定不可能确认联合国所有 51 个会员国的意见,尤其是现在大会已经休会。理事会不是一个专家机构,整个委员会的组成最好由专家决定。因此,他提议,除麻醉药品委员会之外,理事会每个成员都应有权为所有核心委员会提名一名专家。没有哪个国家有义务提名专家,但每个国家都有权这样做。

张先生(中国)宣布,他的提议纯粹是出于实际原因,无意将理事会成员置于特权地位。关于他的提议,应该考虑到两个因素:

(1)理事会认为,挑选专家时不应考虑他们属于哪个国家;并且

(2)他的建议必须被视为过渡措施。

理事会不可能了解代表世界各地的专家,但核心委员会的专家将更有资格提名更多的专家。如果英国代表希望指出,理事会成员可以提名一名不是其本国国民的专家,张先生不反对。

7. 张彭春在经社理事会第一届第12次会议上的发言

联合国经社理事会第一届第12次会议，于1946年2月16日下午3时15分至晚上8时30分，在英国伦敦圣公会总部大楼召开，该次会议的主要议题之一是继续讨论经社理事会核心委员会组成问题。中国代表张彭春参加了本次会议，并在会议上发言，其具体发言内容①会议纪要、纪要影像和纪要译文如下：

【会议纪要】

Mr. CHANG (China) stated that the basic considerations of the matter had already been discussed and he therefore put forward the following proposal which he hoped would enable the Council to arrive at a final decision:

"*The Economic and Social Council*,

Believing that the commissions and their subordinate organs should be composed of highly qualified persons chosen on the basis of their individual qualifications,

Decides,

As an initial step in the procedure, that each member of the Council may designate an expert on any of the four nuclear commissions, and that all members may submit nominations of qualified candidates belonging to any Member of the United Nations on the commissions as they will finally be constituted."

① UN Document: E/1stsess./PV. 1-14, p. 110, p. 112, p. 113.

Mr. CHANG (China) agreed that the nuclear commissions should be as small as possible, and be staffed by experts of world repute.

The proposal of the United States representative that the nuclear commissions be limited to seven members each was then considered and Mr. CHANG (China) moved that the number of members for each commission should be increased to nine.

Decision: *The Council decided that the nuclear Commissions should consist of nine members each.*

The Council agreed to the President's suggestion that the sub-committee which it had been decided to set up should be composed as follows: China, Colombia, Czechoslovakia, France, Greece, Peru, Union of Soviet Socialist Republics, United Kingdom, United States of America.

【纪要影像】

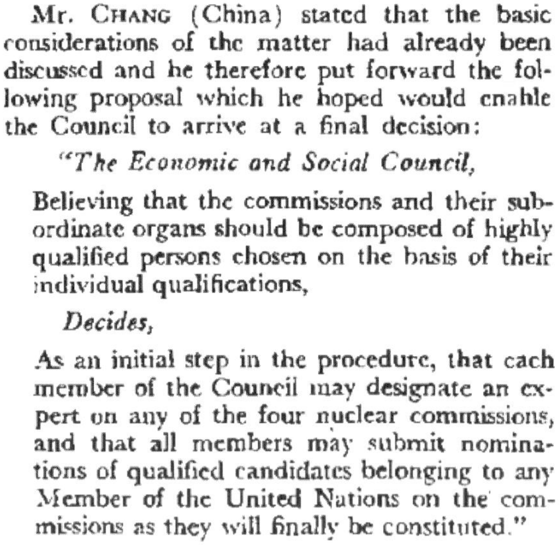

Mr. CHANG (China) stated that the basic considerations of the matter had already been discussed and he therefore put forward the following proposal which he hoped would enable the Council to arrive at a final decision:

"*The Economic and Social Council,*

Believing that the commissions and their subordinate organs should be composed of highly qualified persons chosen on the basis of their individual qualifications,

Decides,

As an initial step in the procedure, that each member of the Council may designate an expert on any of the four nuclear commissions, and that all members may submit nominations of qualified candidates belonging to any Member of the United Nations on the commissions as they will finally be constituted."

图片 1.11　张彭春在经社理事会第一届第 12 次会议发言纪要(1)

Mr. CHANG (China) agreed that the nuclear commissions should be as small as possible, and be staffed by experts of world repute.

The proposal of the United States representative that the nuclear commissions be limited to seven members each was then considered and Mr. CHANG (China) moved that the number of members for each commission should be increased to nine.

Decision: *The Council decided that the nuclear Commissions should consist of nine members each.*

The Council agreed to the President's suggestion that the sub-committee which it had been decided to set up should be composed as follows: China, Colombia, Czechoslovakia, France, Greece, Peru, Union of Soviet Socialist Republics, United Kingdom, United States of America.

图片 1.12　张彭春在经社理事会第一届第 12 次会议发言纪要

【纪要译文】

张先生(中国)说,此事的基本考虑因素已经讨论过,因此他提出以下建议,希望能使理事会作出最终决定:

“经济及社会理事会,

相信各委员会及其附属机构应由根据个人资格挑选的高度称职人员组成,

决定,

作为程序的第一步,理事会每个成员可在四个核心委员会中的任何一个中指定一名专家,所有成员可就最终组成的委员会提名属于联合国任何会员国的合格候选人。”

张先生(中国)同意核心委员会的规模应尽可能小,并应配备具有世界声誉的专家。

随后审议了美国代表提出的每个核心委员会限于七名成员的建议,张先生(中国)提议将每个委员会的成员人数增加到九名。

决定:理事会决定,各个核心委员会应由九名成员组成。

理事会同意主席的建议,决定设立的小组委员会的组成如下:中国、哥伦比亚、捷克斯洛伐克、法国、希腊、秘鲁、苏联、英国和美国。

8. 张彭春在经社理事会第一届第14次会议(闭门会议)上的发言

联合国经社理事会第一届第14次会议,于1946年2月18日晚上6时至7时,在英国伦敦圣公会总部大楼召开,该次会议的主要议题是审议委员会组成小组委员会的报告(E/26号文件)。中国代表张彭春参加了本次会议,并在会议上发言,其具体发言内容[①]会议纪要、纪要影像和纪要译文如下:

【会议纪要】

Mr. CHANG (China) proposed that the name of Mr. John C. H. Wu be added to the list and that "China" be deleted from the last phrase relating to this Commission.

Decision: *The composition of the Commission, with this modification, was approved.*

Mr. CHANG (China) requested that Dr. Franklin L. Ho be added and that "China" be deleted from the last phrase relating to this commission.

Decision: *The composition of the Commission, with this modification, was approved.*

① UN Document: E/1stsess./PV.1-14, p. 120, p. 121.

【纪要影像】

Mr. CHANG (China) proposed that the name of Mr. John C. H. Wu be added to the list and that "China" be deleted from the last phrase relating to this Commission.

Decision: *The composition of the Commission, with this modification, was approved.*

Mr. CHANG (China) requested that Dr. Franklin L. Ho be added and that "China" be deleted from the last phrase relating to this commission.

Decision: *The composition of the Commission, with this modification, was approved.*

图片 1.13　张彭春在经社理事会第一届第 14 次会议发言纪要

【纪要译文】

张先生(中国)建议将 John C. H. Wu(吴经熊)先生的名字列入名单，并从与本委员会有关的最后一句中删除“中国”。

决定:委员会的组成经过这一修改后获得核准。

张先生(中国)要求加上 Franklin L. Ho(何)博士,并从有关本委员会的最后一句中删除“中国”。

决定:委员会的组成经修改后获得批准。

第二章　联合国经社理事会第二届会议

（全文及纪要）

联合国经社理事会第二届会议于1946年5月25日上午10时30分，在美国纽约亨特学院开幕。美国总统杜鲁门致贺信，联合国秘书长亲自参加会议，并发表演讲。本届会议共举行了15次会议，于1946年6月21日结束，18个国家的正式代表参加了会议，并通过了第9(II)号决议，其中接受了核心委员会的报告E/38/Rev.1，并为人权委员会设立职权范围。第9(II)号决议还请秘书长汇编关于现有人权条约的资料、关于纽伦堡和东京审判的人权资料、以及关于人权发展情况的调查以及专门机构和国际组织的计划和宣言。这项任务分配给秘书处人权司，当时由约翰·汉弗莱(John Humphrey)领导。理事会将“落实人权和国际人权法案”①的任务交给新的人权委员会。

图片2.1 联合国经社理事会第二届第1次会议会场图，圆桌自左向右第四位为中国代表张彭春。（该图片1946年5月25日拍摄于纽约亨特学院）

① UN Document：E/RES/9(II)，见网址：http://www.un.org/en/ga/search/view_doc.asp?symbol=E/RES/9(II)。

图片 2.2　联合国经社理事会第二届第 1 次会议会场图,圆桌自左向右第四位为中国代表张彭春。
(该图片 1946 年 5 月 25 日拍摄于纽约亨特学院)

中国代表张彭春参加了本届会议,并在本届第 2 次会议、第 6 次会议、第 7 次会议、第 9 次会议、第 11 次会议、第 12 次会议和第 15 次会议上发表了重要讲话。每次会议档案资料分为两部分:(1)“会议发言全文记录及译文”包括“全文记录”“全文译文”;(2)“会议发言内容纪要”包括“会议纪要”“纪要影像”和“纪要译文”。现根据联合国档案会议记录和会议纪要,将张彭春的具体发言内容整理如下:

1. 张彭春在经社理事会第二届第 2 次会议上的发言

联合国经社理事会第二届第 2 次会议,于 1946 年 5 月 27 日上午 10 时 30 分至下午 1 时 12 分,在美国纽约亨特学院召开。张彭春参加了本次会议,并在会议上做了发言,提议召开国际卫生会议,为促进世界卫生组织的建立大声疾呼。[①] 中国不仅作为世界卫生组织的首倡者,还是力促者,本次会议上的发言无疑具有十分重要的意义。张彭春在本次会议上的部分发言内容也被当时录像记录下来,笔者 2014 年 10 月初在联合国纽约总部音像图书馆获取了这一珍贵的音像资料,但可惜的是,这段音像资料只是本次会议发言的部分内容。

(1) 会议发言全文记录及译文

【全文记录】

Mr. CHANG (China): Mr. President, since the Chinese Delegation, first at San Francisco and then in London had the honor to initiate and present the proposal for an International Health Conference, perhaps I may be permitted to open our discussion today with a few preliminary comments.

I wish, in the first instance, to express that that I feel must be the consen-

① UN Document: E/PV. 2, pp. 31-32. (Verbatim Record of the Second Meeting of the Second Session of the Economic and Social Council)

图片 2.3　根据笔者 2014 年 10 月初在联合国纽约总部音像图书馆所获得的音像资料截图，通过比较研究发现，该相关音像正是 1946 年 5 月 27 日中国代表张彭春在联合国经社理事会第二届第 2 次会议上的发言，也是笔者所掌握的唯一一段有关张彭春的珍贵音像资料。

sus of all members, that the Technical Preparatory Committee in Paris is to be congratulated on the successful conclusion of the task which our Council assigned to it at our first session. I believe that the documents it has prepared form a fully suitable basis for discussion and deliberation by the International Health Conference in June.

I wish also to record the appreciation of the Chinese Delegation in particular, and I also feel of all of us, of the work of the Secretariat in making the necessary preparations for this Conference. Such preparations have had to be made under trying and unusual conditions when the resources and the facilities of the staff have been taxed to the utmost. Considering those difficulties, the Secretariat is to be commented on being able to adhere to the schedule without due undue delay. Our respective governments, I am sure, will wish to facilitate to the fullest possible extent the making of the final preparations for the conference to assemble on June 19th. The Chinese Delegation is especially gratified that a proposal initiated by the Chinese and Brazilian Delegations in San Francisco, and later on presented by the Chinese Delegation in London is now coming to be carried out in action.

We all feel that the United Nations should, as an organization to be supported by the peoples of the world, carry out concrete measures, positive measures, constructive measures for the welfare of all mankind, and this is one of the constructive things that the United Nations will be doing. And it is hoped that this will be done with the idea, as I had the honor to present in London, as the war against the microbes in which we can, as I am sure we will, cooperate as in all warfare. And also, that we shall follow the enemy wherever he goes, in the sense of not regarding overmuch human-made or man-made national demarcations. ①

The Chinese Delegation, therefore, has the honor to support the proposal and to wish that the concrete action will be taken as soon as we planned. Thank you.

上述所收集到的音像材料内容如下：

Mr. CHANG (China): "I had the honor to present in London, as the war against the microbes in which we can, as I am sure we will, cooperate as in all warfare. And also, we shall follow the enemy wherever it goes, in the sense of not regarding overmuch human-made or man-made national demarcations.

The Chinese Delegation, therefore, has the honor in supporting the proposals and in wishing that the concrete action will be taken as soon as we planned. Thank you."

【全文译文】

张先生(中国)：主席先生，由于中国代表团首先在旧金山，随后在伦敦有幸发起并提出了国际卫生会议的建议，也许可以允许我以一些初步的

---

① 针对原文记录文献，通过对比音像资料中张彭春的发言，似乎两者有所不同，录像中有三个词听起来的确有些难以分辨清楚，感谢《中国日报》社高级编审 John Nicholson 先生和北京外国语大学高翻学院的李长栓教授帮助最后确认。幸好，两者之间的差别对内容的理解造成的差异不是太大。值得一提的是，张彭春先生在后面的发言中也引用了《孟子·尽心章句下》中的一句话："尽信《书》，则不如无《书》。"由于种种原因，会议记录中也可能存在某些差错和出入。即便如此，我们却不能否认或贬低原始档案的价值和对研究的意义。

评议开启我们今天的讨论。

首先，我要表示，我认为这必须是所有成员的共识，巴黎的技术筹备委员会将因成功完成我们理事会第一届会议分配给它的任务而受到祝贺。我认为，它准备的文件为6月份的国际卫生会议的讨论和审议提供了一个完全合适的基础。

我还要表示，中国代表团特别赞赏秘书处为本次会议所做的必要准备工作，我也感受到我们全体人员对其的赞赏。当工作人员的资源和设施负担到极致时，这种准备工作必须在艰苦和不寻常的条件下进行。考虑到这些困难，对秘书处能够遵守时间表而未造成不应有的延误将得到应有评价。我相信，我们各自的政府都希望尽可能充分地促进6月19日会议的最后筹备工作。中国代表团特别高兴的是，一项由中国和巴西代表团在旧金山发起的并由中国代表团在伦敦提出的建议，正在付诸实施。

我们都认为，联合国作为一个得到世界各国人民支持的组织，应该为全人类的福祉采取具体措施、积极措施和建设性措施，这是联合国将要做的建设性事情之一。正如我当时有幸在伦敦提出的那样，这是一场对抗微生物的战争，我相信我们会像在所有战争中一样进行合作。而且，无论敌人走到哪里，我们都要追踪到哪里，不要过多地看重人为的国家界限。

因此，中国代表团荣幸地支持这一建议，并希望尽快按计划采取具体行动。谢谢大家。

(2)会议发言内容纪要[①]

【会议纪要】

Mr. CHANG (China) congratulated the members of the Technical Preparatory Committee on the successful conclusion of the tasks assigned to them by the Council; he also desired to record the appreciation of the Chinese delegation for the work accomplished by the Secretariat at those meetings. He was es-

① UN Document: E_2ndsess-SR-1-15-EN, p. 15.

pecially gratified that constructive measures were now being taken on the proposal submitted by the Chinese and Brazilian delegations at San Francisco for the establishment of a single international health organization. He stressed the necessity of international co-operation in the fight against microbes, and expressed the hope that concrete action would be taken without delay.

【纪要影像】

Mr. CHANG (China) congratulated the members of the Technical Preparatory Committee on the successful conclusion of the tasks assigned to them by the Council; he also desired to record the appreciation of the Chinese delegation for the work accomplished by the Secretariat at those meetings. He was especially gratified that constructive measures were now being taken on the proposal submitted by the Chinese and Brazilian delegations at San Francisco for the establishment of a single international health organization. He stressed the necessity of international co-operation in the fight against microbes, and expressed the hope that concrete action would be taken without delay.

图片2.4:张彭春在联合国经社理事会第二届第2次会议发言纪要

【纪要译文】

张先生(中国)祝贺技术筹备委员会成员圆满完成理事会交给他们的任务;他还希望记录中国代表团对秘书处在这些会议上所做工作的赞赏。他特别高兴地看到,中国和巴西代表团在旧金山提出的关于建立一个单一的国际卫生组织的提案正在采取建设性措施。他强调了在防治微生物方面开展国际合作的必要性,并表示希望立即采取具体行动。

2. 张彭春在经社理事会第二届第6次会议上的发言

1946年5月31日下午2时45分至晚上6时3分,联合国经社理事会第二届第6次会议,在美国纽约亨特学院举行。本次会议的主要议题是审议人权委员会的报告、任命两个委员会以审议各委员会的报告、审议临时社会委员会的报告。中国代表张彭春参加了本次会议,并在会议上发言,其具体发言内容如下:

(1)会议发言全文记录[①]及译文

【全文记录】

Mr. CHANG (China): It is far from my wish to speak on the obvious, but I must add a word in regard to the importance of the Commission on Human Rights. The Chinese Delegation has the honor to congratulate the Commission on Human Rights for the most helpful report they have submitted and especially to congratulate the Chairman, Mrs. Roosevelt, for her enlightening and guiding spirit. Concerning the details of the workings of the Commission, such as documentation, draft declarations, methods of implementation and the composition of the Commission and of the Sub-Commission, I will reserve my humble opinion for discussion in the smaller committee. But may I just, in passing comment

① UN Document: E/PV. 6, pp. 19–25. (Verbatim record of the Sixth Meeting of the Second Session of the Economic and Social Council)

briefly on two points: One the perspective, secondly, the motivation. As a matter of fact, all the Commissions are methods of implementation for carrying out the various ideals and ideas implied in the words "human rights". Therefore, while we are thinking on this subject, our works seem to be hollow, our thoughts seem to be vain, if they should only concern the technical matters and detailed consideration.

In regard to the perspective we are actually, as we are all conscious, carrying on a modern trend that started from the Eighteenth Century. From that time on the various impressions for the rights of man had been maintained and fought for under varying conditions. During the Eighteenth Century, fortunately, there was, as a matter fact, for a period, a closer understanding upon the different ways of thinking and perhaps there has been since that time. It was during the Eighteenth Century, for instance, when the humble systems of thought from my own country reached Europe. For instance, in regard to our political thinking and educational and economic thinking, I am not going into that at all at this junction. However, for instance, a sentence like Mencius' saying that in government the people are the most important, institutions come next and Kings are of least importance. That must have been considered quite an atomic bomb in the days when Kings were supposed to be the State themselves and in regard to educational and economic matters, for instance, when we go back to such writers and thinkers like Koenig, Voltaire, Condercet, not to mention half a dozen others like Leibnitz; they all had their ideas on this matter, on the importance of the individual, especially on the importance of an educational system. That, however, is not only in terms of an abstract theory but also in terms of the concretization in the form of a political technique.

What I have in mind, then, is the matter of the free competitive civil service examinations. That will help us one way of getting the equality of talents, so to speak, to reach the administration of this state.

I shall not go on in that spirit but, nevertheless, during the 19th century there was a hundred years or more of what we might call a myopic conceptions concerning relative values. We are very happy that now we are reaching the middle of the 20th century and we look forward, I might say, to the coming of the new humanism. It is not so much only the details but this idea that is most important. A new humanism must prevail. Otherwise, all the various ingenious methods that we may be working out will have no motivation whatsoever.

Now I reach my second point, namely motivation. What is the motivation which is considered on this Commission on Human Rights as well as all the other activities under the Economic and Social Council? The motivation, as we have said again and again, is human freedom or the respect for human dignity, especially the dignity of human individuals. Now we have not time to enter into it in detail. May I just briefly in one sentence comment on this, that after all self-respect must come from mutual respect. In other words, it is a matter of considering the meaning of man. The meaning of man really derives of what we often think of as mutual consideration or, if you like, — if I may be allowed to introduce a Chinese word, "two-man-mindedness" — and that is the consideration always not only in terms of one side but also in regard to how the other man feels in regard to every situation.

Mr. President, I am sorry to have drawn your thought to these questions, but it seems to me that aside from the various details, we must keep in our minds, especially at this stage in the world's history, two things: namely, the perspective not only of the work of the Human Rights Commission but the work of the Economic and Social Council and of the United Nations as a whole; and, secondly, in regard to motivation, after all, the most important thing is to have this motivation or ingenuity cannot work and will not work.

【全文译文】

张先生(中国):就显而易见的问题发言并非我所愿,但我必须补充一句关于人权委员会重要性的话。中国代表团荣幸地祝贺人权委员会提交了最有益的报告,特别是祝贺主席罗斯福夫人的启发和指导精神。关于委员会工作的细节,例如文件、宣言草案、执行方法以及委员会和小组委员会的组成,我将保留我的拙见,供较小的委员会讨论。不过,我只想简单地谈谈两点:一是观点,二是动机。事实上,所有委员会都是实现"人权"一词所隐含的各种理想和理念的执行方法。因此,当我们思考这个问题时,我们的工作似乎是空洞的,我们的思想似乎是徒劳的,如果它们只涉及技术问题和细节考虑的话。

从这个角度来看,我们实际上,正如我们所有人都意识到的那样,正在进行一种始于 18 世纪的现代趋势。从那时起,人们一直保持着对人权的各种印象,并在各种条件下为之奋斗。幸运的是,在 18 世纪,事实上,有一段时间人们对不同的思维方式有了更深入的了解,也许从那时起就如此。例如,在 18 世纪,来自我自己国家的谦卑思想体系传到了欧洲。举例来说,关于我们的政治思想、教育和经济思想,我在这里根本不谈这些。然而,例如孟子的一句话,民为贵,社稷次之,君为轻。在君王被认为是国家本身的时代,在教育和经济问题上,这一定被认为是一颗原子弹,例如,当我们回到像柯尼格、伏尔泰、康德塞特这样的作家和思想家,更不用说像莱布尼茨这样的其他六位作家和思想家了;在这个问题上,他们都有自己的想法,关于个人的重要性,特别是关于教育制度的重要性。然而,这不仅是一种抽象的理论,而且是一种政治技巧形式的具体化。

因此,我心目中的问题是自由竞争的公务员考试。这将是有助于我们实现人才平等的一种方式,可以说,这将有助于我们实现国家行政管理。

我不会继续这样说,但是,在 19 世纪,有一百年或更长的时间,我们可以称之为关于相对价值的短视观念。我们非常高兴,现在我们正进入 20 世纪中叶,我可以说,我们期待着新人文主义的到来。最重要的不仅仅是细节,而是这个理念。新的人文主义必须占上风。否则,我们可能正在研究的各种巧妙的方法将毫无动机。

现在我要谈谈我的第二点,即动机。人权委员会以及经济及社会理事会下的所有其他活动的动机是什么?正如我们一再指出的那样,其动机是人的自由或尊重人的尊严,特别是人的个体尊严。现在我们没有时间详细讨论。请允许我用一句话简单地评论一下,毕竟自尊必须来自相互尊重。换句话说,这是一个考虑人的意义的问题。人的意义实际上来源于我们通常认为的相互体贴,或者,如果你愿意的话,——如果允许我引入一个中文词,"仁"①——这是一种感觉,不仅考虑到一方,而且考虑到另一方对每种情况的感受。

主席先生,很抱歉让你想到这些问题,但在我看来,特别是在世界历史的现阶段,除各种细节之外,我们必须牢记两件事,即不仅是人权委员会的工作视角,而且是经济及社会理事会和整个联合国的工作视角;第二,关于动机,毕竟,最重要的是要有这种动机,否则,创造力就不能起作用,也不会起作用。

(2)会议发言内容纪要②

【会议纪要】

Mr. CHANG (China) congratulated the Commission on Human Rights on behalf of the Chinese delegation, and especially its Chairman, for the results achieved. He suggested that it was important, during the discussion on human

---

① 笔者注:本次会议上首次提到"two-man-mindedness",这是张彭春所造的一个词。根据笔者掌握的材料,1947 年 6 月 17 日,在《世界人权宣言》起草委员会第一届第 8 次会议上,张彭春将儒家思想中的核心理念——"仁"的概念引入起草过程,并提到了这个他本人所造的词。他在后面这次会议上对该词进行了解释,认为"仁"即体现了"两个人之间能够感觉到对方的存在"即"对他人的感觉或同情"。(见 UN Document: E/CN. 4/AC. 1/SR. 8, p. 2.)

② UN Document: E_2ndsess-SR-1-15-EN, pp. 41-42.

rights, not only to consider details of immediate work, but to keep in mind the larger issues which were involved. He pointed out that human rights were too large a concept for one commission and that all other organs of the United Nations were concerned with the carrying out of this concept. He recalled the development of human rights during the last one hundred and fifty years and felt that there existed now a new humanism, as otherwise there would be no incentive for the efforts that were made. Those incentives must be the ideals of human freedom and human dignity.

【纪要影像】

Mr. CHANG (China) congratulated the Commission on Human Rights on behalf of the Chinese delegation, and especially its Chairman, for the results achieved. He suggested that it was important, during the discussion on human rights, not only to consider details of immediate work, but to keep in mind the larger issues which were involved. He pointed out that human rights were too large a concept for one commission and that all other organs of the United Nations were concerned with the carrying out of this concept. He recalled the development of human rights during the last one hundred and fifty years and felt that there existed now a new humanism, as otherwise there would be no incentive for the efforts that were made. Those incentives must be the ideals of human freedom and human dignity.

图片 2.5　张彭春在经社理事会第二届第 6 次会议发言纪要

【纪要译文】

张先生(中国)代表中国代表团祝贺人权委员会特别是其主席所取得的成果。他建议,在人权问题讨论中,重要的是不仅要思考目前工作的细节,而且要铭记涉及的更大问题。他指出,人权对于一个委员会来说是一个太大的概念,联合国所有其他机构都关心这一概念的落实。他回顾了人权在过去 150 年中的发展历程,并认为现在存在着一种新的人道主义,否则的话,就不会有动力去付出所作的一切努力。那些动力肯定是人的自由和人类尊严的理想。

3. 张彭春在经社理事会第二届第7次会议上的发言

1946年6月4日下午2时30分至5时45分,联合国经社理事会第二届第7次会议,在美国纽约亨特学院举行。本次会议的主要议题是通过一项补充议事规则、审议经济和就业委员会的报告。中国代表张彭春参加了本次会议,并在会议上发言,其具体发言内容如下:

(1)会议发言全文记录[①]及译文

【全文记录】

Mr. CHANG (China): Mr. President, we have before us the report of the Economic and Employment Commission. The eminent Members of this nuclear commission are to be congratulated for their constructive and clarifying suggestions and recommendations. The attention given to the problems requiring immediate attention such as the setting up a Sub-commission on Economic and Reconstruction of Devastated Areas is altogether justified and commendable. We are also conscious of the importance and crucial function of the Economic and Social Council in securing continued world economic expansion, economic stability and improved living standards. In the performance of that function the Council will rely essentially on the expert advice of the Economic and Employ-

① UN Document: E/PV. 7, pp. 25-36. (Verbatim record of the Seventh Meeting of the Second Session of the Economic and Social Council) ment Commission, especially as it will be enlarged in membership and supported by Sub-commissions of adequate strength.

The whole world is eagerly awaiting what this Council will do to assist in the much needed economic development, especially in certain areas that are comparatively under-industrialized and to suggest effective means whereby instability and unemployment be minimized, if not avoided in the industrialized area. It is but natural that our economic thinking has been preoccupied with conditions in countries that have attained high degrees of economic achievement. Their significance would not in any way be overlooked and their place in the economic structure of the world of today is potent and pivotal.

Yet, Mr. President, I would like to ask your special indulgence to allow me to draw your attention to the far reaching and deeply stirring significance of what I may call the economically low pressure areas of the world. During our recent war years—that is, the Chinese war years—between 1937 and 1945, I was sent by my Government on roving commissions and diplomatic posts not only in the industrialized areas of Europe and North America but also in the less developed areas in the Middle East and Latin America. Aside from the immediate political and military events that naturally caught my attention, I was particularly struck by the common characteristics of the areas that are under-industrialized. My observations of these economically low pressure areas clarify and illuminc many of thc cxpcricnccs which I havc had in somc parts of thc Far East. I am led to feel that the attention so far given to economically low pressure areas in the world has been altogether inadequate. We are much too strong with respect to the temporary existing contentions and conflicts. We must learn to envisage the world as a whole, giving due consideration to the economically less developed areas not only because of the huge populations and potential resources, not only because they supply the raw materials and furnish the markets for the manufactured goods of the industrialized countries, but also because they serve as the meeting places for conflicts and contention of the industrialized powers. It is in these economically low pressure areas that we can detect and delineate the shape of things to come in international struggles, actual and potential.

Mr. President, time does not allow me to go into details. I shall only comment very briefly on the following points. First, the hunger for industrialization. under-industrialized areas of today are no longer as subdued and overawed as they were before the First World War. I think you understand what I mean. They no longer follow without protest the docile orbits prescribed for them by the powerful industrial nations. They apply especially to those countries which have experience and advanced cultural development at various times and in different aspects before the impact of modern industrialism. This hunger for industrialization is very well illustrated by the following statement: "A country without its own industries is destined to end up as a colony of countries more industrialized than herself. It is manufacturing industry that gives the tone of progress. To process natural riches, whether agricultural or a mineral, amounts to nothing if the country cannot or does not know how to transform them. The mere wealth of materials without an industrious and intelligent population is rather a danger than an advantage. A people which is not capable of producing its own machinery, motors, tools and armaments has no right to call itself independent. This passage, Mr. President, I have taken from a newspaper in Chile, "El Mercurio, Val Paraiso, Chile", that appeared in any paper in the Far East, in the Middle East, or in other less developed areas.

It is realized in certain countries that their economic systems have been encroached upon by the industrial nations and they have been made producers of only raw materials. The industrial revolution which began in Europe towards the end of the eighteenth century gradually submerged them with a flow of cheap machine-made articles, sometimes forced into the country duty free under the favor of so-called Capitulations. These "unequal treaties"—again I do not need to explain—fortunately have been dispensed with in most of the countries where special privileges were maintained by the industrial powers.

There is another phenomenon which might be called specialization in raw material exports. When I traveled and a resided in South America, I was led to observe the admirable new industrial projects in such countries as Brazil, Chile, Colombia, Peru, and others. It is significant that most of the countries in Latin America depend upon exports of a single product such as coffee, petroleum, sugar, meats, copper and other minerals. The single product for export often accounts for fifty per cent or more of the total export values of these countries. This type of economy is most sensitive to shifts in the world market demand and to changes in world prices. Prosperity and depression seem to be altogether outside of the possibility of rational control. These countries with the specialized products for export deserve our sympathetic understanding and support. In the past, the various agricultural, mining, pastoral and forest resources have been exploited to meet the needs of the industrial countries.

Great obstacles and confounding confusion still stand in the way of industrial development in the economically low pressure areas. It is, therefore, the duty of this Council to pay special attention to the problems of industrialization for the benefit of the peoples that live in these areas.

The second point is mutual trade benefit. There are obvious reasons why industrial development of backward areas is desirable for the industrial countries. External investment has been pointed out as a solution for economic stagnation and decline in the so-called mature economies as distinct from the cures for the short-run business fluctuations.

The development of under-industrialized areas presents an investment opportunity to the industrialized countries. That is obvious. The subsequent rise of the income level of the less developed areas will naturally stimulate full employment in the industrialized countries and benefit world trade in general. Economic progress in one area will spur onward the progress in all. A statement such as this seems to me a very significant quotation. "As the countries of the world improve themselves economically, as they increase their productive efficiency, as they expand their purchasing power by developing their resources, the pattern of the world trade will change. There should be no illusion about that. The pattern of world trade will change, but the whole tempo of trade and industrial activity in all areas will increase. The benefits of increased industrialization throughout the world are therefore recognized as applying not only to the areas where such increased industrialization occurs, but also to the world at large, including countries already heavily industrialized." That is the end of the quotation. This quotation was taken from a report of the International Business Conference held at Rye, New York in November, 1944.

The third point, briefly, I call "Ferment and Friction". The first point, "Hunger for Industrialization", the second point, "Mutual Trade Benefits", the third point, "Ferment and Friction". The extension of industrial activities into less developed areas often stirs up an outcry against exploitation and imperialism. Consequently, great care should be given to the manner and method of collaboration between the industrialized countries and the less developed areas. There is always a great temptation on the part of investors to use financial or political strength to seek what is convenient to themselves in the areas where investment takes place. Mr. President, I believe economic imperialism has ceased to be a deliberate policy, but it remains true that concerted international action is necessary to adjust financial and industrial intercourse between nations, it will be desirable to draft a suggested code of international investments, setting down the conditions in lending and borrowing countries that are conducive to such investments. The Council will be tremendously assisted if the Economic and Employment Commission will study these matters and render their expert advice.

Friction also exists between and more industrial powers in their competition for raw materials and markets. Suspension and jealousies thrive and abound. It seems imperative that all such sensitive spots should be closely watched by the Commission—otherwise we will not be doing our duty—and it is hoped, by means of systematic surveying and reporting, the fields of friction, both actual and potential, should be brought to the attention of the Council and of the whole world.

Fourth and lastly, I have just time to comment briefly on Cultural Changes and Cooperation. Changes in economic structure have their effect in many directions—political, social and intellectual. The repercussions often spread beyond national boundaries. New social and economic ideas and institutions replace the old and bring about far-reaching effects. It will be very useful for the Council to be informed by the Economic and Employment Commission on the social and political consequences arising from the efforts in economic development in various parts of the world.

Furthermore, cultural changes in the less developed areas invite cultural cooperation from the more industrialized parts of the world. The training of the new personnel—to take only one instance—needed in the economic transformation can be greatly assisted through international cooperation. Instances are already evident everywhere of such cultural cooperation and exchange.

Mr. President, I confess that I have already taken much time but the world significance of the economically low pressure areas is too pressing to be overlooked. The function of Economic and Employment Commission, as envisaged, includes attention given to the problems of the less developed areas. It is absolutely necessary that a Sub-commission on economic development be set up to advise the Commission on the method of increasing production, productivity and levels of consumption with special attention to the less developed regions of the world.

The Chinese Delegation is inclined to think that the Council might find a Sub-commission inadequate to cope with such a vast program. We, therefore, may in due course wish to propose the enlarging of the Sub-commission into a full commission devoting its concentrated attention to the problems of economic development of the "low pressure" areas, not only for the welfare of the peoples in these areas, but for the betterment of man's estate in all parts of the world. Meanwhile, Mr. President, as the Economic and Employment Commission, in accordance with its terms of reference, is to concern itself with two aspects of the world economy, economic stability and economic development and progress, it seemed to me that in the selection of its members, better distribution should be sought between experts on economic stability and experts on economic development. Nationals from less developed countries should be adequately represented. This question may be discussed in the contemplated Sub-Committee on the Composition of the Commissions.

Mr. President, people all over the world are longing for a standard of living and for some of them a rising standard of living means at present a stay from starvation. The conscience of the world cannot be set at ease unless action is taken towards that goal.

To conclude, as a statement of the idea of economic and social adjustment in the world, please permit me to quote a passage attributed to Confucius formulated some two thousand and five hundred years ago which expresses even today the dream of all mankind. The passage is as follows: "When the Ta Tao or Grand Way prevails, the world is for the welfare of all. Officers are selected because of their virtue and competence. Mutual confidence is promoted and peaceful relations are maintained. People regard not only their own parents as parents not only their own children as children. Provisions are made for the aged; employment is provided for the able-bodied and education is afforded to the young. Widows and widowers, orphans and the childless, the crippled and the deformed are all cared for. Men have their occupations and women have their homes. Surplus goods are not to be wasted; they need not be kept as one's own. Labor is not to be idle; work is not necessarily for self only." Please allow me to repeat these phrases—they seem so modern. "Surplus goods are not to be wasted; they need not be kept as one's own. Labor is not to be idle; work is not necessarily for self only. Scheming and intrigues are repressed, and banditry and rebellion do not arise. As a result there is no need of shutting the house gate at night. Such is the Age of Grant Harmony."

President: Thank you, Dr. Chang, for pointing the Grand Way.

【全文译文】

张先生(中国):主席先生,我们面前有经济和就业委员会的报告。应祝贺该核心委员会的知名成员提出建设性和明确的意见和建议。对需要立即关注的问题给予关注,例如设立一个受破坏地区经济和重建小组委员会,是完全合理和值得赞扬的。我们还意识到经济及社会理事会在确保世界经济持续扩张、经济稳定和生活水平提高方面的重要性和关键作用。在履行这一职能时,理事会将主要依靠经济和就业委员会的专家意见,特别是因为它的成员将增加,并得到有足够实力的小组委员会的支持。

全世界都在急切地等待本理事会将如何协助那些亟需发展经济的特别是某些工业化程度相对较低的地区,并为工业化地区提出有效的方法,如果不能避免的话,也要尽量减少其社会不稳定和失业的状况。很自然,我们对经济的考虑,总是关注那些取得了高度经济成就的国家的状况。它们的重要性绝不会被忽视,它们在当今世界经济结构中的地位是强有力和关键性的。

然而,主席先生,我想请求您特别的恩惠,允许我把你们的注意力转向我所称的世界经济"低压"地区,关注它们对世界经济的深远意义和影响。在 1937 年到 1945 年的战争年代,也是中国抗战的岁月,我受我的政府派遣，不仅在欧洲和北美等发达地区，也在中东和拉美等不发达地区，担任须经常奔走的职务和外交职务。我除了很自然地关注即时的政治事件和军事事件外，还特别注意到那些欠工业化地区的共同特点。对这些经济"低压"地区的观察使我对曾经在远东地区的许多经历有了清楚的认识。使我感到，迄今为止，我们给予世界经济"低压"地区的关注是完全不够的，我们过多地关注临时的争斗和冲突。我们必须学会把世界看成一个整体，给予经济欠发达地区应有的关注。正确看待经济欠发达地区，这不仅仅由于它们拥有众多的人口和潜在的资源，也不仅仅由于它们为工业发达国家的产品提供原材料和市场，还因为它们成为工业化国家冲突与争斗的场所。正是在这些经济"低压"地区，我们能够看到实际的和潜在的国际间的争斗。

主席先生，时间不允许我详述细节。我只能非常简短地阐述以下几点。首先，对工业化的渴望。今天的欠工业化地区不再像第一次世界大战前那样被压制和被吓倒。我想你明白我的意思。它们对工业强国的指令不再唯命是从。那些在现代工业化影响之前，在各个时期和不同方面都曾经历过较高程度的文化发展的国家尤其如此。以下陈述很好地说明了这种对工业化的渴望："一个没有自己工业的国家注定会沦为比她工业化程度更高的国家的殖民地。制造业是进步的基调。如果一个国家不能够或不知道如何改造自然财富，那么拥有自然财富，无论是农业财富还是矿产财富，都毫无意义。只有物质财富而没有勤劳智慧的人民，这与其说是一种优势，不如说是一种危险。一个不能生产自己的机器、汽车、工具和武器的民族，无权自称独立。"我从智利的报纸上摘录下这段话，它登载在 1942 年 3 月 14 日智利瓦尔帕莱索的《信使报》上。同样的陈述也能在远东、中东或其他欠发达地区的报纸上看到。

某些国家认识到，它们的经济体系受到工业国家的侵蚀，它们被当做只生产原材料的生产者。18 世纪末开始于欧洲的工业革命逐渐将这些国家淹没于大量廉价的工业品的汪洋大海中，有时还被迫在所谓投降条约条款的恩惠下成为免税国。这些"不平等条约"——幸运的是，我无需再次解释——在那些工业大国过去维持特权的大多数国家中都已经被废除了。

还有一种现象可以称为原材料出口的专业化。在我旅居南美时,曾在巴西、智利、哥伦比亚、秘鲁和其他国家参观了令人赞叹的新兴工业项目。重要的是,拉丁美洲大多数国家依赖单一产品的出口,如咖啡、石油、糖、肉类、铜和其他矿物。单一出口产品往往占这些国家出口总值的50%或以上。这种类型的经济对世界市场需求的变化和世界价格的变化最为敏感,繁荣和萧条似乎完全超出了理性控制的范围。这些拥有专门出口产品的国家值得我们同情地理解和支持。过去,各种农业、矿产、牧业和森林资源一直为满足工业国家的需求而受到盘剥。

经济"低压"地区的工业发展仍然面临巨大的障碍和混乱。因此,本理事会的职责是:为了居住在这些地区的人民的利益而特别关注这些地区的工业化问题。

第二点是贸易互惠。有很明显的理由说明"落后"地区的工业发展合乎工业国家的需要。与短期医治商业涨落的手段截然不同,对外投资是解决所谓成熟经济中经济停滞或衰退的一种办法。

工业欠发达地区的发展为工业国家提供了投资机会,这是显而易见的。欠发达地区收入水平的上升自然会刺激工业国家的充分就业,并使世界贸易总体受益。一个地区的经济发展将推动整体的发展。在我看来,这段话非常有意义:"随着世界各国经济水平的提高,生产效率的提高,以及通过开发资源扩大购买力,世界贸易的格局将发生变化。对此不应抱有幻想。世界贸易的格局将发生变化,但贸易和工业的整体节奏将发生变化,所有地区的工业活动将增加。因此,全世界工业化程度提高的好处不仅适用于工业化程度提高的地区,而且也适用于整个世界,包括已经高度工业化的国家。"这段话摘自1944年11月在纽约附近的拉伊举行的国际商业大会的报告。

第三点,简而言之,我称之为"骚动与摩擦"。第一点是"工业化的渴望",第二点是"贸易互惠",第三点是"骚动与摩擦"。将工业活动扩展到欠发达地区,常常激起对剥削和帝国主义的强烈抗议。因此,应十分注意工业化国家与欠发达地区之间合作的方式和方法。投资者总是很容易利用财政或政治力量,在进行投资的领域寻求对自己有利的东西。主席先生,我相信经济帝国主义已不再是一种审慎的政策,但确实需要采取协调一致的国际行动,来调整国家间的金融和工业往来,最好建议起草一份国际投资守则,为借贷双方制定有利于此类投资的条件。如果经济和就业委员会研究这些问题并提供专家意见,理事会将受益匪浅。

在工业强国竞争原材料和市场的过程中也存在摩擦,猜忌与嫉妒迅速膨胀。这就迫切需要委员会密切关注这些敏感点,否则我们将无法履行职责。此外,希望通过系统的调查和报告,使实际的和潜在的摩擦能够得到理事会和全世界的关注。

第四,也是最后一点,我有时间简单地谈谈文化变革与合作。经济结构的变化会在政治、社会和智力等多个方面产生影响,其影响往往超越国界。新的社会和经济理念和制度取代旧的理念和制度,并产生深远的影响。经济和就业委员会向理事会通报世界各地经济发展努力所产生的社会和政治结果将非常有益。

此外,欠发达地区的文化变革也吸引了世界上工业化程度较高的地区的文化合作。仅举一例,通过国际合作能够极大地推动经济转化中新型人才的培养。这种文化合作与交流的例子已经随处可见。

主席先生,我承认我已经花了很多时间,但经济“低压”地区的世界意义太紧迫了,不容忽视。按照设想,经济和就业委员会的职能包括关注欠发达地区的问题。绝对有必要设立一个经济发展小组委员会,在特别注意世界上欠发达地区的同时,就提高生产、生产力和消费水平的方法向委员会提供咨询意见。

中国代表团认为,理事会可能觉得一个小组委员会不足以应付如此庞大的项目。因此,我们不妨在适当时候建议将小组委员会扩大为一个完备的委员会,集中注意“低压”地区的经济发展问题。这不仅是为了这些地区人民的福祉,而且是为了改善全世界人民的生存状况。与此同时,主席先生,由于经济和就业委员会根据其职权范围将关注世界经济的两个方面,即经济稳定和经济发展与进步,我认为在挑选其成员时,应寻求经济稳定专家和经济发展专家之间的更好分配。较不发达国家的国民应得到充分代表。这一问题可在拟议的委员会组成小组委员会中讨论。

主席先生,全世界人民都渴望生活水平的提高,对其中一些人来说,生活水平的提高目前意味着他们摆脱饥饿。除非为实现这一目标而采取行动,否则世界的良心就无法得以安宁。

最后,作为对世界经济和社会调整理念的概括,请允许我引用大约2500年前孔子的一段话。它表达了甚至是当今全人类的梦想。这段话如下:

> "大道之行也,天下为公。选贤与能。讲信修睦。故人不独亲其亲,不独子其子,使老有所终,壮有所用,幼有所长。鳏、寡、孤、独、废、疾者皆有所养,男有分,女有归。货恶其弃于地也,不必藏于己;力恶其不出于身也,不必为己。"

请允许我重复一下这些句子——它们看上去是那样的富有现代含义。"货恶其弃于地也,不必藏于己;力恶其不出于身也,不必为己。是故谋闭而不兴,盗窃乱贼而不作,故外户而不闭。是谓大同。"

主席:谢谢张博士,你为我们指引了大道。

(2)会议发言内容纪要①

【会议纪要】

Mr. CHANG (China) congratulated the nuclear Commission on its report; he welcomed, in particular, the suggestion to establish a Sub-commission on Economic Reconstruction of Devastated Areas, and the importance attached to urgent economic problems.

Economic thinking in the past had perhaps been too much preoccupied

① UN Document: E_2ndsess-SR-1-15-EN, pp. 49-50.

with the problems of highly developed countries to the detriment of the economically low-pressure areas. A hunger for industrialization was now manifest in the less developed countries the economic systems of which had often in the past been encroached upon by the industrialized countries.

Special consideration must also be given to the many countries which depended largely upon the export of a single product, since this type of economy was particularly sensitive to fluctuations in demand and in world prices.

The industrialization of the less developed areas would benefit all countries, since it would provide an investment opportunity for the industrialized countries and would, in raising the standard of living of the low-pressure areas, provide additional markets for all.

Great care should, however, be given to the manner of collaboration between industrialized and less developed countries, to avoid the danger of pressure or exploitation. Concerted international action would be required. For instance, a draft code, governing international investments, for lending and borrowing countries should be drawn up.

The Commission should study all these questions and advise the Council. In addition, it should survey and bring to the attention of the Council actual or potential fields of friction between the industrial Powers, resulting from competition for raw materials and markets. It should also keep the Council informed of the social and political consequences arising from the efforts towards economic development in various parts of the world, and should endeavour to provide international cultural co-operation, such as the training of personnel to undertake programmes of industrialization.

The Chinese delegation doubted whether a Sub-commission on Economic Development would prove adequate for such a vast programme; his delegation might, therefore, propose in due course that the Sub-commission be transformed into a full commission, devoting its concentrated attention to the problems of economic development of "low-pressure" areas. In the meantime, since the attention of the Economic and Employment Commission would be devoted to both economic stability and economic development, a better distribution of experts in both types of problems was required, and the less developed countries should be adequately represented there.

【纪要影像】

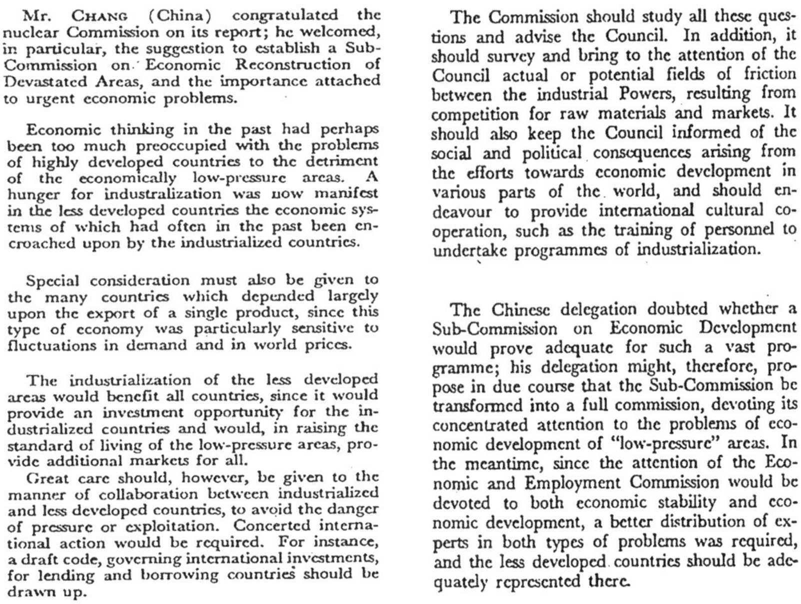

Mr. CHANG (China) congratulated the nuclear Commission on its report; he welcomed, in particular, the suggestion to establish a Sub-Commission on Economic Reconstruction of Devastated Areas, and the importance attached to urgent economic problems.

Economic thinking in the past had perhaps been too much preoccupied with the problems of highly developed countries to the detriment of the economically low-pressure areas. A hunger for industralization was now manifest in the less developed countries the economic systems of which had often in the past been encroached upon by the industrialized countries.

Special consideration must also be given to the many countries which depended largely upon the export of a single product, since this type of economy was particularly sensitive to fluctuations in demand and in world prices.

The industrialization of the less developed areas would benefit all countries, since it would provide an investment opportunity for the industrialized countries and would, in raising the standard of living of the low-pressure areas, provide additional markets for all.

Great care should, however, be given to the manner of collaboration between industrialized and less developed countries, to avoid the danger of pressure or exploitation. Concerted international action would be required. For instance, a draft code, governing international investments, for lending and borrowing countries should be drawn up.

The Commission should study all these questions and advise the Council. In addition, it should survey and bring to the attention of the Council actual or potential fields of friction between the industrial Powers, resulting from competition for raw materials and markets. It should also keep the Council informed of the social and political consequences arising from the efforts towards economic development in various parts of the world, and should endeavour to provide international cultural co-operation, such as the training of personnel to undertake programmes of industrialization.

The Chinese delegation doubted whether a Sub-Commission on Economic Development would prove adequate for such a vast programme; his delegation might, therefore, propose in due course that the Sub-Commission be transformed into a full commission, devoting its concentrated attention to the problems of economic development of "low-pressure" areas. In the meantime, since the attention of the Economic and Employment Commission would be devoted to both economic stability and economic development, a better distribution of experts in both types of problems was required, and the less developed countries should be adequately represented there.

图片 2.6　张彭春在经社理事会第二届第 7 次会议发言纪要

【纪要译文】

张先生(中国)祝贺核心委员会的报告,他特别欢迎关于设立一个灾区经济重建小组委员会的建议,以及对紧迫经济问题的重视。

过去的经济思维可能过于专注于高度发达国家的问题,而损害了经济低压地区的利益。欠发达国家现在表现出对工业化的渴望,这些国家的经济制度过去常常受到工业化国家的侵蚀。

还必须特别考虑到许多主要依赖单一产品出口的国家,因为这类经济对需求和世界价格的波动特别敏感。

欠发达地区的工业化将使所有国家受益,因为它将为工业化国家提供投资机会,并将在提高低压地区生活水平的同时为所有国家提供额外的市场。

然而,应十分注意工业化国家与欠发达国家之间的合作方式,以避免压力或剥削的危险。需要采取协调一致的国际行动。例如,应该为借贷国起草一份管理国际投资的准则草案。

委员会应研究所有这些问题,并向理事会提出建议。此外,它应调查并提请理事会注意工业大国之间因原材料和市场竞争而产生的实际或潜在摩擦领域。它还应随时向理事会通报世界各地经济发展努力所产生的社会和政治后果,并应努力提供国际文化合作,例如培训人员以从事工业化方案。

中国代表团怀疑经济发展小组委员会是否足以执行如此庞大的方案,因此,他的代表团可在适当时候提议将小组委员会转变为一个完整的委员会,集中注意“低压”地区的经济发展问题。与此同时,由于经济和就业委员会的注意力将集中于经济稳定和经济发展,因此需要更好地分配这两类问题方面的专家,欠发达国家应有充分的代表。

4. 张彭春在经社理事会第二届第9次会议上的发言

1946年6月5日下午2时35/45分[①]至5时45分，联合国经社理事会第二届第9次会议，在美国纽约亨特学院举行。本次会议的主要议题是继续审议经济和就业委员会的报告、审议临时交通和通讯委员会的报告等。中国代表张彭春参加了本次会议，并在会议上发言，其具体发言内容如下：

(1)会议发言全文记录[②]及译文

【全文记录】

Mr. CHANG (China): Mr. President, my remarks will be very brief. Yesterday I had the honor of suggesting reasons why the under-industrialized areas should receive due attention from this Council. The Chinese Delegation is extremely gratified for the interest that argument has aroused, and in regard to the measures to be taken, great care naturally should be taken in the means of carrying out this great objective. Just to bring that to a plane which I think would be able to receive sympathetic support from all quarters—we are all interested in the elevation of the standard of living of by far the majority of the people

① 该次会议开始时间在全文记录中是"2时35分"，而在会议纪要中是"2时45分"。

② UN Document: E/PV.9, pp.56-61. (Verbatim record of the Eleventh Meeting of the Second Session of the Economic and Social Council)

of the world who live in so-called under-industrialized or less developed areas.

In regard to the "how", then may I suggest just simply three things. First, there should be a scientific, careful analysis of the inventiveness in that area. In other words, it should not simply go by a matter of coping things from other areas, from patterns and things that have already been done in other part of the world.

Therefore, first of all, there should be a careful study of the condition, of the needs as they are sensitive felt by the people in that area. Secondly, there should be a survey for stimulation and suggestion from experiences. Naturally, the experiences from other parts of the world—its successes as well as failures—should be taken into consideration. And thirdly, naturally—if you will allow me, I will use perhaps a cumbersome phrase, but I think it is necessary, that there should be a liberated inventiveness; there should not be too much of copying. There should be a looking-through, of paying attention, especially to the conditions and circumstances of how various methods have come into being; then we will be able to have a liberated inventiveness not only on the part of the people in areas concerned but also on the part of experts who may be called in to assist.

Consequently by paying attention to these three points, namely a sensitive, careful analysis of the needs felt in the areas concerned; secondly, an extensive, comprehensive survey of methods already worked for stimulation and suggestion, and thirdly, the attitude of liberated inventiveness. It is through this method, I hope, that we shall be able to approach this problem of industrialization of the undeveloped areas.

The reason why I make this point is that I surely see no reason for disagreement whatsoever, because it is something that concerns not only the majority of the population in the less-developed areas but also all the people, including surely the areas where industrialization has already taken place.

We thank, very much, all the fellow Members who have commented most graciously on my inadequate remarks of yesterday.

Thank you.

【全文译文】

张先生(中国):主席先生,我的发言将非常简短。昨天,我荣幸地提出了本理事会应适当关注欠工业化地区的理由。中国代表团对这一论点引起的兴趣感到极为满意,关于将要采取的措施,在实现这一伟大目标的手段上自然应该非常谨慎。为了使这一点达到一个我认为能够得到各方同情支持的水平,我们都对提高世界上大多数生活在所谓欠工业化或欠发达地区的人民的生活水平感兴趣。

关于“如何”的问题,我只想提出三件事。首先,应该对该领域的创造性进行科学、仔细的分析。换言之,它不应该简单地采用其他领域处理事情的方式,也不能简单地依据世界其他地区已经做过的事情或采取的模式。

因此,应该首先仔细研究该地区人民敏感的情况和需求。第二,应进行调查,从经验中获得激励和建议。当然,应该考虑世界其他地区的经验,包括成功和失败。第三,当然,如果允许的话,我可能会用一个笨拙的短语,但我认为有必要,应该有自由的创新;不应该有太多的复制。应该有一个通观,特别是关注各种方法产生的条件和情况;这样,我们将拥有一种自由的创造力,不仅能够体现在相关领域的人们身上,而且能够体现在可能求助的专家身上。

因此,通过关注这三点,既可以对有关地区的需求进行敏感、仔细的分析,又对已有的激励和建议方法进行广泛、全面的调查,再应有自由创新的态度。我希望通过这种方法,我们能够解决欠发达地区工业化的问题。

我提出这一点的原因是,我当然看不出有任何理由存在分歧,因为这不仅关系到欠发达地区的大多数人口,而且也关系到所有人,当然包括已经发生工业化的地区。

我们非常感谢各位同事,他们对我昨天的不充分言论发表了最客气的评论。

感谢大家。

(2)会议发言内容纪要①

【会议纪要】

Mr. CHANG (China) was gratified by the interest which his remarks concerning the development of under-developed areas had aroused. As regards the manner in which this development should be carried out, he suggested that the first step should be a careful, scientific and sympathetic study of the conditions and needs of the people of the area concerned. Secondly, past experience, successes and failures in other parts of the world should be taken into account, and a comprehensive survey should be made of methods already adopted to stimulate develop-

【纪要影像】

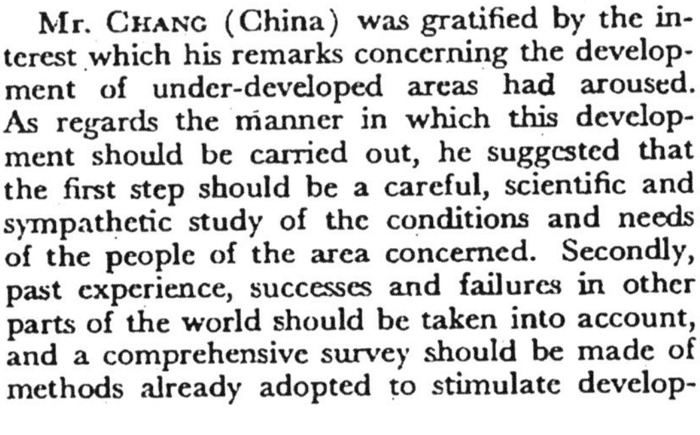
Mr. CHANG (China) was gratified by the interest which his remarks concerning the development of under-developed areas had aroused. As regards the manner in which this development should be carried out, he suggested that the first step should be a careful, scientific and sympathetic study of the conditions and needs of the people of the area concerned. Secondly, past experience, successes and failures in other parts of the world should be taken into account, and a comprehensive survey should be made of methods already adopted to stimulate develop-

图片 2.7　张彭春在经社理事会第二届第 9 次会议发言纪要

① UN Document: E_2ndsess-SR-1-15-EN, pp. 63-64.(值得说明的是本次会议纪要文件缺了第 64 页和第 65 页,正好缺少了张彭春先生在本次会议发言内容的后半部分,即第 64 页的内容。幸好有全文记录可供大家参考。)

【纪要译文】

张先生(中国)对他关于欠发达地区发展的发言引起的兴趣感到满意。关于应实现这一发展的方式,他建议,第一步应该是仔细、科学和富有同情心地研究有关地区人民的条件和需要。第二步应考虑到世界其他地区过去的经验、成功和失败,并对已经采取的促进发展的方法进行全面调查……

5. 张彭春在经社理事会第二届第11次会议上的发言

1946年6月7日下午2时45分至4时(7分)[①],联合国经社理事会第二届第11次会议,在美国纽约亨特学院举行。本次会议的主要议题是继续审议临时交通和通讯委员会的报告、审议统计委员会的报告。中国代表张彭春参加了本次会议,并在会议上发言,其具体发言内容如下:

(1)会议发言全文记录[②]及译文

【全文记录】

Dr. CHANG (China): Mr. President, please permit me to comment briefly on only three points. The first, beside the existing international bodies that deal with transport and communications, the Chinese Delegation would like to see initiated some form of inland transport organization for Asia, which might include, railway, highway and other inland transportation.

My second point is that the composition of the commission as it will be organized ought not to look geographical representation. It seems advisable that the membership should be more than the recommended twelve. I suggest that nine representatives be nominated by governments and six appointed on individ-

① 本次会议结束时间在全文记录中是“4时7分”,而在会议纪要中是“4时”。

② UN Document: E/PV. 11, pp. 25-42. (Verbatim record of the Eleventh Meeting of the Second Session of the Economic and Social Council) ual merits. In both cases, the Council naturally would exercise full powers of appointment. Geographical representation would be particularly important with respect to inland transport which the commission has recommended should, for the time being, remain regional in character.

Experts in one region and in certain technical aspects of one given field should not be expected to know equally well a situation obtaining in another region and having difficulties in certain technical situations.

My third point concerns the establishment of a Permanent Transport and Communications Commission. The Chinese Delegation fully agrees with the Temporary Commission's recommendation that in the ideal of one world a Permanent Commission on Transport and Communication is highly necessary and desirable. Such a Commission should be instrumental in harmonizing and correlating the complex activities of international transport and communications.

Thank you.

【全文译文】

张博士(中国):主席先生,请允许我仅就三点作简要评论。第一,除了处理运输和通信的现有国际机构外,中国代表团希望看到启动某种形式的亚洲内陆运输组织,其中可能包括铁路、公路和其他内陆运输。

第二点是委员会的组成,按照其组织方式,不应该看起来具有地域代表性。成员人数应超过建议的 12 人,这似乎是明智的。我建议 9 名代表由政府提名,6 名根据个人能力任命。在这两种情况下,理事会自然会充分行使任命权。就内陆运输而言,地域代表性尤为重要,委员会已建议内陆运输目前应保持区域性质。

某一个区域和某一特定领域内某些技术方面的专家,不应期待其同样了解另一区域的情况或同样了解在某些技术情况下遇到的困难。

第三点涉及设立一个常设交通运输委员会。中国代表团完全同意临时委员会的建议,即在一个世界的理想中,一个常设的交通运输委员会是非常必要和可取的。这样一个委员会应有助于协调和联络国际运输和通信的复杂活动。

非常感谢。

(2)会议发言内容纪要[①]

【会议纪要】

Mr. CHANG (China) made the following observations:

(1) In addition to the existing international bodies in the field of transport and communications, the Chinese delegation would like to see initiated some form of inland transport organization for Asia.

(2) The Commission should not lose sight of the need for fair geographical representation. In order to attain this purpose, the Chinese delegation thought that the proposed number of members of the full Commission should be increased. The speaker suggested that nine members of the Commission should be nominated by the governments, and six others appointed on the basis of individual merit, subject to the proviso that the Economic and Social Council would retain the right of confirming the appointments or approving the choice. The ultimate composition of the permanent Transport and Communications Commission was particularly important with respect to inland transport, which the nuclear Commission had recommended should remain regional in character. Experts who were familiar with most of the regions in one part of the globe, might very well not be equally familiar with other regions.

(3) The last point concerned the establishment of a permanent Transport and Communications Commission. The Chinese representative fully agreed with the conclusions in the report that such a Commission was highly desirable for the purpose of harmonizing and correlating international communications. The

① UN Document: E_2ndsess-SR-1-15-EN, p. 77.

need for such a Commission was undeniable.

【纪要影像】

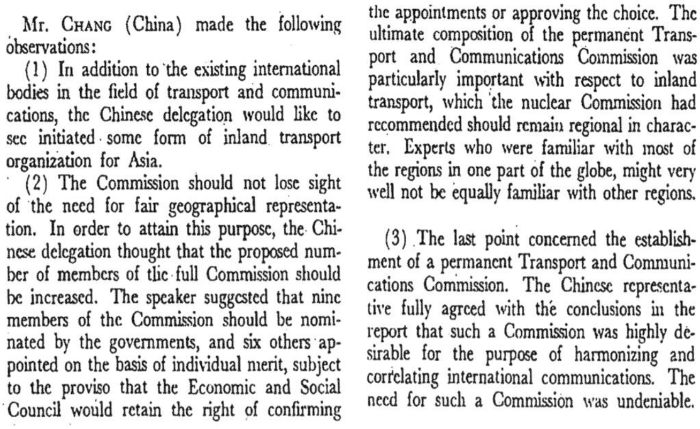

Mr. CHANG (China) made the following observations:

(1) In addition to the existing international bodies in the field of transport and communications, the Chinese delegation would like to see initiated some form of inland transport organization for Asia.

(2) The Commission should not lose sight of the need for fair geographical representation. In order to attain this purpose, the Chinese delegation thought that the proposed number of members of the full Commission should be increased. The speaker suggested that nine members of the Commission should be nominated by the governments, and six others appointed on the basis of individual merit, subject to the proviso that the Economic and Social Council would retain the right of confirming the appointments or approving the choice. The ultimate composition of the permanent Transport and Communications Commission was particularly important with respect to inland transport, which the nuclear Commission had recommended should remain regional in character. Experts who were familiar with most of the regions in one part of the globe, might very well not be equally familiar with other regions.

(3) The last point concerned the establishment of a permanent Transport and Communications Commission. The Chinese representative fully agreed with the conclusions in the report that such a Commission was highly desirable for the purpose of harmonizing and correlating international communications. The need for such a Commission was undeniable.

图片 2.8　张彭春在经社理事会第二届第 11 次会议发言纪要

【纪要译文】

张先生(中国)发表了以下意见:

(1)除了交通运输领域现有的国际机构外,中国代表团希望看到启动某种形式的亚洲内陆运输组织。

(2)委员会不应忽视公平地域代表性的需求。为了达到这一目的,中国代表团认为应该增加整个委员会的拟议成员人数。该发言者建议,委员会的 9 名成员应由各国政府提名,另外 6 名成员应根据个人能力任命,但前提是经济及社会理事会保留确认任命或批准选择的权利。就内陆运输而言,常设交通运输委员会的最终组成特别重要,核心委员会建议内陆运输应保持区域性。熟悉全球某一部分大多数地区的专家,很可能对其他地区没那么熟悉。

(3)最后一点涉及设立一个常设交通运输委员会。中国代表完全同意报告中的结论,即设立这样一个委员会对于协调和联络国际运输是非常可取的。成立这样一个委员会的需求是不可否认的。

6. 张彭春在经社理事会第二届第 12 次会议上的发言

1946 年 6 月 11 日上午 10 时 30 分至下午 1 时 30 分,联合国经社理事会第二届第 12 次会议,在美国纽约亨特学院举行。本次会议的主要议题是审议起草委员会提交的有关健康问题的报告和决议、哥伦比亚代表建立财政委员会的议案、设立一个人口委员会的问题、与在国际联盟主持下发放的某些国际贷款有关的问题。中国代表张彭春参加了本次会议,并在会议上发言,其具体发言内容如下:

(1)会议发言全文记录①及译文

【全文记录】

Dr. CHANG (China): Mr. President, on the establishment of a Fiscal Commission, the Chinese Delegation wishes to concur with the proposal of the Colombian Delegation. The international tax problem is one of the problems which all interested in the development of international trade and investment must tackle. We had, at the early days of our work, conceived of the disability of establishing and international trade organization to study the ways and means for the removal and adjustment of trade barriers, but we must also bear in mind that tax policies, if uncoordinated or unwisely conducted, constitute another

① UN Document: E/PV. 12, pp. 85-91. (Verbatim record of the Twelfth Meeting of the Second Session of the Economic and Social Council)

type of trade barrier. Our work in paving the way for expansion of world economy would not be complete without paying due attention to the tax problems.

Moreover, unstable or cumbersome physical structure in many countries often constitute obstacles to international investment. In my comments on the report of the Economic and Employment Commission I have urged the Council to request the Commission to pay attention to the problem of international investment and to study the conditions in lending and borrowing countries conductive to international investment. Mr. President, I believe a fiscal commission may help to study the fiscal aspects of the problem of international flow of capital.

Mr. President, all the countries in the world today are conscious of the evils of inflation and depression. In so far as inflation and depression arise from varied causes, it is recognized that government finance is an indispensable factor in dealing with such catastrophes. It may also be desirable to study the fiscal techniques, which are of assistance to the prevention of inflation and depression.

It is possible that the work of fiscal commission might overlap, when it is constituted, that of other commissions, especially that of Economic and Employment Commission. It will therefore be useful and necessary to confine the scope of the fiscal commission to purely technical matters, such as legal and administrative aspects of the question.

Subject to reservation on detail points which we must consider carefully later on, I am, in principle, in agreement with the Colombian Delegation in his proposal on the establishment of a fiscal commission.

【全文译文】

张博士(中国):主席先生,关于设立财政委员会,中国代表团同意哥伦比亚代表团的建议。国际税收问题是所有关心国际贸易和投资发展的人都必须解决的问题之一。在我们开展工作的早期,我们曾设想建立一个国际贸易组织来研究消除和调整贸易壁垒的方法和手段是无能为力的,但我们还必须记住,税收政策如果不协调或不明智地实施,将构成另一种贸易壁垒。如果不适当注意税收问题,我们为扩大世界经济铺平道路的工作就不可能完成。

此外,许多国家不稳定或烦琐的实体结构往往对国际投资构成障碍。在我对经济和就业委员会报告的评论中,我敦促理事会要求委员会注意国际投资问题,并研究借贷国有利于国际投资的条件。主席先生,我相信财政委员会可能有助于研究国际资金流动的财政问题。

主席先生,当今世界所有国家都意识到通货膨胀和萧条的危害。鉴于通货膨胀和萧条是由各种原因引起的,人们认识到政府财政是应对这类灾难不可或缺的因素。研究财政技术也是可取的,这有助于防止通货膨胀和萧条。

财政委员会成立后,其工作可能与其他委员会,特别是经济和就业委员会的工作重叠。因此,将财政委员会的范围局限于纯粹的技术性事项,例如该问题的法律和行政方面,将是有益和必要的。

我原则上同意哥伦比亚代表团关于建立一个财政委员会的建议,但对我们必须在以后仔细考虑的细节问题有所保留。

(2)会议发言内容纪要[①]

【会议纪要】

Mr. CHANG (China) supported the proposal for the establishment of a Fiscal Commission. Taxation policies, if unwisely conducted or not coordinated, might constitute a trade barrier.

Moreover, unstable or cumbersome fiscal structures were often obstacles to

---

① UN Document: E_2ndsess-SR-1-15-EN, pp. 86-87.

international investment. The proposed Fiscal Commission might help to study the fiscal aspects of the problem of the international flow of capital.

As for the universally recognized evils of inflation and depression, it was indisputable that governmental finance and taxation were indispensable instruments in dealing with such matters.

At the same time, in order that the work of the Fiscal Commission should not duplicate that of other commissions, it seemed desirable to confine its scope, as suggested in the proposal made by the representative of Colombia, to the technical aspects of public finance.

【纪要影像】

Mr. CHANG (China) supported the proposal for the establishment of a Fiscal Commission. Taxation policies, if unwisely conducted or not co-ordinated, might constitute a trade barrier.

Moreover, unstable or cumbersome fiscal structures were often obstacles to international investment. The proposed Fiscal Commission might help to study the fiscal aspects of the problem of the international flow of capital.

As for the universally recognized evils of inflation and depression, it was indisputable that governmental finance and taxation were indispensable instruments in dealing with such matters.

At the same time, in order that the work of the Fiscal Commission should not duplicate that of other commissions, it seemed desirable to confine its scope, as suggested in the proposal made by the representative of Colombia, to the technical aspects of public finance.

图片 2.9　张彭春在经社理事会第二届第 12 次会议发言纪要

【纪要译文】

张先生(中国)支持设立财政委员会的建议。税收政策如果不明智地实施或不协调,可能构成贸易壁垒。

此外,不稳定或烦琐的财政结构往往是国际投资的障碍。拟议的财政委员会可能有助于研究国际资本流动问题的财政方面。

至于举世公认的通货膨胀和萧条的危害,无可争辩的是,政府财政和税收是处理这类问题不可或缺的工具。

同时,为了使财政委员会的工作不与其他委员会的工作重复,似宜按照哥伦比亚代表的建议,将其范围限于公共财政的技术方面。

7. 张彭春在经社理事会第二届第 15 次会议上的发言

1946 年 6 月 21 日下午 3 时至 22 日凌晨 0 时 10 分，联合国经社理事会第二届第 15 次会议，在美国纽约亨特学院举行。本次会议的议题有 13 个之多，主要是审议各个委员会及小组委员会的决议草案、确定理事会下一届会议日期、会议主席致闭幕词等。中国代表张彭春参加了本次会议，并在会议上发言，其具体发言内容如下：

(1) 会议发言全文记录[①]及译文

【全文记录】

Dr. CHANG (China): Mr. President, my two points are really not so terribly important, but on the other hand, they will clear up the meaning. For one thing, the draft resolution concerning the temporary Sub-commission on the economic reconstruction of devastated areas, the last paragraph, paragraph 4, just add four words. "The Secretary General is authorized to form two working parties made up of members of the Sub-commission ..." The four words "made up of members" in this case—would avoid the ambiguity of forcing the hand of the Secretary General in including the twenty—I don't know how my British colleague got twenty two—in including the twenty members of the Sub-commission. That is a small point but I think it is worthwhile including so that the Sec-

① UN Document: E/PV. 15, pp. 67-72, p. 73, pp. 310-314, pp. 339-344.

retary General will not be so to speak, have his hands forced to include all the twenty into the working parties.

Second, another small thing. It is the matter of logical arrangement. The draft resolution concerning the report of Economic and Employment Commission, Article 1, point (d), in particular, "It shall be the function of the commission to advise the Council on 1, 2, 3..." I would not at this moment advise, let us say, putting the 1 as 3, but I would, however, at this time, advise the change or suggest the amendment of changing the 1 and 2. That is a very obvious one, because we are now organizing a temporary Sub-commission on this subject, while the other two Sub-commissions are still waiting to be acted upon all to be named. So it is only logical to change the point 2 as point 1 and then point 1 as point 2. That is all.

Dr. CHANG (China): Mr. President, I am very ready to concur with your suggestions, if it is a matter of putting on record, the logical arrangement would be, 1—the problems of reconstruction of devastated areas; 2—the promotion of economic development, and 3—the prevention of wide fluctuation. I leave that on the record and withdraw my amendment.

Dr. CHANG (China): I am in favor of the present text.

Dr. CHANG (China): Mr. President, just two words. One is the word of appreciation for the patience, reasonableness, and clarifying devotion of our President. A second word is for the most hard-working efforts of the Secretariat.

【全文译文】

张博士(中国):主席先生,我的两点其实并不那么重要,但另一方面,它们将澄清其含义。首先,关于灾区经济重建临时小组委员会的决议草案,最后一段,第4段,只增加了四个单词。"秘书长有权组成由小组委员会成员组成的两个工作组……""由成员组成"(made up of members)这四个词在这种情况下,可以避免秘书长将 20 名成员强制包括在小组委员会内的模糊性——我不知道我的英国同事是如何得出 22 名。这是一个小问题,但我认为这是值得的,这样秘书长就不会被迫将所有 20 名成员纳入工作组。

第二,另一件小事。这是逻辑安排的问题。关于经济和就业委员会报告的决议草案第 1 条(d)点,特别是,"委员会的职能是就 1、2、3 向理事会提出建议……"。我现在不会建议,比方说,把 1 作为 3,但我现在会建议更改或建议修订 1 和 2。这是一个非常明显的问题,因为我们现在正在组织一个关于这个问题的临时小组委员会,而另外两个小组委员会仍在等待根据任命采取行动。所以把点 2 换成点 1,然后把点 1 换成点 2 才符合逻辑。仅此而已。

张博士(中国):主席先生,我非常愿意同意你的建议,如果要记录在案,那么合乎逻辑的安排是:1. 灾区重建问题;2. 促进经济发展;3. 防止大幅度波动。我将此记录在案,并撤回我的修正案。

张博士(中国):我赞成目前的文本。

张博士(中国):主席先生,就两句话。第一句是,感谢我们主席的耐心、理性和明确的奉献精神。第二句是,感谢秘书处最辛勤的付出。

(2)会议发言内容纪要①

【会议纪要】

Mr. CHANG (China) proposed that the words "made up of members" be added after the words "two working groups" in paragraph 4 of the draft resolution concerning the Temporary Sub-commission on the Economic Reconstruction of Devastated Areas, in order that the Secretary-General might be free not to include all twenty members in each group.

As regards the draft resolution on the Economic and Employment Commis-

① UN Document: E_2ndsess-SR-1-15-EN, p. 119, p. 139.

sion, he proposed that the order of the sub-paragraphs of paragraph 1 (d) be rearranged so that paragraph 1 (d) (i) would deal with questions of economic reconstruction, 1 (d) (ii) with economic development and 1 (d) (iii) with the prevention of wide fluctuations in economic activity and the promotion of full employment. In view of the fact that a Sub-commission on Economic Reconstruction was now being set up, whereas the constitution of the other Sub-commissions was being postponed, he considered it more than ever logical that reconstruction problems be listed first.

Mr. CHANG (China) agreed.

Mr. CHANG (China) expressed the appreciation of the Council for the patience, reasonableness and clarifying devotion, of the President, and the hard-working efforts of the Secretariat.

【纪要影像】

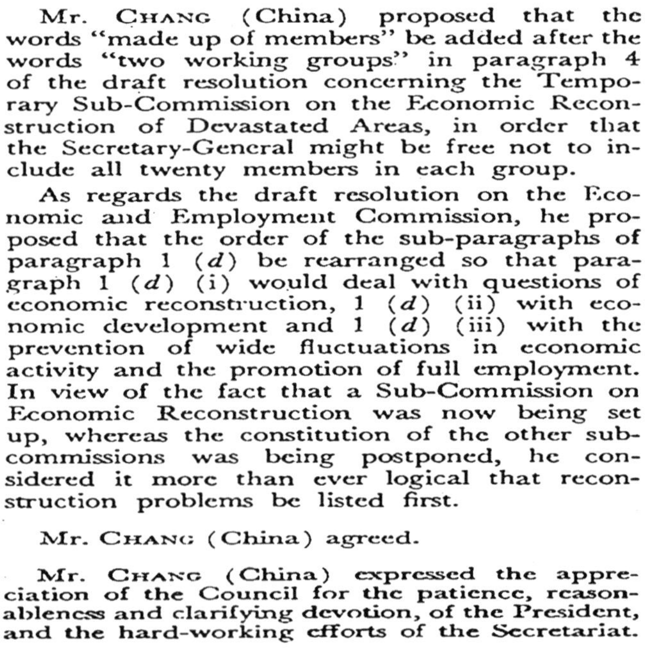

Mr. CHANG (China) proposed that the words "made up of members" be added after the words "two working groups" in paragraph 4 of the draft resolution concerning the Temporary Sub-Commission on the Economic Reconstruction of Devastated Areas, in order that the Secretary-General might be free not to include all twenty members in each group.

As regards the draft resolution on the Economic and Employment Commission, he proposed that the order of the sub-paragraphs of paragraph 1 (*d*) be rearranged so that paragraph 1 (*d*) (i) would deal with questions of economic reconstruction, 1 (*d*) (ii) with economic development and 1 (*d*) (iii) with the prevention of wide fluctuations in economic activity and the promotion of full employment. In view of the fact that a Sub-Commission on Economic Reconstruction was now being set up, whereas the constitution of the other sub-commissions was being postponed, he considered it more than ever logical that reconstruction problems be listed first.

Mr. CHANG (China) agreed.

Mr. CHANG (China) expressed the appreciation of the Council for the patience, reasonableness and clarifying devotion, of the President, and the hard-working efforts of the Secretariat.

图片 2.10：张彭春在联合国经社理事会第二届第 15 次会议发言纪要

【纪要译文】

张先生(中国)建议在关于灾区经济重建临时小组委员会的决议草案第四段中的"两个工作组"之后加上"由成员组成"等字,以便秘书长可以不把每个工作组的所有20名成员都包括在内。

关于经济和就业委员会的决议草案,他提议重新安排第1(d)段各分段的顺序,以便第1(d)(i)段处理经济重建问题,第1(d)(ii)段处理经济发展问题,第1(d)(iii)段处理防止经济活动大幅度波动和促进充分就业问题。鉴于目前正在设立一个经济重建小组委员会,而其他小组委员会的组成却被推迟,他认为将重建问题列在首位比以往任何时候都更符合逻辑。

张先生(中国)表示同意。

张先生(中国)表示理事会感谢主席的耐心、理性和明确的奉献精神,以及感谢秘书处的辛勤付出。

第三章　联合国经社理事会第三届会议

（纪要）

联合国经社理事会第三届第1次会议，于1946年9月11日上午10时30分至下午12时40分，在纽约成功湖举行。至1946年10月3日晚，本届会议共召开21次会议。另外，理事会还于1946年12月10日下午3时至晚上6时，在纽约法拉盛草地公园(Flushing Meadow，当时联合国临时总部)召开了一次特别会议。[1] 本届会议的主要议题有：通过会议日程、讨论经济和就业委员会各小组委员会的职权范围、任命一个审议难民问题的委员会、秘书长关于国际卫生会议的报告、委员会成员的费用支付、审议理事会关于世界卫生组织的决议草案、讨论各委员会的费用问题、审议和讨论国际难民组织决议草案及修正案、讨论国际儿童基金、审议建立人口委员会议案、审议哥伦比亚代表关于建立财政委员会的修正案、国际难民组织特别委员会财政报告、讨论法国代表提交的关于设立联合国研究实验室的决议草案、理事会非政府组织主席报告、讨论理事会第四届会议日期等等。

中国代表张彭春参加了本届会议，并在其中的15次会议上发言，包括本届第1次会议、第2次会议、第3次会议、第5次会议、第6次会议、第7次会议、第12次会议、第14次会议、第15次会议、第17次会议、第18次会议、第19次会议、第20次会议、第21次会议和特别会议上分别发言。

另外，参加本次会议的代表还有施思明先生[2]和杨先生[3]分别参加两

① UN Document: E/SR. 21.

② UN Document: E/SR. 4, p. 34 & E/SR. 9, pp. 59-60.

③ UN Document: E/SR. 8, p. 51 & E/SR. 17, p. 126.

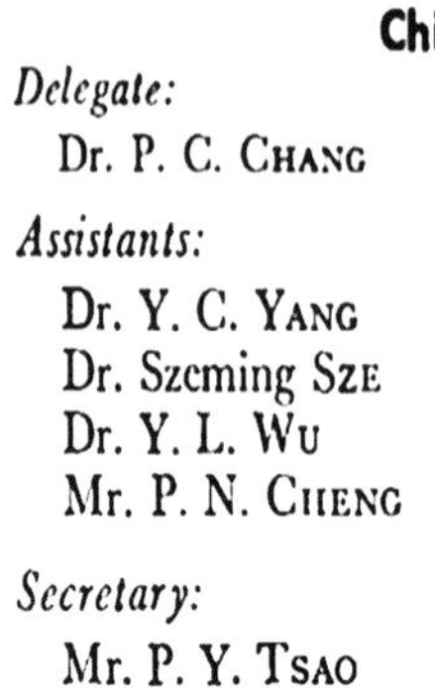

China

Delegate:
Dr. P. C. CHANG

Assistants:
Dr. Y. C. YANG
Dr. Szeming SZE
Dr. Y. L. WU
Mr. P. N. CHENG

Secretary:
Mr. P. Y. TSAO

图片 3.1 联合国经济及社会理事会第三届会议中国代表团名单

次会议。根据有关文件记录,本届会议存有全文记录[①],但令人遗憾的是,联合国正式文件系统目前仍然检索不到,只有会议纪要。虽然经多次与联合国档案馆联系,取得了法语版的全文记录(对应的文件是:E/PV. 16—E/PV. 37),但仍缺少两次会议全文记录,包括 E/PV. 17 和 E/PV. 26 两个文件,而鉴于时间所迫及条件所限,若要把法语版的原文记录包括进来对于笔者来说,除了时间因素之外,还有两个困难,一是法语文字处理困难,包括文字输入和文字翻译;二是若将现有的法语全文记录收入进来,本书整个体例也不统一。因此,本书只好依据"会议发言内容纪要"以"会议纪要""纪要影像"和"纪要译文"呈现本届会议上张彭春先生的发言内容。

① UN Document: E/PV. 38-50, p. 2. ("Note: Verbatim records issued as E/PV. 16 to E/PV. 37.")

1. 张彭春在经社理事会第三届第1次会议上的发言

联合国经社理事会第三届第1次会议,于1946年9月11日上午10时30分至下午12时40分,在纽约成功湖开幕,本次会议的主要议题是通过会议日程。中国代表张彭春率团参加了本次会议,并在会议上发言[①],其发言内容如下:

【会议纪要】

Mr. CHANG (China) agreed with the delegates for Belgium and India. The provisional time table might, however, be modified to comply with the suggestions of the United States and Soviet delegates that item 13 concerning the Demographic Commission be discussed at a later date.

The Council was faced with two categories of problems: organizational problems, such as the setting up of commissions, the election of their members and the payment of their expenses; and current problems such as refugee and health questions and the reconstruction of devastated areas. He agreed that the two types of problems must be dealt with side by side as envisaged in the Secretariat time table.

Mr. CHANG (China) asked that before the meeting rose an understanding should be reached on the programme for the next two or three days. The time

① UN Document: E/SR. 1, pp. 14–15, pp. 15–16.

table proposed by the Secretariat might be adopted with the exception of the postponement of the item referring to the Demographic Commission and possibly of one meeting of the Committee on Refugees. Would items 18 and 19 of the agenda be taken up at the afternoon meeting, after the statement by Mr. La Guardia?

【纪要影像】

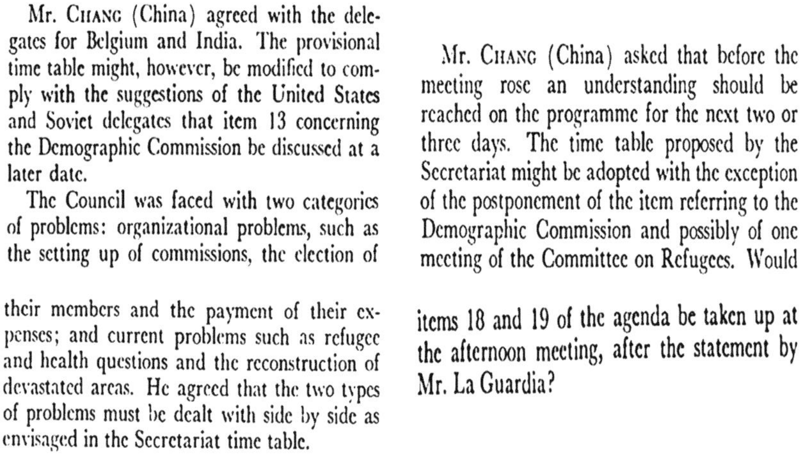

Mr. CHANG (China) agreed with the delegates for Belgium and India. The provisional time table might, however, be modified to comply with the suggestions of the United States and Soviet delegates that item 13 concerning the Demographic Commission be discussed at a later date.

The Council was faced with two categories of problems: organizational problems, such as the setting up of commissions, the election of their members and the payment of their expenses; and current problems such as refugee and health questions and the reconstruction of devastated areas. He agreed that the two types of problems must be dealt with side by side as envisaged in the Secretariat time table.

Mr. CHANG (China) asked that before the meeting rose an understanding should be reached on the programme for the next two or three days. The time table proposed by the Secretariat might be adopted with the exception of the postponement of the item referring to the Demographic Commission and possibly of one meeting of the Committee on Refugees. Would items 18 and 19 of the agenda be taken up at the afternoon meeting, after the statement by Mr. La Guardia?

图片 3.2　　张彭春在经社理事会第三届第 1 次会议发言纪要

【纪要译文】

张先生(中国)同意比利时和印度代表的意见。但是,临时时间表可以修改,以符合美国和苏联代表的建议,即关于人口委员会的项目 13 将在以后讨论。

理事会面临两类问题:组织问题,如设立委员会、选举其成员和支付其费用;以及当前问题如难民和健康问题以及灾区重建等。他同意,这两类问题必须按照秘书处时间表的设想同时处理。

张先生(中国)要求在会议开始之前,就今后两三天的方案达成谅解。

秘书处提议的时间表可以采纳,除人口委员会的项目可能推迟,以及难民委员会可能推迟一次会议之外。在拉·瓜迪亚先生发言之后,下午会议是否会讨论议程项目18和19?

2. 张彭春在经社理事会第三届第 2 次会议上的发言

联合国经社理事会第三届第 2 次会议，于 1946 年 9 月 11 日下午 2 时至 5 时，在纽约成功湖举行，本次会议的主要议程是审议经济和就业委员会各小组委员会的职权范围等。中国代表张彭春率团参加了本次会议，并在会议上发言①，其发言内容如下：

【会议纪要】

Mr. CHANG (China) drew attention to a memorandum on the terms of reference of the Sub-commission on Economic Development (document E/107), which had been distributed. In studying this document, the members of the Council should, he thought, keep before them the following distinction: whereas the organization of the Economic and Employment Commission must, at the higher level, be functional it might, at the executive level, be regional.

He had stressed this distinction because he felt sure the temporary Sub-commission on the Economic Reconstruction of Devastated Areas would ask the Council to establish an Economic Commission for Europe and, in that case, the principle on which he had just laid stress ought to be applied.

With regard to this proposal concerning the terms of reference of the Sub-commission on Economic Development, the Chinese delegation felt bound to make the same reservation as it had made during the second session, namely,

① UN Document: E/SR. 2, pp. 24-25, p. 26.

that in its view a Sub-commission was inadequate to cover such a vast field; it should be enlarged so as to constitute a full commission.

The Chinese delegation would agree to the establishment of a Sub-commission on Economic Development under the authority of the Economic and Employment Commission, if no other suggestions for the establishment of new commissions were submitted, but it reserved the right to raise the question again at the proper time.

Mr. CHANG (China) said the procedure followed at the second session had been to refer the terms of reference of a Sub-commission to a committee, which might be called the Committee on Economic Questions, for the composition of which the representative of Belgium had made a suggestion. He accordingly supported the Norwegian proposal and pointed out that action on these lines would simply imply the continuation of a discussion suspended in June.

On the other hand, as regards the resolution submitted to the Council by the Chinese delegation, members would soon see, if they studied document E/107, page 3, that it proposed only one amendment to the terms of reference which had been drawn up by the Council after a hurried discussion. No new factor had been introduced and the amendment did not affect any principle.

He therefore suggested that this task should be entrusted to the Committee on Economic Questions, which would submit a proposal on the terms of reference to the Council.

He felt sure the Secretariat would be prepared to draw up the terms of reference of the three Sub-commissions and not merely that of the Sub-commission on Economic Development.

【纪要影像】

Mr. CHANG (China) drew attention to a memorandum on the terms of reference of the Sub-Commission on Economic Development (document E/107), which had been distributed. In studying this document, the members of the Council should, he thought, keep before them the following distinction: whereas the organization of the Economic and Employment Commission must, at the higher level, be functional it might, at the executive level, be regional.

He had stressed this distinction because he felt sure the temporary Sub-Commission on the Economic Reconstruction of Devastated Areas would ask the Council to establish an Economic Commission for Europe and, in that case, the principle on which he had just laid stress ought to be applied.

With regard to this proposal concerning the terms of reference of the Sub-Commission on Economic Development, the Chinese delegation felt bound to make the same reservation as it had made during the second session, namely, that in its view a sub-commission was inadequate to cover such a vast field; it should be enlarged so as to constitute a full commission.

The Chinese delegation would agree to the establishment of a Sub-Commission on Economic Development under the authority of the Economic and Employment Commission, if no other suggestions for the establishment of new commissions were submitted, but it reserved the right to raise the question again at the proper time.

Mr. CHANG (China) said the procedure followed at the second session had been to refer the terms of reference of a sub-commission to a committee, which might be called the Committee on Economic Questions, for the composition of which the representative of Belgium had made a suggestion. He accordingly supported the Norwegian proposal and pointed out that action on these lines would simply imply the continuation of a discussion suspended in June.

On the other hand, as regards the resolution submitted to the Council by the Chinese delegation, members would soon see, if they studied document E/107, page 3, that it proposed only one amendment to the terms of reference which had been drawn up by the Council after a hurried discussion. No new factor had been introduced and the amendment did not affect any principle.

He therefore suggested that this task should be entrusted to the Committee on Economic Questions, which would submit a proposal on the terms of reference to the Council.

He felt sure the Secretariat would be prepared to draw up the terms of reference of the three sub-commissions and not merely that of the Sub-Commission on Economic Development.

图片 3.3　张彭春在经社理事会第三届第 2 次会议发言纪要

【纪要译文】

张先生(中国)提请注意已经分发的关于经济发展小组委员会职权范围的备忘录(E/107 号文件)。他认为,在研究这份文件时,理事会成员应注意以下区别:经济和就业委员会的组织在较高一级必须是职能性的,但在执行一级可能是区域性的。

他强调了这一区别,因为他确信灾区经济重建临时小组委员会将要求理事会设立一个欧洲经济委员会,在这种情况下,他刚才强调的原则应该适用。

关于这一涉及经济发展小组委员会职权范围的建议,中国代表团认为有必要作出与第二届会议相同的保留,即认为一个小组委员会不足以涵盖如此广阔的领域;它应该扩大,以便成为一个正式的委员会。

如果没有其他关于设立新委员会的建议提交,中国代表团将同意在经济和就业委员会管辖之下设立经济发展小组委员会,但保留在适当时候再次提出这一问题的权利。

张先生(中国)说,第二届会议遵循的程序是将小组委员会的职权范围提交给一个委员会,该委员会可称为经济问题委员会,比利时代表对其组成提出了建议。据此,他支持挪威的提议,并指出按照这些思路采取行动只会意味着继续进行6月份暂停的讨论。

另一方面,关于中国代表团向理事会提交的决议,如果各位成员研究一下E/107号文件第3页,他们很快就会看到,该决议只对理事会在匆忙讨论后起草的职权范围提出了一项修正。没有引入新的因素,修正案没有影响任何原则。

因此,他建议将这项任务委托给经济问题委员会,该委员会将向理事会提交一份关于职权范围的提案。

他确信秘书处将准备起草三个小组委员会的职权范围,而不仅仅是经济发展小组委员会的职权范围。

3. 张彭春在经社理事会第三届第3次会议上的发言

联合国经社理事会第三届第3次会议，于1946年9月12日上午10时30分至下午1时30分，在纽约成功湖举行。本次会议的主要议题是向联合国转让国际联盟在麻醉药品方面行使的权利、听取了秘书长关于国际卫生会议的报告、讨论了委员会成员费用的支付等。中国代表张彭春率团参加了本次会议，并在会议上发言①，其发言内容如下：

【会议纪要】

Mr. CHANG (China) congratulated the Secretariat on the work it had done, approved the contents of the report presented and recommended the setting up of a small committee to settle certain details of drafting. The representatives of the UNITED STATES OF AMERICA and BELGIUM associated themselves with the views expressed by the Chinese representative.

The representative of INDIA supported what Mr. Chang (China) had said, and stated that his country, being particularly interested in the fight against diseases carried by microbes, considered it necessary that the nations should ratify the Convention and Protocol of the new Organization as a matter of the greatest urgency.

Mr. MARTIN (Canada) pointed out that his country was the first to have formally agreed to the decisions taken at New York.

① UN Document: E/SR. 3, p. 28, p. 29, p. 31.

Replying to a question by the Canadian representative, the CHAIRMAN stated that, up to date, only three nations had ratified the legal instruments of the World Health Organization (Canada, China and the United Kingdom) but he hoped that within a year, the other nations would have signified their approval.

Mr. CHANG (China) pointed out that those commissions had no executive functions; they acted mainly as advisers to the Council. It was a pity that the Council, in altering the composition of the commissions, had not expressed itself sufficiently clearly on this point in its resolution. The Council's attitude was that members of commissions acted in an advisory capacity for the Council; their expenses should therefore be borne by the United Nations.

【纪要影像】

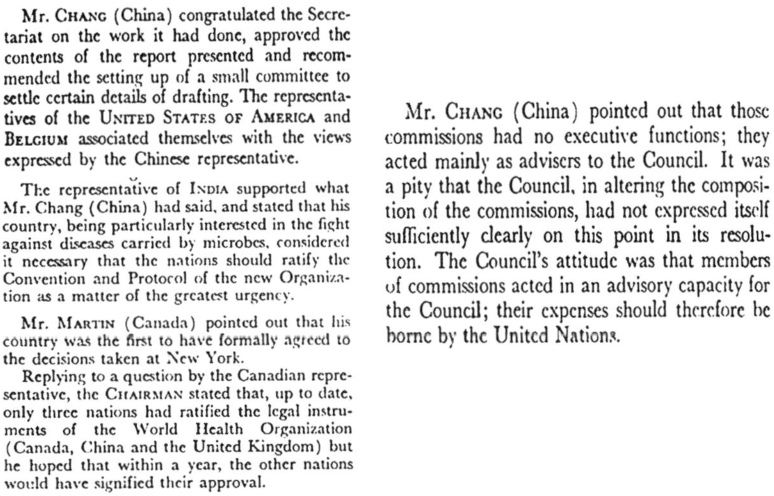

Mr. Chang (China) congratulated the Secretariat on the work it had done, approved the contents of the report presented and recommended the setting up of a small committee to settle certain details of drafting. The representatives of the United States of America and Belgium associated themselves with the views expressed by the Chinese representative.

The representative of India supported what Mr. Chang (China) had said, and stated that his country, being particularly interested in the fight against diseases carried by microbes, considered it necessary that the nations should ratify the Convention and Protocol of the new Organization as a matter of the greatest urgency.

Mr. Martin (Canada) pointed out that his country was the first to have formally agreed to the decisions taken at New York.

Replying to a question by the Canadian representative, the Chairman stated that, up to date, only three nations had ratified the legal instruments of the World Health Organization (Canada, China and the United Kingdom) but he hoped that within a year, the other nations would have signified their approval.

Mr. Chang (China) pointed out that those commissions had no executive functions; they acted mainly as advisers to the Council. It was a pity that the Council, in altering the composition of the commissions, had not expressed itself sufficiently clearly on this point in its resolution. The Council's attitude was that members of commissions acted in an advisory capacity for the Council; their expenses should therefore be borne by the United Nations.

图片 3.4　张彭春在经社理事会第三届第 3 次会议发言纪要

【纪要译文】

张先生(中国)对秘书处所做的工作表示祝贺,同意所提交报告的内容,并建议成立一个小型委员会解决起草工作的某些细节问题。美国和比利时代表赞同中国代表所表达的意见。

印度代表支持张先生(中国)的发言,并指出,印度对防治微生物携带的疾病特别感兴趣,认为各国有必要作为最紧迫的事项批准新组织的公约和议定书。

马丁(Martin)先生(加拿大)指出,加拿大是第一个正式同意在纽约作出的决定的国家。

主席在答复加拿大代表的问题时说,迄今为止,只有三个国家(加拿大、中国和英国)批准了世界卫生组织的法律文书,但他希望在一年内,其他国家会签署同意。

张先生(中国)指出,这些委员会没有行政职能;他们主要担任委员会的顾问。遗憾的是,理事会在改变各委员会的组成时,没有在其决议中就这一点充分明确地表达自己的意见。理事会的态度是,委员会成员以理事会顾问的身份行事;因此,他们的费用应由联合国承担。

4. 张彭春在经社理事会第三届第5次会议上的发言

联合国经社理事会第三届第5次会议，于1946年9月21日上午10时30分下午至1时35分，在纽约成功湖举行。本次会议的主要议题是建议大会授权理事会请求国际法院发表咨询意见、讨论附加议程项目、讨论各个委员会的费用问题等。中国代表张彭春率团参加了本次会议，并在会议上发言①，其发言内容如下：

【全文记录】

M. CHANG (Chine) (interprétation)：La délégation chinoise porte un grand intérêt aux problèmes importants et urgents qui font l'objet de la résolution en question. C'est pourquoi elle appuie la proposition d'inscription de la question à l'ordre du jour.

【记录影像】

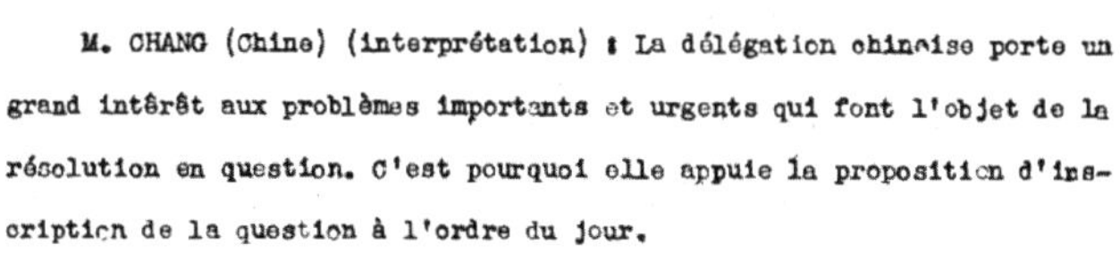
M. CHANG (Chine) (interprétation) : La délégation chinoise porte un grand intérêt aux problèmes importants et urgents qui font l'objet de la résolution en question. C'est pourquoi elle appuie la proposition d'ins-cription de la question à l'ordre du jour.

图片 3.5　张彭春在经社理事会第三届第5次会议发言纪要

① UN Document：E/PV. 20, pp. 32-33.（这是一个法语文本会议全文记录，因联合国正式文件系统，无法获取英语文本，而在会议纪要文件又没有张彭春有关的发言纪要，通过对比法语文献，作为查漏补缺。）

【全文译文】

张先生(中国):中国代表团高度重视决议草案所涉及的重要和紧迫问题。因此,支持将该项目列入议程的建议。

5. 张彭春在经社理事会第三届第6次会议上的发言

联合国经社理事会第三届第6次会议,于1946年9月21日下午2时30分至4时35分,在纽约成功湖举行。本次会议的主要议题是继续讨论委员会成员的费用问题等。中国代表张彭春率团参加了本次会议,并在会议上发言,提出三条建议案①,其发言内容如下:

【会议纪要】

Mr. CHANG (China) considered it advisable to stress the fact that these commissions should be regarded as advisory organs of the Council. It would then be logical for the United Nations to pay the travelling expenses and subsistence allowances of commission members. He suggested, however, that the expenses of the experts accompanying the advisers should not be paid by the United Nations.

Mr. CHANG (China) formulated the three Proposals to be put to the vote:

(1) The proposal that the travelling expenses of members of commissions and Sub-commissions should be paid by the United Nations.

Decision: *This proposal was adopted by seventeen votes to one.*

(2) The proposal that subsistence allowances of members of commissions and Sub-commissions should be borne by the United Nations.

① UN Document: E/SR. 6, p. 42, p. 43.

Decision: *This proposal was adopted by ten votes to eight.*

(3) The proposal that the United Nations should pay the travelling expenses and subsistence allowances of experts attached to a commission or Sub-commission.

Decision: *This proposal was rejected by twelve votes to five, with one abstention.*

【纪要影像】

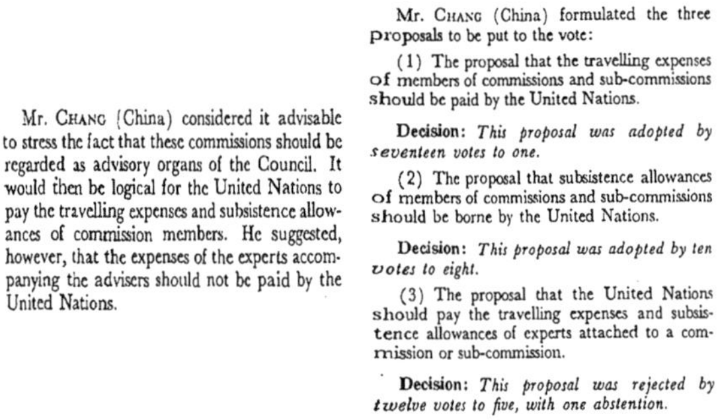

Mr. CHANG (China) considered it advisable to stress the fact that these commissions should be regarded as advisory organs of the Council. It would then be logical for the United Nations to pay the travelling expenses and subsistence allowances of commission members. He suggested, however, that the expenses of the experts accompanying the advisers should not be paid by the United Nations.

Mr. CHANG (China) formulated the three proposals to be put to the vote:

(1) The proposal that the travelling expenses of members of commissions and sub-commissions should be paid by the United Nations.

Decision: *This proposal was adopted by seventeen votes to one.*

(2) The proposal that subsistence allowances of members of commissions and sub-commissions should be borne by the United Nations.

Decision: *This proposal was adopted by ten votes to eight.*

(3) The proposal that the United Nations should pay the travelling expenses and subsistence allowances of experts attached to a commission or sub-commission.

Decision: *This proposal was rejected by twelve votes to five, with one abstention.*

图片 3.6　张彭春在经社理事会第三届第 6 次会议发言纪要

【纪要译文】

张先生(中国)认为应该强调,这些委员会应被视为理事会的咨询机构。因此,联合国支付委员会成员的旅费和生活津贴是合乎逻辑的。但是,他建议,陪同顾问的专家的费用不应由联合国支付。

张先生(中国)提出了三项付诸表决的提案:

(1)委员会和小组委员会成员的旅费应由联合国支付的建议。

决定:该提案以 17 票对 1 票获得通过。

(2)委员会和小组委员会成员的生活津贴应由联合国负担的建议。

决定:该提案以 10 票对 8 票获得通过。

(3)由联合国支付附属于委员会或小组委员会的专家的旅费和生活津贴的建议。

决定:该提案以 12 票对 5 票、1 票弃权被否决。

6. 张彭春在经社理事会第三届第7次会议上的发言

联合国经社理事会第三届第7次会议，于1946年9月23日上午10时30分至下午1时30分，在纽约成功湖举行。本次会议的主要议题是讨论和审议国际难民组织决议草案等。中国代表张彭春率团参加了本次会议，并在会议上发言[①]，其发言内容如下：

【会议纪要】

Mr. CHANG (China), supported by Mr. Martin (Canada), suggested that the words "country of origin" in article II, paragraph 1(a) should be replaced by the words "countries of nationality or former habitual residence."

【纪要影像】

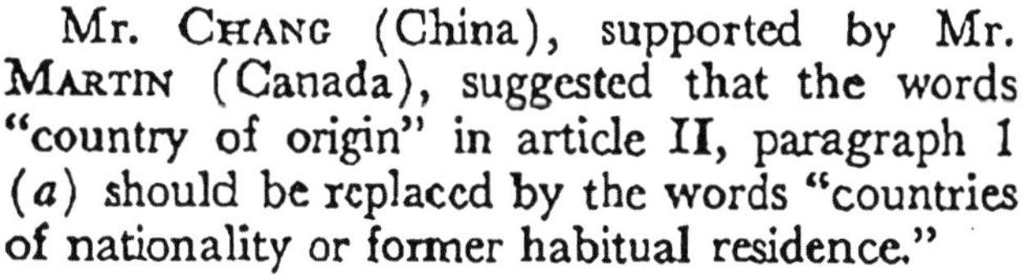

Mr. CHANG (China), supported by Mr. MARTIN (Canada), suggested that the words "country of origin" in article II, paragraph 1 (*a*) should be replaced by the words "countries of nationality or former habitual residence."

图片 3.7　张彭春在经社理事会第三届第7次会议发言纪要

① UN Document: E/SR. 7, p. 46.

【纪要译文】

张先生(中国)在马丁(Martin)先生(加拿大)的支持下建议将第二条第1款(a)项中的“原籍国”改为“国籍国或前惯常居住地国”。

7. 张彭春在经社理事会第三届第12次会议上的发言

联合国经社理事会第三届第12次会议，于1946年9月28日下午2时45分至晚上7时15分，在纽约成功湖举行。本次会议主要议题是讨论苏联代表关于与临时国际航空组织的关系的请求、讨论任命与非政府组织协商安排常设委员会等。中国代表张彭春率团参加了本次会议，并在会议上发言①，其发言内容见如下：

【会议纪要】

Mr. CHANG (China) remarked that the proposal of the Union of Soviet Socialist Republics suggested that negotiations should be suspended, but did not mean that the relationship should be terminated.

Mr. CHANG (China) pointed out that there was already in existence a committee to consider applications for admission from non-governmental organizations, known as the NGO Committee, and he thought that the same committee might well take over both functions.

① UN Document: E/SR. 12, p. 81, p. 82.

【纪要影像】

Mr. CHANG (China) remarked that the proposal of the Union of Soviet Socialist Republics suggested that negotiations should be suspended, but did not mean that the relationship should be terminated.

Mr. CHANG (China) pointed out that there was already in existence a committee to consider applications for admission from non-governmental organizations, known as the NGO Committee, and he thought that the same committee might well take over both functions.

图片 3.8　张彭春在经社理事会第三届第 12 次会议发言纪要

【纪要译文】

张先生(中国)评论,苏维埃社会主义共和国联盟的提案建议暂停谈判,但并不意味着终止这种关系。

张先生(中国)指出,已经存在一个委员会负责审议非政府组织的申请,称为非政府组织委员会,他认为同一个委员会可以很好地同时承担这两项职能。

8. 张彭春在经社理事会第三届第 14 次会议上的发言

联合国经社理事会第三届第 14 次会议，于 1946 年 9 月 30 日下午 2 时 45 分至晚上 7 时 45 分，在纽约成功湖举行。本次会议主要议题是讨论联合国善后救济总署议案开展的与国际儿童应急基金有关的福利工作等。中国代表张彭春率团参加了本次会议，并在会议上发言[①]，其发言内容如下：

【会议纪要】

Mr. CHANG (China) warmly supported the proposals submitted to the Council.

【纪要影像】

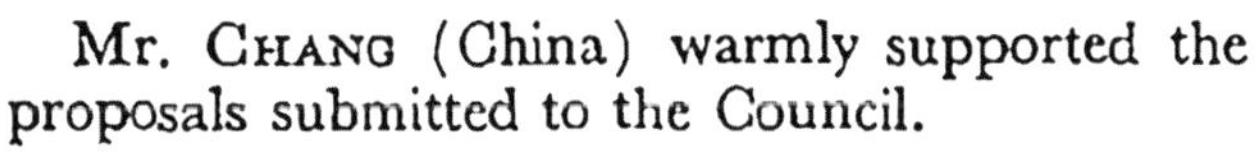
Mr. CHANG (China) warmly supported the proposals submitted to the Council.

图片 3.9　张彭春在经社理事会第三届第 14 次会议发言纪要

【纪要译文】

张先生（中国）热烈支持提交理事会的提案。

---

① UN Document: E/SR. 14, p. 98.

9. 张彭春在经社理事会第三届第 15 次会议上的发言

联合国经社理事会第三届第 15 次会议，于 1946 年 10 月 1 日上午 10 时 30 分至下午 1 时 33 分，在纽约成功湖举行。本次会议主要议题是审议哥伦比亚代表关于建立财政委员会的修正案、审议建立人口委员会的议案等。中国代表张彭春率团参加了本次会议，并在会议上发言[①]，其发言内容如下：

【会议纪要】

Mr. Dávila (Chile) supported the Colombian proposal. It had been on the agenda since the first session of the Council, and prompt action was desirable. Mr. Noel-Baker (United Kingdom) and Mr. Chang (China) also supported this proposal.

【纪要影像】

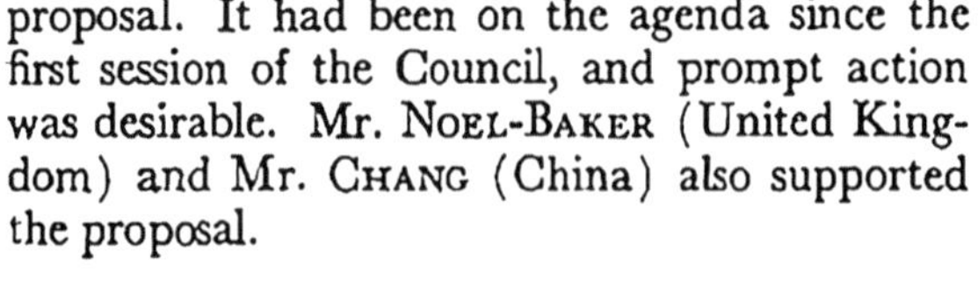
Mr. DÁVILA (Chile) supported the Colombian proposal. It had been on the agenda since the first session of the Council, and prompt action was desirable. Mr. NOEL-BAKER (United Kingdom) and Mr. CHANG (China) also supported the proposal.

图片 3.10　张彭春在经社理事会第三届第 15 次会议发言纪要

① UN Document: E/SR. 15, p. 100.

【纪要译文】

达维拉(Dávila)先生(智利)支持哥伦比亚的提议。自理事会第一届会议以来,它就一直列在议程上,需要立即采取行动。内欧·贝克(Noel Baker)先生(英国)和张先生(中国)也支持这项提议。

10. 张彭春在经社理事会第三届第17次会议上的发言

联合国经社理事会第三届第17次会议,于1946年10月2日上午10时30分至下午1时30分,在纽约成功湖举行。本次会议主要议题是审议特别委员会国际难民组织财政报告等。中国代表张彭春率团参加了本次会议,并在会议上发言①,其发言内容如下:

【会议纪要】

Mr. CHANG (China) suggested that in paragraph 5 (a), page 8, the number of Overseas Chinese, who desired to return to their place of habitual residence, could be reduced to a round figure since that number was based on a rough estimate and changed constantly; on the other hand, the second item, covering Chinese stranded abroad on account of the war and desiring repatriation to China, could be slightly increased.

Mr. Chang accordingly proposed that paragraph 5 (a) should be amended as follows:

> Second line: Change the figure 62,911 to 60,000; change $3,140,550—calculated on the basis of 62,911—to $3,250,000. At the end of the line, add the words: "and 5,000 Chinese stranded abroad on account of the war."

① UN Document: E/SR. 17, pp. 116-117, p. 117.

Fourteenth line: change the figure 62,911 to 60,000. At the end of the paragraph, add the following sentence: "With reference to 10,000 Chinese stranded abroad, the ad hoc Committee is of the opinion that roughly half of them may be transported back to China during the first financial year. Figuring on the lowest average cost of transportation at $50 per person, an item of $250,000 is included in the provisional budget".

Mr. CHANG (China) accepted the correction proposed by the representative of the United States, and suggested that the last line of paragraph 5 (a) should then read: "... is included in the amount of $3,250,000 mentioned above."

【纪要影像】

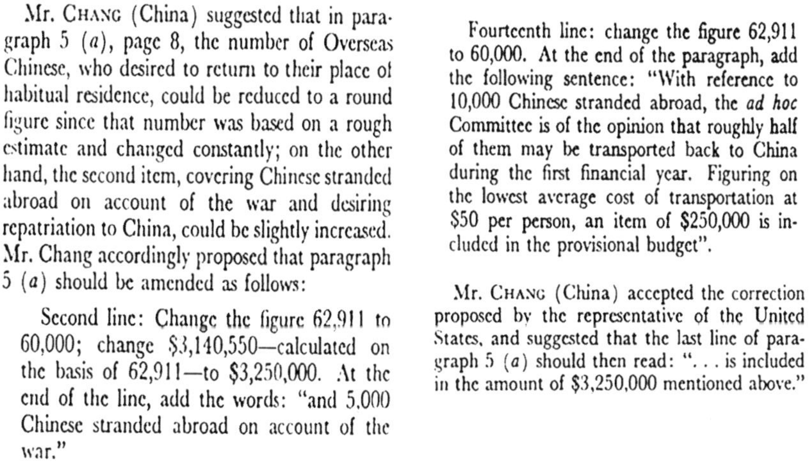
Mr. CHANG (China) suggested that in paragraph 5 (*a*), page 8, the number of Overseas Chinese, who desired to return to their place of habitual residence, could be reduced to a round figure since that number was based on a rough estimate and changed constantly; on the other hand, the second item, covering Chinese stranded abroad on account of the war and desiring repatriation to China, could be slightly increased. Mr. Chang accordingly proposed that paragraph 5 (*a*) should be amended as follows:

Second line: Change the figure 62,911 to 60,000; change $3,140,550—calculated on the basis of 62,911—to $3,250,000. At the end of the line, add the words: "and 5,000 Chinese stranded abroad on account of the war."

Fourteenth line: change the figure 62,911 to 60,000. At the end of the paragraph, add the following sentence: "With reference to 10,000 Chinese stranded abroad, the *ad hoc* Committee is of the opinion that roughly half of them may be transported back to China during the first financial year. Figuring on the lowest average cost of transportation at $50 per person, an item of $250,000 is included in the provisional budget".

Mr. CHANG (China) accepted the correction proposed by the representative of the United States, and suggested that the last line of paragraph 5 (*a*) should then read: ". . . is included in the amount of $3,250,000 mentioned above."

图片 3.11　张彭春在经社理事会第三届第 17 次会议发言纪要

【纪要译文】

张先生(中国)建议,在第 8 页第 5(a)段中,希望返回惯常居住地的海外华侨人数可以减少到一个整数,因为这个数字是根据粗略估计得出的,并且不断变化;另一方面,第二项涉及因战争而滞留国外并希望返回中国的中国人,可能会略微增加。

据此,张先生提议将第5(a)段修改如下:

第二行:将数字62,911改为60,000;将3,140,550美元(根据62,911美元计算)改为3,250,000美元。在这一行的末尾,加上一句“还有5,000名中国人因战争而滞留国外。”

第十四行:将数字62,911改为60,000。在本段末尾,增加如下一句话:“关于滞留海外的10,000中国人,特设委员会认为,其中大约一半可能在第一个财政年度被运回中国。根据每人50美元的最低平均运输成本计算,临时预算中包括25万美元的项目。”。

张先生(中国)接受美国代表提议的更正,并建议将第5(a)段最后一行改为:“……包括在上述3,250,000美元的数额中。”

11. 张彭春在经社理事会第三届第 18 次会议上的发言

联合国经社理事会第三届第 18 次会议,于 1946 年 10 月 2 日下午 2 时 45 分至晚上 7 时 30 分,在纽约成功湖举行。本次会议主要议题是关于粮农组织的法国建议案、法国代表提交的关于设立联合国研究实验室的决议草案、选举委员会成员等。中国代表张彭春率团参加了本次会议,并在会议上发言①,其发言内容如下:

【会议纪要】

Mr. CHANG (China), Mr. Argyropoulos (Greece), Mr. Noel-Baker (United Kingdom) and Mr. Dávila (Chile) supported the French proposal. Mr. Malik (Lebanon) also expressed approval, suggesting, however, that the United Nations research laboratories should be situated in the countries least favourably equipped in that respect.

① UN Document: E/SR. 18, p. 126.

【纪要影像】

Mr. CHANG (China), Mr. ARGYROPOULOS (Greece), Mr. NOEL-BAKER (United Kingdom) and Mr. DÁVILA (Chile) supported the French proposal. Mr. MALIK (Lebanon) also expressed approval, suggesting, however, that the United Nations research laboratories should be situated in the countries least favourably equipped in that respect.

图片 3.12 张彭春在经社理事会第三届第 18 次会议发言纪要

【纪要译文】

张先生(中国)、阿基饶培乐士(Argyropoulos)先生(希腊)、内欧·贝克(Noel Baker)先生(英国)和达维拉(Dávila)先生(智利)支持法国的提案。马利克(Malik)先生(黎巴嫩)也表示赞同,但他建议联合国研究实验室应设在这方面设施最不完善的国家。

12. 张彭春在经社理事会第三届第 19 次会议上的发言

联合国经社理事会第三届第 19 次会议，于 1946 年 10 月 3 日上午 10 时 30 分至下午 1 时 22 分，在纽约成功湖举行。本次会议主要议题是讨论人口委员会决议修正案等。中国代表张彭春率团参加了本次会议，并在会议上发言①，其发言内容如下：

【会议纪要】

Mr. Feonov (Union of Soviet Socialist Republics) proposed that in view of the fact that representatives of the three other commissions were not to be members of the Population Commission, the words "shall also include" should be changed to "shall invite." He also agreed to the suggestion of Mr. CHANG (China) that the words "be entitled to" should be deleted.

Following a suggestion by Sir Girja Shankar Bajpai (India), Mr. CHANG (China) proposed the substitution of the word "shall" by the word "may." The proposal met with no objection.

Mr. Stinebower (United States of America) pointed out that the footnote on page 1 of the resolution (document E/226) was inaccurate, since the Council had made no decision regarding corresponding members.

He proposed the deletion in the text of the words: "corresponding members" and of the footnote itself. Corresponding members were to correspond and

① UN Document: E/SR. 19, p. 137, p. 138.

not to appear in person. Mr. CHANG (China) agreed.

【纪要影像】

Mr. FEONOV (Union of Soviet Socialist Republics) proposed that in view of the fact that representatives of the three other commissions were not to be members of the Population Commission, the words "shall also include" should be changed to "shall invite." He also agreed to the suggestion of Mr. CHANG (China) that the words "be entitled to" should be deleted.

Following a suggestion by Sir Girja Shankar BAJPAI (India), Mr. CHANG (China) proposed the substitution of the word "shall" by the word "may." The proposal met with no objection.

Mr. STINEBOWER (United States of America) pointed out that the footnote on page 1 of the resolution (document E/226) was inaccurate, since the Council had made no decision regarding corresponding members.

He proposed the deletion in the text of the words: "corresponding members" and of the footnote itself. Corresponding members were to correspond and not to appear in person. Mr. CHANG (China) agreed.

图片 3.13　张彭春在经社理事会第三届第 19 次会议发言纪要

【纪要译文】

费奥诺夫(Feonov)先生(苏维埃社会主义共和国联盟)提议,鉴于其他三个委员会的代表不是人口委员会的成员,应将“还应包括”改为“应邀请”。他还同意张先生(中国)的建议,即删除“有权”一词。

根据吉尔拉·山卡尔·巴杰帕伊(Girja Shankar Bajpai)爵士(印度)的建议,张先生(中国)提议将“应”(shall)一词改为“可”(may)。这项提议没有遭到反对。

斯坦鲍尔(Stinebower)先生(美国)指出,决议(E/226 号文件)第 1 页的脚注不准确,因为理事会没有就准成员作出决定。

他建议删除案文中的“准成员”和脚注本身。准成员是采用通信方式,而不是亲自到场。张先生(中国)表示同意。

13. 张彭春在经社理事会第三届第20次会议上的发言

联合国经社理事会第三届第20次会议,于1946年10月3日下午2时45分至晚上7时15分,在纽约成功湖举行。本次会议主要议题是审议关于灾区经济重建临时小组委员会报告的决议草案等。中国代表张彭春率团参加了本次会议,并在会议上发言①,其发言内容如下:

【会议纪要】

Mr. CHANG (China) thought, with regard to resolution VI, that the Temporary Sub-Commission for Economic Reconstruction of Devastated Areas should be raised to the status of a temporary commission, provided such action did not prejudice the establishment of an economic commission for Europe. With regard to resolution III, he expressed gratification that an agency of the United Nations would visit China, and expressed the hope that the Secretary-General would accompany it.

Mr. CHANG (China) supported the suggestion that the matter of PICAO should be submitted to the General Assembly. He would not vote on the USSR proposal, because it raised not a technical, but a political issue.

Mr. CHANG (China) proposed that the question of PICAO should be referred to the General Assembly.

Mr. CHANG (China) replied that one was a matter of signing a protocol,

① UN Document: E/SR. 20, p. 143, p. 146, p. 147.

and the other was a matter of considering PICAO as a technical institution. He pointed out that in the Universal Postal Union there were members who did not agree completely in their political structures.

【纪要影像】

Mr. CHANG (China) thought, with regard to resolution VI, that the Temporary Sub-Commission for Economic Reconstruction of Devastated Areas should be raised to the status of a temporary commission, provided such action did not prejudice the establishment of an economic commission for Europe. With regard to resolution III, he expressed gratification that an agency of the United Nations would visit China, and expressed the hope that the Secretary-General would accompany it.

Mr. CHANG (China) supported the suggestion that the matter of PICAO should be submitted to the General Assembly. He would not vote on the USSR proposal, because it raised not a technical, but a political issue.

Mr. CHANG (China) proposed that the question of PICAO should be referred to the General Assembly.

Mr. CHANG (China) replied that one was a matter of signing a protocol, and the other was a matter of considering PICAO as a technical institution. He pointed out that in the Universal Postal Union there were members who did not agree completely in their political structures.

图片 3.14　张彭春在经社理事会第三届第 20 次会议发言纪要

【纪要译文】

张先生(中国)认为,关于第六号决议,应将灾区经济重建临时小组委员会提升为一个临时委员会,但这种行动不得妨碍欧洲经济委员会的成立。关于第三号决议,他对联合国一个机构将访问中国表示满意,并希望秘书长陪同访问。

张先生(中国)支持将临时国际民用航空组织(PICAO:Provisional International Civil Aviation Organization)问题提交大会的建议。他不会对苏联的提案进行投票,因为它提出的不是技术问题,而是政治问题。

张先生(中国)提议临时国际民用航空组织问题提交大会。

张先生(中国)回答说,一个是签署议定书的问题,另一个是将临时国际民用航空组织视为一个技术机构的问题。他指出,在万国邮政联盟中,有成员在其政治结构方面,并未达成一致意见。

14. 张彭春在经社理事会第三届第 21 次会议上的发言

联合国经社理事会第三届第 21 次会议，于 1946 年 10 月 3 日上午 8 时至 11 时 35 分，在纽约成功湖召开。本次会议主要议题是理事会非政府组织主席报告、讨论理事会会议安排以确认委员会成员、讨论理事会第四届会议日期等。中国代表张彭春率团参加了本次会议，并在会议上发言①，其发言内容如下：

【会议纪要】

Mr. CHANG (China) nominated Dr. Zuleta Angel, representative of Colombia, as Acting Chairman; the nomination was seconded by the representatives of Yugoslavia and Peru, and Dr. Zuleta Angel was unanimously elected.

Mr. CHANG (China), with reference to the suggestion of the Chinese delegation (document E/224), believed these suggestions would facilitate the work of the Council and the eleven commissions. The first proposal was that the Secretary-General should be asked to prepare a calendar of sessions for the coming year, indicating approximately when the meetings of the Council and of the commissions and Sub-Commissions would take place. Secondly, he proposed that the Council should hold four sessions in 1947, in view of the heavy schedule of work with which it had to deal. The sessions, according to his plan, would take place in February, May, August and November, with half of

① UN Document: E/SR. 21, p. 156, pp. 156–157, p. 157.

the commissions meeting before the February and August sessions, and the other half meeting before the May and November sessions. He further suggested that the Council should meet about the middle of February, May, August and November, in order to have one session two to three weeks before the General Assembly.

Mr. CHANG (China) agreed to the acceptance of the first point, and accepted the suggestion of the representative of France that the second point should serve as a basis for consideration.

【纪要影像】

Mr. Chang (China) nominated Dr. Zuleta Angel, representative of Colombia, as Acting Chairman; the nomination was seconded by the representatives of Yugoslavia and Peru, and Dr. Zuleta Angel was unanimously elected.

Mr. Chang (China), with reference to the suggestion of the Chinese delegation (document E/224), believed these suggestions would facilitate the work of the Council and the eleven commissions. The first proposal was that the Secretary-General should be asked to prepare a calendar of sessions for the coming year, indicating approximately when the meetings of the Council and of the commissions and sub-commissions would take place. Secondly, he proposed that the Council should hold four sessions in 1947, in view of the heavy schedule of work with which it had to deal. The sessions, according to his plan, would take place in February, May, August and November, with half of the commissions meeting before the February and August sessions, and the other half meeting before the May and November sessions. He further suggested that the Council should meet about the middle of February, May, August and November, in order to have one session two to three weeks before the General Assembly.

Mr. Chang (China) agreed to the acceptance of the first point, and accepted the suggestion of the representative of France that the second point should serve as a basis for consideration.

图片 3.15　张彭春在经社理事会第三届第21次会议发言纪要

【纪要译文】

张先生(中国)提名哥伦比亚代表祖莱塔·安吉尔(Zuleta Angel)博士为代理主席;南斯拉夫和秘鲁的代表附议了这一提名。祖莱塔·安吉尔博士全票当选。

张先生(中国)提到中国代表团的建议(E/224号文件),认为这些建议将有助于理事会和十一个委员会的工作。第一项提议是,应请秘书长为下一年编制一份会议日历,说明理事会、各委员会和小组委员会会议的大致举行时间。第二,鉴于理事会必须处理繁重的工作日程,他建议理事会在1947年举行四届会议。根据他的计划,这些会议将在2月、5月、8月和11月举行,其中一半的委员会会议在2月和8月的会议之前举行,另一半在5月和11月的会议之前举行。他还建议理事会大约在2月中旬、5月、8月和11月召开会议,以便在大会召开前两至三周举行一届会议。

张先生(中国)同意接受第一点,并接受法国代表的建议,即第二点应作为审议的基础。

15. 张彭春在经社理事会第三届特别会议上的发言

联合国经社理事会第三届特别会议，于 1946 年 12 月 10 日下午 3 时至晚上 6 时，在法拉盛草地公园举行。本次会议的主要议题是确定经社理事会委员会成员任命。中国代表张彭春参加了这次特别会议，并在会议上先后多次发言，其发言内容①如下：

【会议纪要】

Mr. CHANG (China) pointed out that the titles attributed to the candidates proposed by the Chinese Government, in document E/250, were not always correct and asked that the mistakes should be rectified.

Mr. CHANG (China) stated that his Government had submitted precise and detailed lists to the Secretariat, but that the latter had made an arbitrary choice among the qualifications mentioned. He, therefore, proposed that it should be definitely laid down that the Secretariat should consult delegations.

Mr. CHANG (China) proposed the following text:

"Members of Commissions nominated subsequent to the present special meeting and prior to the next session of the Economic and Social Council, after consultation between the Governments concerned and the Secretary-General, in accordance with the Economic and Social Council's decisions of 21 June and 1, 2 and 3 October 1946, may serve provisionally

① UN Document: E/SR. 21, p. 159, p. 162, p. 164, p. 165.

on Commissions pending confirmation by the Economic and Social Council at its next regular session."

Mr. CHANG (China), on behalf of the Economic and Social Council, expressed the gratitude of its members for the successful efforts of the Chairman, who had been kind enough to preside at this meeting, despite his present poor state of health.

【纪要影像】

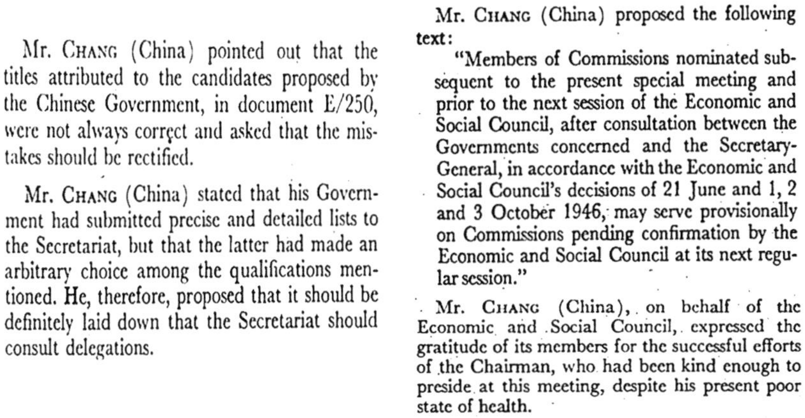

Mr. CHANG (China) pointed out that the titles attributed to the candidates proposed by the Chinese Government, in document E/250, were not always correct and asked that the mistakes should be rectified.

Mr. CHANG (China) stated that his Government had submitted precise and detailed lists to the Secretariat, but that the latter had made an arbitrary choice among the qualifications mentioned. He, therefore, proposed that it should be definitely laid down that the Secretariat should consult delegations.

Mr. CHANG (China) proposed the following text:

"Members of Commissions nominated subsequent to the present special meeting and prior to the next session of the Economic and Social Council, after consultation between the Governments concerned and the Secretary-General, in accordance with the Economic and Social Council's decisions of 21 June and 1, 2 and 3 October 1946, may serve provisionally on Commissions pending confirmation by the Economic and Social Council at its next regular session."

Mr. CHANG (China), on behalf of the Economic and Social Council, expressed the gratitude of its members for the successful efforts of the Chairman, who had been kind enough to preside at this meeting, despite his present poor state of health.

图片 3.16 张彭春在经社理事会第三届特别会议发言纪要

【纪要译文】

张先生(中国)指出,第 E/250 号文件中中国政府提出的候选人的头衔并不总是正确的,他要求纠正错误。

张先生(中国)说,中国政府已向秘书处提交了准确而详细的清单,但秘书处对所提到的资格条件作出了任意选择。因此,他建议明确规定秘书处应与各代表团协商。

张先生(中国)提出以下案文:

在本次特别会议之后、经济及社会理事会下届会议之前，根据经济及社会理事会 1946 年 6 月 21 日和 10 月 1 日、2 日和 3 日的决定，经有关政府和秘书长协商后提名的委员会成员，可暂时在委员会任职，直至经济及社会理事会下届常会确认。

张先生(中国)代表经济及社会理事会表示，理事会成员感谢主席的成功努力，感谢他在目前健康状况不佳的情况下主持了本次会议。

第四章　联合国经社理事会第四届会议

（全文及纪要）

1947 年 2 月 28 日至 3 月 29 日，联合国经社理事会第四届会议，在纽约成功湖召开，本届会议共举行 34 次会议，即第 51 次会议至第 84 次会议。[1] 尽管每一届会议议程安排都会有所不同，但整体来讲，每届会议都十分紧张，所讨论的问题也是当时国际社会所面临的重要问题，本届会议的议题按照会议顺序包括三十多项内容，为了便于了解和研究张彭春对理事会的贡献，这里引证联合国档案记录所罗列的会议日程[2]如下：

1. 通过议程。

2. 修正第 17 号议事规则，以符合关于成员任期的新的大会第 87 号议事规则。

3. 选举主席和副主席。

4. 大会批准的财务条例规定了与理事会决议有关的财务概算。

5. 麻醉品委员会的报告和大会关于麻醉品的决议。

6. 大会关于经济及社会理事会活动的决议：B 部分建议给予世界工会联合会提交临时议程项目的权利，C 部分建议所有 A 类非政府组织应得到平等待遇。

7. 理事会非政府组织委员会的报告。

---

① 值得说明的是：联合国经济及社会理事会经过前三届会议之后，整个会议顺序编号得以规范，即按照理事会所召开的会议总次数计算，因此，从第四届会议首次会议（即第 51 次会议）起，避免了前三届会议次数编号混乱的情况。

② UN Document：E/SR. 51-84，pp. xx-xxi.

8. 秘书长关于协调委员会的报告。

9. 经济和就业委员会的报告。

10. 大会关于重建受破坏地区,包括设立欧洲和远东经济委员会以及调查原材料资源问题的决议。

11. 灾区重建工作组(远东)的报告。

12. 大会关于联合国难民署终止后的救济需要的决议,秘书长的报告。

13. 粮食及农业组织希腊访问团的报告。粮农组织要求的项目。

14. 国际贸易和就业会议筹备委员会的报告:关于在国际贸易组织成立之前就商品问题进行政府间协商和采取行动的决议。

15. 国际贸易和就业会议筹备委员会的报告:关于发展的决议。

16. 秘书长关于粮农组织筹备委员会的报告。

17. 美国关于举行一次关于保存和利用资源的会议的提案。

18. 社会委员会的报告:关于国际紧急儿童基金会的总决议;基金执行委员会报告;大会关于转移联合国善后救济总署福利活动的决议;大会关于移交国际联盟非政治职能的决议。

19. 运输和通讯委员会的报告。

20. 人权委员会的报告;大会关于人权宣言草案的决议;大会关于召开信息自由国际会议的决议。

21. 大会关于大屠杀罪的决议。

22. 统计委员会的报告。

23. 秘书长关于世界统计局赞助船舶的报告。

24. 与专门机构协商委员会的报告。

25. 大会关于与专门机构的协定的决议。

26. 人口委员会的报告。

27. 妇女地位委员会的报告。

28. 大会关于向会员国政府提供专家咨询的决议。

29. 大会关于住房的决议。

30. 大会关于翻译经典著作的决议。

31. 影响理事会程序和组织的问题：

(a)与安全和托管公司协商的安排。

(b)确认委员会成员。

(c)关于委员会成员候补人选的安排。

(d)1947年经济和社会会议日历。

(e)联合国大会理事会报告员问题。

(该会议日程译自联合国文献：E/SR. 51-84, pp. xx-xxi.)

中国代表张彭春参加了本届会议，并在其中的12次会议上发言，包括第51次会议、第59次会议、第62次会议、第69次会议、第70次会议、第72次会议、第73次会议、第78次会议、第79次会议、第81次会议、第82次会议和第84次会议。① 另外，参会人员施思明博士在第52次会议②上发言，杨博士在第54次会议③、第55次会议④、第67次会议⑤、第71次会议⑥、第74次会议⑦和第83次会议⑧上发言。由于本届会议既有全文记录(除第84次会议外)也有会议纪要，本章内容编排与第二章同，即每次会议分为两部分：(1)"会议发言全文记录及译文"包括："全文记录"和"全文译文"；(2)"会议发言内容纪要"包括："会议纪要"、"纪要影像"和"纪

---

① UN Document: E/SR. 84, p. 243. (令人遗憾的是，联合国正式文件系统中由于只有会议纪要文件E/SR. 84，而全文记录文件E/PV. 84，其内容也是会议纪要，虽然能够检索到该文件，但其实仍然缺少本次会议的全文记录内容。)

② UN Document: E/SR. 51-84, pp. 10-11; or UN Document: E/PV. 52, pp. 32-40.

③ UN Document: E/SR. 51-84, p. 23; or UN Document: E/PV. 54, p. 21.

④ UN Document: E/SR. 51-84, pp. 29-30. (说明：联合国文献系统中缺少该次会议的全文记录文献UN Document: E/PV. 55.)

⑤ UN Document: E/SR. 51-84, p. 98; or UN Document: E/PV. 67, pp. 16-21.

⑥ UN Document: E/SR. 51-84, pp. 124-125; or UN Document: E/PV. 71, pp. 41-42. (值得说明的一点：在全文会议记录中，杨博士的姓被错误地打印成Wang，见UN Document: E/PV. 71, p. 41.)

⑦ UN Document: E/SR. 51-84, pp. 147-148, p. 152; or UN Document: E/PV. 74, pp. 36-37, p. 67.

⑧ UN Document: E/SR. 51-84, p. 230; or UN Document: E/PV. 83. pp. 42-43, p. 53, p. 54.

要译文”,并在注释中标明发言内容所在页码。以便研究者分析比较和引用。

CHINA

Representatives
Dr. Tien-fong Cheng
H.E. Dr. P. C. Chang

Alternate
H.E. Dr. Pao Chun-jien

Advisers
Dr. Simon M. Cheng
Mr. K. P. Fengsen
Mr. P. Y. Tsao
Dr. Hsiu Cha
Miss Esme Y. Y. Chu

图片 4.1　联合国经济及社会理事会第四届会议中国代表团名单

1. 张彭春在经社理事会第四届第51次会议上的发言

1947年2月28日上午11时,联合国经社理事会第四届第51次会议,在纽约成功湖召开。本次会议涉及议题:"1. 通过议程。2. 修正第17号议事规则,以符合关于成员任期的新的大会第87号议事规则。3. 选举主席和副主席。"①中国代表张彭春率代表团参加了本次会议,并在会议上发言,其具体发言内容如下:

(1)会议发言全文记录②及译文

【全文记录】

Dr. CHANG (China): Mr. President, first of all, I extend to you our welcome in having you back again with us. Secondly, I am sure that we all would like to take this opportunity of welcoming the new Members who have been admitted to this Council.

In regard to the provisional agenda, I have only one question and a comment.

The question is: Is the order to be decided upon this morning and not to be altered later? I think it may not be wise to have the order definitely decided upon this morning, because as we go on in the discussion we may find that a cer-

① UN Document: E/SR. 51-84, pp. 1-6.

② UN Document: E/PV. 51, pp. 26-35, p. 51.

tain alteration of order—of course, with the consent of the majority of the Council—may be not only wise but also necessary. That is one question which I should like to have the Council think over—whether this matter of the priority of the items on the agenda should be definitely decided upon this morning. My own humble opinion would be that it would be wise for us to keep that matter open for a little while, so that perhaps, after the first four or five days of the session, we should be able to see the situation more clearly as to the order of arrangement on the agenda.

In regard to my comment on the provisional agenda, I think, roughly speaking, all the thirty-odd items can be classified under three categories.

First, there are what we might call some organizational considerations. There are still some—for instance, the organizational consideration under Item 6. That is really part of an organizational consideration and is not yet finished. Some of the five questions listed under Item 31 are really quite important. For instance, this matter of (d) is quite important—the matter of the calendar of the various meetings. If that is left in the air, so to speak, we cannot take very concrete action and we cannot envisage what is going to be done, say, in the next ten months still left of this year. So that is one category on organizational matters.

While I am commenting on this Item 31 (d), I should like provisionally to reserve the right to recommend that this Item should be discussed a little further forward—not necessarily too far forward, but maybe somewhere there could be found a place for it—say about a week or so after the opening of the session. We all like to know what is going to happen afterwards. All of us are shaping our summer programmes, our progammes for the year. We like to know what the general decision of the Council will be in regard to that matter. So I should like to recommend that Item 31 (d)—the calendar for 1947—should be considered, if possible, say about a week or ten days after today, and not push it way, way back to the very end. That would come, it seems to me, a little too late. Furthermore, it seems to me that has to do with our general arrangement on the agenda.

I must come hurriedly to the second category; namely, the Reports of the Commissions and Committees. They are, so to speak, our regular business.

Eight of our nine Commissions have already met. Some of our new Members here may still not be able to repeat the names of all of the nine Commissions. I shall make an attempt at it myself. The Narcotic Commission has met, the Social Commission, the Economic and Employment Commission, the Human Rights Commission, the Status of Women Commission, the Population Commission, the Statistical Commission, and the Transport and Communications Commission. These eight have already met, and we have their Reports. Only one has not met as yet—the Fiscal Commission. According, to the present schedule, it will meet some time late in April. So we have the Reports of the eight Commissions and the Reports of the two permanent Committees; namely, the NGO—which does not mean "No Good Organization," but "Non-Governmental Organizations"—and the Permanent Committee on Negotiations with the Specialized Agencies. They have two important Reports. Therefore, we have the eight Commission Reports and the two Reports of the permanent Committees. They fall under our regular business.

Category 3 would be special business. I think that later on, as we envisage the items on the agenda, we can see them in terms of these three categories; organizational matters, regular business and special business. I think it is much easier when we see it in that simplified form.

With regard to the second, namely, the regular business, the reports of Commissions and Committees; perhaps never will there be another meeting of the Council with so many reports to come before it, all at the same time. It happens that this is the first time when the Council meets that so many Commissions have had their first meetings. So I, personally, would like to suggest that after we discussed the matter of the calendar—that is why I suggest that the calendar should be brought forward somewhat in this matter—we should tackle the reports of the Commissions that will have two meetings this year at this session first, leaving the Commissions that will, according to our judgment when we come to the calendar, have only one meeting this year; those reports to be discussed at our fifth session. That is, you see, a closely related problem. I think it would not be wise to discuss all the eight Commissions' reports and the two Committees' reports. The two committees' reports should be discussed; that is natural. They are Standing Committee reports and perhaps they will not be too long; but the eight Commissions' reports should be reevaluated according to their importance and, furthermore, according to whether or not they will have another meeting before our next session. If they are going to have another meeting, then we should discuss their reports. But if, according to our judgment on the calendar, they will not have another meeting until the next session, their reports may well be postponed until the next session. Otherwise, I fear we have too many things to digest. All of us may suffer from indigestion, which even the W. H. O. may not be able to cure.

In regard to items 10, 11 and 12, I agree with the distinguished representative of the United Kingdom. I do not find that he is always extremely unpopular. I agree with him in his comment on those three items, namely, their importance. And may I remind him, now that he has just come over, that for the last ten days or so we have been discussing the Far Eastern Group, and of that Group I happen to be the humble Chairman, who will produce a report within a very short time, so there is no need of any delay. Therefore, according to his first suggestion, items 10 and 11 should be discussed together. The European devastated conditions and the Asiatic devastated conditions should be discussed at the same time.

Dr. Chang (China): The eminent qualifications of our President need not be reiterated. May I, then, move that the present President be re-elected unanimously.

【全文译文】

张博士(中国):主席先生,首先,我欢迎您再次与我们在一起。第二,我相信我们大家都想借此机会欢迎新成员加入本理事会。

关于临时议程,我只有一个问题和一点意见。

问题是:这个顺序是今天上午决定的,以后不会改变吗?我认为,今天上午就明确决定顺序可能并不明智,因为随着我们讨论的进行,我们可能会发现对顺序的某种改变——当然,要征得理事会大多数成员的同意——可能不仅是明智的,而且是必要的。这是我希望理事会考虑的一个问题——是否应该在今天上午明确决定议程项目的优先次序。我个人的愚见是,我们最好暂时不对这一问题作出决定,这样,也许在会议的头四五天之后,我们应该能够更清楚地看到议程安排顺序的情况。

关于我对临时议程的意见,我认为,粗略地说,所有三十多个项目可以分为三类。

首先,我们可以称之为一些组织审议。还有一些——例如第 6 项下的组织审议。这实际上是组织审议的一部分,尚未完成。在第 31 项下列出的五个问题中,有些确实相当重要。例如,(d)项的问题非常重要——对于各种会议的日程安排问题。可以说,如果这一点悬而未决,我们就无法采取非常具体的行动,也无法设想在今年剩下的 10 个月内会做些什么。这是关于组织事项的一个类别。

在我就 31(d)项发表意见时,我暂时保留建议进一步讨论这一项的权利,不一定前进一大步,但也许可以在某些地方找到讨论的位置——比如在届会开幕后大约一周。我们都想知道之后会发生什么。我们所有人都在制定我们的暑期计划和今年的计划。我们想知道理事会对此时的总体决定。因此,我谨建议,如果可能的话,应该审议项目 31(d)——1947 年的日历——比如说在今天之后一周或十天,而不是把它推到最后。在我看来,这来得有点太晚了。此外,在我看来,这与我们议程上的总体安排有关。

我必须赶紧转到第二类;即各委员会的报告。可以说,它们是我们的日常事务。

我们九个委员会中有八个已经开过会。我们这里的一些新成员可能仍然无法说出所有九个委员会的名称。我将亲自尝试一下。麻醉药品委员会、社会委员会、经济和就业委员会、人权委员会、妇女地位委员会、人口委员会、统计委员会以及交通运输委员会举行了会议。这八个委员会已经开会了,我们有他们的报告。到目前为止,只有一个财政委员会尚未开会。根据目前的时间表,它将在 4 月底的某个时间举行会议。我们有八个委员会的报告和两个常设委员会的报告,两个常设委员会也就是指,非政府组织——不是指“不好的组织”,而是指“非政府组织”——和与专门机构协商常设委员会。他们有两份重要报告。因此,我们有八份委员会报告和两份常设委员会报告。它们属于我们的日常事务范围。

第三类是特殊事务。我认为稍后,当我们设想议程上的项目时,我们可以从这三个类别来看待它们:组织事项、日常事务和特殊事务。我认为,当我们以这种简化的形式来看待它时,会容易得多。

关于第二项,即日常事务,各委员会的报告;也许再也不会有理事会会议同时收到如此多的报告。碰巧,这是理事会第一次遇到如此多的委员会举行第一次会议。因此,我个人想建议,在我们讨论了日程问题之后——这就是为什么我建议在这一问题上,日程应该提前一些——我们应该首先处理今年将在本届会议上举行两次会议的各委员会的报告,留下将要举行会议的各委员会,根据我们在日程上的判断,今年只有一次会议;这些报告将在我们第五届会议上讨论。你看,这是一个密切相关的问题。我认为讨论所有八个委员会的报告和两个常设委员会的报告是不明智的。应该讨论两个常设委员会的报告;这是很自然的。这是常设委会的报告,也许不会太长;但是,八个委员会的报告应根据其重要性,并根据他们是否将在我们下届会议之前举行另一次会议来重新评估。如果他们要再开会，那么我们应该讨论他们的报告。但是，根据我们对日程的判断，如果他们在下一届会议之前不会再开会，他们的报告很可能会推迟到下一届会议。否则，我担心我们要消化的东西太多了。我们所有人都可能患有消化不良，即使是世界卫生组织也可能无法治愈。

关于10、11和12项，我同意尊敬的英国代表的意见。我觉得他并不总是非常不受欢迎。我同意他对这三项的评论，即它们的重要性。我想提醒他，既然他刚过来，在过去十天左右的时间里，我们一直在讨论远东集团，而在该集团中，鄙人恰好是主席，将在很短的时间内提出一份报告，因此没有必要再拖延了。因此，根据他的第一项建议，10和11项应该一起讨论。欧洲的受灾情况和亚洲的受灾情况应该同时讨论。

张博士(中国)：我们主席的杰出资历无需赘述。那么，我谨提议现任主席连任全体一致通过。

(2)会议发言内容纪要①

【会议纪要】

Mr. CHANG (China), after welcoming the President and the new members of the Council, asked whether it might not be possible, in due course, to reconsider the order of items of the provisional agenda. They fell into three groups: (1) organizational questions, (2) regular business reports of commissions and standing committees, and (3) special business. He suggested that item 31 (d) (calendar of economic and social meetings for 1947) should also be placed higher in the agenda, since it affected the entire work of the Council that year. The Council could then take up the reports of the two standing committees and of commissions, having two sessions, leaving less urgent questions

① UN Document: E/SR. 51, pp. 2-3, p. 5 or UN Document: E/SR. 51-84, pp. 2-3, p. 5.

and reports of commissions meeting only once a year until the fifth session of the Council. He agreed with the United Kingdom representative regarding the importance of items 10, 11 and 12, but suggested that since the report for item 11 would be completed shortly, it should be discussed in conjunction with item 10.

Mr. CHANG (China) and Mr. NASH (New Zealand) supported the nomination.

【纪要影像】

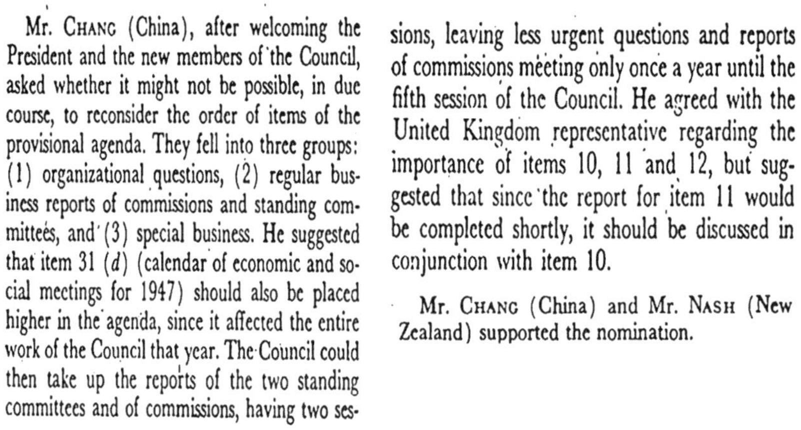

Mr. CHANG (China), after welcoming the President and the new members of the Council, asked whether it might not be possible, in due course, to reconsider the order of items of the provisional agenda. They fell into three groups: (1) organizational questions, (2) regular business reports of commissions and standing committees, and (3) special business. He suggested that item 31 (*d*) (calendar of economic and social meetings for 1947) should also be placed higher in the agenda, since it affected the entire work of the Council that year. The Council could then take up the reports of the two standing committees and of commissions, having two sessions, leaving less urgent questions and reports of commissions meeting only once a year until the fifth session of the Council. He agreed with the United Kingdom representative regarding the importance of items 10, 11 and 12, but suggested that since the report for item 11 would be completed shortly, it should be discussed in conjunction with item 10.

Mr. CHANG (China) and Mr. NASH (New Zealand) supported the nomination.

图片 4.2　张彭春在经社理事会第四届第 51 次会议发言纪要

【纪要译文】

张先生(中国)在欢迎理事会主席和新成员后,询问是否可能在适当时候重新审议临时议程项目的顺序。他们分为三组:(1)组织问题,(2)委员会和常设委员会的日常事务报告,(3)特殊事务。他建议,项目 31(d)(1947 年经济及社会会议日程)也应放在议程的更高位置,因为它影响到理事会当年的整个工作。然后,理事会可以举行两届会议,审议两个常设委员会和各委员会的报告,不太紧迫的问题和每年只举行一次会议的各委员会的报告可以放到理事会第五届会议讨论。他同意英国代表关于项目

10、11 和 12 的重要性的看法，但建议，由于项目 11 的报告将很快完成，因此应与项目 10 一起讨论。

张先生（中国）和奈斯先生（新西兰）支持提名。

2. 张彭春在经社理事会第四届第59次会议上的发言

1947年3月7日下午3时,联合国经社理事会第四届第59次会议,在纽约成功湖召开。本次会议主要讨论经济和就业委员会的报告。中国代表张彭春率代表团参加了本次会议,并在会议上发言,其具体发言内容如下:

(1)会议发言全文记录[①]及译文

【全文记录】

Dr. CHANG (China): Mr. President, may I take this opportunity of reporting to you, sir, that though absent from several of the meetings of this Council, I have not been exactly unemployed. I have, as a matter of fact, enjoyed full employment in the work of the working group on Asia and the Far East under the Temporary Sub-commission on Economic Reconstruction for Devastated Areas.

Those of us who worked in that group for the last three weeks feel at this last hour almost altogether devastated. But fortunately we have produced a re-

① UN Document: E/PV. 59, pp. 61-63.

port, and that report is officially coming to this Council tomorrow, and some[①] I understand Mr. President, are already here.

In discussing that report, I am afraid, sir, I shall have the opportunity of punishing my colleagues on this Council with much verbiage. However, before we conclude the general debate on economic matters, may I just make a very simple comment, that though the delegation of China has not presented any elaborate views during these last two or three meetings, we have contributed our views in past sessions, especially in the second session. There was a speech made by my humble self entitled "World Significance of Economically Low Pressure Areas." If I am not mistaken, that was perhaps a gentle stimulant to the emphasis on under-industrialized or underdeveloped areas.

Instead of rehashing my ideas—that is something that I think we ought not to do—I shall not speak on the same lines, but, if I may, Mr. President, I would like to present to Members of this Council a copy of these very badly-worded comments sometime tomorrow.

Furthermore, on the report on the Economic and Employment Commission, the Chinese delegation has nothing but words of satisfaction and gratification, and in regard to detailed comments, may I take the pleasure of reserving our comments, our views, in the Committee meeting. That, I think, will be

① John Nicholson, a senior copy editor for *China Daily*, says: "One key thing in understanding this is that it appears he is being slightly humorous, first referring to the fact that he has not been idle in recent times but has 'enjoyed full employment'. He then has some fun with a pun, saying that those working with him over the three weeks now feel almost 'devastated'. Strictly speaking one would not use that word to refer to being overwhelmed by work. One is devastated by the loss of a loved one, or a country is devastated by war, for example. But he knowingly uses the word, echoing its use in the title of the report he and his colleagues had been working on. This passage suggests to me that with all the seriousness Chang no doubt brought to his work, that did not prevent him from at times being humorous and even playful. I believe the 'some' refers to the report. It is due officially to arrive at the council in its completed form the next day, but he thinks some copies, or some parts of the report, may already be in the council's hands." (Cited from WeChat communication with Nicholson, February 25, 2022.)

welcome to all here.

In conclusion, I understand there has been some discussion on the relative importance of development and full employment. That seems to be something that requires our attention. May I, in this connection, just read a line here: "The whole tempo of trade and industrial activity in all areas will increase"—that is, with the increasing industrialization of the underdeveloped areas—"The benefits of increased industrialization throughout the world are, therefore, recognized as applying not only to the areas where such increasing industrialization occurs but also to the world at large, including countries already heavily industrialized."

Those words are not mine. They are quoted from a report of the International Business Conference held at Rye, New York, in November, 1944. It was recognized by a group of sound businessmen that industrialization of the underindustrialized areas would spread its benefits (bendits①) to the industrialized countries as well and surely assist in the problem of full employment, whatever that may mean.

Again, in conclusion, these words again are not mine; they appear a little, let us say, stiff. However, allow me to read them: "Mutual confidence is to be promoted, and peaceful relations are to be maintained. People regard not only their parents as parents; not only their own children as children; provisions are made for the aged; employment is provided for the able-bodied; and education is afforded to the young. Widows and widowers, orphans and the childless, the deformed and the diseased are all cared for. Men have their occupations and women have their homes. Surplus good are not to be wasted; they need not be kept as one's own. Labour is not to be idle; work is not necessarily

① 笔者注:括号中的单词是会议全文记录的内容,根据上下文理解,全文记录中的这个词"bendits",估计是打字打错了,应该是"benefits",特此说明和订正,并以其下加下划线的形式呈现出来。

for self only."

The above quotation is from a Chinese text of some 2,500 years ago on this ideal of economic and social adjustment. They seem to out-Beveridge Beveridge. But the last two sentences seem to be particularly appropriate, in view of the philosophical comments of our distinguished colleague of New Zealand. May I just repeat these last two sentences: "Surplus goods are not to be wasted." I understand we are still trying to plow under some sort of thing called potatoes. "Surplus goods are not to be wasted; they need not be kept as one's own. Labour is not to be idle; work is not necessarily for self only."

Sir, I think if we could just but pay a little more attention to selfless effort, humankind, after all, may be benefited.

【全文译文】

张博士(中国):主席先生,请允许我借此机会向你报告,尽管我缺席了本理事会的几次会议,但我并没有真正失业。事实上,我充分参与了灾区经济重建临时小组委员会下属的亚洲和远东问题工作组的工作。

过去三周在该小组工作的我们这些人在这最后的时刻感到几乎完全崩溃了。但幸运的是,我们已经完成了一份报告,该报告将于明天正式提交理事会,据我所知,主席先生,报告的一些内容[①]已经在理事会手里。

主席先生,在讨论该份报告时,我恐怕会有机会用很多言词来惩罚本理事会的同事。然而,在我们结束关于经济问题的一般性辩论之前,请允

① 《中国日报》(*China Daily*)高级文字编辑约翰·尼克尔森表示:"理解这一点的一个关键是,他似乎有点幽默,首先提到的是他最近并没有闲着,而是'享受着充分就业'。然后,他用一句双关语开了个玩笑,说那些和他一起工作了三周的人现在感觉几乎'崩溃'了。严格地说,人们不会用这个词来指被工作压垮。例如,一个人因失去亲人而悲痛欲绝,或者一个国家因战争而满目疮痍。但是他故意用了这个词,在他和他的同事正在做的报告的标题中重复了这个词的用法。这段话让我想到,尽管张对他的工作毫无疑问是严肃的,但这并不妨碍他时而幽默,时而戏谑。我相信'一些'是指报告。该报告的完整形式应于第二天正式提交理事会,但他认为报告的一些副本或部分内容可能已经在理事会手中。"(引自与尼克尔森的微信交流,2022 年 2 月 25 日。)

许我发表一个非常简单的评论，即尽管中国代表团在过去的两三次会议上没有提出任何详细的意见，但我们在过去的几届会议上，特别是在第二届会议上贡献了我们的观点。我发表了一篇题为《经济低压区的世界意义》的演讲。如果我没有弄错的话，这也许是对强调欠工业化或欠发达地区的一种温和的刺激。

我不想重复我的想法——这是我认为我们不应该做的事情——我不会按照同样的思路发言，但是，主席先生，如果可以的话，我想在明天的某个时候向理事会成员提交一份这些措辞非常糟糕的评论的副本。

此外，关于经济和就业委员会的报告，中国代表团只能说满意和欣慰，关于详细的评论，请允许我在委员会会议上保留我们的评论和观点。我认为，这将受到在座各位的欢迎。

总之，我知道对发展和充分就业的相对重要性进行了一些讨论。这似乎是需要我们注意的事情。在这方面，请允许我在这里读一句话："所有地区的贸易和工业活动的整体速度将会加快"——也就是说，随着不发达地区工业化程度的提高——"因此，全世界工业化程度提高的好处被认为不仅适用于工业化程度提高的地区，而且适用于整个世界，包括已经高度工业化的国家。"

那些话不是我说的。它们引自 1944 年 11 月在纽约拉伊举行的国际商务会议的一份报告。一群精明的商人认识到，欠工业化地区的工业化也会给工业化国家带来好处，而且肯定会有助于解决充分就业的问题，不管这意味着什么。

再次，综上，这些话又不是我说的；我们可以说，它们看起来有点古板。然而请允许我读一下："讲信修睦。故人不独亲其亲，不独子其子，使老有所终，壮有所用，幼有所长。鳏、寡、孤、独、废、疾者皆有所养，男有分，女有归。货恶其弃于地也，不必藏于己；力恶其不出于身也，不必为己。"

上述引文来自于大约 2500 年前关于这种经济和社会调整理想的中文

文本。他们似乎胜过了贝弗里奇①。但是，鉴于我们尊敬的新西兰同事富有哲理的评论，最后两句话似乎特别恰当。请允许我重复最后两句话："货恶其弃于地也。"据我所知，我们仍在努力挖掘一种叫做土豆的东西。"货恶其弃于地也，不必藏于己；力恶其不出于身也，不必为己。"

主席先生，我认为如果我们能对无私的努力多一点关注，人类终究会受益。

(2)会议发言内容纪要②

【会议纪要】

Dr. CHANG (China) congratulated the Economic and Employment Commission and confined his remarks to two quotations relating to economic development, one from the words of a business man in 1944, and the other from a Chinese text, which was two thousand years old.

【纪要影像】

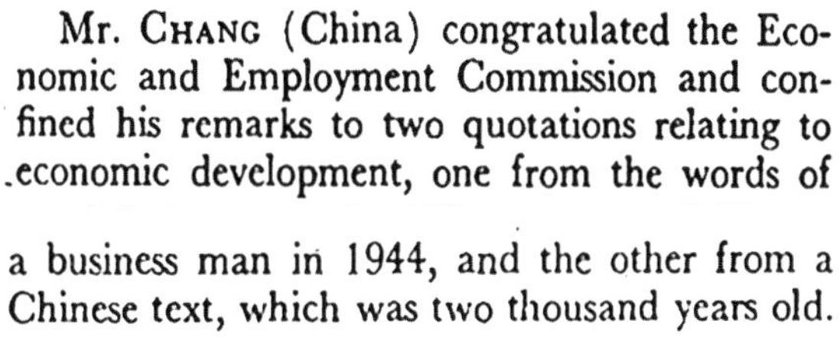
Mr. CHANG (China) congratulated the Economic and Employment Commission and confined his remarks to two quotations relating to economic development, one from the words of a business man in 1944, and the other from a Chinese text, which was two thousand years old.

图片 4.3 张彭春在经社理事会第四届第 59 次会议发言纪要

① 笔者注释：英国战后制定的社会保障计划，由英国著名经济学家威廉·贝弗里奇爵士(Sir William Beveridge)起草了一个报告，称为《贝弗里奇报告》，以消除贫困。正如有关网站介绍的那样："英国政府还要求威廉·贝弗里奇爵士写一份报告，说明帮助低收入人群的最佳方法。1942 年 12 月，贝弗里奇发表了一份报告，建议所有工作年龄的人每周缴纳一次会费。作为回报，福利将支付给生病、失业、退休或丧偶的人。贝弗里奇认为，这一制度将提供最低生活标准，'任何人都不得低于这一标准'。这些措施最终由 1945 年当选的工党政府提出。"(见网址：https://spartacus-educational.com/2WWbeveridgereport.htm，2022 年 1 月 22 日访问。)

② UN Document：E/SR.59，pp.58-59.

【纪要译文】

张先生(中国)向经济和就业委员会表示祝贺,并将其发言限于两段有关经济发展的引语,一段引自于1944年一位商人的话,另一段引自两千年前的中文文本。

3. 张彭春在经社理事会第四届第 62 次会议上的发言

1947 年 3 月 10 日上午 11 时,联合国经社理事会第四届第 62 次会议,在纽约成功湖召开。本次会议主要继续讨论粮农组织将召开的木材会议、讨论交通与通讯委员会的报告、讨论经济项目委员会阶段安排。中国代表张彭春率代表团参加了本次会议,并在会议上发言,其具体发言内容如下:

(1) 会议发言全文记录[①]及译文

【全文记录】

Dr. CHANG (China): Mr. President, my intervention at this juncture will be very brief.

I think that when the honourable representative of Czechoslovakia brought this very important matter to our attention, he had in mind the shortage of timber that has caused a delay in reconstruction and a delay in the economic recovery of Europe. I am sure he did not at all have in mind neglecting, the same condition in Asia and the Far East, because, after all, the world market is closely connected.

May I, then, make this suggestion—that, perhaps, in the first paragraph, beginning: "RECOGNIZING the seriousness of the present timber shortage which is delaying reconstruction and threatening economic recovery"—we then

① UN Document: E/PV. 62, pp. 11-12.

say, "in the war devastated areas." That would include the war devastated areas both in Europe and in Asia.

As to how this would be done, naturally that would be discussed in the Drafting Committee, so I shall not take too much time on that at this juncture. At least, I think something like the following sentence should be added somewhere: "REQUESTS the Secretary-General to call the attention of the Food and Agriculture Organization to the similar shortage of timber in the Far East, and to take adequate measures to ensure equitable supply of timber to the war devastated areas in Asia and the Far East."

I do not think our distinguished colleague from Czechoslovakia would object to any mention of the war devastated areas in Asia and the Far East.

【记录译文】

张博士(中国):主席先生,我在此节点上的发言将非常简短。

我认为,当尊敬的捷克斯洛伐克代表提请我们注意这一非常重要的问题时,他想到的是木材短缺,这种短缺造成了欧洲重建和经济复苏的拖延。我相信他根本没有想要忽视亚洲和远东的同样情况,因为毕竟世界市场是紧密相连的。

那么,请允许我提出这个建议——也许在第一段中,以"认识到目前木材短缺的严重性,这种短缺正在拖延重建并威胁经济复苏"开始——,然后我们说,"在遭受战争破坏的地区。"这将包括欧洲和亚洲遭受战争破坏的地区。

至于如何做到这一点,自然将在起草委员会中进行讨论,因此,我现在不会在这方面花太多时间。至少,我认为应该在某处增加类似下面这句话的内容:"请秘书长提请粮食及农业组织注意远东地区类似的木材短缺,并采取适当措施确保向亚洲和远东受战争破坏地区公平供应木材。"

我想我们尊敬的捷克斯洛伐克同事不会反对提及亚洲和远东遭受战争破坏的地区。

(2)会议发言内容纪要[①]

【会议纪要】

Mr. CHANG (China) thought that though the Czechoslovak representative had had in mind the shortage of timber that had delayed the economic reconstruction and recovery of Europe, he had not intended to ignore similar conditions in Asia and the Far East. Consequently he suggested the insertion of the words "in the war-devastated areas" and of a paragraph pointing out the similar shortage of timber in Asia and the Far East, and stressing the necessity of taking adequate measures to ensure an equitable supply of timber for the war-devasted areas of those regions.

【纪要影像】

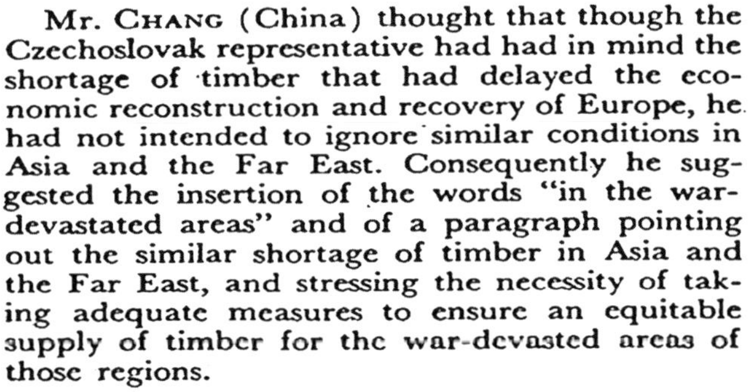

Mr. CHANG (China) thought that though the Czechoslovak representative had had in mind the shortage of timber that had delayed the economic reconstruction and recovery of Europe, he had not intended to ignore similar conditions in Asia and the Far East. Consequently he suggested the insertion of the words "in the war-devastated areas" and of a paragraph pointing out the similar shortage of timber in Asia and the Far East, and stressing the necessity of taking adequate measures to ensure an equitable supply of timber for the war-devasted areas of those regions.

图片 4.4　张彭春在经社理事会第四届第 62 次会议发言纪要

【纪要译文】

张先生(中国)认为,虽然捷克斯洛伐克代表想到的是木材短缺已推迟了欧洲的经济重建和复苏,但他并没有打算忽视亚洲和远东的类似情

① UN Document: E/SR. 51-84, p. 71.

况。因此，他建议插入“在受战争破坏的地区”等字，并插入一个段落，指出亚洲和远东同样缺乏木材，并强调有必要采取足够措施，确保向这些地区受战争破坏的地区公平供应木材。

4. 张彭春在经社理事会第四届第 69 次会议上的发言

1947 年 3 月 14 日下午 2 时 45 分,联合国经社理事会第四届第 69 次会议,在纽约成功湖召开。本次会议主要议题是审议人权委员会的报告。中国代表张彭春率代表团参加了本次会议,并在会议上发言,其具体发言内容如下:

(1)会议发言全文记录[①]及译文

(暂缺。)

(2)会议发言内容纪要[②]

【会议纪要】

Mr. CHANG (China) hoped that after the myopia of the last hundred and fifty years, nations were at last on the threshold of a new humanistic period. The bill envisaged should be based on the aspiration for a new humanism.

The fact that rights of men were included in thirty-five or forty of the world's constitutions indicated that a large measure of agreement was possible in

① 联合国正式文件系统(ODS)中所能检索到的文件 E/PV. 69 系会议纪要而不是全文记录,这是一个文件名错误。也就是说,系统上检索到的全文记录文件 E/PV. 69 与会议纪要文件 E/SR. 69 是同一个文件的内容,都是会议纪要。这样,虽然检索到了两个文件,但却仅有会议纪要的内容。

② UN Document: E/SR. 51-84, p. 110-111.

spite of differences of philosophy or ideology.

In article 18 of the Constitution promulgated in December 1946 by the Constituent Assembly in China a new right was included—the right to take public examination for holding public offices—of which little notice had been taken in the world as a whole. The institution of public civil service examinations and that of representative government had contributed greatly to the promotion of true freedom and equality and formed the basis of social democracy. He hoped that some notice would be taken of the former institution in the bill of rights.

【纪要影像】

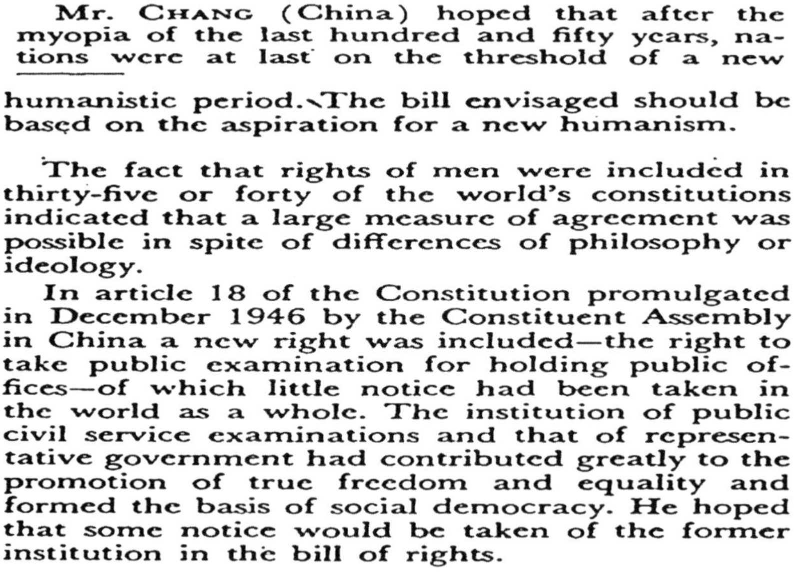
Mr. CHANG (China) hoped that after the myopia of the last hundred and fifty years, nations were at last on the threshold of a new humanistic period. The bill envisaged should be based on the aspiration for a new humanism.

The fact that rights of men were included in thirty-five or forty of the world's constitutions indicated that a large measure of agreement was possible in spite of differences of philosophy or ideology.

In article 18 of the Constitution promulgated in December 1946 by the Constituent Assembly in China a new right was included—the right to take public examination for holding public offices—of which little notice had been taken in the world as a whole. The institution of public civil service examinations and that of representative government had contributed greatly to the promotion of true freedom and equality and formed the basis of social democracy. He hoped that some notice would be taken of the former institution in the bill of rights.

图片 4.5　张彭春在经社理事会第四届第 69 次会议发言纪要

【纪要译文】

张先生(中国)希望,在经历了过去 150 年的短视之后,各国终于进入了一个新的人文时期。设想的法案应基于对新人文主义的渴望。

世界上有35或40部宪法都包含了人权,这一事实表明,尽管哲学或意识形态存在差异,但仍有可能达成很大程度的一致。

中国制宪会议于1946年12月颁布的宪法第18条中包括了一项新的权利——参加公共考试以担任公职的权利——这一权利在整个世界上很少受到注意。公共公务员考试制度和代议制政府制度极大地促进了真正的自由和平等,并构成了社会民主的基础。他希望《人权法案》中会注意到前一个制度。

5. 张彭春在经社理事会第四届第 70 次会议上的发言

1947 年 3 月 15 日上午 10 时 30 分,联合国经社理事会第四届第 70 次会议,在纽约成功湖召开。本次会议主要讨论秘书长关于种族灭绝罪的说明、讨论国际儿童应急基金。中国代表张彭春率团参加了本次会议,并在会议上发言,其具体发言内容如下:

(1) 会议发言全文记录[①]及译文

【全文记录】

Dr. CHANG (China): Mr. President, the Chinese delegation feels that it ought to indicate the grave significance of the problem of genocide. We join with all delegations in moral indignation, and surely something concrete ought to be done.

In regard to the concrete measures, we are very pleased to hear the suggestion of the distinguished representative of the United Kingdom that some legal experts should be called in by the Secretary-General before the next session of the Economic and Social Council to explore the legal aspects of the problem. At the same time, we also feel that there is under the Commission on Human Rights a Sub-commission for the Prevention of Discrimination and Protection of Minorities. It seems to us that after a preliminary study by some legal experts

① UN Document: E/PV. 70, pp. 41-42.

called together by the Secretary-General, and their report to the next session of the Economic and Social Council—after that, the problem may well be turned over to the Sub-commission on the Prevention of Discrimination and the Protection of Minorities.

【全文译文】

张博士(中国):主席先生,中国代表团认为应该表明种族灭绝问题的严重性。我们同所有代表团一道感到道义上的愤慨,当然应该采取一些具体行动。

关于具体措施,我们非常高兴地听到尊敬的英国代表的建议,即秘书长应在经济及社会理事会下届会议之前召集一些法律专家探讨这一问题的法律方面。与此同时,我们还认为,在人权委员会之下有一个防止歧视和保护少数小组委员会。在我们看来,在秘书长召集的一些法律专家进行初步研究并向经济及社会理事会下一届会议提交报告之后,这个问题很可能会移交给防止歧视和保护少数民族委员会。

(2)会议发言内容纪要①

【会议纪要】

Mr. CHANG (China) joined in the general expression of indignation at the crime of genocide, and supported the United Kingdom proposal regarding concrete measures to be taken. However, he felt that after the legal aspect of the question had been thoroughly studied by experts in the Secretariat, the problem might be referred to the Sub-commission on Prevention of Discrimination and Protection of Minorities.

① UN Document: E/SR. 51-84, p. 115.

【纪要影像】

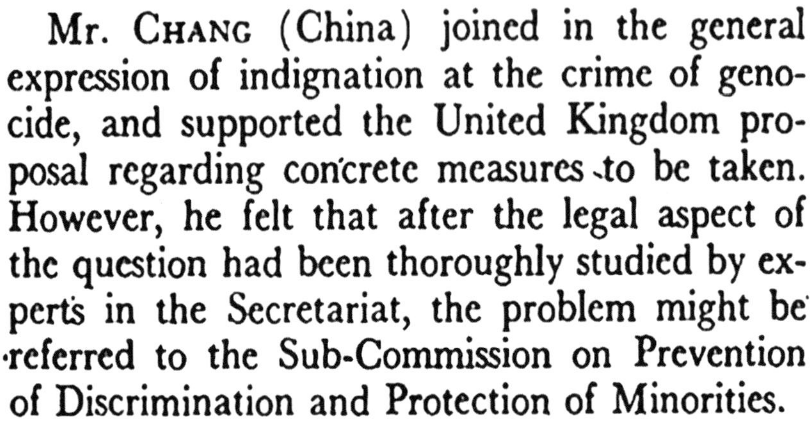

Mr. CHANG (China) joined in the general expression of indignation at the crime of genocide, and supported the United Kingdom proposal regarding concrete measures to be taken. However, he felt that after the legal aspect of the question had been thoroughly studied by experts in the Secretariat, the problem might be referred to the Sub-Commission on Prevention of Discrimination and Protection of Minorities.

图片 4.5　张彭春在经社理事会第四届第 70 次会议发言纪要

【纪要译文】

张先生(中国)也对灭绝种族罪表示愤慨,并支持英国关于采取具体措施的建议。然而,他认为,在秘书处的专家彻底研究了这个问题的法律方面之后,这个问题可能会提交给防止歧视和保护少数民族委员会。

6. 张彭春在经社理事会第四届第72次会议上的发言

1947年3月18日上午11时，联合国经社理事会第四届第72次会议，在纽约成功湖召开。本次会议主要讨论会议日程、继续讨论国际儿童应急基金、讨论亚洲和远东工作组的报告。中国代表张彭春率团参加了本次会议，作为亚洲和远东工作组主席，在会议上做亚洲和远东工作组报告，为亚洲和远东经济委员会的建立做出了重大贡献，其具体发言内容如下：

(1)会议发言全文记录[1]及译文

【全文记录】

Dr. CHANG (China): I beg to ask for a few moments to consider this matter of the timetable for conferences, not only in 1947 but also in 1948. We should look ahead.

Concerning conferences in 1947, I think all of us have this document E/280, Character of Conferences in 1947, which is a memorandum submitted by the Secretary-General. Before we proceed to suggest any concrete timetable, we should naturally have in mind the great responsibility of this Council, the Economic and Social Council, in the United Nations.

It seems to me, Mr. President, that the main problem before the Security Council of our great Organization is conflict; and the main problem before the

① UN Document: E/PV. 72, pp. 2-15, pp. 56-57, pp. 57-62.

Economic and Social Council is confusion. We all mean to do well but we have so many irons in the fire. We have nine Commissions under our direct supervision. We are also interested in the co-ordination of the work of the United Nations and the Specialized Agencies. Under several of our Commissions we have or shall have one or more Sub-commissions. Then, under all these Commissions there will have to be technical committees of an *ad hoc* nature. Furthermore, there will be at least two or three international conferences which will be called under one or another of the Specialized Agencies or one or another of the Commissions under the Council. So we can easily see that without a definite timetable long, long ahead, we shall have confusion with us.

We also realize that this Council, the Economic and Social Council, which has been in operation for the last year and three months, has a great function to perform, especially in the direction of constrictive efforts toward international understanding, co-operation, and peace.

Now, with such a heavy program of work and with such an important objective, we should keep our minds clear. Otherwise, we are apt to have a crowded agenda, as we are having at this Session. At the same time, people will leave with the feeling that we have not given as much time and concentration to the various problems brought before us as we would like to give to them. And I am afraid that in time, Mr. President, the prestige of the Council will be affected if insufficient care is given to problems brought before the Council.

For 1947 we have here a suggested programme with several considerations presented by the Secretary-General. On page 1, considerations one and two, I think, are wholly realistic—namely, the fact that the General Assembly last year at the Second Part of the First Session took a little longer time and did not end until the end of the year. Furthermore, due to the limitations in the Budget, we are not able to have as many meetings as some people would like to have.

In regard to the third consideration, I think there are—as a matter of fact, I have counted altogether—somewhere between five and six delegations, say, which have permanent representatives here, and then seven or eight others who have representatives, if not residing in New York, residing in Washington. So you have a total of twelve to fourteen, all within call either in New York, in Washington, or in another great capital of the world, Ottawa, which is a great capital but still within a night's ride on the train to New York. Consequently, I think there are altogether about twelve to thirteen delegations definitely with representatives in New York or within a short distance of New York; also, there are, I am sure, two or three or more valuable contributions, representatives who come here from other parts of the world, especially for the meetings of the Council.

Nevertheless, I think the third consideration should not be a consideration influencing the Council as a whole, because the so-called distinguished personnel mentioned under the third consideration do not compose more than, at most, one-third of the whole body of the Council. However, I shall not go into details concerning that. We must come to the practical problem of the programme of meetings for 1947.

In regard to this programme suggested by the Secretary-General, I think it is, on the whole, acceptable that in the five months after the closing of this Session of the Council and the beginning of the General Assembly we should, perhaps preferably, have only one ordinary session, perhaps a little longer—instead of three weeks, we could have, say, four weeks. At the same time, I think it is necessary to have a short session at about the same time as the General Assembly, because I am sure there will be problems after the next session which will need to be gone over by the Council as a whole before presentation to the General Assembly. There may be such problems, that is, regarding commission meetings, like the Human Rights Commission. They will have a series of drafting committee jobs between now and the next session of the Council. But I am sure that after the next session of the Council there will still be other work to be done by the Commission on Human Rights, and that report will have to be presented to the Council as a whole before being presented to the General Assembly.

Therefore, the programme as submitted by the Secretary-General seems to me to be acceptable in this sense: that the Council will have a little longer than ordinary session sometime in July, and a short session about the same time as the General Assembly. I think that, as a matter of convenience, the time should be arranged by the Secretariat, as to whether they would like to have it, say, two or three days or three or four days before the General Assembly begins, or just about the same time as the General Assembly. We shall leave that to the wisdom and the practical circumstances of the situation as seen by the Secretary-General.

I said that we ought also to pay attention at this time, though it may seem early, to the possibility of arranging a timetable for 1948. I think we must look ahead, because other specialized agencies lock to this Council for final, let us say, coordination of their programmes. If we have, as we have been having for the last twelve months or so, a sort of tentative arrangement from week to week or from month to month, it is very difficult for other bodies having relations with us to arrange their own meetings; So we should have, also, a provisional 1948 timetable to be presented to our next session of the Council in July, so that we can present it to the General Assembly. This provisional timetable for 1948 may have some connection—and I am sure it will have—with the Budget as a whole. Therefore, we should have a programme planned out for 1948, with these various things in view: First, the financial implications; we should have that before the meeting of the General Assembly. Secondly, how the different commissions, now that they have all had their initial meetings by our next session all of them will have had one meeting and some of them will have had two meetings—should be correlated in regard to their meetings with the meetings of the Council. Thirdly, how to coordinate with the specialized agencies.

In view of that fact, I should like very much, Mr. President, to have the President perhaps appoint an *ad hoc* committee of the Council to cooperate with the Secretary-General in planning a provisional timetable for 1948, to be presented to our next session in July. That is my humble suggestion.

In regard to the place of the meeting, the Secretary-General suggested in this paper, E/280, that the meetings this year, 1947, mostly should be held at the Headquarters. We also agree with this, especially in as much as it is a matter limited by the Budget. But I think, as time goes on, there is a problem to be considered, a problem that is not quite clear as yet—namely, if we are going to have meetings away from Headquarters, should those meetings be of the Council as well as of the commissions, or should those meetings be only of the commissions? It seems to me that this problem is worth considering, because it is much easier for the commissions to meet outside of Headquarters, as they will have a limited part of the Secretariat assisting them and the travel expenses and all other expenses will be much less. But if you have the Council meeting in places other than Headquarters, you will have a much larger staff to travel with you, and more files and materials to go along. Therefore, should it not be a general principle that the Council should meet in the Headquarters, while the commissions may meet in places other than Headquarters? That is just my humble suggestion.

Of course, in conclusion, if we should decide on this programme suggested by the Secretary-General, it may have some influence on the rest of the agenda before this Council, because the reports of commissions that are not going to meet before the next session of the Council may be, either in whole or in part, postponed until our next session. Thank you.

Dr. CHANG (China): Mr. President, you have before you the report of the working group for Asia and the Far East of the Temporary Sub-commission on the Economic Reconstruction of Devastated Areas. As Chairman of that working group, may I briefly comment on the report that is before you.

Devastation in Asia and the Far East was enormous. The working group having in charge the problems involved would indeed itself have been devastated had it not been for the increasingly loyal services of the Secretariat. With their help we continued until 2 a. m. one morning to bring the work to a gratifying conclusion. I hope that the Economic and Social Council will not try to outdo us in our record that evening for prolonging our meeting to the early hours of the morning.

On the whole, I think the Members of the working group regard the report as altogether gratifying and satisfactory. We tried as hard as we could to give an intelligent evaluation of the problems of reconstruction of devastated areas in Asia and the Far East. We carefully analyzed the crucial related problems and needs. We modestly mentioned the methods of organizing international aid and cooperation, and we strongly and unanimously urged the establishment of an Economic Commission for Asia and the Far East during this session, as has been done for Europe.

There were during the debates differences of opinion in certain matters, but the differences were healthy and useful. Some of us were cautious, exceedingly, very cautious, but the caution was by no means unjustified. Our differences never for a moment blinded us to the important task before us or to the urgency of the problem of reconstruction of devastated areas, affecting the lives of a large portion of humanity, perhaps half or more than half of the total population of the globe. As a matter of fact our differences only led us to attain a higher degree of unanimity in purpose, to do something, to get something done. Our caution was the dictate of wisdom, to produce a report acceptable to all in principle.

I myself, Mr. President, am not particularly in favour of the term "Far East". If we look across that peaceful ocean, the Pacific, from the Golden Gate, the Far East will become the Far West, at least to the United States. I make this point now in order to stress the idea that it is dangerous to overemphasize the division of East and West. Historically, the cordon of east and west was, has been and still is only imaginary, a line drawn arbitrarily. Sometimes we wonder where the line is drawn now. Where? As a matter of fact, in China we regard ourselves as living in the center of the earth's surface, and those of you who know Chinese know we call our country the "Middle Country" even today, and we shall continue to call our country the "Middle Country", so we do not belong to any East, wherever you put the line of division.

The President: Or West!

Dr. CHANG (China): Or West—thank you for your correction. In this shrunken world of ours, which is becoming more interdependent economically, and in every other way, such a division can only cloud our thinking in every respect. We cannot afford to divide ourselves into east and west. That is the reason that all along, in our discussion in the group, we stressed the importance of the reconstruction of all devastated areas.

Therefore, we suggest the close cooperation of all the regional Economic Commissions of Reconstruction to be created by the Economic and Social Council. In the report, Mr. President, you will find that emphasis is placed on the free-industrial nature of the methods of production of most of the peoples in the areas under study. If we look at the problem with perspective—that is the word which I humbly stressed again and again—if we look at the problem with perspective we realize that Asia and the Far East say not too far back, some one hundred and fifty years ago, were not too far behind other parts of the world in economic achievement. It is only one hundred and fifty years. We are apt to think the differences are far wider. We are apt to think that at all times the East has been behind the West in industrial achievement. That does not happen to be true. It is only a difference, let us say, of one hundred and, fifty years, and perhaps even much less, and especially it has seemed broader in the last fifty years—in the last fifty years.

It is not necessary to go into all the unpleasant details of what I call again and again the myopic 19th century, so far as China and the Far East are concerned. Suffice it to remind ourselves at this stage of not letting those who are on top now economically be unmindful of the accent of those who are now situated below.

Mr. President, reconstruction must be hastened also in order to make up for the delay in the economic progress—which has been caused by the recent war. The reconstruction of the devastated areas concerned will benefit all the areas, included the areas unscarred by the devastation of war. If international cooperation thus is achieved, it will be beneficial to all. If international aid is to be given the devastated areas in order to put them on their feet, it must not be governed entirely by the immediate results of short-term material goals, but must be motivated by long-term consideration of a more human, or humane basis—on the more human or humane basis which in the long run will benefit and replenish the draining reservoir of goodwill for all.

In regard to the different parts of the report, Mr. President, may I just call your attention to two parts, one of them on page two of the report, namely, the Importance of Asia's Economy to the World. You will find here a statement of the relationship between the economy of Asia and the Far East and the rest of the world.

Under point 2:

> "There are also certain considerations which make the economic reconstruction of these countries a matter of deep concern to the other na-

tions of the world:

(a) First is the fact, which the war so clearly exhibited that the region was one of the chief supplies of vital industrial, medical and household materials, such as rubber, tin, tungsten, quinine, tea, soya beans, hemp and vegetable oils.

(b) Secondly, a substantial rise in the purchasing power of the Asiatic peoples would open up new opportunities for the interchange of goods and services and capital with other regions to the benefit of all.

(c) Conversely, the evil effects of a low standard of living cannot be confined to any one region.

(d) Progress in rebuilding production and trade has hitherto been slow. Such recovery is a prerequisite for sound world trade relations as well as for effecting, on a world-wide basis, that improvement of living standards which is one of the most important objectives of the United Nations. If Asia, with the assistance of other parts of the world, can enter upon a phase of rapid economic progress, its enormous population and resources and its potentially massive production and consumption will make it one of the greatest areas of development in an expanding world economy.

(e) Economically less developed areas have too often in the past served as the meeting place for the conflicts and contentions of the industrialized powers, and their attainment of economic strength will do much to diminish the occasions for such conflicts."

And then, another part, the conclusion—and that is the part we would like very much to call to the attention of the Council, for immediate action. It is the recommendation of the working group, on pages 41 and 42. On page 41, under "D. Conclusions", you will find certain reasons why the working group arrived at the conclusion of recommending an Economic Commission for Asia and the Far East. Then, on page 42, you have the recommendations stated here in very cogent form. Therefore, the working group, appreciating the trust that the Council has given them, now has the honour to present this Report and it is our humble and urgent hope that this Report will be adopted, especially the working part of it, the creation of an Economic Commission for Asia and the Far East.

Thank you.

【全文译文】

张博士(中国):请允许我花一点时间考虑一下会议时间表的问题,不仅是 1947 年的会议时间表,还有 1948 年的会议时间表。我们应该向前看。

关于 1947 年的会议,我认为我们大家都有这份文件 E/280,即 1947 年会议的性质,这是秘书长提交的一份备忘录。在我们开始提出任何具体的时间表之前,我们自然应该铭记理事会——经济及社会理事会在联合国的重大责任。

主席先生,在我看来,我们这个伟大组织的安全理事会面临的主要问题是冲突;经济及社会理事会面临的主要问题是混乱。我们都想做好,但是我们有太多的事情要做。我们有九个委员会在我们的直接监督下。我们还对协调联合国和专门机构的工作感兴趣。在我们的几个委员会下,我们有或将有一个或多个小组委员会。然后,在所有这些委员会之下,必须有特设性质的技术委员会。此外,至少有两三个国际会议将在这个或那个专门机构或理事会下的这个或那个委员会下召开。因此,我们可以很容易地看到,如果没有一个长期的明确时间表,我们将与我们自己产生混乱。

我们还认识到,这个已经运作了一年零三个月的理事会——经济及社会理事会——有着巨大的作用,特别是在促进国际谅解、合作与和平方面。

现在,有如此繁重的工作计划和如此重要的目标,我们应该保持头脑清醒。否则,正如我们在本届会议上所做的那样,我们的议程往往很紧张。与此同时,人们离开时会感到,我们没有给予我们所希望给予他们的时间和精力来解决摆在我们面前的各种问题。主席先生,我担心,如果对提交理事会的问题不给予足够的关注,理事会的威望将受到影响。

在这里,我们提出了 1947 年的拟议方案,其中有秘书长提出的若干考虑因素。在第 1 页,我认为第一和第二项考虑是完全现实的——即大会去年第一届会议第二部分会议花了稍长的时间,直到年底才结束。此外,由于预算的限制,我们不能举行像一些人希望的那么多的会议。

关于第三个考虑,我认为——事实上,我一共数了一下——大约有五六个代表团在这里有常驻代表,然后还有七八个其他代表团有代表,如果不是住在纽约,就是住在华盛顿。所以你总共有 12 到 14 个,都在纽约,在华盛顿,或者在世界上另一个伟大的首都渥太华,这是一个伟大的首都,但仍然可乘坐一个晚上火车到纽约。因此,我认为总共有 12 至 13 个代表团肯定在纽约或离纽约不远的地方有代表;此外,我相信,有两三位或更多有价值的代表从世界其他地方来到这里,特别是出席理事会会议。

然而,我认为第三项考虑不应影响整个理事会,因为第三项考虑中提到的所谓杰出人员最多不超过理事会全体成员的三分之一。然而,我不会详细谈论这个问题。我们必须讨论 1947 年会议日程的实际问题。

关于秘书长建议的这一方案,我认为总的来说可以接受的是,在理事会本届会议结束和大会开始后的五个月内,我们或许最好只举行一届常会,也许会比三周多一点,我们可以有,比如说,四周。与此同时,我认为有必要在大会召开的大约同一时间举行一次简短的会议,因为我相信在下一届会议之后会有一些问题,这些问题需要在提交大会之前由整个理事会审议。可能会有这样的问题,也就是说,关于委员会会议,比如人权委员会。从现在到理事会下届会议期间,他们将有一系列起草委员会的工作。但我相信,在理事会下届会议之后,人权委员会仍将开展其他工作,该报告必须在提交大会之前提交整个理事会。

因此,在我看来,秘书长提交的方案在这个意义上是可以接受的:理事会将在 7 月的某个时候举行比常会稍长一点的会议,并在大约与大会相同的时间举行一次较短的会议。我认为,为方便起见,时间应由秘书处安排,看他们是否希望在大会开始前两三天或三四天，或者正好在大会开始的同时。我们将把这一点留给秘书长以其智慧和他所看到的时局状况来做决策。

我说，我们现在也应该注意为1948年安排一个时间表的可能性，尽管这似乎为时过早。我认为，我们必须向前看，因为其他专门机构将其方案的最终协调交给理事会。如果我们像过去12个月左右那样，每周或每月都有一种临时安排，那么与我们有关系的其他机构很难安排自己的会议；因此，我们也应该有一份1948年的临时时间表，将于7月提交给我们的理事会下届会议，以便我们能够向大会提交。这个1948年的临时时间表可能与整个预算有某种联系——我相信会有。因此，我们应该为1948年制定一个计划，考虑到以下各种问题：第一，财政影响，我们应该在大会开会前拿到。第二，既然到我们下一届会议时，各委员会都已举行了首次会议，所有委员会都将举行一次会议，其中一些委员会将举行两次会议，这些委员会的会议应如何与理事会的会议联系起来。第三，如何与专门机构协调。

鉴于这一事实，主席先生，我非常希望主席或可任命一个理事会特设委员会，与秘书长合作规划1948年的临时时间表，提交给我们7月份的下届会议。这是我的拙见。

关于会议地点，秘书长在E/280号文件中建议，今年1947年的会议大部分应在总部举行。我们也同意这一点，特别是因为这是一个受预算限制的问题。但我认为，随着时间的推移，有一个问题需要考虑，这个问题目前还不太清楚——即如果我们将在总部以外举行会议，这些会议是既是理事会会议也是委员会会议，还是只仅仅是委员会会议？在我看来，这一问题值得考虑，因为各委员会在总部外开会要容易得多，因为它们只有秘书处有限的人员协助它们，旅费和所有其他费用将少得多。但是，如果理事会在总部以外的地方举行会议，将有更多的工作人员随行，还有更多的文件和材料。因此，理事会应在总部开会，而各委员会可在总部以外的地方开会，这难道不是一项一般原则吗？这只是我的拙见。

当然,总之,如果我们就秘书长建议的这一方案作出决定,它可能会对理事会面前的其他议程产生一些影响,因为在理事会下届会议之前不开会的各委员会的报告可能全部或部分推迟到我们下一届会议。非常感谢。

张博士(中国):主席先生,你面前有灾区经济重建临时小组委员会亚洲和远东工作组的报告。作为该工作组主席,请允许我对摆在你面前的报告作简要评论:

亚洲和远东地区的破坏是巨大的。如果不是秘书处日益忠诚的服务,负责处理所涉问题的工作组本身确实会崩溃。在他们的帮助下,我们一直工作到凌晨 2 点才圆满结束。我希望经济及社会理事会不要试图超越我们那天晚上的记录,把我们的会议延长到凌晨。

总的来说,我认为工作组成员认为报告完全令人满意。我们尽最大努力对亚洲和远东灾区重建问题作出明智的评估。我们仔细分析了关键的相关问题和需求。我们谦虚地提到了组织国际援助与合作的方法,我们强烈而一致地敦促在本届会议期间建立一个亚洲和远东经济委员会,正如为欧洲所做的那样。

在辩论期间,在某些问题上存在意见分歧,但这些分歧是有益的。我们中的一些人非常谨慎,及其谨慎,但这种谨慎决不是没有道理的。我们之间的分歧从来没有使我们对摆在我们面前的重要任务视而不见,也没有使我们对重建受破坏地区问题的紧迫性视而不见,这一问题影响到大部分人类的生活,也许是全球总人口的一半或一半以上。事实上,我们的分歧只会使我们在目标、做某事、完成某事上达到更高程度的一致。我们的谨慎是智慧的要求,以编写一份原则上为所有人接受的报告。

主席先生,我本人并不特别赞成"远东"一词。如果我们从金门大桥眺望那片平静的海洋,太平洋,远东将变成遥远的西部,至少对美国来说是如此。我现在提出这一点是为了强调过分强调东西方的划分是危险的。从历史上看,东西方的界限过去、过去和现在都只是想象的,一条任意划定的线。有时我们想知道现在的界线在哪里。哪里?事实上,在中国,我们认为自己生活在地球表面的中心,你们这些懂中文的人知道,即使在今天,我们仍然称我们的国家为"中国",我们将继续称我们的国家为"中国",所以我们不属于任何东方,无论你们把它划分到哪里。

主席:或是西方!

张博士(中国):谢谢你的更正。在我们这个缩小了的世界里,经济上和其他方面都变得越来越相互依赖,这样的分裂只能在各个方面模糊我们的思想。我们不能把自己分成东方和西方。这就是为什么我们在小组讨论中始终强调重建所有灾区的重要性。

因此,我们建议经济及社会理事会设立的所有重建区域经济委员会密切合作。主席先生,在报告中,报告强调了所研究地区大多数民族的生产方式的自由工业性质。如果我们从长远的角度来看问题——这是鄙人一再强调的词——如果我们从长远的角度来看问题,我们会意识到亚洲和远东地区大约150年前,在经济成就方面并不落后于世界其他地区。才仅仅150年。我们倾向于认为差别要大得多。我们倾向于认为,在工业成就方面,东方一直落后于西方。但事实并非如此。我们说,这只是150年的差别,也许更短,特别是在过去50年里,这种差别似乎更大了。

就中国和远东而言,没有必要去探究我一再称之为短视的19世纪的所有令人不快的细节。在这个阶段,只要提醒我们自己不要让那些现在在经济上处于上层的人忽视那些现在处于下层的人的声音就够了。

主席先生,还必须加快重建,以弥补最近战争造成的经济发展的延迟。有关灾区的重建将惠及所有地区,包括未受战争破坏的地区。如果这样实现国际合作,将对所有人都有利。如果向受灾地区提供国际援助,以便使他们重新站立起来,这种援助就不能完全受短期物质目标的眼前结果的支配,而必须是出于对更人道或人道基础的长期考虑——这种更人道或人道的基础从长远来看将有益于并补充所有人枯竭的善意。

主席先生,关于报告的不同部分,请允许我提请你注意报告第2页的两个部分,即亚洲经济对世界的重要性。你可以在这里找到一份关于亚洲、远东和世界其他地区经济关系的声明。

在第2点下:

“还有一些考虑因素使这些国家的经济重建成为世界其他国家深切关注的问题：

(a)首先是这一事实，战争清楚地表明，该地区是重要工业、医疗和家庭材料的主要供应地之一，如橡胶、锡、钨、奎宁、茶、大豆、大麻和植物油。

(b)第二，亚洲人民购买力的大幅度提高将为货物、服务和资本与其他地区的交流创造新的机会，造福于所有人。

(c)相反，低生活水平的有害影响不能局限于任何一个地区。

(d)迄今为止，重建生产和贸易的进展缓慢。这种复苏是健全的世界贸易关系的先决条件，也是在世界范围内实现生活水平提高的先决条件，而生活水平的提高是联合国最重要的目标之一。如果亚洲在世界其他地区的帮助下能够进入一个经济快速发展的阶段，其庞大的人口和资源以及潜在的大规模生产和消费将使其成为不断扩大的世界经济中最重要的发展领域之一。

(e)经济欠发达地区过去常常成为工业化大国冲突和争端的聚集地，它们获得经济实力将大大减少此类冲突的发生。”

然后是结论的另一部分，我们非常希望提请理事会注意这一部分，以便立即采取行动。这是工作组的建议，见第 41 页和第 42 页。在第 41 页的“D. 结论”下，你将找到工作组得出建议成立亚洲和远东经济委员会的结论的某些原因。然后，在第 42 页，有非常有说服力的建议。因此，工作组感谢理事会对他们的信任，现在荣幸地提交这份报告，我们谦卑而迫切地希望这份报告将获得通过，特别是报告的工作部分，即设立亚洲和远东经济委员会。

非常感谢。

(2)会议发言内容纪要[①]

【会议纪要】

Mr. CHANG (China) thought that certain items on the agenda might be postponed until the next session if the Council could decide upon the schedule of conferences for 1947. The work of the Council was so heavy and its fields of interest so varied that only confusion and a resultant lack of prestige could come from failure to decide on a definite time-table well in advance.

Most of the suggestions for 1947 contained in the document entitled "Calendar of conferences in 1947: memorandum by the Secretary-General"[②] seemed satisfactory. Mr. Chang pointed out however that the third consideration given on page 1 of the document, concerning the difficulties delegations had in sending expert personnel to too frequent meetings, would not be applicable to the Economic and Social Council as a whole, since between twelve and fourteen nations had representatives permanently available either in New York or within easy access of United Nations headquarters.

Mr. Chang agreed with the Secretary-General that before the September meeting of the General Assembly there should be one long regular session of the Economic and Social Council, of perhaps four weeks duration, and one short session held at about the same time as the General Assembly, in order to review all the work done by the various commissions following the close of the regular session.

Attention should also be given to the programme for 1948, especially since it would vitally affect the plans of the specialized agencies. Mr. Chang there-

① UN Document: E/SR. 51-84, pp. 127-128, pp. 132-133.

② See document E/280; the Calendar was subsequently amended, see document E/280/Rev. 1 and E/280/Rev. 1/Add. 1.

fore proposed that the President should appoint an *ad hoc* committee of the Council to co-operate with the Secretary-General in planning a provisional timetable for 1948, to be presented to the July session of the Council, and subsequently to be submitted to the General Assembly. Thus the financial implications of the programme could be considered inconnexion with the decision on the budget. Advance planning would also make possible the proper correlation of meetings of the Council and its commissions, as well as better co-ordination with the specialized agencies.

Mr. Chang agreed with the Secretary-General that, because of budget limitations, most meetings in 1947 should be held at headquarters. In the future, however, the question of holding meetings elsewhere would frequently arise. It seemed best that the Council itself should meet regularly at headquarters even though the commissions might meet at other places, for the expenses of servicing the whole Council away from headquarters would be far greater than those incurred for such meetings of the commissions.

Mr. CHANG (China), as Chairman of the Working Group for Asia and the Far East, introduced the report.

Paying tribute to the assistance given by the Secretariat, without which the Working Group itself would have been "devastated", he stated that the report was regarded by members of the Working Group as both gratifying and satisfactory. They had tried to give an intelligent evaluation of the problems of reconstruction of the devastated areas, and to analyse the crucial problems and needs. They had mentioned methods of organizing international aid and co-operation, and had unanimously urged the establishment of an Economic Commission for Asia and the Far East during the current session of the Council, as had been done for Europe.

There had been differences of opinion, but they had been both healthy and useful and had never blinded the Working Group to the importance of the problems which affected the lives of more than half the population of the globe. They had, indeed, only led the Group to a higher degree of unity of purpose to see that something was done soon.

Mr. Chang pointed out the danger of over-emphasizing the difference between East and West. He himself was not in favour of the term "Far East", and in fact China regarded itself as being in the centre of the earth's surface. East and West would become more and more inter-dependent, and such arbitrary divisions could only obscure matters. The world could no longer afford to divide East and West; all devastated areas were in equal need of reconstruction.

Emphasis had been placed on the pre-industrial nature of the methods of production in the areas under consideration, compared with the methods of other countries. If the situation was regarded in the proper perspective, it would be seen that Asia and the Far East were not far behind the West 150 years ago and that the difference was therefore not so old. Those who were on top economically at present should not be allowed to forget those who were now situated below. Reconstruction should be accelerated in order to make up for the delay in economic progress caused by the war. Such reconstruction should be motivated by long-term consideration and benefit all areas, including those which had not been devastated by the war.

Mr. Chang, in particular, drew attention to section A of chapter II of the report, which explained the importance of Asia's economy to the world, to section D of chapter IV, in which the conclusions of the Working Group were summed up and which called the attention of the Council to the need for immediate action, and to chapter V which contained the recommendations of the Working Group. ①

He had the honour to present the report on behalf of the Working Group,

① See Supplement No. 10.

with the hope that it would be adopted by the Council, particularly as concerned the creation of an Economic Commission for Asia and the Far East.

【纪要影像】

Mr. Chang (China) thought that certain items on the agenda might be postponed until the next session if the Council could decide upon the schedule of conferences for 1947. The work of the Council was so heavy and its fields of interest so varied that only confusion and a resultant lack of prestige could come from failure to decide on a definite time-table well in advance.

Most of the suggestions for 1947 contained in the document entitled "Calendar of conferences in 1947: memorandum by the Secretary-General"[1] seemed satisfactory. Mr. Chang pointed out however that the third consideration given on page 1 of the document, concerning the difficulties delegations had in sending expert personnel to too frequent meetings, would not be applicable to the Economic and Social Council as a whole, since between twelve and fourteen nations had representatives permanently available either in New York or within easy access of United Nations headquarters.

Mr. Chang agreed with the Secretary-General that before the September meeting of the General Assembly there should be one long regular session of the Economic and Social Council, of perhaps four weeks duration, and one short session held at about the same time as the General Assembly, in order to review all the work done by the various commissions following the close of the regular session.

Attention should also be given to the programme for 1948, especially since it would vitally affect the plans of the specialized agencies. Mr. Chang therefore proposed that the President should appoint an *ad hoc* committee of the Council to co-operate with the Secretary-General in planning a provisional time-table for 1948, to be presented to the July session of the Council, and subsequently to be submitted to the General Assembly. Thus the financial implications of the programme could be considered in connexion with the decision on the budget. Advance planning would also make possible the proper correlation of meetings of the Council and its commissions, as well as better co-ordination with the specialized agencies.

Mr. Chang agreed with the Secretary-General that, because of budget limitations, most meetings in 1947 should be held at headquarters. In the future, however, the question of holding meetings elsewhere would frequently arise. It seemed best that the Council itself should meet regularly at headquarters even though the commissions might meet at other places, for the expenses of servicing the whole Council away from headquarters would be far greater than those incurred for such meetings of the commissions.

[1] See document E/280; the calendar was subsequently amended, see documents E/280/Rev.1 and E/280/Rev.1/Add.1.

图片 4.6　张彭春在经社理事会第四届第 72 次会议发言纪要(1)

Mr. Chang (China), as Chairman of the Working Group for Asia and the Far East, introduced the report.

Paying tribute to the assistance given by the Secretariat, without which the Working Group itself would have been "devastated", he stated that the report was regarded by members of the Working Group as both gratifying and satisfactory. They had tried to give an intelligent evaluation of the problems of reconstruction of the devastated areas, and to analyse the crucial problems and needs. They had mentioned methods of organizing international aid and co-operation, and had unanimously urged the establishment of an Economic Commission for Asia and the Far East during the current session of the Council, as had been done for Europe.

There had been differences of opinion, but they had been both healthy and useful and had never blinded the Working Group to the importance of the problems which affected the lives of more than half the population of the globe. They had, indeed, only led the Group to a higher degree of unity of purpose to see that something was done soon.

Mr. Chang pointed out the danger of over-emphasizing the difference between East and West. He himself was not in favour of the term "Far East", and in fact China regarded itself as being in the centre of the earth's surface. East and West would become more and more interdependent, and such arbitrary divisions could only obscure matters. The world could no longer afford to divide East and West; all devastated areas were in equal need of reconstruction.

Emphasis had been placed on the pre-industrial nature of the methods of production in the areas under consideration, compared with the methods of other countries. If the situation was regarded in the proper perspective, it would be seen that Asia and the Far East were not far behind the West 150 years ago and that the difference was therefore not so old. Those who were on top economically at present should not be allowed to forget those who were now situated below. Reconstruction should be accelerated in order to make up for the delay in economic progress caused by the war. Such reconstruction should be motivated by long-term consideration and benefit all areas, including those which had not been devastated by the war.

Mr. Chang, in particular, drew attention to section A of chapter II of the report, which explained the importance of Asia's economy to the world, to section D of chapter IV, in which the conclusions of the Working Group were summed up and which called the attention of the Council to the need for immediate action, and to chapter V which contained the recommendations of the Working Group.[1]

He had the honour to present the report on behalf of the Working Group, with the hope that it would be adopted by the Council, particularly as concerned the creation of an Economic Commission for Asia and the Far East.

[1] See Supplement No. 10.

图片 4.7　张彭春在经社理事会第四届第 72 次会议发言纪要(2)

【纪要译文】

张先生(中国)认为,如果理事会能够决定1947年的会议时间表,议程上的某些项目可能会推迟到下届会议。理事会的工作是如此繁重,其关注的领域也是如此多样,如果不提前确定一个明确的时间表,就只能造成混乱和由此造成的威望丧失。

题为"1947年会议日历:秘书长备忘录"①的文件中所载1947年的大多数建议似乎令人满意。然而,张先生指出,文件第1页所述的第三项考虑因素,即各代表团在派遣专家人员参加过于频繁的会议方面遇到的困难,不适用于整个经济及社会理事会,由于有12至14个国家的代表常驻纽约或在联合国总部附近。

张先生同意秘书长的意见,即在大会9月份会议之前,经济及社会理事会应举行一次会期约为四周的长期常会,并在大会召开的大约同一时间举行一次短期常会,以便审查各委员会在常会结束后所做的所有工作。

还应注意1948年的方案,特别是因为它将对各专门机构的计划产生重大影响。因此,张先生提议,主席应任命一个理事会特设委员会,与秘书长合作,规划1948年的临时时间表,提交理事会7月届会,随后提交大会。因此,该方案所涉经费问题可与关于预算的决定联系起来考虑。事先规划还将使理事会及其各委员会的会议能够适当地相互关联,以及与各专门机构更好地协调。

张先生同意秘书长的意见,即由于预算限制,1947年的大多数会议应在总部举行。但是,今后经常会出现在其他地方举行会议的问题。尽管委员会可能在其他地方开会,但理事会本身似乎最好是定期在总部开会,因为在总部以外开会,为整个理事会提供服务的费用将远远高于委员会举行此类会议的费用。

张先生(中国)作为亚洲和远东工作组主席介绍了该报告。

---

① 见文件E/280;日历随后进行了修订,见文件E/280/Rev. 1和E/280/Rev. 1/Add. 1。

他对秘书处提供的协助表示敬意,如果没有这些协助,工作组本身就会“崩溃”,他说,工作组成员认为该报告既令人欣慰又令人满意。他们试图对灾区重建的问题作出明智的评估,并分析关键问题和需求。他们提到了组织国际援助和合作的方法,并一致敦促在理事会本届会议期间建立亚洲和远东经济委员会,就像在欧洲所做的那样。

虽然存在意见分歧,但这些分歧是健康的和有益的,从未使工作组忽视影响到全球一半以上人口生活的问题的重要性。事实上,他们只是让小组达到了更高程度的目标一致,以确保很快完成一些工作。

张先生指出过分强调东西方差异的危险。他本人并不赞成“远东”一词,事实上,中国认为自己处于地球表面的中心。东西方将变得越来越相互依赖,这种武断的划分只会混淆视听。世界再也承受不起分裂东方和西方的代价;所有受灾地区都同样需要重建。

与其他国家的方法相比,重点放在审议地区前工业化生产方法上。如果从正确的角度看待这一情况,就会发现,150 年前亚洲和远东地区并不落后于西方,因此这种差异并不太大。不应允许那些目前在经济上处于领先地位的人忘记那些现在处于劣势的人。应当加快重建,以弥补战争造成的经济发展的延迟。这种重建应以长期考虑为动力,并惠及所有地区,包括那些没有受到战争破坏的地区。

张先生特别提请注意报告第二章 A 节,其中解释了亚洲经济对世界的重要性;提请注意第四章 D 节,其中总结了工作组的结论,并提请理事会注意需要立即采取行动,并注意包含工作组建议的第五章。[①]

他荣幸地代表工作组提出该报告,希望理事会采的该报告,特别是关于设立亚洲和远东经济委员会的部分。

① 见补编第 10 号。

7. 张彭春在经社理事会第四届第 73 次会议上的发言

1947 年 3 月 18 日下午 3 时,联合国经社理事会第四届第 73 次会议,在纽约成功湖召开。本次会议继续讨论亚洲和远东工作组的报告,讨论过程中,张彭春在第 72 次会议上的报告,得到了与会各国代表的充分肯定和高度赞赏,印度代表认为,中国代表作为工作组主席其智慧和努力在相当程度上为报告的制作做出了贡献①;荷兰代表认为设立亚洲和远东经济委员会是必须的也是机遇②;英国代表认为设立亚洲和远东经济委员会至少与设立欧洲经济委员会一样急迫和重要③;秘鲁代表、法国代表、新西兰代表、智利代表均表示支持;而美国代表则表示完全支持④;加拿大代表不仅表达了对张彭春杰出才能的高度赞赏,还肯定了秘书处对工作组的支持⑤;黎巴嫩代表马利克表示完全支持⑥;最后表决结果,理事会一致通过了设立亚洲和远东经济委员的决议。⑦ 在本次会议上,中国代表张彭春的具体发言内容如下:

---

① UN Document: E/SR. 51-84, p. 133.
② UN Document: E/SR. 51-84, p. 134.
③ UN Document: E/SR. 51-84, p. 134.
④ UN Document: E/SR. 51-84, p. 137.
⑤ UN Document: E/PV. 73, p. 36.
⑥ UN Document: E/PV. 73, p. 42.
⑦ UN Document: E/SR. 51-84, p. 139.

(1)会议发言全文记录[①]及译文

【全文记录】

Dr. CHANG (China): May I just say a few words in appreciation of all the statements of approval, as well as of concern, in regard to this Report. Especially do we appreciate the general agreement on the importance and the urgency of the area; and also the general agreement concerning the establishment of an Economic Commission for Asia and the Far East.

Now, in regard to certain suggestions concerning the carrying on of studies, if I may say so, the general temper of this humble Report is caution. For any one who reads it, I think that would probably be the general impression. If we turn to the Recommendations, it is put as (a), under 1, in the guiding principles:

> "make or sponsor such investigations and studies of economic and technological problems and developments in countries of Asia and the Far East (as enumerated in this Report and subject to review by the Economic and Social Council)"—that is just a little incident of the caution, the spirit in which the thing was phrased—"as it deems appropriate, including the collect on, evaluation, dissemination and publication of economic, technological and statistical information."

If I may say so, perhaps the principal motivation for the immediate establishment of such a commission is study the investigation for more facts.

In that respect, perhaps this emphasis is somewhat different from the emphasis for the establishment of on Economic Commission for Europe. There perhaps coordination is the first function in the minds of most people, while here investigation is, you might say, of primary importance among the functions en-

① UN Document: E/PV. 73, p. 47-52

visaged.

In regard to a suggestion that field studies should be carried on, that matter was discussed, and on page 2 you will find it stated clearly, on the left-hand side: "Sufficient material, however, is available now to enable us to make an analysis of the crucial reconstruction problems and needs of the area in the present report, and to advance certain specific recommendations which appear in Chapter V. We have also embodied in those recommendations our view that field studies and investigations would be periodic or continuous and should be sponsored by the permanent agency which we propose." That point has already been brought to our attention by the distinguished representative of Canada.

In our discussion I think we have realized that the situation in most of the countries in the Far East is such that statistical studies are not so available as in most of the countries, let us say, in Europe; furthermore, things also change, so that you may have a study carried out during the next three months, say, and then in another three to six months conditions may again change. Therefore, the most valuable result that can be expected would be brought about if the nature of the study and investigation were continuous. The most practical way, it seems to me, in the carrying out of the investigations would be to have the investigations carried out under this new agency. We all seem to agree that this Commission should be set up as soon as possible, and if we should agree, as we seem to agree, that this Commission should be set up as soon as possible, and if we can answer some of those questions which, naturally, we all want answered and also fix the areas of investigation for this Commission—that is, certain facts that ought to be investigated, that can be left to the Commission when it is constituted—then it seems to us, in agreeing on that general procedure, perhaps we shall be able to proceed to get the work done in time. However, the working group; as I was able to interpret its general desire, was to have this Commission established during this Session and also set to function as soon as possible, especially to carry out the investigations—the continuous and periodic investigations—which we believe are needed in this area. Thank you.

【全文译文】

张博士(中国):请允许我说几句话,感谢所有对这份报告表示赞同和关注的发言。我们尤其赞赏对该地区的重要性和紧迫性的普遍一致意见,以及普遍同意关于设立亚洲和远东经济委员会的建议。

现在,关于进行研究的某些建议,如果我可以这样说的话,这份简陋的报告的总基调是谨慎。对于任何一个读过它的人来说,我认为这可能是一个普遍的印象。如果我们看一下建议,它被放在《指导原则》第 1 项下的(a)中:

> “对亚洲和远东国家的经济和技术问题及发展进行或赞助此类调查和研究(如本报告所列举的,并须经经济及社会理事会审查)”——这只是一个谨慎的小事件,这种谨慎的精神是这样表述的——“在它认为适当的情况下,包括收集、评估、传播和发布经济、技术和统计信息。”

如果我可以这样说的话,也许立即成立这样一个委员会的主要动机是研究调查更多的事实。

在这方面,这一重点可能与建立欧洲经济委员会的重点有所不同。在大多数人的头脑中,协调也许是第一个功能,而在这里,你可以说,调查是设想的功能中最重要的。

关于应该进行实地研究的建议,这一问题已经讨论了,在第 2 页,你会发现在左手边有明确的说明:“然而,现在已有足够的材料,使我们能够在本报告中分析该地区的关键重建问题和需求,并提出第五章中提出的某些具体建议。我们还在这些建议中体现了我们的观点,即实地研究和调查将是定期或持续的,应由我们提议的常设机构赞助。”尊敬的加拿大代表已经提请我们注意这一点。

在我们的讨论中，我认为我们已经意识到，远东大多数国家的情况是，统计研究不像欧洲大多数国家那样可用；此外，情况也会发生变化，比如说，你可能会在接下来的三个月内进行一项研究，然后在接下来的三到六个月内，情况可能会再次发生变化。因此，如果研究和调查的性质是持续的，那么最有价值的结果就会出现。在我看来，在进行调查时，最实际的方法是在这个新机构下进行调查。我们似乎都同意这个委员会应该尽快成立，如果我们同意，就像我们似乎同意的那样，这个委员会应该尽快成立，如果我们能够回答一些我们都想回答的问题，并确定该委员会的调查领域——即应该调查的某些事实，这可以留待委员会成立时去做——然后，在我们看来，在商定一般程序时，我们也许将能够着手及时完成工作。然而，正如我能够解释其通常愿望的那样，工作组希望在本届会议期间设立该委员会，并尽快开始运作，特别是进行调查——持续和定期的调查——我们认为这方面需要这些调查。非常感谢。

(2)会议发言内容纪要①

【会议纪要】

Mr. CHANG (China) appreciated the general agreement concerning the importance and urgency of the problems of the area under consideration and the consensus regarding the establishment of an Economic Commission for Asia and the Far East. The main reason for the immediate creation of the Commission was the necessity of obtaining more information. That was somewhat different from the case of the Economic Commission for Europe, where co-ordination might be considered the primary function; in the case of Asia, investigation was the most important concern.

The suggestion that field studies should be conducted had been fully taken

① UN Document: E/SR. 51-84, pp. 138-139.

into consideration in the report.

Statistical studies in the countries of Asia and the Far East were not so readily available as in Europe. Furthermore, the situation was constantly changing and therefore most valuable results would be obtained if the study were continuous. It had been the desire of the Working Group to have the Commission established during the current session and to set it in operation as soon as possible, especially in the field of continuous and periodic investigations.

【纪要影像】

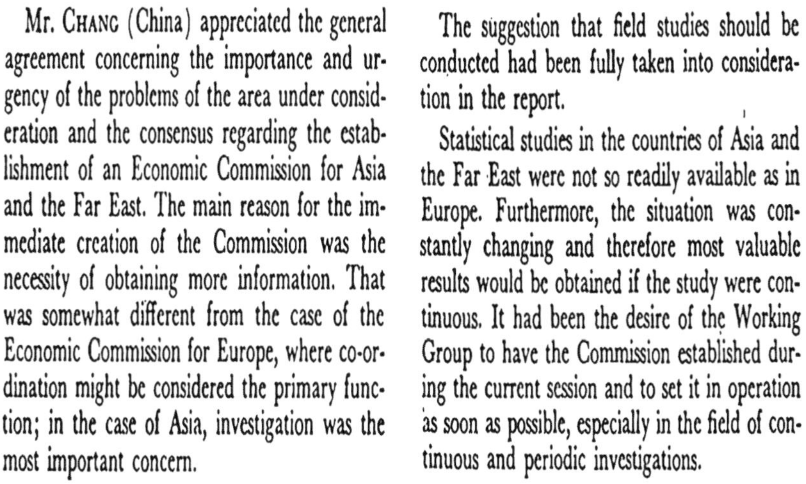

Mr. CHANG (China) appreciated the general agreement concerning the importance and urgency of the problems of the area under consideration and the consensus regarding the establishment of an Economic Commission for Asia and the Far East. The main reason for the immediate creation of the Commission was the necessity of obtaining more information. That was somewhat different from the case of the Economic Commission for Europe, where co-ordination might be considered the primary function; in the case of Asia, investigation was the most important concern.

The suggestion that field studies should be conducted had been fully taken into consideration in the report.

Statistical studies in the countries of Asia and the Far East were not so readily available as in Europe. Furthermore, the situation was constantly changing and therefore most valuable results would be obtained if the study were continuous. It had been the desire of the Working Group to have the Commission established during the current session and to set it in operation as soon as possible, especially in the field of continuous and periodic investigations.

图片 4.7　张彭春在经社理事会第四届第 73 次会议发言纪要

【纪要译文】

张先生(中国)赞赏就审议中的地区问题的重要性和紧迫性达成的普遍一致意见,以及就设立亚洲和远东经济委员会达成的共识。立即设立该委员会的主要原因是需要获得更多信息。这与欧洲经济委员会的情况有所不同,欧洲经济委员会的主要职能可能是协调;就亚洲而言,调查是最重要的问题。

报告充分考虑了应进行实地研究的建议。

亚洲和远东国家的统计研究不像欧洲那样容易获得。此外,情况在不断变化,因此,如果继续进行研究,将获得最有价值的结果。工作组一直希望在本届会议期间设立委员会,并尽快使其开始运作,特别是在持续和定期调查领域。

8. 张彭春在经社理事会第四届第 78 次会议上的发言

1947 年 3 月 24 日上午 10 时，联合国经社理事会第四届第 78 次会议，在纽约成功湖召开。本次会议主要讨论美国关于举行资源养护和利用会议的提案、讨论大会关于翻译经典著作的决议、讨论非联合国会员国加入教科文组织的申请等。中国代表张彭春率代表团参加了本次会议，并在会议上发言，具体发言内容如下：

(1) 会议发言全文记录[①]及译文

【全文记录】

Dr. CHANG (China): Mr. President, due to the extent and potentiality of the natural resources of China, my Government is vitally interested in the problem of scientific utilization and conservation. Therefore, we are heartily in favour of the United States proposal.

Inasmuch as our timetable is already heavily laden, the Chinese delegation would not oppose holding the conference in 1948 instead of 1947.

I am just speaking two sentences in order to encourage the habit of brief interventions.

Dr. CHANG (China): Mr. President, up to 150 years ago, books published in Chinese outnumbered books published in all the languages together.

① UN Document: E/PV. 78, pp. 47–50, pp. 71–75, p. 76.

Naturally, the Chinese delegation is interested in this problem of the translation of the classics. But there was a saying by that man, Mencius, whose other saying I quoted a few days ago, namely: that in government, people are the most important institutions; countries and kings are of less importance.① That same man also said: If all historical records are believed in, it would be better to be without the records. Therefore, for a people that have valued the records, we also have the proper critical point of view.

Some thirteen hundred years ago, a Chinese scholar went to India and collected all the records on Buddhism, all the philosophical studies. He came back and translated them in his lifetime. Many of those records in the original Sanskrit had been lost in India, but the Chinese translations remained, and during the last fifteen years, efforts have been made to retranslate them from the Chinese to Sanskrit. So, you can easily see that for people like the Chinese who have valued classics, valued the preservation of thought forms, that we are in favour of a study of this type.

Furthermore, Leibnitz, in Europe, in drawing up the terms — not terms of reference, Mr. President — for the Prussian Academy — that is a hateful word now and non-existent in our political dictionary because it has been ruled out, Prussia does not exist — but about two hundred years ago there was such an attempt by Leibnitz, and in drawing up the provisional constitution, let us say, of the Prussian Academy, he suggested all things of value in the world at that time to him — which was probably Europe, I suppose — should be preserved in Chinese translations because the Chinese language happens to be the one language that has remained with comparatively fewer changes for the longest period

---

① 笔者检索了前面张彭春有关发言的记录,在经社理事会第二届第6次会议上,张彭春曾讲到孟子的这句格言:"In government the people are the most important, institutions come next and Kings are of least importance."而对照这里的记录,似乎感觉到这次会议的记录有点问题,值得大家探讨。但为了尊重联合国档案会议记录的真实性,这里保持原记录所使用的语言。

in history, because things written 2500 years or 3000 years ago can still be read with only a slightly modified script. However, I am not advocating, Mr. President, that all the world's classics should be translated into Chinese today. But if there should be; such a suggestion, I would naturally support it.

I am not going to go on, to follow my habit of encouraging the brevity of interventions, but I think I have not said things that have already been said by other Members of this Council. In general, I am in favour of the translation of the classics, but naturally, I would like to have the question critically evaluated, and I shall in committee propose changes to this resolution, while I approve the proposal in principle.

Thank you.

Dr. CHANG (China): May I, Mr. President, just say one sentence: The Lights were on when I was talking. I hope it was not particularly in favour of what I spoke, that it was not exactly symbolic, and I hope it will not be prejudicial to others who will now speak after me with the lights off.

【全文译文】

张博士(中国):主席先生,鉴于中国自然资源的丰富和潜力,我国政府对科学利用和保护问题很感兴趣。因此,我们衷心支持美国的建议。

由于我们的时间表已经排得很满,中国代表团不会反对在 1948 年而不是 1947 年举行会议。

我说两句话是为了鼓励人们养成简短发言的习惯。

张博士(中国):主席先生,直到 150 年前,以中文出版的书籍数量超过其他所有语言出版的书籍总数。当然,中国代表团对古典文学的翻译问题很感兴趣。但是孟子有一句话,我几天前引用了他的另一句话,那就是:“民为贵,社稷次之,君为轻。”[1]这个人还说:“尽信书,则不如无书。”[2]因

① 笔者注:该句出自《孟子 · 尽心章句下》

② 笔者注:该句出自《孟子 · 尽心章句下》

此,对于一个重视记录的民族来说,我们也有适当的批评观点。

大约 1300 年前,一位中国学者去了印度,收集了所有关于佛教的记录,所有的哲学研究。他回来后,在有生之年翻译了它们。许多原始梵文的记录在印度丢失了,但是中文译本保留了下来,在过去的 15 年里,人们努力将它们从中文重新翻译成梵文。所以,你可以很容易地看到,对于像中国人这样重视经典、重视保存思想形式的人来说,我们赞成这种类型的研究。

此外,在欧洲,莱布尼茨在为普鲁士学院起草条款时——不是职权范围,主席先生——这现在是一个令人憎恶的词,在我们的政治词典中不存在,因为它已经被排除了,普鲁士不存在了——但大约 200 年前,莱布尼茨有过这样的尝试,在起草普鲁士学院的临时章程时,他建议,当时世界上所有对他有价值的东西——我想可能是欧洲——都应该保留在中文译本中,因为中文恰好是历史上最长时期内变化相对较少的一种语言,因为 2500 年或 3000 年前写的东西只需稍加修改就可以阅读。但是,主席先生,我并不是主张今天世界上所有的经典都应该翻译成中文。但是如果应该有的话;这样的建议,我自然会支持。

我不打算继续沿用我鼓励发言简短的习惯,但我想我没有说过本理事会其他成员已经说过的话。总的来说,我赞成翻译经典著作,但我自然希望对这个问题进行批判性的评估,我将在委员会中提出对这项决议的修改建议,同时原则上同意这项建议。

非常感谢。

张博士(中国):主席先生,我只想说一句话:我发言时灯是亮着的。我希望这并不特别有利于我的发言,这并不完全是象征性的,我希望现在关灯这不会对在我之后发言的其他人产生不利影响。

(2)会议发言内容纪要①

【会议纪要】

Mr. CHANG (China) favoured the United States proposal because his Government was vitally interested in the problem of scientific utilization and conservation. Concerning the date of the conference, the Chinese delegation was inclined to agree with 1948.

Mr. CHANG (China) favoured the translation of the classics but wished to have the question critically assessed. He referred to historical examples manifesting continued Chinese interest in the preservation of the classics and of forms of thought.

【纪要影像】

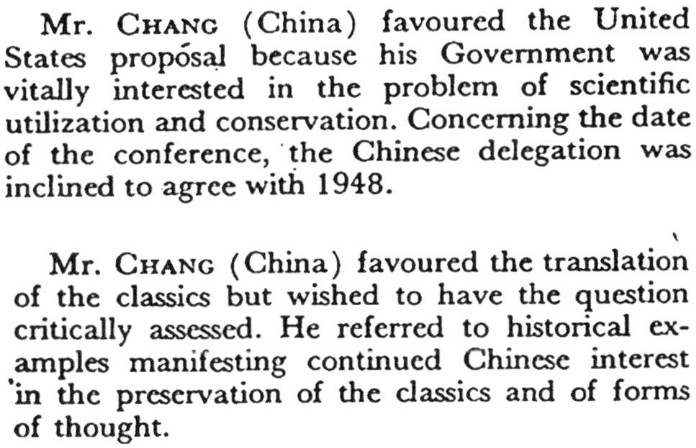
Mr. CHANG (China) favoured the United States proposal because his Government was vitally interested in the problem of scientific utilization and conservation. Concerning the date of the conference, the Chinese delegation was inclined to agree with 1948.

Mr. CHANG (China) favoured the translation of the classics but wished to have the question critically assessed. He referred to historical examples manifesting continued Chinese interest in the preservation of the classics and of forms of thought.

图片 4.8　张彭春在经社理事会第四届第 78 次会议发言纪要

【纪要译文】

张先生(中国)赞成美国的提案,因为中国政府对科学利用和保护问

① UN Document: E/SR. 51-84, p. 184, p. 186.

题极为感兴趣。关于会议日期,中国代表团倾向于同意 1948 年。

张先生(中国)赞成经典作品的翻译,但希望对这一问题进行批判性的评估。他提到了一些历史例子,这些例子表明中国人对保存经典和思想形式一直很感兴趣。

9. 张彭春在经社理事会第四届第79次会议上的发言

1947年3月24日下午3时,联合国经社理事会第四届第79次会议,在纽约成功湖召开。本次会议主要讨论关于通过世界日历的决议草案、讨论世界工会联合会提交的关于保障行使和发展工会权利的决议和美国劳工联合会提交的备忘录等。中国代表张彭春率代表团参加了本次会议,并在会议上发言,具体发言内容如下:

(1)会议发言全文记录[①]及译文

【全文记录】

Dr. CHANG (China): Mr. President, is it in order to comment very briefly on the Peruvian proposal?

The PRESIDENT: Yes, I think so.

Dr. CHANG (China): I thought I heard a point of order was raised. If it is in order, I will comment briefly. If not, I will obey your ruling.

The PRESIDENT: I think it is in order to comment briefly on the merits of the proposal.

Dr. CHANG (China): Good, very good.

Mr. President, it is very clear to all the world that the Gregorian Calendar was not even considered by China in 1582, when it was first promulgated.

---

① UN Document: E/PV. 79, p. 12, pp. 12-13.

In 1912, China adopted it. By that time, certain defects of the Gregorian Calendar became clear. It lacked a certain degree of stability, order and permanence.

The matter has been studied recently, especially during the last half-century and particularly the last thirty years — by experts all over the world. A calendar that may be improved is surely desirable for the world as a whole. The League of Nations began its studies of the calendar revision some years ago, and China sent a fully accredited representative to participate in their discussions. The result of the studies was shown in China's favourable reply to the League of Nations inquiry when the League submitted the draft on the World Calendar to Member and non-Member States.

China believes that the question of adopting the World Calendar should at least, receive careful consideration by this Council.

【全文译文】

张博士(中国):主席先生,对秘鲁的提案作非常简短的评论是否符合规程?

主席:是的,我想是的。

张博士(中国):我想我听到有人提出一个程序问题。如果符合规程,我将简要评论一下。如果不符合,我将服从你的裁决。

主席:我认为对这一提案的优点作非常简短的评论符合规程。

张博士(中国):很好,非常好。

主席先生,全世界都很清楚,公历在 1582 年首次颁布时,中国甚至没有考虑过公历。

1912 年,中国采用了它。到那个时候,公历的某些缺陷变得明显了。它缺乏一定程度的稳定、秩序和持久性。

世界各地的专家最近对这一问题进行了研究,特别是在过去半个世纪,尤其是过去三十年。一个可以改进的日历对全世界来说无疑是可取的。国际联盟几年前就开始研究日历的修订,中国派出了一名完全认可的代表参加了他们的讨论。当国际联盟向成员国和非成员国提交世界日历草案时,中国对国际联盟的调查给予了肯定的答复,这一答复显示了研究的结果。

中国认为,采用世界日历的问题至少应得到本理事会的认真审议。

(2)会议发言内容纪要[①]

【会议纪要】

Mr. CHANG (China) said that the Gregorian calendar was faulty in many respects, and that China had collaborated with the League of Nations in a study of the proposed world calendar. He felt that the subject deserved careful consideration by the Council.

【纪要影像】

Mr. Chang (China) said that the Gregorian calendar was faulty in many respects, and that China had collaborated with the League of Nations in a study of the proposed world calendar. He felt that the subject deserved careful consideration by the Council.

图片 4.9　张彭春在经社理事会第四届第 79 次会议发言纪要

【纪要译文】

张先生(中国)说,公历在许多方面存在缺陷,中国与国际联盟合作研究了拟议的世界日历。他认为这个问题值得理事会认真审议。

① UN Document:E/SR. 51-84,p. 190.

10. 张彭春在经社理事会第四届第81次会议上的发言

1947年3月28日上午11时,联合国经社理事会第四届第81次会议,在纽约成功湖召开。本次会议主要议题是继续讨论欧洲经济委员会职权范围草案、关于设立亚洲和远东经济委员会的讨论、讨论关于运输和通信委员会报告的决议草案、讨论关于经济和就业委员会报告和相关项目的决议草案、讨论社会事务委员会关于麻醉药品委员会报告的第一次报告等。中国代表张彭春率代表团参加了本次会议,并在会议上先后多次发言,具体发言内容如下:

(1)会议发言全文记录[①]及译文

【全文记录】

Dr. CHANG (China): Mr. President, your last expression is something which the Chinese delegation would like to see happen, namely, without unnecessary prolonged debate, to have both amendments adopted.

As to the possibility of rewording, that can easily be arranged. In other words, now that we have already acted upon the establishment of a Commission for the Asia and the Far East, while we agree that whenever the permanent headquarters of the United Nations in the Far East is decided, naturally the

① UN Document: E/PV. 81, pp. 27-28-A, pp. 35-36, p. 37, p. 41, pp. 43-44, p. 45, p. 45A, p. 47.

Commission should have its headquarters there. But now that the Commission has been established, it is but natural that the Commission should meet in the Far East, inasmuch as the chief work of the Commission in its preliminary stages will be surveys, investigations, and studies. But studies of what Mr. President, it is but natural that we should study the instructions and the suggestions of the General Assembly; namely, the study of the effects and efforts in connection with war devastation and reconstruction. If that is so, it is but natural that the temporary headquarters should be near the places where there has been most devastation from the war. So I think it is very simple, Mr. President.

Furthermore, in order to show the spirit of compromise—which I think the Chinese delegation, for once, can take pleasure in saying for itself because I think many of us, all of us, realize that the Chinese delegation has done certain things without claiming credit—but in this case I think we have shown that spirit here in modifying it even further.

Will you please look at the qualified amendments, E/376. The temporary headquarters are not only qualified by the fact that whenever the permanent headquarters of the United Nations is established in Asia and the Far East, there will then be a charge, but also qualified by this: "... subject to review by the Economic and Social Council at its first session in 1948." Even the temporary headquarters will be subject to review. In other words, the temporary headquarters, after the first meeting of the Commission in Shanghai, will proceed with the work of investigation, and in six months' time it will produce a report to the Council. By that time the Council will have a chance to review whether the temporary headquarters should be in Shanghai, in case by that time the question of the permanent headquarters will not have been decided, or discussed, let us say.

Furthermore, it is again qualified by the amendment to the draft resolution 3 (b). Referring to the last five lines of this document, E/376, it reads: "to appoint a Committee of the whole to meet at the interim headquarters of the United Nations ... " That sounds awfully cumbersome, but we have been advised that is the term for Lake Success. If you prefer a shorter phrasing, just say "to meet at Lake Success". But I understand this is the official way of saying "Lake Success": "... to meet at the interim headquarters of the United Nations to consider the question rising under paragraph 1"—that is, concerning the discussion on terms of reference and other matters—"... and to submit its recommendations to the Fifth Session of the Economic and Social Council." In other words, we recognize there were good reasons for the discussion on terms of references taking place in Lake Success, because of the various matters that are easily within reach here at the headquarters of the United Nations. In other words, the temporary headquarters in Shanghai is really qualified by these three points I have already mentioned.

I hope, Mr. President, in view of the shortness of our time and in view of the general good spirit so far prevailing in the Working Group and in the discussions of the Economic Commission in Committee, that we shall have a happy solution.

Dr. CHANG (China): Mr. President, I really think that we deeply appreciate the kind expressions of interest, concern and support of Shanghai. I am not one of those who wish to have a strong fight on this issue. I am still trying to get some sort of thing that may work unanimously. I think we can still do so. As I see it, the United States delegation's point of view is that if there should be the meeting of the Commission in Shanghai—that is agreed—then there must be some sort of a Secretariat to serve it, and furthermore, if the investigation that is already agreed upon to take place, that will also have to have a Secretariat to serve it. Therefore, while I appreciate all the expressions of support for Shanghai as the temporary headquarters, in case you think that the Chinese delegation has not yet compromised enough, I am willing to go one step further.

But before I go, I would like to know that will actually receive unanimous support. Let us step wrangling about this. I hate to say harsh words, words that may be said which are obvious—what is the use? Let us be very reasonable. I think I will just come down to this, and I hope it will receive the support of our United States colleague as well as others, that not to prejudice the question, I will just change one word. Instead of "temporary" headquarters, because "headquarters" may imply a headquarters, I will just change that to "temporary offices of the Commission shall be located at Shanghai", because you will have to have offices to serve the meeting as well as to serve the conference.

Furthermore, in pursuance of that opinion, may I just call your attention to the last paragraph on paper E/376: "The Commission, in assuming its work under paragraphs 1 and 2, (a) to convene at its temporary headquarters in the Far East ..." delete those words and say "to convene in Shanghai" in order to avoid any possibility of misunderstanding that it is something that may prejudice the direction of choosing a headquarters.

I do hope that will receive unanimous support, and I am not going into this question. I think our Indian representative already said very well that mere expenses should not be taken into consideration.

Furthermore, so far as we know, the exchange rates are now much better than two or threc wccks ago, and the expenses will gradually be shifted. Moreover, inasmuch as it will be a Secretariat of only, say, fifteen or twenty people, the signing of the contract and all those things would not be so cumbersome. Really, it is a very simple thing: fifteen, twenty people—a city with a population of—I do not know the exact number: three million or four—to get a house to, accommodate twenty. I can say almost definitely that it can be done.

In regard to the accessibility, sir, I beg to differ from our distinguished representative of the United Kingdom. Shanghai is the most accessible place in all the areas of the Far East. There is no question in regard to flying trips and airmail, and other facilities. Surely, I think, that is not exactly an argument against it. So, sir, if that should be the case, may I offer just one more suggestion, and I hope that will meet with the approval of all. Of course, I will have to ask the consent of all my friends who have supported the words "temporary headquarters", to permit me to make a further amendment, to change "headquarters" into "offices", if they kindly agree.

Mr. CHANG (China): Mr. President, I am extremely sorry to hear that, because my use of English is extremely inadequate, but I think there is a difference between headquarters and offices. As to the proper distinction, I would not go into that. At least one would suggest temporary offices. In other words, you have to have two or three rooms where you have to have people to service the investigations to be done by Members of the Commission and assisted by proper secretariat people.

Friends, the Commission for Asia in the Far East has been set up. It must do some work, and the work can only be done in the field. And after having yielded one, two, three, and four steps, I think a decision must be made.

The PRESIDENT: I think, also, the decision must be made.

I am now going to put to the vote the propositions that are before me. Does the Chinese representative want to put "offices" instead of "headquarters"?

Mr. CHANG (China): Yes.

Dr. CHANG (China): I did not quite follow it, please. Where would it come?

Dr. CHANG (China): Mr. President, it seems as though it is not wise to open a thing which has already been passed. The Commission can discuss the matter of headquarters, naturally, at any time it likes, and it may not be necessary for us to provide any special item here, but in case we should like to, we can put that at some place. Naturally, they may have other meetings, especially to receive the reports of investigations.

It seems to me that with everything uncertain, nothing can be done in regard to investigations. At least, the Secretariat will know there will be a six-month period of certainty. Then, there will be two things: first, the meeting of the Commission, secondly, the carrying on of the investigations. They will bring in the report, within, say, three or four months, and then the Commission, as I envisage, will probably have a second meeting to go over the report of the field study, and then present their reports to the first meeting in 1948, in January 1948, to the Council.

It seems to me that the matters of headquarters or offices after that should come naturally together with the reports to be submitted to the Council at that time. Of course, the Commission can be discussing temporary suggestions and things whenever they meet, but it seems to me that inasmuch as we have already passed the other phrase—namely, "subject to review at that session"—we should give the Commission a chance to study the matter more carefully, because, after all, suppose they should meet in June; they will meet for, say, only a week or ten days. They will not have a chance to look over this matter of temporary offices, to revise it, or to review it.

It seems to me it is only reasonable that we should give them a chance to review it and study it and then to present their views to the first meeting of the Council in 1948. Furthermore, sir, I have not had time to comment on this fact, the great concern of the distinguished representative of New Zealand for the other Members of the Commission on the views of the site. It seems as though we did that thing without consulting all the Members for other Commissions, as well as for meeting places of other bodies under this Council.

I think it is a little too technical to say that those three absent members should be consulted concerning this on every step of our decision of the Council. While of course their views will have great weight when the Commission will formally meet, and it seems only reasonable that we ought to give the Commission a little more time to consider the thing, rather than to force them or to require them to submit a definite proposal to the Fifth Session—namely, the July meeting of the Council — it seems to me it is just a reasonableness in getting the work in order and then provide for the Secretariat, a sort of small staff to service the meeting, as well as to service the investigations, and then have the whole matter reviewed by the Council at its first session in 1948.

I think the Secretariat, if they should go out there, will go out there with that understanding—for six months—and then that it is to be reviewed in January.

Dr. CHANG (China): Thank you.

Dr. CHANG (China): Mr. President, if you look at the Chinese amendment, it says: "to appoint a committee of the Whole to meet at the interim headquarters of the United Nations to consider the questions arising under paragraph 1". In other words, paragraph 1, (a), (b), (c) and (d) will be considered in New York. If that is the case, then the Commission Members proper, not the Committee of the Whole, will have no chance to deal with it.

I think, if we are going to insert this at all, we ought to let the Commission in plenary session discuss this, because that was the great concern of our distinguished representative of New Zealand. If we put it under (d), it will only be discussed by the Committee of the Whole and not by the Commission in plenary session. If we want that inserted, I think we should have some other way of doing it. I think you can have another l and 2, my 3, and then add a 4, request the Commission to submit their views to the first session of the Council in 1948 concerning headquarters, because you do not have to say "temporary". It will really be that we have decided on temporary temporarily.

May I just suggest that instead of adding this sentence at (d), which would bring the matter to the Committee of the Whole in New York only, add a

4 after my 3, that the Commission shall be requested to submit its views on the question of headquarters to the first session of the Economic and Social Council in 1948.

The PRESIDENT: It will still be temporary, Dr. Chang, because the permanent headquarters has been decided upon as the permanent headquarters of the United Nations in the Far East.

Dr. CHANG (China): That is good. Then, I will admit your amendment, sir.

Dr. CHANG (China): Mr. President, in saying the Commission will appoint the Committee of the Whole, it does not at all imply that all the personnel will travel from Shanghai to New York. They may appoint other representatives from their own respective governments to represent them at the Committee of the Whole discussion here at Lake Success.

The PRESIDENT: The further proposal is that a clause (c) shall be added that the Commission shall make recommendations regarding a temporary headquarters to the Economic and Social Council.

Dr. CHANG (China): It is a fresh sentence. At the First Session of 1948.

【全文译文】

张博士(中国):主席先生,你最后一句话表达的是中国代表团希望看到的,即在不进行不必要的冗长辩论的情况下,通过这两项修正案。

至于重新措辞的可能性,这很容易安排。换言之,既然我们已经就设立亚洲和远东委员会采取了行动,同时我们同意,无论何时决定联合国在远东的常设总部,该委员会的总部自然应该设在那里。但现在委员会已经成立,委员会自然应该在远东举行会议,因为委员会在其初步阶段的主要工作将是调查、调研和研究。但是,主席先生,我们应该研究大会的指示和建议,这是很自然的;即研究战争破坏和重建的影响和努力。如果是这样的话,那么临时总部应该设在遭受战争破坏最严重的地方,这是很自然的。因此,我认为这很简单,主席先生。

此外,为了显示妥协精神——我想中国代表团这一次可以高兴地为自己这样说,因为我想我们中的许多人,我们所有人,都意识到中国代表团做了某些事情而没有邀功——但在这种情况下,我想我们已经展示了这种精神,在这里对它作了进一步的修改。

请你看看合格的修正案,E/376。临时总部的限定条件不仅是,无论何时在亚洲和远东设立联合国常设总部,都会有一笔费用,而且还包括:"……须经经济及社会理事会 1948 年第一届会议审查。"甚至临时总部也将受到审查。换言之,在委员会在上海举行第一次会议之后,临时总部将继续进行调查工作,并在六个月后向理事会提交一份报告。我们可以说,如果到那时,常设总部的问题还没有决定或讨论,届时理事会将有机会审查临时总部是否应设在上海。

此外,它再次受到决议草案第 3(b)段修正案的资格判定。关于这份文件 E/376 的最后五行,它写道:"任命一个全体委员会在联合国临时总部开会……"这听起来非常累赘,但我们被建议这是成功湖的说法。如果你喜欢较短的措辞,就说"在成功湖会面"。但我知道这是"成功湖"的正式说法:"……在联合国临时总部开会,审议根据第 1 段提出的问题"——即关于职权范围和其他事项的讨论——"并向经济及社会理事会第五届会议提交其建议。"换句话说,我们认识到在成功湖进行关于职权范围的讨论是有充分理由的,因为在联合国总部,各种问题触手可及。换句话说,上海的临时总部,就我已经提到的这三点来说,确实是合格的。

主席先生,我希望,鉴于我们的时间紧迫,且鉴于工作组和经济委员会在委员会的讨论中迄今普遍存在的良好精神,我们将找到一个令人满意的解决办法。

张博士(中国):主席先生,我确实认为我们非常感谢上海对我们的兴趣、关心和支持。我不是那些希望在这个问题上激烈争论的人之一。我仍在努力找到某种可能会一致奏效的方法。我认为我们仍然可以这样做。

在我看来,美国代表团的观点是,如果委员会在上海举行会议——这是已经商定的——那么就必须有个秘书处为其服务,此外,如果已经商定进行调查,也必须有一个秘书处为其服务。因此,虽然我感谢所有表示支持上海作为临时总部的观点,但如果你认为中国代表团妥协程度还不够,我愿意再让一步。

但在我离开之前,我想知道它是否会得到一致支持。让我们停止争论这件事。我讨厌说刺耳的话,那些可能会说的话显而易见——有什么用呢?我们要非常理智。我想我就说到这一点,我希望这将得到我们的美国同事以及其他人的支持,为了不影响这个问题,我将只改变一个词。“总部”可能意味着一个总部,所以我不使用“临时”总部,而是将它改为“委员会的临时办事处将设在上海”,因为你必须有办事处为会面和会议服务。

此外,根据这一意见,我谨提请大家注意 E/376 号文件最后一段:“委员会在根据第 1 和第 2 段开展工作时,(a)在其远东临时总部召开会议……”删除这些词语,并说“在上海召开会议”,以避免误解,认为这可能会影响选择总部的方向。

我确实希望这将得到一致支持,我不打算讨论这个问题。我认为我们的印度代表已经说得很好,不应该仅仅考虑费用。

此外,据我们所知,现在的汇率比两三个星期前要好得多,开支也会逐渐转变。此外,由于秘书处只有,比方说,15 或 20 人,所以合同的签署和所有这些事情就不会那么麻烦了。事实上,这是一件非常简单的事情:15 或 20 人——在一个人口为三百万或四百万的城市,我不知道确切的数字——买一所房子,住 20 个人。我几乎可以肯定地说,这是可以做到的。

关于可及性,主席先生,我不敢苟同尊敬的英国代表的意见。上海是远东所有地区中最通达的地方。飞行和航空邮件以及其他设施都没有问题。当然,我认为,这不完全是反对它的理由。因此,主席先生,如果是这样的话,请允许我再提出一个建议,我希望这将得到所有人的赞同。当然,我必须征得所有支持“临时总部”一词的朋友的同意,如果他们同意的话,允许我作进一步的修正,将“总部”改为“办事处”。

张先生(中国):主席先生,听到这个消息,我感到非常遗憾,因为我的英语使用极为匮乏,但我认为总部和办事处之间存在差异。至于适当的区别,我不想深究。至少有人会建议设立临时办公室。换言之,你必须有两三个房间,在那里你必须有人为委员会成员进行的调查提供服务,并由适当的秘书处人员协助。

朋友们,远东和亚洲委员会已经成立。它必须做一项工作,且这项工作只能在实地进行。在做出一、二、三、四个步骤之后,我认为必须做出决定。

主席:我也认为必须作出决定。

我现在将把摆在我面前的提议付诸表决。中方代表是否希望用“办事处”代替“总部”?

张先生(中国):是的。

张博士(中国):我不太明白你的意思。它会出现在哪里?

张博士(中国):主席先生,重启一个已经通过的事情似乎是不明智的。委员会当然可以在它喜欢的任何时候讨论总部问题,我们可能没有必要在这里提供任何特殊项目,但如果我们愿意,我们可以把它放在某个地方。当然,他们可能会有其他会议,特别是接收调查报告。

在我看来,由于一切都不确定,在调查方面什么也做不了。至少,秘书处会知道将有六个月的确定期。然后,将有两件事:第一,委员会的会议,第二,调查的进行。他们将在三四个月内提交报告,然后,正如我设想的那样,委员会可能会举行第二次会议,审查实地研究的报告,然后在 1948 年 1 月的第一次会议上向理事会提交报告。

在我看来,此后总部或办事处的事项自然应与届时将提交理事会的报告一并审议。当然,委员会可以随时会面讨论临时建议和事项,但在我看来由于我们已经通过了另一个短语,即“在该届会议上进行审查”,我们应该给委员会一个更仔细地研究这个问题的机会,因为毕竟,假设他们应该在 6 月份开会;比如说,他们只会会面一周或十天。他们将没有机会检查、修改或审查临时办公室的问题。

在我看来,我们应该给他们一个机会来审查和研究它,然后向1948年的理事会第一次会议提出他们的意见,这是完全合理的。此外,主席先生,我还没有时间评论这一事实,尊敬的新西兰代表对委员会其他成员对该地点的看法表示极大关注。我们这样做似乎没有咨询其他委员会的所有成员,也没有咨询本理事会其他机构的会议地点。

我认为,在理事会决定的每一步时都应就此问题征求这三位缺席成员的意见,这有点技术性太强了。虽然在委员会正式开会时,他们的意见当然会有很大的分量,而且我们应该给委员会多一点时间考虑这个问题,而不是强迫他们或要求他们向第五届会议——即理事会7月份的会议——提交一份明确的提案,这似乎是合理的,我认为这样做只是为了使工作井然有序,然后为秘书处提供少量工作人员,以便为会议提供服务并为调查提供服务,进而让理事会在1948年第一届会议上审查整个问题。

我认为,如果秘书处应该到那里去,可以理解为,他们将到那里去六个月,然后在1月份对其进行审查。

张博士(中国):谢谢你。

张博士(中国):主席先生,如果你看一下中国的修正案,它说"任命一个全体委员会在联合国临时总部开会,审议第1款引起的问题"。换言之,第1款(a)、(b)、(c)和(d)项将在纽约审议。如果是这样,那么委员会成员本身,而不是全体委员会,将没有机会处理这个问题。

我认为,如果我们要插入这一点,我们应该让委员会全体会议讨论这一点,因为这是我们尊敬的新西兰代表非常关切的问题。如果我们把它放在(d)下,它将只由全体委员会讨论,而不是由委员会全体会议讨论。如果我们想插入,我想我们应该有其他的方法。我想你可以再有一个1和2,我的3,然后再加上一个4,要求委员会向1948年第一届理事会提交他们关于总部的观点,因为你不必说"临时"。这真的是我们临时决定的。

我谨建议,不要在(d)处加上这句话,否则将使该问题只提交纽约的全体委员会,而是在我的3后面加上4,请委员会向经济及社会理事会1948年第一届会议提交其有关总部问题的意见。

主席:张博士,这仍然是暂时的,因为永久总部已被确定为联合国在远东的永久总部。

张博士(中国):这很好。那么,主席先生,我会接纳你的修正案。

张博士(中国):主席先生,说委员会将任命全体委员会,并不意味着所有人员都将从上海前往纽约。他们可以任命各自政府的其他代表,代表他们出席在成功湖举行的全体委员会的讨论。

主席:进一步的建议是,应增加一项条款(c),即委员会应向经济及社会理事会提出关于临时总部的建议。

张博士(中国):这是一个新的句子。在1948年第一届会议上。

(2)会议发言内容纪要[①]

【会议纪要】

Mr. CHANG (China) said that he would like to see both amendments approved. After the seat of the permanent headquarters of the United Nations in Asia and the Far East had been decided, the Commission should take up its headquarters there. In the meantime, it was necessary that the Commission should meet in the Far East, in order to be able to carry out surveys and studies of war devastation and of reconstruction needs. Its temporary headquarters should be close to the area which had suffered the greatest devastation. In a spirit of compromise, the Chinese delegation had made even the temporary headquarters subject to review by the Council at its first session in 1948, and had suggested that a committee of the whole should meet at the United Nations interim headquarters, at Lake Success.

Mr. CHANG (China), in the interests of obtaining unanimous agreement, proposed that the words "temporary headquarters" in his amendment

① UN Document: E/SR. 51-84, p. 206, p. 208, p. 210, p. 210-211.

should be changed to "temporary offices", and that in his proposed paragraph 3 (a) the words "at Shanghai" should replace the phrase "at its temporary headquarters in the Far East". The words "temporary headquarters" would thus be avoided. He said that Shanghai was one of the most accessible cities in the Far East, and that there would be little difficulty in finding accommodation there for a small secretariat group.

Mr. CHANG (China) declared that there was indeed a difference between "temporary headquarters" and "temporary offices". If the Commission were to hold a meeting, offices would be required for the staff servicing the meeting and carrying out investigations. He pointed out that now the Economic Commission for Asia and the Far East had been set up, it had to proceed with its task, and that it was absolutely essential that its work should be carried out in the field. He urged the Council to come to a decision.

Mr. CHANG (China) considered that the previous decision should not be reopened. The Commission would require time to study the question and to take into account the views of all its members.

Mr. CHANG (China) proposed that if the words "including recommendations on the temporary headquarters of the Commission" were to be included in the resolution, they should be added after the additional paragraphs 3(a) and (b) proposed by the Chinese delegation.

The committee of the whole envisaged in paragraph 3(b) would meet at Lake Success to consider questions arising under paragraph 1, whereas the question of the Commission's headquarters would obviously be discussed in plenary session by all the members of the Commission, who might not be the same persons as those attending the committee of the whole in New York.

【纪要影像】

Mr. Chang (China) said that he would like to see both amendments approved. After the seat of the permanent headquarters of the United Nations in Asia and the Far East had been decided, the Commission should take up its headquarters there. In the meantime, it was necessary that the Commission should meet in the Far East, in order to be able to carry out surveys and studies of war devastation and of reconstruction needs. Its temporary headquarters should be close to the area which had suffered the greatest devastation. In a spirit of compromise, the Chinese delegation had made even the temporary headquarters subject to review by the Council at its first session in 1948, and had suggested that a committee of the whole should meet at the United Nations interim headquarters, at Lake Success.

Mr. Chang (China), in the interests of obtaining unanimous agreement, proposed that the words "temporary headquarters" in his amendment should be changed to "temporary offices", and that in his proposed paragraph 3 (*a*) the words "at Shanghai" should replace the phrase "at its temporary headquarters in the Far East". The words "temporary headquarters" would thus be avoided. He said that Shanghai was one of the most accessible cities in the Far East, and that there would be little difficulty in finding accommodation there for a small secretariat group.

Mr. Chang (China) declared that there was indeed a difference between "temporary headquarters" and "temporary offices". If the Commission were to hold a meeting, offices would be required for the staff servicing the meeting and carrying out investigations. He pointed out that now the Economic Commission for Asia and the Far East had been set up, it had to proceed with its task, and that it was absolutely essential that its work should be carried out in the field. He urged the Council to come to a decision.

Mr. Chang (China) considered that the previous decision should not be reopened. The Commission would require time to study the question and to take into account the views of all its members.

Mr. Chang (China) proposed that if the words "including recommendations on the temporary headquarters of the Commission" were to be included in the resolution, they should be added after the additional paragraphs 3(*a*) and (*b*) proposed by the Chinese delegation.

The committee of the whole envisaged in paragraph 3(*b*) would meet at Lake Success to consider questions arising under paragraph 1, whereas the question of the Commission's headquarters would obviously be discussed in plenary session by all the members of the Commission, who might not be the same persons as those attending the committee of the whole in New York.

图片 4.10　张彭春在经社理事会第四届第 81 次会议发言纪要

【纪要译文】

张先生(中国)说,他希望两项修正案都获得通过。在联合国亚洲和远东常设总部所在地确定后,委员会应将其总部设在那里。同时,委员会有必要在远东开会,以便能够对战争破坏和重建需求进行调查和研究。其临时总部应该靠近受灾最严重的地区。本着妥协的精神,中国代表团甚至让临时总部接受理事会 1948 年第一届会议的审查,并建议全体委员会在成功湖的联合国临时总部开会。

张先生(中国)为了获得一致同意,提议将其修正案中的"临时总部"改为"临时办事处",并在其提议的第 3(a)段中,将"远东临时总部"改为"上海"。因此,将避免使用"临时总部"一词。他说,上海是远东地区交通最便利的城市之一,在那里为一个小型秘书处小组找到住处不会有什么困难。

张先生(中国)宣称,"临时总部"和"临时办公室"之间确实有区别。如果委员会要举行会议,将需要为会议提供服务和进行调查的工作人员提供办公室。他指出,现在亚洲和远东经济委员会已经成立,它必须继续执行其任务,它的工作必须在实地进行。他敦促理事会作出决定。

张先生(中国)认为不应重新审议先前的决定。委员会需要时间来研究这个问题,并考虑所有成员的意见。

张先生(中国)提议,如果在决议中列入"包括关于委员会临时总部的建议",则应在中国代表团提议补充的第3(a)和(b)段之后加上。

第3(b)段设想的全体委员会将在成功湖开会,审议第1段提出的问题,而委员会总部的问题显然将由委员会所有成员在全体会议上讨论,这些成员可能不都是出席纽约全体委员会的那些人。

11. 张彭春在经社理事会第四届第82次会议上的发言

1947年3月28日下午2时45分,联合国经社理事会第四届第82次会议,在纽约成功湖召开。本次会议主要讨论关于理事会及其各委员会和小组委员会届会的决议等。中国代表张彭春率代表团参加了本次会议,并在会议上做了十多次发言,具体发言内容如下:

(1)会议发言全文记录[①]及译文

【全文记录】

Dr. CHANG (China): Mr. President, I am just wondering whether we might not proceed from the top down. By the time you reach the last paragraph that is in this Document E/389, by the time you reach the bottom of page one, I think we may then bring up this Chinese amendment.

Dr. CHANG (China): I thought the best way would be to proceed from the top down. If we are now beginning from the bottom up, it is a little confusing, is it not?

Dr. CHANG (China): You do not mean to this so-called Chinese amendment?

The VICE-PRESIDENT: That is it.

---

① UN Document: E/PV. 82, p. 91, p. 93, p. 94, p. 95, p. 96, p. 101, p. 102, p. 103, p. 112, p. 113, p. 118.

Dr. CHANG (China): Are you discussing it now?

The VICE-PRESIDENT: Well, we are ready.

Dr. CHANG (China): Or would you like to vote on the other inasmuch as we discussed the other so much?

The VICE-PRESIDENT: After we agree on this, we will vote on the whole.

I understand there is no objection to adding another paragraph to the text as it is. Then we will vote on the whole of it if we agree on your end of it.

Dr. CHANG (China): All right. Then my amendment really was the result of some talks with certain members of the Secretariat in considering the meetings of the different commissions. As the text of this paper E/389 reads, you will see the last paragraph on page 1 invites the Secretary-General to make arrangements with regard to the dates of commission sessions so that the reports of these commissions would normally be sent to the Members of the Council not later than six weeks before the session of the Council at which they will be examined.

The emphasis here is to invite the Secretary-General in making arrangements with regard to dates of commission sessions in such and such a manner. Now, if this is followed, let us suppose there will be three sessions of the Council, each one lasting roughly four weeks. Then, six weeks before that would be ten weeks for each session. Consequently, it will amount up to thirty weeks of the whole year, when it is not likely that the Secretary-General, following these instructions, will be able to arrange any meetings of the commissions.

Furthermore, there will be at least eight weeks taken up by the General Assembly. So you will have thirty-eight weeks taken from the possibility of arranging meetings for commissions. Fifty-two minus thirty eight—you will have only fourteen weeks left to arrange for two sessions of from four to six of the commissions and then one session from two to six, including the Sub-commissions.

You can easily see that the Secretary-General will meet with a very difficult situation. For instance, this noon I was talking with the Secretary in charge of the Human Rights Commission. If this should be carried out, then the Human Rights Commission's last date would be the end of May. Therefore, a meeting should be called around the 12th or the 15th of May in order to finish by the end of May, leaving six weeks for the documents to be sent to people in order that whatever the Human Rights Commission may present to the Council may be considered at the next session.

The same thing applies to the other three or four commissions. I think it makes it impossible. Consequently, the suggestion here in this amendment really has two things practically non-controversial, with only one little point that may be considered controversial. The non-controversial thing is to turn the phraseology around—this is a verbal change—to comply with the former intent of the Article; namely, the intent of the Article is that reports should be considered carefully and should be sent out. That was the important thing. It is not so much to limit the Secretary-General in arranging the meetings.

Therefore, it is a verbal modification, that the reports of commissions will normally be considered by the Council. That is where you begin, after they have been sent to the Members of the Council, not later than so many weeks. That "four" is a little substantial change from our consideration yesterday. I should like to have that voted separately, if people should object, before the session of the Council at which they will be examined.

Now, the next phrase, as I understood yesterday during our discussion, was included by the President, but somehow it was omitted from the final draft as we have it. The President did say it with the exception of the two newly created regional commissions in 1947. I think that was the approximate wording that the President used. This morning we decided there was something to be presented by one of the commissions to the Council at its first session in 1948, so the last clause was added in order to clarify the situation with the exception of those—that means of the reports of the regional commissions to be presented to the Council up to and including its first session in 1948. That is, after that, the regional commissions should also obey the general rule.

That is my simple proposal.

Dr. CHANG (China): Yes, Mr. President, it seems to me that the first suggestion here implied would, I think, be accepted by all, namely the verbal change. Instead of simply restricting the Secretary-General in arranging the meetings, what we are interested in is to see that the reports must reach our hands. Therefore, that verbal change should be accepted by all. That is one thing.

Secondly, whether there should be four or six: that deserves to be voted upon. That is another matter.

Now as to the amendment to my amendment, just presented by the representative of the United Kingdom — would he be satisfied by deleting all the words after "to be presented" in my amendment? That is, "... with the exception of those of the Regional Commissions." Would that be acceptable, because if so I make that withdrawal of the last line "with the exception of those of the Regional Commissions." But the thing may still be voted on three times, if you like it.

Dr. CHANG (China): As amended by the United States representative — "... will normally not be considered by the Council unless they have been ..."

Dr. CHANG (China): Mr. President, may I clarify the matter? I think a vote is needed on the word "four" or "six": That needs a vote. We will leave that question aside. The others are merely verbal changes which I think we all agree are helpful in clarifying the situation. If so, may I read it? If as I understand it, after accepting all amendments to my amendments, the things will read: "... that the reports of commissions (except the Regional Commissions) will normally not be considered by the Council unless they have been sent to the Members of the Council at least so many weeks before the session of the Council at which they will be examined." Delete all the rest, and then that "so many"—four or six—we will have to vote on that. Naturally I favour four weeks.

The VICE-PRESIDENT: There is an amendment of the Chinese representative that "six weeks" should be replaced by "four weeks".

Dr. CHANG (China): That is right.

Mr. CHANG (China): From the point of view of the attention that the Chinese Government would like to give it, I think we should suggest ten weeks because of the longer distance. The reason I made this was really in the interest of arranging of the meetings by the Secretariat. We shall have about twenty-odd meetings of the commissions and Sub-commissions, all to be arranged within a possible period of fourteen weeks. Out of the fourteen weeks you will have to take some time out—two weeks out for the Christmas holidays—so you will have only twelve weeks. Now, the Secretariat is signaling me—they want me to speak for them. Of course, they are public servants and they do not want to speak. I am not at all in this case presenting the needs of my Government, which would be ten weeks, but I refuse to submit that now as an amendment. I should say ten weeks. But it is really in the public interest—some of us will have to think of the public interest, even though our public servants do not feel exactly in the position to insist on their needs.

You have about fourteen weeks, and if you take out two weeks for Christmas, you have about twelve weeks for arranging twenty-odd meetings.

I think that is really an impossibility.

Dr. CHANG (China): May I make a reservation that I made the proposal for four weeks not in the interest of my Government but in the interest of the

Secretariat. That ought to be recorded.

Dr. CHANG (China): Mr. President, I did not mean to intervene, but I think that instead of meetings in Geneva you might have meant not Shanghai but Shangri-La. I think it is altogether unwise to fix a general principle in regard to this. I am in favour of the present text as printed and then the Council may decide on, naturally, the proposal of the commissions concerned, and then in consultation with the Secretary-General, to hold the meeting in Shangri-La if necessary.

【全文译文】

张博士先生(中国):主席先生,我想知道我们是否可以不自上而下地进行。当你看到 E/389 号文件的最后一段时,当你看到第一页的底部时,我想我们可以提出中国的修正案。

张博士(中国):我认为最好的办法是自上而下进行。如果我们现在从下往上开始,那就有点混乱了,不是吗?

张博士(中国):你不是指这项所谓的中国修正案吗?

副主席:就是这样。

张博士(中国):你现在正在讨论这个问题吗?

副主席:我们准备好了。

张博士(中国):还是你愿意就另一个问题投票,因为我们已经讨论了那么多其它问题了?

副主席:在我们就这一点达成一致意见之后,我们将对整体进行表决。据我所知,没有人反对在原文中增加另一段。那么,如果我们同意你的观点,我们将对整体进行表决。

张博士(中国):好的。那么,我的修正案实际上是与秘书处某些成员在审议不同委员会会议时进行了一些会谈的结果。正如 E/389 号文件的案文所述,你将看到第 1 页最后一段请秘书长就委员会届会的日期作出安排,以便这些委员会的报告通常不迟于理事会审议这些报告的届会之前六周送交理事会成员。

这里的重点是请秘书长以这种方式就委员会届会的日期作出安排。现在,如果这样做,让我们假设理事会将举行三届会议,每届会议大约持续四周。那么,在这之前的六个星期,每届会都是十个星期。因此,全年将有多达30周的时间,而根据这些指示秘书长不可能安排委员会的任何会议。

此外,大会将至少占用八周时间。所以你将有38周的时间不可能安排委员会会议。52减去38——你只有14周的时间来安排两届由4至6个委员会参加的会议,然后是一届由2至6个委员会参加的会议,包括小组委员会。

你可以很容易地看到,秘书长将面临一个非常困难的局面。例如,今天中午我与负责人权委员会的秘书交谈。如果这样执行,那么人权委员会的最后日期将是5月底。因此,应在5月12日或15日左右召集一次会议,以便在5月底之前结束,留出6周时间将文件发给人们,以便人权委员会可能向理事会提交的任何文件都可以在下一届会议上得到审议。

同样的事情也适用于其他三个或四个委员会。我认为这是不可能的。因此,这项修正案中的建议实际上有两点没有争议,只有一点可能会引起争议。无争议的事情是改变措辞——这是一个文字上的改变——以符合条款的原意;也就是说,该条的意图是,应该仔细审议报告,并且应该发出报告。这是重要的事情。限制秘书长安排会议并不那么重要。

因此,这是一个文字修改,即委员会的报告通常将由理事会审议。你就从这里开始,在这些文件送交理事会成员之后,不迟于这么多个星期。这个“四”与我们昨天的考虑相比有一点实质性的变化。如果有人反对,我希望在理事会审议这些提案的会议之前,将其进行单独表决。

现在,正如我昨天在讨论中所理解的那样,主席列入了下一个表述,但不知何故,它从我们现有的最后草案中被省略了。除了1947年新成立的两个区域委员会外,主席确实说过这句话。我认为这是主席使用的近似措辞。今天上午,我们决定其中一个委员会向理事会1948年第一届会议提交一些东西,因此,增加最后一条是为了澄清情况,区域委员会在1948年理事会第一届会议之前(包括第一届会议之前)将向理事会提交的报告所述情况除外。也就是说,在此之后,各区域委员会也应遵守一般规则。

这是我的简单提议。

张博士(中国):是的,主席先生,在我看来,我认为这里暗示的第一个建议会被所有人接受,即文字上的改动。我们感兴趣的不是简单地限制秘书长安排会议,而是确保报告必须送到我们手中。因此,文字上的改变应该被所有人接受。这是一件事。

第二,应该有四个还是六个:这值得投票表决。那是另一回事。

至于英国代表刚才提出的对我的修正案的修正案,他是否就删除了我的修正案中“将要提出”之后的所有文字表示了满意?也就是说,“……各区域委员会除外。”这是否可以接受,因为如果是这样的话,我会撤回最后一行“区域委员会除外”但如果你喜欢的话,这件事可能会被投票三次。

张博士(中国):经美国代表修正——“……通常不会由理事会审议,除非它们已经……”

张博士(中国):主席先生,我可否澄清此事?我认为需要就“四”或“六”这个词投票表决:这需要投票表决。我们将把这个问题放在一边。其他只是文字上的改变,我认为我们都同意这有助于澄清情况。如果是这样,我可以读一下吗?据我所知,在接受对我的修正案的所有修正案后,内容如下:“……各委员会(区域委员会除外)的报告通常不会由理事会审议,除非这些报告已在理事会审议这些报告的届会之前至少数周送交理事会成员。”删除所有其余的,然后“数量”　　四周还是六周,我们将不得不投票。我当然喜欢四周。

副主席:中国代表提出一项修正案,将“六周”改为“四周”。

张博士(中国):是的。

张先生(中国):从中国政府希望给予它的关注的角度来看,我认为我们应该建议十周,因为距离更长。我这样做的原因实际上是为了秘书处安排会议。我们将举行大约二十多次委员会和小组委员会会议,所有会议都将在可能的14周内安排。在这14周中,你必须抽出一些时间——两周圣诞节假期——所以你只有 12 周的时间。现在,秘书处向我发出信号——希望我代表他们发言。当然,他们是公务员,他们不想发言。在这种情况下,我根本不是为了提出我国政府的需要,即 10 周,但我现在拒绝将其作为一项修正案提交。我应该说是 10 周。但是,这确实符合公众利益——我们中的一些人将不得不考虑公众利益,尽管我们的公务员并不感到完全有资格坚持他们的需要。

你有大约 14 周的时间,如果你抽出两周的时间过圣诞节,你就有大约 12 周的时间安排二十多个会议。

我认为这真的是不可能的。

张博士(中国):请允许我作出保留,即我提出这项建议的四周时间不是为了我国政府,而是为了秘书处。这应该被记录下来。

张博士(中国):主席先生,我不是有意干预,但我认为你可能不是指在日内瓦开会,而是指在香格里拉。我认为在这方面确定一个一般原则是完全不明智的。我同意印出的案文,然后理事会自然可以就有关委员会的提议作出决定,然后与秘书长协商,在必要时在香格里拉举行会议。

(2)会议发言内容纪要[①]

【会议纪要】

Mr. CHANG (China) suggested that the words "six weeks" be replaced by "four weeks".

Decision: *This proposal was rejected.*

① UN Document: E/SR. 51-84, p. 220.

【纪要影像】

Mr. CHANG (China) suggested that the words "six weeks" be replaced by "four weeks".

Decision: *This proposal was rejected.*

图片 4.11　张彭春在经社理事会第四届第 82 次会议发言纪要

【纪要译文】

张先生(中国)建议将"六周"改为"四周"。

决定:该提案被否决。

12. 张彭春在经社理事会第四届第84次会议上的发言

1947年3月29日上午10时30分,联合国经社理事会第四届第84次会议,在纽约成功湖召开。本次会议主要讨论法国代表团提交的关于移徙问题的决议草案、讨论关于妇女地位委员会报告的决议草案、讨论关于苏联代表团关于保证行使和发展贸易的提案、讨论1947年会议日历、会议主席致闭幕词。中国代表张彭春率代表团参加了本次会议,并在会议上发言,但联合国文件检索系统由于文件命名出现差错,有会议纪要文件(E/SR. 84),而全文记录文件(E/PV. 84)其内容与会议纪要文件完全相同。因此本次会议只能检索到会议纪要,而没有全文记录。张彭春在本次会议上的具体发言内容如下:

(1)会议发言全文记录及译文

(暂缺。)

(2)会议发言内容纪要[1]

【会议纪要】

Dr. CHANG (China) recalled the decision which had been taken that all documents to be considered by the Council had to be in the hands of the different Governments six weeks before the time of the meeting. This would obviously

---

[1] UN Document: E/SR. 84, p. 243.

prohibit a June commission meeting.

【纪要影像】

Dr. CHANG (China) recalled the decision which had been taken that all documents to be considered by the Council had to be in the hands of the different Governments six weeks before the time of the meeting. This would obviously prohibit a June commission meeting.

图片 4.12　张彭春在经社理事会第四届第 84 次会议发言纪要

【纪要译文】

张博士回顾了已作出的决定,即理事会审议的所有文件必须在会议召开前六周交给各国政府。这显然会阻止委员会在 6 月举行的会议。

第五章　联合国经社理事会第五届会议

（全文及纪要）

1947 年 7 月 19 日至 8 月 16 日，联合国经社理事会第五届会议在纽约成功湖召开，本届会议共召开了 37 次会议，即第 85 次会议至第 121 次会议。中国代表张彭春率团(见图片 5.1 名单)参加了本届会议，并在其中的 17 次会议上发言，包括第 85 次会议、第 87 次会议、第 88 次会议、第 90 次会议、第 94 次会议、第 95 次会议、第 100 次会议、第 101 次会议、第 105 次会议、第 106 次会议、第 107 次会议、第 110 次会议、第 112 次会议、第 113 次会议、第 117 次会议、第 120 次会议和第 121 次会议。第 121 次会议于 1947 年 8 月 16 日晚上 8 时 15 分开始一直开到 17 日凌晨 1 时 30 分，本届会议才圆满结束。

本届会议取得了圆满的成功，大会决定召开两个重要国际会议，一是贸易与就业国际会议，另一个是新闻和出版自由国际会议。会议确定了五个重要的特别机构，包括万国邮政联盟(the International Post Union)、世界卫生组织(the World Health Organization)、国际通讯联盟(the International Telecommunication Union)、国际重建与发展银行(the International Bank of Reconstruction and Development)和国际货币基金组织(the International Monetary Fund)。本届会议还审议通过了几个委员会的报告，尤其是报告涉及两个重要区域：一个是欧洲经济委员会的报告，另一个是亚洲和远东经济委员会的报告。

根据现有的联合国文献检索系统，这些会议，除了第 113 次会议和第 117 次会议只有会议纪要外，其余会议均有会议纪要和全文记录。本届会议发言内容遵循第二届和第四届会议相关内容的编写体例及编排方式，每次会议分为两部分：(1)“会议发言全文记录及译文”包括：“全文记录”和“全文译文”；(2)“会议发言内容纪要”包括：“会议纪要”“纪要影像”和“纪要译文”。

CHINA

Representative

H.E. Dr. P. C. Chang.

Assistants

Dr. Szeming Sze.
Dr. T. Y. Wu.
Professor Y. T. Sun.
Dr. Hsiu Cha.
Dr. H. K. Sang.

图片 5.1　中国代表团参加联合国经社理事会第五届会议名单

1. 张彭春在经社理事会第五届第85次会议上的发言

1947年7月19日上午11时,联合国经社理事会第五届首次会议(即第85次会议),在纽约成功湖召开。本次会议主要议题就是开幕式和通过会议日程。中国代表张彭春率团参加了本次会议,并在会议上提出会议日程议案,由于所提议案得到了其他代表(如加拿大等国代表)的支持,会议最后通过了张彭春先生提出的会议日程议案。张彭春在本次会议上先后三次发言,其具体发言内容全文、纪要及其译文等如下:

(1)会议发言全文记录[①]及译文

【全文记录】

Dr. CHANG (China): We are now at the beginning of the Fifth Session of the Economic and Social Council. I have had the honour to attend the four prior sessions. We are beginning to face the problems and activities of the Council in what might be described as a better-organized condition. During the first three sessions of the Council the chief problem was the actual organization of the various commissions and committees. At the last session of the Council we dealt with the reports of the first sessions of eight of the commissions under the Council.

At this session, we have already had at least one meeting of all the com-

① UN Document: E/PV. 85, pp. 56-60, pp. 71-75, p. 86.

missions under the Council. We may say that this is the first session at which we can tackle problems as they arise. It has been commented that some of the items on the agenda have not been properly dealt with by the appropriate commissions and other agencies. That may be true in regard to some, but if so, it is hoped that proper attention will be given to the procedure, and that items which should be dealt with by the commissions should be referred to the commissions so as to be included in their reports as they are presented to the Council.

We are all struck by the volume of items on the agenda. It has been commented that it is not necessary for us to have full-dress debates on them all, but even so the number is still quite formidable. If we do not do good, conscientious and careful work, work which will be respected by the world, we shall not be satisfied ourselves. The task before the Council is altogether too serious. That being the case, we feel that the number of items on the agenda is still too large. However, there is one point which perhaps only old timers will remember—it has not been commented on yet — it is that this is only our second session this year, and according to our rules of procedure we are supposed to have three or more sessions. Because of the fact that we had a late session of the General Assembly last year, and because of the various other matters in regard to organization, we have been compelled to have only two sessions. It may be necessary to have a third session; perhaps we shall be able to decide when we reach a later stage of this session.

Therefore, I do not think it is wise for us to force ourselves to finish all the items just in order to have them finished and done with. We should not be restricted in our debates in regard to these items just because we happen to have had only two sessions of the Council this year. So far as I remember, this question was not decided at the last session of the Council, and therefore it is still open to us to have another session this year. If my impression on that subject is wrong, I shall no doubt be corrected by the Secretariat.

In regard to the items listed on pages 8 and 9 of the Report of the Agenda Committee, it does not really seem as if we have had enough time to go over them at all. We have had two previous notices, but I think several items are quite new. In regard to the arrangement of the items also, some of us may wish to have time for a little more thought. At the last session the items of the agenda were not definitively adopted at the first meeting, and it may not be wise for us to adopt definitively today the items listed. It may be wise for us to think the matter over until some time early next week — not, I hope, with a view to adding any more, but to see whether we have any suggestions in regard to the arrangement.

There may be certain items from the Fourth Session which will have to be brought up here and which are not yet included. I have in mind especially the question of the meetings and meeting places of the commissions, not only in 1948 as already covered by item 39, but also during the rest of this year. There may be still one or two points to be considered by the Council in that connection.

Consequently, I should like to see a general item relating to unfinished business from the last session included, if not definitely in black and white, at least tacitly.

Dr. CHANG (China): I move that the agenda as recommended by the Agenda Committee in its Report on pages 8 and 9 be provisionally adopted, leaving, however, the first three days of next week for any adjustments that may be made. If there are any adjustments, I think they can be made with the President of the Council, according to our custom. After that, the President may make the adjustment, and if he feels he should call the attention of the Council to any changes that need the decision of the Council, he will be free to do so.

In regard to the suggestion made that the Agenda Committee should be consulted again, I rather doubt whether this is included in the terms of reference of the Agenda Committee, which provide: "The Agenda Committee shall prior to each session consider the provisional agenda..."

Now that the session has begun, I think we may leave the matter of the agenda to the Council as a whole, with the President representing the Council in dealing with matters of the agenda, as entrusted to him by the Council.

As we all realize, the chief problem of the Security Council is conflict and the chief problem of the Economic and Social Council is confusion, and we shall tackle this problem of confusion in a very speedy manner. Therefore, I beg to move that the agenda as proposed by the Agenda Committee in its Report on pages 8 and 9 be provisionally adopted, and that three days of next week be given for readjustment with the President of the Council. If necessary, the President of the Council may call the attention of the Council to any necessary changes.

Dr. CHANG (China): I must apologize for not having expressed myself clearly, especially with regard to my appreciation of the work done by the Agenda Committee. I was one of those who were in favour of the creation of the Agenda Committee. Now that the work of the Agenda Committee has been completed, we should express our appreciation for what it has contributed.

With regard to the wording of the motion, I did not say this should be considered as a provisional agenda. I did say that this agenda may be adopted provisionally, but if even that word should cast any doubt concerning the value of the work of the Agenda Committee, I am ready to modify it. I am ready to propose that the agenda, as proposed by the Agenda Committee, be adopted. If any adjustments are to be made, the President of the Council may report back to the Council within the first three days of next week. I hope that will meet the objections of the Canadian representative. I also think that will meet the situation presented by the Cuban representative.

【全文译文】

张博士(中国):我们现在开始经济及社会理事会第五届会议。我有幸出席了之前的四届会议。我们正开始面对理事会的问题和活动,可以说是组织得更有序。在理事会前三届会议期间,主要问题是各类委员会和事务委员会的实际组织。在理事会上届会议上,我们处理了理事会下属八个委员会第一届会议的报告。

在本届会议上,理事会所有下属委员会至少举行了一次会议。我们可以说,这是我们能够在出现问题时解决问题的第一次会议。有评论说,议程上的一些项目没有得到适当的委员会和其他机构的妥善处理。对某些人来说可能确实如此,但如果是这样,希望将适当注意这一程序,该由各委员会处理的项目应该交给各委员会,以便在提交理事会的报告中包括这些项目。

我们都对议程上的项目数量感到吃惊。有评论说,我们没有必要对所有这些问题进行全面的辩论,但即使如此,数目仍然很大。如果我们不认真细致地做好这项将受到全世界尊重的工作,我们自己都不会满意。理事会面前的任务太重了。在这种情况下,我们认为议程上的项目仍然太多。然而,有一点也许只有老前辈才会记得——这一点尚未得到评论——那就是,这只是我们今年的第二届会议,根据我们的议事规则,我们应该有三届或更多届会。由于去年我们的大会届会开得很晚,而且由于组织方面的各种其他问题,我们不得不只举行两届会议。可能有必要举行第三届会议;也许我们将能够在本届会议的后一阶段作出决定。

因此,我不认为我们只是为了完成和了结它们而强迫自己完成所有项目是明智的。我们不应仅仅因为今年理事会只举行了两届会议,就限制我们就这些项目进行辩论。据我记忆所及,这一问题在理事会上届会议上没有作出决定,因此,我们仍然可以在今年举行另一届会议。如果我对这个问题的印象是错误的,秘书处无疑将纠正我的错误。

关于议程委员会报告第 8 页和第 9 页所列的项目,我们似乎根本没有足够的时间来审议这些项目。我们之前收到过两份通知,但我认为有几项很新。另外,关于项目的安排,我们中的一些人可能希望抽出时间多考虑一下。在上届会议上,第一次会议没有明确通过议程项目,我们今天明确通过所列项目可能并不明智。我们最好在下周初的某个时候再考虑这个问题——我希望不是为了增加任何内容,而是看看我们对这一安排是否有任何建议。

第四届会议的某些项目可能必须在此提出,但尚未包括在内。我尤其记得的是各委员会的会议和开会地点问题,不仅在项目 39 已经涉及的 1948 年,而且在今年剩下的时间里。在这方面,理事会可能仍有一两点需要审议。

因此,我希望看到一个与上届会议未完成的工作有关的一般性项目被列入议程,如果不是绝对白纸黑字的话,至少是心照不宣的。

张博士(中国):我提议临时采纳议程委员会在其报告第 8 页和第 9 页中建议的议程,但将下周前三天留给可能作出的任何调整。如果有任何调整,我认为可以根据我们的习惯,与理事会主席一起进行。在这之后,主席可以作出调整,如果他认为他应该提请理事会注意需要理事会作出决定的任何变化,他将可以这样做。

关于建议再次审议议程委员会的建议,我很怀疑这是否包括在议程委员会的职权范围内,其中规定:“议程委员会应在每一届会议之前审议临时议程……”

既然会议已经开始,我认为我们可以把议程问题留给整个理事会,由主席代表理事会处理理事会委托他处理的议程问题。

众所周知,安全理事会的主要问题是冲突,经济及社会理事会的主要问题是混乱,我们将以非常迅速的方式处理这一混乱问题。因此,我谨动议临时采纳议程委员会在其报告第 8 页和第 9 页中提出的议程,并在下周的三天内与理事会主席一起重新调整议程。如有必要,理事会主席可提请理事会注意任何必要的变动。

张博士(中国):我必须为没有明确表达自己的意见而致歉,特别是关于我对议程委员会所做工作的赞赏。我是赞成设立议程委员会的人之一。既然议程委员会的工作已经完成,我们应该对它所做的贡献表示赞赏。

关于议案的措辞,我没有说这应被视为临时议程。我确实说过,这一议程可以暂时采纳,但如果连这个词都对议程委员会工作的价值产生任何疑问,我乐意修改它。我准备提议通过议程委员会提议的议程。如果需要进行任何调整,理事会主席可在下周前三天内向理事会报告。我希望这将打消加拿大代表的反对意见。我还认为,这将符合古巴代表提出的情况。

(2)会议发言内容纪要①

【会议纪要】

Mr. CHANG (China) drew attention to the fact that as the Council now faced its work in a more organized fashion, the fifth session would be the first in which it would be possible for it to tackle problems as they arose.

There obviously could not be a full debate on every item of the voluminous agenda, but unless it worked conscientiously, the Council would be the first to be dissatisfied. According to the rules of procedure, there was still a possibility that a third session might be held this year. It would be unwise to expedite consideration of the items on the agenda just for the sake of disposing of them.

There had not been enough time to study all the items on the agenda. It would therefore be wiser to postpone its final adoption for a few days.

Mr. Chang reminded the Council that there were still one or two items discussion of which had not been completed at the last session. He considered that they should be comprised in a special item, or at least brought to the attention of the President and the Vice-Presidents.

Mr. CHANG (China) moved that the agenda as recommended by the Agenda Committee should be adopted provisionally, leaving to the President of

① UN Document: E/SR. 85, p. 16, p. 17. p. 18.

the Council two or three days for possible readjustment. The President could, if necessary, call the attention of the Council to any changes.

He considered that it would not be possible to hold another meeting of the Agenda Committee, as suggested by the representative of Cuba, since it would be contrary to the rules of procedure of the Council.

Mr. CHANG (China), after having expressed his appreciation of the work of the Agenda Committee, modified his previous motion and suggested that the agenda, as proposed by the Agenda Committee, should be adopted; if any adjustments were necessary, the President should report to the Council within the first three days of the coming week.

Mr. DAVIDSON (Canada) supported the amended motion of the representative of China, and pointed out that it provided an opportunity for the representative of Cuba to explain his point of view to the President of the Council.

Mr. PÉREZ CISNEROS (Cuba) accepted the motion as presented by Mr. Chang (China) and supported by Mr. Davidson (Canada).

Decision: *The agenda was adopted as proposed by the representative of China.*

【纪要影像】

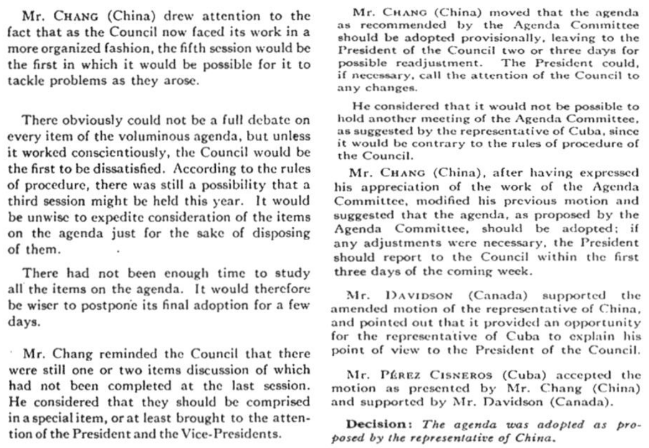

Mr. CHANG (China) drew attention to the fact that as the Council now faced its work in a more organized fashion, the fifth session would be the first in which it would be possible for it to tackle problems as they arose.

There obviously could not be a full debate on every item of the voluminous agenda, but unless it worked conscientiously, the Council would be the first to be dissatisfied. According to the rules of procedure, there was still a possibility that a third session might be held this year. It would be unwise to expedite consideration of the items on the agenda just for the sake of disposing of them.

There had not been enough time to study all the items on the agenda. It would therefore be wiser to postpone its final adoption for a few days.

Mr. Chang reminded the Council that there were still one or two items discussion of which had not been completed at the last session. He considered that they should be comprised in a special item, or at least brought to the attention of the President and the Vice-Presidents.

Mr. CHANG (China) moved that the agenda as recommended by the Agenda Committee should be adopted provisionally, leaving to the President of the Council two or three days for possible readjustment. The President could, if necessary, call the attention of the Council to any changes.

He considered that it would not be possible to hold another meeting of the Agenda Committee, as suggested by the representative of Cuba, since it would be contrary to the rules of procedure of the Council.

Mr. CHANG (China), after having expressed his appreciation of the work of the Agenda Committee, modified his previous motion and suggested that the agenda, as proposed by the Agenda Committee, should be adopted; if any adjustments were necessary, the President should report to the Council within the first three days of the coming week.

Mr. DAVIDSON (Canada) supported the amended motion of the representative of China, and pointed out that it provided an opportunity for the representative of Cuba to explain his point of view to the President of the Council.

Mr. PÉREZ CISNEROS (Cuba) accepted the motion as presented by Mr. Chang (China) and supported by Mr. Davidson (Canada).

Decision: *The agenda was adopted as proposed by the representative of China.*

图片5.2 张彭春在经社理事会第五届第85次会议发言纪要

【纪要译文】

张先生(中国)提请注意这样一个事实,即由于理事会现在以一种更有条理的方式面对其工作,第五届会议将是理事会能够处理出现的问题的第一届会议。

显然,不可能对冗长议程中的每个项目都进行充分辩论,但除非认真履职,否则理事会将第一个感到不满。根据议事规则,今年仍有可能举行第三届会议。仅仅为了处理议程上的项目而加速审议这些项目是不明智的。

没有足够的时间研究议程上的所有项目。因此,明智的做法是将其最后通过日期推迟几天。

张先生提醒理事会,在上届会议上仍有一两个项目的讨论尚未完成。他认为,这些问题应列入一个特别项目,或至少提请主席和副主席注意。

张先生(中国)动议临时通过议程委员会建议的议程,留给理事会主席两三天时间进行可能的调整。如有必要,主席可提请理事会注意任何变化。

他认为,不可能按照古巴代表的建议再举行一次议程委员会会议,因为这将违反理事会议事规则。

张先生(中国)在对议程委员会的工作表示赞赏后,修改了他先前的动议,并建议通过议程委员会提议的议程;如果需要任何调整,主席应在下一周的前三天内向理事会报告。

戴维森先生(加拿大)支持中国代表的修正动议,并指出这为古巴代表向理事会主席解释其观点提供了机会。

佩雷斯·西塞罗斯先生(古巴)接受了张先生(中国)提出并得到戴维森先生(加拿大)支持的动议。

决议:通过了中国代表提议的议程。

2. 张彭春在经社理事会第五届第 87 次会议上的发言

1947 年 7 月 21 日下午 2 时 30 分,联合国经社理事会第五届第 87 次会议,在纽约成功湖召开。本次会议主要议题就是讨论财政委员会的报告。中国代表张彭春率团参加了本次会议,并在会议上的发言,其具体发言内容全文、纪要及其译文等如下:

(1) 会议发言全文记录[①]及译文

【全文记录】

Mr. CHANG (China): The Chinese delegation to congratulate the Members of the Fiscal Commission on their useful and helpful Report. In general we share the Commission's attitude that a careful study of the problem should be made before any action is taken.

The Chinese delegation particularly wishes to endorse paragraph (b) on page 4 of this Report, which states:

"Make appropriate arrangements so as to be equipped to give, on request, technical advice, information and assistance on fiscal matters coming within the terms of reference of the Fiscal Commission, to the Economic and Social Council, other commissions and organs of the United Nations, the specialized agencies and Member Governments. Apart from other important advantages this ad-

① UN Document: E/PV. 87, pp. 21-25.

vice on fiscal matters would be particularly useful to economically less advanced countries as a means of facilitating their development and raising their standards of living."

The Fiscal Commission also directed our attention to the problem of international taxation. The problem of international double taxation is a very complicated one, especially because of the fact that nations of the world are at very various stages of economic development. Some are advanced economically and industrially, while others are not so advanced. Some principle has to be worked out that would be fair and acceptable to the economically advanced, as well as the less advanced countries of the world. The under-developed country may well feel that if it has nothing to say or little to say in regard to the economic activities of corporations or individuals working in that country, there is a threatened infringement of its sovereign rights.

However, whatever principles the Council will be able to work out, we should constantly have in mind that such principles should contain the interests of both the economically advanced and economically under-developed countries. In this respect I was particularly pleased to hear the representative of Canada paying, as usual, his gracious attention to the under-developed countries in the world. We all appreciate that. Whatever action we may arrive at, it should be fair and should contribute to the economic welfare of the world as a whole.

【全文译文】

张先生(中国):我谨请中国代表团祝贺财政委员会成员提交了有助益的报告。总的来说,我们同意委员会的态度,即在采取任何行动之前,应仔细研究该问题。

中国代表团特别希望赞同本报告第4页(b)段,其中指出:

作出适当安排,以便能够应要求,就财政委员会职权范围内的财政事项向经济及社会理事会、联合国其他委员会和机关、专门机构和会员国政府提供技术咨询、信息和援助。除了其他重要的益处之外,这种关于财政问题的建议对于经济欠发达的国家特别有用,可以促进它们的发展,提高它们的生活水平。

财政委员会还提请我们注意国际税收问题。国际双重征税问题是一个非常复杂的问题,特别是因为世界各国正处于非常不同的经济发展阶段。一些国家在经济和工业方面都很先进,而另一些国家则不那么先进。必须制定一些对世界上经济发达国家和欠发达国家都公平和可接受的原则。欠发达国家可能会觉得,如果它深感在该国工作的公司或个人的经济活动无话可说或几乎无话可说,那么它的主权权利就有可能受到侵犯。

然而,无论理事会能够制定出什么原则,我们都应始终牢记,这些原则应包含经济发达国家和经济欠发达国家的利益。在这方面,我特别高兴地听到加拿大代表一如既往地对世界上欠发达国家给予亲切的关注。我们都很感激。无论我们可能采取什么行动,都应该是公平的,并且应该有助于整个世界的经济福利。

(2)会议发言内容纪要①

【会议纪要】

Mr. CHANG (China) commended the report in particular the recommendations regarding technical help to be given to economically less advanced countries, and supported the view that a careful study be made of the report before any action was taken.

① UN Document: E/SR. 85, p. 27.

【纪要影像】

Mr. CHANG (China) commended the report, in particular the recommendations regarding technical help to be given to economically less advanced countries, and supported the view that a careful study be made of the report before any action was taken.

图片 5.3　张彭春在经社理事会第五届第 87 次会议发言纪要

【纪要译文】

张先生(中国)赞扬该报告,特别是关于向经济较不发达国家提供技术援助的建议,并支持在采取任何行动之前对该报告进行仔细研究的观点。

3. 张彭春在经社理事会第五届第 88 次会议上的发言

1947 年 7 月 22 日上午 11 时，联合国经社理事会第五届第 88 次会议，在纽约成功湖召开。本次会议主要议题就是审议将联合国某些资产移交世界卫生组织临时委员会的问题、讨论国际儿童紧急救助基金会[①]的临时报告。中国代表张彭春率团参加了本次会议，并在会议上讨论国际儿童紧急救助基金会的临时报告时先后四次发言(会议纪要概述了三个发言)，其具体发言内容全文、纪要及其译文等如下：

(1) 会议发言全文记录[②]及译文

【全文记录】

Mr. CHANG (China): I have only two words to say. The first is appreciation. On behalf of my Government and the Chinese delegation, I express profound gratitude for what the Fund has already done, and also appreciation for the devoted services of the Director, Mr. Pate, who has given so much of his energy and time and most just consideration in regard to the needs of the various

① 联合国国际儿童紧急救助基金会(United Nations International Children's Emergency Fund, 简称 UNICEF)，现名联合国儿童基金会，于 1946 年 12 月 11 日创建，其目的是满足战后欧洲与中国儿童的紧急需求。1950 年起，它的工作扩展到满足全球所有发展中国家儿童和母亲的长期需求。1953 年，UNICEF 成为联合国系统的永久成员，隶属联合国系统，受联合国大会的委托，致力于实现全球各国儿童的生存、发展、受保护和参与的权利。

② UN Document: E/PV. 88, p. 61, pp. 72-73, p. 77, p. 82.

countries.

The second word is the word perspective. I think we are going to discuss some problems in which we may have differences of opinion, but in regard to this problem, the needs of children all over the world, I am sure all of us are at one. Therefore, in a world where there are so many conflicts, we have this one thing in which we all agree.

In conclusion, I shall quote one sentence from an old Chinese proverb: "Great man is he who does not lose his heart of a child." Therefore, in considering this matter we hope we shall all keep the children's heart. So, with that perspective in view, I sincerely hope that the Report will receive the unanimous support of the Council.

Mr. CHANG (China): Mr. President, may I just ask a question through you, whether the representatives of the Fund would feel that a brief resolution on the part of the Council, in the spirit of appreciation and encouragement, especially as stated by the representative of the United States, encouraging not only governments but also private institutions and individuals to give. Would such a short resolution be of any use or any help to the Fund? If so, I think the Council will be only too glad to have such a resolution drafted and passed.

Mr. CHANG (China): In connection with the question of the form of the resolution, I think it may be quite easy to entrust the matter to the Secretariat which, in consultation with the representatives of the Fund, would draft some form for the resolution. One or two sentences, at least, seem to be necessary; otherwise it will appear as though this matter were discussed and no conclusion whatever was reached. We cannot easily refer people to the verbatim reports.

It seems to me that one or two sentences of approval or encouragement are necessary. If the Fund desires something longer than that to show definite approval on the part of the Council, then that would have to be suggested by the representatives of the Fund.

Therefore, I suggest that we pass on to the next point on the agenda, leaving this matter to the Secretariat which will prepare a short resolution expressing our approval and encouragement. The Secretariat will be able to secure the aid of the representatives of the Fund for that task.

Mr. CHANG (China): I agree with the President's suggestion. As a matter of fact, it is a way to bring our discussion to a conclusion.

This is what is proposed, as I understand it: The Council, having considered the Report of the Fund, wishes to show its appreciation for the work done by the Fund, and hopes that governments and voluntary agencies will be able to contribute to the Fund as much as possible, and that the discussion hold by the Council will be referred to the Fund for its attention. Is that the meaning of the proposal?

The PRESIDENT: That is the meaning of my proposal.

I consider the report approved, and all suggestions made during this meeting will be referred to the Fund.

【全文译文】

张先生(中国):我只有两个词要说。第一个是感谢。我代表我国政府和中国代表团,对基金会已经做的工作表示深切的感谢,并对总干事佩特先生的热诚服务表示赞赏,他付出了如此多的精力和时间,并对各国的需要给予了最公正的考虑。

第二个词是视角。我想我们将要讨论一些我们可能有不同意见的问题,但是关于这个问题,全世界儿童的需要,我相信我们所有人的意见是一致的。因此,在一个有如此多冲突的世界里,我们有一件我们达成共识的事情。

最后,我将引用中国古老谚语中的一句话:"大人者,不失其赤子之心者也。"[1]因此,在考虑这件事时,我们希望大家都能保持一颗赤子之心。

---

① 笔者注:该句出自《孟子·离娄章句下》。

因此,从这个角度来看,我真诚地希望该报告将得到理事会的一致支持。

张先生(中国):主席先生,我只想通过你问一个问题,基金会代表是否会认为,理事会本着赞赏和鼓励的精神,特别是如美国代表所说的那样,通过一项简短的决议,不仅鼓励各国政府,也鼓励私人机构和个人捐助。这样一个简短的决议会对基金有任何用处或帮助吗?如果是这样,我认为理事会将非常高兴起草并通过这样一项决议。

张先生(中国):关于决议的形式问题,我认为将此事委托秘书处可能相当容易,秘书处将与基金会代表协商,起草某种形式的决议。至少一两句话似乎是必要的;否则,这件事似乎已经讨论过了,而且没有得出任何结论。我们不能轻易地让人们查阅逐字记录报告。

在我看来,一两句赞许或鼓励是必要的。如果基金会希望有比这更长的时间来表明理事会的明确批准,则必须由基金会代表提出建议。

因此,我建议我们继续讨论议程上的下一问题,把这个问题留给秘书处,秘书处将准备一份简短的决议,表示我们的赞同和鼓励。秘书处将能够确保基金会代表为这项任务提供援助。

张先生(中国):我同意主席的建议。事实上,这是结束我们讨论的一种方式。

据我理解,这就是提议的内容:理事会在审议了基金会的报告后,希望对基金会所做的工作表示感谢,并希望各国政府和志愿机构能够尽所能向基金会捐款,理事会进行的讨论将提交基金会,以引起其注意。这就是提议的含义吗?

主席:这就是我提议的含义。

我认为这份报告已获批准,所有在会议期间提出的建议将被提交给基金会。

(2)会议发言内容纪要①

【会议纪要】

Mr. CHANG (China) thanked Mr. Pate for all the time and work he had devoted to the Children's Fund. In the course of international debate there were often problems on which countries disagreed, but the question of children was one which they had most at heart and in which agreement was essential. He recalled the saying of a Chinese thinker: "Great man is he who does not lose his heart of a child." He hoped that the report would be adopted unanimously by the Council.

Mr. CHANG (China) asked Mr. Alexander whether a short resolution with a view to encouraging Governments and private associations to assist the Children's Fund would not be a good thing.

Mr. CHANG (China) agreed with what had been said and expressed the hope that Governments and voluntary bodies would continue, in an increasingly generous manner, to assist in the work already accomplished by the Children's Fund.

① UN Document: E/SR. 88, p. 33, p. 34, p. 35.

【纪要影像】

Mr. CHANG (China) thanked Mr. Pate for all the time and work he had devoted to the Children's Fund. In the course of international debate there were often problems on which countries disagreed, but the question of children was one which they had most at heart and in which agreement was essential. He recalled the saying of a Chinese thinker: "Great man is he who does not lose his heart of a child." He hoped that the report would be adopted unanimously by the Council.

Mr. CHANG (China) asked Mr. Alexander whether a short resolution with a view to encouraging Governments and private associations to assist the Children's Fund would not be a good thing.

Mr. CHANG (China) agreed with what had been said and expressed the hope that Governments and voluntary bodies would continue, in an increasingly generous manner, to assist in the work already accomplished by the Children's Fund.

图片 5.4　张彭春在经社理事会第五届第 88 次会议发言纪要

【纪要译文】

张先生(中国)感谢佩特先生为儿童基金会投入的所有时间和工作。在国际辩论过程中,经常会出现各国意见不一致的问题,但儿童问题是他们最关心的问题,达成一致意见是至关重要的。他回顾了一位中国思想家的话:“大人者,不失其赤子之心者也。”[①]他希望理事会一致通过该报告。

张先生(中国)问亚历山大先生,一项旨在鼓励各国政府和私人协会协助儿童基金会的简短决议是不是一件好事。

张先生(中国)同意所说的话,并表示希望各国政府和志愿机构继续以越来越慷慨的方式协助儿童基金会已经完成的工作。

① 笔者注:该句出自《孟子·离娄章句下》。该句的译文核对,承蒙山东菏泽学院中文系邵子华教授的指点,笔者表示感谢。

4. 张彭春在经社理事会第五届第90次会议上的发言

1947年7月23日上午11时,联合国经社理事会第五届第90次会议,在纽约成功湖召开。本次会议主要议题就是讨论经济和就业委员会第二届会议的报告。中国代表张彭春率团参加了本次会议,并在会议上发言,其具体发言内容全文、纪要及其译文等如下:

(1)会议发言全文记录[①]及译文

【全文记录】

Dr. CHANG (China): While approving in general the Report of the second session of the Economic and Employment Commission, the Chinese delegation would like to stress the point that there should be proper attention given to the harmony of interests of the under-developed areas and of the industrially more developed areas in the world.

We should make clear our main assumption, that the industrially more advanced areas can maintain economic stability and full employment only if the other parts of the world which are less developed also increase their economic activities in the form of industrial and agricultural development.

The world is eagerly awaiting what this Council will do to assist in the much needed economic development of certain areas that are comparatively un-

① UN Document: E/PV.90, pp. 66-67.

der-industrialized, as well as to suggest effective means whereby instability and unemployment may be minimized, if not avoided, in the industrialized areas. It is but natural that our economic thinking has been preoccupied with conditions in countries that have attained high degrees of economic achievement. Their significance should in no way be overlooked, and their place in the economic structure of the world of today is potent and pivotal.

We must, however, give due consideration to the economically less developed areas not only because of the huge populations and potential resources, not only because they supply the materials and furnish the markets for the manufactured goods of the industrialized countries, but also because the less industrialized areas served as the meeting places for conflicts and contentions of the industrialized powers. It is in these economically low-pressure areas that we can detect and delineate the shape of things to come—the international struggles, actual and potential.

I really have been quoting from a humble speech of mine made during the Second Session of the Economic and Social Council in New York on 4 June 1946.

Attention should be called to the significance of the under-industrialized areas, not only from the point of view of the economic angle, but also of the political and other significance in regard to these areas being the points at which the different industrialized powers have cause to show conflict. Let us not in any way give the impression to the under-industrialized areas that their problems and desires have not been given due consideration by the Council.

In these areas there is a persistent eagerness for industrialization. In order partly to meet this persistent eagerness, the Chinese delegation has proposed that the Secretariat should arrange so undertake the study of the patterns of industrialization so that the under-industrialized areas can benefit from the experience of the industrialized countries during the last one hundred fifty years. That historical perspective should be kept in view.

The Chinese delegation therefore hopes that the Council will continue to direct the Economic and Employment Commission, as well as the Secretariat, to give due consideration to the problems of the under-industrialized areas without of course prejudicing the recommendations to be given to the problems of economic stability and full employment.

In regard to detailed recommendations, the Chinese delegation will bring them to the attention of the Economic Committee of the Whole when it comes to discuss the problem.

【全文译文】

张博士(中国):中国代表团在总体上同意经济和就业委员会第二届会议报告的同时,要强调一点,即应适当注意世界上欠发达地区和工业较发达地区利益的协调。

我们应该明确我们的主要假设,即只有世界上其他欠发达地区也以工农业发展的形式增加其经济活动,工业较发达的地区才能保持经济稳定和充分就业。

全世界都在急切地等待理事会将采取什么行动,以协助某些工业化程度相对较低的地区实现急需的经济发展,并提出有效的办法,使工业化地区的不稳定和失业现象,如果不能避免的话,尽可能减少。我们的经济思维总是自然而然地关注那些取得了高度经济成就的国家的状况。它们的重要性不容忽视,它们在当今世界经济结构中的地位强大而关键。

然而,我们必须适当考虑经济欠发达地区,这不仅是因为人口众多和潜在资源丰富,不仅是因为它们为工业化国家的制成品提供材料和市场,而且还因为欠工业地区是工业化大国冲突和争夺的场所。正是在这些经济低压的地区,我们可以发现并描绘出未来的情况——实际的和潜在的国际斗争。

我确实一直在引用我 1946 年 6 月 4 日在纽约举行的经济及社会理事

会第二届会议上所发表的拙见。

应当提请注意欠工业化地区的重要性,不仅从经济角度来看,而且从政治和其他方面来看,这些地区是各工业大国引起冲突的地方。我们不要以任何方式给欠工业化地区留下这样的印象,即理事会没有适当考虑他们的问题和愿望。

在这些地区,人们一直渴望实现工业化。为了部分满足这种持续的渴望,中国代表团建议秘书处作出安排,对工业化模式进行研究,以便欠工业化地区能够从工业化国家过去 150 年的经验中受益。应该牢记这一历史观点。

因此,中国代表团希望理事会将继续指示经济和就业委员会以及秘书处适当考虑欠工业化地区的问题,当然不影响对经济稳定和充分就业问题提出的建议。

关于详细建议,中国代表团将在讨论该问题时提请全体经济事务委员会注意。

(2)会议发言内容纪要①

【会议纪要】

Mr. CHANG (China), quoting from an address he delivered before the second session of the Council, called attention to the harmony of economic interest between under-developed and developed countries. He emphasized that world stability must be achieved through international co-operation. He believed that consideration should be given to the less developed areas, not only because of their large populations and resources, and their role as markets for the more industrialized nations, but also because those areas were often the location of conflict between advanced nations.

The Chinese representative expressed the hope that the Council would not

① UN Document: E/SR. 90, p. 46.

give the impression that the problems of the under-industrialized countries were not accorded due consideration. He felt that a historical perspective of the development of economically advanced nations would be of inestimable value to under-developed countries.

【纪要影像】

Mr. CHANG (China), quoting from an address he delivered before the second session of the Council, called attention to the harmony of economic interest between under-developed and developed countries. He emphasized that world : tability must be achieved through international co-operat'on. He believed that conside-ation should be given to the less developed areas, not only because of their large populations and resources, and their role as markets for the more industrialized nations, but also because those areas were often the location of conflict between advanced nations.

The Chinese representative expressed the hope that the Council would not give the impression that the problems of the under-industrialized countries were not accorded due consideration. He felt that a historical perspective of the development of economically advanced nations would be of inestimable value to under-developed countries.

图片 5.5　张彭春在经社理事会第五届第 90 次会议发言纪要

【纪要译文】

张先生(中国)引用了他在理事会第二届会议上的发言,呼吁注意欠发达国家和发达国家之间经济利益的协调。他强调世界稳定必须通过国际合作来实现。他认为,应当考虑较不发达地区,这不仅是因为这些地区人口众多、资源丰富,是工业化程度较高的国家的市场,而且因为这些地区往往是发达国家之间发生冲突的地方。

中国代表表示希望理事会不要给人留下一种印象,认为欠工业化国家的问题没有得到应有的考虑。他认为,从历史角度看待经济发达国家的发展,对欠发达国家具有不可估量的价值。

5. 张彭春在经社理事会第五届第 94 次会议上的发言

1947 年 7 月 25 日上午 11 时,联合国经社理事会第五届第 94 次会议,在纽约成功湖召开。本次会议主要议题是讨论新闻和出版自由小组委员会的报告。中国代表张彭春率团参加了本次会议,并在会议上发言;另有一位张先生(P. H. Chang)也参加了本次会议并作为新闻和出版自由小组委员会的临时报告员在会议上做报告。两位张先生的具体发言内容全文、纪要及其译文等如下:

(1)会议发言全文记录[1]及译文

【全文记录】

Mr. CHANG (Member, Sub-commission on Freedom of Information and the Press): On behalf of the Sub-commission of Freedom of Information and the Press, and in place of Mr. Ferguson, the elected Rapporteur, who is unable to be here today, I have the honour to submit for your consideration the Report of the Sub-commission's First Session.

With your permission, I shall not read the Report, copies of which have been distributed and are before you. I shall merely remind you of the acts and interests taken by the Council which has led to the creation of the Sub-commission, and to point out the salient features and the outstanding recommendations contained in the Report.

On 14 December 1946 the United Nations General Assembly, acting in the spirit of paragraphs 3 and 4 of Article 1 of the Charter, resolved to authorize the holding of a conference of all Members of the United Nations on the freedom of information.

---

① UN Document: E/PV.94, pp.31-36, pp.78-81.(注释:根据对经济及社会理事会小组委员会之一的新闻和出版自由小组委员会的会议记录,中国参加该小组的成员也是一位张先生,其名字是 P.H. Chang,他因为该小组报告员缺席,担任代理报告员,其后当选为该小组的报告员。另外,在研究人权的过程中,印象上加拿大汉弗莱曾经说过在小组委员会中,还有一位与张彭春同姓的中国代表一事。据此,本人查阅了新闻和出版自由小组委员会五届会议共计 112 次会议的全文记录,看到汉弗莱作为秘书处人权司司长,也参加了这个小组委员会的会议,可以认定这位中国的报告员不是张彭春先生,而是另一位张先生 P.H. Chang。但是在经济及社会理事会第五届第 94 次会议上,两位张先生在一起开会并发言,给联合国会议记录带来了一个小难题,如何区别两位张先生,这也是现在西方学界在注释和参考文献中出现的一个问题。为了真实地记录这个小插曲,这里将两位张先生的发言内容完整呈现出来,从而更能展现中国代表对国际新闻和出版自由的贡献。无独有偶的是,张彭春作为中国代表团首席代表出席了 1948 年在日内瓦召开的联合国新闻和出版自由会议,并在会议上慷慨陈词,国内新闻报业多有报道,值得大家关注。)

In this resolution, the General Assembly defined freedom of information as implying the right to gather, transmit, and publish news which, anywhere and everywhere without being bettered, which, as the Resolution says, it is an essential factor in any serious effort to promote peace and progress in the world.

The General Assembly approved the resolution, and instructed the Economic and Social Council to undertake the convocation of such a World Conference on Freedom of Information, The Sub-commission was created under the Council's Commission on Human Rights, which itself is concerned with freedom of information and similar matters.

The terms of references embodied in the Resolution of the Economic and Social Council, adopted on 28 March 1947, gave the Sub-commission two tasks to perform. The first task was to prepare an agenda for the proposed world conference, and, the second, to examine or analyze the concepts of freedom of information.

The Sub-commission has prepared an agenda, and this will be found in Chapter III of the Report. The Council may approve this now, or it may decide to postpone its decision until its Sixth Session, in order that Member States and specialized agencies may have a longer time in which to prepare suggestions.

In this connection, I wish to call attention to the fact that the Sub-commission tried to consider only the inclusion or exclusion of items on the agenda. That is to say, it only tried to answer the question: What should the Conference discuss? It did not attempt to go into the final substance of the items themselves, which, of course, is for the Council to decide.

Therefore, it seems to me, and also to my colleagues on the Sub-commission, that, comparatively speaking, it is an easy matter for the Council to decide.

The second, and the most important, task assigned to the Sub-commission was the examination of the concepts of freedom of information. This was also undertaken but it was not completed, as will be seen from Charter IV of the Report. Certain members of the Sub-commission made short speeches, and these speeches are reported in the separate document. Therefore, the Sub-commission requests the permission of the Council to hold another meeting before the Conference, which will be devoted principally to the analysis of the concept of freedom of information. Now I come to the recommendations.

1. The Sub-commission recommends that the Council request the General Assembly to take such action and will permit the Conference to be held in 1948 instead of in 1947.

This is necessary because of scheduling and because of the importance of adequate preparation. The Sub-commission recommends that the Conference be scheduled for March or April 1948, and the Council may wish to state these dates as limits, and to request the Secretary-General to fix and exact date at the Six Session of Economic and Social Council

2. The Sub-commission recommends that non-member States be invited, as the problems to be discussed are universal, and that the precedent of the World Health Conference be used as a basis.

It further recommends that non-member States that are invited have full privileges of participation and vote.

3. The Sub-commission recommends further that the Conference be held in Europe.

Although three cities were mentioned in our discussion, namely, Paris, Prague and Geneva, the final choice was not made. We felt that the occupied European nations which suffered so seriously from the restriction of information, should know that the United Nations is concerned with the problem of the freer flow of information.

4. The Sub-commission has made recommendations concerning the machinery or the structure of the Conference, and has prepared draft rules of pro-

cedure.

5. The Sub-commission has recommended that the Council requested the Secretary-General to prepare a request the States invited for information to be used as the basis for documentation of the Conference. This information should be brief and follow closely the proposed agenda, and it is recommended that the Secretary-General be requested to consult UNESCO in this connection.

It is our aim that the Conference should have a comprehensive picture of the existing information policies, practices and regulations.

The last recommendation is as follow:

The Sub-commission has recommended that the Council should, as the matter of urgency, institute a study of the shortage of news-print material, especially as it affects the war devastated areas. Without papers it is impossible adequately to inform the public. We have recommended that a study be made, and that action be taken on the basis of such a study.

There is another point which I wish to bring to the attention of the Council before closing. The Sub-commission wishes to inform the International Telecommunications Union of its interest in the work of the Union and of its hope and recommendation that the Union shall be asked to participate in the Conference. Since the Union was in session at Atlantic City during the session of the Sub-commission, the Sub-commission took the liberty of requesting the Secretary-General to communicate with the Union. We hope that this action meets with your approval.

Dr. CHANG (China): I should first like to say that I give general support to the Report of the Sub-commission.

When the Acting Rapporteur reported on the shortage of newsprint, I felt that somehow China was responsible. As we all know, China contributed to the invention of printing and of paper. If the Chinese had never done that, we would never have had to bother with this question at all. Especially there would not be the consumption of tons of paper and printing by the United Nations at all its meetings.

With respect to the three concrete questions, I am very much in favour of the suggestions made by the representative of the United States, With respect to the exact time, I am very much in favour, generally speaking, of holding the Conference as early as possible in 1948.

With respect to the exact time, I think it might be wise to leave the matter to the time when we come to discuss the proposed programme of meetings. I hope that will not be too late, and that it will not be put at the end of the session, as we did before.

In regard to the place of the Conference, this is an occasion for me to make of record that, for certain purposes and specific reasons, the place at which the Conference is held should be outside the Headquarters of the United Nations. Therefore, while I — and, I hope, many of my colleagues also, — shall be against the holding of the meetings of the Economic and Social Council outside the Headquarters for very specific reasons which I hope I shall have the chance to present, in regard to the location at which this specific Conference is to be held, I think Europe would be preferable.

I should like to make my position clear. In regard to the holding of this Conference which we are discussing, I am in favour of Europe. As for the different places in Europe at which the Conference could be held, inasmuch as the representative of Czechoslovakia did not particularly make any suggestion to hold the Conference in Prague — I believe he was rather indefinite in his proposal — and inasmuch as I have not heard any specific place mentioned and it has been stated that facilities are available in Geneva, I believe we should decide on Geneva as the place to hold the Conference.

In regard to the membership of the Conference, I am also favour of the suggestion by the Sub-commission to include non-Member States, especially those non-Member States which took part in the WHO Conference.

【全文译文】

张先生[1](新闻和出版自由小组委员会成员):我谨代表新闻和出版自由小组委员会,并以当选报告员弗格森先生的名义提交小组委员会第一届会议的报告,供你们审议。

如果你们允许,我将不宣读这份报告,报告的副本已经分发并摆在大家面前。我只想提醒大家,注意理事会采取的导致设立小组委员会的行动和关心的问题,并指出报告中的突出特点和尚未落实的建议。

1946 年 12 月 14 日,联合国大会本着《宪章》第一条第三款至第四款的精神,决定授权召开一次联合国全体会员国新闻自由会议。

在这项决议中,大会将新闻自由定义为意味着有权在任何所有地方收集、传播和发布新闻,而不必加以粉饰。正如该决议所诉,这对促进世界和平与进步的任何严肃努力是一个基本因素。

大会批准了这项决议,并指示经济及社会理事会召开这样一次新闻自由问题世界会议。小组委员会是在理事会人权委员会之下设立的,该委员会本身负责新闻自由和类似问题。

1947 年 3 月 28 日通过的经济及社会理事会决议所载职权范围赋予小组委员会两项任务。第一项任务是为拟议的世界会议拟定议程,第二项任务是审查或分析新闻自由的概念。

小组委员会准备了一份议程,该议程将载于报告第三章。理事会可以现在批准,也可以推迟到第六届会议再作决定,以便会员国和专门机构有更多的时间编写建议。

在这方面,我想提醒大家注意,小组委员会只考虑列入或排除议程上的项目。也就是说,它只是试图回答一个问题:会议应该讨论什么? 它没有试图讨论这些项目本身的最终实质,当然,这应由理事会决定。

---

① 如前一个注释所述,这位张先生是 P. H. Chang,而不是张彭春(P. C. Chang),但他的发言全文内容也收集在此。

因此,在我和小组委员会的同事看来,相对而言,理事会作出决定是一件容易的事情。

分配给小组委员会的第二项也是最重要的任务是审查新闻自由的概念。这项工作也已进行,但尚未完成,从报告第四章可以看出这一点。小组委员会的某些成员作了简短发言,这些发言载于单独的文件。因此,小组委员会请理事会允许在会议之前举行另一次会议,主要用于分析新闻自由的概念。现在我来谈谈建议。

1. 小组委员会建议理事会请大会采取这种行动,并允许会议在 1948 年而不是 1947 年举行。

这是必要的,因为日程安排和充分准备的重要性。小组委员会建议会议定于 1948 年 3 月或 4 月举行,理事会不妨将这些日期列为限制日期,并请秘书长在经济及社会理事会第六届会议上确定确切日期。

2. 小组委员会建议邀请非成员国参加,因为所讨论的问题具有普遍性,并以世界卫生会议的先例为基础。

它进一步建议,被邀请的非成员国充分享有参与和投票特权。

3. 小组委员会进一步建议会议在欧洲举行。

虽然在我们的讨论中提到了三个城市,即巴黎、布拉格和日内瓦,但没有作出最后的选择。我们认为,受新闻限制之害如此严重的被占领欧洲国家应该知道,联合国关心的是新闻更自由流动的问题。

4. 小组委员会就会议的机制或结构提出了建议,并拟订了议事规则草案。

5. 小组委员会建议理事会请秘书长编写一份请求,请被邀请的国家提供资料,作为会议文件的基础。这些资料应简短,并严格遵循拟议议程,建议请秘书长就此与教科文组织协商。

我们的目标是,会议应全面了解现有的新闻政策、做法和条例。

最后一项建议如下:

小组委员会建议理事会作为紧急事项,对新闻印刷材料短缺问题进行研究,特别是因为它影响到受战争破坏的地区。没有报纸,就不可能充分地向公众通报情况。我们建议进行一项研究,并在这项研究的基础上采取行动。

在结束发言之前,我还要提请理事会注意另一点。小组委员会通知国际电信联盟,它对该联盟的工作感兴趣,并希望和建议邀请该联盟参加会议。由于此联盟在小组委员会届会期间在大西洋城开会,小组委员会冒昧地请秘书长与此联盟联系。我们希望这一行动得到您的同意。

张博士[①](中国):首先,我要说,我总体上支持小组委员会的报告。

当代理报告员报告新闻纸短缺时,我觉得中国多少应负责任。众所周知,中国对印刷术和纸张的发明做出了贡献。如果中国人从来没有这么做,我们根本就不必为这个问题烦恼。特别是,联合国将不能在其所有会议上消耗成吨的纸张和印刷品。

关于这三个具体问题,我非常赞成美国代表提出的建议。关于确切时间,总的来说,我非常赞成在 1948 年尽早举行会议。

关于确切的时间,我认为将这个问题留给我们来讨论拟议的会议方案时再处理可能是明智的。我希望这不会太晚,也不会像我们以前那样,到本届会议结束时提出。

关于会议地点,我借此机会记录在案,出于某些目的和具体原因,会议地点应在联合国总部以外。因此,虽然我——我希望,我的许多同事也是如此——将反对在总部以外举行经济及社会理事会会议,我希望我将有机会提出非常具体的理由,关于举行这次会议的具体地点,我认为欧洲会更好。

我想表明我的立场。关于举行我们正在讨论的这次会议,我赞成欧洲。至于在欧洲不同的地方举行会议,由于捷克斯洛伐克代表没有特别提出在布拉格举行会议的任何建议——我认为他的建议相当不明确——而且由于我没有听到提到任何具体地点,而且据说日内瓦设施可用,我认为我们应该决定把日内瓦作为举行会议的地点。

① 这位发言人张博士就是张彭春先生,从发言的内容和所使用的语言风格也可以断定这一位是张彭春先生。

关于会议成员，我也赞成小组委员会的建议，即包括非成员国，特别是参加世界卫生组织会议的非成员国。

(2)会议发言内容纪要[①]

【会议纪要】

Mr. CHANG (China), in the absence of the Rapporteur of the Sub-commission, presented the Sub-commission's report to the Council and referred to General Assembly resolution 59 (I) recommending the convening of a United Nations Conference on Freedom of Information. He said that the Sub-commission had devoted itself mainly to formulating recommendations for the organization of the Conference on Freedom of Information, and had temporarily to postpone defining the rights, obligations and practices inherent in the concept of freedom of information.

The Sub-commission had decided to recommend the Council to ask the General Assembly to amend its resolution so that the United Nations Conference on Freedom of Information could be held in March or April, 1948. It recommended that the Conference be held in Europe, at Prague, Geneva or Paris. The Sub-commission was also anxious that the Conference should be attended by non-Member States who would have full rights to take part in the discussion and to vote. The Sub-commission likewise asked that certain specialized agencies, inter-governmental organizations, and non-governmental organizations should be

① UN Document: E/SR. 94, pp. 66–67, p. 70.（说明：会议纪要中将两位张先生，都写成了 Mr. Chang，其实对比研究发现，在全文记录中，前面的一个使用的称呼是张先生，后面的一个称呼是张博士，且前面的一个在其后的括号中标明了是新闻和出版自由小组委员会成员，后面的一个在其后面标明了是中国代表。这样看来，在会议全文记录中，记录人注意到了中国两位不同的张先生，而在会议纪要中却忽略了两人的不同。这里只好由笔者加上本注释加以说明，以便引起人们的注意。然而为了尊重历史档案记录，这里仍然按照联合国文献会议纪要整理，并附相应纪要译文。）

invited to participate in the preparations for the Conference, and to attend it.

The Sub-commission had laid down the procedure and indicated the principal commissions of the Conference, and had decided that the Secretary-General should ask the Governments of States participating in the Conference to supply data concerning freedom of information; this might be done jointly with UNESCO.

Finally, Mr. Chang stressed the seriousness of the shortage of newsprint, and emphasized the Sub-commission's desire to collaborate with the International Telecommunications Union.

Mr. CHANG (China) approved the report in general. In his opinion, however, the exact date of the Conference should be discussed later, when the dates of all the 1947 and 1948 meetings included on the Council's agenda were being examined. He agreed that the Conference should be held in Europe and, more specifically, at Geneva, but this should be considered as an exception.

【纪要影像】

Mr. CHANG (China), in the absence of the Rapporteur of the Sub-Commission, presented the Sub-Commission's report to the Council and referred to General Assembly resolution 59 (I) recommending the convening of a United Nations Conference on Freedom of Information. He said that the Sub-Commission had devoted itself mainly to formulating recommendations for the organization of the Conference on Freedom of Information, and had had temporarily to postpone defining the rights, obligations and practices inherent in the concept of freedom of information.

The Sub-Commission had decided to recommend the Council to ask the General Assembly to amend its resolution so that the United Nations Conference on Freedom of Information could be held in March or April, 1948. It recommended that the Conference be held in Europe, at Prague, Geneva or Paris. The Sub-Commission was also anxious that the Conference should be attended by non-member States who would have full rights to take part in the discussion and to vote. The Sub-Commission likewise asked that certain specialized agencies, intergovernmental organizations, and non-governmental organizations should be invited to participate in the preparations for the Conference, and to attend it.

The Sub-Commission had laid down the procedure and indicated the principal commissions of the Conference, and had decided that the Secretary-General should ask the Governments of States participating in the Conference to supply data concerning freedom of information; this might be done jointly with UNESCO.

Finally, Mr. Chang stressed the seriousness of the shortage of newsprint, and emphasized the Sub-Commission's desire to collaborate with the International Telecommunications Union.

图片 5.6　张先生(P. H. Chang)在联合国经社理事会第五届第94次会议发言纪要(1)

Mr. CHANG (China) approved the report in general. In his opinion, however, the exact date of the Conference should be 'iscussed later, when the dates of all the 1947 and 1948 meetings included on the Council's agenda were being examined. He agreed that the Conference should be held in Europe and, more specifically, at Geneva, but this should be considered as an exception.

图片 5.7　张彭春(P. C. Chang)在联合国经社理事会第五届第94次会议发言纪要(2)

【纪要译文】

张先生(中国),在小组委员会报告员缺席的情况下,向理事会介绍了小组委员会的报告,并提到了建议召开联合国新闻自由会议的大会第59(I)号决议。他说,小组委员会主要致力于拟订关于组织新闻自由会议的建议,并不得不暂时推迟界定新闻自由概念所固有的权利、义务和做法。

小组委员会决定建议理事会请大会修改其决议,以便联合国新闻自由会议可以在 1948 年 3 月或 4 月举行。它建议会议在欧洲布拉格、日内瓦或巴黎举行。小组委员会还迫切希望非成员国出席会议,他们将有充分的权利参加讨论和投票。小组委员会同样要求邀请某些专门机构、政府间组织和非政府组织参加会议的筹备工作,并出席会议。

小组委员会制定了程序,指明了会议的主要委员会,并决定秘书长应要求参加会议的各国政府提供有关新闻自由的数据;这可以与教科文组织联合行动。

最后,张先生强调了新闻纸短缺的严重性,并强调了小组委员会与国际电信联盟合作的愿望。

张先生(中国)总体上同意该报告。但是,他认为,会议的确切日期应稍后讨论,届时将审查安理会议程上所列的所有 1947 年和 1948 年会议的日期。他同意会议应在欧洲举行,更具体地说,应在日内瓦举行,但这应被视为例外。

6. 张彭春在经社理事会第五届第 95 次会议上的发言

1947 年 7 月 25 日下午 3 时，联合国经社理事会第五届第 95 次会议，在纽约成功湖召开。本次会议主要议题是讨论新闻和出版自由小组委员会的报告。中国代表张彭春（P. C. Chang）率团参加了本次会议，并在会议上发言。另有一位张博士（P. H. Chang）也参加了本次会议并在会议上发言，他们的具体发言内容全文、纪要及其译文等如下：

(1) 会议发言全文记录[①]及译文

【全文记录】

Dr. P. H. CHANG (Acting Rapporteur of the Sub-commission on Freedom of Information and of the Press): Having listened to the speeches made by the Members of the Council, I, as the Acting Rapporteur and as a Member of the Sub-commission, feel that I am in the position of a cook partly happy because he has cooked some good dishes which have pleased his guests, and partly unhappy because he has cooked some bad ones which did not suit their palates.

① UN Document: E/PV. 95, pp. 71-75, pp. 86-90, p. 101.（值得说明的是，本次会议三次发言中，后两次为张彭春先生的发言，这一点从对发言内容的关联上也能看出来，如在第二个发言中提出了决议草案，第三个发言中的内容与此决议草案有明确的衔接和关联。）

As a Member of the Sub-commission and as its Acting Rapporteur, I wish, first of all, to express my gratitude for some rather complimentary remarks made with regard to certain aspects of the work of the Sub-commission. I also wish to express regret for the imperfections which may be found in the work of the Sub-commission.

The Report of the Sub-commission represents the composite effort of some eleven Members, and it is certainly not up to me to add or detract from this Report. If there are any flaws in the Report, then it is up to the Members of this Council to remove them. I was asked to play the acting role of Rapporteur at rather short notice. If I had l known that I would have such duties, I would have made copious notes from the very beginning and would have been in a much better position to answer your questions and reply to some of the comments made. Under the present circumstances, however, I will make some very brief remarks on some three or four points only with the aid of material that I can lay my hands on, and relying mostly upon my memory.

First, let us take up the question why the category of books has been omitted from our definition. You will note the definition that appears on page 12: "By information, for the purposes of the Conference, is meant the following means of bringing current situations, events and opinions thereon to the knowledge of the public: newspapers, news periodicals, radio broadcasts and newsreels." Books are not included.

Here I wish merely to call your attention to the fact that this was neither an omission nor an oversight. Members of the Sub-commission were divided on this particular point, and in fact we were so serious-minded about this that the Sub-commission had to appoint a Sub-Committee to discuss and determine the scope of the information for the purpose of the Conference of Freedom of Information. That Sub-Committee was under the Chairmanship of the French representative Mr. Andre Geraud, and after due deliberations the Sub-Committee "kicked the ball" back to the Sub-commission and stated that it was for the Sub-commission to decide whether or not books should be included. After a rather heated debate, we adopted the definition as it is found in the Report. That is one explanation. Another explanation of reasons for omitting the category of books was given by the representative of the United States. If you include books, you will certainly have other questions, more complicated ones, for instance the question of copyrights. In order not to overburden the Conference and not to make the question more complicated, we finally decided to leave out the category of books.

The second remark I wish to make is with regard to the concept of freedom. It seemed to me that the Sub-commission did not do a perfect job because that part of the task is certainly an important one, and we merely touched upon it, not completing it. The reason for that was the urgency of preparing for the Conference. The Sub-commission met on 19 May, and it was rather late. We thought we should devote our time, first of all, to the preparation of the agenda so that the preparation of the Conference could go on. That is the reason why the Sub-commission recommended to the Council that a second session of the Sub-commission should be held; that additional time be given to the Members of the Sub-commission so that they could devote further efforts to defining the concept of freedom of information. In fact, if you do give the Sub-commission a second session, I think the discussion of the substantive matters on that topic will be of great benefit to the Conference when the Conference is called.

Thirdly, I come to the responsibility of the press for the prevention of abuses. The Sub-commission was created with the title, "The Sub-commission on Freedom of Information and of the Press." You did not say "Sub-commission on the Restrictions of Abuses of the Freedom of Information." Naturally, the Members of the Sub-commission were led to lay far more emphasis on the positive side of the issue rather than the negative side. However, the negative side was by no means neglected. If you will refer to page 15, you will see under heading (c) (iii) Counteracting false information through

(1) The study of measures for counteracting the persistent spreading of demonstrably false or tendentious reports which confuse the peoples of the world, aggravate relations between nations or otherwise interfere with the growth of international understanding, peace and security against a recurrence of Nazi, Fascist or Japanese aggression;

(2) the study of the various laws of libel with a view to recommending the removal of anomalies in the legislation in different countries;

(3) the study of the possible universal adoption of the right of reply;

(4) the study of the dissemination through domestic news channels of official denials, particularly with respect to matters of concern to another nation.

It can be observed, therefore, that the Sub-commission did emphasize the negative side of the issue.

Finally, with regard to the voting for absent Members, one representative, if I understand him correctly, apparently objected on the ground that the Sub-commission does not possess the power or the right to decide that a substitute shall be appointed by Members, feeling that such power belongs to the Economic and Social Council.

May I call the Council's attention to the fact that this matter was not treated very lightly by the Members of the Sub-commission. This matter was also referred to the special study of a Sub-Committee under the Chairmanship of the United States Member, Professor Chafee. After due deliberations, we thought that, if the three absent Members, particularly the two representing the United Kingdom and France, were not given the right to vote, these experts, whose varied background and traditions of thought gave balance to the representation on the Sub-commission, would not be able to give greater importance to the deliberations of the Sub-commission. We also consulted a resolution passed by the

Economic and Social Council which states that, when a Member of the Commission is unavoidably prevented from attending a session, an alternate shall be designated, and that an alternate so designated shall have the same status as a Member of the Commission, including the right to vote.

Of course, our Sub-commission is a Sub-commission and not a Commission. We do not know whether that particular resolution would equally apply to us, but we did try to solve a very unpleasant problem and tried to make the best of a bad bargain. We had no intention of overstepping the limits granted to us by the Economic and Social Council, and it was certainly not done with disrespect.

I think that is all I can say in reply to some of the comments that have been made.

I should like to add that I did not know I would have this extra duty of Acting Rapporteur and had made no provision for it. My other duties require my constant presence in office, and, therefore, I regret to say that I shall not be able to attend the subsequent meetings of the Council when the Report of the Sub-commission is discussed, but I shall be most happy to furnish the Council with a written reply if it will ask me questions in writing and send them to my office.

Mr. P. C. CHANG (China): Today has been a very happy day for all of us, and this happy day must be concluded happily. It is now my happy duty to present a happy resolution to be attached to the happy document before us. The document is happy because it brings good news.

The significance of the help that was made available by Resolution 58 of the General Assembly—I hope that Resolution number will be long remembered—is clearly stated on page 3 of the Progress Report, document E/458. I shall quote two or three sentences from this statement, which was originally contained in the Report of the Social Commission:

"The significance of the General Assembly resolution"—the famous Resolution 58; I hope it will be famous—"goes beyond the continuance of UNRRA activities. It is the first experiment by the United Nations in rendering practical field service to the people of the different nations. The development of these advisory services in the field of social welfare therefore provides a most important opportunity of demonstrating in a practical manner the interest and concern of the United Nations itself in meeting human needs through an effective service provided by its Secretariat. ..."

The significance, then, is very clear. It goes far beyond the mere continuation of UNRRA activities. The General Assembly Resolution actually marks not only an ending and a transition, but also a new beginning.

Furthermore, I must compliment the Secretariat—I think I am expressing the views of all of us when I say this—for having performed marvelously. The Secretariat has made the requests, and it has already carried out some of the items which were included—for instance, the supply of experts, the initiation of fellowships, and the promulgation of publications.

Moreover, it is not just the few countries that have benefited from UNRRA which will be affected. Page 20 of the Progress Report before us refers to "a seminar for the training of social welfare workers in Latin American countries ..." Accordingly, many countries are benefited by this Report in many parts of the world.

Lastly, the effect of the good work that has been done is clearly seen if one refers to the sentence on page 27 of the document we are discussing which reads:

"The Governments have generally shown interest in all phases of the programme; however, all Governments which have requested services have assistance in training their been predominantly interested in receiving assistance in training their own nationals to carry on social welfare programmes ..." In other words, this is a way of encouraging those who help themselves after receiving this badly needed assistance. Therefore, I have this happy draft resolution to propose:

> "The Economic and Social Council notes the progress made by the Secretary-General in providing advisory welfare services and requests that, in view of the urgent need for such services, as indicated by requests from Governments, the Secretary-General make provision in the budget which he submits to the General Assembly for continuing such services in 1948, and also requests the Social Commission, at its next session, to review the Report of the Secretary-General and make further recommendations concerning this programme."

I think this is a happy note on which to conclude our happy day. The Economic and Social Council is supposed to encourage constructive, cooperative activities. People by nature develop interest in, support of, and devotion to an organization after having experienced positive benefits derived from being members of that organization. Therefore, what we are doing—and I hope will continue to do—will be a very vital part in initiating and promoting a new loyalty essential to the very existence of the United Nations itself.

Dr. CHANG (China): May I just ask one question and then offer a suggestion.

The question concerns the fact that we do not especially wish to commit ourselves when we come to the General Assembly. It was in that spirit, I think, that the draft resolution which I humbly submitted was made, and I am wondering whether I should ask through the President if the distinguished representative of the United States meant that the proposed draft resolution is at least in line with what he had in mind. That is the first question.

Secondly, inasmuch as the hour is rather late, and we all wish to conclude the day happily, and this is too important a matter to be hurried, I think it may be referred to the Social Committee.

【全文译文】

张博士(新闻和出版自由小组委员会代理报告员):在听取了理事会成员的发言后,作为代理报告员和小组委员会成员,我感到我扮演了一个厨师,有些高兴是因为他做了一些客人喜欢的好菜,有些不高兴是因为他做了一些不合他们口味的坏菜。

作为小组委员会成员及其代理报告员,我首先要感谢就小组委员会工作的某些方面所作的一些相当恭维的评论。我还要对小组委员会工作中可能存在的不完善之处表示遗憾。

小组委员会的报告代表了大约 11 名成员的合力,我当然不能增加或减少这份报告的内容。如果报告中有任何缺陷,则应由本理事会成员予以移除。我在很仓促的状况下被要求担任代理报告员。如果我知道我会有这样的职责,我会从一开始就做大量的笔记,并且会更好地回答你们的问题和回答一些评论。不过,在目前的情况下,我仅借助我能掌握的材料,主要依靠我的记忆,就三、四点作一些非常简短的评论。

首先,让我们讨论一下为什么在我们的定义中省略了图书类别的问题。你会注意到第 12 页上的定义:“就会议而言,新闻是指使公众了解当前情况、事件和意见的以下手段:报纸、新闻期刊、广播和新闻短片。”书籍不包括在内。

在此,我只想提请你们注意,这既不是疏忽,也不是失察。小组委员会成员在这一点上存在意见分歧,事实上,我们对此非常认真,小组委员会不得不任命一个小组委员会来讨论和确定新闻自由会议的新闻范围。该小组委员会由法国代表安德烈·杰拉德先生担任主席,经过适当的审议后,小组委员会将球“踢”回小组委员会,并表示应由小组委员会决定是否应列入书籍。经过相当激烈的辩论,我们采纳了报告中的定义。这是一种解释。美国代表对省略图书类别的原因作了另一种解释,如果包括图书,肯定会有其他问题,更复杂的问题,例如版权问题。为了不让会议负担过重,也不让问题变得更复杂,我们最后决定不包括书籍这一类别。

我想说的第二点是关于自由的概念。在我看来,小组委员会的工作似乎并不完美,因为这部分任务肯定是一项重要的任务,我们只是触及它,而不是完成它。原因是会议筹备工作的紧迫性。小组委员会于 5 月 19 日举行会议,时间相当晚。我们认为,我们首先应该把时间花在议程的准备上,以便会议的准备工作能够继续下去。这就是小组委员会向理事会建议举行小组委员会第二届会议的原因;应给予小组委员会成员更多的时间,以便他们能够进一步努力界定新闻自由的概念。事实上,如果你确实让小组委员会举行第二届会议,我认为在召开会议时讨论关于该议题的实质性事项将对会议大有裨益。

第三,我谈到新闻界在防止滥用方面的责任。小组委员会的名称是“新闻和出版自由小组委员会”你说的不是“限制滥用新闻自由小组委员会”。自然,小组委员会成员被引导更多地强调问题的积极方面,而不是消极方面。然而,消极方面并没有被忽视。如果你参阅第 15 页,你会看到标题(c)(iii)下通过如下方式对抗虚假新闻

(1)研究各种措施,抵制持续传播明显虚假或有倾向性的报道,这些报道混淆世界人民的视听,恶化国家间的关系,或以其他方式干扰国际谅解、和平与安全的发展,防止纳粹、法西斯或日本侵略重演;

(2)研究各种诽谤法,以期建议消除不同国家立法中的异常现象;

(3)研究是否可能普遍采用回应权;

(4)研究通过国内新闻渠道传播的官方否认新闻,特别是关于另一个国家关注的问题。

因此,可以看出,小组委员会确实强调了问题的消极方面。

最后,关于对缺席成员的表决,一位代表(如果我理解正确的话)明确反对,理由是小组委员会没有权力或权利决定由成员任命一名替代者,认为这种权力属于经济及社会理事会。

请允许我提请理事会注意这样一个事实,即小组委员会成员并未轻视这个问题。这个问题也被提交给由美国成员查菲教授担任主席的一个小

组委员会进行特别研究。经过适当的审议后,我们认为,如果三名缺席的成员,特别是代表英国和法国的两名成员无权投票,这些专家的不同背景和思想传统使他们在小组委员会中的代表性得到平衡,将无法对小组委员会的审议给予更大的重视。我们还审议了经济及社会理事会通过的一项决议,该决议规定,当委员会成员不可避免地被阻止出席某届会议时,应指定一名候补成员,并且如此指定的候补成员应具有与委员会成员相同的地位,包括投票权。

当然,我们的小组委员会是一个小组委员会,而不是一个委员会。我们不知道这项决议是否同样适用于我们,但我们确实设法解决了一个非常令人不快的问题,并试图在一次糟糕的讨价还价中尽力而为。我们无意超越经济及社会理事会给予我们的权限,这当然不是不尊重。

我想这就是我对一些评论的回应。

我想补充一点,我不知道我会有代理报告员的这一额外职责,也没有为此作出安排。我的其他职责要求我经常待在办公室,因此,我遗憾地说,我将无法出席理事会随后讨论小组委员会报告时的会议,但是,如果理事会以书面形式向我提出问题,并将其送交我的办公室,我将非常乐意向理事会提供书面答复。

张彭春先生(中国):今天对我们所有人来说都是非常快乐的一天,这快乐的一天必须愉快地结束。现在,我高兴地有责任提出一项令人愉快的决议,附在我们面前的令人愉快文件之后。这份文件令人高兴,因为它带来了好消息。

进展报告 E/458 号文件第 3 页清楚地说明了大会第 58 号决议提供的帮助的重要性——我希望决议编号将被长期铭记。我将引述社会委员会报告中最初所载的这一发言中的两三句话:

“大会决议的意义”——著名的第 58 号决议;我希望它会出名——“这超出了联总[①]活动的持续性。这是联合国在向不同国家人民提供实际

① 笔者注:联合国善后救济总署,简称“联总”;英语名称 United Nations Relief and Rehabilitation Administration,英文简称 UNRRA。

实地服务方面的第一次试验。因此,在社会福利领域发展这些咨询服务提供了一个非常重要的机会,以实际的方式展示了联合国本身对通过其秘书处提供的有效服务来满足人类需求的兴趣和关切……"

因此,其意义非常明确。它远远超出了联合国善后救济总署活动的单纯延续。大会决议实际上不仅标志着一个结束和过渡,而且标志着一个新的开始。

此外,我必须赞扬秘书处——因为它的表现非常出色——我认为我说这番话是表达了我们所有人的观点。秘书处提出了这些要求,并已执行了其中的一些项目,例如,提供专家、发起研究金以及发布出版物。

此外,受影响的不仅仅是从联总中受益的少数国家。我们面前的进度报告第 20 页提到"拉丁美洲国家社会福利工作者培训研讨会……"因此,世界许多地区的许多国家都受益于这份报告。

最后,如果提到我们正在讨论的文件第 27 页上的一句话,就可以清楚地看到所做的出色工作的效果:

> "各国政府总体上对该方案的所有阶段都表现出兴趣;然而,所有要求提供服务的政府都获得援助,主要是在培训本国国民开展社会福利方案方面有兴趣获得援助的人……"换言之,这是一种鼓励那些在获得急需援助后自助的人的方式。因此,我要提出这项令人高兴的决议草案:
>
> "经济及社会理事会注意到秘书长在提供咨询福利服务方面取得的进展,并请秘书长根据各国政府的请求,鉴于这种服务的迫切需要,在 1948 年提交大会的预算中为继续提供这种服务编列经费,并请社会委员会下届会议审查秘书长的报告,并就这一方案提出进一步建议。"

我认为这是一个快乐的音符,来结束我们的快乐一天。经济及社会理事会应该鼓励建设性的合作活动。人们在经历了作为组织成员所带来的积极利益后,自然会对组织产生兴趣、给予支持和做出奉献。因此,我们正在做的和我希望将继续做的工作,将对发起和促进对联合国本身的生存至关重要的新的忠诚来说,是一个非常重要的部分。

张博士(中国):请允许我提出一个问题,然后提出一个建议。

问题涉及这样一个事实,即我们并不特别希望在大会上作出承诺。我认为,正是本着这种精神,我谦恭地提出了这项决议草案。我想知道,我是否应该通过主席询问,尊敬的美国代表的意思是,拟议的决议草案至少符合他的想法。这是第一个问题。

第二,由于时间已经很晚了,我们都希望愉快地结束这一天,而且这件事太重要了,不能匆忙处理,我认为可以把它提交给社会委员会。

(2)会议发言内容纪要①

【会议纪要】

Mr. CHANG (Acting Rapporteur of the Sub-commission on Freedom of Information and of the Press) explained that no reference had been made to "books" in section 2 of Chapter III owing to the additional complications, such as the question of copyright, which would arise if this item appeared in a list of media of information.

There had been little discussion on the concept of freedom because prior consideration had been given to the agenda of the Conference by reason of its urgency. If the Sub-commission were to be allowed to hold a second session, it would be able to give thorough attention to that subject.

① UN Document: E/SR. 95, pp. 75-76, pp. 76-77. (值得说明的是:本次会议发言内容纪要与前面的全文记录一样,第一个张先生指的是 P. H. Chang,而后面的张先生指的是张彭春,即 P. C. Chang。他们二人所讲的内容在纪要影像中以两张单独的图片呈现,以示区别。)

The question of the restriction of abuses had been touched upon in paragraph 5 (c) (ii), of the provisional draft agenda[1] but as the Council had called attention specifically to the positive side of the whole subject of freedom of information, that aspect had been stressed by the Sub-commission.

Alternates had been granted the right to vote on the basis of the rules of procedure of the Council. There had been no intention of exceeding the competence of the Sub-commission.

In conclusion Mr. Chang stated that he would be happy to furnish a written reply to any further queries which might be forthcoming.

Mr. CHANG (China) pointed out that resolution 58 (I) went beyond the mere continuation of the advisory social welfare activities of UNRRA. Further, the aid to be given would not be limited to only a few countries. The United Nations was expected to encourage constructive ideas and such assistance would have the effect of promoting a new loyalty to the ideal of international co-operation.

He congratulated the Secretariat on the work which had already been carried out, and proposed the following resolution:

> "The Economic and Social Council
>
> "Notes the progress made by the Secretary-General in providing advisory welfare services and
>
> "Requests that, in view of the urgent need for such services, as indicated by requests from Governments, the Secretary-General make provision in the budget which he submits to the General Assembly for continuing such services in 1948, and also
>
> "Requests the Social Commission, at its next session, to review the report of the Secretary-General and make further recommendations concerning this programme."

【纪要影像】

Mr. CHANG (China), in the absence of the Rapporteur of the Sub-Commission, presented the Sub-Commission's report to the Council and

referred to General Assembly resolution 59 (I) recommending the convening of a United Nations Conference on Freedom of Information. He said that the Sub-Commission had devoted itself mainly to formulating recommendations for the organization of the Conference on Freedom of Information, and had had temporarily to postpone defining the rights, obligations and practices inherent in the concept of freedom of information.

The question of the restriction of abuses had been touched upon in paragraph 5 (*c*) (iii), of the provisional draft agenda[1] but as the Council had called attention specifically to the positive side of the whole subject of freedom of information, that aspect had been stressed by the Sub-Commission.

Alternates had been granted the right to vote on the basis of the rules of procedure of the Council. There had been no intention of exceeding the competence of the Sub-Commission.

In conclusion Mr. Chang stated that he would be happy to furnish a written reply to any further queries which might be forthcoming.

图片 5.8　张先生(P. H.　Chang)在经社理事会第五届第 95 次会议发言纪要

Mr. CHANG (China) pointed out that resolution 58 (I) went beyond the mere continuation of the advisory social welfare activities of UNRRA. Further, the aid to be given would not be limited to only a few countries. The United Nations was expected to encourage constructive ideas and such assistance would have the effect of promoting a new loyalty to the ideal of international co-operation.

He congratulated the Secretariat on the work which had already been carried out, and proposed the following resolution:

"*The Economic and Social Council*

"*Notes* the progress made by the Secretary-General in providing advisory welfare services and

"*Requests* that, in view of the urgent need for such services, as indicated by requests from Governments, the Secretary-General make provision in the budget which he submits to the General Assembly for continuing such services in 1948, and also

"*Requests* the Social Commission, at its next session, to review the report of the Secretary-General and make further recommendations concerning this programme."

图片 5.9　张彭春(P. C.　Chang)在经社理事会第五届第 95 次会议发言纪要

【纪要译文】

张先生(新闻和出版自由小组委员会代理报告员)解释说,第三章第 2 节中没有提到"书籍",因为如果这一项目出现在新闻媒体清单中,会产生额外的复杂问题,例如版权问题。

对自由概念的讨论很少,因为会议议程因其紧迫性而被优先考虑。如果允许小组委员会举行第二届会议,它将能够彻底关注这一问题。

临时议程草案 1 第 5(c)(ii)段提到限制滥用的问题,但由于理事会特别提请注意整个新闻自由问题的积极方面,小组委员会强调了这一方面。

候补委员已根据理事会议事规则获得表决权。没有超越小组委员会权限的意图。

最后,张先生表示,他很乐意就可能提出的任何进一步问题提供书面答复。

张先生(中国)指出,第58(I)号决议超越了联合国善后救济总署的社会福利咨询活动的单纯延续。此外,提供的援助将不仅限于少数几个国家。人们期望联合国鼓励建设性的想法,这种援助将产生促进对国际合作理想的新的忠诚的效果。

他祝贺秘书处已经开展的工作,并提出以下决议:

"经济及社会理事会:注意到秘书长在提供咨询和福利服务方面取得的进展,请秘书长考虑到各国政府所表示的对这种服务的迫切需要,在他提交大会的预算中为在1948年继续提供这种服务编列经费,并请社会委员会下届会议审查秘书长的报告,并就此方案提出进一步建议。"

7. 张彭春在经社理事会第五届第100次会议上的发言

1947年7月31日上午11时,联合国经社理事会第五届第100次会议,在纽约成功湖召开。本次会议继续讨论联合国贸易和就业会议筹备委员会第二届会议的临时报告。中国代表张彭春率团参加了本次会议,并在会议上非常简短地表达了自己的意见,其具体发言内容全文、纪要及其译文等如下:

(1)会议发言全文记录[①]及译文

【全文记录】

Dr. CHANG (China): I am in favour of the President's ruling.

【全文译文】

张博士(中国):我同意主席的裁决。

(2)会议发言内容纪要[②]

【会议纪要】

Mr. CHANG (China) agreed.

---

① UN Document: E/PV.100, p.46.

② UN Document: E/SR.100, p.112.

【纪要影像】

Mr. CHANG (China) agreed.

图片 5.10　张彭春在经社理事会第五届第 100 次会议发言纪要①

【纪要译文】

张先生(中国)同意。

---

① 值得说明的是,这恐怕是最为简单的会议纪要了,当时由于一些国家的代表没有参加会议,有人提出推迟对有争议的事项进行讨论,会议主席表示同意推迟,张彭春先生借机也表达了他的意见。

8. 张彭春在经社理事会第五届第 101 次会议上的发言

1947 年 7 月 31 日下午 3 时,联合国经社理事会第五届第 101 次会议,在纽约成功湖召开。本次会议主要议题是继续讨论亚洲和远东经济委员会第一届会议的报告和全体委员会的报告。中国代表张彭春率团参加了本次会议,在会议上先后四次发言并提交议案,其具体发言内容全文、纪要及其译文等如下:

(1) 会议发言全文记录[①]及译文

【全文记录】

Dr. CHANG (China): My first word is one of gratification that, after the Working Group of the Sub-commission dealing with the devastated areas produced their Report, the Economic Commission for Asia and the Far East has already been formally constituted.

We are, therefore, extremely gratified that the work has progressed so far, since it is work which affects one half of the human race. How little time we have given to that half of the human race! Let us be frank, and realise our past neglect.

The Chinese delegation is especially gratified that the Report of the Working Group for Asia and the Far East was received, commended and supported

① UN Document: E/PV. 101, pp. 71-80, pp. 91-92, p. 96, pp. 101-102.

by the Commission.

On Page 9 of the Report it states: "The Commission affirms its full agreement with, and support of, the general principles enunciated in the Report, especially in Chapters III and IV." Chapter III of the Report deals with the analysis of the reconstruction problems, and Chapter IV deals with methods of organizing international aid.

After the mountains of material that have been studied in recent weeks, it is indeed gratifying to hear the favourable comments made upon the Report, and I think that if there is anyone who has not yet read the document he ought to do so, since it is worthy of attention.

After all, this is a constructive analysis, made after hard work in studying a problem which is not only of interest to one half of the human race, but is also of interest to the whole world. It is an analysis that gives us a practical and constructive method of approach.

We are also gratified that there has been such a large measure of agreement. We have heard speeches dealing with different parts of the two Reports, but so far the disagreement only concerns the matter of membership.

There has been some comment made on the character of our discussion, especially concerning what we might call the political character of some of the contributions. But may I say, in this connection, that while we realise there is another agency of the United Nations which, strictly and formally, deals with political problems, yet we feel that in dealing with social and economic problems as this Council has the duty to do, we cannot get very far in dealing with any problem unless we include the larger human meaning of self-respect and freedom.

The Chinese Delegation, therefore, feels that great care should be taken in criticising suggestions as political whenever a problem arises concerning the feelings for freedom and self-respect of peoples, especially the peoples of Asia.

Technical and formal, problems may be considered to be political, but attention should be given to a desire for freedom and self-respect.

With regard to the problem of membership, I wish to state that the Chinese Delegation is not completely satisfied with the final recommendation of the Committee of the Whole of the Commission. Yet we feel that, as so much has already been done, we may direct our efforts into concrete, constructive directions, at the same time realising that adjustments can and will be made continuously and progressively.

The Chinese Delegation, therefore, will not make detailed criticisms at this juncture. There are points which we would like to discuss, but, taking into consideration the fact that attention has been drawn to this most important problem concerning half the human race, the fact that the Secretariat has only just been organised, and the fact that we are satisfied with the general procedure so far followed and the work that has already been done, let us give the Commission our moral support and then proceed with the work.

In other words, we should reserve our suggestion on detailed points until a later session of the Commission and a later session of the Council.

We should therefore like to make the following suggestion: First, with regard to the Report of the First Session of the Economic Commission for Asia and the Far East, that may be dealt with by means of a brief resolution, as follows: "The Economic and Social Council notes the Report of the First Session of the Economic Commission for Asia and the Far East, expresses its appreciation, and approves the preparatory arrangements made by the Commission for the carrying out of its functions."

With regard to the Report of the Committee of the Whole, there are two draft resolutions submitted for our approval, one appearing on page 10 and the other appearing on pages 8 and 9. In view of the fact that hours have been spent in discussing these topics — and that is particularly true of the subject matter contained in the resolution on pages 8 and 9, dealing with membership — and in view of the further fact that we can make suggestions later which will bring the situation more nearly in line with the spirit of human freedom and self-respect, the Chinese delegation believes that these resolutions should be approved now.

I therefore formally suggest that the three resolutions be taken in this order: first, the brief resolution approving the Report of the First Session of the Commission; second, the resolution on the extension of the terms of reference, appearing on page 10 of the Report of the Committee of the Whole; third, the resolution in regard to membership, appearing on pages 8 and 9 of that Report.

Dr. CHANG (China): I just was waiting to be asked if I would accept the amendment. May I say that I would accept it on this understanding. There is a slight difference between this case and other cases; in all cases, there were differences of opinion. In this case, there happens to be only one expression of opinion which is in the glorious language which we do not understand. We have not as yet received the French, English or Chinese translation; therefore, this case is slightly different.

On the other hand, I am very happy that the representative of the United Kingdom made his very significant and short speech. We now have heard two opinions: one, the opinion of the representative of the Soviet Union, and the other, the opinion of the representative of the United Kingdom saying that, in Shanghai, the Commission did discuss the matter and did turn it down, and this transferring of all the records of the opinions would, in a sense, not affect the decision of the Commission. Therefore, as we do have two different opinions on record, I think a mere transmission, as suggested by the President, would not have any definite loaded weight on either side.

Dr. CHANG (China): My friends have agreed to your suggestion for me, so I also agree.

Dr. CHANG (China): May I just follow this happy agreement with a suggestion which I hope will also be unanimously accepted. We do have in front of us a draft programme of meetings for 1948. I think that is a matter of great importance. If we do not pay attention to all these various meeting dates, we may have further occasions for confusion.

Consequently, I think the point will be accepted by all the Members that we refer this matter to a committee for consideration, before it comes to the plenary session of the Council. Inasmuch as it is too much of a bother to create another committee, may I suggest that this matter of the draft programme of meetings for 1948 be referred to the existing *ad hoc* Committee on Rules of Procedure, because after all it is a matter of procedure and most of us will be interested in it. We can refer this matter to the Committee on Rules of Procedure, with this prevention—again, the matter of saving time—in case any Member of the Council should be interested in this problem, he can easily make his suggestion to the President to have him added to the Committee. In other words, it is not a matter of making the committee altogether a closed one. In case any Member should be particularly interested in the problem, I believe the President of the Council as a whole will all be too glad to have him added to that Committee on Rules of Procedure, so as to discuss this matter of the draft programme of meetings for 1948.

【全文译文】

张博士(中国):我首先感到欣慰的是,在处理灾区问题的小组委员会工作组提出报告之后,亚洲和远东经济委员会已经正式成立。

因此,我们对这项工作迄今为止取得的进展极为满意,因为这项工作影响到了一半的人类。我们给那一半人类的时间是多么少啊! 我们要坦率地承认过去的疏忽。

中国代表团尤其感到高兴的是,亚洲和远东工作组的报告得到了委员会的接受、赞扬和支持。

报告第9页指出:“委员会申明完全同意并支持报告中阐述的一般原则,特别是第三章和第四章中阐述的一般原则。”报告第三章涉及对重建问题的分析,第四章涉及组织国际援助的方法。

在最近几周研究了堆积如山的材料之后,听到对该报告的好评确实令人高兴。我认为,如果有人尚未阅读该文件,他应该去读一读,因为它值得注意。

毕竟,这是一个建设性的分析,是在努力研究一个不仅关系到一半人类,而且关系到整个世界的问题之后作出的。这种分析为我们提供了一种实用和建设性的方法。

我们还感到满意的是已经达成了如此多的共识。我们听到了关于两份报告不同部分的发言,但迄今为止,分歧只涉及成员问题。

对于我们讨论的性质,特别是关于我们可以称之为某些贡献的政治性质,已经有一些评论。不过,在这方面,我想指出,虽然我们知道联合国还有另一个机构严格而正式地处理政治问题,但我们认为,在本理事会处理社会和经济问题时,我们有责任这样做,除非我们包括自尊和自由这一更广泛的人类含义,否则我们无法在处理任何问题方面取得很大进展。

因此,中国代表团认为,每当出现涉及各国人民,特别是亚洲人民的自由和自尊的问题时,都应该非常谨慎地将这些批评性建议视为政治性的。

技术上和形式上的问题可能被认为是政治问题,但应该注意对自由和自尊的渴望。

关于成员问题,我想指出,中国代表团对委员会全体委员会的最后建议并不完全满意。然而,我们认为,正如已经做了的这些工作,我们可以将我们的努力引向具体和建设性的方向,同时认识到可以且将不断和逐步地进行调整。

因此,中国代表团不会在这个时候提出详细的批评。有几点我们想讨论,但考虑到人们已经注意到这一涉及一半人类的最重要问题,考虑到秘书处刚刚成立,我们对迄今为止遵循的一般程序和已经完成的工作感到满意,让我们给予委员会道义上的支持,然后继续工作。

换句话说,我们应该将我们对细节问题的建议保留到委员会和理事会的下一届会议。

因此,我们谨提出以下建议:第一,关于亚洲和远东经济委员会第一届会议的报告,可以通过一项简短的决议加以处理,如下:“经济及社会理事会注意到亚洲和远东经济委员会第一届会议的报告,表示赞赏,并核准委员会为履行其职能所作的筹备安排。”

关于全体委员会的报告,有两项决议草案提交我们核准,一项在第 10 页,另一项在第 8 和第 9 页。鉴于人们花了数小时讨论这些议题,尤其是第 8 页和第 9 页决议中所载关于成员资格问题的主题——鉴于我们可以在以后提出建议,使情况更符合人类自由和自尊的精神,中国代表团认为这些决议现在应该获得批准。

因此,我正式建议按以下顺序通过三项决议:第一,批准委员会第一届会议报告的简要决议;第二,全体委员会报告第 10 页所载关于延长职权范围的决议;第三,该报告第 8 页和第 9 页所载关于成员资格的决议。

张博士(中国):我只是在等待有人问我是否会接受修正案。请允许我说,基于这一理解,我将接受它。这种情况与其他情况略有不同,在所有情况下,都存在意见分歧。在这种情况下,只有一种观点的表达是用我们不理解的华丽词藻表达的。我们尚未收到法文、英文或中文译本,因此,这种情况略有不同。

另一方面,我很高兴英国代表作了非常重要且简短的发言。我们现在听到了两种意见:一种是苏联代表的意见,另一种是英国代表的意见,他说,在上海,委员会确实讨论了这一问题,并拒绝了这一问题,这种转移所有意见记录的做法在某种意义上不会影响委员会的决定。因此,由于我们有两种不同的意见记录在案,我认为,正如主席所建议的那样,仅仅是一次传输,对任何一方都不会产生任何明确的影响。

张博士(中国):我的朋友们已经同意你们给我的建议,所以我也同意。

张博士(中国):请允许我在达成这一令人愉快的协议之后提出一项建议,我希望这项建议也将得到一致接受。我们面前确实有一份 1948 年会议计划草案。我认为这是一个非常重要的问题。如果我们不注意所有这些不同的会议日期,我们可能会有更多的混乱。

因此,我认为所有成员都会接受这样一个观点,即在理事会全体会议召开之前,我们将此事提交一个委员会审议。鉴于设立另一个委员会太麻烦,我是否可以建议将 1948 年会议计划草案的这一事项提交现有的议事规则特设委员会处理,因为毕竟这是一个程序问题,我们大多数人都会对此感兴趣。我们可以把这件事提交议事规则委员会,有了这一预防措施——也是为了节省时间——万一理事会任何成员对这一问题感兴趣,他可以很容易地向主席提出建议,让他加入委员会。换句话说,这不是一个使委员会完全封闭的问题。如果有任何成员对这一问题特别感兴趣,我相信理事会主席整体上都会非常高兴他加入议事规则委员会,以便讨论 1948 年会议计划草案的这一事项。

(2)会议发言内容纪要①

【会议纪要】

Mr. CHANG (China) expressed his gratification at the way in which the report of the Working Group had been received, and praised the report as a constructive analysis of interest to the whole world.

Regarding the accusations of political bias in the discussions of the Commission, he said that great care should be taken not to criticize suggestions on the grounds that they were political whenever a problem arose with regard to the desire for freedom and self-respect of peoples, and in particular the peoples of Asia.

---

① UN Document: E/SR. 101, pp. 123-124, p. 125.

As regards membership, the Chinese delegation was not completely satisfied with the recommendations of the Committee of the Whole, but since he felt that adjustments could be made as the work of the Commission progressed, he did not wish to make any detailed criticisms at the present juncture; he would reserve his suggestions until a later meeting of the Commission and of the Council.

He proposed the adoption of the following resolution:

"The Economic and Social Council

"Notes the report of the first session of the Economic Commission for Asia and the Far East;

"Expresses its appreciation, and approves the preparatory arrangements made by the Commission for the carrying out of its functions."

In addition, he proposed that a vote should be taken without further discussion on the two draft resolutions concerning terms of reference and membership contained in the report of the Committee of the Whole.

Mr. CHANG (China) and Mr. THORP (United States of America) approved the proposal made by the President on, the grounds that it would leave the Commission complete freedom of action.

Decisions:

1. *The resolution proposed by the representative of China, as amended by the President, was adopted.*

Decisions:

1. *The Council agreed that the Commission on Human Rights should meet in Geneva as soon after the close of the session of the General Assembly as possible.*

2. *On the proposal of Mr. Chang (China) it was decided to refer the* 1948 *programme of meetings to the Committee on Procedural Questions.*

【纪要影像】

Mr. CHANG (China) expressed his gratification at the way in which the report of the Working Group had been received, and praised the report as a constructive analysis of interest to the whole world.

Regarding the accusations of political bias in the discussions of the Commission, he said that great care should be taken not to criticize suggestions on the grounds that they were political whenever a problem arose with regard to the desire for freedom and self-respect of peoples, and in particular the peoples of Asia.

As regards membership, the Chinese delegation was not completely satisfied with the recommendations of the Committee of the Whole, but since he felt that adjustments could be made as the work of the Commission progressed, he did not wish to make any detailed criticisms at the present juncture; he would reserve his suggestions until a later meeting of the Commission and of the Council.

He proposed the adoption of the following resolution:

"*The Economic and Social Council*

"*Notes* the report of the first session of the Economic Commission for Asia and the Far East;

"*Expresses its appreciation, and approves* the preparatory arrangements made by the Commission for the carrying out of its functions."

In addition, he proposed that a vote should be taken without further discussion on the two draft resolutions concerning terms of reference and membership contained in the report of the Committee of the Whole.

Mr. CHANG (China) and Mr. THORP (United States of America) approved the proposal made by the President on the grounds that it would leave the Commission complete freedom of action.

Decisions:

1. *The resolution proposed by the representative of China, as amended by the President, was adopted.*

Decisions:

1. *The Council agreed that the Commission on Human Rights should meet in Geneva as soon after the close of the session of the General Assembly as possible.*

2. *On the proposal of Mr. Chang (China) it was decided to refer the 1948 programme of meetings to the Committee on Procedural Questions.*

图片 5.11　张彭春在联合国经社理事会第五届第 101 次会议发言纪要

【纪要译文】

张先生(中国)对收到的工作组报告的方式表示满意,并赞扬该报告是对全世界感兴趣的建设性分析。

关于对委员会讨论中的政治偏见的指控,他说,应当非常小心,不要在各国人民,特别是亚洲人民渴望自由和自尊方面出现问题时,以建议是政治性的为由批评这些建议。

关于成员组成,中国代表团对全体委员会的建议并不完全满意,但由于他认为随着委员会工作的进展可以作出调整,他不想在目前这个阶段提出任何详细的批评;他将保留他的建议到委员会和理事会以后的会议上再提出。

他提议通过以下决议:

“经济及社会理事会:注意到亚洲和远东经济委员会第一届会议的报告;“表示赞赏并核准委员会为履行其职能所作的筹备安排。”

此外,他提议在不进一步讨论全体委员会报告中所载的关于职权范围和成员资格的两项决议草案的情况下进行表决。

张先生(中国)和索普先生(美国)同意主席提出的建议,理由是这将使委员会享有完全的行动自由。

决定:

1. 中国代表提出的决议经主席修正后获得通过。

决定:

1. 理事会同意人权委员会应在大会届会结束后尽快在日内瓦举行会议。

2. 根据张先生(中国)的提议,决定将1948年的会议方案提交程序问题委员会。

9. 张彭春在经社理事会第五届第105次会议上的发言

1947年8月5日上午11时,联合国经社理事会第五届第105次会议,在纽约成功湖召开。本次会议主要议题是继续讨论拟议的拉丁美洲经济委员会。中国代表张彭春率团参加了本次会议,并在会议上先后三次发言,其具体发言内容全文、纪要及其译文等如下:

(1)会议发言全文记录①及译文

【全文记录】

Dr. CHANG (China): This problem before us is one of the most significant problems that has come before this session of the Council, because it touches the fundamental organizational issue of the Council: How far are we going to proceed in this matter of initiating and establishing regional commissions?

We appreciate deeply the moving proposal of the representative of Chile. I, for one, feel profound sympathy, and I may say, some slight understanding of the problems before the Latin American countries in the economic field. I have had the pleasure and the honour of residing and travelling in South America for some months, where you do meet with some peculiar characteristics of economic situations.

There is this fact that has already been commented upon, namely, that in

① UN Document: E/PV. 105, pp. 41–55, pp. 77–85, p. 92.

most of the countries of Latin America, in regard to exports, they depend upon a single product, such as coffee, petroleum, sugar, beets, copper or other minerals. The single product for export often accounts for fifty per cent or more of the total export values of these countries. This type of economy is most sensitive, naturally, to shifts in world market demands, and to changes in world prices. Prosperity and depression seem to be altogether outside of the possibility of rational control. These countries, therefore, with their specialized products for export, deserve our sympathetic support and understanding.

Furthermore, there has been in South America, as in other parts of the world that are under-industrialized, such as the Far East and the Middle East, a situation that is described in this sentence taken from the Chilean newspaper "El Mercurio" in Valparaso, dated 14 May 1942.

This situation shows how closely linked the countries of the Far East, the Middle East, Eastern Europe, and all the under industrialized countries are to South America.

The quotation reads: "A country without its own industries is destined to end up as a colony of countries more industrialized than herself. It is manufacture and industry that gives the tone of progress. To possess natural riches whether agricultural and mineral amounts to nothing if the country cannot or does not know how to transform them. The mere wealth of materials without an industrious and intelligent population is rather a danger than an advantage. A people which is not capable of producing its own machinery, motors, tools and armaments, has no right to call itself independent."

Whether we agree with all the sentiments implied in that statement we do feel a certain eagerness in it, a certain hunger for independence, for self respect, for industrialization. Therefore, we feel particularly grateful to our colleague from Chile for bringing this matter to our attention.

There is another reason for instance, why the study of economic problems in this part of the world is most urgent. This problem is what we might call the matter of handicrafts mechanical habits, and certain leanings in leadership. I noticed when I travelled in South America, as well as in the Middle East, that most of these countries did not have a very long and fervent tradition in the handicrafts. Handicrafts have rather been looked down upon. The leadership has been mainly in the direction of literary cultivation. To elevate himself in society, a man must go up the bureaucratic ladder. I know in certain countries in the Far East also, that they have suffered from the same mistake, but nevertheless handicrafts surely have played an important part in the patterns of industrialization. This matter has already been noted by keen analysis in Latin American countries themselves, and I just wanted to draw the Council's attention to this as one of the important elements to be studied: how to provide not only industrial equipment, but also the necessary trained personnel.

All these various aspects of the characteristics of the economy of Latin America would convince us that we, from the point of view of the United Nations, should pay particular attention to the economic problems of this area.

So the problem is not simply one of being in favour of establishing an Economic Commission for Latin America or of not being in favour. That is the reason why we ought not simply to put this to a vote without having studied it more carefully. That is the reason why I feel that, while some of us may not be ready to vote in favour, none of us is quite ready to vote against it.

That is the fundamental attitude towards a proposition of this kind. I think that a three-point procedure should be adopted, although I have not yet found the necessary words. I feel that those of us who are talking on this matter of economic development, and who handle words, should be ashamed, because we should get down to the dirty work. The trouble with most of these countries is that the so-called leaders have gone too far in the direction of literary leanings and the polishing of language instead of using their hands. I will use rough and rugged words, and leave them to be polished afterwards.

The first point is to state, in a sentence or two, our appreciation of the Chilean proposal and the great vision implied in the speech of the Chilean representative. We should state we recognize the needs in Latin America. That would be the first paragraph or sentence in the resolution.

The second paragraph would contain a request to the Secretary-General to study and report on the general needs and the economic characteristics of Latin America, collecting material from all the countries concerned. Then the various countries would know that the United Nations was doing something.

I am not at all in favour of postponing action; I think that something ought to be done now. This session must do something, and not simply form some sort of committee of investigation. That does not satisfy anyone, and if we could get this study started, then in three to six months' time a report, even more suggestive, promising and useful than the Report of the Working Group on the situation in Asia and the Far East, could be produced.

I hope the report would be more illuminating and more useful than that Report, because in the creation of the European Commission the intention was the practical one of making use of the existing agencies and coordinating them. Creating the Economic Commission for the area of the Far East entailed an analysis of the effects of the war, with a keen consciousness of the special characteristics of the economics of that area. I hope that the background of this report, which I think can be produced within three to six months, will be one of the most suggestive yet produced under the auspices of this Council.

The question of personnel is one of the most important questions. Fortunately, in the production of the Report on Asia and the Far East we secured the services of such men as Professor Eugene Staley, and Professor T. Y. Wu from China, and experts from the United Kingdom, France and other countries. In three months these experts were able to gather together the fundamental material on which the Working Group of this Council based its Report.

I think the personnel should start gathering materials from Latin America right away, and I hope that the Secretariat will be able to get two, three or four experts and send out a proper questionnaire. If necessary, they could travel to various places to collect this material by field observations.

The Council could then appoint a small committee to examine the material and then — I now reach the third point — request the Secretary-General to suggest effective machinery for the carrying out of our objectives, including the possibility of establishing an economic commission for Latin America.

In other words, the matter should not be voted upon immediately; we should give it a thorough study, and then we can devise the machinery. That really touches upon one of the fundamental matters before this Council. We are interested in doing effective work, and we should view all our machinery as machinery or as tools. We have the purpose; we have the motivation; we want to do something, and the machinery is something for our use.

Merely because one has one kind of machinery somewhere, does not mean another region should have similar machinery, though I do not say that an economic regional commission would not be the proper form for the Latin American area.

For some months I resided in the Middle East; I very much enjoyed the experience, and I learned something of the problems of the under-industrialized parts of the world.

Should we be faced at the next session with a proposal for the creation of an economic commission for the Middle East, then we shall have other regional problems. Are we going to do it in that way, or are we going to review the whole matter of economic regional commissions? It may not be at our next session, but I hope it will be within the next year or two at the outside. For instance, from the very beginning I have not been in favour of creating regional commissions. I have always maintained that there should be commissions on an international or a world basis, with regional offices, regional research staff, and, if necessary, regional executive staff. But the commissions should all be in one, and it should all be done from headquarters.

However, these two commissions having been created for specific reasons, we should pause, and ponder whether we should create another regional commission or not. In saying that we should study the problem, it does not mean that we deny the urgency of the problem. That is why I have avoided taking part in this discussion without suggesting something concrete to do immediately as to whether we must create a commission or create a special group.

But we must face this matter from the problem to the procedure, and from the motivation to the machinery, and not *vice verse*, We must not say we want the machinery, and leave to the next step the question of whether the machinery will be able to do the work or not. We must set a goal immediately, and then devise the proper machinery to reach it.

I advocated the same idea when we discussed the creation of a commission for Europe. It was discussed at one or two sessions and at one Assembly. A commission was finally created, but I wonder whether it is being used. However that is another question.

In regard to the matter before us, it touches a very vital point in this Council. We must maintain the authority of this Council. This Council must do something concrete. From motivation, through machinery we proceed to what? To what I would call methods and means. That is, this machinery should be able to suggest and devise concrete methods and means of doing things. After that, we get something accomplished; namely, the making and mending of economic devises in all countries. That is where the concrete results will be produced.

There is still another "M". I have been using words starting with the letter

"M" such as motivation, machinery, methods and means, making and mending; and there is another "M", namely men. We must have the right sort of men, and the right sort of men can be obtained through the right type of example and the right type of education.

That is what a Council of this type should do. It must have the motivation. Then it must have the daring, the courage, and the vision to create the right type of machinery through which to produce results and means that may be reached; and then actually bring about those things in the world by making and mending through men of worth.

This, therefore, is my humble suggestion. It consists of three steps. The first step is the appreciation of the proposal and the recognition of the needs. The second step is to request the Secretary-General to study and report, and then gather the material immediately from all the countries concerned. The third step is to request the Secretary-General to suggest the most effective machinery for carrying out the results of the study, including the possibility of establishing an Economic Commission for Latin America. I forgot to mention one thing in connection with the third point. That is, the Secretary-General, in performing this function, should make contact with all organizations and agencies both within the United Nations and outside the United Nations. In other words, from the United Nations point of view we can simply say organizations and agencies within the United Nations. That would mean our commissions and specialized agencies which have contact with us. Outside the United Nations would include those agencies that have not yet had any formal contact with the United Nations.

These are the three suggestions which I make. As to the wording, that may be polished by others.

Dr. CHANG (China): We are very happy to see this proposal by the delegation of Cuba because it does bring the matter to some concrete issue. However, it may require something of a study and perhaps a drafting committee would be needed. Furthermore, certain points may be involved which are seemingly beyond a drafting committee. By that I mean there are certain principles involved. But if we agree on those principles, then perhaps a drafting committee will be sufficient. In that event there would be no need of referring the matter to the Committees of the Whole.

The first two paragraphs of the proposal are merely a statement of the importance and significance of the problems, as we realize the need for co-operative measures. The operative part is the establishment of an *ad hoc* committee. How is that to be placed in regard to our commissions, Sub-commissions regional commissions and committees?

I think that requires a little consideration.

I am not opposed to the establishment of an *ad hoc* committee, but if we are going to do that, the terms of its establishment should be gone over.

The first point of the proposal states: "The Committee shall prepare an analysis regarding the establishment of an economic commission..." If I understand that correctly, that is the same thing as my third point, namely, the studying of the possibilities. It does not deal definitely with the matter. There may be other means of doing the job, but this is surely one of the ways. There should be a preparation of the arguments both for and against, by the Secretariat. That is what I meant. I was going to suggest that to combine this with my third point would be very appropriate and very simple. That is, the Secretariat would do the job, but would allow another body to supervise and permit it to use the means and facilities available to the United Nations.

As to the second point of the proposal, I think there should be a committee created by the Council to bring its report to the attention of some other organ, but it is rather awkward. I think we should say that the committee should consult the Ninth International Conference of American States convening in Bogota.

That is another matter. The report will have to come back here. The matter of a report, not considered by the Council, being sent to some body outside the Council, is something that requires consideration.

The third point of the proposal seems to me to be too long. Suppose we put it this way: "The committee shall consult" such and such, "and report at the following session of the Economic and Social Council". That is all. Then, "present to the Council recommendations for action by the Council," really is a phrase to be attached to the first point instead of to the third point. In other words if it is attached to the third point, it means that the action of the Council is made conditional to some body outside the Council. I think that point requires a little consideration. Therefore, we should split the third point into two, deleting whether it is available or not, and leaving it as a matter to be reported; that is all. We might just say "The committee shall consult" and so forth, "and shall report at the following session of the Economic and Social Council, the result of the consultation," naturally.

Then the other matter might be added to point (1) as follows: "shall prepare an analysis," and so forth, "and present to the Economic and Social Council recommendations for action." "Recommendations for action" really belongs to point (1) in regard to the study of the whole matter and the recommending of the action to be taken. Then in the meantime the committee shall consult any other body that happens to be intensely interested in the matter.

As regards the fourth point, I think that is again some organizational point, and it is an important one. Shall this Council create a regional group outside the Council? So far we have created regional groups for regional action, and this is a matter within the Council itself. Shall we create a committee outside the Council, composed of regional members? I am not definitely against it, but I should like to raise the question from the organizational point of view.

I am glad to note that the general opinion is that we think the problem is serious. That means we must pay attention to it and do something about it. I understand that my Cuban colleague agrees that something must be done immediately, so the second point of my proposal can be incorporated.

The proposal will still have three points. The first will be "realizing the importance" and so forth—the preamble, really. The true purpose of point (1) is to ask the Secretary-General to do some studying immediately. I know that it will be done immediately and in an effective way. The Secretariat, with expert consultants, can produce a good document, and that will be very useful.

The third point deals with the creation of the committee. I am not against it, but I should like to have the whole organizational problem considered by all of us, because we are getting ourselves more and more confused. The matter before the Economic and Social Council is confused. We should consider that aspect. If we want to have a committee, then what are we going to do?

It seems to me that the terms of reference are really two-fold. However, it is really not a matter of the terms of reference; it is the composition of the committee. The composition is one thing. You may call it an *ad hoc* committee, or call it whatever you like. If you call it an *ad hoc* committee, then in effect you say that it is composed of so many members. You may then say that the members shall comprise Members of the Council, but if you say that the members shall be so and so, that is another method.

The two items are quite clear. The first is to make an analysis with the assistance of the Secretariat, and then to present it to the Council with recommendations for action. The second point is to consult such and such. As a matter of fact, I should like to see that point widened a little to include the suggestions of the representative of New Zealand. The committee has not only to consult this Conference which is outside the United Nations. There are organizations and agencies within the United Nations which should not be neglected, and we should include in this second item of the terms of reference the matter of the consultation.

If you wish to separate the items to give this point due importance, I do not object. That is a matter for others to decide.

However, the organizations, specialized agencies, commissions and Sub-commissions in the field, which are interested, may have something to say. Therefore I should like them included in the consultation provisions.

I suggest that there should be some general statement like this: "The committee shall consist of agencies and organizations in and outside the United Nations, especially the Ninth International Conference of American States convening in Bogota," That is my humble suggestion.

Dr. CHANG (China): If we turn this matter over to a drafting committee, it means we would agree in principle. Now, with regard to the principle, we all agreed on a general preamble recognizing the needs. We all agreed on making some studies immediately.

We also agreed to have some *ad hoc* committee to study the possibilities and consult other agencies, but there is one point of principle that is important, that is, the membership of the *ad hoc* committee.

I have just consulted with the representative of Cuba on this and he agrees with me in thinking that the membership should not be exclusively coming from one region, because it touches something very vital in regard to the organization of the Council as a whole. He has agreed to that principle. I think we are ready to go on to a drafting committee.

【全文译文】

张博士(中国):我们面前的这个问题是理事会本届会议面临的最重要问题之一,因为它涉及理事会的根本组织问题:我们在发起和设立区域委员会这一事项上要走多远?

我们非常赞赏智利代表令人感动的提议。就我个人而言,我对拉丁美洲国家在经济领域面临的问题深表同情,也可以说略有了解。我有幸在南美洲居住和旅行了几个月,在那里你确实遇到一些特殊的经济情况。

有一个事实已经得到了评论,即在大多数拉丁美洲国家,就出口而言,它们依赖单一产品,如咖啡、石油、糖、甜菜、铜或其他矿物。单一出口产品往往占这些国家出口总值的50%或更多。这类经济自然对世界市场需求的变化和世界价格的变化最为敏感。繁荣和萧条似乎完全超出了理性控制的范围。因此,这些专门出口产品的国家,值得我们同情、理解和支持。

此外,正如在世界其他欠工业化地区,如远东和中东一样,南美洲也出现了这种情况,这句话摘自1942年5月14日在智利瓦尔帕莱索出版的一份报纸《信使报》。

这种情况表明,远东、中东、东欧和所有欠工业化国家与南美洲的联系是多么紧密。

这句引语是这样写的:“一个没有自己工业的国家注定会沦为比她工业化程度更高的国家的殖民地。制造业和工业是进步的基调。如果一个国家不能够或不知道如何改造自然财富,那么拥有自然财富,无论是农业财富还是矿产财富,都毫无意义。只有物质财富而没有勤劳智慧的人民,这与其说是一种优势,不如说是一种危险。一个不能生产自己的机器、汽车、工具和武器的民族,无权自称独立。”

不管我们是否同意这句话中隐含的所有观点,我们确实感觉到其中的某种渴望,对独立、自尊和工业化的某种渴望。因此,我们特别感谢我们的智利同事提请我们注意这个问题。

还有另一个原因,例如,为什么研究世界这一地区的经济问题是最迫切的。这个问题就是我们可以称之为手工艺、机械习惯和某些领导阶层倾向的问题。当我在南美和中东旅行时,我注意到这些国家大多没有悠久而热忱的手工艺品传统。手工艺品颇被人瞧不起。领导才能一直以文学修养为导向。一个人要想提高自己的社会地位,就必须在官僚阶层中往上爬。我知道在远东的一些国家也犯了同样的错误,但是手工业确实在工业化模式中发挥了重要作用。拉丁美洲国家本身的敏锐分析已经注意到这一问题，我只想提请理事会注意这一问题，将其作为需要研究的重要内容之一：如何不仅提供工业设备，而且提供必要的训练有素的人员。

拉丁美洲经济特点的所有这些方面都将使我们相信，从联合国的角度来看，我们应该特别注意这一地区的经济问题。

因此，问题不仅仅是赞成或不赞成成立拉丁美洲经济委员会。这就是为什么我们不应该在没有更仔细研究的情况下就简单地把它付诸表决。这就是为什么我认为，虽然我们中的一些人可能还不准备投赞成票，但我们中没有人准备投反对票。

这是对这种主张的基本态度。我认为应该采用三点程序，尽管我还没有找到必要的措辞。我觉得我们这些谈论经济发展问题的人，以及那些处理文字的人，应该感到惭愧，因为我们应该脚踏实地干。大多数这些国家的问题是，所谓的领导人在文学倾向和语言修饰方面走得太远，而不是用他们的手实干。我会用粗糙、简陋的文字，留待事后打磨。

第一点是用一两句话说明我们对智利提案和智利代表讲话中所隐含的伟大愿景的赞赏。我们应该声明我们认识到拉丁美洲的需求。这将是决议的第一段或第一句话。

第二段将请秘书长研究和报告拉丁美洲的一般需求和经济特点，从所有有关国家收集材料。然后各国就会知道联合国正在行动。

我完全不赞成推迟行动；我认为现在应该做点什么。本届会议必须有所作为，而不仅仅是成立某种调查委员会。这不能使任何人满意，如果我们能够开始这项研究，那么在三到六个月的时间内，就可以编写一份报告，比亚洲和远东局势工作组的报告更具指导性、更有希望且更有用。

我希望该报告将比那份报告更具启发性和更有用，因为在创建欧洲委员会时，本意是实际地利用现有机构并协调它们的实际意图。设立远东地区经济委员会需要对战争的影响进行分析，同时敏锐地意识到该地区经济的特点。我希望这份报告的背景，我认为可以在三至六个月内完成，将是在本理事会主持下完成的最具指导性的报告之一。

人事问题是最重要的问题之一。幸运的是，在编写《亚洲和远东报告》的过程中,我们获得了尤金·斯塔利教授和来自中国的吴德耀教授以及来自英国、法国和其他国家的专家的帮助。在三个月内,这些专家收集了本理事会工作小组报告所依据的基本资料。

我认为,工作人员应该立即开始从拉丁美洲收集材料,我希望秘书处能够找到两名、三名或四名专家,并发出一份适当的调查问卷。如果有必要,他们可以到不同的地方通过实地观察来收集这些资料。

理事会然后可以任命一个小型委员会来审查这些材料,然后——我现在谈到第三点——请秘书长提出实现我们目标的有效机制,包括设立拉丁美洲经济委员会的可能性。

换句话说,不应立即就此事进行表决;我们应该对它进行彻底的研究,然后才能设计出机制。这确实涉及本理事会面前的一项基本问题。我们对做有效的工作感兴趣,我们应该把我们所有的机制都视为机制或工具。我们有目的;我们有动力;我们想做点什么,机制是供我们用的。

仅仅因为某个地区有一种机制,并不意味着另一个地区也应该有类似的机制,尽管我并不是说经济区域委员会对拉丁美洲地区而且并不是。

我在中东住了几个月,我非常享受这段经历,并且我了解到世界上欠工业化地区的一些问题。

如果我们在下一届会议上面临设立中东经济委员会的建议,那么我们将面临其他区域问题。我们是要这样做,还是要审查整个经济区域委员会的问题?它可能不会在我们的下一届会议上进行,但我希望它最迟将在未来一两年内举行。例如,我从开始就不赞成设立区域委员会。我一直主张,应该在国际或世界范围内设立委员会,设立区域办事处、配备区域研究人员,必要时还应配备区域执行人员。但是,这些委员会应该合而为一,而且都应该在总部进行。

然而,这两个委员会的设立有其特定的原因,我们应该停下来思考是否应该设立另一个区域委员会。说我们应该研究这个问题,并不意味着我们否认这个问题的紧迫性。这就是为什么我在没有就我们是否必须设立一个委员会或设立一个特别小组提出立即采取具体行动的建议时避免参与讨论。

但是,我们必须从问题到程序,从动机到机制,而不是相反,面对这个问题,我们不能说我们想要机制,而把机制是否能够完成工作的问题留给下一步。我们必须立即制定一个目标,然后设计适当的机制来实现它。

在我们讨论成立欧洲委员会时,我也提出了同样的想法。在一两届会议和一次大会上讨论了这一问题。一个委员会终于成立了,但我想知道它是否正在使用中。然而,那是另一个问题。

关于摆在我们面前的问题,它涉及理事会中一个非常重要的问题。我们必须维护本理事会的权威。本理事会必须做一些具体事情。从动机,通过机制,我们能做什么?我称之为方法和手段。也就是说,这一机制应该能够提出和设计具体的做事方法和手段。在那之后,我们完成了一些事情;也就是说,所有国家的经济计划的制定和修补。这是产生具体结果之处。

还有一个"M"。我一直在使用以字母"M"开头的单词,如动机(motivation)、机制(machinery)、方法(methods)和手段(means)、制造(making)和修补(mending);还有另一个"M",即男人(men)。我们必须有合适的人,而合适的人可以通过合适的实例(example)和合适的教育(education)获得。

这就是这类理事会应该做的事情。它必须有动机。然后,它必须有胆识、勇气和远见来创造正确的机制,通过这种机制产生可能达到的结果和手段;然后通过有价值的人的创造和修补,在这个世界上实现这些事情。

因此,这是我的拙见。它包括三个步骤。第一步是对提案的赞赏和对需求的认识。第二步是请秘书长研究并提出报告,然后立即从所有有关国家收集材料。第三步是请秘书长提出执行研究结果的最有效机制,包括设立拉丁美洲经济委员会的可能性。关于第三点,我忘了提一件事。也就是说,秘书长在履行这一职能时,应与联合国内外的所有组织和机构接触。换言之,从联合国的角度来看,我们可以简单地说是联合国内的组织和机构。这将意味着我们的委员会和与我们有联系的专门机构。联合国以外的机构将包括那些尚未与联合国进行任何正式接触的机构。

这些就是我提出的三项建议。至于措辞,其他人可能会加以润色。

张博士(中国):我们非常高兴地看到古巴代表团的这一建议,因为它确实使这一问题涉及一些具体问题。然而,这可能需要进行一些研究,也许还需要一个起草委员会。此外,可能涉及起草委员会似乎无法处理的某些问题。我的意思是说,这涉及到某些原则。但是,如果我们在这些原则上达成一致,那么也许成立一个起草委员会就足够了。在这种情况下,没有必要将此事提交全体委员会。

建议的前两段只是说明问题的重要性和意义,因为我们认识到需要采取合作措施。执行部分是设立一个特设委员会。我们的委员会、小组委员会和区域委员会如何看待这一点?

我认为这需要考虑一下。

我不反对设立一个特设委员会,但如果我们要这样做,就应该回顾一下设立该委员会的条件。

该建议的第一点指出:"委员会应就设立经济委员会编写一份分析报告。"如果我理解正确的话,这与我的第三点是一样的,即研究的可能性。它没有明确处理这件事。也许还有其他方法可以做这项工作,但这肯定是其中一种方法。秘书处应准备好赞成和反对的理由。这就是我的意思。我想说的是,把这一点和我的第三点结合起来是非常恰当和简单的。也就是说,秘书处将负责这项工作,但将允许另一个机构监督并允许它使用联合国现有的手段和设施。

至于建议的第二点,我认为理事会应该设立一个委员会,提请其他机构注意其报告,但这相当尴尬。我认为我们应该说,委员会应与在波哥大召开的第九次美洲国家国际会议进行磋商。那是另一回事。报告必须回到这里。一份未经理事会审议的报告被送交理事会以外的某个机构,这是一个需要审议的问题。。

在我看来,建议的第三点似乎太长了。假设我们这样说:"委员会将咨询'某某人',并向经济及社会理事会下届会议提出报告"。仅此而已。

那么,“向理事会提出供理事会采取行动的建议”这句话实际上是附属于第一点而不是第三点的短语。换言之,如果附属于第三点,则意味着理事会的行动是以理事会以外的某个机构为条件的。我认为这一点需要稍加考虑一下。因此,我们应将第三点一分为二,不管它是否可用,删除并将其作为报告的问题;仅此而已。我们可以说“委员会将进行磋商”等等,“并将在经济及社会理事会下届会议上报告磋商结果”,这是理所当然的。

那么,另一个问题可以添加到第(1)点中,内容如下:“应编写一份分析报告”,等等,“并向经济及社会理事会提出行动建议。”“行动建议”实际上属于第(1)点,即研究整个问题并建议采取行动。那么在此期间,委员会应与碰巧对此事有强烈兴趣的任何其他机构进行磋商。

关于第四点,我认为这也是一个组织问题,而且是一个重要问题。本理事会是否应在理事会以外设立一个区域组织?迄今为止,我们已经为区域行动建立了区域组织,这是理事会内部事务。我们是否应该在理事会之外设立一个由区域成员组成的委员会?我并非绝对反对,但我想从组织的角度提出这个问题。

我高兴地注意到,一般意见是,我们认为这个问题很严重。这意味着我们必须关注它并对此采取行动。我的理解是,我的古巴同事同意必须立即采取行动,因此可以纳入我提议的第二点。

这项建议仍有三点。第一个点是“意识到重要性”等等——实际上是序言。第(1)点的真正目的是请秘书长立即进行一些研究。我知道这将立即以有效的方式完成。秘书处在专家顾问的帮助下,可以编写一份很好的文件,这将非常有用。

第三点涉及事务委员会的设立。我并不反对,但我希望所有人都能考虑整个组织问题,因为我们越来越困惑。摆在经济及社会理事会面前的问题是混乱的。我们应该考虑这个方面。如果我们想成立一个事务委员会,那我们该怎么办?

在我看来,职权范围实际上是双重的。不过,这并非职权范围的问题;这是委员会的组成。组成是一回事。你可以称之为特设委员会,也可以随意称呼它。如果你称它为一个特设委员会,那么实际上你说它是由这么多成员组成的。你可以说成员由理事会成员组成,但如果你说成员是某某某,那是另一种方法。

这两项内容非常清楚。第一是在秘书处的协助下进行分析,然后向理事会提出行动建议。第二是咨询某某某。事实上,我希望这一点扩大一点,以纳入新西兰代表的建议。事务员会不仅要与联合国以外的这类会议进行磋商。联合国内有一些组织和机构不应被忽视,我们应在职权范围的第二个项目中列入协商事项。

如果你想把这些项目分开,以突出这一点,我不反对。那是一个由其他人决定的事情。

然而,领域内感兴趣的组织、专门机构、委员会和小组委员会可能有话要说。因此,我希望这些建议能纳入咨询条文内。

我建议应该有这样的一般性发言,"事务委员会应由联合国内外的机构和组织组成,特别是在波哥大召开的第九届美洲国家国际会议",这是我的拙见。

张博士(中国):如果我们把这个问题交给起草委员会,这意味着我们将原则上同意。现在,关于这项原则,我们都同意一项承认需要的一般性序言。我们一致同意立即进行一些研究。

我们还同意设立一个特设委员会来研究各种可能性并咨询其他机构,但有一点原则很重要,那就是特设委员会的成员组成。

我刚刚就此征求了古巴代表的意见,他同意我的看法,认为成员不应只来自一个区域,因为这涉及整个理事会组织的一些非常重要的问题。他已同意这一原则。我认为我们已经准备好成立一个起草委员会。

(2)会议发言内容纪要①

【会议纪要】

Mr. CHANG (China) said that he regarded the proposal as one of the most significant presented to the present session of the Council, because it raised the question as to the advisability of establishing additional regional organizations.

He recalled his residence and travels in Latin America and expressed his deep sympathy with the Latin American problems, particularly those connected with their economic dependence on external market conditions caused by monoproduction in several countries. He also read a quotation from a Chilean newspaper dated 14 May 1942 as an illustration and expression of Latin American desire for industrialization and economic independence.

Mr. Chang called attention to the handicap imposed upon Latin America, as well as on the Middle and Far East economy by long concentration of leadership in intellectual as opposed to craft activities; he noted the need for qualified personnel.

He believed that no member of the Council would oppose the proposal although some members were not prepared to give their immediate approval. He, therefore, suggested that a proposal should be formulated which would:

(1) state the Council's approval of the Chilean proposal and its recognition of the needs of Latin America; (2) request the Secretary-General to study those needs and report upon them; and (3) request the Secretary-General to suggest effective measures for the realization of the objects of the proposal.

He believed that this procedure would indicate the Council's sympathy with the aims of the Chilean proposal and would fulfil the requirement for con-

---

① UN Document: E/SR. 105, pp. 149-150, p. 153.

crete action. He hoped that the resultant report might be even more useful than that which had been submitted on Asia and the Far East, which had, in turn, excelled that on Europe, because it would consider means to incorporate the machinery designed for the special problems of Latin America into the framework of the United Nations. Emphasizing the importance of qualified personnel, he expressed hope that all facilities, including the necessary travel facilities, would be available, and thought a report should be completed in three to six months. The report would include suggestions to meet the objections raised against the establishment of the proposed commission.

He recalled that he had not previously favoured the creation of regional bodies, but rather the establishment of regional branches of a central organization. However, he maintained an open mind on the matter pending closer study and emphasized that the purposes to be achieved rather than existent organization or precedent should be the first consideration. He believed that qualified men were of paramount importance.

He thought that the Secretary-General should consult all interested organizations both within and without the United Nations.

Mr. CHANG (China) suggested that a drafting committee might be needed to study the Cuban proposal, but felt that there were some points which involved principles beyond the sphere of competence of a drafting committee. However, if the Council was in agreement on those principles, a drafting committee would be sufficient.

He thought that the first point of the proposal was similar to his earlier suggestion. The Secretariat could study the possibilities of establishing a commission, but the Secretariat's work would be supervised by another body such as the proposed *ad hoc* committee.

He suggested that the second point of the proposal should be redrafted so as to state that the *ad hoc* committee should consult with the Ninth Inter-American Conference rather than bring a report, which had not been considered by the Council, to the attention of some outside body. Provision should also be made for the committee to consult United Nations organs such as the specialized agencies and commissions interested in the problem.

With regard to the third point, he suggested that only the first part, dealing with the consultation to be carried on between the committee and the Conference, should stand. The latter part dealing with recommendations for action should be added to the first point of the proposal. He felt that by redrafting the third point as he had suggested, any implication that the Council's action depended on the decisions of an outside body would be avoided.

With respect to the last paragraph of the proposal dealing with the composition of the committee, he did not think that the members of the *ad hoc* committee should be drawn exclusively from one region, since the problem with which they would deal was of vital importance to the Council as a whole.

【纪要影像】

Mr. CHANG (China) said that he regarded the proposal as one of the most significant presented to the present session of the Council, because it raised the question as to the advisability of establishing additional regional organizations.

He recalled his residence and travels in Latin America and expressed his deep sympathy with the Latin American problems, particularly those connected with their economic dependence on external market conditions caused by mono-production in several countries. He also read a quotation from a Chilean newspaper dated 14 May 1942 as an illustration and expression of Latin American desire for industrialization and economic independence.

Mr. Chang called attention to the handicap imposed upon Latin America, as well as on the Middle and Far East economy by long concentration of leadership in intellectual as opposed to craft activities; he noted the need for qualified personnel.

He believed that no member of the Council would oppose the proposal although some members were not prepared to give their immediate approval. He, therefore, suggested that a proposal should be formulated which would: (1) state the Council's approval of the Chilean proposal and its recognition of the needs of Latin America; (2) request the Secretary-General to study those needs and report upon them; and (3) request the Secretary-General to suggest effective measures for the realization of the objects of the proposal.

He believed that this procedure would indicate the Council's sympathy with the aims of the Chilean proposal and would fulfil the requirement for concrete action. He hoped that the resultant report might be even more useful than that which had been submitted on Asia and the Far East, which had, in turn, excelled that on Europe, because it would consider means to incorporate the machinery designed for the special problems of Latin America into the framework of the United Nations. Emphasizing the importance of qualified personnel, he expressed hope that all facilities, including the necessary travel facilities, would be available, and thought a report should be completed in three to six months. The report would include suggestions to meet the objections raised against the establishment of the proposed commission.

图片 5.12　张彭春在经社理事会第五届第 105 次会议发言纪要(1)

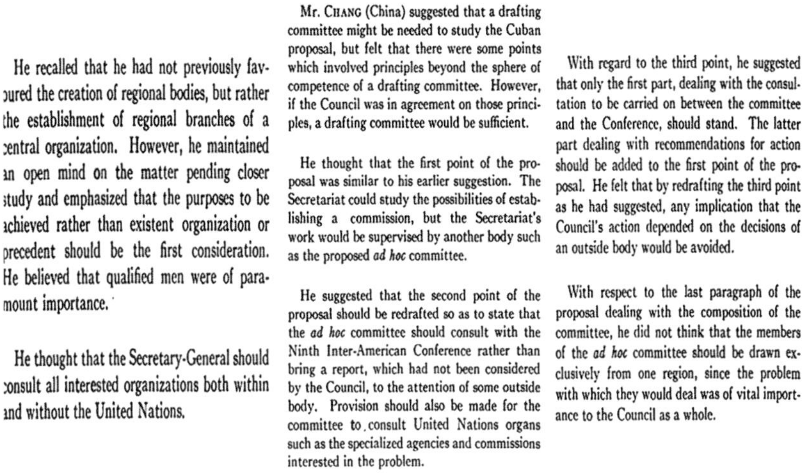
He recalled that he had not previously favoured the creation of regional bodies, but rather the establishment of regional branches of a central organization. However, he maintained an open mind on the matter pending closer study and emphasized that the purposes to be achieved rather than existent organization or precedent should be the first consideration. He believed that qualified men were of paramount importance.

He thought that the Secretary-General should consult all interested organizations both within and without the United Nations.

Mr. CHANG (China) suggested that a drafting committee might be needed to study the Cuban proposal, but felt that there were some points which involved principles beyond the sphere of competence of a drafting committee. However, if the Council was in agreement on those principles, a drafting committee would be sufficient.

He thought that the first point of the proposal was similar to his earlier suggestion. The Secretariat could study the possibilities of establishing a commission, but the Secretariat's work would be supervised by another body such as the proposed *ad hoc* committee.

He suggested that the second point of the proposal should be redrafted so as to state that the *ad hoc* committee should consult with the Ninth Inter-American Conference rather than bring a report, which had not been considered by the Council, to the attention of some outside body. Provision should also be made for the committee to consult United Nations organs such as the specialized agencies and commissions interested in the problem.

With regard to the third point, he suggested that only the first part, dealing with the consultation to be carried on between the committee and the Conference, should stand. The latter part dealing with recommendations for action should be added to the first point of the proposal. He felt that by redrafting the third point as he had suggested, any implication that the Council's action depended on the decisions of an outside body would be avoided.

With respect to the last paragraph of the proposal dealing with the composition of the committee, he did not think that the members of the *ad hoc* committee should be drawn exclusively from one region, since the problem with which they would deal was of vital importance to the Council as a whole.

图片 5.13　张彭春在经社理事会第五届第 105 次会议发言纪要(2)

【纪要译文】

张先生(中国)说,他认为该提案是提交理事会本届会议的最重要的提案之一,因为它提出了设立更多区域组织是否可取的问题。

他回顾了他在拉丁美洲的居住和旅行经历,并对拉丁美洲的问题深表同情,特别是与几个国家因生产单一造成的经济依赖外部市场条件有关的问题。他还宣读了 1942 年 5 月 14 日智利一家份报纸中的一段引文,作为拉丁美洲工业化和经济独立愿望的说明和表达。

张先生提请注意长期以来领导阶层集中在知识领域而不是手工业领域对拉丁美洲以及中东和远东经济造成的不利影响;他注意到对合格人员的需求。

他相信理事会没有任何成员会反对这项提议,尽管一些成员不准备立即予以批准。因此,他建议拟订一项提案,该提案将:

(1)说明理事会批准智利提案并承认拉丁美洲的需要;(2)请秘书长研究这些需求,并就此提出报告;(3)请秘书长提出实现该提案目标的有效措施。

他认为,这一程序将表明理事会对智利提案的目标表示同情,并将满足采取具体行动的要求。他希望咨询报告可以比亚洲和远东提交的报告更有用,而亚洲和远东提交的报告又优于欧洲,因为它将考虑如何把为拉丁美洲的特殊问题设计的机制纳入联合国的框架。他强调合格人员的重要性,表示希望所有设施,包括必要的旅行设施,都将齐备,并认为应在三至六个月内完成一份报告。该报告将包括解决反对设立拟议委员会意见的建议。

他回顾说,他以前并不赞成设立区域机构,而是赞成设立一个中央组织的区域分支机构。然而,他对此事持开放态度,等待进一步研究,并强调应首先考虑的是要实现的目标,而不是现有的组织或先例。他认为合格的人至关重要。

他认为秘书长应该与联合国内外所有感兴趣的组织协商。

张先生(中国)建议,可能需要一个起草委员会来研究古巴的提案,但认为有些问题涉及的原则超出了起草委员会的职权范围。然而,如果理事会同意这些原则,一个起草委员会就足够了。

他认为提案的第一点与他早先的建议相似。秘书处可以研究设立一个委员会的可能性,但秘书处的工作将由另一个机构监督,如拟议的特设委员会。

他建议重新起草提案的第二点,以便说明特设委员会应与第九次美洲会议协商,而不是将一份未经理事会审议的报告提请某个外部机构注意。还应规定委员会与联合国机构协商,如对该问题感兴趣的专门机构和委员会。

关于第三点,他建议只保留第一部分,即关于委员会和会议之间进行协商的部分。关于行动建议的后一部分应添加到提案的第一点中。他认为,按照他的建议重新起草第三点,就可以避免任何关于理事会的行动取决于外部机构决定的任何含义。

关于提案中涉及委员会组成的最后一段,他认为特设委员会的成员不应完全来自一个区域,因为他们将处理的问题总体上对理事会至关重要。

10. 张彭春在经社理事会第五届第 106 次会议上的发言

1947 年 8 月 5 日下午 3 时,联合国经社理事会第五届第 106 次会议,在纽约成功湖召开。本次会议主要议题是继续讨论亚洲和远东经济委员会第一届会议的报告和全体委员会的报告等。中国代表张彭春率团参加了本次会议,并在会议上发言,其具体发言内容全文、纪要及其译文等如下:

(1)会议发言全文记录①及译文

【全文记录】

Dr. CHANG (China): I am in favour of your suggestion, Mr. President, of taking a vote immediately in as much as we have had very long discussions on this subject.

【全文译文】

张博士(中国):主席先生,我赞成你关于立即进行表决的建议,因为

① UN Document: E/PV. 106, pp. 28-30.(值得说明的是:按照一般情况来说,全文记录应该更能全面而准确地体现具体发言内容,而会议纪要则是摘要记录,一般会比较短。比如说,在全文发言中发言的内容长并且发言次数多,而在会议纪要中,摘要记录的短且次数少等,因为全文记录中有发言不被会议纪要记录的情况。对比本次会议的全文记录和会议纪要,发现全文记录中张彭春先生只有一个简短的发言,而查先生也有一个较长一些的发言,在该全文记录的第 61-66 页,但并未涉及加拿大代表。然而奇怪的是,会议纪要中只有张彭春先生的发言纪要,而且是两次,这与全文记录并不一致。)

我们已经就此问题进行了很长时间的讨论。

(2)会议发言内容纪要①

【会议纪要】

Mr. CHANG (China) was in favour of the President's earlier proposal to take an immediate vote.

Mr. CHANG (China) agreed with the Canadian representative's proposal.

【纪要影像】

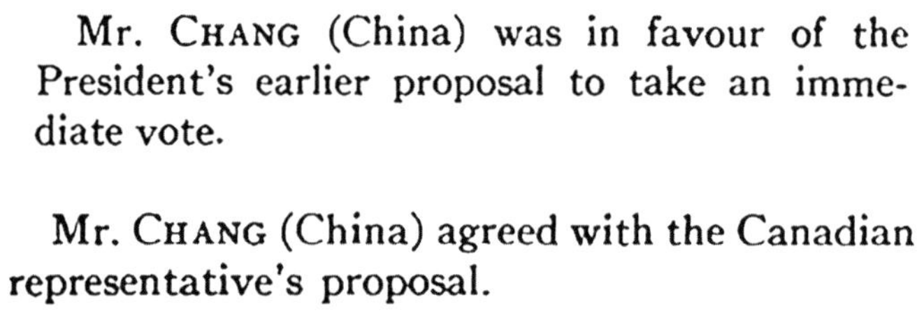

Mr. CHANG (China) was in favour of the President's earlier proposal to take an immediate vote.

Mr. CHANG (China) agreed with the Canadian representative's proposal.

图片 5.14　张彭春在经社理事会第五届第 106 次会议发言纪要

【纪要译文】

张先生(中国)赞成主席早些时候提出的立即进行表决的提议。

张先生(中国)同意加拿大代表的提议。

---

① UN Document: E/SR. 106, p. 156, p. 158.

11. 张彭春在经社理事会第五届第 107 次会议上的发言

1947 年 8 月 6 日上午 11 时,联合国经社理事会第五届第 107 次会议,在纽约成功湖召开。本次会议继续讨论秘书长关于联大第 58(I)号决议执行情况的进度报告,该决议涉及将联合国难民署的社会福利咨询职能移交给联合国。中国代表张彭春率团参加了本次会议,并在会议上发言,其具体发言内容全文、纪要及其译文等如下:

(1)会议发言全文记录[①]及译文

【全文记录】

Mr. CHANG (China): Having heard the changed version proposed by the representative of New Zealand, I am more convinced than before that we should stick to the unsatisfactory proposal, because if we try to redraft the whole thing we shall arrive at something which is just as unsatisfactory. It is in that spirit that I shall vote for the second paragraph, though that paragraph itself may be criticized. Perhaps several other Members may also vote for it, as it is in the interest of saving time.

Mr. CHANG (China): I feel that one remark is necessary. While I appreciate the ruling made by the President, with which I agreed, I think the suggestion to reconsider any paragraph surely was made quite seriously by the repre-

① UN Document: E/PV. 107, p. 46, p. 62.

sentative of Lebanon and in a very mature manner.

【全文译文】

张先生(中国):在听取了新西兰代表提出的修改后的版本后,我比以前更加确信,我们应该坚持这份不尽人意的提案,因为如果我们试图重新起草整个提案,我们会得出同样不尽人意的提案。正是本着这种精神,我将投票赞成第二段,尽管该段本身可能会受到批评。也许其他几个成员也会投赞成票,为了节省时间。

张先生(中国):我认为有必要说一句。虽然我赞赏主席所作的裁决,我也同意这一裁决,但我认为,重新审议任何段落的建议肯定是由黎巴嫩代表以非常成熟的方式非常认真地提出的。

(2)会议发言内容纪要①

【会议纪要】

Mr. CHANG (China) pointed out that the resolution of the General Assembly was for the continuation of the services initiated by and carried on by UNRRA only, and this did not mean that any Member State had enjoyed any special privileges unduly. He recognized that the resolution was not entirely satisfactory, but inasmuch as it represented several points of view and had already been to a drafting committee, he proposed its adoption.

① UN Document: E/SR. 107, p. 162.

【纪要影像】

Mr. CHANG (China) pointed out that the resolution of the General Assembly was for the continuation of the services initiated by and carried on by UNRRA only, and this did not mean that any Member State had enjoyed any special privileges unduly. He recognized that the resolution was not entirely satisfactory, but inasmuch as it represented several points of view and had already been to a drafting committee, he proposed its adoption.

图片 5.15　张彭春在经社理事会第五届第 107 次会议发言纪要

【纪要译文】

张先生(中国)指出,大会的决议只是为了使由联合国善后救济总署发起和开展的服务持续下去,这并不意味着任何会员国不适当地享有任何特权。他承认该决议并不完全令人满意,但鉴于它代表了几种观点,并且已经提交起草委员会,他建议通过该决议。

12. 张彭春在经社理事会第五届第110次会议上的发言

1947年8月11日上午11时,联合国经社理事会第五届第110次会议,在纽约成功湖召开。本次会议继续讨论拟议的是拉丁美洲经济委员会。中国代表张彭春率团参加了本次会议,并在会议上发言,其具体发言内容全文、纪要及其译文等如下:

(1)会议发言全文记录①及译文

【全文记录】

Mr. CHANG (China): I should like to speak with regard to the implementation of the proposal itself, Document E/531/Add. 1 contains the implementation to the resolution which we just passed, that is, the estimate of expenses.

There appears to be a very interesting verbal difficulty in paragraph 3 of document E/531/Add. 1. The ninth line of that paragraph reads "... as are strictly relevant to making a decision concerning the disability." There seems to be something wrong with the word "disability."

The PRESIDENT: That is a mistake; the word should be "desirability."

Mr. CHANG (China): Besides that, there is something there we should pay attention to. The part of this paragraph dealing with research was not meant to be closely related to the *ad hoc* Committee's work. After all, the type of re-

① UN Document: E/PV. 110, p. 87, pp. 87–88.

search that will be initiated—even though it will be of a preliminary nature—will be of use far beyond the decision of the *ad hoc* Committee with regard to the desirability of establishing the Commission for Latin America.

May I just say for the record—and not to be debated on—that perhaps this sentence cannot be interpreted exactly because of the way it is written. By that I mean, it should not be limited only to the decision itself. It should be limited in the preliminary stages to defining and analyzing the economic problems of Latin America. "Should initiate" does not necessarily mean that the commencement of the work may require a dozen people.

I think some money may be saved with regard to the transportation of Members of the *ad hoc* Committee, because most of the Members, if not all, will probably be in New York. Money can be saved, if that is the case.

The report of this Committee should not only be made with respect to the specific problem, but could also be of great use in other respects concerning the study of the problems of Latin America.

【全文译文】

张先生(中国):我想就提案本身的执行情况发言,E/531/Add. 1 号文件载有对我们刚刚通过的决议的执行情况,即费用概算。

E/531/Add. 1 号文件第三段似乎有一个非常有趣的文字障碍。该段第九行的内容是,"……与作出有关残疾的决定密切相关。""残疾"(disability)这个词似乎有点不对劲。

主席:这是一个错误;这个词应该是"可取性"(desirability)。

张先生(中国):除此之外,还有一点我们应该注意。该段涉及研究的部分并不意味着与特设委员会的工作密切相关。毕竟,将要开始的研究类型——尽管是初步性质的——将远远超出特设委员会就设立拉丁美洲委员会的可取性所作的决定。

请允许我正式指出——而不是就此进行辩论——也许这句话因其书

写方式而无法准确解释。我的意思是,它不应仅限于决定本身。在初步阶段,它应限于界定和分析拉丁美洲的经济问题。"应该开始"并不一定意味着工作的开始可能需要十几个人。

我认为在特设委员会成员的交通方面可以节省一些钱,因为大多数成员,如果不是全部的话,可能都在纽约。如果是这样的话,钱可以省下来。

这个委员会的报告不仅针对具体问题,而且在研究拉丁美洲问题的其他方面也会大有用处。

(2)会议发言内容纪要①

【会议纪要】

Mr. CHANG (China) suggested that the money allocated for transportation in the Secretary-General's estimate might not need to be listed under that heading, since most of the members of the Committee were probably already in New York. The sum might, therefore, be used for the purposes set out in paragraph 3. In addition, he pointed out that the work to be carried out in connexion with a survey of the economic problems of Latin America would be of great use for purposes other than the question of whether or not there was to be an economic commission for Latin America.

① UN Document: E/SR. 110, p. 188.

【纪要影像】

Mr. CHANG (China) suggested that the money allocated for transportation in the Secretary-General's estimate might not need to be listed under that heading, since most of the members of the Committee were probably already in New York. The sum might, therefore, be used for the purposes set out in paragraph 3. In addition, he pointed out that the work to be carried out in connexion with a survey of the economic problems of Latin America would be of great use for purposes other than the question of whether or not there was to be an economic commission for Latin America.

图片 5.16　张彭春在经社理事会第五届第 110 次会议发言纪要

【纪要译文】

张先生(中国)建议,秘书长概算中用于交通的拨款可能不需要列在该标题下,因为委员会的大多数成员可能已经在纽约。因此,这笔钱可以用于第三段所述的目的。此外,他指出,在拉丁美洲经济问题调查方面将要进行的工作,除是否将设立一个拉丁美洲经济委员会的问题之外,对于其他目的也很有用。

13. 张彭春在经社理事会第五届第112次会议上的发言

1947年8月12日上午10时30分，联合国经社理事会第五届第112次会议，在纽约成功湖召开。本次会议继续讨论世界石油资源的国际管制问题。中国代表张彭春率团参加了本次会议，并在会议上发言，其具体发言内容全文、纪要及其译文等如下：

(1)会议发言全文记录[①]及译文

【全文记录】

Dr. CHANG (China): This is not the time to comment on substance. The Chinese delegation was struck by a certain refreshing attitude in the proposal — the suggestion that this large problem of oil should be tackled in some way. I think that what our distinguished friend from Lebanon commented on was quite appropriate, that other matters should also be studied. Therefore, I am just wondering whether, at this hour of our discussion, we might not add a clause to the suggested resolution—as we have done before — which would draw the attention of the Commission to the discussions of the Council; in other words, all the various problems that have been brought up due to the complexity of the subject. For instance, there is another problem for which I have always had a great deal of sympathy on the negative side; namely, that we have already un-

① UN Document: E/PV. 112, pp. 51-52, p. 71.

dertaken a great many problems.

We should do our work well. I do not know whether we shall be able to do this well at all as it is such a large problem. I think that opinion has been expressed and that also should go to the Commission. Anyway, it does not seem as though we should simply say that this matter should be postponed. I think I would agree with our colleague from Norway. Surely the Council should not leave it aside. Therefore, the suggested resolution with that added clause may be the most appropriate measure in order to bring this matter to the Commission with all the various criticisms and comments and observations. That may give the measure its proper place for consideration.

Dr. CHANG (China): I did not comment on the substance of this problem, and in case the resolution which was suggested by the President should be considered at all, I thought that the addition of calling the attention of the Commission to all the varied opinions would perhaps improve the structure of the resolution itself. But if there should be a fundamental question as to whether we should have a resolution of that type at all, then that would throw the debate completely open.

In regard to that point, the Chinese delegation would like to reserve its own attitude with regard to the substance. It was a mere suggestion to facilitate the acceptance of that resolution. That point was added in order not to commit the opinion of the Council.

【全文译文】

张博士(中国):现在不是评论实质性问题的时候。中国代表团对提案中某种令人耳目一新的态度印象深刻——建议以某种方式解决石油这一大问题。我认为,我们尊敬的黎巴嫩朋友的评论是非常恰当的,其他问题也应该加以研究。因此,我只是在想,在我们讨论的这个时刻,我们是否可以像我们以前所做的那样,在建议的决议中增加一个条款,提请委员会注意理事会的讨论;换句话说,所有由于主题的复杂性而提出的各种问题。例如,还有另一个问题,我一直对它的消极面深表同情;也就是说,我们已经承担了许多问题。

我们应该把工作做好。我不知道我们是否能够做好这件事,因为这是一个如此大的问题。我认为已经表达了这种意见,这种意见也应该提交给委员会。无论如何,我们似乎不应该简单地说这件事应该推迟。我想我会同意我们挪威同事的看法。理事会当然不应该把它搁置一边。因此,所建议的增加了这一条款的决议可能是最适当的措施,以便将这一带有各种批评、评论和意见的问题提交给委员会。这可能会给这项措施以适当的考虑机会。

张博士(中国):我没有评论这一问题的实质,如果主席建议的决议应该得到审议,我认为增加提请委员会注意所有不同意见的内容可能会改进决议本身的结构。但是,如果有一个根本性的问题,即我们是否应该有一项这种类型的决议,那么这将使辩论完全开放。

关于这一点,中国代表团愿保留自己对实质内容的态度。这只是一个促进接受该决议的建议。增加这一点是为了不让理事会做出承诺。

(2)会议发言内容纪要①

【会议纪要】

Mr. CHANG (China) said that he did not wish to comment on the substance of the problem at this stage. He thought the suggestion of the Lebanese representative, that international control of raw materials other than oil should also be studied, was appropriate, and proposed the addition to the draft resolution of a clause drawing the attention of the Economic and Employment Commission to the discussion in the Council.

① UN Document: E/SR. 112, p. 200.

【纪要影像】

Mr. CHANG (China) said that he did not wish to comment on the substance of the problem at this stage. He thought the suggestion of the Lebanese representative, that international control of raw materials other than oil should also be studied, was appropriate, and proposed the addition to the draft resolution of a clause drawing the attention of the Economic and Employment Commission to the discussion in the Council.

图片 5.17　张彭春在经社理事会第五届第 112 次会议发言纪要

【纪要译文】

张先生(中国)说,他不想在现阶段评论问题的实质。他认为黎巴嫩代表的建议是合适的,即也应研究对石油以外原材料的国际管制,并建议在决议草案中增加一项条款,提请经济和就业委员会注意理事会的讨论。

14. 张彭春在经社理事会第五届第113次会议上的发言

1947年8月12日下午3时,联合国经社理事会第五届第113次会议,在纽约成功湖召开。本次会议继续讨论程序问题委员会的报告。中国代表张彭春率团参加了本次会议,并在会议上发言,其具体发言内容全文、纪要及其译文等如下:

(1)会议发言全文记录及译文

(暂缺。)

(2)会议发言内容纪要①

【会议纪要】

Mr. CHANG (China) thought that the Council should consider the question of holding a short session during the General Assembly, in order to review the reports of the specialized agencies. If it was decided not to have a short session, he thought provision should be made for liaison between the General Assembly and the Council.

Mr. CHANG (China) seconded the motion of the representative of the United States of America.

① UN Document: E/SR. 113, p. 212, p. 213.

【纪要影像】

Mr. Chang (China) thought that the Council should consider the question of holding a short session during the General Assembly, in order to review the reports of the specialized agencies. If it was decided not to have a short session, he thought provision should be made for liaison between the General Assembly and the Council.

Mr. Chang (China) seconded the motion of the representative of the United States of America.

图片 5.18　张彭春在经社理事会第五届第 113 次会议发言纪要

【纪要译文】

张先生(中国)认为,理事会应考虑在大会期间举行一期短期届会的问题,以便审查专门机构的报告。如果决定不举行短期届会,他认为应为大会和理事会之间的联络作出规定。

张先生(中国)附议了美国代表的动议。

15. 张彭春在经社理事会第五届第 117 次会议上的发言

1947 年 8 月 14 日下午 3 时，联合国经社理事会第五届第 117 次会议，在纽约成功湖召开。本次会议讨论程序问题委员会的临时报告。中国代表张彭春率团参加了本次会议，并在会议上发言，其具体发言内容全文、纪要及其译文等如下：

(1) 会议发言全文记录及译文

(暂缺。)

(2) 会议发言内容纪要[①]

【会议纪要】

Mr. CHANG (China) said that the draft resolution represented a compromise solution on the question of holding two or three sessions of the Council in 1948. The wider question of improving the effectiveness of meetings required examination. He pointed out that the Council had not yet held three sessions in a year, which might make it possible to have less items on the agenda of each session. He also considered that the functions of the commissions and the Council required clarification: to date all the commissions had met for a period of two weeks with a varying number of sessions and he thought this method of pro-

① UN Document: E/SR. 117, pp. 245-246.

cedure might be reconsidered.

The function of the Council was very different from that of a conference. It was not a body dealing with colourful critical problems all the time, which attracted a great deal of attention, but one which was a permanent part of an organization and which must continue meeting on the problems it had before it. All the delegations should consider carefully the whole question of the organization of the Council, and the question could then be examined at the sixth or seventh session.

Mr. Chang said he approved of the compromise solution submitted in the draft resolution, which left the final decision on a third session to the second session in 1948. With regard to the second paragraph of the draft resolution, he proposed its deletion, as he thought it would be sufficient to put on record the recommendation it contained to exercise added caution when considering the possibility of a third session.

【纪要影像】

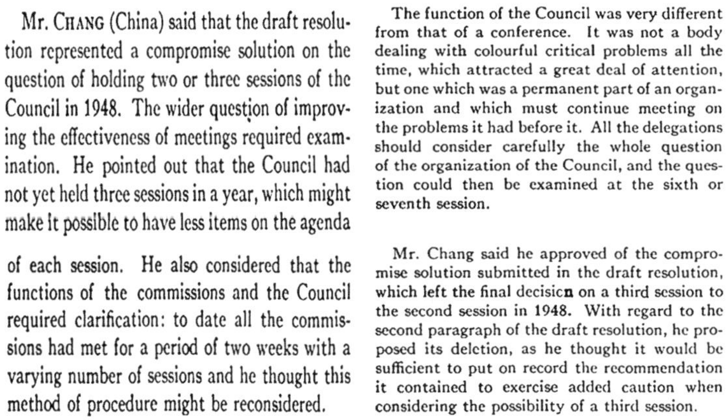

Mr. CHANG (China) said that the draft resolution represented a compromise solution on the question of holding two or three sessions of the Council in 1948. The wider question of improving the effectiveness of meetings required examination. He pointed out that the Council had not yet held three sessions in a year, which might make it possible to have less items on the agenda of each session. He also considered that the functions of the commissions and the Council required clarification: to date all the commissions had met for a period of two weeks with a varying number of sessions and he thought this method of procedure might be reconsidered.

The function of the Council was very different from that of a conference. It was not a body dealing with colourful critical problems all the time, which attracted a great deal of attention, but one which was a permanent part of an organization and which must continue meeting on the problems it had before it. All the delegations should consider carefully the whole question of the organization of the Council, and the question could then be examined at the sixth or seventh session.

Mr. Chang said he approved of the compromise solution submitted in the draft resolution, which left the final decision on a third session to the second session in 1948. With regard to the second paragraph of the draft resolution, he proposed its deletion, as he thought it would be sufficient to put on record the recommendation it contained to exercise added caution when considering the possibility of a third session.

图片 5.19　张彭春在经社理事会第五届第 117 次会议发言纪要

【纪要译文】

张先生(中国)说,该决议草案代表了在1948年举行两届或三届理事会会议问题上的折衷解决办法。提高会议效率这一更广泛的问题需要审查。他指出,理事会尚未在一年内举行过三届会议,而举行三届会议可能使每届会议议程上的项目减少。他还认为,委员会和理事会的职能需要厘清:迄今为止,所有委员会都举行了为期两周的会议,会议次数不一,他认为可以重新考虑这种议程方式。

理事会的职能与会议的职能大不相同。它不是一个一直在处理各种各样的备受瞩目的关键问题的机构,而是作为一个组织的永久性组成部分,它必须继续就它面前的问题举行会议。所有代表团都应认真审议理事会组织的整个问题,然后在第六届或第七届会议上审查这个问题。

张先生说,他赞成决议草案中提出的折衷解决办法,该办法将第三届会议的最终决定留给1948年的第二届会议。关于决议草案第二段,他提议删除该段,因为他认为在考虑召开第三届会议的可能性时,将其中所载的更加谨慎的建议记录在案就足够了。

16. 张彭春在经社理事会第五届第120次会议上的发言

1947年8月16日下午3时30分,联合国经社理事会第五届第120次会议,在纽约成功湖召开。本次会议继续讨论日程委员会两个成员的选举。中国代表张彭春率团参加了本次会议,并在会议上发言,其具体发言内容全文、纪要及其译文等如下:

(1)会议发言全文记录[①]及译文

【全文记录】

Dr. CHANG (China): I have the honour to second the motion of the representative of the United States. I think the suggestion is altogether fitting, and if we follow the suggestion we will have a good Committee. At the same time, we shall have a Second Vice-President who is eminently qualified for the post.

【全文译文】

张博士(中国):我荣幸地附议美国代表的动议。我认为这个建议是完全合适的,如果我们遵循这个建议,我们将得到一个有益的委员会。同时,我们将有第二位副主席,他完全有资格担任这一职务。

① UN Document: E/PV. 120, pp. x–xx, p. x.

(2)会议发言内容纪要[①]

【会议纪要】

Mr. CHANG (China) and Mr. SEN (India) supported the proposals of the United States representative.

【纪要影像】

Mr. CHANG (China) and Mr. SEN (India) supported the proposals of the United States representative.

图片 5.20　张彭春在经社理事会第五届第 120 次会议发言纪要

【纪要译文】

张先生(中国)和森先生(印度)支持美国代表的提议。

① UN Document: E/SR. 120, pp. 245-246.

17. 张彭春在经社理事会第五届第121次会议上的发言

1947年8月16日晚上8时15分至17日凌晨1时30分，联合国经社理事会第五届第121次会议，在纽约成功湖召开，这次会议也是本届会议的最后一次会议。中国代表张彭春参加了本次会议，就委员会程序问题在会议上先后10次发言，其具体发言内容全文、纪要及其译文等如下：

(1) 会议发言全文记录[①]及译文

【全文记录】

Dr. CHANG (China): Is it the President's ruling that we discuss this item paragraph by paragraph, and vote paragraph by paragraph. If so, I wish to speak on the first paragraph.

The PRESIDENT: I should prefer to have it adopted without any discussion, but we have proposals concerning paragraph 3, so perhaps the best way to dispose of it would be by discussing it paragraph by paragraph.

Dr. CHANG (China): I am completely in agreement with that, except with regard to paragraph 1 and except for a simple little word. If that could be amended, I would accept the whole report. That one word is a very important word; it is a word that represents something most beautiful, most charming,

① UN Document: E/PV. 121, p. 16, pp. 16-25, p. 26, pp. 32-35, p. 46, pp. 48-51, p. 61, p. 151.

and most attractive. As a matter of fact, I am so afraid of it that it may be fascination as the first stage, separation, the second stage, and divorce the third stage.

I am proposing an amendment in the interests of only one word, and one word only—stability—the amendment being to paragraph 1 of the report, deleting "on 5 July at Geneva," and adding the words "at the seat of the United Nations."

Naturally, the word stability is a very simple word, yet it is a word which all of us in the world, at the present stage, would long to have. We are moving about a great deal; the changes have been so much that we always need some point around which we can make our place. There is a Chinese symbol, the stars of the Dipper which surround the North Pole star. So, in everything, I think we should keep the word stability in view, and it is in the interests of stability that I speak these few words.

I am not against holding special sessions of the Council away from the Headquarters when there are strictly limited agendas, and Geneva would be one of the most attractive places for such meetings. So my position should be made very clear. If we had more time for discussion, we might have agreed on two regular sessions at Lake Success at the seat of the United Nations, and one special session, with limited interests and items for discussion, perhaps, somewhere away from the United Nations Headquarters. If so, surely Geneva would have the first priority.

But to have a regular session of one of the chief organs of the United Nations held away from the seat of the United Nations seems to me to be not quite along the line of stability and the encouragement of stability. The Council should not be peripatetic. The regular sessions should be held at the seat of the United Nations, and I hope that general principle is agreed upon.

One can imagine how much would be involved in regard to personnel, and in regard to expenses. The personnel for a regular session involves not only the personnel of the Division of Economic Stability and Development and the Department of Social Affairs, but other Departments as well, because this Council deals with very many problems and very many items. Consequently, it has been calculated that not counting the stenographic staff serving the conference and not counting the regular conference staff, but only the executive and more responsible staff, a great number is involved. This number has not been definitely calculated, but some of the responsible members of the Secretariat inform me that it would be around forty. That is a fairly large number of the executive people from the Secretariat to move to another place.

That is a fairly large number of executive people from the departments of the Secretariat that will have to move to another place.

If we look at the tentative draft schedule drawn up by the Secretariat, with the supposition that at that time in April there would be a session of the Economic and Social Council in Geneva, we will find that the other side on the Headquarters Staff would be left completely open for about two months. It would mean that when a Council meeting would be held in Geneva, this place would be practically deprived of the assistance of a large number of the responsible people on the Secretariat. That is one point.

The second point is naturally the expenses, the traveling expenses, the other expenses. I understand that some estimates have been made. I would not introduce that into the debate, but the number has been called this sum and that sum. But I think that all depends on our point of view. If we are inclined to go there, then we calculate the expense, according to one way of doing things, and make the figure very attractively small. But if we are against going there, we make it oppositely large. In any event, there is the extra expense.

Thirdly, there is the really fundamental influence on the permanent delegations. There are permanent delegations here which are prepared to service the representatives to the Council and also representatives to the Commissions. Then, with such a moving around from one place to another, it will mean that practically the whole set of the delegations will have to go elsewhere.

Furthermore, there is the matter of mere physical filing cabinets. I happen to have five steel cases which I refer to from time to time by telephone back to my office. I do not know what amount I shall have to carry for my own delegation. Shall I make special boxes? This Council deals with thirty or forty items at each of the regular sessions. Do you not think there is a problem to be considered?

I am not going to speak too long. It may be argued that we need to go there because Europe is particularly important to this juncture, with which statement I agree. With great respect I would point out that modern civilization had its beginnings in Europe. I have the highest admiration for Europe. I have visited Europe dozens of times. I would not be surprised that people would like to visit Europe. All that is out of question.

But we are the Economic and Social Council. We do not attract too much attention. That is altogether to our credit. Because we do quiet work, we do the type of work that is colorless. It is even crisisless because it is not critical. It is without crises, and because of that we attract less attention, I think we should be satisfied to do the colorless jobs.

For the specific tackling of work of political importance in Europe, why not ask the Security Council to go there and have a month session. I think it would be much more effective. Also, fever Members of the Secretariat would be involved, because after all their departments are more or less specialized, while here we have a wide range of people whom we would have to have along with us.

I have spoken very briefly. It is a matter of stability. I have thought, thought and thought of one thing to agree with my French colleague. I have thought and thought, but again and again it occurs to me should we at this Juncture or at this stage of the organization of the United Nations add instability, or should we not encourage stability? I have thought and thought again, but I cannot help coming back to the point that we should encourage stability.

May I just say this final word, because I have, so much respect and so much hope for this Council. Our President Ramaswami Mudaliar once said that he hoped very much that this Council will make itself so useful that perhaps the Security Council will have very little work to do. I think that is what all of us hope. It is by improving the economic and social conditions of the world by this slow, colorless, patient method, we will be able to achieve so much stability in the world that security will be guaranteed and there will be fewer conflicts.

Therefore, with the world as it is today, and having in mind the present conditions and stage of the United Nations, which is so close to our hearts and souls, may I say, this, that even if one organ of the United Nations should happen to suffer a period of suspended animation may this organ continue to carry on the thread of the hope of humanity.

Mr. CHANG (China): I deeply appreciate the attention given to my proposal. The vote on it was very close. However, even if the vote had been in favour of my proposal, I should not have felt very happy about it, because the division was too close and people would surely have thought that I had prevented them from spending time in Geneva. With the decision now made, and with those Members who are in favour of Geneva being made happy, I should like to introduce another amendment: that at the end of paragraph 1, after the words "at Genera," there be added the words "without prejudice to the proposition that regular sessions of the Council should be held at the seat of the United Nations." It will thereby be made clear to the world that the Council's regular sessions should be held at the seat of the United Nations, and that the particular situation involved here is merely an exception.

Dr. CHANG (China): I have very high esteem for my colleague from France, but the fact that he commented on my amendment seems to indicate that there is some necessity for it. But I will not start a long argument; this is too late an hour.

I shall simply state that I will accept the amendment suggested by the representative of the United States.

Dr. CHANG (China): There is no particular objection indeed to the suggested amendment of the representative of the United Kingdom, because in considering the programme of the Council, we do not so much have reference to the Commissions and the Sub-commissions. But even there, there may be some relationship with the specialized agencies. Therefore, I think it is quite proper to include "in co-operation with the Secretary-General and the Co-ordination Commission."

Therefore, I second the amendment.

Dr. CHANG (China): I do not think it is profitable at this moment to prolong the debate, but may I just suggest that the second paragraph does not stop with "to collect and classify." It is really to "to collect and classify for a report with comments and recommendations." The emphasis is on the last part, the comments and recommendations to be included in the report, and the collection and classifying is to serve only as a process. To collect and classify is a very simple Secretariat job, but to report with comments and recommendations, it seems very natural, should belong to responsible Members of this Council.

Furthermore, there have been suggestions concerning the improvement of our meetings, some of them making suggestions on how to streamline and increase the efficiency both of the meetings of the Council and of those of the Commissions. Consequently, it was thought that we might be able to gather together some of these observations and suggestions and bring them forward for discussion by the Council at the next session. Therefore, if there is any doubt concerning the usefulness of the second paragraph, we should read the first two lines together. It is not only "to collect and classify", but "to collect and classify for report with comments and recommendations".

Dr. CHANG (China): We were talking about the terms of reference, but it seems as though you are asking us to vote on the first paragraph with regard to the number of members. If this is so, may I just say a word in favour of eleven members, because Members of the Council have spoken in favour of a smaller number. The Committee discussed this thoroughly and, finally, the number of eleven was arrived at by a majority decision, because it was not considered that the Council should be represented by a small number, and it was thought that eleven members would be able to make readjustments to the programme by representing views of a greater number of delegations. It would facilitate the work of such a small group if more opinions were represented, and eleven members are by no means difficult to call together.

Mr. CHANG (China): What are we voting for?

The PRESIDENT: The amendment of the representative of India, agreed to by the representative of the United Kingdom.

The amendment was adopted by nine votes in favour.

Dr. CHANG (China): I understood that we delayed voting on the first matter because we were waiting for the result of the vote on the terms of reference. Now that the terms of reference are decided, I wonder whether that will change some opinions, because it has more to do with this matter than paragraph 1. Therefore the number of eleven would be much more desired in this case. That is all.

Dr. CHANG (China): May I express, on behalf of the Chinese delegation our whole-hearted gratitude to you Mr. President, and I am in agreement with all the compliments made. I know they are all very sincere. And may I, on the part of the Chinese delegation, add one more quality which you highly deserve in great measure, namely, your good humour.

Furthermore, we also join, especially with the views of the representative of the Soviet Union, in expressing our appreciation for the efficient and most faithful service on the part of the Secretariat and their staff. I have only one complaint against the Secretary-General on this occasion, namely, the representative of Czechoslovakia awhile ago, reminded us, and reminded me especially, that at Hunter College the Secretary-General prepared sandwiches for us, and I should like very much to have sandwiches tonight. But aside from that, I think there are also three or four Members of the Council who deserve special appreciation. I must mention them, especially the very devoted and hardworking Chairman of the Social Committee, the representative of Norway; furthermore the most clear-headed, selfless and most competent Chairman of the Committee on Procedural Questions, Mr. Davidson, as well as others whom I have not had the personal privilege of working with. But I am sure all the Chairmen who have done their work deserve our hearty gratitude.

【全文译文】

张博士(中国):主席是否裁定我们逐段讨论这项内容,并逐段表决。如果是,我想就第一段发言。

主席:我更希望它不经任何讨论就获得通过,但是我们有关于第三段的建议,因此处理它的最好办法也许是逐段讨论。

张博士(中国):我完全同意这一点,除了关于第一段和一个简单的词。如果可以修改,我将接受整个报告。这一个词是一个非常重要的词;这是一个代表最美丽、最迷人、最有吸引力的事物的词。事实上,我是很害怕它,它可能会是第一阶段的迷恋、第二阶段的分居和第三阶段的离婚。

我提议的修正案仅为了一个词,一个词——“稳定”,即对报告第一段的修正案,删除“7 月 5 日在日内瓦”,并添加“在联合国所在地”。

当然,“稳定”是一个非常简单的词,但在现阶段,它是我们世界上所有人都渴望拥有的。我们到处走动；变化如此之大，以至于我们总是需要一个点来确定我们的位置。有一个中国符号，围绕着北极星的北斗七星。因此，在任何事情上，我认为我们都应该牢记稳定这个词，我说这几句话是为了稳定。

我不反对在议程受到严格限制的情况下，在总部以外举行理事会特别会议，日内瓦将是举行这种会议的最有吸引力的地方之一。所以我的立场应该说得很清楚。如果我们有更多的时间进行讨论，我们可能已经商定在联合国所在地成功湖举行两次常会，并在联合国总部以外的某个地方举行一次讨论限定的兴趣和项目的特别会议。如果是这样的话，日内瓦无疑将是第一优先选项。

但是，在联合国所在地之外举行联合国主要机关之一的常会，在我看来似乎不太符合稳定和鼓励稳定的原则。理事会不应该流动工作。常会应在联合国所在地举行，我希望就这一总的原则达成一致。

可以想象在人员和费用方面会涉及多少。一次常会的人员不仅涉及经济稳定和发展司和社会事务部的人员，还涉及其他部门，因为本理事会所处理的问题和项目很多。因此，据计算，不包括为会议服务的速记工作人员，也不包括常会工作人员，而只包括行政人员和更多负责的工作人员，涉及的人数很多。这一数字尚未明确计算出来，但秘书处一些负责人员告诉我，大约为 40 人。即相当多的行政人员从秘书处转移到另一个地方。

秘书处各部门的相当多的行政人员将不得不搬到另一个地方。

如果我们看一下秘书处拟定的暂定时间表草案，并假设在 4 月份的那个时候，经济及社会理事会将在日内瓦举行一届会议，我们将发现总部工作人员的另一方将有大约两个月完全没有时间。这将意味着，当理事会在日内瓦举行会议时，这个地方将实际上得不到秘书处许多负责人的协助。这是一点。

第二点当然是费用，差旅费，其他费用。我知道已经作出了一些估计。我不想在辩论中提出这个问题，但这个数字被称为这个总数和那个总数。但我认为这一切都取决于我们的观点。如果我们倾向于去那里，那么我们根据一种做事方式来计算费用,并使这个数字非常诱人的小。但如果我们反对去那里,我们就把它做得大一些。无论如何,都有额外的费用。

第三,对常驻代表团有着真正根本性的影响。这里有常驻代表团,随时准备为理事会代表和各委员会代表提供服务。然后,随着这样一个从一个地方转移到另一个地方,这意味着整个代表团将实际上不得不去其他地方。

此外,还有一个仅仅是实体文件柜的问题。我碰巧有五个钢制箱子,我会不时通过电话到办公室查询。我不知道我要为我自己的代表团带多少钱。我要做特殊的盒子吗?本理事会在每届常会处理三十或四十个项目。你不认为这是一个需要考虑的问题吗?

我不会讲太久。有人可能会说,我们需要去那里,因为欧洲在这一关头特别重要,我同意这种说法。我怀着极大的敬意指出,现代文明起源于欧洲。我对欧洲有最深的敬意。我去过欧洲几十次。人们愿意访问欧洲,我并不感到惊讶。那毫无疑问。

但我们是经济及社会理事会。我们不会吸引太多的注意力。这完全归功于我们。因为我们做的是默默无闻的工作,我们做的是没有色彩的工作。它甚至没有批判性,因为它不是批判性的。它没有危机,正因为如此,我们吸引的注意力更少,我认为我们应该满足于做那些没有色彩的工作。

为了具体处理在欧洲具有政治重要性的工作,为什么不请安全理事会去那里举行一次为期一个月的会议。我认为这样会更有效。此外,秘书处的热忱成员也将参与,因为毕竟他们的部门或多或少都是专业的,而我们这里有各种各样的人,我们必须与他们在一起。

我已经非常简要地讲了。这是一个稳定的问题。我想了又想,想了又想,终于同意了我的法国同事的观点。我想了又想,但我一次又一次地想到,在联合国组织的这个关头或这个阶段,我们是应该增加不稳定,还是不应该鼓励稳定?我想了又想,但我不得不回到我们应该鼓励稳定这一点上来。

请允许我说最后一句话,因为我对本理事会充满敬意和希望。我们主席拉马斯瓦米·穆达利亚尔曾说,他非常希望本理事会将使自己变得非常有用,也许安全理事会将没有多少工作要做。我认为这是我们所有人的希望。正是通过这种缓慢、平淡、耐心的方法改善世界的经济和社会状况,我们才能在世界上实现如此多的稳定,从而确保安全,减少冲突。

因此,在当今世界的情况下,考虑到联合国目前的状况和所处的阶段,它如此贴近我们的心灵,我想说,即使联合国的一个机构碰巧经历了一段时间的停滞不前,也愿这个机构继续延续人类的希望。

张先生(中国):我非常感谢大家对我的建议的关注。投票结果非常接近。然而,即使投票赞成我的建议,我也不会对此感到非常高兴,因为分歧太大,人们肯定会认为我妨碍了他们在日内瓦花费时间。现在作出决定,赞成日内瓦的成员感到高兴,我谨提出另一项修正案:在第一段末尾,在“在日内瓦”之后加上“不妨碍在联合国所在地举行理事会常会的提议”。这将向全世界表明,理事会的常会应该在联合国所在地举行,这里所涉及的特殊情况只是一个例外。

张博士(中国):我非常尊重我的法国同事,但他对我的修正案发表意见这一事实似乎表明,这一修正案有一定的必要性。但我不会展开长篇大论;这已经晚了一个小时。

我只想说,我将接受美国代表提出的修正案。

张博士(中国):事实上,没有人特别反对英国代表提出的修正案,因为在审议理事会的方案时,我们没有过多地提到委员会和小组委员会。但即使如此,也可能与专门机构有某种关系。因此,我认为包含“与秘书长和协调委员会合作”是相当恰当的。

因此,我支持修正案。

张博士(中国):我不认为此时延长辩论是有益的,但我谨建议第二段不要止于“收集和分类”。这实际上是“收集和分类,形成一份附有评论和建议的报告。”重点是最后一部分,即报告中应包含的评论和建议,收集和分类只是一个过程。收集和分类是秘书处一项非常简单的工作,但提出评论和建议的报告似乎很自然,应该属于本理事会负责的成员。

此外,有人建议改进我们的会议,其中一些人就如何精简和提高理事会和各委员会会议的效率提出了建议。因此,有人认为,我们或许能够收集其中一些意见和建议,并将其提交理事会下届会议讨论。因此,如果对第二段的有用性有任何疑问,我们应该一起阅读前两行。它不仅是“收集和分类”,而且是“收集和分类,以便提出评论和建议”。

张博士(中国):我们在讨论职权范围,但你似乎要求我们就关于成员人数的第一段进行表决。如果是这样的话,我只想说一句支持11名成员,因为理事会成员已经发言支持较少的成员人数。委员会对此进行了彻底的讨论,最后,11人的数目是以多数票决定的,因为它认为理事会不应由少数成员代表,而且它认为11名成员将能够通过代表更多代表团的意见对方案进行重新调整。如果能代表更多的意见,这将有助于这样一个小组的工作,召集11名成员绝非难事。

张先生(中国):我们投什么票?

主席:经英国代表同意的印度代表的修正案。

修正案以九票赞成获得通过。

张博士(中国):我的理解是,我们推迟了对第一个问题的表决,因为我们在等待关于职权范围的表决结果。现在职权范围已经决定,我不知道这是否会改变一些意见,因为它与这个问题的关系比第一段更大。因此,在这种情况下,11这个数字会更理想。仅此而已。

张博士(中国):主席先生,请允许我代表中国代表团向你表示衷心的感谢,我同意所有的称赞。我知道他们都很真诚。请允许我,就中国代表团而言,再补充一点你非常值得称赞的品质,那就是你的幽默感。

此外,我们也特别赞同苏联代表的观点,对秘书处及其工作人员的高效和最忠实的服务表示赞赏。在这一场合,我对秘书长只有一条抱怨,即捷克斯洛伐克代表刚才提醒我们,特别是提醒我,秘书长在亨特学院为我们准备了三明治,我今晚非常想吃三明治。但除此之外,我认为还有三四个理事会成员值得特别感谢。我必须提到他们,特别是非常敬业和勤奋的社会委员会主席挪威代表;此外,程序问题委员会最清醒、最无私和最有能力的主席戴维森先生,以及我个人未有幸与之共事的其他人。但我相信,所有完成工作的主席都值得我们衷心感谢。

(2)会议发言内容纪要[①]

【会议纪要】

Mr. CHANG (China) thought that paragraph 1 should be amended to read "seat of the United Nations" instead of "Geneva". He said he was not against holding a special session of the Council with a strictly limited agenda away from headquarters, and as a place, Geneva would have first priority, but in the interests of stability he was against regular sessions of any of the principal organs of the United Nations being held away from headquarters. He drew attention to the expense involved especially in the transfer of Secretariat personnel, particularly executive staff, and the transfer of practically all permanent delegation staffs. He recognized the political importance of Europe at the present time, but thought the Economic and Social Council on the whole dealt with problems which did not attract too much attention, and did not give rise to very striking crises; for political reasons, it would be preferable to hold a series of meetings of the Security Council in Europe, for at the same time, it would require a smaller number of Secretariat personnel to service it.

Decision: *The proposal of the representative of China to hold the second session of the Economic and Social Council in* 1948 *at Lake Success was rejected by seven votes to five with six abstentions.*

Mr. CHANG (China) proposed the addition to paragraph 1 of the words: "without prejudice to the proposition that regular sessions of the Council should be held at the seat of the United Nations".

---

① UN Document: E/SR. 121, pp. 277-278, p. 278, p. 279, p. 280, p. 281.

Mr. CHANG (China) said he would withdraw his amendment in favour of the United States alternative wording.

Mr. CHANG (China) supported that proposal.

Mr. CHANG (China) said that the emphasis in paragraph 2 was on the words: "for a report with comments and recommendations ... for improving and stabilizing the programme ..." rather than on the words " to collect and classify ... observations and suggestions".

Mr. CHANG (China) said that the number of members of the interim committee had been fully discussed in the Committee on Procedural Questions, which had finally decided in favour of eleven as representing the views of a greater number of delegations, which would facilitate the work of the Committee if readjustments to the calendar were needed.

【纪要影像】

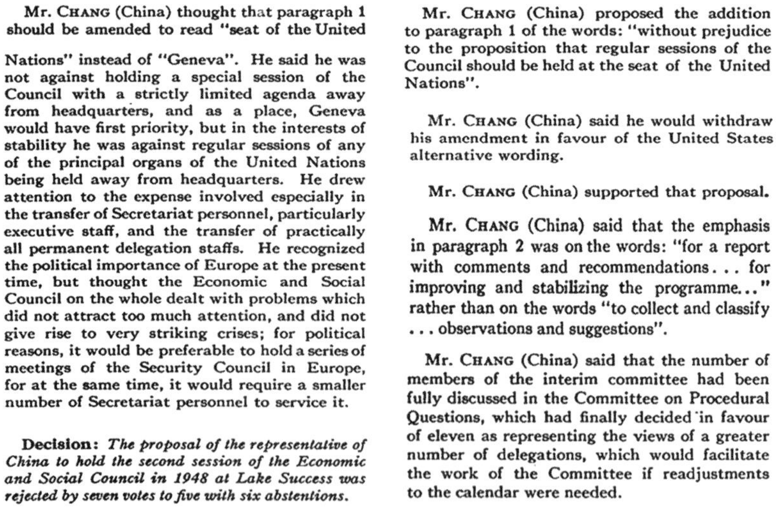

Mr. CHANG (China) thought that paragraph 1 should be amended to read "seat of the United Nations" instead of "Geneva". He said he was not against holding a special session of the Council with a strictly limited agenda away from headquarters, and as a place, Geneva would have first priority, but in the interests of stability he was against regular sessions of any of the principal organs of the United Nations being held away from headquarters. He drew attention to the expense involved especially in the transfer of Secretariat personnel, particularly executive staff, and the transfer of practically all permanent delegation staffs. He recognized the political importance of Europe at the present time, but thought the Economic and Social Council on the whole dealt with problems which did not attract too much attention, and did not give rise to very striking crises; for political reasons, it would be preferable to hold a series of meetings of the Security Council in Europe, for at the same time, it would require a smaller number of Secretariat personnel to service it.

Decision: *The proposal of the representative of China to hold the second session of the Economic and Social Council in 1948 at Lake Success was rejected by seven votes to five with six abstentions.*

Mr. CHANG (China) proposed the addition to paragraph 1 of the words: "without prejudice to the proposition that regular sessions of the Council should be held at the seat of the United Nations".

Mr. CHANG (China) said he would withdraw his amendment in favour of the United States alternative wording.

Mr. CHANG (China) supported that proposal.

Mr. CHANG (China) said that the emphasis in paragraph 2 was on the words: "for a report with comments and recommendations. . . for improving and stabilizing the programme..." rather than on the words "to collect and classify . . . observations and suggestions".

Mr. CHANG (China) said that the number of members of the interim committee had been fully discussed in the Committee on Procedural Questions, which had finally decided in favour of eleven as representing the views of a greater number of delegations, which would facilitate the work of the Committee if readjustments to the calendar were needed.

图片 5.21　张彭春在经社理事会第五届第 121 次会议发言纪要

【纪要译文】

张先生(中国)认为第1款应将“日内瓦”修改为“联合国所在地”。他说,他不反对在总部以外举行议程受到严格限制的理事会特别会议,作为一个地方,日内瓦将是第一优先选项,但为了稳定,他反对在总部以外举行联合国任何主要机构的常会。他提请注意尤其是转运秘书处人员、特别是执行人员以及所有实际常驻代表团工作人员所涉及的费用。他承认欧洲目前的政治重要性,但认为经济及社会理事会总体上处理的问题没有引起太多的注意,也没有引起非常显著的危机;出于政治原因,最好在欧洲举行一系列安全理事会会议,因为与此同时,需要为其提供服务的秘书处人员较少。

决定:中国代表关于1948年在成功湖举行经济及社会理事会第二届会议的提议以7票对5票、6票弃权被否决。

张先生(中国)提议在第1段中增加以下内容:“在不影响理事会常会应在联合国所在地举行这一提议的情况下”。

张先生(中国)说,他将撤回他的修正案,赞成美国的备选措辞。

张先生(中国)支持该建议。

张先生(中国)说,第二段的重点是:“对于一份载有评论和建议的报告……改进和稳定方案……”而不是“收集和分类……意见和建议”。

张先生(中国)说,程序问题委员会已就临时委员会的成员人数进行了充分讨论,最后决定11名成员代表了更多代表团的意见,如果需要调整会议日历,这将有利于委员会的工作。

第六章　联合国经社理事会第六届会议

（纪要）

1948年2月2日至3月11日，联合国经社理事会第六届会议在纽约成功湖召开，本届会议共召开了53次会议，即第122次会议至第174次会议。本届会议主要议题是讨论通过会议日程、讨论联合国海事会议表决权问题、讨论人口委员会的报告、讨论麻醉药品委员会的报告、讨论临时委员会关于拉丁美洲经济委员会建议案、讨论亚洲和远东经济委员会报告、讨论男女同工同酬原则、讨论关于在联合国总部举行经社理事会第七届会议的建议案、讨论与协调有关的事宜、讨论世界经济状况与趋势调查、讨论缅甸与锡兰参加联合国新闻自由会议、讨论经济委员会(第二届会议)报告、讨论理事会非政府组织报告、讨论专门机构的报告、讨论人口委员会(第二届会议)报告等，本届会议将宣言草案和公约草案的审议推迟到下届会议，以便委员会有机会根据各国政府提出的意见审查宣言草案和公约草案。理事会1948年3月2日第116(VI)F号决议“指示人权委员会通过其起草委员会并在其下届会议上特别注意《人权法案》的执行方面”。

图片6.1　联合国经社理事会第六届会议开幕式全景图，圆桌自右向左第四位：张彭春(该图片拍摄于1948年2月2日拍摄于纽约成功湖)。

中国代表张彭春率团参加了本届会议，并在其中的20次会议上发言，包括第122次会议、第123次会议、第124次会议、第125次会议、第128次会议、第130次会议、第133次会议、第134次会议、第135次会议、第140次会议、第141次会议、第144次会议、第145次会议、第148次会议、第151次会议、第153次会议、第154次会议、第155次会议、第165次会议和第171次会议。另外，萧(蘧)先生、吴(德耀)先生和查(修)先生分别参加了本届会议，其中，萧先生在第137次会议①、第139次会议②和第153次会议③上发言，吴先生在第157次会议④、第159次会议⑤、第160次会议⑥、第161次会议⑦、第162次会议⑧和第164次会议⑨上发言，查先生在第174次会议⑩上发言。根据现有的联合国文献检索系统，自本届会议起，之后所有的会议只有会议纪要。现将会议发言内容纪要以“会议纪要”“纪要影像”和“纪要译文”的形式，呈现中国代表张彭春在相关会议上的发言内容。

图片6.2　联合国经济及社会理事会第六届会议开幕前，苏联候补代表阿马萨普·阿鲁蒂乌尼安(Amazasp A. Arutiunian)教授(左)和亚历山大·莫罗佐夫(Alexander p. Morozov)教授(中)分别与中国代表张彭春博士交谈(该图片拍摄于1948年2月2日)。

① UN Document: E/SR. 137, pp. 123-124, p. 126, p. 127.
② UN Document: E/SR. 139, p. 134.
③ UN Document: E/SR. 153, p. 262.
④ UN Document: E/SR. 157, p. 302.
⑤ UN Document: E/SR. 159, p. 318, p. 319.
⑥ UN Document: E/SR. 160, p. 325.
⑦ UN Document: E/SR. 161, pp. 335-336.
⑧ UN Document: E/SR. 162, p. 338, p. 340, p. 344, p. 346.
⑨ UN Document: E/SR. 164, p. 360.
⑩ UN Document: E/SR. 174, p. 492.

1. 张彭春在经社理事会第六届第122次会议上的发言

1948年2月2日上午11时,联合国经社理事会第六届第122次会议,在纽约成功湖举行。本次会议是本届会议的首次会议,主要议题就是本届会议开幕、选举主席和副主席、会议主席讲话等。中国代表张彭春率代表团参加了本次会议,并在会议上发言①,其具体发言内容会议纪要及译文等如下:

【会议纪要】

The PRESIDENT pointed out that there remained only one candidate—namely, Mr. Santa Cruz.

Mr. CHANG (China) congratulated the representatives of Poland and the U.S.S.R. on the noteworthy attitude they had observed, which had made it possible for the officers of the Council to be elected unanimously. He warmly supported the candidature of the Chilean representative.

He asked the representative of Poland to agree to be Second Vice-President. He thought, incidentally, that the question of rank, as between First and Second Vice-President, was not so important; both would assist the President in the discharge of his duties. It was absolutely necessary that there should be a unanimous decision at the very beginning of the Council's work.

① UN Document: E/SR.122, p.4.

【纪要影像】

The PRESIDENT pointed out that there remained only one candidate—namely, Mr. Santa Cruz.

Mr. CHANG (China) congratulated the representatives of Poland and the U.S.S.R. on the noteworthy attitude they had observed, which had made it possible for the officers of the Council to be elected unanimously. He warmly supported the candidature of the Chilean representative.

He asked the representative of Poland to agree to be Second Vice-President. He thought, incidentally, that the question of rank, as between First and Second Vice-President, was not so important; both would assist the President in the discharge of his duties. It was absolutely necessary that there should be a unanimous decision at the very beginning of the Council's work.

图片 6.3 张彭春在经社理事会第六届第 122 次会议发言纪要

【纪要译文】

主席指出,现在只剩下一名候选人,即桑塔·克鲁兹先生。

张先生(中国)祝贺波兰和苏联代表所表现出的值得注意的态度,这使理事会主席团成员得以一致同意当选。他热烈支持智利代表的候选资格。

他请波兰代表同意担任第二副主席。此外,他认为第一副主席和第二副主席之间的级别问题并不那么重要;两者都将协助主席履行职责。绝对有必要在理事会工作一开始就作出一致决定。

2. 张彭春在经社理事会第六届第 123 次会议上的发言

1948 年 2 月 2 日下午 3 时，联合国经社理事会第六届第 123 次会议，在纽约成功湖举行。本次会议主要议题就是讨论和通过会议日程。中国代表张彭春率代表团参加了本次会议，并在会议上发言①，其具体发言内容会议纪要及译文等如下：

【会议纪要】

Mr. CHANG (China) stated that the work of the Council, though often unspectacular and unexciting, was basic for the establishment of economic, social and moral freedoms throughout the world.

He urged adoption of the agenda as a whole, for in his opinion, each and every item merited careful consideration. If all the items could not be disposed of satisfactorily during the current session, they should be referred to the next session, and if necessary, the Council should arrange to have more than two, or even more than three, sessions a year, preferably lasting three or three and a half weeks each. It should take constructive action on matters before it, and should eliminate the all too frequent use of the formula "The Council takes note of ..."

Mr. CHANG (China) and Mr. SARPER (Turkey) felt that there was no basic contradiction between the two methods, for final decision was always

① UN Document: E/SR. 123, p. 14, p. 15.

taken on separate items individually.

【纪要影像】

Mr. CHANG (China) stated that the work of the Council, though often unspectacular and unexciting, was basic for the establishment of economic, social and moral freedoms throughout the world.

He urged adoption of the agenda as a whole, for in his opinion, each and every item merited careful consideration. If all the items could not be disposed of satisfactorily during the current session, they should be referred to the next session, and if necessary, the Council should arrange to have more than two, or even more than three, sessions a year, preferably lasting three or three and a half weeks each. It should take constructive action on matters before it, and should eliminate the all too frequent use of the formula " The Council takes note of . . ."

Mr. CHANG (China) and Mr. SARPER (Turkey) felt that there was no basic contradiction between the two methods, for final decision was always taken on separate items individually.

图片 6.4 张彭春在经社理事会第六届第 123 次会议发言纪要

【纪要译文】

张先生(中国)说,虽然理事会的工作往往不引人注目,也不令人兴奋,但却是在全世界建立经济、社会和道德自由的基础。

他敦促采纳整个议程,因为他认为,每一个项目都值得认真审议。如果在本届会议期间未能令人满意地处理所有项目,则应将其提交下届会议,如有必要,理事会应安排每年举行两届以上,甚至三届以上的会议,最好每次为期三周或三周半。理事会应就其面前的事项采取建设性行动,并应消除过于频繁地使用“理事会注意到……”的说法。

张先生(中国)和莎颇先生(土耳其)认为,这两种方法之间没有根本的矛盾,因为最终决定总是分别就各个项目作出的。

3. 张彭春在经社理事会第六届第124次会议上的发言

1948年2月3日上午11时,联合国经社理事会第六届第124次会议,在纽约成功湖举行。本次会议主要议题是讨论联合国海事会议表决权问题。中国代表张彭春率代表团参加了本次会议,并在会议上发言[①],其具体发言内容会议纪要及译文等如下:

【会议纪要】

Mr. CHANG (China) supported the representative of the United States and recalled the political difficulties that might arise if the principle of full voting rights were adopted.

Non-Member States were given the right to express and develop their views; those views would be recorded and the Conference would be invited to take them into consideration before voting. A formal distinction should, however, at all times be made between Member and non-Member States.

① UN Document: E/SR. 124, p. 21.

【纪要影像】

Mr. CHANG (China) supported the representative of the United States and recalled the political difficulties that might arise if the principle of full voting rights were adopted.

Non-member States were given the right to express and develop their views ; those views would be recorded and the Conference would be invited to take them into consideration before voting. A formal distinction should, however, at all times be made between Member and non-member States.

图片 6.5 张彭春在经社理事会第六届第 124 次会议发言纪要

【纪要译文】

张先生(中国)支持美国代表的意见,并回顾如果采用完全投票权原则可能会产生的政治困难。

非成员国有权表达和展开自己的观点;这些意见将被记录下来,并请会议在表决前加以考虑。然而,在任何时候,都应该正式区分成员国和非成员国。

4. 张彭春在经社理事会第六届第125次会议上的发言

1948年2月3日下午3时,联合国经社理事会第六届第125次会议,在纽约成功湖举行。本次会议主要议题是讨论暂停执行议事规则第35条和第50条的问题。中国代表张彭春率代表团参加了本次会议,并在会议上发言①,其具体发言内容会议纪要及译文等如下:

【会议纪要】

In answer to a question asked by Mr. CHANG (China) concerning the number and importance of similar States, Mr. FELLER (Secretariat) stated that it was customary to include San Marino, Liechtenstein and the Republic of Andorra in the same category as Monaco.

【纪要影像】

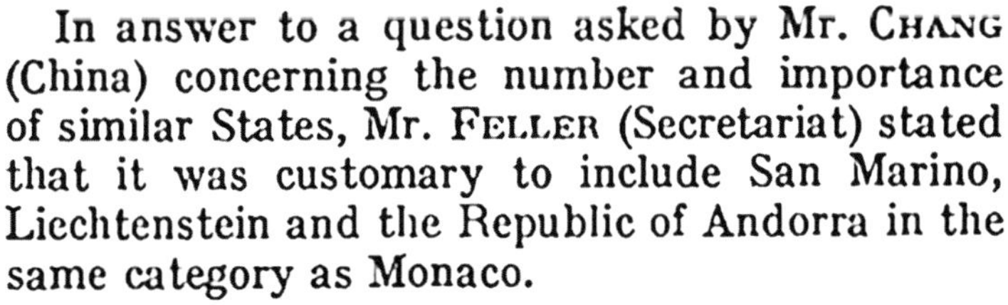
In answer to a question asked by Mr. CHANG (China) concerning the number and importance of similar States, Mr. FELLER (Secretariat) stated that it was customary to include San Marino, Liechtenstein and the Republic of Andorra in the same category as Monaco.

图片6.6 张彭春在经社理事会第六届第125次会议发言纪要

① UN Document: E/SR.125, p.26.

【纪要译文】

费勒先生(秘书处)在回答张先生(中国)提出的关于类似国家的数量和重要性的问题时说,按照惯例,圣马力诺、列支敦士登和安道尔共和国与摩纳哥属于同一类别。

5. 张彭春在经社理事会第六届第128次会议上的发言

1948年2月5日上午11时，联合国经社理事会第六届第128次会议，在纽约成功湖举行。本次会议主要议题是对人权委员会第二届会议的报告进行总辩论。中国代表张彭春率代表团参加了本次会议，并在会议上发言①，其具体发言内容会议纪要及译文等如下：

【会议纪要】

Mr. CHANG (China) congratulated the Commission on Human Rights on its work and thanked the Secretariat for its contribution to that work, emphasizing the great importance given to the formulation of the declaration and covenant by his country.

Mr. CHANG (China) seconded the motion.

The motion was adopted.

Mr. CHANG (China) proposed the adjournment of the meeting. The whole report should then be handed to the Committee, and the Australian resolution could be considered there.

Mr. CHANG (China) withdrew his motion for adjournment, and supported the Canadian proposal.

The Canadian proposal was adopted unanimously.

---

① UN Document: E/SR. 128, p. 47, p. 48, p. 49.

【纪要影像】

Mr. CHANG (China) congratulated the Commission on Human Rights on its work and thanked the Secretariat for its contribution to that work, emphasizing the great importance given to the formulation of the declaration and covenant by his country.

Mr. CHANG (China) seconded the motion.

The motion was adopted.

Mr. CHANG (China) proposed the adjournment of the meeting. The whole report should then be handed to the Committee, and the Australian resolution could be considered there.

Mr. CHANG (China) withdrew his motion for adjournment, and supported the Canadian proposal.

The Canadian proposal was adopted unanimously.

图片 6.7　张彭春在经社理事会第六届第 128 次会议发言纪要

【纪要译文】

张先生(中国)祝贺人权委员会的工作,并感谢秘书处为这项工作所做的贡献,强调了中国高度重视《宣言》和《公约》的拟订。

张先生(中国)附议该动议。

该动议获得通过。

张先生(中国)提议休会。随后,整个报告应提交给委员会,澳大利亚的决议可在那里审议。

张先生(中国)撤回其休会动议,并支持加拿大的提案。

加拿大的提案获得一致通过。

6. 张彭春在经社理事会第六届第 130 次会议上的发言

1948 年 2 月 6 日上午 11 时 15 分，联合国经社理事会第六届第 130 次会议，在纽约成功湖举行。本次会议主要议题是讨论麻醉药品委员会的报告。中国代表张彭春率代表团参加了本次会议，并在会议上发言①，其具体发言内容会议纪要及译文等如下：

【会议纪要】

Mr. CHANG (China) emphasized that the control of narcotic drugs was one of the constructive activities of the United Nations. That activity, carried on through the intermediary of the Economic and Social Council, offered a field for moral agreement, the importance of which should not be underestimated.

The Chinese delegation wished to congratulate the Narcotics Commission on its admirable report. The Commission had not merely supervised the application of the existing conventions; it had also turned its attention to new problems such as that created by the manufacture of synthetic drugs, the effect of which might prove even more harmful than that of hitherto known drugs.

Mr. Chang was glad that the Protocol regarding the transfer to the United Nations of the functions of the League of Nations had come into force, thereby enabling the United Nations to exercise control of drug traffic on a sound legal basis. It was for the governments to take the necessary steps to make their re-

① UN Document: E/SR. 130, p. 60.

spective ratifications effective.

He emphasized that the Permanent Central Opium Board was one of the essential parts of the machinery set up to control narcotic drugs, and for that reason the Chinese delegation attached great importance to the composition of that body.

Lastly, he remarked that the Permanent Central Opium Board had to make sure that Japan could never again act as a centre for the manufacture and distribution of drugs and would thus be prevented from again engaging in the harmful activities of the past directed against the population of neighbouring countries.

【纪要影像】

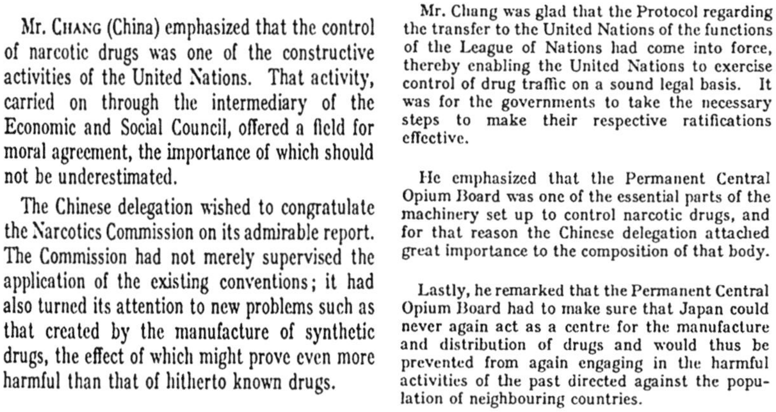

Mr. CHANG (China) emphasized that the control of narcotic drugs was one of the constructive activities of the United Nations. That activity, carried on through the intermediary of the Economic and Social Council, offered a field for moral agreement, the importance of which should not be underestimated.

The Chinese delegation wished to congratulate the Narcotics Commission on its admirable report. The Commission had not merely supervised the application of the existing conventions; it had also turned its attention to new problems such as that created by the manufacture of synthetic drugs, the effect of which might prove even more harmful than that of hitherto known drugs.

Mr. Chang was glad that the Protocol regarding the transfer to the United Nations of the functions of the League of Nations had come into force, thereby enabling the United Nations to exercise control of drug traffic on a sound legal basis. It was for the governments to take the necessary steps to make their respective ratifications effective.

He emphasized that the Permanent Central Opium Board was one of the essential parts of the machinery set up to control narcotic drugs, and for that reason the Chinese delegation attached great importance to the composition of that body.

Lastly, he remarked that the Permanent Central Opium Board had to make sure that Japan could never again act as a centre for the manufacture and distribution of drugs and would thus be prevented from again engaging in the harmful activities of the past directed against the population of neighbouring countries.

图片 6.8　张彭春在经社理事会第六届第 130 次会议发言纪要

【纪要译文】

张先生(中国)强调,麻醉药品管制是联合国的建设性活动之一。这项活动是通过经济及社会理事会的中介机构进行的,为达成道德共识提供了一个领域,其重要性不应低估。

中国代表团祝贺禁毒委员会提交了令人钦佩的报告。委员会不仅监督了现有公约的适用;它还将注意力转向新的问题,例如合成药物的制造所造成的问题,其影响可能比迄今已知的药物更为有害。

张先生感到高兴的是,关于向联合国移交国际联盟职能的议定书已经生效,从而使联合国能够在健全的法律基础上对毒品贩运进行管制。各国政府应采取必要步骤,使其各自的批准生效。

他强调,常设中心鸦片委员会是为管制麻醉药品而设立的机制的重要组成部分之一,因此,中国代表团高度重视该机构的组成。

最后,他说,常设中心鸦片委员会必须确保日本永远不能再充当毒品制造和分销中心,从而防止日本再次从事过去针对邻国人口的有害活动。

7. 张彭春在经社理事会第六届第 133 次会议上的发言

1948 年 2 月 9 日下午 3 时,联合国经社理事会第六届第 133 次会议,在纽约成功湖举行。本次会议主要议题是讨论"特设"委员会关于设立拉丁美洲经济委员会提案的报告。中国代表张彭春率代表团参加了本次会议,并在会议上发言①,其具体发言内容会议纪要及译文等如下:

【会议纪要】

Mr. CHANG (China) said that his Government warmly supported the Latin American countries' efforts to develop their economies. As it had already stated, however, the Chinese delegation was not without doubts as to the virtue of regional commissions.

He agreed with the representatives of New Zealand and Canada that it would be important clearly to define the relationship between functional and regional commissions. In view of the fact that the organization of regional commissions was to be reviewed "not later than 1951", it was essential that the organization of the economic commission for Latin America should not be over-elaborated. It was also essential that the commission should work closely with related agencies.

① UN Document: E/SR. 133, pp. 91-92.

【纪要影像】

Mr. CHANG (China) said that his Government warmly supported the Latin American countries'

efforts to develop their economies. As it had already stated, however, the Chinese delegation was not without doubts as to the virtue of regional commissions.

He agreed with the representatives of New Zealand and Canada that it would be important clearly to define the relationship between functional and regional commissions. In view of the fact that the organization of regional commissions was to be reviewed " not later than 1951 ", it was essential that the organization of the economic commission for Latin America should not be over-elaborated. It was also essential that the commission should work closely with related agencies.

图片 6.9 张彭春在经社理事会第六届第 133 次会议发言纪要

【纪要译文】

张先生(中国)说,中国政府热烈支持拉丁美洲国家发展经济的努力。然而,正如已经指出的那样,中国代表团对区域委员会的优点并非没有疑问。

他同意新西兰和加拿大代表的意见,即明确界定职司委员会和区域委员会之间的关系显然是重要的。鉴于将“不迟于 1951 年”对区域委员会的组织进行审查,至关重要的是,拉丁美洲经济委员会的组织不应过于详细。委员会还必须与有关机构密切合作,这一点也至关重要。

8. 张彭春在经社理事会第六届第134次会议上的发言

1948年2月10日上午10时45分，联合国经社理事会第六届第134次会议，在纽约成功湖举行。本次会议主要议题是讨论亚洲和远东经济委员会的报告。中国代表张彭春率代表团参加了本次会议，并在会议上发言①，其具体发言内容会议纪要及译文等如下：

【会议纪要】

Mr. CHANG (China) gave a brief historical account of the creation of the Economic Commission for Asia and the Far East and expressed his satisfaction at the progress it had made in a period of eight months in dealing with what he knew was an immense and complicated task.

The Commission's work had two aspects: that of organization and that of executive measures properly so-called. The Commission's provisional Bureau had been established in Shanghai, and, while making contact with the specialized agencies and authorities concerned, the Commission had taken the necessary steps to ensure the future functioning of the organization.

The problem of admitting to the Commission countries which were not Members of the United Nations and non-autonomous territories had been settled, and the Council had before it a recommendation approving the admission of New Zealand as a member of the Commission.

① UN Document: E/SR. 134, p. 103.

With regard to executive measures, during its second session, which had taken place at Baguio, the Commission had adopted more than ten resolutions dealing with such questions as the development of industry and commerce, the production of foodstuffs, flood control etc. Although it might eventually take months or even years to complete the task envisaged in those resolutions, the Commission had, nevertheless, taken some excellent practical steps.

He submitted for consideration by the Council a draft resolution (E/644) dealing with the establishment of a bureau of flood control for Asia and the Far East.

【纪要影像】

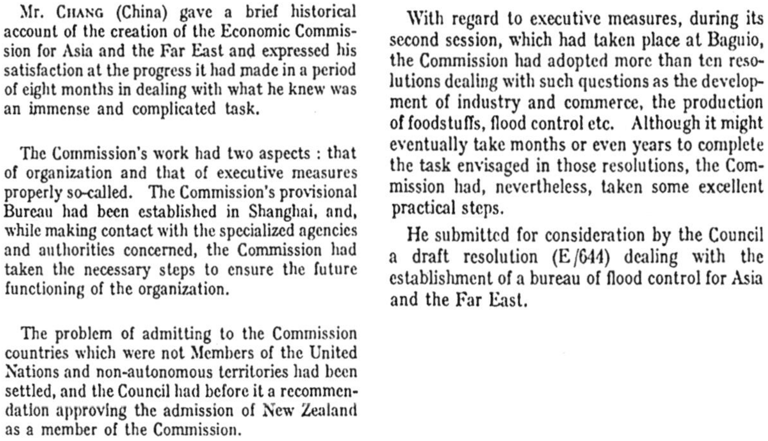

Mr. CHANG (China) gave a brief historical account of the creation of the Economic Commission for Asia and the Far East and expressed his satisfaction at the progress it had made in a period of eight months in dealing with what he knew was an immense and complicated task.

The Commission's work had two aspects : that of organization and that of executive measures properly so-called. The Commission's provisional Bureau had been established in Shanghai, and, while making contact with the specialized agencies and authorities concerned, the Commission had taken the necessary steps to ensure the future functioning of the organization.

The problem of admitting to the Commission countries which were not Members of the United Nations and non-autonomous territories had been settled, and the Council had before it a recommendation approving the admission of New Zealand as a member of the Commission.

With regard to executive measures, during its second session, which had taken place at Baguio, the Commission had adopted more than ten resolutions dealing with such questions as the development of industry and commerce, the production of foodstuffs, flood control etc. Although it might eventually take months or even years to complete the task envisaged in those resolutions, the Commission had, nevertheless, taken some excellent practical steps.

He submitted for consideration by the Council a draft resolution (E/644) dealing with the establishment of a bureau of flood control for Asia and the Far East.

图片 6.10　张彭春在经社理事会第六届第 134 次会议发言纪要

【纪要译文】

张先生(中国)简要介绍了成立亚洲和远东经济委员会的历史,并对该委员会在八个月的时间里在处理他所知道的艰巨而复杂的任务方面取得的进展表示满意。

委员会的工作有两个方面:组织方面和所谓的执行措施方面。委员会的临时办事处设在上海,在与各专门机构和有关当局联系的同时,委员会已采取必要步骤,确保本组织今后的运作。

接纳非联合国会员国和非自治领土加入委员会的问题已经解决,理事会面前有一项建议,批准接纳新西兰为委员会成员。

关于执行措施,在碧瑶举行的委员会第二届会议期间,委员会通过了十多项决议,涉及工商业的发展、食品生产、防洪等问题,虽然最终可能需要几个月甚至几年才能完成这些决议中设想的任务,但委员会已经采取了一些出色的实际步骤。

他提交了一项关于设立亚洲和远东防洪局的决议草案(E/644)供理事会审议。

9. 张彭春在经社理事会第六届第135次会议上的发言

1948年2月10日下午2时30分,联合国经社理事会第六届第135次会议,在纽约成功湖举行。本次会议主要议题是讨论亚洲和远东经济委员会的报告。中国代表张彭春率代表团参加了本次会议,并在会议上发言①,其具体发言内容会议纪要及译文等如下:

【会议纪要】

Mr. CHANG (China) expressed his appreciation of the interest that the Commission's report had aroused and the general support the Council had given to his resolution.

In reply to the statement by the U. S. S. R. representative that the question of the admission of the colonies to associate membership of the Commission had been circumvented, he said that the Chinese delegation had had no such intention, but had merely referred in its resolution (E/644) to the recommendations contained in the Commission's resolutions on the admission of New Zealand to membership of the Commission and on the establishment of a bureau of flood control (E/606, annexes, part I, pages 10 and 17).

He agreed to substitute the words "takes note of" for "notes with approval" in the third paragraph of his resolution, in compliance with the request by the U. S. S. R. representative (134th meeting).

---

① UN Document: E/SR. 135, p. 108.

He also agreed to add the words "seventh session of the" before the word "Council" at the end of the resolution.

In regard to the proposal of the Netherlands representative, he agreed with the representative of the United States that the Secretariat should be asked to study the question of the time limit imposed.

【纪要影像】

Mr. CHANG (China) expressed his appreciation of the interest that the Commission's report had aroused and the general support the Council had given to his resolution.

In reply to the statement by the U.S.S.R. representative that the question of the admission of the colonies to associate membership of the Commission had been circumvented, he said that the Chinese delegation had had no such intention, but had merely referred in its resolution (E/644) to the recommendations contained in the Commission's resolutions on the admission of New Zealand to membership of the Commission and on the establishment of a bureau of flood control (E/606, annexes, part I, pages 10 and 17).

He agreed to substitute the words "takes note of" for "notes with approval" in the third paragraph of his resolution, in compliance with the request by the U.S.S.R. representative (134th meeting).

He also agreed to add the words "seventh session of the" before the word "Council" at the end of the resolution.

In regard to the proposal of the Netherlands representative, he agreed with the representative of the United States that the Secretariat should be asked to study the question of the time limit imposed.

图片 6.11　张彭春在经社理事会第六届第 135 次会议发言纪要

【纪要译文】

张先生(中国)对委员会的报告引起的关注以及理事会对其决议的普遍支持表示赞赏。

在回答苏联代表关于接纳殖民地为委员会准成员的问题被回避的声明时,他说,中国代表团没有这样的意图,但在其决议(E/644)中仅仅提到了委员会关于接纳新西兰为委员会成员和设立防洪局的决议(E/606,附件,第一部分,第 10 页和第 17 页)中所载的建议。

他同意按照苏联代表的要求(第 134 次会议),将其决议第三段中的"注意并同意"替换为"注意到"。

他还同意在决议末尾的“理事会”一词之前加上“第七届”。

关于荷兰代表的建议,他同意美国代表的意见,即应请秘书处研究所规定的时限问题。

10. 张彭春在经社理事会第六届第140次会议上的发言

1948年2月13日上午10时30分,联合国经社理事会第六届第140次会议,在纽约成功湖举行。本次会议主要议题是讨论种族灭绝问题。中国代表张彭春率代表团参加了本次会议,并在会议上发言①,其具体发言内容会议纪要及译文等如下:

【会议纪要】

Mr. CHANG (China), recalling the tragic history of the Chinese people's long years of oppression under Japanese imperialism, and pointing out that final victory had not been accompanied by any reprisals on the part of the Chinese, drew attention to the fact that, in addition to whole sale massacres—pure and simple acts of genocide—the Japanese Government had made use of narcotics in its attempts to exterminate the Chinese people. He therefore thought that narcotic sought to be clearly mentioned in the draft convention as a means of genocide.

He regretted having to point out the tendency in the Press in recent months to recreate an idyllic picture of Japan and the Japanese people. He did not wish to investigate the purposes of such a manœuvre, but thought it necessary to beware of so dangerous a tendency if all possibility of repetition of the tragic past was to be avoided.

① UN Document: E/SR. 140, p. 145.

The Chinese delegation supported the draft resolutions submitted by the United States (E/662 /Add. 1) and Venezuela (E/663).

【纪要影像】

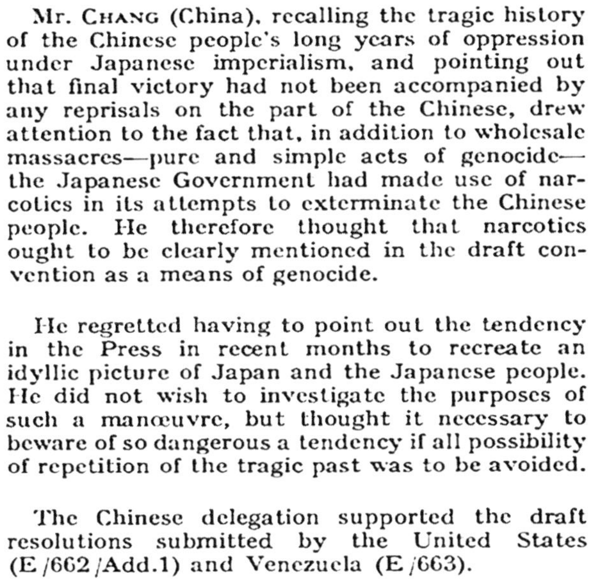
Mr. CHANG (China), recalling the tragic history of the Chinese people's long years of oppression under Japanese imperialism, and pointing out that final victory had not been accompanied by any reprisals on the part of the Chinese, drew attention to the fact that, in addition to wholesale massacres—pure and simple acts of genocide—the Japanese Government had made use of narcotics in its attempts to exterminate the Chinese people. He therefore thought that narcotics ought to be clearly mentioned in the draft convention as a means of genocide.

He regretted having to point out the tendency in the Press in recent months to recreate an idyllic picture of Japan and the Japanese people. He did not wish to investigate the purposes of such a manœuvre, but thought it necessary to beware of so dangerous a tendency if all possibility of repetition of the tragic past was to be avoided.

The Chinese delegation supported the draft resolutions submitted by the United States (E/662/Add.1) and Venezuela (E/663).

图片6.12　张彭春在经社理事会第六届第140次会议发言纪要

【纪要译文】

张先生(中国)回顾了中国人民在日本帝国主义统治下长期遭受压迫的悲惨历史,并指出最后的胜利并没有伴随着中国人的任何报复,他提请注意以下事实:除了纯粹进行种族灭绝的整个屠杀事件外,日本政府还利用麻醉品企图消灭中国人民。因此,他认为,公约草案应当明确提到麻醉品是种族灭绝的一种手段。

他很遗憾不得不指出,近几个月来,媒体倾向于再现日本和日本人民的田园风光。他不想调查这一花招目的,但认为如果要避免过去悲剧重演的一切可能性,就有必要提防这种危险的倾向。

中国代表团支持美国(E/662/Add. 1)和委内瑞拉(E/663)提交的决议草案。

11. 张彭春在经社理事会第六届第141次会议上的发言

1948年2月13日下午3时，联合国经社理事会第六届第141次会议，在纽约成功湖举行。本次会议主要议题是讨论关于在联合国总部举行经社理事会第七届的议案、讨论与协调有关的事宜。中国代表张彭春率代表团参加了本次会议，并在会议上发言①，其具体发言内容会议纪要及译文等如下：

【会议纪要】

Mr. CHANG (China), while agreeing with Mr. Stinebower, wished nevertheless to clarify certain points that had been raised during the discussion.

He suggested that the speech of each representative should be limited to five minutes.

The PRESIDENT and Mr. STINEBOWER (United States of America) agreed.

Mr. CHANG (China) felt that the decision of the General Assembly to hold its third session in Europe was a factor of sufficient weight to warrant reconsideration of the Council's previous decision, a view that had prompted the United Kingdom representative, wisely and with complete justification, to submit his draft resolution, which had China's full support.

The Council's prestige would suffer through the frequent displacement of

① UN Document: E/SR.141, p.152, p.153, p.154, p.155.

its meetings, and a high standard of efficiency could be maintained only through the presence of permanent representatives in one place, where they could benefit, in their own thorough preparations, by the existence of permanent facilities and the work of a permanent secretariat.

Mr. CHANG (China) suggested that the Polish proposal to postpone the seventh session of the Council for three weeks should be referred to the Interim Committee on Programme of Meetings.

Mr. CHANG (China) concurred with that view, emphasizing that only the time and not the place of the session would be under discussion.

Mr. CHANG (China) supported Mr. Stinebower's proposal.

【纪要影像】

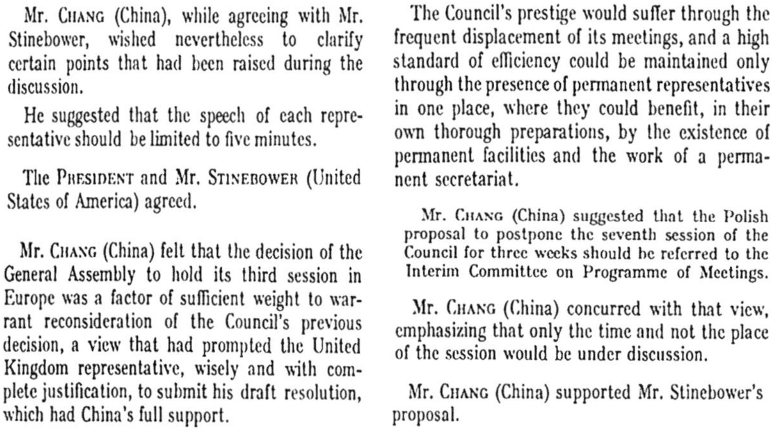

Mr. CHANG (China), while agreeing with Mr. Stinebower, wished nevertheless to clarify certain points that had been raised during the discussion.

He suggested that the speech of each representative should be limited to five minutes.

The PRESIDENT and Mr. STINEBOWER (United States of America) agreed.

Mr. CHANG (China) felt that the decision of the General Assembly to hold its third session in Europe was a factor of sufficient weight to warrant reconsideration of the Council's previous decision, a view that had prompted the United Kingdom representative, wisely and with complete justification, to submit his draft resolution, which had China's full support.

The Council's prestige would suffer through the frequent displacement of its meetings, and a high standard of efficiency could be maintained only through the presence of permanent representatives in one place, where they could benefit, in their own thorough preparations, by the existence of permanent facilities and the work of a permanent secretariat.

Mr. CHANG (China) suggested that the Polish proposal to postpone the seventh session of the Council for three weeks should be referred to the Interim Committee on Programme of Meetings.

Mr. CHANG (China) concurred with that view, emphasizing that only the time and not the place of the session would be under discussion.

Mr. CHANG (China) supported Mr. Stinebower's proposal.

图片 6.13　张彭春在经社理事会第六届第 141 次会议发言纪要

【纪要译文】

张先生(中国)虽然同意斯坦鲍尔先生的意见,但希望澄清讨论中提出的某些要点。

他建议每位代表的发言应限于五分钟。

主席和斯坦鲍尔先生(美国)表示同意。

张先生(中国)认为,大会关于在欧洲举行第三届会议的决定是一个足够重要的因素,有理由重新审议理事会以前的决定,这一观点促使英国代表明智地、有充分理由地提交了他的决议草案,这得到了中国的全力支持。

理事会的威望将因其会议的频繁撤换而受损,只有通过常驻代表在一个地方的存在才能保持高标准的效率,在那里,他们在自己进行充分的准备中,可以从永久设施的存在和常设秘书处的工作中受益。

张先生(中国)建议,波兰关于将理事会第七届会议推迟三周的建议应提交会议日程临时委员会。

张先生(中国)同意这一观点,强调要讨论的只是会议的时间而不是地点。

张先生(中国)支持斯坦鲍尔先生的建议。

12. 张彭春在经社理事会第六届第 144 次会议上的发言

1948 年 2 月 17 日上午 10 时 30 分,联合国经社理事会第六届第 144 次会议,在纽约成功湖举行。本次会议主要议题是讨论与协调有关的事宜。中国代表张彭春率代表团参加了本次会议,并在会议上发言①,其具体发言内容会议纪要及译文等如下:

【会议纪要】

Mr. CHANG (China) said that the work of the Economic and Social Council required clarification and simplification. Ever since the fourth session of the Council he had observed that, while the danger facing the Security Council was that of conflict, the danger facing the Economic and Social Council was that of confusion.

In dealing with the problem of co-ordination, the Council should bear three points in mind. First of all, it should have a clear vision of its objectives. The mere compilation of statistics, figures, charts and the like could not in itself replace the Council's main function as laid down by the Charter, which was to inspire and unify the activities of the various commissions and specialized agencies in accordance with current needs.

The second point which the Council had to keep in mind was the necessity of properly timing the schedules and programmes of those various organizations,

① UN Document: E/SR. 144, pp. 176-177.

rather than concern itself with duplication.

The third point was the need for specialization and the proper distribution of functions and attributions.

Only if those three points were kept in mind, and only if the Council performed its inspirational and unifying function, could the confusion be avoided.

The two *ad hoc* committees proposed by the United States (E/647) might be better differentiated if one were called "Committee on matters relating to Co-ordination", and the other "*Ad Hoc* Committee of the Council on Co-ordination Problems".

Mr. Chang welcomed the proposal to reconsider the terms of reference of the commissions of the Council, especially those of the functional commissions. The terms of reference of some of the Commissions were inadequate to enable them to do the work assigned to them. The nature of their work was such that they could serve no useful purpose by meeting for two or three weeks only in a year; moreover, it was impossible to secure the services of highly qualified men for so short a period.

In conclusion, Mr. Chang said that the terms of reference of the commissions should not be rigid but should be adaptable to changing circumstances.

【纪要影像】

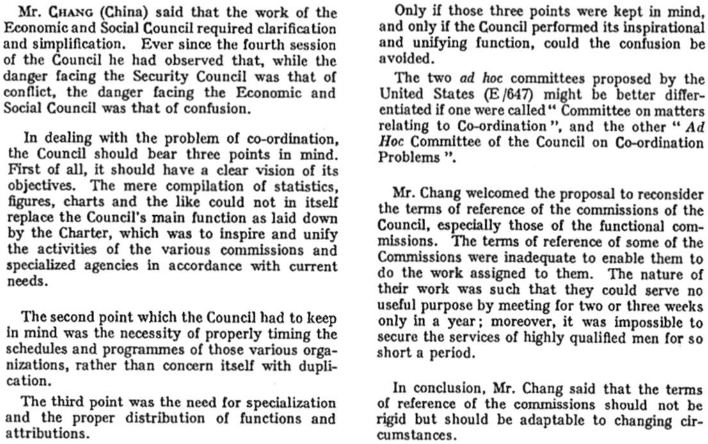
Mr. CHANG (China) said that the work of the Economic and Social Council required clarification and simplification. Ever since the fourth session of the Council he had observed that, while the danger facing the Security Council was that of conflict, the danger facing the Economic and Social Council was that of confusion.

In dealing with the problem of co-ordination, the Council should bear three points in mind. First of all, it should have a clear vision of its objectives. The mere compilation of statistics, figures, charts and the like could not in itself replace the Council's main function as laid down by the Charter, which was to inspire and unify the activities of the various commissions and specialized agencies in accordance with current needs.

The second point which the Council had to keep in mind was the necessity of properly timing the schedules and programmes of those various organizations, rather than concern itself with duplication.

The third point was the need for specialization and the proper distribution of functions and attributions.

Only if those three points were kept in mind, and only if the Council performed its inspirational and unifying function, could the confusion be avoided.

The two *ad hoc* committees proposed by the United States (E/647) might be better differentiated if one were called "Committee on matters relating to Co-ordination", and the other "*Ad Hoc* Committee of the Council on Co-ordination Problems".

Mr. Chang welcomed the proposal to reconsider the terms of reference of the commissions of the Council, especially those of the functional commissions. The terms of reference of some of the Commissions were inadequate to enable them to do the work assigned to them. The nature of their work was such that they could serve no useful purpose by meeting for two or three weeks only in a year; moreover, it was impossible to secure the services of highly qualified men for so short a period.

In conclusion, Mr. Chang said that the terms of reference of the commissions should not be rigid but should be adaptable to changing circumstances.

图片 6.14　张彭春在经社理事会第六届第 144 次会议发言纪要

【纪要译文】

张先生(中国)说,经济及社会理事会的工作需要澄清和简化。自从理事会第四届会议以来,他就注意到,尽管安全理事会面临的危险是冲突,经济及社会理事会面临的危险是混乱。

在处理协调问题时,本理事会应考虑三点。首先,它应该对其目标有一个明确的构想。仅仅汇编统计数据、数字、图表等本身不能取代《宪章》规定的理事会的主要职能,即根据目前的需要激励和统一各委员会和专门机构的活动。

理事会必须铭记的第二点是适当安排这些不同组织的时间表和方案的必要性,而不是单纯对重复的担心。

第三点是需要专门化以及职能和属性的适当分配。

只有牢记这三点,只有理事会履行其鼓舞人心和统一的职能,才能避免混乱。

美国提议的两个特设委员会(E/647)如果一个被称为"协调事项委员会",另一个被称为"理事会协调问题特设委员会",可能会更好地加以区分。

张先生欢迎重新审议理事会各委员会,特别是职司委员会职权范围的建议。一些委员会的职权范围不足以使它们能够完成分配给它们的工作。它们工作的性质决定了它们一年只开两三个星期的会是没有用的;此外,不可能在如此短的时间内获得高素质人员的服务。

最后,张先生说,委员会的职权范围不应僵化,而应适应不断变化的情况。

13. 张彭春在经社理事会第六届第 145 次会议上的发言

1948 年 2 月 17 日下午 3 时 10 分,联合国经社理事会第六届第 145 次会议,在纽约成功湖举行。本次会议主要议题是讨论与协调有关的事宜。中国代表张彭春率代表团参加了本次会议,并在会议上发言①,其具体发言内容会议纪要及译文等如下:

【会议纪要】

Mr. CHANG (China) offered a tentative suggestion that Australia should be added to the committee, on the strict understanding that no further additions should be made.

Mr. CHANG (China) noted that it was the first time that the Council had received so many reports from the specialized agencies. Moreover, the reports had so many aspects that he doubted whether a general debate would do justice to them.

He suggested that the Committee on Matters relating to Co-ordination should decide upon the method of considering the reports. The Council should instruct the committee to deal with the question at the earliest possible moment.

It was so agreed.

① UN Document: E/SR. 145, p. 181, p. 182.

【纪要影像】

Mr. Chang (China) offered a tentative suggestion that Australia should be added to the committee, on the strict understanding that no further additions should be made.

Mr. Chang (China) noted that it was the first time that the Council had received so many reports from the specialized agencies. Moreover, the reports had so many aspects that he doubted whether a general debate would do justice to them.

He suggested that the Committee on Matters relating to Co-ordination should decide upon the method of considering the reports. The Council should instruct the committee to deal with the question at the earliest possible moment.

It was so agreed.

图片 6.15 张彭春在经社理事会第六届第 145 次会议发言纪要

【纪要译文】

张先生(中国)提出应将澳大利亚加入委员会的一项初步建议,但有一项严格的谅解,即不应再增加。

张先生(中国)注意到,这是理事会第一次从专门机构收到如此多的报告。此外,这些报告有许多方面,他怀疑一般性辩论是否会公正对待它们。

他建议协调事项委员会决定审议这些报告的方法。理事会应指示委员会尽早处理这一问题。

就这样达成了同意。

14. 张彭春在经社理事会第六届第148次会议上的发言

1948年2月19日上午10时40分,联合国经社理事会第六届第148次会议,在纽约成功湖举行。本次会议主要议题是讨论世界经济状况及趋势调查。中国代表张彭春率代表团参加了本次会议,并在会议上发言①,其具体发言内容会议纪要及译文等如下:

【会议纪要】

Mr. CHANG (China) considered the report commendable as a whole. The general arrangement was clear; the analysis of facts, valuable; the presentation of problems, suggestive; the warning of imminent dangers, thoughtful.

Certain matters had however been omitted which might have made the description of the economic situation more complete. War had brought about certain economic changes such as the nationalization of banks, land reform, redistribution of income of which something more than passing reference might have been made in the report. An adequate background of such changes would be helpful in understanding world economic conditions.

Mr. Chang pointed out the varying importance that the Economic Report assigned to various countries and territories. The economic problems of industrial countries, for example, received chief attention; yet under-industrialized countries were important too in a discussion of world economic conditions, and

① UN Document: E/SR. 148, pp. 218-219.

should not be passed over. At least 65 per cent of the world's population was contained in such areas. At the second session of the Council, in 1946, he had called attention, in a statement on the world significance of economically "low-pressure" areas, to the importance of the development of under-industrialized countries[①]. Development of under-industrialized areas would not only allow higher standards of living in the areas but would also give a clue to the solution of the problem of stability and full employment in industrialized countries. Hence it should be given emphasis in the report. Out of a total of 290 pages of the report, only one chapter had been devoted to that subject. In part II, where regional economic conditions were discussed, the report gave 21 pages out of 156 to a description of Asia and the Far East; and the picture it presented was vague and misleading. Page 248 contained only six lines to cover the whole topic of China's development, although ample data about China were available and could easily have been procured for use in the report. As a result of the inadequate consideration given to under-industrialized areas, the account of the world economic situation was ill-balanced. The proportion of space given in the report had not been evenly distributed between description and interpretation.

Mr. Chang was in agreement with the main conclusions of the report, although he could not but agree with the representative of Canada (146th meeting) that the interpretation of facts presented too sharp a contrast of black and white; more grey shades were desirable.

① See *Official Records of the Economic and Social Council*, Second Session, 7th meeting.

【纪要影像】

Mr. CHANG (China) considered the report commendable as a whole. The general arrangement was clear; the analysis of facts, valuable; the presentation of problems, suggestive; the warning of imminent dangers, thoughtful.

Certain matters had however been omitted which might have made the description of the economic situation more complete. War had brought about certain economic changes such as the nationalization of banks, land reform, redistribution of income of which something more than passing reference might have been made in the report. An adequate background of such changes would be helpful in understanding world economic conditions.

Mr. Chang pointed out the varying importance that the *Economic Report* assigned to various countries and territories. The economic problems of industrial countries, for example, received chief attention; yet under-industrialized countries were important too in a discussion of world economic conditions, and should not be passed over. At least 65 per cent of the world's population was contained in such areas. At the second session of the Council, in 1946, he had called attention, in a statement on the world significance of economically "low-pressure" areas, to the importance of the development of under-industrialized countries[1]. Development of under-industrialized areas would not only allow higher standards of living in the areas but would also give a clue to the solution of the problem of stability and full employment in industrialized countries. Hence it should be given emphasis in the report. Out of a total of 290 pages of the report, only one chapter had been devoted to that subject. In part II, where regional economic conditions were discussed, the report gave 21 pages out of 156 to a description of Asia and the Far East; and the picture it presented was vague and misleading. Page 248 contained only six lines to cover the whole topic of China's development, although ample data about China were available and could easily have been procured for use in the report. As a result of the inadequate consideration given to under-industrialized areas, the account of the world economic situation was ill-balanced. The proportion of space given in the report had not been evenly distributed between description and interpretation.

Mr. Chang was in agreement with the main conclusions of the report, although he could not but agree with the representative of Canada (146th meeting) that the interpretation of facts presented too sharp a contrast of black and white; more grey shades were desirable.

[1] See *Official Records of the Economic and Social Council, Second Session*, 7th meeting.

图片 6.16　张彭春在经社理事会第六届第 148 次会议发言纪要

【纪要译文】

张先生(中国)认为整个报告值得赞扬。总体布局明确;对事实的分析有价值;提出问题具有启发性;对迫在眉睫的危险有所警告,考虑周到。

然而,某些事项被忽略了,而这些事项可能使对经济状况的描述更加完整。战争带来了某些经济变化,如银行国有化、土地改革、收入再分配,可能已经超出报告中所提及的范围。了解这些变化的充分背景将有助于了解世界经济状况。

张先生指出,《经济报告》对不同国家和地区的重视程度不同。例如,工业国家的经济问题受到主要关注;然而,欠工业化的国家在讨论世界经济状况时也很重要,不应被忽略。至少 65%的世界人口居住在这些地区。在 1946 年理事会第二届会议上,他在一份关于经济"低压"地区的世界意义的声明中,提请注意欠工业化国家发展的重要性①。欠工业化地区的发

① 见《经济及社会理事会正式记录》,第二届,第 7 次会议。

展不仅可以提高这些地区的生活水平,而且还可以为工业化国家稳定和充分就业问题的解决提供线索。因此,应该在报告中予以强调。在总共 290 页的报告中,只有一章专门讨论这个问题。在讨论区域经济状况的第二部分中,报告从 156 页起用 21 页描述了亚洲和远东地区;它所呈现的画面模糊不清,具有误导性。第 248 页只有六行内容,涵盖了中国发展的整个主题,尽管有大量关于中国的数据可供获取,并且可以很容易地用于报告中。由于对欠工业化地区考虑不足,对世界经济形势的描述是不平衡的。报告中给出的篇幅比例在描述和解释之间分配不均。

张先生同意报告的主要结论,尽管他不得不同意加拿大代表(第 146 次会议)的看法,即对事实的解释呈现出太鲜明的黑白对比;需要更多的灰色阴影。

15. 张彭春在经社理事会第六届第 151 次会议上的发言

1948 年 2 月 24 日下午 3 时，联合国经社理事会第六届第 151 次会议，在纽约成功湖举行。本次会议主要议题是讨论建立一个培训公共管理人员国际中心。中国代表张彭春率代表团参加了本次会议，并在会议上发言①，其具体发言内容会议纪要及译文等如下：

【会议纪要】

Mr Chang (China) supported the Brazilian draft resolution and did not share the doubts expressed by the Canadian representative.

【纪要影像】

Mr. CHANG (China) supported the Brazilian draft resolution and did not share the doubts expressed by the Canadian representative.

图片 6.17　张彭春在经社理事会第六届第 151 次会议发言纪要

【纪要译文】

张先生（中国）支持巴西的决议草案，不同意加拿大代表表示的质疑。

① UN Document：E/SR. 151，p. 252.

16. 张彭春在经社理事会第六届第 153 次会议上的发言

1948 年 2 月 25 日下午 3 时，联合国经社理事会第六届第 153 次会议，在纽约成功湖举行。本次会议主要议题是讨论缅甸和锡兰参加联合国新闻自由会议的事宜。中国代表张彭春率代表团参加了本次会议，并在会议上发言①，其具体发言内容会议纪要及译文等如下：

【会议纪要】

Mr. CHANG (China) thought that the vote should be limited to the question whether the Council wished to consider the participation of Burma and Ceylon in the Conference.

【纪要影像】

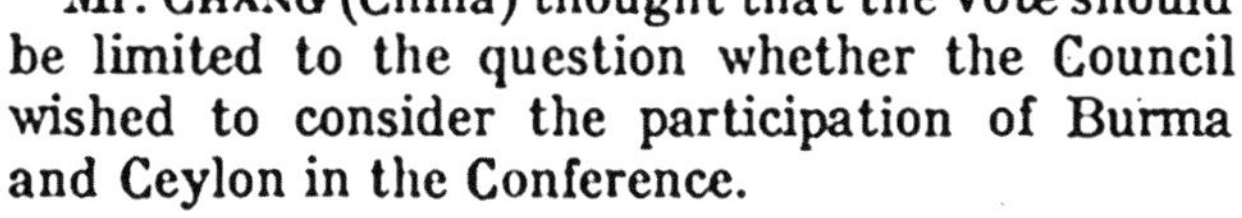
Mr. CHANG (China) thought that the vote should be limited to the question whether the Council wished to consider the participation of Burma and Ceylon in the Conference.

图片 6.18　张彭春在经社理事会第六届第 153 次会议发言纪要

① UN Document: E/SR. 153, p. 269.

【纪要译文】

张先生(中国)认为,投票应限于理事会是否希望考虑缅甸和锡兰在会议中的参与问题。

17. 张彭春在经社理事会第六届第154次会议上的发言

1948年2月26日上午11时20分,联合国经社理事会第六届第154次会议,在纽约成功湖举行。本次会议主要议题是讨论1948年会议日程草案。中国代表张彭春率代表团参加了本次会议,并在会议上发言①,其具体发言内容会议纪要及译文等如下:

【会议纪要】

Mr. CHANG (China) regretted that the note by the Secretary-General (E/700), which had specified the difficulties raised by the holding of the seventh session of the Council at Geneva, had not been published before the vote had been taken on the United Kingdom representative's proposal to hold the seventh session at Lake Success. The decision had been taken, however, and could not be revoked.

Because of the difficulties to which the decision had given rise, especially the necessity for delegations to increase their personnel, he suggested, in order to shorten the sojourn in Europe, that the date of the opening of the seventh session of the Council should be postponed until 26 July, keeping in mind the possibility of convening an eighth session at Lake Success before the end of the year, if the Council considered that to be necessary.

With regard to the number of meetings per day, he thought that more than

① UN Document: E/SR. 154, p. 270, p. 271, pp. 275-276.

three concurrent meetings should not be contemplated.

Mr. CHANG (China) greeted with satisfaction the proposal put forward by the United States representative that the Council should itself draw up and approve at the end of each session the report to be submitted to the General Assembly. This method might be adopted, if not at the current session, at least during the following sessions.

He thanked the French delegation for its attitude towards the proposal that the opening date of the seventh session should be postponed. He pointed out that the Council had taken no formal decision to hold only two sessions in 1948. It should be understood that if an additional session appeared necessary at the end of the seventh session, the Council should not be prevented in advance from taking such a decision.

As regards the number of meetings to be held by the Council and its committees per day, he thought that the practice established at Lake Success might be continued, and the President might be left to decide on the programme of meetings. Without binding itself to hold three concurrent meetings, that is, six meetings a day, the Council should not exclude the possibility of having occasional recourse to that method of working.

He failed to see any difficulties that would prevent the opening of the session being delayed for two weeks; an earlier date might, on the other hand, cause real difficulties for the representatives of permanent delegations.

【纪要影像】

Mr. CHANG (China) regretted that the note by the Secretary-General (E/700), which had specified the difficulties raised by the holding of the seventh session of the Council at Geneva, had not been published before the vote had been taken on the United Kingdom representative's proposal to hold the seventh session at Lake Success. The decision had been taken, however, and could not be revoked.

Because of the difficulties to which the decision had given rise, especially the necessity for delegations to increase their personnel, he suggested, in order to shorten the sojourn in Europe, that the date of the opening of the seventh session of the Council should be postponed until 26 July, keeping in mind the possibility of convening an eighth session at Lake Success before the end of the year, if the Council considered that to be necessary.

With regard to the number of meetings per day, he thought that more than three concurrent meetings should not be contemplated.

Mr. CHANG (China) suggested that a vote should first of all be taken on the question of postponing the opening date of the session. The Secretariat could later on deal with any modifications which might be necessary with regard to the number of meetings to be held each day.

Mr. CHANG (China) greeted with satisfaction the proposal put forward by the United States representative that the Council should itself draw up and approve at the end of each session the report to be submitted to the General Assembly. This method might be adopted, if not at the current session, at least during the following sessions.

He thanked the French delegation for its attitude towards the proposal that the opening date of the seventh session should be postponed. He pointed out that the Council had taken no formal decision to hold only two sessions in 1948. It should be understood that if an additional session appeared necessary at the end of the seventh session, the Council should not be prevented in advance from taking such a decision.

As regards the number of meetings to be held by the Council and its committees per day, he thought that the practice established at Lake Success might be continued, and the President might be left to decide on the programme of meetings. Without binding itself to hold three concurrent meetings, that is, six meetings a day, the Council should not exclude the possibility of having occasional recourse to that method of working.

He failed to see any difficulties that would prevent the opening of the session being delayed for two weeks; an earlier date might, on the other hand, cause real difficulties for the representatives of permanent delegations.

图片 6.19　张彭春在经社理事会第六届第 154 次会议发言纪要

【纪要译文】

张先生(中国)感到遗憾的是,在就英国代表关于在成功湖举行理事会第七届会议的提议进行表决之前,没有公布秘书长的说明(E/700),该说明具体说明了在日内瓦举行理事会第七届会议带来的困难。然而,决定已经作出,不能撤销。

由于该决定引起的困难,特别是各代表团需要增加人员,他建议,为了缩短在欧洲的逗留时间,理事会第七届会议的开幕日期应推迟到 7 月 26 日,同时考虑到如果理事会认为有必要,有可能在年底前在成功湖召开第八届会议。

关于每天的会议次数,他认为不应考虑超过三场的平行会议。

张先生(中国)满意地欢迎美国代表提出的建议,即理事会应在每届会议结束时自行起草并批准提交大会的报告。即使不是在本届会议上,至少在以后的会议上,也可以采用这种方法。

他感谢法国代表团对推迟第七届会议开幕日期的建议所持的态度。他指出,理事会没有正式决定在 1948 年只举行两届会议。应当理解为,如果在第七届会议结束时似乎有必要再举行一届会议,不应事先阻止理事会作出这样的决定。

关于理事会及其各委员会每天举行的会议次数,他认为,在成功湖建立的做法可能会继续下去,会议日程可能由主席决定。理事会不应强迫自己举行三场平行会议,意味着每天六次会议,不排除偶尔采用这种工作方法的可能性。

他未看到有任何困难会阻止会议推迟两周开幕;另一方面,较早的日期可能会给常驻代表团的代表带来实际困难。

18. 张彭春在经社理事会第六届第155次会议上的发言

1948年2月27日上午10时50分，联合国经社理事会第六届第155次会议，在纽约成功湖举行。本次会议主要议题就是讨论1948年会议日程草案。中国代表张彭春率代表团参加了本次会议，并在会议上发言①，具体发言内容会议纪要及译文如下：

【会议纪要】

Mr. CHANG (China) thought that the fewer days spent away from United Nations headquarters, the better. To move away from headquarters not only necessarily caused some inefficiency in the Secretariat but also interfered with the vital task of building up the permanent national delegations. The Chinese delegation believed that the educative value of meetings in Europe would be more than offset by the loss in efficiency to the Secretariat and to the permanent delegations. There was a difference between meetings of a conference and meetings of the Council. A conference might profitably move to other places; the Council should not.

Mr. CHANG (China) replied that it was important that the necessary papers should reach the delegations before the Council's session. What governments needed was the decisions of the Council, and no great time was required to forward them after the session.

① UN Document: E/SR. 155, p. 280, p. 284.

Mr. CHANG (China) agreed that the Council should do its utmost not to prolong its session beyond the time limit of 5 March. Upon that condition only would it be justifiable to postpone the consideration of the items mentioned.

Mr. CHANG pointed out that the Council was working under great strain and he wondered whether two sessions a year were enough to enable the Council to carry out its responsibilities conscientiously.

Mr. CHANG (China) joined with Mr. Mayhew (United Kingdom) in expressing his regret that some items had to be postponed more or less arbitrarily at the last moment. Such postponement had no justification unless the Council decided to terminate its work promptly by 5 March.

He requested the President to inform the Council, by 4 March at the latest, of the date on which the sixth session would come to a close and what further items, if any, had to be dropped.

【纪要影像】

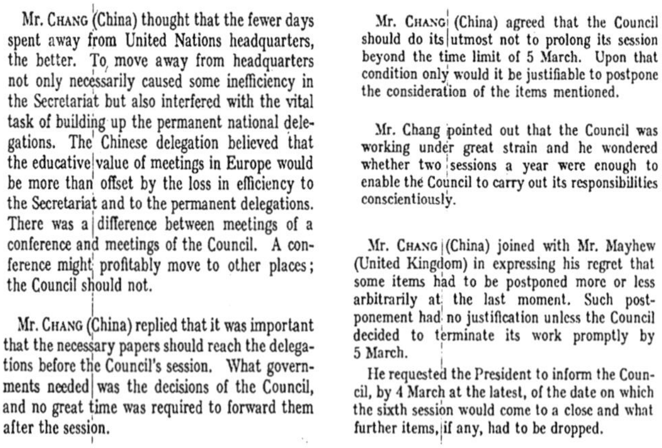

Mr. CHANG (China) thought that the fewer days spent away from United Nations headquarters, the better. To move away from headquarters not only necessarily caused some inefficiency in the Secretariat but also interfered with the vital task of building up the permanent national delegations. The Chinese delegation believed that the educative value of meetings in Europe would be more than offset by the loss in efficiency to the Secretariat and to the permanent delegations. There was a difference between meetings of a conference and meetings of the Council. A conference might profitably move to other places; the Council should not.

Mr. CHANG (China) replied that it was important that the necessary papers should reach the delegations before the Council's session. What governments needed was the decisions of the Council, and no great time was required to forward them after the session.

Mr. CHANG (China) agreed that the Council should do its utmost not to prolong its session beyond the time limit of 5 March. Upon that condition only would it be justifiable to postpone the consideration of the items mentioned.

Mr. Chang pointed out that the Council was working under great strain and he wondered whether two sessions a year were enough to enable the Council to carry out its responsibilities conscientiously.

Mr. CHANG (China) joined with Mr. Mayhew (United Kingdom) in expressing his regret that some items had to be postponed more or less arbitrarily at the last moment. Such postponement had no justification unless the Council decided to terminate its work promptly by 5 March.

He requested the President to inform the Council, by 4 March at the latest, of the date on which the sixth session would come to a close and what further items, if any, had to be dropped.

图片 6.20　张彭春在经社理事会第六届第 155 次会议发言纪要

【纪要译文】

张先生(中国)认为,离开联合国总部的日子越少越好。离开总部不仅必然导致秘书处效率低下,而且干扰了建立常驻国家代表团的重要任务。中国代表团认为,在欧洲举行会议的教育价值将被秘书处和常驻代表团的效率损失所抵消。大会的会议与理事会的会议是有区别的。大会可能会有益地转移到其他地方;理事会不应该这样做。

张先生(中国)回答说,重要的是,在理事会届会之前将必要的文件送达各代表团。各国政府需要的是理事会的决定,在届会结束后提交这些决定不需要太多时间。

张先生(中国)同意,理事会应尽最大努力不将其届会延长到3月5日的时限之后。只有在这一条件下,才有理由推迟对上述项目的审议。

张先生指出,理事会工作压力很大,他想知道一年两届会议是否足以使理事会认真履行其职责。

张先生(中国)与梅休先生(英国)一道对某些项目在最后一刻或多或少被任意推迟表示遗憾。除非理事会决定在3月5日前迅速结束其工作,否则这种推迟是没有理由的。

他请主席最迟在3月4日之前通知理事会第六届会议的闭幕日期,以及还有哪些项目需要舍弃。

19. 张彭春在经社理事会第六届第165次会议上的发言

1948年3月5日下午3时,联合国经社理事会第六届第165次会议,在纽约成功湖举行。本次会议主要议题是讨论专门机构的报告。中国代表张彭春率代表团参加了本次会议,并在会议上发言①,其具体发言内容会议纪要及译文等如下:

【会议纪要】

Mr. CHANG (China) requested that in future, instead of a general discussion, there should be a debate on each of the reports of the specialized agencies. He stressed that there should be a real debate and that general statements were not enough.

【纪要影像】

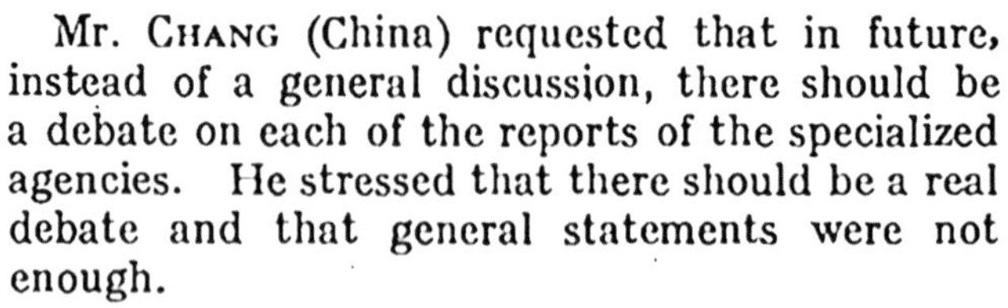
Mr. CHANG (China) requested that in future, instead of a general discussion, there should be a debate on each of the reports of the specialized agencies. He stressed that there should be a real debate and that general statements were not enough.

图片6.21 张彭春在经社理事会第六届第165次会议发言纪要

① UN Document: E/SR. 165, p. 371.

【纪要译文】

张先生(中国)要求今后对专门机构的每一份报告进行辩论,而不是进行一般性讨论。他强调,应该进行真正的辩论,一般性发言是不够的。

20. 张彭春在经社理事会第六届第171次会议上的发言

1948年3月10日上午11时,联合国经社理事会第六届第171次会议,在纽约成功湖举行。本次会议主要议题是讨论协调委员会与协调相关的问题。中国代表张彭春率代表团参加了本次会议,并在会议上发言①,其具体发言内容会议纪要及译文等如下:

【会议纪要】

Mr. CHANG (China) seconded the proposal.

Mr. CHANG (China) added that at its seventh session the Council would have full opportunities of judging the results obtained by the newly established body.

Mr. CHANG (China) seconded the proposal.

Mr. CHANG (China) wanted an explanation of the word "re-establishing" in the addition proposed by the United Kingdom. He asked whether the idea was that the Committee's work would end and then begin again later, and wondered whether it would not be better to speak of "maintaining" rather than re-establishing the committee.

Mr. CHANG (China) said he was satisfied and seconded the United Kingdom proposal.

---

① UN Document: E/SR. 171, p. 439, p. 445, p. 446, p. 447.

【纪要影像】

Mr. CHANG (China) seconded the proposal.

Mr. CHANG (China) added that at its seventh session the Council would have full opportunities of judging the results obtained by the newly established body.

Mr. CHANG (China) seconded the proposal.

Mr. CHANG (China) wanted an explanation of the word "re-establishing" in the addition proposed by the United Kingdom. He asked whether the idea was that the Committee's work would end and then begin again later, and wondered whether it would not be better to speak of "maintaining" rather than re-establishing the committee.

Mr. CHANG (China) said he was satisfied and seconded the United Kingdom proposal.

图片 6.22　张彭春在经社理事会第六届第 171 次会议发言纪要

【纪要译文】

张先生(中国)附议这项提案。

张先生(中国)补充说,理事会第七届会议将有充分的机会对新成立的机构取得的成果进行评判。

张先生(中国)附议这项提案。

张先生(中国)希望对英国提议的补充中的"重建"一词作出解释。他询问这一想法是否是委员会的工作将结束,稍后再开始,他想知道,与其重新设立委员会,说"维持"委员会是否更好。

张先生(中国)说,他对英国的建议感到满意,并表示赞同。

第七章　联合国经社理事会第七届会议

（纪要）

联合国经社理事会第七届会议,于1948年7月19日至1948年8月28日,在日内瓦万国宫举行。本届会议共召开51次会议,即从第175次会议到第225次会议。本届会议主要议题是讨论了亚洲和远东经济委员会的报告、讨论麻醉药品委员会(第三届会议)的报告、讨论欧洲经济委员会的报告、讨论人口委员会和社会委员会(第三届会议)的报告、讨论秘书长和经社理事会关于在成员国学校中开展有关联合国的目的、原则、结构和活动教育的报告、审议国际劳工组织的报告、讨论会议日程安排、讨论拉丁美洲经济委员会的报告等。

中国代表张彭春率团参加了本届会议(中国代表团名单见图片7.1),并在其中的23次会议上发言[1],包括第175次、第176次、第177次、第178次、第179次、第180次、第187次、第188次、第189次、第190次、第191次、第192次、第198次、第199次、第200次、第201次、第202次、第203次、第206次、第209次、第216次、第217次和第221次会议。另外,参加本届会议的还有中国代表团顾问萧蘧教授(Prof. Hsiao[2])和三位代表助理

① UN Document: E/SR. 175-225.

② 萧蘧教授作为本届会议中国代表团顾问参加了会议,并在第224次会议上发言,发言内容见:UN Document: E/SR. 175-225, p. 798.

发言,这三位代表助理是曹保颐先生①、吴德耀先生②和查修先生③。代表团中两位秘书是沈叔勤先生和张树柏先生。现将会议发言内容纪要以“会议纪要”“纪要影像”和“纪要译文”的形式,呈现中国代表张彭春在相关会议上的发言内容。

CHINA

Representative
H.E. Dr. P. C. Chang, Ambassador, Permanent Representative of China to the United Nations

Adviser
Professor C. Hsiao

Assistants
Mr. P. Y. Tsao
Dr. T. Y. Wu
Mr. H. Cha

Secretaries
Mr. S. C. Shen
Mr. S. P. Chang

图片 7.1　联合国经社理事会第七届会议中国代表团成员名单④

① 曹保颐(P. Y. Tsao)先生为本届会议中国代表助理,参加了本届会议,并在第 181 次会议上发言,发言内容见:UN Document: E/SR. 175-225, pp. 80-82, p. 82.

② 吴德耀(T. Y. Wu)先生为本届会议中国代表助理,参加了本届会议,并在第 225 次会议上发言,发言内容见:UN Document: E/SR. 175-225, p. 814, p. 822.

③ 查修(H. Cha)先生为本届会议中国代表助理,参加了本届会议,并在第 210 次会议和第 218 次会议上发言,发言内容见:UN Document: E/SR. 175-225, p. 577; pp. 708-709.

④ UN Document: E/SR. 175-225, p. xiv.

1. 张彭春在经社理事会第七届第175次会议上的发言

1948年7月19日上午11时，联合国经社理事会第七届第175次会议，在日内瓦万国宫举行，本次会议的主要议题是本届会议开幕，并讨论会议日程。中国代表张彭春率团参加了本次会议，并在会议上发言[①]，相关会议纪要、纪要影像及纪要译文如下：

【会议纪要】

Mr. P. C. CHANG (China) seconded the proposal, particularly as it would afford representatives time properly to digest the wise and inspiring speech they had heard from the Chair.

【纪要影像】

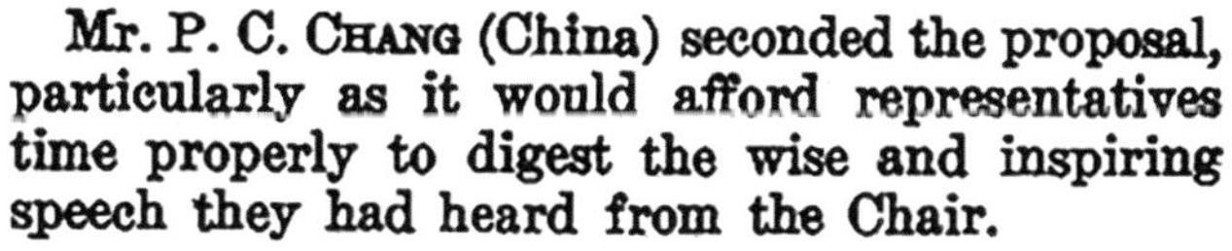

Mr. P. C. CHANG (China) seconded the proposal, particularly as it would afford representatives time properly to digest the wise and inspiring speech they had heard from the Chair.

图片7.2　张彭春在经社理事会第七届第175次会议发言纪要

【纪要译文】

张彭春先生（中国）附议这项建议，特别是因为这将使各位代表有时间适当地消化他们从主席那里听到的明智而富有启发性的发言。

---

① UN Document: E/SR. 175-225, p. 6.

2. 张彭春在经社理事会第七届第176次会议上的发言

1948年7月19日下午3时,联合国经社理事会第七届第176次会议,在日内瓦万国宫举行,本次会议的主要议题是继续讨论会议日程。中国代表张彭春率团参加了本次会议,并在会议上发言①,相关会议纪要、纪要影像及纪要译文如下:

【会议纪要】

Mr. P. C. CHANG (China) supported the proposal made by the Australian representative. Referring to the number of committees to be set up by the Council, he agreed with the suggestion of the New Zealand representative, that a committee of the whole on human rights should be appointed to consider the Final Act of the United Nations Conference on Freedom of Information, the draft Convention on the Crime of Genocide and the Report of the Commission on Human Rights. There would thus be four committees of the whole: Economic, Social, Matters relating to Co-ordination, and Human Rights. A committee on procedure might also be set up, consisting of those members of the Council who were interested in such matters. He felt that the question of the number of committees to be established, should be discussed before the Council considered which items should be referred to individual committees.

Referring to the proposal of the Soviet Union representative that the agenda

① UN Document: E/SR. 175-225, p. 10. (注意:本次会议纪要缺少第8-9页内容。)

should be discussed item by item, he suggested that after the Council had decided on the number of committees to be set up, and which questions should be referred to individual committees, it should discuss the various items listed in the Report of the Agenda Committee and decide which of them were to be postponed or deleted.

【纪要影像】

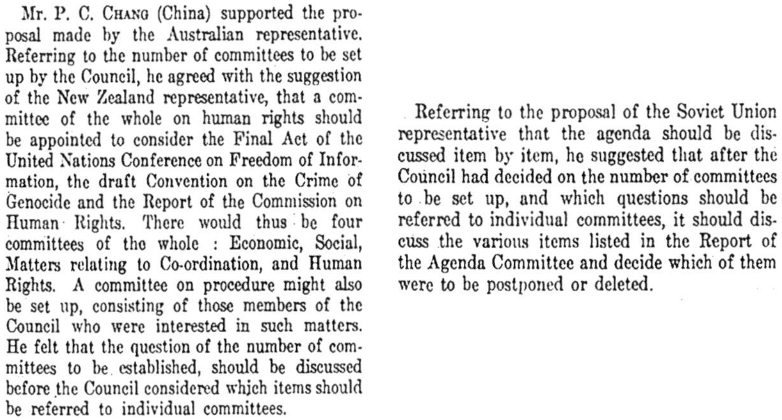

Mr. P. C. CHANG (China) supported the proposal made by the Australian representative. Referring to the number of committees to be set up by the Council, he agreed with the suggestion of the New Zealand representative, that a committee of the whole on human rights should be appointed to consider the Final Act of the United Nations Conference on Freedom of Information, the draft Convention on the Crime of Genocide and the Report of the Commission on Human Rights. There would thus be four committees of the whole : Economic, Social, Matters relating to Co-ordination, and Human Rights. A committee on procedure might also be set up, consisting of those members of the Council who were interested in such matters. He felt that the question of the number of committees to be established, should be discussed before the Council considered which items should be referred to individual committees.

Referring to the proposal of the Soviet Union representative that the agenda should be discussed item by item, he suggested that after the Council had decided on the number of committees to be set up, and which questions should be referred to individual committees, it should discuss the various items listed in the Report of the Agenda Committee and decide which of them were to be postponed or deleted.

图片 7.3　张彭春在经社理事会第七届第 176 次会议发言纪要

【纪要译文】

张彭春先生(中国)支持澳大利亚代表提出的建议。根据理事会拟设立的委员会的数目,他同意新西兰代表的建议,即应任命一个人权问题全体委员会,审议联合国新闻自由会议的最后文件、灭绝种族罪公约草案和人权委员会的报告。因此,将有四个全体委员会:经济委员会、社会委员会、协调事务委员会和人权委员会。还可以设立一个程序委员会,由对这些事项感兴趣的理事会成员组成。他认为,在理事会审议哪些项目应提交各委员会之前,应先讨论拟设立的委员会数目问题。

关于苏联代表提出的议程应逐项讨论的建议,他建议,在理事会决定了要设立的委员会的数量以及哪些问题应提交给各个委员会后,它应讨论议程委员会报告中列出的各个项目,并决定哪些项目应推迟或删除。

3. 张彭春在经社理事会第七届第177次会议上的发言

1948 年 7 月 20 日上午 10 时，联合国经社理事会第七届第 177 次会议，在日内瓦万国宫举行，本次会议的主要议题是继续讨论会议日程。中国代表张彭春率团参加了本次会议，并在会议上发言[①]，相关会议纪要、纪要影像及纪要译文如下：

【会议纪要】

Mr. P. C. CHANG (China) supported the proposal. In the absence of the representative of Peru, such a decision was the only one which could rightly be taken by the Council.

【纪要影像】

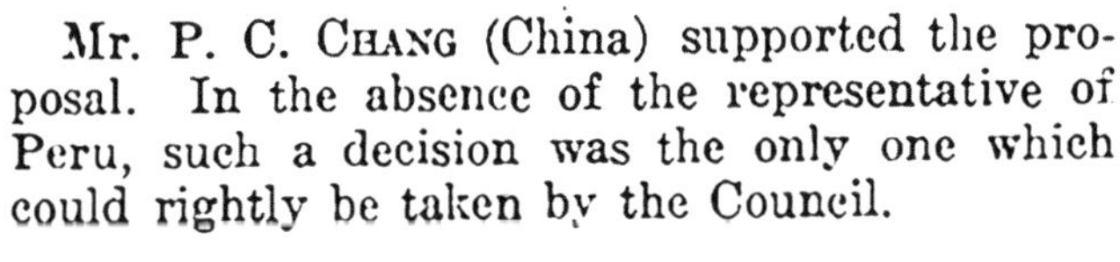
Mr. P. C. CHANG (China) supported the proposal. In the absence of the representative of Peru, such a decision was the only one which could rightly be taken by the Council.

图片 7.4 张彭春在经社理事会第七届第 177 次会议发言纪要

【纪要译文】

张彭春先生（中国）支持该提案。在秘鲁代表缺席的情况下，这样一项决定是理事会能够正确作出的唯一决定。

① UN Document: E/SR. 175-225, p. 29.

4. 张彭春在经社理事会第七届第 178 次会议上的发言

1948 年 7 月 20 日下午 3 时，联合国经社理事会第七届第 178 次会议，在日内瓦万国宫举行，本次会议的主要议题是继续讨论会议日程。中国代表张彭春率团参加了本次会议，并在会议上发言①，相关会议纪要、纪要影像及纪要译文如下：

【会议纪要】

Mr. P. C. CHANG (China) observed that the Council remained seized of the problem by the General Assembly's resolution. Any reaction to it should come after the item had been placed on the agenda.

Mr. P. C. CHANG (China) announced that he also would oppose the French proposal. In the narrower sense of the word, the item was one of the few constructive measures before the Council. It was not in the same category as the question of rules for calling international conferences. There might later be a lengthier report on it, but a more definitive report could not be expected. It was in any case essential to keep world attention constantly focused on the United Nations.

① UN Document: E/SR. 175-225, p. 42, p. 43.（注意：本次会议纪要缺少第 40—41 页内容。）

【纪要影像】

Mr. P. C. Chang (China) observed that the Council remained seized of the problem by the General Assembly's resolution. Any reaction to it should come after the item had been placed on the agenda.

Mr. P. C. Chang (China) announced that he also would oppose the French proposal. In the narrower sense of the word, the item was one of the few constructive measures before the Council. It was not in the same category as the question of rules for calling international conferences. There might later be a lengthier report on it, but a more definitive report could not be expected. It was in any case essential to keep world attention constantly focused on the United Nations.

图片 7.5 张彭春在经社理事会第七届第 178 次会议发言纪要

【纪要译文】

张彭春先生(中国)注意到,理事会仍然抓着大会决议处理这一问题。对该项目的任何反应都应在该项目列入议程之后作出。

张彭春先生(中国)宣布,他也将反对法国的提案。从狭义上讲,该项目是理事会面前为数不多的建设性措施之一。但这与召开国际会议的规则问题不属于同一类别。稍后可能会有一份更长的报告,但不能指望会有一份更明确的报告。无论如何,让世界的注意力持续集中在联合国是至关重要的。

5. 张彭春在经社理事会第七届第 179 次会议上的发言

1948 年 7 月 21 日上午 10 时，联合国经社理事会第七届第 179 次会议，在日内瓦万国宫举行，本次会议的主要议题是新闻发布、继续讨论会议日程和讨论会议工作安排。中国代表张彭春率团参加了本次会议，并在会议上先后多次发言①，相关会议纪要、纪要影像及纪要译文如下：

【会议纪要】

Mr. P. C. CHANG (China) also pointed out that the brief statement he had made in support or the Brazilian representative's proposal had been omitted from the Press release. It was undesirable that Press releases should be drawn up on the basis of length of speeches, rather than of their content.

Mr. P. C. CHANG (China) pointed out that at the previous session it had been agreed to set up a Committee on Matters relating to Co-ordination, but that no decision had been taken as to its composition, although several representatives had urged that it should be a committee of the whole. The Economic Committee, the Social Committee and the Human Rights Committee should also be committees of the whole.

Mr. P. C. CHANG (China) urged that in that case the Economic, Social, and Human Rights Committees, at least, should be committees of the whole, that the other two committees should be composed as the President had

① UN Document: E/SR. 175-225, p. 46, p. 56, p. 56, p. 59.

suggested, and that the President himself should determine, in consultation with other representatives, which members it was particularly desirable to appoint to those committees.

Mr. P. C. CHANG (China) proposed that the Council should vote immediately on the establishment of the proposed committees.

【纪要影像】

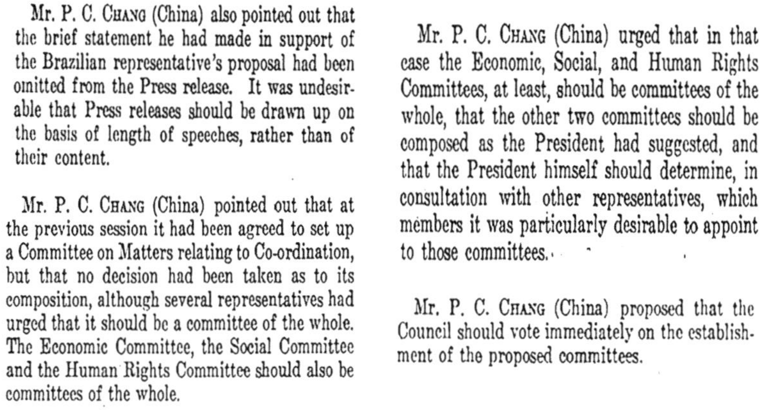
Mr. P. C. Chang (China) also pointed out that the brief statement he had made in support of the Brazilian representative's proposal had been omitted from the Press release. It was undesirable that Press releases should be drawn up on the basis of length of speeches, rather than of their content.

Mr. P. C. Chang (China) pointed out that at the previous session it had been agreed to set up a Committee on Matters relating to Co-ordination, but that no decision had been taken as to its composition, although several representatives had urged that it should be a committee of the whole. The Economic Committee, the Social Committee and the Human Rights Committee should also be committees of the whole.

Mr. P. C. Chang (China) urged that in that case the Economic, Social, and Human Rights Committees, at least, should be committees of the whole, that the other two committees should be composed as the President had suggested, and that the President himself should determine, in consultation with other representatives, which members it was particularly desirable to appoint to those committees.

Mr. P. C. Chang (China) proposed that the Council should vote immediately on the establishment of the proposed committees.

图片 7.6　张彭春在经社理事会第七届第 179 次会议发言纪要

【纪要译文】

张彭春先生(中国)还指出,新闻稿中省略了他为支持巴西代表的提案而作的简短发言。根据发言的长度而不是内容来起草新闻稿,这是不可取的。

张彭春先生(中国)指出,在上届会议上已商定设立一个协调事项委员会,但尚未就其组成作出决定,尽管有几位代表敦促该委员会应是一个全体委员会。经济委员会、社会委员会和人权委员会也应是全体委员会。

张彭春先生(中国)敦促,在这种情况下,经济、社会和人权委员会至少应是全体委员会,其他两个委员会应按照主席的建议组成,主席本人应与其他代表协商,决定哪些成员特别适合任命为这些委员会的成员。

张彭春先生(中国)提议,理事会应立即就设立拟议委员会进行表决。

6. 张彭春在经社理事会第七届第180次会议上的发言

1948年7月21日下午3时,联合国经社理事会第七届第180次会议,在日内瓦万国宫举行,本次会议的主要议题是继续讨论会议工作安排。中国代表张彭春率团参加了本次会议,并在会议上先后多次发言①,相关会议纪要、纪要影像及纪要译文如下:

【会议纪要】

Mr. P. C. CHANG (China) and Mr. WILGRESS (Canada) supported the Venezuelan representative's view.

Mr. P. C. CHANG (China) supported the United States amendment, with the proviso that other interested delegations should be allowed to serve on the committee if they notified the President within twenty-four hours of its establishment.

Mr. P. C. CHANG (China) pointed out that related problems might be considered in different committees, and that it would be preferable that such committees should not meet simultaneously. He would prefer that the Social and the Human Rights Committees, for example, should not meet simultaneously.

Mr. P. C. CHANG (China) said that the procedure advocated in the New Zealand proposal and the Australian and United States amendments was nothing

① UN Document: E/SR. 175-225, p. 61, p. 62, p. 62, p. 65, p. 71, p. 72, p. 73, p. 73.(注意:本次会议纪要缺少第40—41页内容。)

really new. It was important to remember the difference between a conference and the Council. A conference was convened to discuss specific problems, on which plenary discussion might be generally desirable. The Council, on the other hand, was a body in continuous function. Matters came before it that had arisen previously, and in such cases he could see no impropriety in referring them to committees at once.

He suggested, first, that any subject which had not come up before, should be discussed by the Council before reference to a committee, whereas questions that had already been dealt with at previous sessions could be referred directly to committee.

He wished also to support the Soviet Union proposal that the vote should be taken item by item. Though he agreed in principle with the New Zealand proposal and the Australian and United States amendments, there might well be slight differences of opinion over specific items.

He further suggested that, after the vote had been taken, the President should name the committee to which the item in question was to be referred.

The PRESIDENT was in full agreement with the suggestions made by the representative of China.

Mr. P. C. CHANG (China) agreed with the remarks of the United Kingdom representative.

Mr. P. C. CHANG (China) asked whether item 10 could not be considered in plenary together with items 7, 8 and 9.

Mr. P. C. CHANG (China) suggested that the various problems referred to in the reports of the specialized agencies should be simultaneously submitted to the Economic, Social and Co-ordination Committees.

Mr. P. C. CHANG (China) supported the proposal of the United Kingdom representative.

【纪要影像】

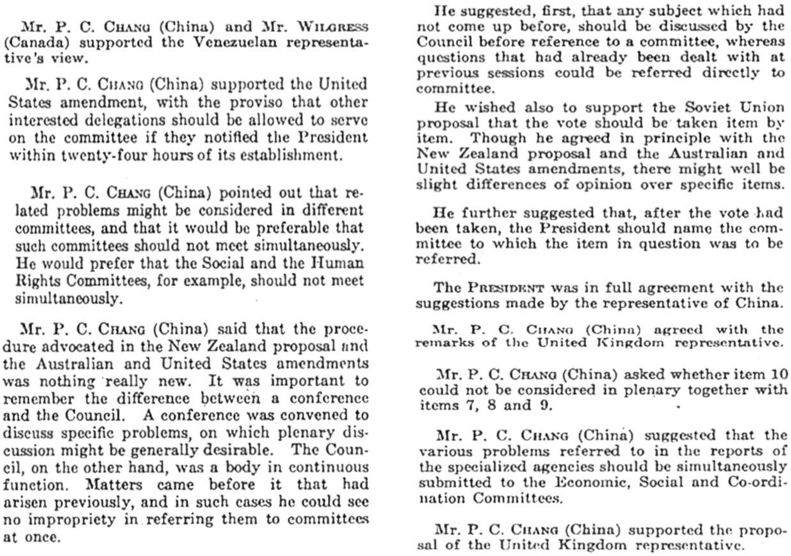
Mr. P. C. CHANG (China) and Mr. WILGRESS (Canada) supported the Venezuelan representative's view.

Mr. P. C. CHANG (China) supported the United States amendment, with the proviso that other interested delegations should be allowed to serve on the committee if they notified the President within twenty-four hours of its establishment.

Mr. P. C. CHANG (China) pointed out that related problems might be considered in different committees, and that it would be preferable that such committees should not meet simultaneously. He would prefer that the Social and the Human Rights Committees, for example, should not meet simultaneously.

Mr. P. C. CHANG (China) said that the procedure advocated in the New Zealand proposal and the Australian and United States amendments was nothing really new. It was important to remember the difference between a conference and the Council. A conference was convened to discuss specific problems, on which plenary discussion might be generally desirable. The Council, on the other hand, was a body in continuous function. Matters came before it that had arisen previously, and in such cases he could see no impropriety in referring them to committees at once.

He suggested, first, that any subject which had not come up before, should be discussed by the Council before reference to a committee, whereas questions that had already been dealt with at previous sessions could be referred directly to committee.

He wished also to support the Soviet Union proposal that the vote should be taken item by item. Though he agreed in principle with the New Zealand proposal and the Australian and United States amendments, there might well be slight differences of opinion over specific items.

He further suggested that, after the vote had been taken, the President should name the committee to which the item in question was to be referred.

The PRESIDENT was in full agreement with the suggestions made by the representative of China.

Mr. P. C. CHANG (China) agreed with the remarks of the United Kingdom representative.

Mr. P. C. CHANG (China) asked whether item 10 could not be considered in plenary together with items 7, 8 and 9.

Mr. P. C. CHANG (China) suggested that the various problems referred to in the reports of the specialized agencies should be simultaneously submitted to the Economic, Social and Co-ordination Committees.

Mr. P. C. CHANG (China) supported the proposal of the United Kingdom representative.

图片 7.7　张彭春在经社理事会第七届第 180 次会议发言纪要

【纪要译文】

张彭春先生(中国)和威尔格雷斯先生(加拿大)支持委内瑞拉代表的观点。

张彭春先生(中国)支持美国的修正案,但附带条件是,如果其他感兴趣的代表团在委员会成立 24 小时内通知主席,则应允许他们在委员会任职。

张彭春先生(中国)指出,相关问题可以在不同的委员会中审议,最好不要同时举行会议。例如,他希望社会委员会和人权委员会不要同时开会。

张彭春先生(中国)说,新西兰提案以及澳大利亚和美国修正案中主张的程序其实并无新意。重要的是要记住会议和理事会之间的区别。召开了一次会议讨论具体问题,一般来说,全体会议讨论这些问题是可取的。另一方面,理事会是一个持续运作的机构。摆在它面前的事情,在先前就已提出在这种情况下,他看不出立即将它们提交委员会有什么不妥。

他建议,首先,任何以前没有提出来的问题都应在提交委员会之前由理事会讨论,而在前几届会议上已经处理过的问题可以直接提交委员会。

他还希望支持苏联的提议,即应该逐项进行表决。尽管他原则上同意新西兰的提案以及澳大利亚和美国的修正案,但在具体项目上可能会有细微的意见分歧。

他还建议,在进行表决后,主席应指定该项目将提交哪个委员会。

主席完全同意中国代表提出的建议。

张彭春先生(中国)同意英国代表的意见。

张彭春先生(中国)问,项目 10 是否不能与项目 7、8 和 9 一起在全体会议上审议。

张彭春先生(中国)建议,各专门机构报告中提到的各种问题应同时提交经济、社会和协调委员会。

张彭春先生(中国)支持英国代表的提案。

7. 张彭春在经社理事会第七届第 187 次会议上的发言

1948 年 7 月 31 日上午 10 时,联合国经社理事会第七届第 187 次会议,在日内瓦万国宫举行,本次会议的议题主要是讨论亚洲和远东经济委员会的报告。中国代表张彭春率团参加了本次会议,并作为亚洲国家唯一一位代表,在会议上发言[①],相关会议纪要、纪要影像及纪要译文如下:

【会议纪要】

Mr. P. C. CHANG (China) suggested that, in order to save the time of the technical experts, those items which were referred to the Economic Committee should be placed before all other questions already on the agenda of that committee.

The PRESIDENT said that he would take up the matter with the Chairman of the Economic Committee.

Mr. P. C. CHANG (China), as the representative of the only Asiatic State that was a member of the Council, thanked members for the interest they had shown in the Report of the Economic Commission for Asia and the Far East. The Chinese delegation appreciated the comments and constructive proposals which had been made in the general debate on that Report by the representative of Canada, and was also grateful for the statements made by the representatives of France, the Netherlands, and the United Kingdom.

---

① UN Document: E/SR. 175-225, pp. 192-193, pp. 193-194, p. 194.

Referring to the remarks of the Soviet Union representative, he agreed that there were great differences between under-industrialized countries in different parts of the world, which were due mainly to natural and social conditioning factors of various types. One of the most interesting factors was handicraft habits and traditions, which varied a great deal in the so-called under-industrialized areas.

He emphasized that all countries wishing to adopt modern technology should first analyse their needs and resources, as well as their past patterns of life and experiences. It might be necessary to bring about changes in social tradition before applying modern technological methods. The peoples of the under-industrialized countries, including China, should be given the chance of doing their own thinking, assessing their own needs, making their own analyses and benefiting from experiences in other parts of the world.

Turning to the estimates, presented by the Secretary-General, of financial implications of the resolutions approved by the Economic Commission for Asia and the Far East (E/839/Add. 1), he said it was imperative that a point in connexion with paragraph 6 of that document, concerning the Bureau of Flood Control, should be cleared up if the Chinese delegation was to continue taking part in the debates. In that paragraph it was stated that "no indication is given, however, as to the items which were excluded from the budget drawn up by the officers of the Chinese Ministry of Water Conservancy in order to arrive at the reduced figure". It was further stated that "in view of the considerable expense involved and the fact that the benefits of the proposed Bureau are likely to fall unequally between either Members of the United Nations as a whole or members of the Commission, the Secretary-General would appreciate the advice of the Council as to how this considerable expenditure should be financed". He asked how the benefits could be equally shared, and how the estimates drawn up by the officers of the Chinese Ministry of Water Conservancy could have anything to do with the document before the Council. He requested that the matter should be elucidated immediately by a responsible member of the Secretariat.

Mr. P. C. CHANG (China), said that the reference to the officers of the Chinese Ministry of Water Conservancy should not appear in the document, as it placed the Chinese delegation in a very embarrassing position.

【纪要影像】

Mr. P. C. CHANG (China) suggested that, in order to save the time of the technical experts, those items which were referred to the Economic Committee should be placed before all other questions already on the agenda of that committee.

The PRESIDENT said that he would take up the matter with the Chairman of the Economic Committee.

Mr. P. C. CHANG (China), as the representative of the only Asiatic State that was a member of the Council, thanked members for the interest they had shown in the Report of the Economic Commission for Asia and the Far East. The Chinese delegation appreciated the comments and constructive proposals which had been made in the general debate on that Report by the representative of Canada, and was also grateful for the statements made by the representatives of France, the Netherlands, and the United Kingdom.

Referring to the remarks of the Soviet Union representative, he agreed that there were great differences between under-industrialized countries in different parts of the world, which were due mainly to natural and social conditioning factors of various types. One of the most interesting factors was handicraft habits and traditions, which varied a great deal in the so-called under-industrialized areas.

He emphasized that all countries wishing to adopt modern technology should first analyse their needs and resources, as well as their past patterns of life and experiences. It might be necessary to bring about changes in social tradition before applying modern technological methods. The peoples of the under-industrialized countries, including China, should be given the chance of doing their own thinking, assessing their own needs, making their own analyses and benefiting from experiences in other parts of the world.

图片 7.8　张彭春在经社理事会第七届第 187 次会议发言纪要(1)

Turning to the estimates, presented by the Secretary-General, of financial implications of the resolutions approved by the Economic Commission for Asia and the Far East (E/839/Add.1), he said it was imperative that a point in connexion with paragraph 6 of that document, concerning the Bureau of Flood Control, should be cleared up if the Chinese delegation was to continue taking part in the debates. In that paragraph it was stated that "no indication is given, however, as to the items which were excluded from the budget drawn up by the officers of the Chinese Ministry of Water Conservancy in order to arrive at the reduced figure". It was further stated that "in view of the considerable expense involved and the fact that the benefits of the proposed Bureau are likely to fall unequally between either Members of the United Nations as a whole or members of the Commission, the Secretary-General would appreciate the advice of the Council as to how this considerable expenditure should be financed". He asked how the benefits could be equally shared, and how the estimates drawn up by the officers of the Chinese Ministry of Water Conservancy could have anything to do with the document before the Council. He requested that the matter should be elucidated immediately by a responsible member of the Secretariat.

Mr. P. C. CHANG (China), said that the reference to the officers of the Chinese Ministry of Water Conservancy should not appear in the document, as it placed the Chinese delegation in a very embarrassing position.

图片 7.9　张彭春在经社理事会第七届第 187 次会议发言纪要(2)

【纪要译文】

张彭春先生（中国）建议，为了节省技术专家的时间，提交经济事务委员会的项目应放在该委员会议程上所有其他问题之前。

主席说他将与经济事务委员会主席讨论此事。

张彭春先生（中国）作为理事会成员中唯一一位亚洲国家的代表，感谢各成员对亚洲和远东经济委员会的报告所表现出的兴趣。中国代表团赞赏加拿大代表在关于该报告的一般性辩论中提出的评论和建设性议案，并感谢法国、荷兰和英国代表的发言。

关于苏联代表的发言，他同意世界不同地区的欠工业化国家之间存在巨大差异，这主要是由于各种自然和社会条件因素造成的。最有趣的因素之一是手工艺习惯和传统，在所谓的欠工业化地区，手工艺习惯和传统差异很大。

他强调，所有希望采用现代技术的国家都应首先分析它们的需求和资源，以及它们过去的生活方式和经验。在应用现代技术方法之前，可能有必要改变社会传统。包括中国在内的欠工业化国家的人民应该有机会进行自己的思考，评估自己的需要，进行自己的分析，并从世界其他地区的经验中获益。

谈到秘书长提出的关于亚洲和远东经济委员会批准的决议所涉经费问题的估计（E/839/Add. 1），他说，与该文件第六段有关的关于防洪局的一点至关重要，如果中国代表团要继续参加辩论，就应该澄清。在该段中指出，“但是，没有说明中国水利部官员为了达到减少的数字而从预算中排除的项目。”有人进一步指出，“鉴于所涉费用巨大，而且拟议防洪局的利益很可能在整个联合国会员国或委员会成员之间不平等，秘书长希望理事会就如何筹措这笔可观的开支提供咨询意见，”他询问如何平等分享利益，以及中国水利部官员拟定的估算与委员会面前的文件有何关系。他要求秘书处的一名负责成员立即澄清此事。

张彭春先生（中国）说，文件中不应出现中国水利部的官员，因为这使中国代表团处于非常尴尬的境地。

8. 张彭春在经社理事会第七届第 188 次会议上的发言

1948 年 8 月 2 日下午 3 时,联合国经社理事会第七届第 188 次会议,在日内瓦万国宫举行,本次会议的议题是继续讨论亚洲和远东经济委员会的报告。中国代表张彭春率团参加了本次会议,并作为亚洲国家唯一一位代表,在会议上先后多次发言[①],相关会议纪要、纪要影像及纪要译文如下:

【会议纪要】

Mr. P. C. CHANG (China) appreciated the co-operative spirit shown by the Secretariat, and asked the Executive Secretary of the Economic Commission for Asia and the Far East to express the thanks of the Chinese delegation to the Assistant Secretary-General in charge of Economic Affairs.

He had further comments to make on the second part of paragraph 6, but with regard to the first part he wished to raise two points concerning the mention of the source of estimates and also to call the Council's attention to a further point of procedure.

He thought it was generally understood at any international conference that if a delegation introduced material supplied by a department or ministry of its government and incorporated it in a document or resolution, from that moment it

① UN Document: E/SR. 175-225, p. 195, p. 196, p. 208, p. 209, pp. 209-210, p. 211.

was a document of the delegation and no longer of the department or ministry.

Again, if a draft resolution was adopted by a definite body it immediately became that body's resolution and no longer the delegation's. He would like the Secretariat to observe that usage. There might of course be exceptions as, for instance, when a document had, by its nature, to be referred to a particular source.

Mr. P. C. CHANG (China), referring to the resolution on the establishment of a Bureau of Flood Control,① adopted by the Commission on 10 June 1948, was glad to note that there was no division of opinion as to the necessity or urgency of establishing the Bureau, but only as to certain constitutional and administrative aspects of the problem. Six Asian and seven non-Asian countries were represented on the Commission, but he was the only representative of an Asian country at that session of the Council. That made his position rather difficult, as he did not know the views of the representatives of the other five Asian countries. As far as he understood, and as far as the record showed, of the seven non-Asian countries represented on the Commission, one had expressed opposition to the proposal, another had indicated some objection to a point in the arrangements, and the other five had not shown any opposition. He expected that his non-Asian colleagues, who had either supported, or, to say the least, had not objected to the proposal, would support the recommendations of the Commission in the Council.

He thought it would be inappropriate to refer the question of flood control to the Economic Committee; the discussion should rather be completed in plenary. It was not possible at that time to deal with all the technical ramifications of flood control. The necessary experts were not present and, from that point of view, the Economic Committee was no better qualified to examine the matter

① *See Supplement No.* 12, *page* 19.

than the Council itself. He suggested that matters on which a Council decision was required should be discussed first, and that there might then be an expression of views by members.

Mr. P. C. CHANG (China) suggested that in view of the Chilean representative's last observation it might be desirable to consider his amendment at the same time as the Soviet Union proposal.

Mr. P. C. CHANG (China) accepted both amendments.

The Chinese draft resolution (*E/*890), *as amended*, *was adopted unanimously*.

Mr. P. C. CHANG (China) remarked that of all countries China should have most to say about Japan since she had suffered most from Japanese aggression. The fact that the Chinese delegation had not made a statement on the matter yet was not because it had nothing to say, but because there were other places where such things should be said. There were two points to be considered. As the Australian representative had said, consideration of the resolution might lead to a legalistic debate. It might also lead to a debate on the question of substance of what to do with Japan. He therefore proposed that the Council should take no action in the matter at the current session. That would be in accordance with the line taken by the Commission itself, which had not expressed a desire for action but merely a pious wish.

Mr. P. C. CHANG (China) wished it to be noted that in proposing to defer consideration of the matter the Chinese delegation had in no way committed itself to the substance of the Commission's resolution.

【纪要影像】

Mr. P. C. Chang (China) appreciated the co-operative spirit shown by the Secretariat, and asked the Executive Secretary of the Economic Commission for Asia and the Far East to express the thanks of the Chinese delegation to the Assistant Secretary-General in charge of Economic Affairs.

He had further comments to make on the second part of paragraph 6, but with regard to the first part he wished to raise two points concerning the mention of the source of estimates and also to call the Council's attention to a further point of procedure.

He thought it was generally understood at any international conference that if a delegation introduced material supplied by a department or ministry of its government and incorporated it in a document or resolution, from that moment it was a document of the delegation and no longer of the department or ministry.

Again, if a draft resolution was adopted by a definite body it immediately became that body's resolution and no longer the delegation's. He would like the Secretariat to observe that usage. There might of course be exceptions as, for instance, when a document had, by its nature, to be referred to a particular source.

Mr. P. C. Chang (China), referring to the resolution on the establishment of a Bureau of Flood Control,[1] adopted by the Commission on 10 June 1948, was glad to note that there was no division of opinion as to the necessity or urgency of establishing the Bureau, but only as to certain constitutional and administrative aspects of the problem. Six Asian and seven non-Asian countries were represented on the Commission, but he was the only representative of an Asian country at that session of the Council. That made his position rather difficult, as he did not know the views of the representatives of the other five Asian countries. As far as he understood, and as far as the record showed, of the seven non-Asian countries represented on the Commission, one had expressed opposition to the proposal, another had indicated some objection to a point in the arrangements, and the other five had not shown, any opposition. He expected that his non-Asian colleagues, who had either supported, or, to say the least, had not objected to the proposal, would support the recommendations of the Commission in the Council.

[1] See Supplement N° 12, page 19.

图片 7.10　张彭春在经社理事会第七届第 188 次会议发言纪要(1)

He thought it would be inappropriate to refer the question of flood control to the Economic Committee; the discussion should rather be completed in plenary. It was not possible at that time to deal with all the technical ramifications of flood control. The necessary experts were not present and, from that point of view, the Economic Committee was no better qualified to examine the matter than the Council itself. He suggested that matters on which a Council decision was required should be discussed first, and that there might then be an expression of views by members.

Mr. P. C. Chang (China) suggested that in view of the Chilean representative's last observation it might be desirable to consider his amendment at the same time as the Soviet Union proposal.

Mr. P. C. Chang (China) accepted both amendments.

The Chinese draft resolution (E/890), as amended, was adopted unanimously.

Mr. P. C. Chang (China) remarked that of all countries China should have most to say about Japan since she had suffered most from Japanese aggression. The fact that the Chinese delegation had not made a statement on the matter yet was not because it had nothing to say, but because there were other places where such things should be said. There were two points to be considered. As the Australian representative had said, consideration of the resolution might lead to a legalistic debate. It might also lead to a debate on the question of substance of what to do with Japan. He therefore proposed that the Council should take no action in the matter at the current session. That would be in accordance with the line taken by the Commission itself, which had not expressed a desire for action but merely a pious wish.

Mr. P. C. Chang (China) wished it to be noted that in proposing to defer consideration of the matter the Chinese delegation had in no way committed itself to the substance of the Commission's resolution.

图片 7.11　张彭春在经社理事会第七届第 188 次会议发言纪要(2)

【纪要译文】

张彭春先生(中国)赞赏秘书处表现出的合作精神,并请亚洲和远东经济委员会执行秘书向主管经济事务助理秘书长表示中国代表团的感谢。

他对第6段第二部分有进一步的评论,但关于第一部分,他希望就提及概算来源提出两点意见,并提请理事会注意另一个更深入的程序问题。

他认为,人们普遍认为,在任何一次国际会议上,如果一个代表团介绍了其政府某个部门或部委提供的材料,并将其纳入一份文件或决议,从那一刻起,它就是该代表团的文件,而不再是该部门或部委的文件。

同样,如果一项决议草案由一个明确的机构通过,它立即成为该机构的决议,而不再是代表团的决议。他希望秘书处遵守这一惯例。当然也可能有例外,例如,当一份文件从本体上涉及某个特定的来源时。

张彭春先生(中国)提到委员会1948年6月10日通过的关于设立防洪局的决议,①他高兴地注意到,对于设立该局的必要性或紧迫性没有意见分歧,只是在这个问题的某些章程和行政方面有分歧。六个亚洲国家和七个非亚洲国家派代表出席了委员会,但他是出席理事会该届会议的唯一一个亚洲国家的代表。这使他的立场相当困难,因为他不知道其他五个亚洲国家代表的意见。据他所知,而且根据记录显示,在委员会有代表的七个非亚洲国家中,一个表示反对这项提议,另一个表示反对安排中的某一点,另外五个没有表示反对。他希望他的非亚洲同事支持或至少不反对该提案,他们将在理事会支持委员会的建议。

他认为把防洪问题提交经济事务委员会是不合适的;讨论应该在全体会议上完成。当时不可能处理洪水控制的所有技术问题。必要的专家不在场,从这个角度来看,经济事务委员会并不比理事会本身更有资格审查这个问题。他建议首先讨论需要理事会作出决定的事项,然后成员们可以发表意见。

张彭春先生(中国)建议,鉴于智利代表的最后一点意见,最好在苏联提议的同时考虑他的修正案。

张彭春先生(中国)接受这两项修正案。

经修正的中国决议草案(E/890)获得一致通过。

---

① 见补编第12号,第19页。

张彭春先生(中国)说,在所有国家中,中国应该对日本有最多的发言权,因为它在日本侵略中受害最深。中国代表团尚未就此事发表声明,并不是因为它无话可说,而是因为还有其他地方应该说这些话。有两点需要考虑。正如澳大利亚代表所说,对该决议的审议可能会导致死抠法律条文的辩论。这也可能导致一场关于如何对待日本的实质性问题的辩论。因此,他建议理事会在本届会议上不对该事项采取任何行动。这将符合委员会本身采取的方针,委员会并没有表示采取行动的意愿,而只是一种虔诚的愿望。

张彭春先生(中国)希望注意,中国代表团在提议推迟审议这一事项时,根本没有对委员会决议的实质内容作出承诺。

9. 张彭春在经社理事会第七届第 189 次会议上的发言

1948 年 8 月 3 日上午 10 时,联合国经社理事会第七届第 189 次会议,在日内瓦万国宫召开,本次会议的议题是讨论麻醉药品委员会第三届会议的报告。张彭春参加了本次会议,并在会议上先后多次发言①,相关会议纪要、纪要影像及纪要译文如下:

【会议纪要】

Mr. P.C. CHANG (China) said that there was a clear summary of the views of the Chinese delegation on the Protocol in the Social Committee's report (E/902). For obvious reasons, the delegation of China was not in favour of the permanent continuation of the colonial system, which, in his opinion, was then in a stage of transition. Consequently, the Government of China was not at all interested in the retention of article 8. However, the moral necessity and urgent need to apply the Protocol universally as soon as possible made it advisable to retain article 8 in the form recommended by the Social Committee.

He inquired whether the adoption of the Protocol would mean that all narcotic drugs with the exception of those listed in article 4 would be controlled. He further inquired whether, apart from the constitutional issues, there was any safeguard against loopholes in the control. Was the moral feeling of the world

① UN Document: E/SR. 175-225, p. 215, p. 216, p. 220, p. 223, pp. 223-224, p. 224.

sufficient to provide such a safeguard?

Mr. P. C. CHANG (China) said that he was naturally interested in the statement, for which he thanked Mr. Steinig. From the humanitarian point of view he wished the control to be universal, and he was glad to hear that there was no territory which could, in practice, remain unaffected by the application of the Protocol. Pointing out that subparagraphs 2 (a) and (b), and in particular (c) and (d), of the draft resolution, as well as the third paragraph of the preamble to the draft Protocol, stressed the need to apply the Protocol as soon as possible, he expressed the hope that such early application would be universal. The most effective instrument for making control really effective was the conscience of mankind, and the Council should mobilize it to that end.

Mr. P. C. CHANG (China) was surprised that the Council could not unanimously adopt draft resolution E. It merely requested "the Secretary-General to initiate studies and inquiries on the desirability of convening a Conference ... for the purpose of reaching an interim commodity agreement limiting the production and exports of opium ..." There were several steps which the Council might take in that field. It might arrange for the immediate drafting of an International Convention on the production and export of opium; he hoped that such a convention would eventually come into force. It might take steps to ensure that an interim commodity agreement was concluded, or merely convene a conference to discuss the possibility of concluding such an agreement. But all that was recommended in the draft resolution was simply that the Secretary General be requested to initiate studies "... on the desirability of convening a conference ... for the purpose of reaching an interim commodity agreement. ..." Such studies could not be discussed by the Commission on Narcotic Drugs until the following spring, which meant that the Council itself would not discuss the desirability of convening a conference for yet another year. The preparation of the studies would involve no extra expenditure and they would be of use in the future, even if the Council decided, a year later, that the proposed conference, which he presumed would not take place until 1950 at the earliest, was inappropriate.

The recommendation in resolution E was the fourth of a series of compromises and had finally been adopted, not by a narrow majority of the Committee, but by 11 votes to 4;① it represented the most restricted line of action contemplated, and to reject it would be no compliment to the Committee's good intentions. Since it normally took from four to eight years to bring an international convention into being, he hoped that the Council would at least request the Secretary-General to initiate studies on the desirability of convening the proposed conference.

Mr. P. C. CHANG (China) suggested that if it were decided to refer the Canadian draft resolution to the Committee on Procedure, that Committee should be asked to examine it as soon as possible in order to reduce to a minimum the period of enforced absence from Headquarters, or from their home countries, of certain members of the Secretariat and of some delegations.

Mr. P. C. CHANG (China) felt that paragraph (2) of the Canadian draft resolution raised a question which the Council might not be prepared to examine at that session. A number of amendments to the terms of reference or rules of procedure of the functional commissions might well be desirable; the President had, however, wisely suggested that all those questions should not be dealt with at the current session. But if the question of revision of the rules of procedure of the Commission on Narcotic Drugs were raised, there was no logical reason why all other related questions should not be raised too. He suggested, therefore, that the Committee on Procedure be instructed to examine the implications of paragraph (2) of the Canadian draft resolution and to report back to the eighth session of the Council. He agreed with the United States representative that

---

① *See document E/AC. 7/SR.* 45, *page* 14.

paragraph (1) could be easily disposed of in plenary.

Mr. P. C. Chang (China) asked what were the views of the Secretariat and the Chairman of the Commission on Narcotic Drugs.

【纪要影像】

Mr. P. C. CHANG (China) said that there was a clear summary of the views of the Chinese delegation on the Protocol in the Social Committee's report (E/902). For obvious reasons, the delegation of China was not in favour of the permanent continuation of the colonial system, which, in his opinion, was then in a stage of transition. Consequently, the Government of China was not at all interested in the retention of article 8. However, the moral necessity and urgent need to apply the Protocol universally as soon as possible made it advisable to retain article 8 in the form recommended by the Social Committee.

He inquired whether the adoption of the Protocol would mean that all narcotic drugs with the exception of those listed in article 4 would be controlled. He further inquired whether, apart from the constitutional issues, there was any safeguard against loopholes in the control. Was the moral feeling of the world sufficient to provide such a safeguard?

Mr. P. C. CHANG (China) said that he was naturally interested in the statement, for which he thanked Mr. Steinig. From the humanitarian point of view he wished the control to be universal, and he was glad to hear that there was no territory which could, in practice, remain unaffected by the application of the Protocol. Pointing out that subparagraphs 2 (*a*) and (*b*), and in particular (*c*) and (*d*), of the draft resolution, as well as the third paragraph of the preamble to the draft Protocol, stressed the need to apply the Protocol as soon as possible, he expressed the hope that such early application would be universal. The most effective instrument for making control really effective was the conscience of mankind, and the Council should mobilize it to that end.

图片 7.12　张彭春在经社理事会第七届第 189 次会议发言纪要(1)

Mr. P. C. CHANG (China) was surprised that the Council could not unanimously adopt draft resolution E. It merely requested "the Secretary-General to initiate studies and inquiries on the desirability of convening a Conference . . . for the purpose of reaching an interim commodity agreement limiting the production and exports of opium..." There were several steps which the Council might take in that field. It might arrange for the immediate drafting of an International Convention on the production and export of opium; he hoped that such a convention would eventually come into force. It might take steps to ensure that an interim commodity agreement was concluded, or merely convene a conference to discuss the possibility of concluding such an agreement. But all that was recommended in the draft resolution was simply that the Secretary General be requested to initiate studies" . . . on the desirability of convening a conference . . . for the purpose of reaching an interim commodity agreement . . .". Such studies could not be discussed by the Commission on Narcotic Drugs until the following spring, which meant that the Council itself would not discuss the desirability of convening a conference for yet another year. The preparation of the studies would involve no extra expenditure and they would be of use in the future, even if the Council decided, a year later, that the proposed conference, which he presumed would not take place until 1950 at the earliest, was inappropriate.

The recommendation in resolution E was the fourth of a series of compromises and had finally been adopted, not by a narrow majority of the Committee, but by 11 votes to 4;[2] it represented the most restricted line of action contemplated, and to reject it would be no compliment to the Committee's good intentions. Since it normally took from four to eight years to bring an international convention into being, he hoped that the Council would at least request the Secretary-General to initiate studies on the desirability of convening the proposed conference.

[2] See document E/AC.7/SR.45, page 14.

图片 7.13　张彭春在经社理事会第七届第 189 次会议发言纪要(2)

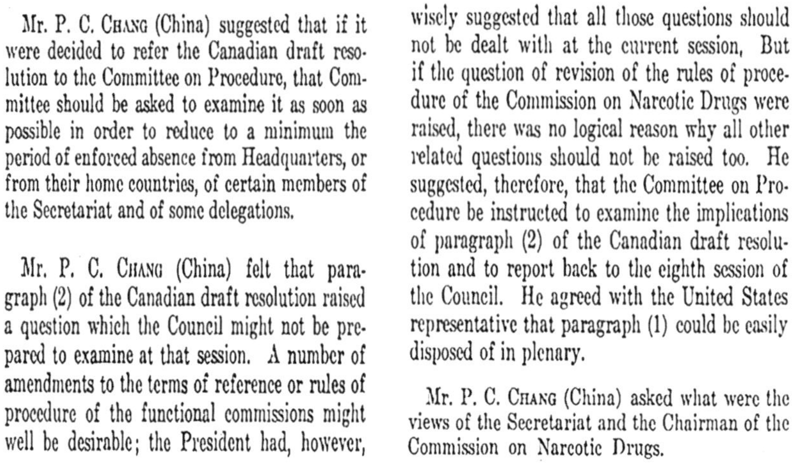

Mr. P. C. Chang (China) suggested that if it were decided to refer the Canadian draft resolution to the Committee on Procedure, that Committee should be asked to examine it as soon as possible in order to reduce to a minimum the period of enforced absence from Headquarters, or from their home countries, of certain members of the Secretariat and of some delegations.

Mr. P. C. Chang (China) felt that paragraph (2) of the Canadian draft resolution raised a question which the Council might not be prepared to examine at that session. A number of amendments to the terms of reference or rules of procedure of the functional commissions might well be desirable; the President had, however, wisely suggested that all those questions should not be dealt with at the current session. But if the question of revision of the rules of procedure of the Commission on Narcotic Drugs were raised, there was no logical reason why all other related questions should not be raised too. He suggested, therefore, that the Committee on Procedure be instructed to examine the implications of paragraph (2) of the Canadian draft resolution and to report back to the eighth session of the Council. He agreed with the United States representative that paragraph (1) could be easily disposed of in plenary.

Mr. P. C. Chang (China) asked what were the views of the Secretariat and the Chairman of the Commission on Narcotic Drugs.

图片 7.14　张彭春在经社理事会第七届第 189 次会议发言纪要(3)

【纪要译文】

张彭春先生(中国)说,社会事务委员会的报告(E/902)中明确概述了中国代表团对议定书的看法。出于显而易见的原因,中国代表团不赞成殖民制度的永久延续,他认为当时殖民制度正处于过渡阶段。因此,中国政府对保留第 8 条毫无兴趣。然而,尽快普遍适用议定书的道德必要性和迫切需要使得以社会事务委员会建议的形式保留第 8 条是可取的。

他询问议定书的通过是否意味着除第 4 条所列麻醉药品外的所有麻醉药品都将受到管制。他进一步询问,除了章程问题外,是否有任何保障措施防止管制漏洞。世界的道德感是否足以提供这样的保障?

张彭春先生(中国)说,他当然对该发言感兴趣,为此他感谢斯特尼格先生。从人道主义的角度来看,他希望控制具有普遍性,他高兴地听到,实际上没有任何领土能够不受议定书适用的影响。他指出,决议草案第 2(a)和(b)分段,特别是(c)和(d)分段,以及议定书草案序言部分第三段,都强调了尽快适用议定书的必要性,并表示希望这种早日适用将具有普遍性。使控制真正有效的最有效工具是人类的良知,理事会应为此目的动员它。

张彭春先生（中国）对理事会未能一致通过决议草案E感到惊讶。它只是要求“秘书长就召开一次会议……以达成一项限制鸦片生产和出口的临时商品协定……的可取性进行研究和调查。”理事会在这方面可以采取若干步骤。它可以安排立即起草一项关于鸦片生产和出口的国际公约；他希望这样一项公约最终能够生效。它可以采取步骤以确保缔结一项临时商品协定，或者仅仅召开一次会议讨论缔结这种协定的可能性。但决议草案中建议的只是请秘书长开始研究“……是否适宜召开一次会议……以达成一项临时商品协定……”麻醉药品委员会要到次年春天才能讨论这类研究，这意味着理事会本身在下一年之前不会讨论召开一次会议的可取性。准备这些研究报告将不涉及额外开支，并且在将来也会有用。即使理事会在一年后决定，他认为拟议会议最早要到1950年才会举行，这是不合适的。

决议草案E中的建议是一系列折衷方案中的第四项，并最终以11票对4票获得通过，而不是以委员会微弱多数获得通过；[①]它代表了所设想的最受限制的行动路线，拒绝它并不是对委员会良好意图的恭维。由于制定一项国际公约通常需要四至八年的时间，他希望理事会至少请秘书长着手研究召开拟议会议的可取性。

张彭春先生（中国）建议，如果决定将加拿大的决议草案提交程序委员会，应要求该委员会尽快审查该决议草案，以便将秘书处某些成员和一些代表团的代表被迫离开总部或祖国的时间减少到最低。

张彭春先生（中国）认为，加拿大决议草案第（2）段提出了一个理事会可能不准备在该届会议上审议的问题。对职司委员会的职权范围或议事规则进行若干修正可能是可取的；然而，主席明智地建议，不应在本届会议上处理所有这些问题。但是，如果有人提出修订麻醉药品委员会议事规则的问题，那么就没有符合逻辑之理由不提出所有其他相关问题。因此，他建议指示程序委员会审查加拿大决议草案第（2）段所涉及的问题，并向理事会第八届会议提出报告。他同意美国代表的意见，即第（1）款可以很容

① 见文件：*E/AC. 7/SR. 45*, *page* 14.

易地在全体会议上处理。

张彭春先生(中国)询问秘书处和麻醉药品委员会主席有何看法。

10. 张彭春在经社理事会第七届第 190 次会议上的发言

1948 年 8 月 4 日上午 10 时，联合国经社理事会第七届第 190 次会议，在日内瓦万国宫召开，本次会议的议题是继续讨论欧洲经济委员会的报告和亚洲和远东经济委员会的报告。张彭春参加了本次会议，并在会议上就亚洲和远东经济委员会的报告发言①，相关会议纪要、纪要影像及纪要译文如下：

【会议纪要】

Mr. P. C. CHANG (China) said that it would be appropriate for a representative of one of the countries in the area under consideration to comment on the discussion at that stage. He quoted the following passage: "A country without its own industries is destined to end up as a colony of countries more industrialized than itself. It is manufacturing industry that gives the tone of progress. To possess natural riches, whether agricultural or mineral, amounts to nothing if a country cannot or does not know how to transform them. Mere wealth of materials without an industrious and intelligent population is rather a danger than an advantage. A people which is not capable of producing its own machinery, motor vehicles, tools and armaments has no right to call itself independent." Some might think that that passage came from a work published in the Union of Soviet Socialist Republics. In fact, it was from a newspaper called *El Mercurio*,

① UN Document: E/SR. 175-225, pp. 244-246, p. 249.

published in Valparaiso, Chile, and had appeared in the issue of 14 May 1942. It showed that the importance of industrialization for the development of under-developed countries was widely realized. He could cite several passages from publications issued in Latin America and the Middle East, regions in which he had had the honour to represent his country, to show that the views expressed in the newspaper he had quoted were general. He did not permit himself to disregard local conditions. It was very important to establish priorities and techniques for development, but that would take time. Further discussion of such matters could not be effective until certain definitions had been established.

He pointed out that the question of rehabilitation and development of the countries of Asia and the Far East had not been neglected before the Economic Commission for Asia and the Far East came into being. Practically all the arguments advanced during the current debate had been discussed by the Working Group for Asia and the Far East (Temporary Sub-commission on Economic Reconstruction of Devastated Areas), of which he had had the honour to be Chairman, and on which had been represented many members of the Commission and of the Council, such as France, the Netherlands, New Zealand, the Union of Soviet Socialist Republics, the United Kingdom, and the United States of America.

The discussions of the Working Group had been very interesting, and at one time it had appeared that agreement could not be reached; but a final agreement had eventually been reached, and should be regarded as the preliminary agreement on the subject under discussion. The relevant passage was recorded in document E/307/Rev. 1,[①] page 63, and read as follows:

> "In order to achieve those 'conditions of stability and well-being' which the United Nations Charter envisages, there is need for a new and much more rapid and comprehensive effort to modernize production meth-

---

① See *Official Records of the Economic and Social Council*, second year, fourth session, Supplement No. 10.

ods throughout Asia and the Far East, with the object of bringing the tools of modern technology within the reach of all the people. This would imply increased industrialization, the fabrication of more of the region's resources within the region for use locally or for trade, and the building up of new and equitable economic relations with the rest of the world. We suggest, in short, that reconstruction in Asia and the Far East must be regarded as the first step in a vast readjustment whereby the people of the region, with such assistance as the United Nations can give, would undertake the systematic application of modern technology, adapted as necessary to local needs, as rapidly as may be feasible, to all departments of their economic life. It is not overlooked that reconstruction efforts can at the outset be most effectively directed towards existing industries and agriculture, upon which the life of the people depends, and upon export industries for which there are established markets."

The principles in the first sentence were well stated, using, in part, the words of the Charter, and surely there could be no objection to them. They were clearly what the Council wished to say. Could anyone honestly disagree with the suggestion contained in the passage? He hoped that it would be studied by all members of the Secretariat of the Economic Commission for Asia and the Far East, and by the members of its working parties in their task of forwarding the aims for which the Commission had been established.

Mr. P. C. CHANG (China) thought it would be difficult for the representative of Chile to withdraw from the Drafting Committee, as it was his delegation that had put forward one of the two draft resolutions which had been referred to that committee. Although he himself would like to withdraw, he felt that as the only representative present of a country which formed such a large part of the area under discussion he, in turn, might also find it rather difficult to do so.

【纪要影像】

Mr. P. C. Chang (China) said that it would be appropriate for a representative of one of the countries in the area under consideration to comment on the discussion at that stage. He quoted the following passage: "A country without its own industries is destined to end up as a colony of countries more industrialized than itself. It is manufacturing industry that gives the tone of progress. To possess natural riches, whether agricultural or mineral, amounts to nothing if a country cannot or does not know how to transform them. Mere wealth of materials without an industrious and intelligent population is rather a danger than an advantage. A people which is not capable of producing its own machinery, motor vehicles, tools and armaments has no right to call itself independent." Some might think that that passage came from a work published in the Union of Soviet Socialist Republics. In fact, it was from a newspaper called *El Mercurio*, published in Valparaiso, Chile, and had appeared in the issue of 14 May 1942. It showed that the importance of industrialization for the development of under-developed countries was widely realized. He could cite several passages from publications issued in Latin America and the Middle East, regions in which he had had the honour to represent his country, to show that the views expressed in the newspaper he had quoted were general. He did not permit himself to disregard local conditions. It was very important to establish priorities and techniques for development, but that would take time. Further discussion of such matters could not be effective until certain definitions had been established.

图片 7.15:张彭春在经社理事会第七届第190次会议发言纪要(1)

He pointed out that the question of rehabilitation and development of the countries of Asia and the Far East had not been neglected before the Economic Commission for Asia and the Far East came into being. Practically all the arguments advanced during the current debate had been discussed by the Working Group for Asia and the Far East (Temporary Sub-Commission on Economic Reconstruction of Devastated Areas), of which he had had the honour to be Chairman, and on which had been represented many members of the Commission and of the Council, such as France, the Netherlands, New Zealand, the Union of Soviet Socialist Republics, the United Kingdom, and the United States of America.

The discussions of the Working Group had been very interesting, and at one time it had appeared that agreement could not be reached; but a final agreement had eventually been reached, and should be regarded as the preliminary agreement on the subject under discussion. The relevant passage was recorded in document E/307/Rev.1,[1] page 63, and read as follows:

"In order to achieve those 'conditions of stability and well-being' which the United Nations Charter envisages, there is need for a new and much more rapid and comprehensive effort to modernize production methods throughout Asia and the Far East, with the object of bringing the tools of modern technology within the reach of all the people. This would imply increased industrialization, the fabrication of more of the region's resources within the region for use locally or for trade, and the building up of new and equitable economic relations with the rest of the world. We suggest, in short, that reconstruction in Asia and the Far East must be regarded as the first step in a vast readjustment whereby the people of the region, with such assistance as the United Nations can give, would undertake the systematic application of modern

1 See *Official Records of the Economic and Social Council*, second year, fourth session, Supplement No. 10.

图片 7.16　张彭春在经社理事会第七届第190次会议发言纪要(2)

technology, adapted as necessary to local needs, as rapidly as may be feasible, to all departments of their economic life. It is not overlooked that reconstruction efforts can at the outset be most effectively directed towards existing industries and agriculture, upon which the life of the people depends, and upon export industries for which there are established markets."

The principles in the first sentence were well stated, using, in part, the words of the Charter, and surely there could be no objection to them. They were clearly what the Council wished to say. Could anyone honestly disagree with the suggestion contained in the passage ? He hoped that it would be studied by all members of the Secretariat of the Economic Commission for Asia and the Far East, and by the members of its working parties in their task of forwarding the aims for which the Commission had been established.

Mr. P. C. Chang (China) thought it would be difficult for the representative of Chile to withdraw from the Drafting Committee, as it was his delegation that had put forward one of the two draft resolutions which had been referred to that committee. Although he himself would like to withdraw, he felt that as the only representative present of a country which formed such a large part of the area under discussion he, in turn, might also find it rather difficult to do so.

图片 7.17　张彭春在经社理事会第七届第 190 次会议发言纪要(3)

【会议译文】

张彭春先生(中国)说,审议所涉地区的一个国家的代表宜对该阶段的讨论发表意见。他引用了以下段落:“一个没有自己工业的国家注定会沦为比她工业化程度更高的国家的殖民地。制造业和工业是进步的基调。如果一个国家不能够或不知道如何改造自然财富,那么拥有自然财富,无论是农业财富还是矿产财富,都毫无意义。只有物质财富而没有勤劳智慧的人民,这与其说是一种优势,不如说是一种危险。一个不能生产自己的机器、汽车、工具和武器的民族,无权自称独立。”有人可能会认为,这段话出自苏维埃社会主义共和国联盟出版的一部著作。事实上,它来自于1942 年 5 月 14 日在智利瓦尔帕莱索出版的一份名为《信使报》的报纸。这表明工业化对欠发达国家发展的重要性已得到广泛认识。他可以引用在拉丁美洲和中东发表的出版物中的几段话,以表明他所引用的报纸上表达的观点是一般性的,在这些地区他有幸代表他的国家。他不允许自己无视当地条件。确定发展的优先事项和技术非常重要,但这需要时间。在明确定义达成之前,对这些事项的进一步讨论不可能有效。

他指出,在亚洲和远东经济委员会成立之前,亚洲和远东国家的复兴和发展问题没有被忽视。实际上,亚洲和远东工作组(灾区经济重建临时小组委员会)在当前辩论中讨论了先前提出的所有论点,他有幸担任该工作组的主席,委员会和理事会的许多成员国都派代表出席,例如法国、荷兰、新西兰、苏联、英国和美国。

工作组的讨论非常有趣,一度似乎无法达成一致意见;但最后达成了一项最终协议,并应被视为就正在讨论的主题达成的初步协议。有关段落记录在 E/307/Rev. 1 号文件[①]中第 63 页,内容如下:

> "为了实现《联合国宪章》所设想的'稳定和幸福的条件',有必要作出新的、更加迅速和全面的努力,使整个亚洲和远东的生产方式现代化,目的是让所有人都能获得现代技术工具。这将意味着加强工业化,在区域内制造更多的本区域资源供当地使用或用于贸易,并与世界其他地区建立新的公平的经济关系。简而言之,我们建议,亚洲和远东的重建必须被视为大规模调整的第一步,该地区的人民将在联合国能够提供的援助下,尽快在经济生活的所有部门有系统地应用现代技术,必要时根据当地需要进行调整。不容忽视的是,重建努力在一开始可以最有效地针对人民生活所依赖的现有工业和农业,以及有既定市场的出口工业。"

第一句中的原则已经很好地阐述,部分使用了《宪章》的措辞,当然没有人反对这些原则。这些显然是理事会希望说的话。有谁会真的不同意条款中的建议?他希望亚洲和远东经济委员会秘书处的所有成员以及其工作组的成员,在推进该委员会设立的目标的任务时,都能对该报告进行研究。

张彭春先生(中国)认为智利代表很难退出起草委员会,因为智利代表团提出了提交该委员会的两项决议草案之一。虽然他本人想退出,但他认为,作为一个在讨论的地区中占如此大比重的国家的唯一代表,他反过来也可能觉得很难这样做。

---

① 见《经济及社会理事会正式记录》,第二年,第四届会议,补编第 10 号。

11. 张彭春在经社理事会第七届第191次会议上的发言

1948年8月6日下午3时，联合国经社理事会第七届第191次会议，在日内瓦万国宫召开，本次会议的议题是继续亚洲和远东经济委员会的报告。张彭春参加了本次会议，并在会议上先后多次发言①，相关会议纪要、纪要影像及纪要译文如下：

【会议纪要】

Mr. P. C. CHANG (China) submitting the Chinese proposal, said that he had not yet had an opportunity of commenting on it fully. In discussing that proposal three factors must be borne in mind.

The first of those factors was the problem itself, which, for once, was concrete. It was not necessary to make analyses like the economic analyses of purposes and policies of industrialization — a necessarily abstract, somewhat vague and understandably controversial problem, which each might envisage in his own way. The problem of flood control was not abstract; there could be no difference of opinion as to the true end to be achieved.

Moreover, the problem was unique, because the rivers of East and South Asia flowed through areas which were geologically comparatively young. Consequently, the courses of those rivers were not stable. That only made the prob-

① UN Document: E/SR. 175-225, pp. 250-251, pp. 252-253, p. 257, pp. 257-258, p. 260, p. 262.

lem more serious and more urgent. If a concrete, constructive and co-operative effort were made, the interest of the peoples of Asia in the United Nations would at once be stimulated, and those peoples would be brought to support the United Nations with new zeal.

The second factor was the tool to be employed, which must clearly be sufficiently effective to produce the desired results. Simple and direct technical methods must be used. It was for that reason that having carefully studied the initial proposals, the Commission had decided, after long deliberation, to establish a Bureau of Flood Control to perform the tasks which all its members considered to be indispensable.

With regard to the organization of the Bureau, he would like to ask the Executive Secretary of the Commission briefly to explain the reasons for which the recommendations submitted to the Council had been adopted, and the organizational implications of the proposed Bureau. He hoped that after an objective statement by the Executive Secretary on the gradual crystallization of the Commission's recommendation, the doubts of certain members of the Council would be dispelled, and it would be possible to reach a satisfactory decision.

Mr. P. C. CHANG (China) thanked the Executive Secretary of the Commission and pointed out that the number of experts to be appointed to the Bureau had given rise to lengthy discussion. He reminded the Council that, as the representative of Australia had said, it would be advisable to confine themselves to simple directives and go straight to the goal, without entering into details, since the Commission was more competent to consider organizational arrangements. That would obviate possible duplication of work and loss of time.

The draft resolution had been adopted almost unanimously, only one delegation having raised objections and one other having made reservations on certain specific aspects of the problem. He did not think there was any doubt but that members of the Council who were also members of the Economic Commission for Asia and the Far East would support the draft resolution submitted by the Commission. He stressed the fact that the plans suggested by the Bureau would naturally be carried out by Governments themselves. He also pointed out that the Bureau would submit reports, and that the Commission and the Council would be in a position to supervise its work.

The establishment of a semi-independent Bureau was the only means by which the problem could be tackled effectively. Any other procedure would be very much slower and more gradual, and would therefore be inadequate to solve a problem of such magnitude as that of the floods in Asia and the Far East, which should be considered a technical problem. They must use imagination to find the right solution and not adhere slavishly to current methods.

Finally he turned to the last of the three factors he had mentioned in his opening remarks, namely, the will. Pointing out that "where there's a will there's a way", he asked the Council whether it wished to support the proposal to organize flood control. He emphasized that floods in Asia were an extensive and pivotal problem. Its solution might bring about a radical change in the economic and social conditions of life. From the most remote times, a Chinese school of thought had maintained that the economic and social evolution of China at any given period was always bound up with the system of waterways and with floods.

He observed that it was not a question of creating a costly permanent service, but of finding specialists who would serve only for six months or a year; first-class experts on flood control were exceedingly rare and would certainly not be able to accept long appointments. The Council was called upon to show whether it really desired to do useful work in Asia and the Far Fast in a spirit of full collaboration. Unfortunately, the importance of that region was not yet fully recognized; that was shown by the membership of the Council, which contained only one representative of Asia. The elimination of floods might permit the countries of Asia and the Far Fast to take their proper place in the world.

To those who were afraid of establishing a new permanent organization because of all the expense it entailed, he would point out that the status of the regional commissions would be reviewed before 1951, which would allow them to reconsider the question of the Bureau; but he had already indicated that it was mainly a job for experts and one of short duration. He felt assured of the support of the six non-Asiatic members of the Economic Commission for Asia and the Far East who were taking part in the Council's work.

Mr. P. C. CHANG (China) thanked members of the Council for the interest and concern they had shown in the problem of flood control, and expressed his gratitude to the Netherlands Government for the invitation extended to Chinese engineers.

The statements made had been constructive, and he felt the debate would prove of great value to the Economic Commission for Asia and the Far East. It was gratifying to note that the representatives of France and of the Soviet Union supported the recommendations of the Commission. He asked the Executive Secretary whether the words "semi-autonomous" had been used by members of the Economic Commission for Asia and the Far East when the establishment of a Bureau of Flood Control had been discussed. He understood that the Food and Agriculture Organization, when consulted by the Executive Secretary, had not objected to the proposal regarding the Bureau of Flood Control.

Mr. P. C. CHANG (China), resuming, said that the organizational relationship could surely be worked out to the satisfaction of all concerned. The important thing was to set out with good will on all sides.

All that the Council required was a simple resolution approving the formation of a unit such as the Bureau of Flood Control, to be appointed by the Secretary-General, to be responsible to the Secretary-General through the Executive Secretary of the Commission and with which the Executive Secretary would co-operate. Such a unit would give its main attention to technical matters and would no doubt come to certain conclusions which would have to be approved by the Executive Secretary and then transmitted to the Commission.

The Canadian proposal and the observations of the United States, the Netherlands and the Soviet Union delegations need not be considered at that stage, but could be referred to the next session of the Commission, which was to be held in Australia in November. They could then be further considered at the next session of the Economic and Social Council in January 1949. Meanwhile, the Secretary-General would have had the necessary time to obtain the services of the suitable experts.

He saw no reason why the Council should not take decisions on the establishment of particular units, and on the size of such units. It had, in fact, already done so, by setting up commissions and similar bodies. The final decision on such matters would in any case rest with the General Assembly, and more especially with the Fifth Committee. Similarly, it would be for the General Assembly and the Fifth Committee to decide whether the Economic Commissions for Europe and for Asia and the Far East should have one comprehensive budget, from which particular projects could be financed. The Chinese delegation would have no objection to such a decision.

Mr. P. C. CHANG (China) replied that the two operative paragraphs in the Chinese resolution were an abbreviation of the Commission's own resolution. He believed that they should be adopted forthwith and then transmitted to the Commission at its next session, together with a report of the Council's discussions.

The Chinese delegation had not withdrawn its resolution, but hoped for immediate action on the general principle.

Mr. P. C. CHANG (China) thanked the New Zealand representative for the expression of his country's interest in assisting Chinese engineers. China had always met in New Zealand a splendid spirit of co-operation, not only in engineering but also in other fields. He also thanked the New Zealand representative for raising the question of the Secretary-General's report on the financial implications of the scheme, to which the Assistant Secretary-General had adequately replied.

The Assistant Secretary-General's statement had been helpful and the Chinese delegation would at any rate tentatively withdraw the words to which he had referred, subject to further consideration by the Commission.

It was understood that the Bureau would be a unit under the Commission, and the relationship would be that the broader administrative policies would pass through the Executive Secretary to the Commission.

He requested the Executive Secretary and the Assistant Secretary-General in charge of Economic Affairs to examine all the available material and provide the Council with a rough estimate; for a bureau of three to five experts, he thought it would not amount to more than $180,000 a year. He was sure that the Council could then reach agreement, and that even those who had spoken against the scheme would agree on the expenditure required.

【纪要影像】

Mr. P. C. Chang (China) submitting the Chinese proposal, said that he had not yet had an opportunity of commenting on it fully. In discussing that proposal three factors must be borne in mind.

The first of those factors was the problem itself, which, for once, was concrete. It was not necessary to make analyses like the economic analyses of purposes and policies of industrialization — a necessarily abstract, somewhat vague and understandably controversial problem, which each might envisage in his own way. The problem of flood control was not abstract; there could be no difference of opinion as to the true end to be achieved.

Moreover, the problem was unique, because the rivers of East and South Asia flowed through areas which were geologically comparatively young. Consequently, the courses of those rivers were not stable. That only made the problem more serious and more urgent. If a concrete, constructive and co-operative effort were made, the interest of the peoples of Asia in the United Nations would at once be stimulated, and those peoples would be brought to support the United Nations with new zeal.

The second factor was the tool to be employed, which must clearly be sufficiently effective to produce the desired results. Simple and direct technical methods must be used. It was for that reason that having carefully studied the initial proposals, the Commission had decided, after long deliberation, to establish a Bureau of Flood Control to perform the tasks which all its members considered to be indispensable.

With regard to the organization of the Bureau, he would like to ask the Executive Secretary of the Commission briefly to explain the reasons for which the recommendations[1] submitted to the Council had been adopted, and the organizational implications of the proposed Bureau. He hoped that after an objective statement by the Executive Secretary on the gradual crystallization of the Commission's recommendation, the doubts of certain members of the Council would be dispelled, and it would be possible to reach a satisfactory decision.

图片 7.18 张彭春在经社理事会第七届第 191 次会议发言纪要(1)

Mr. P. C. Chang (China) thanked the Executive Secretary of the Commission and pointed out that the number of experts to be appointed to the Bureau had given rise to lengthy discussion. He reminded the Council that, as the representative of Australia had said, it would be advisable to confine themselves to simple directives and go straight to the goal, without entering into details, since the Commission was more competent to consider organizational arrangements. That would obviate possible duplication of work and loss of time.

The draft resolution had been adopted almost unanimously, only one delegation having raised objections and one other having made reservations on certain specific aspects of the problem. He did not think there was any doubt but that members of the Council who were also members of the Economic Commission for Asia and the Far East would support the draft resolution submitted by the Commission. He stressed the fact that the plans suggested by the Bureau would naturally be carried out by Governments themselves. He also pointed out that the Bureau would submit reports, and that the Commission and the Council would be in a position to supervise its work.

The establishment of a semi-independent Bureau was the only means by which the problem could be tackled effectively. Any other procedure would be very much slower and more gradual, and would therefore be inadequate to solve a problem of such magnitude as that of the floods in Asia and the Far East, which should be considered a technical problem. They must use imagination to find the right solution and not adhere slavishly to current methods.

Finally he turned to the last of the three factors he had mentioned in his opening remarks, namely, the will. Pointing out that "where there's a will there's a way", he asked the Council whether it wished to support the proposal to organize flood control. He emphasized that floods in Asia were an extensive and pivotal problem. Its solution might bring about a radical change in the economic and social conditions of life. From the most remote times, a Chinese school of thought had maintained that the economic and social evolution of China at any given period was always bound up with the system of waterways and with floods.

图片 7.19 张彭春在经社理事会第七届第 191 次会议发言纪要(2)

He observed that it was not a question of creating a costly permanent service, but of finding specialists who would serve only for six months or a year; first-class experts on flood control were exceedingly rare and would certainly not be able to accept long appointments. The Council was called upon to show whether it really desired to do useful work in Asia and the Far East in a spirit of full collaboration. Unfortunately, the importance of that region was not yet fully recognized; that was shown by the membership of the Council, which contained only one representative of Asia. The elimination of floods might permit the countries of Asia and the Far East to take their proper place in the world.

To those who were afraid of establishing a new permanent organization because of all the expense it entailed, he would point out that the status of the regional commissions would be reviewed before 1951, which would allow them to reconsider the question of the Bureau; but he had already indicated that it was mainly a job for experts and one of short duration. He felt assured of the support of the six non-Asiatic members of the Economic Commission for Asia and the Far East who were taking part in the Council's work.

Mr. P. C. Chang (China) thanked members of the Council for the interest and concern they had shown in the problem of flood control, and expressed his gratitude to the Netherlands Government for the invitation extended to Chinese engineers.

The statements made had been constructive, and he felt the debate would prove of great value to the Economic Commission for Asia and the Far East. It was gratifying to note that the representatives of France and of the Soviet Union supported the recommendations of the Commission. He asked the Executive Secretary whether the words "semi-autonomous" had been used by members of the Economic Commission for Asia and the Far East when the establishment of a Bureau of Flood Control had been discussed. He understood that the Food and Agriculture Organization, when consulted by the Executive Secretary, had not objected to the proposal regarding the Bureau of Flood Control.

图片 7.19　张彭春在经社理事会第七届第 191 次会议发言纪要(3)

Mr. P. C. Chang (China), resuming, said that the organizational relationship could surely be worked out to the satisfaction of all concerned. The important thing was to set out with goodwill on all sides.

All that the Council required was a simple resolution approving the formation of a unit such as the Bureau of Flood Control, to be appointed by the Secretary-General, to be responsible to the Secretary-General through the Executive Secretary of the Commission and with which the Executive Secretary would co-operate. Such a unit would give its main attention to technical matters and would no doubt come to certain conclusions which would have to be approved by the Executive Secretary and then transmitted to the Commission.

The Canadian proposal and the observations of the United States, the Netherlands and the Soviet Union delegations need not be considered at that stage, but could be referred to the next session of the Commission, which was to be held in Australia in November. They could then be further considered at the next session of the Economic and Social Council in January 1949. Meanwhile, the Secretary-General would have had the necessary time to obtain the services of the suitable experts.

He saw no reason why the Council should not take decisions on the establishment of particular units, and on the size of such units. It had, in fact, already done so, by setting up commissions and similar bodies. The final decision on such matters would in any case rest with the General Assembly, and more especially with the Fifth Committee. Similarly, it would be for the General Assembly and the Fifth Committee to decide whether the Economic Commissions for Europe and for Asia and the Far East should have one comprehensive budget, from which particular projects could be financed. The Chinese delegation would have no objection to such a decision.

图片 7.20　张彭春在经社理事会第七届第 191 次会议发言纪要(4)

Mr. P. C. CHANG (China) replied that the two operative paragraphs in the Chinese resolution were an abbreviation of the Commission's own resolution. He believed that they should be adopted forthwith and then transmitted to the Commission at its next session, together with a report of the Council's discussions.

The Chinese delegation had not withdrawn its resolution, but hoped for immediate action on the general principle.

M. P. C. CHANG (China) thanked the New Zealand representative for the expression of his country's interest in assisting Chinese engineers. China had always met in New Zealand a splendid spirit of co-operation, not only in engineering but also in other fields. He also thanked the New Zealand representative for raising the question of the Secretary-General's report on the financial implications of the scheme, to which the Assistant Secretary-General had adequately replied.

The Assistant Secretary-General's statement had been helpful and the Chinese delegation would at any rate tentatively withdraw the words to which he had referred, subject to further consideration by the Commission.

It was understood that the Bureau would be a unit under the Commission, and the relationship would be that the broader administrative policies would pass through the Executive Secretary to the Commission.

He requested the Executive Secretary and the Assistant Secretary-General in charge of Economic Affairs to examine all the available material and provide the Council with a rough estimate; for a bureau of three to five experts, he thought it would not amount to more than $180,000 a year. He was sure that the Council could then reach agreement, and that even those who had spoken against the scheme would agree on the expenditure required.

图片 7.21　张彭春在经社理事会第七届第 191 次会议发言纪要(5)

【纪要译文】

张彭春先生(中国)在提交中国的提案时说,他还没有机会对提案作充分评论。在讨论该建议时,必须铭记三个因素。

这些因素中的第一个是问题本身,这一次是具体的。没有必要像对工业化的目的和政策进行经济分析那样进行分析——这是一个必然抽象的、有点模糊的、可以理解的有争议的问题,每个人都可能以自己的方式设想。防洪问题不是抽象的;对于要达到的真正目的,意见不可能有分歧。

此外,这个问题是独特的,因为东亚和南亚的河流流经地质上相对年轻的地区。因此,这些河流的河道并不稳定。这只会使问题更加严重和紧迫。如果作出具体、建设性和合作的努力,亚洲各国人民对联合国的兴趣将立即得到激发,这些人民将以新的热情支持联合国。

第二个因素是要使用的工具,它显然必须足够有效,以产生预期的结果。必须使用简单直接的技术方法。正是由于这个原因,委员会在仔细研究了初步建议后,经过长期审议,决定设立一个防洪局,以执行其所有成员认为不可或缺的任务。

关于防洪局的组织,他想请委员会执行秘书简要解释提交理事会的建议获得通过的原因，以及拟议防洪局的组织影响。他希望，在执行秘书就委员会建议的逐步明晰化发表客观声明后，理事会某些成员的疑虑将得到消除，并有可能作出令人满意的决定。

张彭春先生（中国）感谢委员会执行秘书，并指出将被任命为防洪局成员的专家人数引起了长时间的讨论。他提醒理事会，正如澳大利亚代表所说的那样，最好将自己局限于简单的指令，直接进入目标，而不是细节，因为委员会更有能力考虑组织安排。这将避免可能的重复工作和时间损失。

决议草案几乎一致通过，只有一个代表团提出反对，另一个代表团对问题的某些具体方面提出保留。他不认为有任何疑问，但同时也是亚洲和远东经济委员会成员的理事会成员将支持委员会提出的决议草案。他强调，防洪局建议的计划自然将由各国政府自己执行。他还指出，防洪局将提交报告，委员会和理事会将能够监督其工作。

设立一个半独立的防洪局是有效解决这一问题的唯一手段。任何其他程序都将非常缓慢和更加渐进，因此不足以解决亚洲和远东洪水这样规模的问题，这一问题应被视为一个技术问题。他们必须运用想象力找到正确的解决方案，而不是死守现有方法。

最后，他谈到他在开幕词中提到的三个因素中的最后一个，即意愿。他指出“有志者事竟成”，并询问理事会是否愿意支持组织防洪的提议。他强调，亚洲的洪水是一个广泛而关键的问题。它的解决方案可能会带来经济和社会生活条件的根本改变。从很久以前，一个中国学派就坚持认为，中国在任何特定时期的经济和社会发展都与水道系统和洪水有关。

他指出，这不是建立一个昂贵的长期服务的问题，而是寻找只服务六个月或一年的专家的问题；一流的防洪专家极为罕见，肯定无法接受长期任命。理事会被要求表明，它是否真的愿意本着充分合作的精神，在亚洲和非洲开展有益的工作。不幸的是，该区域的重要性尚未得到充分承认；这一点在理事会成员国组成上得以表明，即只包含一名亚洲代表。洪水的消除可能会允许亚洲国家和远东在世界上占据适当的位置。

对于那些由于所需费用而害怕建立一个新的常设组织的人，他指出，将在 1951 年之前审查各区域委员会的地位，这将使它们能够重新考虑防洪局的问题；但他已经表示，这主要是专家的工作，而且是短期的工作。他确信，参加理事会工作的亚洲和远东经济委员会六个非亚洲成员将给予支持。

张彭春先生(中国)感谢理事会成员对防洪问题的兴趣和关注，并感谢荷兰政府向中国工程师发出邀请。

所作的发言是建设性的，他认为这次辩论将证明对亚洲和远东经济委员会具有重大价值。令人欣慰地注意到，法国和苏联代表支持委员会的建议。他问执行秘书，在讨论设立防洪局时，亚洲和远东经济委员会成员是否使用了"半自治"一词。他理解，执行秘书征求粮食及农业组织的意见时，该组织没有反对关于防洪局的建议。

张彭春先生(中国)再次发言时说，组织关系的建立肯定能使所有有关方面满意。重要的是要带着各方的善意出发。

理事会所需要的只是一项简单的决议，批准成立一个单位，例如由秘书长任命的防洪局，通过委员会执行秘书向秘书长负责，执行秘书将与之合作。该单位将主要关注技术事项，并毫无疑问将得出某些结论，这些结论必须得到执行秘书的批准，然后转交委员会。

加拿大的提案以及美国、荷兰和苏联代表团的意见在该阶段无需审议，但可提交定于 11 月在澳大利亚举行的委员会下届会议。然后可在 1949 年 1 月经济及社会理事会下届会议上进一步审议。同时，秘书长本来有所必要的时间获得适当专家的服务。

他认为理事会没有理由不就设立特定单位和这些单位的规模作出决定。事实上，它已经通过设立委员会和类似机构这样做了。无论如何，关于这些事项的最后决定将取决于大会，尤其是第五委员会。同样，应由大会和第五委员会决定欧洲经济委员会、亚洲和远东经济委员会是否应该有一个全面预算，以便为特定项目提供资金。中国代表团不反对这一决定。

张彭春先生(中国)答复说，中国决议执行部分的两段是委员会自己决议的缩写。他认为,这些建议应立即获得通过,然后连同理事会讨论情况的报告提交委员会下届会议。

中国代表团没有撤回其决议,但希望立即就一般原则采取行动。

张彭春先生(中国)感谢新西兰代表表示他的国家有兴趣协助中国工程师。中国在新西兰一直感受到非常好的合作精神,不仅在工程领域,而且在其他领域。他还感谢新西兰代表提出秘书长关于该计划所涉经费问题的报告的问题,助理秘书长已对此作出了充分答复。

助理秘书长的发言很有帮助,中国代表团无论如何都将暂时撤回他提到的措辞,但须经委员会进一步审议。

据了解,防洪局将是委员会下的一个单位,其关系是更广泛的行政政策将通过执行秘书转交给委员会。

他请执行秘书和主管经济事务助理秘书长审查所有现有材料,并向理事会提供粗略估计;对于一个由三到五名专家组成的机构,他认为每年的费用不会超过 18 万美元。他确信,届时理事会能够达成协议,甚至那些反对该计划的人也会同意所需的支出。

12. 张彭春在经社理事会第七届第192次会议上的发言

1948年8月7日上午10时，联合国经社理事会第七届第192次会议，在日内瓦万国宫召开，本次会议的议题是继续亚洲和远东经济委员会的报告。张彭春参加了本次会议，并在会议上先后十多次发言①，相关会议纪要、纪要影像及纪要译文如下：

【会议纪要】

Mr. P. C. CHANG (China) said that the spirit of cordiality underlying the Canadian representative's proposals was deeply appreciated by the delegation of China. The Council was dealing with a matter in which, he believed, something concrete, unique and imaginative would be done to meet a specific situation. He had studied the Canadian representative's new suggestion closely, and it seemed to him to be the tail end of the original proposal; it was not an attack on the problem itself, but a proposal to transfer responsibility to the Secretariat. In ordinary circumstances, the approach suggested by the Canadian representative might be a wise one; but the Council had before it a special case, for it was rarely confronted with an international problem so immediate, so uncontroversial and so "pivotal". That being so, the matter should be dealt with adequately. It should be tackled with the right tools. The main task should be

① UN Document: E/SR. 175-225, pp. 264-266, p. 267, p. 268, p. 269, p. 270, p. 271, p. 272, p. 273, p. 275.

tackled adequately from the outset, in a bold manner; well begun was half done. The tail end of the task could be gathered up, after getting expert advice, and attached to the Secretariat after the bold initial attack. A gradual accretion of staff to carry out the task, as proposed by the representative of Canada, was not adequate. He appreciated the attempt made by the latter to enable the Council to reach agreement, but the new Canadian proposal was a weakening of the Commission's approach to the problem.

He proposed that the third paragraph of his draft resolution (E/893) should be amended by substituting the words "millions of" for the words "over half a billion", since the word "billion" had different meanings in the United States of America and the United Kingdom. It had been pointed out that the words "and that the Executive Secretary of the ECAFE shall assist and collaborate with the bureau in all necessary ways in its organization and operation", contained in the final paragraph, were not in accordance with normal Council practice in issuing directives, and he therefore proposed their deletion. He further proposed that a new final paragraph should be added, reading: "Recommends that a progress report on plans of activities and of organization of the Bureau be submitted by the Economic Commission for Asia and the Far East to the Council at its eighth session." That wording was straightforward, and preferable to the instructions to "consider further" embodied in the Canadian amendment (E/936). He felt that the draft resolution he had submitted, amended as he had just proposed, covered every aspect of the problem in a proper and mature way.

He further proposed that the following recommendations be appended to the resolution for the guidance of the Commission:

> "It is recommended that the ECAFE take into account the views of the Council, including the following:
>
> "(1) That the Bureau approach the problem of flood control in a bold

manner by providing itself with highly qualified experts, and by providing plenty of temporary services of experienced consultants and other technical assistance;

"(2) That the Bureau may act directly in approaching various governmental departments and research facilities in regard to technical matters that the relationships of the Bureau to the Commission and its administrative facilities shall be under the general direction of the Secretary-General through the Executive-Secretary of the ECAFE;

"(3) That the Bureau should maintain close co-operation with the FAO and other specialized agencies and related organs of the United Nations;

"(4) That in the selection of experts and consultants for the Bureau, the Secretary-General may in the former category pay due attention to expert knowledge of local conditions, and in the latter category modern technological experience should serve as criterion."

With regard to the first paragraph of those recommendations, he believed that the United States representative agreed with him concerning the temporary services of experienced consultants. The recommendation in the second paragraph was in conformity with the statement made by the Assistant Secretary-General on organization. The recommendation in the third paragraph would show that the Council expected a progress report from the Bureau on its co-operation with the Food and Agriculture Organization and with other specialized agencies and related organs of the United Nations. The fourth paragraph should be considered only as a suggestion, not binding on the Secretary-General; but he believed that it would assist the Secretary-General in selecting experts and consultants for the Bureau. He assumed that the consultants would outnumber the experts by about three to one and that their services would only be required for three or four months. He had no doubt that the Council would be able to accept those recommendations.

Any attempt, such as that implicit in the Canadian amendment, to minimize the approach pro-posed by the Commission, would detract from the initial effort. The United Nations should start the ball rolling boldly.

Mr. P. C. CHANG (China) said that it would have been preferable to have had the estimate earlier, but the fault, perhaps, was partly his. However, the Council's earlier doubts had been resolved, it had agreed that the project should be carried out, and he was grateful for the estimate just submitted by the Assistant Secretary-General. The appointment of the five permanent experts envisaged in the estimate was bound up with the provision of sufficient consultants to ensure that the project was properly carried out. He was glad that the Assistant Secretary-General had suggested that the five more permanent posts should be allotted to experts, most of whom should have local knowledge, and that he had not excluded the possibility of such experts being drawn from the region itself. Few were available, but they could be found. Perhaps he was going too far, but he thought that the omission of any statement on the nationality of the experts might be taken to imply something with which he did not agree. It was important that everything should be done to ensure satisfactory results.

Finally, he suggested that the amount allocated for consultants'fee should be doubled, and that a further $10,000 should be allowed for their travel expenses, since they would mainly be drawn from other parts of the world.

Mr. P. C. CHANG (China) requested the Council to take no decision until the recommendations he had proposed for guidance of the Commission had been circulated in writing. ①

Mr. P. C. CHANG (China) requested that each paragraph of the Canadian proposal should be voted on separately. He proposed that the second paragraph should be replaced by the paragraph which he had proposed as an addi-

---

① See *document E/893/Add.* 1

tion to his own resolution—namely, "Recommends that a progress report on plans of activities and of organization of the Bureau be submitted by the Economic Commission for Asia and the Far East to the Council at its eight session".

Mr. P. C. CHANG (China) said that since the Canadian amendments consisted of paragraphs to be substituted for paragraphs in the Chinese draft resolution, he also had the right to propose the substitution of a paragraph for one of those in the Canadian amendment. He urged the rejection of the whole of the Canadian amendment, since it eliminated the recommendations of the Commission for the establishment of a Bureau of Flood Control.

Mr. P. C. CHANG (China) pointed out that the debate on the substance of the proposal had not yet been closed.

The PRESIDENT stated that the Chinese representative had withdrawn the amendment he had proposed to his own resolution with a view to submitting it as a sub-amendment to the Canadian amendment. That was the only procedure possible. The Chinese representative had requested the Council to vote separately on the two paragraphs of the Canadian amendment.

Mr. P. C. CHANG (China) did not think the first paragraph of the Canadian proposal should be voted on before he had had an opportunity to state his objections to it.

The PRESIDENT pointed out that he had not formally declared the discussion closed, but as no representative had wished to speak, he had thought the Council might proceed to vote.

Mr. P. C. CHANG (China) said that he objected to the Canadian proposal since it simply side-tracked the Commission's recommendations for the establishment of a Bureau of Flood Control. The words "in conformity with the principles laid down in General Assembly resolution 52 (I) and Economic and Social Council resolution 51 (IV)," would so restrict action on the project as to produce the direst results. The Commission, on which many members of the Council were represented, had definitely decided to recommend the establishment of the Bureau. The Canadian proposal was unworthy of the debate that had so far taken place, and would be quite unacceptable to the Commission and to those representatives who desired bold action on the project to be initiated forthwith.

Mr. P. C. CHANG (China) proposed that the following text be substituted for the first paragraph of the Canadian proposal: "Resolves that a bureau of flood control be formed of from three to five properly qualified experts, to be appointed by the Secretary-General, to carry out the tasks proposed by ECAFE at its third session, for the areas within the geographical scope of ECAFE". Such an amendment would test the feelings of the Council on whether appropriate action should be taken, whereas adoption of the Canadian proposal would mean that the project would be dealt with in a gradual manner which would eventually kill it.

Mr. P. C. CHANG (China), accepting the ruling, said he was glad that the President had made it clear that adoption of the Canadian amendment would be a negation of the Chinese proposal.

Mr. P. C. CHANG (China) said that the discussion was gradually crystallizing. He felt that sufficient progress had been made to indicate what structure should be adopted for the proposed machinery of flood control. He still supported the recommendation of the Economic Commission for Asia and the Far East, and hoped that all non-Asian members of that Commission would also continue to support it.

Mr. P. C. CHANG (China) regretted the dissipation, as a result of procedural argument, of the atmosphere of harmony and support for his draft resolution, which had prevailed at the previous meeting.

He felt, however, that a drafting committee of four or five members, taking into account the strong support for the Chinese draft resolution expressed during the debate, might well stand a better chance of success than an informal meeting of only two representatives, held before that support was voiced.

Mr. P. C. CHANG (China) supported that view and proposed the addition to the Drafting Committee of the United States representative, whose delegation had been in consistent but friendly opposition to the view held by his own.

【纪要影像】

Mr. P. C. CHANG (China) said that the spirit of cordiality underlying the Canadian representative's proposals was deeply appreciated by the delegation of China. The Council was dealing with a matter in which, he believed, something concrete, unique and imaginative would be done to meet a specific situation. He had studied the Canadian representative's new suggestion closely, and it seemed to him to be the tail end of the original proposal; it was not an attack on the problem itself, but a proposal to transfer responsibility to the Secretariat. In ordinary circumstances, the approach suggested by the Canadian representative might be a wise one; but the Council had before it a special case, for it was rarely confronted with an international problem so immediate, so uncontroversial and so "pivotal". That being so, the matter should be dealt with adequately. It should be tackled with the right tools. The main task should be tackled adequately from the outset, in a bold manner; well begun was half done. The tail end of the task could be gathered up, after getting expert advice, and attached to the Secretariat after the bold initial attack. A gradual accretion of staff to carry out the task, as proposed by the representative of Canada, was not adequate. He appreciated the attempt made by the latter to enable the Council to reach agreement, but the new Canadian proposal was a weakening of the Commission's approach to the problem.

He proposed that the third paragraph of his draft resolution (E/893) should be amended by substituting the words "millions of" for the words "over half a billion", since the word "billion" had different meanings in the United States of America and the United Kingdom. It had been pointed out that the words "and that the Executive Secretary of the ECAFE shall assist and collaborate with the bureau in all necessary ways in its organization and operation", contained in the final paragraph, were not in accordance with normal Council practice in issuing directives, and he therefore proposed their deletion. He further proposed that a new final paragraph should be added, reading: "*Recommends* that a progress report on plans of activities and of organization of the Bureau be submitted by the Economic Commission for Asia and the Far East to the Council at its eighth session." That wording was straightforward, and preferable to the instructions to "consider further" embodied in the Canadian amendment (E/936). He felt that the draft resolution he had submitted, amended as he had just proposed, covered every aspect of the problem in a proper and mature way.

图片 7.22　张彭春在经社理事会第七届第 192 次会议发言纪要(1)

He further proposed that the following recommendations be appended to the resolution for the guidance of the Commission :

"It is recommended that the ECAFE take into account the views of the Council, including the following :

"(1) That the Bureau approach the problem of flood control in a bold manner by providing itself with highly qualified experts, and by providing plenty of temporary services of experienced consultants and other technical assistance;

"(2) That the Bureau may act directly in approaching various governmental departments and research facilities in regard to technical matters that the relationships of the Bureau to the Commission and its administrative facilities shall be under the general direction of the Secretary-General through the Executive-Secretary of the ECAFE;

"(3) That the Bureau should maintain close co-operation with the FAO and other specialized agencies and related organs of the United Nations;

"(4) That in the selection of experts and consultants for the Bureau, the Secretary-General may in the former category pay due attention to expert knowledge of local conditions, and in the latter category modern technological experience should serve as criterion."

With regard to the first paragraph of those recommendations, he believed that the United States representative agreed with him concerning the temporary services of experienced consultants. The recommendation in the second paragraph was in conformity with the statement made by the Assistant Secretary-General on organization. The recommendation in the third paragraph would show that the Council expected a progress report from the Bureau on its co-operation with the Food and Agriculture Organization and with other specialized agencies and related organs of the United Nations. The fourth paragraph should be considered only as a suggestion, not binding on the Secretary-General; but he believed that it would assist the Secretary-General in selecting experts and consultants for the Bureau. He assumed that the consultants would outnumber the experts by about three to one and that their services would only be required for three or four months. He had no doubt that the Council would be able to accept those recommendations.

图片 7.23 张彭春在经社理事会第七届第 192 次会议发言纪要(2)

Any attempt, such as that implicit in the Canadian amendment, to minimize the approach proposed by the Commission, would detract from the initial effort. The United Nations should start the ball rolling boldly.

Mr. P. C. Chang (China) said that it would have been preferable to have had the estimate earlier, but the fault, perhaps, was partly his. However, the Council's earlier doubts had been resolved, it had agreed that the project should be carried out, and he was grateful for the estimate just submitted by the Assistant Secretary-General. The appointment of the five permanent experts envisaged in the estimate was bound up with the provision of sufficient consultants to ensure that the project was properly carried out. He was glad that the Assistant Secretary-General had suggested that the five more permanent posts should be allotted to experts, most of whom should have local knowledge, and that he had not excluded the possibility of such experts being drawn from the region itself. Few were available, but they could be found. Perhaps he was going too far, but he thought that the omission of any statement on the nationality of the experts might be taken to imply something with which he did not agree. It was important that everything should be done to ensure satisfactory results.

Finally, he suggested that the amount allocated for consultants' fees should be doubled, and that a further $10,000 should be allowed for their travel expenses, since they would mainly be drawn from other parts of the world.

Mr. P. C. Chang (China) requested the Council to take no decision until the recommendations he had proposed for guidance of the Commission had been circulated in writing.[1]

[1] See document E/893/Add.1.

Mr. P. C. Chang (China) requested that each paragraph of the Canadian proposal should be voted on separately. He proposed that the second paragraph should be replaced by the paragraph which he had proposed as an addition to his own resolution — namely, "*Recommends* that a progress report on plans of activities and of organization of the Bureau be submitted by the Economic Commission for Asia and the Far East to the Council at its eight session".

Mr. P. C. Chang (China) said that since the Canadian amendments consisted of paragraphs to be substituted for paragraphs in the Chinese draft resolution, he also had the right to propose the substitution of a paragraph for one of those in the Canadian amendment. He urged the rejection of the whole of the Canadian amendment, since it eliminated the recommendations of the Commission for the establishment of a Bureau of Flood Control.

图片 7.24 张彭春在经社理事会第七届第 192 次会议发言纪要(3)

Mr. P. C. CHANG (China) pointed out that the debate on the substance of the proposal had not yet been closed.

The PRESIDENT stated that the Chinese representative had withdrawn the amendment he had proposed to his own resolution with a view to submitting it as a sub-amendment to the Canadian amendment. That was the only procedure possible. The Chinese representative had requested the Council to vote separately on the two paragraphs of the Canadian amendment.

Mr. P. C. CHANG (China) did not think the first paragraph of the Canadian proposal should be voted on before he had had an opportunity to state his objections to it.

The PRESIDENT pointed out that he had not formally declared the discussion closed, but as no representative had wished to speak, he had thought the Council might proceed to vote.

Mr. P. C. CHANG (China) said that he objected to the Canadian proposal since it simply side-tracked the Commission's recommendations for the establishment of a Bureau of Flood Control. The words "in conformity with the principles laid down in General Assembly resolution 52 (I) and Economic and Social Council resolution 51 (IV)," would so restrict action on the project as to produce the direst results. The Commission, on which many members of the Council were represented, had definitely decided to recommend the establishment of the Bureau. The Canadian proposal was unworthy of the debate that had so far taken place, and would be quite unacceptable to the Commission and to those representatives who desired bold action on the project to be initiated forthwith.

图片 7.25　张彭春在经社理事会第七届第 192 次会议发言纪要(4)

Mr. P. C. CHANG (China) proposed that the following text be substituted for the first paragraph of the Canadian proposal: "*Resolves* that a bureau of flood control be formed of from three to five properly qualified experts, to be appointed by the Secretary-General, to carry out the tasks proposed by ECAFE at its third session, for the areas within the geographical scope of ECAFE". Such an amendment would test the feelings of the Council on whether appropriate action should be taken, whereas adoption of the Canadian proposal would mean that the project would be dealt with in a gradual manner which would eventually kill it.

Mr. P. C. CHANG (China), accepting the ruling, said he was glad that the President had made it clear that adoption of the Canadian amendment would be a negation of the Chinese proposal.

Mr. P. C. CHANG (China) said that the discussion was gradually crystallizing. He felt that sufficient progress had been made to indicate what structure should be adopted for the proposed machinery of flood control. He still supported the recommendation of the Economic Commission for Asia and the Far East, and hoped that all non-Asian members of that Commission would also continue to support it.

Mr. P. C. CHANG (China) regretted the dissipation, as a result of procedural argument, of the atmosphere of harmony and support for his draft resolution, which had prevailed at the previous meeting.

He felt, however, that a drafting committee of four or five members, taking into account the strong support for the Chinese draft resolution expressed during the debate, might well stand a better chance of success than an informal meeting of only two representatives, held before that support was voiced.

Mr. P. C. CHANG (China) supported that view and proposed the addition to the Drafting Committee of the United States representative, whose delegation had been in consistent but friendly opposition to the view held by his own.

图片 7.26　张彭春在经社理事会第七届第 192 次会议发言纪要(5)

【纪要译文】

张彭春先生(中国)说,中国代表团对加拿大代表的提案所体现的热诚精神深表赞赏。他认为,理事会正在处理一个问题,在这个问题上,将采取具体、独特和富有想象力的行动,以应付具体情况。他仔细研究了加拿大代表的新建议,在他看来,这似乎是原来建议的收尾;这不是对问题本身的应对,而是将责任移交给秘书处的建议。在一般情况下,加拿大代表建议的办法可能是明智的;但理事会面前有一个特殊情况,因为它很少遇到如此紧迫、如此无争议和如此"关键"的国际问题。既然如此,这件事应该得到妥善处理。应该用正确的工具来解决这个问题。主要任务应该从一开始就以大胆的方式充分处理;良好的开端是成功的一半。在获得专家建议后,任务的收尾工作可以集中起来,并在大胆的初步全力处理后将其归属秘书处。按照加拿大代表的建议,逐步增加工作人员来执行这项任务是不够的。他赞赏后者为使理事会能够达成协议所作的努力,但加拿大的新提议削弱了委员会处理这一问题的方法。

他提议对其决议草案(E/893)第三段进行修正,将"5亿多"改为"数百万",因为"十亿"一词在美国和英国有不同的含义。有人指出,最后一段中所载的"以及亚洲和远东经委会执行秘书应在防洪局的组织和运作中以一切必要方式给予其协助和配合"等字不符合理事会发布指令的正常惯例,因此他建议删除这些字。他还建议增加一个新的最后段落,内容如下:"建议亚洲和远东经济委员会向理事会第八届会议提交一份关于防洪局活动计划和组织安排的进度报告。"这种措辞是直截了当的,而且比加拿大修正案(E/936)中体现的"进一步考虑"的指令更为可取。他认为,他提交的决议草案,经他刚才提议的修正,以适当和成熟的方式涵盖了问题的各个方面。

他还提议将下列建议附在决议之后,作为委员会的指南:

"建议亚洲和远东经济委员考虑理事会的意见,包括:

“(1)该防洪局大胆处理防洪问题，为自己提供高素质的专家，并提供大量经验丰富的顾问的临时服务和其他技术援助；

“(2)防洪局可就技术事项直接与各政府部门和研究机构接洽，防洪局与委员会及其行政机构的关系应在秘书长通过欧洲经委会执行秘书总体领导下；

“(3)防洪局应与粮农组织和联合国其他专门机构及有关机关保持密切合作；

“(4)在为防洪局选择专家和顾问时，秘书长可在前一类中适当注意当地情况的专门知识，在后一类中，现代技术经验应作为标准。”

关于这些建议的第一段，他认为美国代表同意他关于经验丰富的顾问的临时服务的意见。第二段中的建议符合助理秘书长关于组织的发言。第三段中的建议将表明，理事会期望一份由防洪局就其与粮食及农业组织以及与联合国其他专门机构和有关机关合作的进度报告。第四段只应视为一项建议，对秘书长没有约束力；但他认为，这将有助于秘书长为防洪局挑选专家和顾问。他假设顾问的人数将以大约三比一超过专家人数，他们的服务只需要三到四个月。他毫不怀疑理事会将能够接受这些建议。

任何试图尽量减少委员会提出的办法的企图，例如加拿大修正案中隐含的企图，都会减损最初的努力。联合国应该大胆地开始行动。

张彭春先生(中国)说，早点作出估计更好，但可能部分是他的错。然而，理事会早些时候的疑虑已经解决，它同意该项目应当实施，他感谢助理秘书长刚才提出的估计数。概算中设想的五名常设专家的任命与提供足够的顾问有关，以确保项目得到适当执行。他感到高兴的是，助理秘书长建议将五个以上的常设员额分配给专家，其中大多数应具有当地知识，他并没有排除从该区域本身抽调这些专家的可能性。科技的专家很少，但可以找到。也许他离题太远了，但他认为，遗漏关于专家国籍的任何声明可能被视为暗示了他不同意的东西。必须尽一切努力确保取得令人满意的结果。

最后,他建议,分配给顾问费的数额应增加一倍,并应为他们的旅费再留出 10000 美元,因为他们主要来自世界其他地方。

张彭春先生(中国)请理事会在他提出的指导委员会的建议以书面形式分发之前不要作出决定。[①]

张彭春先生(中国)要求对加拿大提案的每一段分别进行表决。他提议将第二段改为他作为自己决议的补充而提议的段落,即"建议亚洲和远东经济委员会向理事会第八届会议提交一份关于防洪局活动计划和组织安排的进度报告"。

张彭春先生(中国)说,由于加拿大的修正案包括将取代中国决议草案段落的段落,他也有权提议用一段取代加拿大修正案中的一段。他敦促否决整个加拿大修正案,因为该修正案取消了委员会关于设立防洪局的建议。

张彭春先生(中国)指出,关于提案实质内容的辩论尚未结束。

主席说,中国代表撤回了他对自己的决议提出的修正案,以期将其作为加拿大修正案的附属修正案提交。这是唯一可能的程序。中国代表要求理事会就加拿大修正案的两段分别进行表决。

张彭春先生(中国)认为,加拿大提案的第一段不应在他有机会对其提出反对意见之前进行表决。

主席指出,他尚未正式宣布讨论结束,但由于没有代表希望发言,他认为理事会可以开始表决。

张彭春先生(中国)说,他反对加拿大的提案,因为它只是偏离了委员会关于设立防洪局的建议。"按照大会第 52(Ⅰ)号决议和经济及社会理事会第 51(Ⅳ)号决议规定的原则"这几个字将限制对该项目采取行动,从而产生直接的结果。理事会许多成员派代表参加的委员会明确决定建议设立防洪局。加拿大的提案不值得进行到目前为止的辩论,委员会和那些希望立即就项目采取大胆行动的代表将无法接受加拿大的提案。

张彭春先生(中国)提议用以下案文取代加拿大提案的第一段:"决议

---

① 见文件:E/893/Add. 1.

由秘书长任命的三至五名具有适当资格的专家组成一个防洪局,负责执行亚洲和远东经济委员会第三届会议提出的任务,在亚洲和远东经济委员会地理范围内的地区执行这些任务。”这样一项修正案将考验理事会对是否应采取适当行动的感受,而加拿大提案的通过将意味着该项目将以渐进的方式处理,这最终将扼杀该项目。

张彭春先生(中国)接受这一裁决,他说,他很高兴主席明确表示,加拿大修正案的通过将是对中国提案的否定。

张彭春先生(中国)说,讨论逐渐有了结果。他认为已经取得了足够的进展,以表明拟定的防洪机制应采用何种结构。他仍然支持亚洲和远东经济委员会的建议,并希望该委员会的所有非亚洲成员也将继续支持该建议。

张彭春先生(中国)感到遗憾的是,由于程序上的争论,在上次会议上盛行的和谐气氛和对其决议草案的支持消失了。

然而,他认为,考虑到辩论期间对中国决议草案表示的强烈支持,一个由四五名成员组成的起草委员会,可能比在表示支持之前举行的只有两名代表的非正式会议更有可能取得成功。

张彭春先生(中国)支持这一观点,并建议在起草委员会中增加美国代表,美国代表团一贯但友好地反对他所持观点。

13. 张彭春在经社理事会第七届第 198 次会议上的发言

1948 年 8 月 13 日下午 3 时,联合国经社理事会第七届第 198 次会议,在日内瓦万国宫召开,本次会议的主要议题是讨论秘书长和经社理事会关于在成员国学校中开展有关联合国的目的、原则、结构和活动教育的报告、审议关于社会委员会第三届会议的报告。张彭春参加了本次会议,并在会议上先后多次发言①,相关会议纪要、纪要影像及纪要译文如下:

【会议纪要】

Mr. P. C. CHANG (China) pointed out that the publicity currently given to any event appeared to be in direct proportion to the amount of controversy it aroused. Any measure which was passed without violent opposition was regarded as obvious or unrealistic. There was a very real danger that the Chinese draft resolution, which could give rise to no vehement controversy, would for that very reason fall into oblivion.

Yet the question it dealt with lay at the very heart of human aspiration. While the need for a realistic and effective approach to education in the ways of international co-operation was universally recognized, the belief in such a possibility was too often regarded as a kind of well-intentioned, wishful thinking.

To be effective, all educational endeavour had to begin with humility and a clear realization of deeply felt needs. The second step was a comprehensive a-

① UN Document: E/SR. 175-225, p. 368, p. 369, p. 375, p. 376.

nalysis of means to meet educational needs; the existence of more than one attitude to education, and indeed to life itself, must be recognized; if any sure foundation for co-operation was to be laid.

The final consideration, realization of which he suggested would lend more weight to the Chinese proposal, was that education, in the narrow sense of dissemination of information, often aroused a natural opposition; it would not, therefore, be the most effective way of promoting international co-operation, which could be better encouraged by the provision of opportunities to settle controversy through constructive co-operation on tangible and worth-while projects.

Mr. P. C. CHANG (China) stated that he would accept the French amendment. He proposed, however, that the words "and its specialized agencies" should be added after the words "of the United Nations"; that would be in accordance with the customary wording.

Mr. P. C. CHANG (China) pointed out that the resolution had been discussed at length both in the Social Committee and in the Social Commission. It seemed unnecessary, therefore, to re-open discussion on it, particularly as the United States representative had said that he would vote in favour of it, with reservations as to paragraph (d). He therefore thought it wise to retain the resolution as it stood.

Mr. P. C. CHANG (China) repeated that the resolution should remain as it stood, because it represented a definite opinion which could, nevertheless, be changed by the Fifth Committee of the General Assembly. It would be unwise for the Council not to commit itself on the point.

【纪要影像】

Mr. P. C. CHANG (China) pointed out that the publicity currently given to any event appeared to be in direct proportion to the amount of controversy it aroused. Any measure which was passed without violent opposition was regarded as obvious or unrealistic. There was a very real danger that the Chinese draft resolution, which could give rise to no vehement controversy, would for that very reason fall into oblivion.

Yet the question it dealt with lay at the very heart of human aspiration. While the need for a realistic and effective approach to education in the ways of international co-operation was universally recognized, the belief in such a possibility was too often regarded as a kind of well-intentioned, wishful thinking.

To be effective, all educational endeavour had to begin with humility and a clear realization of deeply felt needs. The second step was a comprehensive analysis of means to meet educational needs; the existence of more than one attitude to education, and indeed to life itself, must be recognized, if any sure foundation for co-operation was to be laid.

The final consideration, realization of which he suggested would lend more weight to the Chinese proposal, was that education, in the narrow sense of dissemination of information, often aroused a natural opposition; it would not, therefore, be the most effective way of promoting international co-operation, which could be better encouraged by the provision of opportunities to settle controversy through constructive co-operation on tangible and worth-while projects.

Mr. P. C. CHANG (China) stated that he would accept the French amendment. He proposed, however, that the words "and its specialized agencies" should be added after the words "of the United Nations"; that would be in accordance with the customary wording.

Mr. P. C. CHANG (China) pointed out that the resolution had been discussed at length both in the Social Committee and in the Social Commission. It seemed unnecessary, therefore, to re-open discussion on it, particularly as the United States representative had said that he would vote in favour of it, with reservations as to paragraph (*d*). He therefore thought it wise to retain the resolution as it stood.

Mr. P. C. CHANG (China) repeated that the resolution should remain as it stood, because it represented a definite opinion which could, nevertheless, be changed by the Fifth Committee of the General Assembly. It would be unwise for the Council not to commit itself on the point.

图片 7.27　张彭春在经社理事会第七届第 198 次会议发言纪要

【纪要译文】

张彭春先生（中国）指出，目前对任何活动的宣传似乎与其引起的争议量成正比。任何在没有强烈反对的情况下通过的措施都被认为是显而易见的或不现实的。中国的决议草案可能不会引起激烈的争论，因此有可能会被遗忘。

然而，它所处理的问题正是人类渴望的核心。虽然需要以国际合作的方式对教育采取现实和有效的做法是一项普遍共识，但对这种可能性的信念往往被视为一种善意的、一厢情愿的想法。

要想取得成效，所有教育努力都必须始于谦逊和对深切感知的需求的明确认识。第二步是全面分析满足教育需求的手段；必须承认对教育，甚至对生活本身存在着不止一种态度；如果要为合作打下坚实的基础的话。

最后一个考虑因素是，从狭义的信息传播角度来看，教育往往会引起自然的反对，他认为认识到这一点会使中国的建议更有分量；因此，这并不是促进国际合作的最有效方法，而通过在有形和有价值的项目上进行建设性合作，提供解决争议的机会，可以更好地促进国际合作。

张彭春先生（中国）说，他将接受法国的修正案。但是，他建议在“联合国”之后加上“及其专门机构”：这将符合习惯用语。

张彭春先生（中国）指出，社会事务委员会和社会委员会都对该决议进行了详细讨论。因此，似乎没有必要重新开始讨论这一问题，特别是因为美国代表说，他将投票赞成这一问题，但对（d）段有所保留。因此，他认为保留现有决议是明智的。

张彭春先生（中国）重申，该决议应保持原状，因为它代表了一种明确的意见，尽管如此，大会第五委员会仍可对其进行修改。理事会不在这一点上作出承诺是不明智的。

14. 张彭春在经社理事会第七届第199次会议上的发言

1948年8月14日上午9时30分,联合国经社理事会第七届第199次会议,在日内瓦万国宫召开,本次会议继续讨论会议工作安排及国际劳工组织的报告。张彭春参加了本次会议,并在会议上发言①,相关会议纪要、纪要影像及纪要译文如下:

【会议纪要】

Mr. P. C. CHANG (China) pointed out that the Council would actually continue to sit until the Human Rights Committee had completed its work, since a plenary session had to be held to adopt the necessary resolutions. He thought that the solution recommended by the representative of Canada would have been acceptable if the Council had been meeting at Headquarters; but in the existing situation it would entail a heavy financial burden on delegations, and the continuation of services which the Secretariat might not be able to maintain. Although the total number of representatives called upon to remain could be substantially reduced, the smaller delegations would still need to keep the majority of their staffs at Geneva.

The Human Rights Committee was dealing with several conventions, and the smaller delegations often entrusted the study of each convention to a different person. They would not be able to meet the expenditure entailed by the Ca-

① UN Document: E/SR. 175-225, pp. 382-383, p. 387, p. 395.

nadian suggestion. The Secretariat should provide an estimate of the cost of prolonging the session for an additional two, and perhaps even four weeks.

It should be frankly admitted that the Human Rights Committee could not achieve much at that time, however many meetings it might hold. It had met more frequently than the other Committees, and in the last seven meetings it had examined only four articles of one convention.

He thought that the Committee should aim at finishing discussion of each item in a set number of meetings and report to the Council on the stage then reached, even if it had been unable to reach any decision; it should also submit suggestions for further action on each item. In order to gain time the Committee could limit the number of interventions and apply the five-minute rule.

The practice of holding sessions of some six weeks' duration was not doing justice to the business of the Council. Fifty items could not be examined in so short a time, particularly when the variety of subjects was taken into account. He reminded the Council of the proposals he had previously made that the session should be divided, so as to deal with economic, social, procedural and other questions in turn. In addition to the opportunities that method of work would afford for thorough examination of each item, it would permit a reduction of the staff required by delegations at any particular time, although the whole session would last longer.

It might be possible to hold one such session from the middle of January to the middle or end of April, to sit again in July and to hold a short session before the General Assembly.

In conclusion, he suggested that the Human Rights Committee be instructed to take a decision at once on the matters before it, and to report to the Council on the action to be taken.

Mr. P. C. CHANG (China) pointed out that no decision could be taken on the Canadian or any other suggestion before a comprehensive plan dealing with the work as a whole was put before the Council. The Soviet Union representative had rightly pointed out that if one Committee continued to sit, that meant prolonging the session of the whole Council.

He stressed the great importance his delegation had always attached to the work of the Council. Items must be adequately, not hurriedly discussed, and there should be no suggestion of limiting the debates, which would lower the prestige of the Council.

In conclusion, he pointed out that the original date set for the end of the session was 20 August, not 25 August as stated by the Soviet Union representative. The session might be extended by three days, thus ending on 23 August. He was opposed to further extension, though he did not wish to adopt an inflexible attitude on the subject.

Mr. P. C. CHANG (China) supported the President's views. The Council had a tendency to adopt short resolutions, simply taking note of reports, which lowered its prestige. Provision should be made for the careful consideration of all documents submitted to the Council.

【纪要影像】

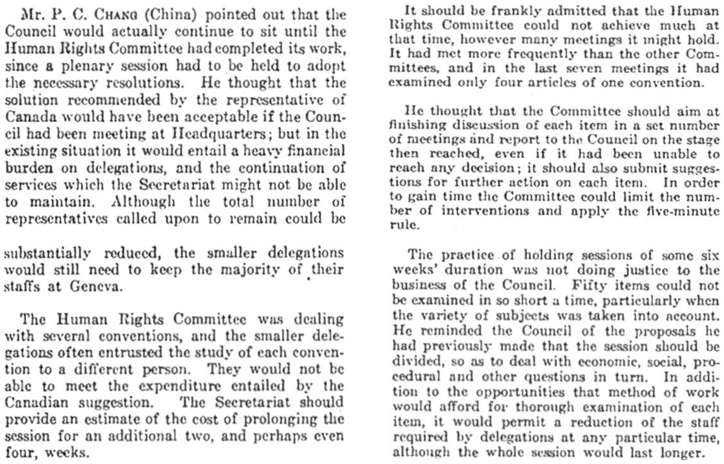

Mr. P. C. CHANG (China) pointed out that the Council would actually continue to sit until the Human Rights Committee had completed its work, since a plenary session had to be held to adopt the necessary resolutions. He thought that the solution recommended by the representative of Canada would have been acceptable if the Council had been meeting at Headquarters; but in the existing situation it would entail a heavy financial burden on delegations, and the continuation of services which the Secretariat might not be able to maintain. Although the total number of representatives called upon to remain could be substantially reduced, the smaller delegations would still need to keep the majority of their staffs at Geneva.

The Human Rights Committee was dealing with several conventions, and the smaller delegations often entrusted the study of each convention to a different person. They would not be able to meet the expenditure entailed by the Canadian suggestion. The Secretariat should provide an estimate of the cost of prolonging the session for an additional two, and perhaps even four, weeks.

It should be frankly admitted that the Human Rights Committee could not achieve much at that time, however many meetings it might hold. It had met more frequently than the other Committees, and in the last seven meetings it had examined only four articles of one convention.

He thought that the Committee should aim at finishing discussion of each item in a set number of meetings and report to the Council on the stage then reached, even if it had been unable to reach any decision; it should also submit suggestions for further action on each item. In order to gain time the Committee could limit the number of interventions and apply the five-minute rule.

The practice of holding sessions of some six weeks' duration was not doing justice to the business of the Council. Fifty items could not be examined in so short a time, particularly when the variety of subjects was taken into account. He reminded the Council of the proposals he had previously made that the session should be divided, so as to deal with economic, social, procedural and other questions in turn. In addition to the opportunities that method of work would afford for thorough examination of each item, it would permit a reduction of the staff required by delegations at any particular time, although the whole session would last longer.

图片 7.28 张彭春在经社理事会第七届第 199 次会议发言纪要(1)

It might be possible to hold one such session from the middle of January to the middle or end of April, to sit again in July and to hold a short session before the General Assembly.

In conclusion, he suggested that the Human Rights Committee be instructed to take a decision at once on the matters before it, and to report to the Council on the action to be taken.

Mr. P. C. CHANG (China) pointed out that no decision could be taken on the Canadian or any other suggestion before a comprehensive plan dealing with the work as a whole was put before the Council. The Soviet Union representative had rightly pointed out that if one Committee continued to sit, that meant prolonging the session of the whole Council.

He stressed the great importance his delegation had always attached to the work of the Council. Items must be adequately, not hurriedly discussed, and there should be no suggestion of limiting the debates, which would lower the prestige of the Council.

In conclusion, he pointed out that the original date set for the end of the session was 20 August, not 25 August as stated by the Soviet Union representative. The session might be extended by three days, thus ending on 23 August. He was opposed to further extension, though he did not wish to adopt an inflexible attitude on the subject.

M. P. C. CHANG (China) supported the President's views. The Council had a tendency to adopt short resolutions, simply taking note of reports, which lowered its prestige. Provision should be made for the careful consideration of all documents submitted to the Council.

图片 7.29　张彭春在经社理事会第七届第 199 次会议发言纪要(2)

【纪要译文】

张彭春先生(中国)指出,理事会实际上将继续开会,直到人权事务委员会完成其工作为止,因为必须举行全体会议才能通过必要的决议。他认为,如果理事会在总部开会,加拿大代表建议的解决办法是可以接受的;但在目前的情况下,这将给各代表团带来沉重的财政负担,并使秘书处无法继续提供服务。虽然被要求留任的代表总数可以大幅度减少,但较小的代表团仍需要将其大多数工作人员留在日内瓦。

人权事务委员会正在处理几项公约,较小的代表团往往将每项公约的研究委托给不同的人。他们将无法支付加拿大建议所带来的开支。秘书处应提供一份估计成本,说明将届会再延长两周甚至可能是四周的费用。

应当坦率地承认,当时人权事务委员会无论举行多少次会议,都无法取得多大成果。它比其他委员会开会更频繁,在过去的七次会议中,它只审议了一项公约的四个条款。

他认为,委员会的目标应该是在规定次数的会议上完成对每个项目的讨论,并向理事会报告当时达到的阶段,即使它无法作出任何决定;它还应就每个项目提出进一步行动的建议。为了争取时间,委员会可以限制发言次数并适用五分钟规则。

举行为期约六周的届会的做法不利于理事会的工作。50 个项目不可能在这么短的时间内审查,特别是在考虑到各种主题的情况下。他提醒理事会注意他以前提出的建议,即会议应分次举行,以便依次处理经济、社会、程序和其他问题。这种工作方法除了有机会彻底审查每个项目外,还将允许减少各代表团在任何特定时间所需的工作人员,尽管整个届会将持续更长时间。

也许可以在 1 月中旬至 4 月中旬或 4 月底举行一届这样的会议,在 7 月再次举行会议,并在大会之前举行一届简短的会议。

最后,他建议指示人权事务委员会立即就其面前的事项作出决定,并向理事会报告将要采取的行动。

张彭春先生(中国)指出,在向理事会提交一项涉及整个工作的全面计划之前,不能就加拿大的建议或任何其他建议作出决定。苏联代表恰当地指出,如果一个委员会继续开会,就意味着延长整个理事会的会议。

他强调,他的代表团一贯高度重视理事会的工作。必须充分而不是仓促地讨论项目,不应建议限制辩论,因为这会降低理事会的威望。

最后,他指出,最初确定的会议结束日期是 8 月 20 日,而不是苏联代表所说的 8 月 25 日。会议可能延长三天,因而于 8 月 23 日结束。他反对进一步延长,尽管他不希望在这个问题上采取不变通的态度。

张彭春(中国)支持主席的观点。理事会通过简短的决议、仅仅注意到报告的倾向,降低了它的威望。应为仔细审议提交理事会的所有文件作出规定。

15. 张彭春在经社理事会第七届第200次会议上的发言

1948年8月16日上午10时,联合国经社理事会第七届第200次会议,在日内瓦万国宫召开,本次会议的议题是继续讨论亚洲和远东经济委员会的报告。张彭春参加了本次会议,并在会议上发言①,相关会议纪要、纪要影像及纪要译文如下:

【会议纪要】

Mr. P.C. CHANG (China) said that the attitude of the Chinese Government towards State sovereignty had already been made clear in the debate. It was unnecessary for the Council to discuss the matter further; a theoretical analysis of it had already been undertaken by the working group which had preceded the setting-up of the Economic Commission for Asia and the Far East. The current debate had added nothing to what was contained in the report of that working group. He explained that as China was affected, he would abstain on all votes taken.

[1] Working Group for Asia and the Far East; see *Official Records of the Economic and Social Council*, second year, forth session, supplement No. 10 (E/307/Rev. 1)

① UN Document: E/SR. 175-225, p. 404.

【纪要影像】

Mr. P. C. CHANG (China) said that the attitude of the Chinese Government towards State sovereignty had already been made clear in the debate. It was unnecessary for the Council to discuss the matter further; a theoretical analysis of it had already been undertaken by the working group [1] which had preceded the setting-up of the Economic Commission for Asia and the Far East. The current debate had added nothing to what was contained in the report of that working group. He explained that as China was affected, he would abstain on all votes taken.

1 Working Group for Asia and the Far East; see *Official Records of the Economic and Social Council,* second year, fourth session, supplement No. 10 (E/307/Rev.1).

图片 7.30　张彭春在经社理事会第七届第 200 次会议发言纪要

【纪要译文】

张彭春先生(中国)说,中国政府对国家主权的态度在辩论中已经明确。理事会没有必要进一步讨论此事;在亚洲和远东经济委员会成立之前,工作组已经对其进行了理论分析。目前的辩论对该“工作组[1]”的报告所载内容没有任何补充。他解释说,由于中国受到影响,他将对所有投票投弃权票。

[1] 亚洲和远东工作组;见《经济及社会理事会正式记录》,第二年,第四届会议,补编第10 号文件(E/307/Rev. 1)。

16. 张彭春在经社理事会第七届第201次会议上的发言

1948年8月17日上午9时30分,联合国经社理事会第七届第201次会议,在日内瓦万国宫召开,本次会议的议题是继续讨论会议工作安排。张彭春参加了本次会议,并在会议上发言①,相关会议纪要、纪要影像及纪要译文如下:

【会议纪要】

Mr. P. C. CHANG (China) said that the procedure to be followed by the Human Rights Committee had been discussed by the Committee itself, but that had not resulted in any reduction of the numerous amendments and copious comments on the conventions under consideration. There was no chance of finishing the work by 20 August, which was still the scheduled date for closing the session. In view of the large number of amendments already submitted, he greatly doubted whether the Committee would be able to finish its work on items 17, 18 and 19 by 27 August, even if three meetings a day were held. He wished to see the Council's work properly carried out, not spoiled by over-hasty action, and it could not be completed properly in the limited time available.

He was not formally proposing that there should be another session, but he pointed out that the Council could well hold one, as there had only been two sessions during the current year.

---

① UN Document: E/SR. 175-225, p. 415.

He could not pass over, without comment, the suggestion that Committees of the Council should transmit documents directly to the Assembly. While appreciating the reasons for which the United Kingdom representative had made that suggestion, he hesitated to accept it, both on constitutional grounds and because its adoption would lower the dignity of the Council.

Since it did not seem possible to complete the work adequately by 27 August, the Council could only adopt course A. Many members wished to see the conventions on matters relating to human rights submitted to the forthcoming session of the General Assembly, and course A did not preclude that possibility. Although course A was unsatisfactory, it seemed the most desirable and practicable one. He agreed with the Netherlands representative's suggestion regarding resolution No. 39 on freedom of information. The Council should take a decision on resolutions concerning the draft conventions which it submitted to the General Assembly.

【纪要影像】

Mr. P. C. CHANG (China) said that the procedure to be followed by the Human Rights Committee had been discussed by the Committee itself, but that had not resulted in any reduction of the numerous amendments and copious comments on the conventions under consideration. There was no chance of finishing the work by 20 August, which was still the scheduled date for closing the session. In view of the large number of amendments already submitted, he greatly doubted whether the Committee would be able to finish its work on items 17, 18 and 19 by 27 August, even if three meetings a day were held. He wished to see the Council's work properly carried out, not spoiled by over-hasty action, and it could not be completed properly in the limited time available.

He was not formally proposing that there should be another session, but he pointed out that the Council could well hold one, as there had only been two sessions during the current year.

He could not pass over, without comment, the suggestion that Committees of the Council should transmit documents directly to the Assembly. While appreciating the reasons for which the United Kingdom representative had made that suggestion, he hesitated to accept it, both on constitutional grounds and because its adoption would lower the dignity of the Council.

Since it did not seem possible to complete the work adequately by 27 August, the Council could only adopt course A. Many members wished to see the conventions on matters relating to human rights submitted to the forthcoming session of the General Assembly, and course A did not preclude that possibility. Although course A was unsatisfactory, it seemed the most desirable and practicable one. He agreed with the Netherlands representative's suggestion regarding resolution No. 39 on freedom of information. The Council should take a decision on resolutions concerning the draft conventions which it submitted to the General Assembly.

图片 7.31　张彭春在经社理事会第七届第 201 次会议发言纪要

【纪要译文】

张彭春先生(中国)说,人权事务委员会将遵循的程序已经由委员会本身讨论过,但这并没有导致对正在审议的公约的众多修正案和大量评论的减少。在 8 月 20 日之前完成工作是不可能的,因为 8 月 20 日仍然是会议闭幕的预定日期。鉴于已经提交了大量修正案,他极为怀疑,即使每天举行三次会议,委员会是否能够在 8 月 27 日之前完成关于项目 17、18 和 19 的工作。他希望看到理事会的工作得到适当的执行,而不是被过于仓促的行动所破坏,且不能在有限的时间内妥善完成。

他没有正式提议举行另一届会议,但他指出,理事会完全可以举行一届会议,因为今年只有两届会议。

他不能不加评论地提出理事会各委员会应直接向大会转交文件的建议。尽管他赞赏英国代表提出这一建议的理由,但出于章程的依据以及通过这一建议会降低理事会的尊严,他对接受这一建议有所犹豫。

由于似乎不可能在 8 月 27 日之前充分完成工作,理事会只能通过方案 A。许多成员希望看到有关人权事项的公约提交给即将举行的大会届会,方案 A 并不排除这种可能性。虽然方案 A 并不令人满意,但它似乎是最可取和可行的方案。他同意荷兰代表关于新闻自由的第 39 号决议的建议。理事会应就其提交大会的有关公约草案的决议作出决定。

17. 张彭春在经社理事会第七届第 202 次会议上的发言

1948 年 8 月 17 日下午 3 时，联合国经社理事会第七届会议第 202 次会议，在日内瓦万国宫举行，本次会议的主要议题是讨论职司委员会三分之一成员的选举、继续讨论会议工作安排。中国代表张彭春率团参加了本次会议，并在会议上发言①，相关会议纪要、纪要影像及纪要译文如下：

【会议纪要】

Mr. P. C. CHANG (China) explained that he had made two informal proposals: (1) to examine in plenary, and not in the Human Rights Committee, first the draft Declaration on Human Rights and then the draft Convention on the Crime of Genocide; (2) to decide that the Human Rights Committee should work at a normal pace, holding one or two meetings a day. After the two items he had mentioned had been withdrawn from its agenda, the Committee should endeavour to complete its examination of the first draft convention contained in the Final Act of the Conference on Freedom of Information; if it succeeded in so doing, it should then procced to the second and third draft conventions and should transmit them to the Council two days, or at least one day, before the end of the session, irrespective of the stage reached. That would be on 23 or 24 August. The Council, in plenary, would then deal with those draft conventions in the same way as with the draft Convention on the Crime of Genocide and the

① UN Document: E/SR. 175-225, p. 435, pp. 436-437, p. 441.

draft Declaration on Human Rights, and transmit them to the General Assembly. The Council should not sit later than 26 August.

Mr. P. C. CHANG (China) observed that he was mainly concerned to see the Committee finish the first draft convention which it had undertaken to examine. He would not object to a ruling that it might consider the other questions if it had time to do so.

Mr. P. C. CHANG (China) wondered whether the Canadian proposal should not be considered as an amendment to course C described in document E/979 rather than an amendment to the whole of the document.

He had comments to make on the substance of the Canadian proposal. It left some matters to a rather late hour; indeed it implied that the Council might decide, on the morning of 25 August, to revert to the original Canadian suggestion (E/965) and prolong the meetings of the Human Rights Committee. The Council could not work by such methods of work, nor could the Secretariat. The closing date of the session must be determined forthwith. A week or more could not be allowed to pass without any decision. Moreover, the Canadian representative had suggested that the Human Rights Committee should continue to work at its previous pace; he (Mr. Chang) did not think it would be likely to accomplish anything by following that method. It was clear that the difficulties which had arisen were due to the slow progress so far achieved.

He suggested that a vote should be taken first on course A, then on course B, then on the new Canadian proposal (E/984), to be considered as an amendment to course C, and, finally, on course C itself.

Mr. P. C. CHANG (China) suggested that the items returned to plenary from the Human Rights Committee should be considered in the following order: (1) human rights; (2) genocide; (3) the three draft conventions on freedom of information.

He proposed that the directive to the Human Rights Committee should be worded as follows: "The Human Rights Committee should do its utmost to finish consideration of the draft Convention on the Gathering and International Transmission of News within three four meetings".

【纪要影像】

Mr. P. C. CHANG (China) explained that he had made two informal proposals : (1) to examine in plenary, and not in the Human Rights Committee, first the draft Declaration on Human Rights and then the draft Convention on the Crime of Genocide; (2) to decide that the Human Rights Committee should work at a normal pace, holding one or two meetings a day. After the two items he had mentioned had been withdrawn from its agenda, the Committee should endeavour to complete its examination of the first draft convention contained in the Final Act of the Conference on Freedom of Information; if it succeeded in so doing, it should then proceed to the second and third draft conventions and should transmit them to the Council two days, or at least one day, before the end of the session, irrespective of the stage reached. That would be on 23 or 24 August. The Council, in plenary, would then deal with those draft conventions in the same way as with the draft Convention on the Crime of Genocide and the draft Declaration on Human Rights, and transmit them to the General Assembly. The Council should not sit later than 26 August.

Mr. P. C. CHANG (China) observed that he was mainly concerned to see the Committee finish the first draft convention which it had undertaken to examine. He would not object to a ruling that it might consider the other questions if it had time to do so.

Mr. P. C. CHANG (China) wondered whether the Canadian proposal should not be considered as an amendment to course C described in document E/979 rather than an amendment to the whole of the document.

He had comments to make on the substance of the Canadian proposal. It left some matters to a rather late hour; indeed it implied that the Council might decide, on the morning of 25 August, to revert to the original Canadian suggestion (E/965) and prolong the meetings of the

图片 7.32　张彭春在经社理事会第七届第 202 次会议发言纪要(1)

Human Rights Committee. The Council could not work by such methods of work, nor could the Secretariat. The closing date of the session must be determined forthwith. A week or more could not be allowed to pass without any decision. Moreover, the Canadian representative had suggested that the Human Rights Committee should continue to work at its previous pace; he (Mr. Chang) did not think it would be likely to accomplish anything by following that method. It was clear that the difficulties which had arisen were due to the slow progress so far achieved.

He suggested that a vote should be taken first on course A, then on course B, then on the new Canadian proposal (E/984), to be considered as an amendment to course C, and, finally, on course C itself.

Mr. P. C. CHANG (China) suggested that the items returned to plenary from the Human Rights Committee should be considered in the following order : (1) human rights; (2) genocide; (3) the three draft conventions on freedom of information.

He proposed that the directive to the Human Rights Committee should be worded as follows : "The Human Rights Committee should do its utmost to finish consideration of the draft Convention on the Gathering and International Transmission of News within three four meetings".

图片 7.33　张彭春在经社理事会第七届第 202 次会议发言纪要(2)

【纪要译文】

张彭春先生(中国)解释说,他提出了两项非正式建议:(1)在全体会议上,而不是在人权事务委员会上,首先审议人权宣言草案,然后审议灭绝种族罪公约草案;(2)决定人权事务委员会应以正常速度工作,每天举行一至两次会议。在他提到的两个项目从其议程中撤回后,委员会应努力完成对新闻自由会议最终文件所载公约草案的审查;如果它成功地做到这一点,那么它应着手审议第二和第三项公约草案,并应在届会结束前两天,或至少一天,将其转交理事会,而不论所处的阶段如何。那将是8月23日或24日。理事会随后将在全体会议上以处理灭绝种族罪公约草案和人权宣言草案的同样方式处理这些公约草案,并将其转交大会。理事会不应迟于8月26日开会。

张彭春先生(中国)说,他主要关心的是委员会完成其承诺审查的第一份公约草案。他不会反对这样一个裁决:如果有时间的话,它可能会考虑其他问题。

张彭春先生(中国)想知道,加拿大的提案是否不应被视为对E/979号文件所述方案C的修正,而应被视为对整个文件的修正。

他对加拿大提案的实质内容有意见。它把一些事项留到了相当晚的时间;事实上,这意味着理事会可能在8月25日上午决定恢复加拿大原来的建议(E/965号文件),延长人权事务委员会的会议。理事会不能以这种工作方法开展工作,秘书处也不能。必须立即确定会议的闭幕日期。做出决定不得超过一周或更长的时间。此外,加拿大代表建议,人权事务委员会应继续按照以前的速度工作;他(张先生)认为,采用这种方法不太可能取得任何成果。显然,出现的困难是由于迄今取得的进展缓慢。

他建议首先对方案A进行表决,然后对方案B进行表决,然后对加拿大的新提案(E/984)进行表决,将其视为对方案C的修正,最后对方案C本身进行表决。

张彭春先生(中国)建议,人权事务委员会返回全体会议的项目应按以下顺序审议:(1)人权;(2)灭绝种族;(3)关于新闻自由的三项公约草案。

他提议,给人权事务委员会的指示的措辞应如下:“人权事务委员会应尽最大努力在三至四次会议内完成对关于新闻收集和国际传播公约草案的审议”。

18. 张彭春在经社理事会第七届第203次会议上的发言

1948年8月18日上午10时，联合国经社理事会第七届第203次会议，在日内瓦万国宫举行，本次会议的主要议题是继续讨论会议工作安排。中国代表张彭春率团参加了本次会议，并在会议上发言[①]，相关会议纪要、纪要影像及纪要译文如下：

【会议纪要】

Mr. P. C. CHANG (China) said that he was again prepared to run the risk of being called unrealistic in order to defend an idealistic endeavor. He opposed deferment of the item, especially as it could be quickly disposed of.

Mr. P. C. CHANG (China) said that he was opposed to deferment of that important question, consideration of which would not in any case take much time.

① UN Document: E/SR. 175-225, p. 454, p. 457.

【纪要影像】

Mr. P. C. CHANG (China) said that he was again prepared to run the risk of being called unrealistic in order to defend an idealistic endeavour. He opposed deferment of the item, especially as it could be quickly disposed of.

Mr. P. C. CHANG (China) said that he was opposed to deferment of that important question, consideration of which would not in any case take much time.

图片 7.34　张彭春在经社理事会第七届第 203 次会议发言纪要

【纪要译文】

张彭春先生(中国)说,为了捍卫理想的努力,他再次准备冒被称为不现实的风险。他反对推迟该项目,特别是因为它可以很快处理掉。

张彭春先生(中国)说,他反对推迟审议这一重要问题,因为审议这一问题无论如何不会花费太多时间。

19. 张彭春在经社理事会第七届第206次会议上的发言

1948年8月19日下午3时，联合国经社理事会第七届第206次会议，在日内瓦万国宫举行，本次会议的议题是继续讨论职司委员会三分之一成员的选举、继续讨论亚洲和远东经济委员会的报告和讨论联合国资源保护和利用科学大会。中国代表张彭春率代表团参加了本次会议，并在会议上发言①，相关会议纪要、纪要影像及纪要译文如下：

【会议纪要】

Mr. P.C. CHANG (China), speaking as a representative of one of the countries on the Economic Commission for Asia and the Far East, expressed his great appreciation of the friendly concern shown throughout the debate and especially for the work done on the Drafting Committee by the representatives of Canada, France, New Zealand, the Soviet Union, the United States of America and Venezuela.

He could not agree that alternative B was substantially the same as the original recommendation. If members turned to document E/893, in which the Chinese delegation had reproduced the Commission's original proposal, they would see that there were a number of significant differences. Document E/893 referred to a Bureau of Flood Control to be composed of not more than five experts appointed from a panel of names to be submitted by Member Govern-

① UN Document: E/SR. 175-225, pp. 508-509, p. 510.

ments. There was also a chairman to be appointed from among the experts. All those features in the original proposal, to which objections had been raised, were absent from alternative B. Alternative B provided for the formation of the Bureau by the Secretary-General and for it to be responsible to the Economic Commission for Asia and the Far East. The proposal was limited to the formation of a technical group which could no longer be regarded as semi-autonomous or independent of the Secretary-General.

With regard to the view that the Council should not instruct the Secretary-General how many experts to engage, he did not believe that argument was entirely valid. Only a few days before, in discussing the report of the Social Commission,① it had been decided that a group of not more than seven persons should survey problems of crime. A recommendation on the number of experts for the Bureau of Flood Control would not, therefore, be the first of its kind.

He agreed with the New Zealand representative that the Council should not encourage the formation of new agencies. But there was no question of a precedent; flood control was a unique problem and the word "bureau" had been used, not in order to set a precedent, but in order to avoid increasing the United Nations Secretariat.

Neither alternative A nor alternative B as amended by the New Zealand delegation provided the immediate tool that was required. The adoption of either would mean delay in dealing with a most urgent problem.

Mr. P. C. CHANG (China) said that the use of the word "or" in the first part of the New Zealand amendment implied a doubt. That was quite unnecessary in view of the words "formed by the Secretary-General", which were perfectly clear.

---

① See *supra*, 198th meeting.

【纪要影像】

Mr. P. C. CHANG (China), speaking as a representative of one of the countries on the Economic Commission for Asia and the Far East, expressed his great appreciation of the friendly concern shown throughout the debate and especially for the work done on the Drafting Committee by the representatives of Canada, France, New Zealand, the Soviet Union, the United States of America and Venezuela.

He could not agree that alternative B was substantially the same as the original recommendation. If members turned to document E/893, in which the Chinese delegation had reproduced the Commission's original proposal, they would see that there were a number of significant differences. Document E/893 referred to a Bureau of Flood Control to be composed of not more than five experts appointed from a panel of names to be submitted by Member Governments. There was also a chairman to be appointed from among the experts. All those features in the original proposal, to which objections had been raised, were absent from alternative B. Alternative B provided for the formation of the Bureau by the Secretary-General and for it to be responsible to the Economic Commission for Asia and the Far East. The proposal was limited to the formation of a technical group which could no longer be regarded as semi-autonomous or independent of the Secretary-General.

With regard to the view that the Council should not instruct the Secretary-General how many experts to engage, he did not believe that argument was entirely valid. Only a few days before, in discussing the report of the Social Commission,[1] it had been decided that a group of not more than seven persons should survey problems of crime. A recommendation on the number of experts for the Bureau of Flood Control would not, therefore, be the first of its kind.

He agreed with the New Zealand representative that the Council should not encourage the formation of new agencies. But there was no question of a precedent; flood control was a unique problem and the word "bureau" had been used, not in order to set a precedent, but in order to avoid increasing the United Nations Secretariat.

Neither alternative A nor alternative B as amended by the New Zealand delegation provided the immediate tool that was required. The adoption of either would mean delay in dealing with a most urgent problem.

[1] See *supra*, 198th meeting.

Mr. P. C. CHANG (China) said that the use of the word "or" in the first part of the New Zealand amendment implied a doubt. That was quite unnecessary in view of the words "formed by the Secretary-General", which were perfectly clear.

图片 7.35　张彭春在经社理事会第七届第 206 次会议发言纪要

【纪要译文】

张彭春先生（中国）作为亚洲和远东经济委员会一个成员国的代表发言，他表示非常感谢加拿大、法国、新西兰、苏联、美国和委内瑞拉代表在整个辩论期间所表现的友好关切，特别是对起草委员会所做的工作。

他不同意备选案文 B 与原建议基本相同。如果各位成员看一下 E/893 号文件，其中中国代表团复制了委员会的原始提案，他们会发现有一些重大差异。E/893 号文件提到防洪局由不超过五名专家组成，这些专家从成员国政府提交的名单中任命。还将从专家中任命一名主席。原提案中受到反对意见的所有这些特点，备选案文 B 中都没有了。备选案文 B 规定由秘书长组织防洪局，并向亚洲和远东经济委员会负责。该提案仅限于成立一个技术小组，该小组不能再被视为半自治或独立于秘书长。

关于理事会不应指示秘书长聘用多少专家的观点，他认为这一论点是完全站不住脚的。就在几天前,在讨论社会委员会的报告[1]时,决定由不超过七人的小组调查犯罪问题。因此,关于防洪局专家人数的建议并非第一次。

他同意新西兰代表的意见,即理事会不应鼓励成立新的机构。但没有先例的问题;防洪是一个独特的问题,使用“局”一词不是为了开创先例,而是为了避免增加联合国秘书处的人数。

经新西兰代表团修正的备选方案 A 和备选方案 B 均未提供所需的直接工具。采用这两种方法都将意味着推迟处理最紧迫的问题。

张彭春先生(中国)说,新西兰修正案第一部分中使用“或”一词意味着怀疑。这是完全没有必要的,因为“由秘书长组织”这几个字非常清楚。

① 见:同上,第 198 次会议。

20. 张彭春在经社理事会第七届第209次会议上的发言

1948年8月21日上午10时，联合国经社理事会第七届第209次会议，在日内瓦万国宫举行，本次会议的议题是继续讨论拉丁美洲经济委员会的报告。中国代表张彭春率团参加了本次会议，并在会议上发言①，相关会议纪要、纪要影像及纪要译文如下：

【会议纪要】

Mr. P. C. CHANG (China) said that when he had heard the Chilean representative speak of the enthusiastic atmosphere that had reigned at Santiago during the first session of the Commission, he had been reminded of the two pleasant years he had spent in one of the most hospitable cities in the world.

On that occasion, he had gone to South America from China by way of the Middle East. In those three areas, he had found the same hunger for industrialization, the same lack of machinery and modern capital goods, the same over-emphasis on agricultural products or even on one agricultural product, and the same approach to capital investment.

All those areas, which were striving for industrial modernization, needed to exchange the fruits of their experience. China, for example had developed a primitive method of extracting nitrates, and it was a source of gratification that the most eminent Chinese scientist in that field had been twice invited to Bra-

① UN Document: E/SR. 175-225, pp. 572-573.

zil. Similarly, Chile had received information on the experiments carried out in China in small-scale steel production. Lack of vision had as yet prevented full realization of the potential benefits of such pooling of experience by areas which were going through analogous experiences.

During the past 150 years, it might be that too much attention had been paid to material factors in themselves, and not enough to human factors. In the under-developed countries, the higher strata of the population had tended to literary-mindedness. They might naturally resent any criticism to the effect that they were lacking in practical genius. Scientific aptitude was as much innate in one people as in another. But it could not be denied that it needed to be developed among the peoples of the under-developed countries, and especially among their leaders.

Moreover, there was a tendency to be fascinated by the latest "gadget", without troubling to grasp the processes of development that had finally resulted in the current stage of mechanical advancement; there was interest in the latest machines, but a lack of interest in how they came into being. If the less developed countries were ever to achieve new creative developments of their own, they must study how each progressive material advance had gone a stage further to meet an existing need, so that they could criticize and improve on the latest stage of development reached.

【纪要影像】

Mr. P. C. CHANG (China) said that when he had heard the Chilean representative speak of the enthusiastic atmosphere that had reigned at Santiago during the first session of the Commission, he had been reminded of the two pleasant years he had spent in one of the most hospitable cities in the world.

On that occasion, he had gone to South America from China by way of the Middle East. In those three areas, he had found the same hunger for industrialization, the same lack of machinery and modern capital goods, the same over-emphasis on agricultural products or even on one agricultural product, and the same approach to capital investment.

All those areas, which were striving for industrial modernization, needed to exchange the fruits of their experience. China, for example had developed a primitive method of extracting nitrates, and it was a source of gratification that the most eminent Chinese scientist in that field had been twice invited to Brazil. Similarly, Chile had received information on the experiments carried out in China in small-scale steel production. Lack of vision had as yet prevented full realization of the potential benefits of such pooling of experience by areas which were going through analogous experiences.

During the past 150 years, it might be that too much attention had been paid to material factors in themselves, and not enough to human factors. In the under-developed countries, the higher strata of the population had tended to literary-mindedness. They might naturally resent any criticism to the effect that they were lacking in practical genius. Scientific aptitude was as much innate in one people as in another. But it could not be denied that it needed to be developed among the peoples of the under-developed countries, and especially among their leaders.

Moreover, there was a tendency to be fascinated by the latest "gadget", without troubling to grasp the processes of development that had finally resulted in the current stage of mechanical advancement; there was interest in the latest machines, but a lack of interest in how they came into being. If the less developed countries were ever to achieve new creative developments of their own, they must study how each progressive material advance had gone a stage further to meet an existing need, so that they could criticize and improve on the latest stage of development reached.

图片 7.36　张彭春在经社理事会第七届第 209 次会议发言纪要

【纪要译文】

张彭春先生(中国)说,当他听到智利代表谈到委员会第一届会议期间圣地亚哥的热烈气氛时,他想起了他在世界上最热情好客的城市之一度过的愉快的两年。

当时,他从中国经中东前往南美洲。在这三个区域,他发现了同样的工业化渴望,同样的机械和现代资本货物的缺乏,同样的对农产品甚至一种农产品的过度强调,以及同样的资本投资方法。

所有这些正在努力实现工业现代化的区域都需要交流经验成果。例如,中国开发了一种提取硝酸盐的原始方法,该领域最杰出的中国科学家两次被邀请到巴西,这让人感到欣慰。同样,智利也收到了关于在中国进行的小规模钢铁生产试验的信息。迄今为止,由于缺乏远见,正在经历类似经验的区域,还无法充分领会这种经验汇集的潜在好处。

在过去的 150 年中,可能是对物质因素本身的关注太多,而对人为因素的关注不够。在欠发达国家,较高层次的人口倾向于文学意识。他们自然会对任何批评感到不满,认为他们缺乏实践天赋。科学天赋在一个人和另一个人身上都是天生的。但不可否认的是,它需要在欠发达国家的人民之间,特别是在他们的领导人之间得到发展。

此外,有一种趋势是对最新的“小玩意”着迷,而没有费心去掌握最终导致现阶段机械进步的发展过程;人们对最新的机器感兴趣,但对它们是如何产生的缺乏兴趣。如果较不发达国家要实现自己的新的创造性发展,它们必须研究每一个向前的物质进步是如何进一步满足现有需求的,这样它们就可以在最新发展阶段的基础上进行批评和改进。

21. 张彭春在经社理事会第七届第216次会议上的发言

1948年8月25日下午3时,联合国经社理事会第七届第216次会议,在日内瓦万国宫举行,本次会议的主要议题是讨论1949年会议日程草案等。中国代表张彭春率团参加了本次会议,并在会议上先后多次发言[①],相关会议纪要、纪要影像及纪要译文如下:

【会议纪要】

Mr. P. C. CHANG (China) felt that it would be necessary to consider all three of those important questions at reasonable length before anyone of them could be voted on.

They were discussing not the meeting of a Conference, but the sessions of a Council with definite responsibilities which, in many most important respects, had not been fully discharged at the current session. The Council must find some method of discharging its responsibilities more adequately. He believed that it should make provision for fuller consideration of the weighty questions with which it had to deal. The first of the sessions to be held in 1949 should last at least 8 or 9, and possibly 12 weeks. The Trusteeship Council, which had a much narrower field of responsibility, had recently been sitting in New York for as long as, if not longer than, the Economic and Social Council at Geneva. A long, continuous session was necessary to ensure a consistent level of

① UN Document: E/SR. 175-225, p. 661, p. 665, p. 666, p. 667.

productive work. The length of time for which various experts were required to be present could be lessened by dividing up the session according to the nature of items, one third being devoted to economic questions, one third to social questions, and one third to questions of co-ordination and procedure.

It was not necessary for the Council to decide, at that stage, whether there should be two sessions or three. If the work were not completed by the close of the second session, a third, shorter session might be necessary.

At the sixth session of the Council, the Chinese delegation had formulated its objections to holding sessions away from Headquarters.① Other delegations had argued that the holding of the seventh session in Europe would give representatives greater knowledge of European conditions. That contention had proved over-optimistic, to say the least. The President had rightly said that if the Council performed its functions well in the economic and social fields, political and military problems would fade more and more into the background. Yet the Council was apparently envisaging without alarm an unnecessary loss of working efficiency. He wished to place on record his Government's conviction that the Council, as one of the principal organs of the United Nations—perhaps the organ with the greatest promise for the future—, should not move away from Headquarters.

He therefore proposed that the first session of the Council in 1949 should be held at Lake Success, should continue for a period of 8 to 12 weeks, and should be divided into three equal parts for the consideration of economic questions, social questions, and questions relating to co-ordination and procedure respectively.

Mr. P. C. CHANG (China) thought the Secretariat could confirm that when the Council had been asked by the United Kingdom delegation, at its

① See *Official Records of the Economic and Social Council*, third year, sixth session, 141st meeting.

sixth session, to reverse the decision to hold the seventh session in Europe,[①] both that proposal and the estimated financial implications had been circulated well over twenty-four hours in advance of the discussion.

He himself had until that morning been quite unaware that any proposal would be introduced to hold the second session of the Council in 1949 away from Headquarters.

Mr. P. C. CHANG (China) pointed out that if representatives had been at Lake Success, they could easily have had access to those financial estimates. The point gave an excellent example of the inconvenience of holding sessions away from Headquarters.

Mr. P. C. CHANG (China) felt that the President's interpretation of rule 30 was casuistical Before the Council could begin serious and intelligent consideration of the Chilean proposal, it had to have before it estimates of the financial implications of that proposal.

【纪要影像】

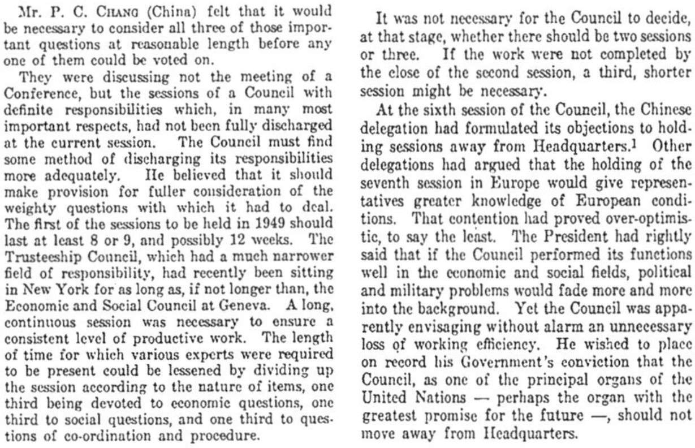

Mr. P. C. CHANG (China) felt that it would be necessary to consider all three of those important questions at reasonable length before any one of them could be voted on.

They were discussing not the meeting of a Conference, but the sessions of a Council with definite responsibilities which, in many most important respects, had not been fully discharged at the current session. The Council must find some method of discharging its responsibilities more adequately. He believed that it should make provision for fuller consideration of the weighty questions with which it had to deal. The first of the sessions to be held in 1949 should last at least 8 or 9, and possibly 12 weeks. The Trusteeship Council, which had a much narrower field of responsibility, had recently been sitting in New York for as long as, if not longer than, the Economic and Social Council at Geneva. A long, continuous session was necessary to ensure a consistent level of productive work. The length of time for which various experts were required to be present could be lessened by dividing up the session according to the nature of items, one third being devoted to economic questions, one third to social questions, and one third to questions of co-ordination and procedure.

It was not necessary for the Council to decide, at that stage, whether there should be two sessions or three. If the work were not completed by the close of the second session, a third, shorter session might be necessary.

At the sixth session of the Council, the Chinese delegation had formulated its objections to holding sessions away from Headquarters.[1] Other delegations had argued that the holding of the seventh session in Europe would give representatives greater knowledge of European conditions. That contention had proved over-optimistic, to say the least. The President had rightly said that if the Council performed its functions well in the economic and social fields, political and military problems would fade more and more into the background. Yet the Council was apparently envisaging without alarm an unnecessary loss of working efficiency. He wished to place on record his Government's conviction that the Council, as one of the principal organs of the United Nations — perhaps the organ with the greatest promise for the future —, should not move away from Headquarters.

图片 7.37　张彭春在经社理事会第七届第 216 次会议发言纪要(1)

① See *Official Records of the Economic and Social Council*, third year, sixth session, 140th meeting.

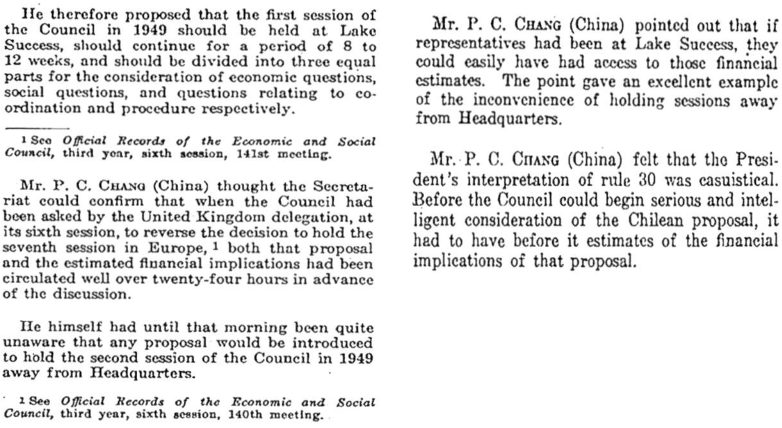

He therefore proposed that the first session of the Council in 1949 should be held at Lake Success, should continue for a period of 8 to 12 weeks, and should be divided into three equal parts for the consideration of economic questions, social questions, and questions relating to co-ordination and procedure respectively.

[1] See *Official Records of the Economic and Social Council*, third year, sixth session, 141st meeting.

Mr. P. C. CHANG (China) thought the Secretariat could confirm that when the Council had been asked by the United Kingdom delegation, at its sixth session, to reverse the decision to hold the seventh session in Europe, [1] both that proposal and the estimated financial implications had been circulated well over twenty-four hours in advance of the discussion.

He himself had until that morning been quite unaware that any proposal would be introduced to hold the second session of the Council in 1949 away from Headquarters.

[1] See *Official Records of the Economic and Social Council*, third year, sixth session, 140th meeting.

Mr. P. C. CHANG (China) pointed out that if representatives had been at Lake Success, they could easily have had access to those financial estimates. The point gave an excellent example of the inconvenience of holding sessions away from Headquarters.

Mr. P. C. CHANG (China) felt that the President's interpretation of rule 30 was casuistical. Before the Council could begin serious and intelligent consideration of the Chilean proposal, it had to have before it estimates of the financial implications of that proposal.

图片 7.38　张彭春在经社理事会第七届第 216 次会议发言纪要(2)

【纪要译文】

张彭春先生(中国)认为,在任何人都可以投票表决之前,有必要将这三个重要问题以合理的长度考虑在内。

他们讨论的不是一次会议,而是一个具有明确责任的理事会的届会,在许多最重要的方面,本届会议还没有充分履行这些责任。理事会必须找到某种更充分地履行其职责的方法。他认为,它应作出规定,以便更充分地审议它必须处理的重大问题。1949 年举行的第一届会议应至少持续 8 或 9 周,可能 12 周。托管理事会的职责范围要窄得多,它最近在纽约的会议时间与经济及社会理事会在日内瓦的会议时间一样长,如果不是更长的话。为了确保持续的生产性工作水平,有必要举行一次长时间、连续的会议。各专家出席会议的时间可以缩短,办法是根据项目的性质划分会议,三分之一专门讨论经济问题,三分之一专门讨论社会问题,三分之一专门讨论协调和程序问题。

在这一阶段,理事会没有必要决定是举行两届会议还是三届会议。如果工作在第二届会议结束时仍未完成,则可能需要举行第三届较短的会议。

在理事会第六届会议上,中国代表团反对在总部以外举行会议。[1] 其他代表团认为,在欧洲举行第七届会议将使代表们更多地了解欧洲的情况。至少可以说,这一争论被证明过于乐观了。主席直接地说,如果理事会在经济和社会领域很好地履行其职能,政治和军事问题将越来越淡出人们的视线。然而,理事会显然正在毫无顾忌地设想不必要的工作效率损失。他希望将其政府的信念记录在案,即理事会作为联合国的主要机构之一——也许是对未来最有希望的机构——不应离开总部。

因此,他建议 1949 年理事会第一届会议应在成功湖举行,会期为 8 至 12 周,并应平分为三部分,分别审议经济问题、社会问题以及与协调和程序有关的问题。

张彭春先生(中国)认为秘书处可以确认,当英国代表团在其第六届会议上要求理事会撤销在欧洲举行第七届会议的决定[2]时,该提案和估计所涉经费已在讨论前 24 小时内分发。

直到那天上午,他本人还完全不知道会提出任何在总部以外举行理事会 1949 年第二届会议的建议。

张彭春先生(中国)指出,如果代表们在成功湖,他们很容易就能得到这些财务估计数。这一点为在总部以外举行会议带来的不便提供了一个极好的例子。

张彭春先生(中国)认为,主席对第 30 条的解释是随意的,在理事会能够开始认真和明智地审议智利的提案之前,它必须有关于该提案所涉经费问题的估计。

① 《经济及社会理事会正式记录》第三年,第六届,第 141 次会议。

② 《经济及社会理事会正式记录》第三年,第六届,第 140 次会议。

22. 张彭春在经社理事会第七届第217次会议上的发言

1948年8月26日上午10时,联合国经社理事会第七届第217次会议,在日内瓦万国宫举行,本次会议的主要议题是继续讨论1949年会议日程草案。中国代表张彭春率团参加了本次会议,并在会议上发言①,相关会议纪要、纪要影像及纪要译文如下:

【会议纪要】

Mr. P. C. CHANG (China) did not wish to claim the vain glory of defending a lost cause. He had, however, some observations to make both on the substance of the proposals and on the manner in which they had been submitted.

The Chinese delegation had already been complimented on the consistency of its attitude regarding the Council's place of meeting. It was no doubt because of that consistency that it had not been approached, even informally, about the proposed change of place for the next session. It would have been gratifying if the Chinese delegation had also been paid the compliment of an assumption that it could change its mind. He hoped that in future any proposal to change the Council's place of meeting would be considered as a major item on the agenda and be subject to notice in advance under the six-weeks rule.

With regard to the substance of the question, the Chinese delegation was

① UN Document: E/SR. 175-225, pp. 678-679.

not in principle opposed to the holding of special sessions on special matters at places other than United Nations Headquarters. From the point of view of efficiency, however, such sessions were undesirable. They entailed the absence of members of the Secretariat from their offices at Lake Success, and a consequent interruption of the normal progress of work. It had been said that it was important to hold sessions in Europe, because Europe was important politically. That might be true, but there were important countries, and even important problems, outside Europe. Moreover, the Council was not a political body, and if political importance were to be taken as a criterion for determining the meeting place of United Nations organs, the proper course would surely be to suggest that the Security Council, rather than the Economic and Social Council, should meet in Europe.

Few of the items on the Council's agenda concerned Europe, and the Council itself had contributed little to the European scene by meeting in Geneva. It had been said that people from all over Europe would attend its meetings. If that were the case, the audience seemed to have failed in its duty that morning. A year ago, when Geneva had first been proposed as a meeting place for the Council, he had said that although the name Geneva fascinated him, fascination might well be only the first stage, leading next to separation and finally to divorce. He did not, however, wish the United Nations to be divorced from its Headquarters. The Chinese delegation maintained its previous attitude, though had it been informed earlier of the proposed change of venue, it might have asked its Government whether it could agree to such a change.

The Canadian and Netherlands representatives had suggested that it would be unwise to fix a time-limit for the Council's sessions. He agreed, and hoped that the first session in 1949 would continue until it had finished its work. It was undesirable that discussion of certain items should be repeatedly deferred. At its current session the Council should have considered the Declaration of Human Rights, the three conventions on freedom of information, and the Convention on Genocide. It had not done so, and to that extent had failed in its duty.

He would make no formal motion, but would suggest that the Committee on Matters relating to Coordination should be asked to consider whether, in 1949, the Council should not be given an opportunity to remain in session until its work was completed.

【纪要影像】

Mr. P. C. CHANG (China) did not wish to claim the vain glory of defending a lost cause. He had, however, some observations to make both on the substance of the proposals and on the manner in which they had been submitted.

The Chinese delegation had already been complimented on the consistency of its attitude regarding the Council's place of meeting. It was no doubt because of that consistency that it had not been approached, even informally, about the proposed change of place for the next session. It would have been gratifying if the Chinese delegation had also been paid the compliment of an assumption that it could change its mind. He hoped that in future any proposal to change the Council's place of meeting would be considered as a major item on the agenda and be subject to notice in advance under the six-weeks rule.

With regard to the substance of the question, the Chinese delegation was not in principle opposed to the holding of special sessions on special matters at places other than United Nations Headquarters. From the point of view of efficiency, however, such sessions were undesirable. They entailed the absence of members of the Secretariat from their offices at Lake Success,

and a consequent interruption of the normal progress of work. It had been said that it was important to hold sessions in Europe, because Europe was important politically. That might be true, but there were important countries, and even important problems, outside Europe. Moreover, the Council was not a political body, and if political importance were to be taken as a criterion for determining the meeting place of United Nations organs, the proper course would surely be to suggest that the Security Council, rather than the Economic and Social Council, should meet in Europe.

图片 7.39 张彭春在经社理事会第七届第 217 次会议发言纪要(1)

【纪要译文】

张彭春先生(中国)不希望因捍卫一项失败的事业而赢得虚名。然而,他对提案的实质内容和提交方式都有一些看法。

中国代表团在理事会会议地点问题上的一贯态度已经得到赞扬。毫无疑问,由于这种一致性,没有人就下一届会议拟议的地点变更问题与它进行接恰,甚至是非正式接恰。如果中国代表团也得到一种恭维,认为它可能会改变主意,那将是令人欣慰的。他希望今后任何改变理事会会议地点的提案都将被视为议程上的一个主要项目,并根据六周规则提前通知。

关于问题的实质,中国代表团原则上不反对在联合国总部以外的地点

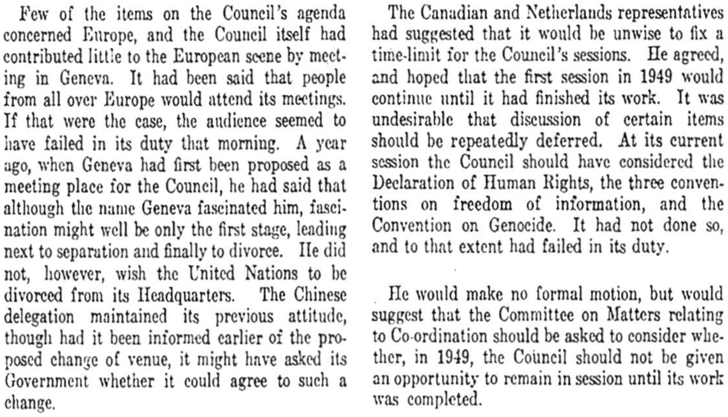

Few of the items on the Council's agenda concerned Europe, and the Council itself had contributed little to the European scene by meeting in Geneva. It had been said that people from all over Europe would attend its meetings. If that were the case, the audience seemed to have failed in its duty that morning. A year ago, when Geneva had first been proposed as a meeting place for the Council, he had said that although the name Geneva fascinated him, fascination might well be only the first stage, leading next to separation and finally to divorce. He did not, however, wish the United Nations to be divorced from its Headquarters. The Chinese delegation maintained its previous attitude, though had it been informed earlier of the proposed change of venue, it might have asked its Government whether it could agree to such a change.

The Canadian and Netherlands representatives had suggested that it would be unwise to fix a time-limit for the Council's sessions. He agreed, and hoped that the first session in 1949 would continue until it had finished its work. It was undesirable that discussion of certain items should be repeatedly deferred. At its current session the Council should have considered the Declaration of Human Rights, the three conventions on freedom of information, and the Convention on Genocide. It had not done so, and to that extent had failed in its duty.

He would make no formal motion, but would suggest that the Committee on Matters relating to Co-ordination should be asked to consider whether, in 1949, the Council should not be given an opportunity to remain in session until its work was completed.

图片 7.40　张彭春在经社理事会第七届第 217 次会议发言纪要(2)

举行关于特殊事项的特别会议。然而,从效率的角度来看,这种会议是不可取的。这导致秘书处成员不在成功湖的办公室,从而中断正常的工作进展。有人说,在欧洲举行会议很重要,因为欧洲在政治上很重要。这可能是真实的,但在欧洲以外还有一些重要的国家,甚至是重要的问题。此外,理事会不是一个政治机构,如果要将政治重要性作为确定联合国各机构开会地点的标准,正确的做法肯定是建议安全理事会而不是经济及社会理事会在欧洲开会。

理事会议程上几乎没有涉及欧洲的项目,而理事会本身在日内瓦开会对欧洲情况贡献甚微。据说来自欧洲各地的人都会参加会议。如果是这样的话,听众那天早上似乎没有履行职责。一年前,当日内瓦第一次被提议作为理事会的会议地点时,他曾说,尽管日内瓦这个名字让他着迷,但迷恋很可能只是第一个阶段,接着是分居,最后是离婚。然而,他并不希望联合国脱离其总部。中国代表团保持其先前的态度,但如果早些时候通知它拟议的地点变更,它可能会询问其政府是否同意这样的变更。

加拿大和荷兰代表建议,为理事会届会确定一个时限是不明智的。他同意这一点,并希望 1949 年第一届会议将继续举行,直到完成其工作为止。对某些项目的讨论一再推迟是不可取的。理事会本届会议应审议《人权宣言》、关于新闻自由的三项公约和《灭绝种族罪公约》。它没有这样做,故在这一层面没有尽到责任。

他将不作正式的动议,但会建议要求协调事项委员会考虑,是否在1949年,在完成其工作前理事会不应该给予继续召开届会的机会。

23. 张彭春在经社理事会第七届第221次会议上的发言

1948年8月27日下午3时，联合国经社理事会第七届会议第221次会议，在日内瓦万国宫举行，本次会议的主要议题是继续讨论新闻自由法案终稿。中国代表张彭春率团参加了本次会议，并在会议上发言①，相关会议纪要、纪要影像及纪要译文如下：

【会议纪要】

Mr. P. C. CHANG (China) also felt that it was much to be regretted that, chiefly owing to shortage of time, the Council had been unable to deal with all the three draft Conventions in a proper and befitting manner. The fact should be carefully borne in mind when the Council came to consider the future discharge of its duties.

The Chinese delegation reserved the right to comment on the three draft Conventions at the appropriate time.

① UN Document: E/SR. 175-225, p. 753.

【纪要影像】

Mr. P. C. Chang (China) also felt that it was much to be regretted that, chiefly owing to shortage of time, the Council had been unable to deal with all the three draft Conventions in a proper and befitting manner. The fact should be carefully borne in mind when the Council came to consider the future discharge of its duties.

The Chinese delegation reserved the right to comment on the three draft Conventions at the appropriate time.

图片 7.41 张彭春在经社理事会第七届第 221 次会议发言纪要

【纪要译文】

张彭春先生(中国)还感到非常遗憾的是,主要由于时间不足,理事会未能以适当和合适的方式处理所有三项公约草案。当理事会考虑未来履行职责时,必须认真考虑这一事实。

中国代表团保留了在适当的时候对三项公约草案的评论权。

第八章　联合国经社理事会第八届会议

（纪要）

1949年2月7日上午11时,联合国经社理事会第八届会议开幕,从1949年2月7日至3月18日,本届共召开了57次会议,分别从第226次会议至第282次会议。本届会议讨论了一系列有关经济社会等问题,包括会议日程安排、联大关于人权的决议、新闻和出版小组委员会的问题、人权委员会第三届会议的报告、锡兰加入联合国教科文组织的事宜、经典著作的翻译问题、非政府组织委员会的报告、男女同工同酬的原则、强迫劳动调查及其废除措施、特殊机构的关系与合作、世界经济形势、麻醉药品委员会成员选举的程序问题、欧洲经济委员会的报告、欠发达地区的经济发展问题、理事会工作的组织和理事会程序规则的修订、亚洲和远东经济委员会的报告、亚洲和远东经济委员会的临时报告、有关经济和社会建议的落实,以及选举理事会第九届日程委员会成员等。

中国代表张彭春率团参加了本届会议,并在本届20次会议上进行了大会发言,包括第227次会议、第229次会议、第230次会议、第231次会议、第232次会议、第234次会议、第235次会议、第240次会议、第242次会议、第243次会议、第244次会议、第259次会议、第260次会议、第261次会议、第268次会议、第269次会议、第270次会议、第272次会议、第273次会议和第282次会议。另外,代表团代表助理查修先生和吴德耀先生分别参与了本届会议,其中查先生在第236次会议[①]和第269次会议[②]

① UN Document: E/SR. 236, pp. 99-100.

② UN Document: E/SR. 269, p. 530, pp. 530-531.

上发言，吴德耀先生在第 258 次会议[①]、第 272 次会议[②]、第 275 次会议[③]、第 278 次会议[④]和第 279 次会议[⑤]上发言。其中，张彭春先生的发言内容如下：

① UN Document: E/SR. 258, p. 400.
② UN Document: E/SR. 272, p. 574.
③ UN Document: E/SR. 275, p. 596.
④ UN Document: E/SR. 278, p. 619, p. 623, p. 624.
⑤ UN Document: E/SR. 279, p. 632.

1. 张彭春在经社理事会第八届第227次会议上的发言

1949年2月7日下午3时，联合国经社理事会第八届第227次会议，在纽约成功湖召开。本次会议继续讨论会议日程。中国代表张彭春率团参加了本次会议，并在会议上发言①，其发言内容纪要及其译文等如下：

【会议纪要】

Mr. CHANG (China) stated that if item 51 remained on the agenda, his delegation would have the pleasure of defending the measure. It was certain that if the present decision were maintained the representative of France would raise the question of holding the eleventh session of the Council in Geneva at the ninth session; if discussion were permitted now, however, the Chinese delegation thought it would be able to present convincing arguments against holding sessions away from headquarters.

Mr. Chang hoped therefore that the Council would permit the presentation of a brief but telling argument on the point.

Mr. CHANG (China), in reply to the representative of Denmark, stated that his delegation wished to include the item on the agenda for the purpose of explaining the reasons in favour of holding the next session of the Council at headquarters. The Chinese delegation did not feel that to reconsider the question would decrease the prestige of the Council.

① UN Document: E/SR. 227, pp. 17-18, p. 18.

【纪要影像】

Mr. CHANG (China) stated that if item 51 remained on the agenda, his delegation would have the pleasure of defending the measure. It was certain that if the present decision were maintained the representative of France would raise the question of holding the eleventh session of the Council in Geneva at the ninth session; if discussion were permitted now, however, the Chinese delegation thought it would be able to present convincing arguments against holding sessions away from headquarters.

Mr. Chang hoped therefore that the Council would permit the presentation of a brief but telling argument on the point.

Mr. CHANG (China), in reply to the representative of Denmark, stated that his delegation wished to include the item on the agenda for the purpose of explaining the reasons in favour of holding the next session of the Council at headquarters. The Chinese delegation did not feel that to reconsider the question would decrease the prestige of the Council.

图片 8.1　张彭春在经社理事会第八届第 227 次会议发言纪要

【纪要译文】

张先生(中国)说,如果议程上保留项目 51,中国代表团将很高兴为这项措施辩护。可以肯定的是,如果维持本决定,法国代表将会提出在第九届会议期间在日内瓦举行理事会第十一届会议的问题;然而,如果现在允许进行讨论,中国代表团认为它将能够提出令人信服的理由,来反对在总部以外举行会议。

因此,张先生希望理事会允许就这一点提出简短而有力的论点。

张先生(中国)在答复丹麦代表时说,中国代表团希望将该项目列入议程,以便解释赞成在总部举行理事会下届会议的理由。中国代表团认为,重新审议这个问题不会降低理事会的威望。

2. 张彭春在经社理事会第八届第229次会议上的发言

1949年2月8日下午3时,联合国经社理事会第八届第229次会议,在纽约成功湖召开。本次会议讨论并通过了会议日程、讨论届会的工作安排。中国代表张彭春率团参加了本次会议,并在会议上先后多次发言[①],其发言内容纪要及其译文等如下:

【会议纪要】

Mr. CHANG (China) also felt that the useful recommendations made by the Agenda Committee should be accepted in principle. Members of the Council, however, should not bind themselves by a formal vote for, otherwise, they would have to take a formal decision each time they wished to alter the order of consideration.

Mr. CHANG (China) pointed out there was no need for a formal vote; the Council would merely proceed for the next two days as suggested by the President.

Mr. CHANG (China) expressed the Council's gratitude to the President for his helpful suggestions. He pointed out that if the Economic Committee did not begin its work until items 16 and 17 had been discussed in plenary session, the work of that Committee would be considerably delayed and a very short period would be left for the consideration of the many items on its agenda. He won-

① UN Document: E/SR. 229, p. 29, p. 31, p. 33, p. 34, p. 35.

dered if it would not be possible for the Economic Committee to initiate discussion on some of the items on its agenda before consideration of item 16 had been concluded in plenary session. He also wondered whether the Social Committee could not start its work as soon as possible even though the discussion of items 28, 29 and 27 in plenary session had not been concluded.

Mr. CHANG (China) agreed that, theoretically, every item was closely connected with any conclusions reached in regard to the world economic situation. There were some items, however, on which the Council was agreed in principle, as, for example, with regard to item 4 concerning the establishment of an economic commission for the Middle East. In view of the Economic Committee's heavy agenda and since all economic items had to be returned to the Council, it seemed impossible that the Committee would conclude its work in time.

He would therefore request the Secretariat to render an opinion as to whether the Committee could start its work on certain other items of the agenda before the Council had concluded its first debate on items 16 and 17 in plenary session.

Mr. CHANG (China) reminded the Council that its manner of work and its time-table had always been a problem. The real solution would be for the Council to sit continuously. He did not, however, wish to go into that question at that time. Nevertheless, in the interests of the work of the Council, he thought that it would be advisable to start meetings at 10. 30 a. m. and rise earlier. He would propose as a compromise solution, in view of the other opinions which had been expressed, that meetings should start at 11 a. m. and finish at 5. 30 p. m.

【纪要影像】

Mr. CHANG (China) also felt that the useful recommendations made by the Agenda Committee should be accepted in principle. Members of the Council, however, should not bind themselves by a formal vote for, otherwise, they would have to take a formal decision each time they wished to alter the order of consideration.

Mr. CHANG (China) pointed out there was no need for a formal vote; the Council would merely proceed for the next two days as suggested by the President.

Mr. CHANG (China) expressed the Council's gratitude to the President for his helpful suggestions. He pointed out that if the Economic Committee did not begin its work until items 16 and 17 had been discussed in plenary session, the work of that Committee would be considerably delayed and a very short period would be left for the consideration of the many items on its agenda. He wondered if it would not be possible for the Economic Committee to initiate discussion on some of the items on its agenda before consideration of item 16 had been concluded in plenary session. He also wondered whether the Social Committee could not start its work as soon as possible even though the discussion of items 28, 29 and 27 in plenary session had not been concluded.

Mr. CHANG (China) agreed that, theoretically, every item was closely connected with any conclusions reached in regard to the world economic situation. There were some items, however, on which the Council was agreed in principle, as, for example, with regard to item 4 concerning the establishment of an economic commission for the Middle East. In view of the Economic Committee's heavy agenda and since all economic items had to be returned to the Council, it seemed impossible that the Committee would conclude its work in time.

He would therefore request the Secretariat to render an opinion as to whether the Committee could start its work on certain other items of the agenda before the Council had concluded its first debate on items 16 and 17 in plenary session.

Mr. CHANG (China) reminded the Council that its manner of work and its time-table had always been a problem. The real solution would be for the Council to sit continuously. He did not, however, wish to go into that question at that time. Nevertheless, in the interests of the work of the Council, he thought that it would be advisable to start meetings at 10.30 a.m. and rise earlier. He would propose as a compromise solution, in view of the other opinions which had been expressed, that meetings should start at 11 a.m. and finish at 5.30 p.m.

图片 8.2　张彭春在经社理事会第八届第 229 次会议发言纪要

【纪要译文】

张先生(中国)还认为,原则上应接受议程委员会提出的有益建议。然而,理事会成员不应通过正式投票来约束自己,否则,他们将不得不在每次希望改变审议顺序时作出正式决定。

张先生(中国)指出,没有必要进行正式表决;理事会将按照主席的建议在今后两天内继续工作。

张先生(中国)表示理事会感谢主席提出了有益的建议。他指出,如果经济事务委员会在全体会议讨论了项目 16 和 17 之后才开始工作,该委员会的工作将大大推迟,留给审议其议程上许多项目的时间将会很短。他想知道,在全体会议结束对项目 16 的审议之前,经济事务委员会是否可能就其议程上的一些项目展开讨论。他还想知道,即使全体会议对项目 28、29 和 27 的讨论尚未结束,社会事务委员会是否能够尽快开始工作。

张先生(中国)同意,从理论上讲,每个项目都与就世界经济形势得出的任何结论密切相关。然而,理事会原则上同意了一些项目,例如关于设立中东经济委员会的项目4。鉴于经济事务委员会议程繁重,而且所有经济项目都必须返回理事会,委员会似乎不可能及时完成其工作。

因此,他请秘书处在理事会全体会议结束关于项目16和17的第一次辩论之前,就委员会是否可以开始其关于议程上某些其他项目的工作提出意见。

张先生(中国)提醒理事会,其工作方式和时间表一直是个问题。真正的解决办法是理事会继续开会。然而,他当时不想讨论这个问题。尽管如此,为了理事会的工作,他认为最好在上午10时30分开始开会,早点起床。考虑到所表达的其他意见,他将提出一项折衷解决办法,即会议应在上午11时开始,下午5时30分结束。

3. 张彭春在经社理事会第八届第230次会议上的发言

1949年2月9日上午11时，联合国经社理事会第八届第230次会议，在纽约成功湖召开。本次会议讨论联大关于人权的决议、讨论新闻和出版自由小组委员会的问题。中国代表张彭春率团参加了本次会议，并在会议上发言①，其发言内容纪要及其译文等如下：

【会议纪要】

Mr. CHANG (China) pointed out that a short text would result in savings in printing and publication.

Mr. CHANG (China) pointed out that when in plenary session, the Council should confine itself to general discussion of the question and should entrust the Social Committee with a detailed study of both the draft resolution drawn up by the Secretary-General and of the amendment submitted by the United States. Mr. Chang therefore proposed that item 29 should be referred to the Social Committee.

① UN Document: E/SR. 230, p. 39, pp. 42-43.

【纪要影像】

Mr. CHANG (China) pointed out that a short text would result in savings in printing and publication.

Mr. CHANG (China) pointed out that when in plenary session, the Council should confine itself to general discussion of the question and should entrust the Social Committee with a detailed study of both the draft resolution drawn up by

the Secretary-General and of the amendment submitted by the United States. Mr. Chang therefore proposed that item 29 should be referred to the Social Committee.

图片 8.3　张彭春在经社理事会第八届第 230 次会议发言纪要

【纪要译文】

张先生(中国)指出,简短的案文将节省印刷和出版费用。

张先生(中国)指出,在全体会议上,理事会应仅限于对问题的一般性讨论,并应委托社会事务委员会,对秘书长起草的决议草案和美国提交的修正案进行详细研究。因此,张先生提议将项目 29 提交社会事务委员会。

4. 张彭春在经社理事会第八届第231次会议上的发言

1949年2月9日下午3时,联合国经社理事会第八届第231次会议,在纽约成功湖召开。本次会议继续讨论人权委员会第三届会议的报告。中国代表张彭春率团参加了本次会议,并在会议上先后多次发言①,其发言内容纪要及其译文等如下:

【会议纪要】

Mr. CHANG (China) stated that when the matter had been brought before the Commission on Human Rights; it had been with the intention of broadening the understanding of human rights and how those rights were being put into practice. If the Yearbook included only legislative codes no concrete idea would be gained of how those rights were actually being upheld. That information could be gained if court decisions were included in the Yearbook but he wondered whether it would be practicable to initiate such a programme at that time. The project was a complicated one since all human rights were in some way involved in all court decisions and therefore the Council ought to consider the matter carefully before taking a decision.

The Council should bear in mind that the difficulties of the plan would be increased because various systems of jurisprudence and different social philosophies would be reflected in those court decisions.

---

① UN Document: E/SR. 231, pp. 51-52, p. 54.

He considered that the Council's task should be to improve man's moral sensitiveness and not to expand the areas of contention amongst nations. The Council should aim at educational improvement and moral discipline. He considered it would be extremely difficult for the Secretary-General to attempt to handle such a programme unless further guidance could be forthcoming from the Council.

It would be difficult to define the range of human rights involved in court decisions which should be included in the Yearbook. He thought it might be wiser therefore to postpone taking a final decision until the following session of the Council. The Secretariat could proceed on an experimental basis, however, compiling two or three pilot papers which would comprise decisions on human rights handed down in two or three countries over a period of two or three years. With those studies before it, the Council could form a concrete idea of exactly how the project would be carried out. It could determine whether those studies would lead to a better understanding of human rights and moral discipline and would also indicate whether the scope of the project should be limited.

He therefore proposed that the Council should postpone taking a decision on the second draft resolution regarding the inclusion of court decisions relating to human rights in the Yearbook on Human Rights until the ninth session of the Council, and furthermore that the Secretariat should prepare for presentation to the ninth session of the Council three or four pilot papers which would illustrate what was meant by court decisions.

Mr. CHANG (China) thought that it would not be necessary to institute a new research programme. His intention had been to utilize correspondents already appointed, who, he was sure, would be glad to co-operate in such a vitally important programme.

Mr. CHANG (China) thought that it was not a question of shirking a duty but rather a matter of scientific approach. He thought the suggestion to include court decisions in the Yearbook was a valuable one but that before taking a decision the Council should have some information on the type of work which would be done. He therefore maintained his proposal.

Mr. CHANG (China) agreed with that procedure.

【纪要影像】

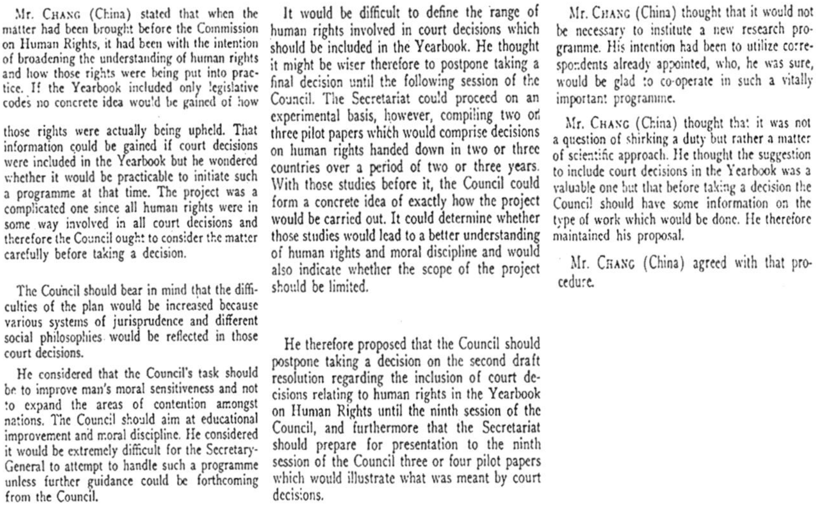

Mr. CHANG (China) stated that when the matter had been brought before the Commission on Human Rights, it had been with the intention of broadening the understanding of human rights and how those rights were being put into practice. If the Yearbook included only legislative codes no concrete idea would be gained of how those rights were actually being upheld. That information could be gained if court decisions were included in the Yearbook but he wondered whether it would be practicable to initiate such a programme at that time. The project was a complicated one since all human rights were in some way involved in all court decisions and therefore the Council ought to consider the matter carefully before taking a decision.

The Council should bear in mind that the difficulties of the plan would be increased because various systems of jurisprudence and different social philosophies would be reflected in those court decisions.

He considered that the Council's task should be to improve man's moral sensitiveness and not to expand the areas of contention amongst nations. The Council should aim at educational improvement and moral discipline. He considered it would be extremely difficult for the Secretary-General to attempt to handle such a programme unless further guidance could be forthcoming from the Council.

It would be difficult to define the range of human rights involved in court decisions which should be included in the Yearbook. He thought it might be wiser therefore to postpone taking a final decision until the following session of the Council. The Secretariat could proceed on an experimental basis, however, compiling two or three pilot papers which would comprise decisions on human rights handed down in two or three countries over a period of two or three years. With those studies before it, the Council could form a concrete idea of exactly how the project would be carried out. It could determine whether those studies would lead to a better understanding of human rights and moral discipline and would also indicate whether the scope of the project should be limited.

He therefore proposed that the Council should postpone taking a decision on the second draft resolution regarding the inclusion of court decisions relating to human rights in the Yearbook on Human Rights until the ninth session of the Council, and furthermore that the Secretariat should prepare for presentation to the ninth session of the Council three or four pilot papers which would illustrate what was meant by court decisions.

Mr. CHANG (China) thought that it would not be necessary to institute a new research programme. His intention had been to utilize correspondents already appointed, who, he was sure, would be glad to co-operate in such a vitally important programme.

Mr. CHANG (China) thought that it was not a question of shirking a duty but rather a matter of scientific approach. He thought the suggestion to include court decisions in the Yearbook was a valuable one but that before taking a decision the Council should have some information on the type of work which would be done. He therefore maintained his proposal.

Mr. CHANG (China) agreed with that procedure.

图片 8.4　张彭春在经社理事会第八届第 231 次会议发言纪要

【纪要译文】

张先生(中国)说,当此事提交人权委员会时,它的目的是扩大对人权的理解以及如何将这些权利付诸实践。如果《年鉴》只包括法律法规,就无法具体了解这些权利实际上是如何得到维护的。如果法院判决列入《年鉴》,就可以获得这方面的信息,但他想知道在那个时候启动这样一个方案是否可行。该项目是一个复杂的项目,因为所有法院判决都以某种方式涉及所有人权,因此理事会在作出决定之前应该仔细审议这件事。

理事会应铭记,该计划的困难将增加,因为这些法院判决将反映各种判例制度和不同的社会哲学。

他认为,理事会的任务应该是提高人们的道德敏感性,而不是扩大各国之间的争议领域。该理事会应致力于改善教育和道德纪律。他认为,除非理事会能够提供进一步指导,否则秘书长将极难设法处理这一方案。

很难界定应列入《年鉴》的法院判决所涉及的人权范围。因此,他认为推迟到理事会下一届会议再作出最后决定可能更为明智。不过,秘书处可以在试验的基础上着手编写两份或三份试点文件,其中包括两个或三个国家在两三年内作出的关于人权的决定。有了这些研究报告,理事会可以就如何确切执行该项目形成一个具体的想法。它可以确定这些研究是否有助于更好地了解人权和道德纪律,还将表明项目的范围是否应受到限制。

因此,他提议理事会推迟到理事会第九届会议再就关于将与人权有关的法院判决列入《人权年鉴》的第二项决议草案作出决定,此外,秘书处应准备向理事会第九届会议提交三份或四份试点文件,说明法院裁决的含义。

张先生(中国)认为没有必要制订新的研究方案。他的意图是利用已经任命的通讯员,他确信,这些通讯员将乐于在如此重要的项目中合作。

张先生(中国)认为,这不是一个推卸责任的问题,而是一个科学方法的问题。他认为在《年鉴》中列入法院判决这一建议很有价值,但在作出决定之前,理事会应了解将要做的工作类型。因此,他坚持他的提议。

张先生(中国)同意这一程序。

5. 张彭春在经社理事会第八届第232次会议上的发言

1949年2月10日上午11时,联合国经社理事会第八届第232次会议,在纽约成功湖召开。本次会议讨论锡兰加入联合国教科文组织的事宜、讨论联合国善后救济总署物质销售程序。中国代表张彭春率团参加了本次会议,并在会议上先后多次发言①,其发言内容纪要及其译文等如下:

【会议纪要】

Mr. CHANG (China) suggested that, in view of the twenty-four hour rule for the submission of documents and in view of the objections which had been raised to the text of their resolution, the delegations of India and the United Kingdom should withdraw their joint draft resolution in favour of the draft included in document E/W. 5.

Mr. CHANG (China) endorsed the statement of the representative of Chile.

Mr. CHANG (China) suggested that the Council should adopt the text of document E/W. 8 as presented by the Secretariat and request the Secretary-General to take note of the statements made in the course of the discussion.

Mr. CHANG (China) withdrew his suggestion but reserved the right to re introduce it if the discussion became prolonged.

---

① UN Document: E/SR. 232, p. 63, p. 64, p. 65.

【纪要影像】

Mr. CHANG (China) suggested that, in view of the twenty-four hour rule for the submission of documents and in view of the objections which had been raised to the text of their resolution, the delegations of India and the United Kingdom should withdraw their joint draft resolution in favour of the draft included in document E/W.5.

Mr. CHANG (China) endorsed the statement of the representative of Chile.

Mr. CHANG (China) suggested that the Council should adopt the text of document E/W.8 as presented by the Secretariat and request the Secretary-General to take note of the statements made in the course of the discussion.

Mr. CHANG (China) withdrew his suggestion but reserved the right to reintroduce it if the discussion became prolonged.

图片 8.5　张彭春在经社理事会第八届第 232 次会议发言纪要

【纪要译文】

张先生(中国)建议,鉴于提交文件的 24 小时规则以及对其决议案文提出的反对意见,印度和英国代表团应撤回其联合决议草案,支持 E/W. 5 号文件中的草案。

张先生(中国)赞同智利代表的发言。

张先生(中国)建议理事会通过秘书处提交的 E/W. 8 号文件的案文,并请秘书长注意在讨论过程中所作的发言。

张先生(中国)撤回了他的建议,但如果讨论被延长,他保留重新提出建议的权利。

6. 张彭春在经社理事会第八届第234次会议上的发言

1949年2月11日上午11时，联合国经社理事会第八届第234次会议，在纽约成功湖召开。本次会议讨论锡兰加入联合国教科文组织的事宜、讨论经典的翻译问题。中国代表张彭春率团参加了本次会议，并在会议上发言[①]，其发言内容纪要及其译文等如下：

【会议纪要】

Mr. CHANG (China) said that as perhaps the only Buddhistic member of the Council, he was particularly pleased to welcome Ceylon as an important centre of the religion of Buddha. The rich cultural heritage of Ceylon would constitute a significant contribution to the work of UNESCO.

Mr. CHANG (China) doubted whether the USSR proposal was a substitute for that of Lebanon. The subject matter of the two draft resolutions was not mutually exclusive, one resolution dealing with the selection of works for translation and the other with questions of finance. The Council might therefore decide to amalgamate the two resolutions. On the other hand, it was possible that UNESCO had already adopted a procedure similar to that suggested in the USSR draft resolution.

Mr. CHANG (China), referring to the resolution adopted by the General Conference of UNESCO in Beirut the previous year (E/823/Add. 1, page 1),

① UN Document: E/SR. 234, p. 79, p. 80, p. 83.

pointed out that it was not clear whether the member States mentioned in that resolution were member States of UNESCO only. He thought it important that the Director-General of UNESCO should approach not only the member States of UNESCO but all States which were Members of the United Nations.

Referring to the Agreement concluded between UNESCO and the Lebanese Government on the establishment of a regional foundation in the Lebanon for the translation of classics, Mr. Chang suggested that the experiment should be allowed to develop and that the Council should not take any far-reaching action in the meantime.

He suggested that the Secretariat might be asked to draw up a brief draft resolution, commending the work of UNESCO and recommending that it should continue on the same lines. UNESCO would of course report to the Council on the progress of its work.

【纪要影像】

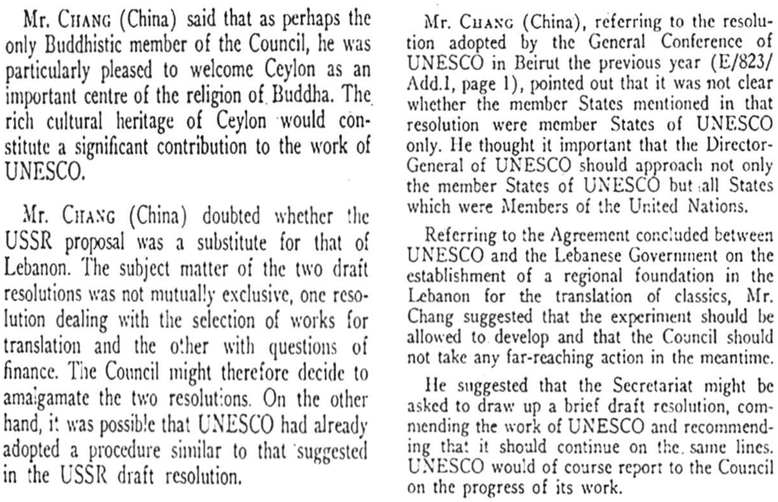

Mr. CHANG (China) said that as perhaps the only Buddhistic member of the Council, he was particularly pleased to welcome Ceylon as an important centre of the religion of Buddha. The rich cultural heritage of Ceylon would constitute a significant contribution to the work of UNESCO.

Mr. CHANG (China) doubted whether the USSR proposal was a substitute for that of Lebanon. The subject matter of the two draft resolutions was not mutually exclusive, one resolution dealing with the selection of works for translation and the other with questions of finance. The Council might therefore decide to amalgamate the two resolutions. On the other hand, it was possible that UNESCO had already adopted a procedure similar to that suggested in the USSR draft resolution.

Mr. CHANG (China), referring to the resolution adopted by the General Conference of UNESCO in Beirut the previous year (E/823/Add.1, page 1), pointed out that it was not clear whether the member States mentioned in that resolution were member States of UNESCO only. He thought it important that the Director-General of UNESCO should approach not only the member States of UNESCO but all States which were Members of the United Nations.

Referring to the Agreement concluded between UNESCO and the Lebanese Government on the establishment of a regional foundation in the Lebanon for the translation of classics, Mr. Chang suggested that the experiment should be allowed to develop and that the Council should not take any far-reaching action in the meantime.

He suggested that the Secretariat might be asked to draw up a brief draft resolution, commending the work of UNESCO and recommending that it should continue on the same lines. UNESCO would of course report to the Council on the progress of its work.

图片 8.6　张彭春在经社理事会第八届第 234 次会议发言纪要

【纪要译文】

张先生(中国)说,作为理事会中可能是唯一的佛教徒成员,他特别高兴地欢迎锡兰成为佛教的重要中心。锡兰丰富的文化遗产将对教科文组织的工作作出重大贡献。

张先生(中国)怀疑苏联的提案是否可以替代黎巴嫩的提案。这两项决议草案的主题并不是相互排斥的,一项决议涉及翻译作品的选择,另一项决议涉及财务问题。因此,理事会可能决定合并这两项决议。另一方面,教科文组织可能已经通过了类似于苏联在决议草案中所建议的程序。

张先生(中国)提到前一年在贝鲁特举行的教科文组织大会通过的决议(E/823/Add. 1,第1页),他指出,不清楚该决议中提到的成员国是否只是教科文组织的成员国。他认为,重要的是,教科文组织总干事不仅应与教科文组织成员国接触,而且应与联合国所有会员国接触。

在联合国教科文组织与黎巴嫩政府缔结的关于在黎巴嫩设立一个古典翻译经典的区域基金会达成的协议中,张先生建议,应该允许这项实验继续进行,理事会不应同时采取任何长臂管辖行动。

他建议,可以请秘书处起草一份简短的决议草案,赞扬教科文组织的工作,并建议教科文组织继续按照同样的思路开展工作。教科文组织当然将向理事会报告其工作进展情况。

7. 张彭春在经社理事会第八届第235次会议上的发言

1949年2月14日上午11时，联合国经社理事会第八届第235次会议，在纽约成功湖召开。本次会议讨论非政府组织委员会的报告。中国代表张彭春率团参加了本次会议，并在会议上发言①，其发言内容纪要及其译文等如下：

【会议纪要】

Mr. CHANG (China) suggested that the New Zealand representative might withdraw his amendment and agree to the deletion of the second paragraph as proposed by the representative of Denmark.

【纪要影像】

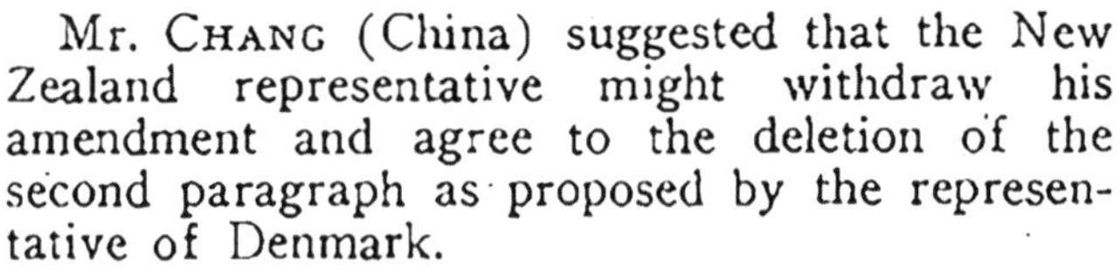
Mr. CHANG (China) suggested that the New Zealand representative might withdraw his amendment and agree to the deletion of the second paragraph as proposed by the representative of Denmark.

图片8.7　张彭春在经社理事会第八届第235次会议发言纪要

① UN Document: E/SR. 235, p. 89.

【纪要译文】

张先生(中国)建议新西兰代表撤回其修正案,并同意按照丹麦代表的建议删除第二段。

8. 张彭春在经社理事会第八届第240次会议上的发言

1949年2月16日下午3时，联合国经社理事会第八届第240次会议，在纽约成功湖召开。本次会议讨论非政府组织委员会的报告。中国代表张彭春率团参加了本次会议，并在会议上发言①，其发言内容纪要及其译文等如下：

【会议纪要】

Mr. CHANG (China) said that in his opinion the summary record of the Council's preceding meeting was not complete insofar as the question under discussion was concerned. He asked that the Secretariat should prepare a verbatim record of the part of the Council's 239th meeting which concerned that question from the sound track.

Mr. CHANG (China) did not think the members of the Council could be expected to reach a considered decision at that meeting. He therefore formally proposed that the meeting should be adjourned.

---

① UN Document: E/SR. 240, p. 137, p. 138.

【纪要影像】

Mr. CHANG (China) said that in his opinion the summary record of the Council's preceding meeting was not complete insofar as the question under discussion was concerned. He asked that the Secretariat should prepare a verbatim record of the part of the Council's 239th meeting which concerned that question from the soundtrack.

Mr. CHANG (China) did not think the members of the Council could be expected to reach a considered decision at that meeting. He therefore formally proposed that the meeting should be adjourned.

图片 8.8　张彭春在经社理事会第八届第 240 次会议发言纪要

【纪要译文】

张先生(中国)说,就所讨论的问题而言,他认为理事会上次会议的简要记录并不完整。他要求秘书处从录音带中逐字记录理事会第 239 次会议有关该问题的部分。

张先生(中国)认为,不可能指望理事会成员在那次会议上作出深思熟虑的决定。因此,他正式提议休会。

9. 张彭春在经社理事会第八届第 242 次会议上的发言

1949 年 2 月 17 日下午 3 时,联合国经社理事会第八届第 242 次会议,在纽约成功湖召开。本次会议讨论特殊机构的关系与合作。中国代表张彭春率团参加了本次会议,并在会议上发言①,其发言内容纪要及其译文等如下:

【会议纪要】

Mr. CHANG (China) suggested that the doubts expressed by the Danish representative might be solved by the deletion of the final paragraph of the United States draft resolution.

【纪要影像】

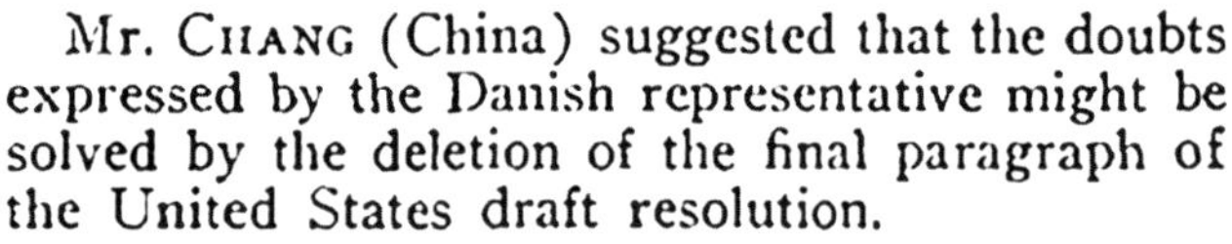
Mr. CHANG (China) suggested that the doubts expressed by the Danish representative might be solved by the deletion of the final paragraph of the United States draft resolution.

图片 8.9　张彭春在经社理事会第八届第 242 次会议发言纪要

【纪要译文】

张先生(中国)建议,删除美国决议草案的最后一段,以解决丹麦代表提出的疑问。

① E/SR. 242, p. 162.

10. 张彭春在经社理事会第八届第 243 次会议上的发言

1949 年 2 月 18 日上午 11 时,联合国经社理事会第八届第 243 次会议,在纽约成功湖召开。本次会议继续讨论男女同工同酬的原则等。中国代表张彭春率团参加了本次会议,并在会议上发言①,其发言内容纪要及其译文等如下:

【会议纪要】

Mr. CHANG (China) quoted article 63, paragraph 2, of the Universal Declaration of Human Rights, and the last paragraph of the preamble to that Declaration. He pointed out that the USSR draft resolution reproduced the actual provisions of the Declaration. Moreover, that Declaration had been solemnly adopted by the General Assembly and it would be most ill-advised of the Council to repeat the terms of such a Declaration, as it would seem to be taking a decision of the General Assembly lightly.

① UN Document: E/SR. 243, p. 165.

【纪要影像】

Mr. CHANG (China) quoted article 63, paragraph 2, of the Universal Declaration of Human Rights, and the last paragraph of the preamble to that Declaration. He pointed out that the USSR draft resolution reproduced the actual provisions of the Declaration. Moreover, that Declaration had been solemnly adopted by the General Assembly and it would be most ill-advised of the Council to repeat the terms of such a Declaration, as it would seem to be taking a decision of the General Assembly lightly.

图片 8.10　张彭春在经社理事会第八届第 243 次会议发言纪要

【纪要译文】

张先生(中国)引用了《世界人权宣言》第 63 条第 2 款[①]以及该宣言序言的最后一段。他指出,苏联的决议草案复制了《宣言》的实际规定。此外,该宣言已由大会庄严通过,理事会重复该宣言的条款是极不明智的,因为这似乎是轻率地对待大会的决定。

---

① 笔者注:这里会议纪要文字中有一个明显的错误,正确的内容应该为“引用了《世界人权宣言》第 23 条第 2 款”,请读者明鉴。

11. 张彭春在经社理事会第八届第244次会议上的发言

1949年2月18日下午3时，联合国经社理事会第八届第244次会议，在纽约成功湖召开。本次会议讨论强迫劳动调查及其废除措施。中国代表张彭春率团参加了本次会议，并在会议上发言①，其发言内容纪要及其译文等如下：

【会议纪要】

Mr. CHANG (China) thought that the Australian amendment might place the Secretary-General in a somewhat delicate and awkward position. He inquired whether in the present stages of the building up of the United Nations Secretariat, the Secretary-General would have at his disposal adequate machinery to implement the Australian amendment. He also asked what financial implications it might entail. In general, the United States resolution was the most adequate measure, since it called for reports from all countries.

The representative of China expressed the hope that the Australian delegation would reconsider its amendment.

① UN Document: E/SR. 244, p. 180.

【纪要影像】

Mr. CHANG (China) thought that the Australian amendment might place the Secretary-General in a somewhat delicate and awkward position. He inquired whether in the present stages of the building up of the United Nations Secretariat, the Secretary-General would have at his disposal adequate machinery to implement the Australian amendment. He also asked what financial implications it might entail. In general, the United States resolution was the most adequate measure, since it called for reports from all countries.

The representative of China expressed the hope that the Australian delegation would reconsider its amendment.

图片 8.11　张彭春在经社理事会第八届第 244 次会议发言纪要

【纪要译文】

张先生(中国)认为,澳大利亚的修正案可能使秘书长处于某种微妙和尴尬的境地。他询问目前联合国秘书处的建设阶段,秘书长是否拥有执行澳大利亚修正案的适当机制。他还询问这可能涉及哪些财政问题。总的来说,美国的决议是最适当的措施,因为它要求所有国家提交报告。

中国代表表示希望澳大利亚代表团重新考虑其修正案。

12. 张彭春在经社理事会第八届第259次会议上的发言

1949年3月3日上午11时,联合国经社理事会第八届第259次会议,在纽约成功湖召开。本次会议讨论欠发达地区经济发展问题。中国代表张彭春率团参加了本次会议,并在会议上进行了长篇发言①,其发言内容纪要及其译文等如下:

【会议纪要】

Mr. CHANG (China) praised the constructive character and high standard of the debate on economic development; it had given him great satisfaction to hear the numerous and interesting statements so far made by members of the Council. He simply wished to add some observations on the question of the economic development of under-developed regions.

The whole of those observations might be summed up in three phrases: the exact appraisal of facts, the various angles from which the problem should be viewed, and methods of application.

Obviously, the importance of under-developed regions of the world had been estimated correctly: the proof was that the Economic and Social Council had begun to discuss that question as early as its second session in June 1946. In that connexion, he thanked the representative of Lebanon for recalling in his recent statement the role which the Chinese delegation had played at that time.

---

① UN Document: E/SR. 259, pp. 419–423.

World economy should be viewed as a whole, special consideration being given to under-developed regions, not only because of the importance of their population or their natural resources, because they provided raw materials and formed outlets for the manufactured goods of industrialized countries, but also because the conflicts between industrialized Powers originated in those regions.

It was in those areas that the nature which future international conflicts would assume could be foreseen. The regions industrially least developed were today no longer under the subjection of the rest of the world, as they had been before the First World War; they no longer obeyed without protest the orders of powerful industrialized nations. That was particularly true of countries which had been culturally developed long before modern industrialization. Some of them had realized that the industrial nations had kept under-developed countries in the inferior position of suppliers of raw materials. Following the industrial revolution which had occurred in Europe towards the close of the eighteenth century, the less developed areas had little by little been deluged with cheap manufactured articles; in particular, certain arrangements such as the system of capitulations had allowed manufactured goods to enter those areas duty-free. It was easy to understand why the industrial development of those regions was desirable from the point of view of manufacturing nations.

It had already been emphasized that investments in under-developed areas prevented economic stagnation and the decline of more developed economies. Those regions could play such a part for a long period of time, and in so doing would not act merely as reabsorbing agents in a brief economic crisis. In fact, investments caused a rise in the standard of living of the countries concerned which, in turn, promoted full employment in the industrialized countries and benefited world trade as a whole. The economic progress of one region stimulated economic advancement throughout the world. It was often said, however, that the industrialization of less developed countries was a form of exploitation and imperialism. For that reason, it was advisable to pay special attention to the methods of collaboration between industrialized countries and less developed areas. Capitalists had always been tempted to use financial and political power to promote their own interests in the areas where they had investments. The representative of China thought that economic imperialism was no longer a policy deliberately pursued; it was, none the less, true that concerted international action was needed to ensure good financial and industrial relations between nations. Furthermore, the race for raw materials and markets led to friction between the industrial Powers, and it was therefore important to study carefully all the regions where such disagreements might arise. Any such study should be brought to the attention of the Council.

The representative of China pointed out that, in the statement which he had just made, he had recalled some sentences from a speech which he had delivered before the Council on 4 June 1946.① Since then the delegations and the Secretariat had carried out some interesting analyses of the question. The regional economic commissions had been created and the Economic and Social Council as well as the General Assembly had adopted constructive measures, of which the note of the Secretary-General (E/1119) gave a useful summary. Finally, in the course of the present session, the representative of the United States had pointed out the great importance of "low-pressure" economic areas.

Mr. Chang then examined the aspects from which the problem should be considered. Several delegations had stressed the importance of industrial equipment and of capital investments for the economic development of under-developed regions. The social and human points of view should also be taken into consideration. In that connexion, the representative of the World Health Organization would speak to the Council on the important questions of hygiene

---

① See *Official Records of the Economic and Social Council*, first year, second session, 7th meeting.

and food. The problem should be envisaged from three angles, but he wished to stress only the historical aspect of economic development. Most people perhaps were inclined to think that economic development had taken place at an even pace throughout the centuries. He wondered, however, whether the modern world was not characterized, on the contrary, by an acceleration in the rhythm of progress.

Some people thought that the scientific spirit had always prevailed in Europe. It was often asserted that the origins of science dated from ancient Greece and that since then there had been uninterrupted scientific progress in Europe. But the gap between ancient Greece and the modern era was a wide one. Such an over-simplified hypothesis was reminiscent of the parvenu who attempted to endow his family with a large family tree. In fact, the scientific progress of the modern world had been made possible as a result of the development of knowledge based on the study of objective facts. Supposing, for example, that some people had, from the time of their birth, never left the room they lived in and had before them a model of a chair. They would acquire a certain perfectly clear concept of a chair. Should the walls of that room collapse one day, they might on leaving the room behold a dozen different models of chairs. They would then realize that their concept of a chair no longer fitted those new models, of the existence of which they had been unaware. That example was a rather good illustration of the way in which the world had made scientific discoveries. In the modern world, the bounds of people's lives were forever widening; they were consequently aspiring to a kind of new paradise. That aspect of the question was of particular interest to peoples who had lived within narrower limits and who had attained a very high level of civilization before the industrial era. Some of those people might unconsciously think that they were unable to adapt themselves to technique and science. That was not true, however, in all areas. In the space of one generation eminent scientists had appeared in regions which until then had made no contributions to scientific progress.

One was thus led to wonder how the various under-developed countries would manage to put themselves on the level of industrialized regions. Certain conjectures had already been made as regards agriculture, industry, hygiene and other essential forms of activity, For the moment, however, Mr. Chang did not wish to labour that point. He wondered whether the problem was not being viewed from only two angles at the present time, a fact which would impede progressive and creative adaptation. There was no doubt that, of the three principal elements of economic development, the adaptation of man was the most essential. In that connexion, the three attitudes adopted by the countries which had benefited from industrial development should be noted. Some, wishing to be self-sufficient, had aimed too high, for no people could remain isolated. Others had, without due consideration, adopted certain methods of work which had served them well for a time. The true solution, however, lay in creative adaptation, a solution for which there must be three prerequisites: firstly, the needs to be satisfied must be determined; secondly, creative ideas must be stimulated; lastly, an entirely unfettered spirit of inventiveness must prevail.

The representative of China stressed the fact that in his actions man was guided by habit and tradition. He was dissatisfied whenever he discovered that his traditional ways of acting no longer precisely corresponded to reality. To understand that, it was essential to know and analyse accurately the nature of the traditions which had thus been respected; those traditions and the causes of man's dissatisfaction were often not understood. It was there that the danger lay of using all the modern technical processes without knowing whether they could wholly meet man's needs.

In the second place, it was advisable to proceed to an exhaustive study of creative ideas and elements of a stimulative nature.

Lastly, the period of "liberated inventiveness" freed from ancient inertia and ancient forms, had been reached. In other words, to formulate a method of action, the determining conditions should be borne in mind. Without an examination of those conditions, there could be no real liberation; without liberation, there would be no spirit of inventiveness.

Mr. Chang stated that many suggestions had been made as to the methods to be followed to achieve completely the aims the Council had set itself. He reserved the right to return to that point in committee. He wished to emphasize, however, that without the necessary equipment, the modernization of an under-developed country could not be ensured. Though he had stressed the human aspect of the problem, he did not underestimate the importance of the role played by equipment goods, thanks to which it would be possible for all the countries concerned to avoid economic instability and unemployment and to improve the lot of the countries which were least advanced.

The Secretary-General had been requested, through the Administrative Committee on Co-ordination, to prepare a comprehensive plan for an expanded co-operative programme of technical assistance for economic development. Such a programme should be prepared on the initiative of the under-developed countries themselves; otherwise, the programme would lack a guiding principle and the whole would prove ineffective.

The representative of China concluded by saying that the goal which the Council had set for itself could stir the imagination. There was no cause either for over-optimism or for despair. Mankind today could not afford too many set-backs in its realization of constructive ideas.

【纪要影像】

Mr. CHANG (China) praised the constructive character and high standard of the debate on economic development; it had given him great satisfaction to hear the numerous and interesting statements so far made by members of the Council. He simply wished to add some observations on the question of the economic development of under-developed regions.

The whole of those observations might be summed up in three phrases: the exact appraisal of facts, the various angles from which the problem should be viewed, and methods of application.

Obviously, the importance of under-developed regions of the world had been estimated correctly: the proof was that the Economic and Social Council had begun to discuss that question as early as its second session in June 1946. In that connexion, he thanked the representative of Lebanon for recalling in his recent statement the role which the Chinese delegation had played at that time.

World economy should be viewed as a whole, special consideration being given to under-developed regions, not only because of the importance of their population or their natural resources, because they provided raw materials and formed outlets for the manufactured goods of industrialized countries, but also because the conflicts between industrialized Powers originated in those regions.

It was in those areas that the nature which future international conflicts would assume could be foreseen. The regions industrially least developed were today no longer under the subjection of the rest of the world, as they had been before the First World War; they no longer obeyed without protest the orders of powerful industrialized nations. That was particularly true of countries which had been culturally developed long before modern industrialization. Some of them had realized that the industrial nations had kept under-developed countries in the inferior position of suppliers of raw materials. Following the industrial revolution which had occurred in Europe towards the close of the eighteenth century, the less developed areas had little by little been deluged with cheap manufactured articles; in particular, certain arrangements such as the system of capitulations had allowed manufactured goods to enter those areas duty-free. It was easy to understand why the industrial development of those regions was desirable from the point of view of manufacturing nations.

图片 8.12　张彭春在经社理事会第八届第 259 次会议发言纪要(1)

It had already been emphasized that investments in under-developed areas prevented economic stagnation and the decline of more developed economies. Those regions could play such a part for a long period of time, and in so doing would not act merely as reabsorbing agents in a brief economic crisis. In fact, investments caused a rise in the standard of living of the countries concerned which, in turn, promoted full employment in the industrialized countries and benefited world trade as a whole. The economic progress of one region stimulated economic advancement throughout the world. It was often said, however, that the industrialization of less developed countries was a form of exploitation and imperialism. For that reason, it was advisable to pay special attention to the methods of collaboration between industrialized countries and less developed areas. Capitalists had always been tempted to use financial and political power to promote their own interests in the areas where they had investments. The representative of China thought that economic imperialism was no longer a policy deliberately pursued; it was, none the less, true that concerted international action was needed to ensure good financial and industrial relations between nations. Furthermore, the race for raw materials and markets led to friction between the industrial Powers, and it was therefore important to study carefully all the regions where such disagreements might arise. Any such study should be brought to the attention of the Council.

The representative of China pointed out that, in the statement which he had just made, he had recalled some sentences from a speech which he had delivered before the Council on 4 June 1946.[1] Since then the delegations and the Secretariat had carried out some interesting analyses of the question. The regional economic commissions had been created and the Economic and Social Council as well as the General Assembly had adopted constructive measures, of which the note of the Secretary-General (E/1119) gave a useful summary. Finally, in the course of the present session, the representative of the United States had pointed out the great importance of "low-pressure" economic areas.

Mr. Chang then examined the aspects from which the problem should be considered. Several delegations had stressed the importance of industrial equipment and of capital investments for the economic development of under-developed regions. The social and human points of view should also be taken into consideration. In that connexion, the representative of the World Health Organization would speak to the Council on the important questions of hygiene and food. The problem should be envisaged from three angles, but he wished to stress only the historical aspect of economic development. Most people perhaps were inclined to think that economic development had taken place at an even pace throughout the centuries. He wondered, however, whether the modern world was not characterized, on the contrary, by an acceleration in the rhythm of progress.

图片 8.13　张彭春在经社理事会第八届第 259 次会议发言纪要(2)

Some people thought that the scientific spirit had always prevailed in Europe. It was often asserted that the origins of science dated from ancient Greece and that since then there had been uninterrupted scientific progress in Europe. But the gap between ancient Greece and the modern era was a wide one. Such an over-simplified hypothesis was reminiscent of the parvenu who attempted to endow his family with a large family tree. In fact, the scientific progress of the modern world had been made possible as a result of the development of knowledge based on the study of objective facts. Supposing, for example, that some people had, from the time of their birth, never left the room they lived in and had before them a model of a chair. They would acquire a certain perfectly clear concept of a chair. Should the walls of that room collapse one day, they might on leaving the room behold a dozen different models of chairs. They would then realize that their concept of a chair no longer fitted those new models, of the existence of which they had been unaware. That example was a rather good illustration of the way in which the world had made scientific discoveries. In the modern world, the bounds of people's lives were forever widening; they were consequently aspiring to a kind of new paradise. That aspect of the question was of particular interest to peoples who had lived within narrower limits and who had attained a very high level of civilization before the industrial era. Some of those people might unconsciously think that they were unable to adapt themselves to technique and science. That was not true, however, in all areas. In the space of one generation eminent scientists had appeared in regions which until then had made no contributions to scientific progress.

[1] See *Official Records of the Economic and Social Council*, first year, second session, 7th meeting.

One was thus led to wonder how the various under-developed countries would manage to put themselves on the level of industrialized regions. Certain conjectures had already been made as regards agriculture, industry, hygiene and other essential forms of activity. For the moment, however, Mr. Chang did not wish to labour that point. He wondered whether the problem was not being viewed from only two angles at the present time, a fact which would impede progressive and creative adaptation. There was no doubt that, of the three principal elements of economic development, the adaptation of man was the most essential. In that connexion, the three attitudes adopted by the countries which had benefited from industrial development should be noted. Some, wishing to be self-sufficient, had aimed too high, for no people could remain isolated. Others had, without due consideration, adopted certain methods of work which had served them well for a time. The true solution, however, lay in creative adaptation, a solution for which there must be three prerequisites: firstly, the needs to be satisfied must be determined; secondly, creative ideas must be stimulated; lastly, an entirely unfettered spirit of inventiveness must prevail.

图片 8.14　张彭春在经社理事会第八届第 259 次会议发言纪要(3)

The representative of China stressed the fact that in his actions man was guided by habit and tradition. He was dissatisfied whenever he discovered that his traditional ways of acting no longer precisely corresponded to reality. To understand that, it was essential to know and analyse accurately the nature of the traditions which had thus been respected; those traditions and the causes of man's dissatisfaction were often not understood. It was there that the danger lay of using all the modern technical processes without knowing whether they could wholly meet man's needs.

In the second place, it was advisable to proceed to an exhaustive study of creative ideas and elements of a stimulative nature.

Lastly, the period of "liberated inventiveness", freed from ancient inertia and ancient forms, had been reached. In other words, to formulate a method of action, the determining conditions should be borne in mind. Without an examination of those conditions, there could be no real liberation; without liberation, there would be no spirit of inventiveness.

Mr. Chang stated that many suggestions had been made as to the methods to be followed to achieve completely the aims the Council had set itself. He reserved the right to return to that point in committee. He wished to emphasize, however, that without the necessary equipment, the modernization of an under-developed country could not be ensured. Though he had stressed the human aspect of the problem, he did not underestimate the importance of the role played by equipment goods, thanks to which it would be possible for all the countries concerned to avoid economic instability and unemployment and to improve the lot of the countries which were least advanced.

The Secretary-General had been requested, through the Administrative Committee on Co-ordination, to prepare a comprehensive plan for an expanded co-operative programme of technical assistance for economic development. Such a programme should be prepared on the initiative of the under-developed countries themselves; otherwise, the programme would lack a guiding principle and the whole would prove ineffective.

The representative of China concluded by saying that the goal which the Council had set for itself could stir the imagination. There was no cause either for over-optimism or for despair. Mankind today could not afford too many setbacks in its realization of constructive ideas.

图片 8.15　张彭春在经社理事会第八届第 259 次会议发言纪要(4)

【纪要译文】

张先生(中国)赞扬关于经济发展的辩论的建设性和高标准;他非常满意地听到理事会成员迄今所作的许多有趣的发言。他只是想就欠发达区域的经济发展问题补充一些意见。

所有这些观察结果可以归纳为三个短语:对事实的准确评估、看待问题的各种角度,以及应用方法。

显然,对世界欠发达区域的重要性的估计是正确的:证据是经济及社会理事会早在1946年6月第二届会议上就开始讨论这个问题。在这方面,他感谢黎巴嫩代表在最近的发言中回顾了中国代表团当时发挥的作用。

应将世界经济视为一个整体,对欠发达地区给予特别考虑,这不仅是因为它们的人口或自然资源的重要性,因为它们为工业化国家的制成品提供了原材料并形成了销路,还因为工业化大国之间的冲突起源于这些地区。

正是在这些区域,可以预见未来国际冲突的性质。工业上最不发达的地区今天不再像第一次世界大战前那样受制于世界其他地区;他们不再毫无抗议地服从强大的工业化国家的命令。对于那些在现代工业化之前很久就文化发达的国家来说,情况尤其如此。其中一些国家已经意识到,工业国家使欠发达国家处于原材料供应国的劣势地位。在18世纪末欧洲发生工业革命之后,欠发达地区逐渐充斥着廉价制成品;特别是,某些安排,如投降制度,允许制成品免税进入这些地区。从制造业国家的角度来看,很容易理解为什么这些地区的工业发展是可取的。

已经强调,对欠发达地区的投资可以防止经济停滞和较发达经济体的衰退。这些地区可以在很长一段时间内发挥这样的作用,这样做不会仅仅在短暂的经济危机中充当再吸收者。事实上,投资提高了有关国家的生活水平,从而促进了工业化国家的充分就业,并使整个世界贸易受益。一个地区的经济进步刺激了全世界的经济进步。然而,人们经常说,欠发达国家的工业化是剥削和帝国主义的一种形式。因此,应当特别注意工业化国家与欠发达地区之间的合作方式。资本家总是受到诱惑,利用金融和政治权力在他们有投资的领域促进自己的利益。中国代表认为,经济帝国主义不再是一种蓄意推行的政策;尽管如此,确实需要协调一致的国际行动来确保国家间良好的金融和工业关系。此外,对原材料和市场的争夺导致了工业大国之间的摩擦,因此,仔细研究可能出现这种分歧的所有地区非常重要。任何此类研究都应提请理事会注意。

中国代表指出,在他刚才的发言中,他回顾了他 1946 年 6 月 4 日在理事会发言中的一些句子。[①] 自那时以来,各代表团和秘书处对这个问题进行了一些有趣的分析。各区域经济委员会已经成立,经济及社会理事会和大会已经采取了建设性措施,秘书长的说明(E/1119)对这些措施作了有益的总结。最后,在本届会议期间,美国代表指出了“低压”经济地区的重要性。

张先生接着探讨了应该从哪些方面来考虑这个问题。一些代表团强调了工业设备和资本投资对欠发达区域经济发展的重要性。还应考虑到社会和人的观点。在这方面,世界卫生组织的代表将就卫生和食品等重要问题向理事会发言。应该从三个角度考虑这个问题,但他只想强调经济发展的历史方面。大多数人可能倾向于认为,经济发展在几个世纪中一直以平稳的速度进行。然而,他想知道,现代世界是否正相反地以进步节奏的加快为特征。

有些人认为科学精神在欧洲一直盛行。人们常常断言,科学的起源可以追溯到古希腊,从那时起,欧洲的科学进步就从未间断过。但是古希腊和现代之间的差距很大。这种过于简化的假设让人想起了那种试图给他的家族建立一个庞大家谱的暴发户。事实上,现代世界的科学进步是基于对客观事实研究的知识发展的结果。例如,假设有些人从出生时起就从未离开过他们居住的房间,他们面前有一个椅子模型。他们会对椅子有一个非常清晰的概念。如果有一天房间的墙壁倒塌,他们离开房间时可能会看

① 见《经济及社会理事会正式记录》,第一年,第二届会议,第 7 次会议。

到十几种不同型号的椅子。然后,他们会意识到,他们的椅子概念不再适合那些他们不知道存在的新模型。这个例子很好地说明了世界科学发现的方式。在现代世界,人们的生活范围不断扩大,因此,他们渴望一种新的乐土。这个问题的这一方面对那些在工业时代之前生活在狭窄范围内并达到高度文明的人民特别有意义。其中一些人可能会无意识地认为自己无法适应技术和科学。然而,并非所有区域都是如此。在一代人的时间里,杰出的科学家出现在那些之前对科学进步没有贡献的区域。

因此,人们不禁想知道,各种欠发达国家将如何设法使自己处于工业化区域的水平。关于农业、工业、卫生和其他基本活动形式,已经有人作出了某些推测,但张先生暂时不想再详述这一点。他想知道目前是否只从两个角度看待这个问题,这一事实将阻碍进步和创造性的适应。毫无疑问,在经济发展的三大要素中,人的适应是最基本的。在这方面,应当指出受益于工业发展的国家采取的三种态度。有些人希望自给自足,但目标太高,因为没有人能够保持孤立。其他人在没有适当考虑的情况下采用了某些工作方法,这些方法在一段时间内对他们很有用。然而,真正的解决办法在于创造性的适应,这一解决办法必须有三个先决条件:首先,必须确定需要满足的需求;第二,必须激发创造性的想法;最后,一种完全不受束缚的创新精神必须占上风。

中国代表强调了这样一个事实,即人的行动受习惯和传统的指导。每当他发现自己传统的行为方式不再完全符合现实时,他就会感到不满。为了理解这一点,必须准确地了解和分析受到尊重的传统的性质;那些传统和人类不满的原因经常不被理解。正是在这一点上,使用所有的现代技术方法而不知道它们是否能完全满足人类的需求是危险的。

第二,着手彻底研究创造性的想法和具有激励性质的因素是明智的。

最后,从古老的惰性和古老的形式中解放出来的“解放的创造性”时期已经到来。换句话说,要制定一个行动的方法,必须牢记决定性的条件。没有对这些条件的检查,就不可能有真正的解放;没有解放,就没有创新精神。

张先生说,已经就完全实现理事会为自己确定的目标应采取的方法提出了许多建议。他保留在委员会讨论这一问题的权利。然而,他希望强调,如果没有必要的设备,就无法确保欠发达国家的现代化。虽然他强调了问题的人的方面,但他没有低估设备货物所发挥的作用的重要性,因为有了设备货物,所有有关国家才有可能避免经济不稳定和失业,并改善最不发达国家的命运。

已通过行政协调委员会请秘书长为扩大经济发展技术援助合作方案拟订一项全面计划。这种方案应根据欠发达国家本身的倡议制定;否则,该方案将缺乏指导原则,整个方案将被证明没有效果 。

中国代表最后说,理事会为自己确定的目标可以激发想象力。没有理由过分乐观或绝望。今天的人类在实现建设性理念的过程中承受不起太多的挫折。

13. 张彭春在经社理事会第八届第 260 次会议上的发言

1949 年 3 月 3 日下午 3 时，联合国经社理事会第八届第 260 次会议，在纽约成功湖召开。本次会议继续讨论欠发达地区经济发展问题。中国代表张彭春率团参加了本次会议，并在会议上先后多次发言①，其发言内容纪要及其译文等如下：

【会议纪要】

Mr. CHANG (China) endorsed the remarks of the United Kingdom representative. At the previous meeting, the Chinese delegation had already suggested the advisability of referring the matter to the Economic Committee. In view of the fact that the Chilean proposal would not be voted upon immediately, Mr. Chang suggested that both the United States and the Chilean draft resolutions be referred to the Committee for further consideration.

Mr. CHANG (China) felt that the ideas put forward by the representative of the WHO were of great importance and that the members of the Council should be given an opportunity to ponder over them and perhaps make further constructive suggestions. He was strongly of the opinion that the Council should give further consideration to the whole question of economic development in under-developed countries.

Mr. CHANG (China) felt that the United States draft resolution required

① UN Document: E/SR. 260, p. 439, p. 440, p. 441.

careful study and that the members of the Council should be given further opportunity to submit amendments if they wished.

Mr. CHANG (China) also wished to submit an oral amendment to insert the words "and in co-operation with an advisory committee to be appointed by the Council and composed of the representatives of" after the words "through the Administrative Committee on Co-ordination" in paragraph 5 of the United States draft resolution. Mr. Chang explained that he thought it would be useful that representatives of countries closely affected by the problem should work in close co-operation with the Secretary-General in the preparation of his report. He suggested that the number could be limited to three or four members, but that the matter could be discussed further at the following meeting.

Mr. STINEBOWER (United States of America) and Mr. CHANG (China) said that they would submit their amendments in writing at the following meeting.

【纪要影像】

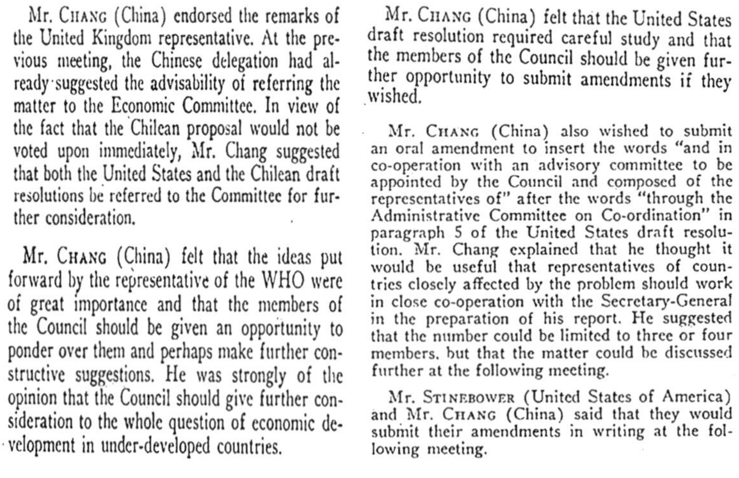

Mr. CHANG (China) endorsed the remarks of the United Kingdom representative. At the previous meeting, the Chinese delegation had already suggested the advisability of referring the matter to the Economic Committee. In view of the fact that the Chilean proposal would not be voted upon immediately, Mr. Chang suggested that both the United States and the Chilean draft resolutions be referred to the Committee for further consideration.

Mr. CHANG (China) felt that the ideas put forward by the representative of the WHO were of great importance and that the members of the Council should be given an opportunity to ponder over them and perhaps make further constructive suggestions. He was strongly of the opinion that the Council should give further consideration to the whole question of economic development in under-developed countries.

Mr. CHANG (China) felt that the United States draft resolution required careful study and that the members of the Council should be given further opportunity to submit amendments if they wished.

Mr. CHANG (China) also wished to submit an oral amendment to insert the words "and in co-operation with an advisory committee to be appointed by the Council and composed of the representatives of" after the words "through the Administrative Committee on Co-ordination" in paragraph 5 of the United States draft resolution. Mr. Chang explained that he thought it would be useful that representatives of countries closely affected by the problem should work in close co-operation with the Secretary-General in the preparation of his report. He suggested that the number could be limited to three or four members, but that the matter could be discussed further at the following meeting.

Mr. STINEBOWER (United States of America) and Mr. CHANG (China) said that they would submit their amendments in writing at the following meeting.

图片 8.16 张彭春在经社理事会第八届第 260 次会议发言纪要

【纪要译文】

张先生(中国)赞同英国代表的发言。在上次会议上,中国代表团已经建议将此事提交经济事务委员会。鉴于智利的提案不会立即付诸表决,张先生建议将美国和智利的决议草案提交事务委员会进一步审议。

张先生(中国)认为,世界卫生组织代表提出的想法非常重要,理事会成员应该有机会思考这些想法,或许可以提出进一步的建设性建议。他强烈认为,理事会应进一步审议欠发达国家经济发展的整个问题。

张先生(中国)认为,美国的决议草案需要仔细研究,如果理事会成员愿意,应进一步给予他们提交修正案的机会。

张先生(中国)还希望提交一项口头修正案,在美国决议草案第5段中的"通过行政协调委员会"等字之后插入"并与理事会任命的、由……代表组成的咨询委员会合作"等字。张先生解释说,他认为受这一问题密切影响的国家的代表应就报告拟写与秘书长密切合作。他建议将成员人数限制在三至四名,但这一问题可在下次会议上进一步讨论。

斯坦鲍尔先生(美国)和张先生(中国)说,他们将在下次会议上以书面形式提交修正案。

14. 张彭春在经社理事会第八届第261次会议上的发言

1949年3月4日上午11时,联合国经社理事会第八届第261次会议,在纽约成功湖召开。本次会议继续讨论欠发达地区经济发展问题。中国代表张彭春率团参加了本次会议,并在会议上先后多次发言[①],其发言内容纪要及其译文等如下:

【会议纪要】

Mr. CHANG (China) supported the French amendment. He regretted having proposed an amendment (E/1211) too hastily and as the Chinese delegation had never supported any proposal to establish new organs, he would replace the text of his proposed addition to the United States resolution by the following sentence: "and taking into account the suggestions of the Governments of Member States of the United Nations who were especially interested."

That proposal did not, of course, imply that a very thorough investigation should be undertaken but simply that the members of the Council who had shown special interest in the problem should express their views in order to simplify the task of the Secretary-General.

Mr. CHANG (China) replied that in the main he had had in mind suggestions which had already been made in the course of the present discussion, but that fact did not prevent Member States from making further suggestions. "Gov-

① UN Document: E/SR. 261, p. 446, p. 447, pp. 447-448.

ernments...especially interested" meant under-developed countries as well as all States which were in a position to help such countries. It was clear that once a definite programme had been established, practically all Member States of the United Nations would be concerned in the matter, but during the actual preparation phase of the programme, the Chinese representative felt that only certain countries could be considered as being directly interested.

Mr. CHANG (China) accepted that suggestion but expressed the fear that the remainder of his amendment might be interpreted in too broad a manner.

Mr. CHANG (China) said that his main intention was to ensure that too many Governments did not send suggestions to the Secretary-General who might otherwise be snowed under, and, secondly, to make sure that the Secretary-General would take into account all suggestions sent to him.

【纪要影像】

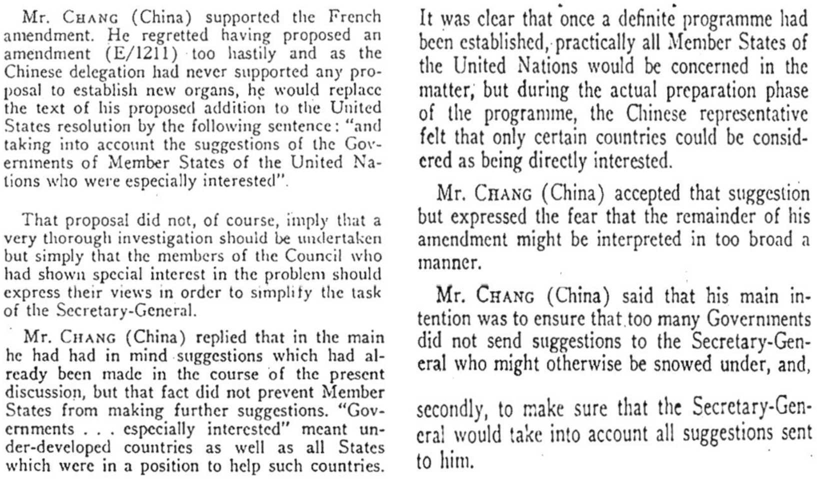
Mr. CHANG (China) supported the French amendment. He regretted having proposed an amendment (E/1211) too hastily and as the Chinese delegation had never supported any proposal to establish new organs, he would replace the text of his proposed addition to the United States resolution by the following sentence: "and taking into account the suggestions of the Governments of Member States of the United Nations who were especially interested".

That proposal did not, of course, imply that a very thorough investigation should be undertaken but simply that the members of the Council who had shown special interest in the problem should express their views in order to simplify the task of the Secretary-General.

Mr. CHANG (China) replied that in the main he had had in mind suggestions which had already been made in the course of the present discussion, but that fact did not prevent Member States from making further suggestions. "Governments . . . especially interested" meant under-developed countries as well as all States which were in a position to help such countries. It was clear that once a definite programme had been established, practically all Member States of the United Nations would be concerned in the matter, but during the actual preparation phase of the programme, the Chinese representative felt that only certain countries could be considered as being directly interested.

Mr. CHANG (China) accepted that suggestion but expressed the fear that the remainder of his amendment might be interpreted in too broad a manner.

Mr. CHANG (China) said that his main intention was to ensure that too many Governments did not send suggestions to the Secretary-General who might otherwise be snowed under, and, secondly, to make sure that the Secretary-General would take into account all suggestions sent to him.

图片 8.17 张彭春在经社理事会第八届第 261 次会议发言纪要

【纪要译文】

张先生(中国)支持法国的修正案。他对过于仓促地提出一项修正案(E/1211)表示遗憾,因为中国代表团从未支持任何设立新机构的提议,他将把他提议对美国决议的补充案文改为以下句子:“并考虑到特别感兴趣的联合国成员国政府的建议。”

当然,这项建议并不意味着应该进行非常彻底的调查,而只是意味着对这一问题表现出特别兴趣的理事会成员应该发表意见,以简化秘书长的任务。

张先生(中国)回答说,他主要考虑的是在本次讨论过程中已经提出的建议,但这一事实并不妨碍成员国提出进一步的建议。“各国政府……特别感兴趣”是指欠发达国家以及所有能够帮助这些国家的国家。很明显,一旦确定了一个明确的方案,实际上所有联合国成员国都将关注此事,但在方案的实际筹备阶段,中国代表认为只有某些国家可以被视为直接感兴趣。

张先生(中国)接受这一建议,但表示担心对其修正案其余部分的解释方式可能过于宽泛。

张先生(中国)说,他的主要意图是确保不会有太多的国家政府向秘书长提出建议,否则秘书长可能会被压得喘不过气来,其次,确保秘书长将能考虑向他提出的所有建议。

15. 张彭春在经社理事会第八届第268次会议上的发言

1949年3月9日下午3时，联合国经社理事会第八届第268次会议，在纽约成功湖召开。本次会议讨论关于理事会工作的组织和讨论理事会程序规则的修订。中国代表张彭春率团参加了本次会议，并在会议上进行了长篇发言①，其发言内容纪要及其译文等如下：

【会议纪要】

Mr. CHANG (China) thanked the representative of Lebanon for having made such a useful contribution to the debate. The document presented by the Lebanese delegation (E/1227) contained a great many elements which would prove extremely useful in the course of the discussion.

He realized that the subject was an extremely important one but it was advisable to view it with a certain skepticism. The essential thing was to know what the Council wished to do. Where there was a will there was a way. Consequently, the first question was to determine what the Council wanted to do. Mr. Chang thought that account should be taken of the fact that the situation was continually developing: no one knew what would be the position of the Economic and Social Council and of the United Nations in two or three years and consequently those who were deeply devoted to the mission and work of the Council should adopt not a fixed but, on the contrary, a dynamic attitude towards the

① UN Document: E/SR. 268, pp. 524-527.

substance of the problem.

He thought that the members of the Council should be frank with themselves. The text which would finally be adopted for rule 1 of the rules of procedure should not be too rigid; that was one reason why Mr. Chang would oppose the substitution of the word "normally" for the words "in principle". The current situation could hardly be considered to be normal.

He thought that there was a fundamental difference between an organ like the Economic and Social Council, which was of a permanent nature, and an international conference. The sessions of the General Assembly, in contrast to those of the Council, could be considered as international conferences. The representatives of the Member States at the sessions of the General Assembly were persons responsible in their respective countries for the formulation and execution of a policy. The Economic and Social Council had an entirely different character and that was one aspect of the problem which it would be wise to consider realistically.

In view of the organization of its work, the Council functioned as a conference during about half of its sessions and as a council, in the strict sense of the word, during the other half. The second part of its work comprised questions which called for careful preparation and attentive and prolonged examination; the application of decisions taken in their respect should be closely observed. Most of the latter type of work, i. e. from eighty to ninety per cent, could be done by the permanent representatives of the States members of the Council; the remaining ten percent, which represented the political aspect of that work, could be the subject of communications between the permanent delegations to the United Nations and the national Governments. Furthermore, he thought that, in any case, it might be possible for the commissions to meet at the same time as the Council. Generally speaking, that type of work could be carried on by the permanent delegation officials of diplomatic rank.

On the other hand, the relative importance of the type of work accomplished by a conference could vary according to the direction taken by the various international policies. The Council dealt with such a great number of topics that its work could not be given the importance it deserved if only one person with ministerial rank was sent. Mr. Chang thought that if they wished to give their full support to the work of the Council, the Governments should send to the Council two or three ministers in succession who would each represent their country for a week or two.

The result of such a method, if it were adopted. would be that the Council would sit almost permanently and would spend most of its time on slow and detailed work, which would be interrupted every year by a few brief periods during which the Council would function as an international conference, the Governments members of the Council being represented by responsible ministers.

He thought that the moment had not yet come to make a formal proposal to that effect but he requested the members of the Council to advise their respective Governments to remember the fundamental difference between the work of a council and that of a conference. If they were confused, both would be fruitless: for example, for the work of a council properly speaking, it would certainly not be necessary to work at the current pace of two meetings a day; only one or two meetings a week could be held, between which the members would have time to study carefully the questions on the agenda.

If that difference were taken into account the decisions of the Council would have much more weight; decisions on questions within the competence of a council strictly speaking would be more fully considered (for example the examination of the revision of the Council's rules of procedure would take about a month): working groups, for example, could be set up to study a particular question. The "conference" periods would be settled in advance and the agenda of those conferences would include only certain items appearing on the agenda of the Council. There again the representative of China would abstain from making a formal proposal which would not be realistic in existing circumstances.

Mr. Chang thought that, for the time being, the members of the Council should concentrate on clarifying their thoughts and not on laying down definitive rules of procedure for the Council. He thought that rule 1 of the rules of procedure could be considered as a temporarily satisfactory solution in a changing situation; he would not oppose the retention of that rule.

All the proposals which had been made with regard to rule 1 corresponded to one aspect of the problem. The first question to be decided was whether the Council should hold a definite number of sessions of limited duration each year or whether it should sit in almost permanent session. Once that decision had been made, a study should be undertaken of the work to be carried out by the Council and of the best method of doing it. About seventy per cent of the examination of reports submitted by specialized agencies should therefore consist of a detailed study of each paragraph of those reports and of the problems which they raised and only thirty percent of general decisions which should be taken by responsible political persons.

It might be an advantage for at least some of the Council's commissions to meet at the same time as the Council so as to be able to submit interim reports, which would avoid delays in the examination of reports and the adoption of decisions.

He wondered whether, putting aside all question of prestige, it was really necessary for all the Council's commissions to meet invariably once or twice a year. A much more flexible system might be devised whereby the commissions would meet only when they had to consider a question falling within their competence. They would then sit as long as it was necessary in order to study the question thoroughly.

In conclusion, he stated that the most important thing was that an effort should be made to see clearly what was needed. The United Nations was still at an experimental stage and it was difficult to say exactly where its development would end. The members of the Council should show proof of great mental flexibility and should above all avoid having fixed ideas. It should be remembered that methods were meant to serve man and men were not meant to be slaves of method.

【纪要影像】

Mr. CHANG (China) thanked the representative of Lebanon for having made such a useful contribution to the debate. The document presented by the Lebanese delegation (E/1227) contained a great many elements which would prove extremely useful in the course of the discussion.

He realized that the subject was an extremely important one but it was advisable to view it with a certain scepticism. The essential thing was to know what the Council wished to do. Where there was a will there was a way. Consequently, the first question was to determine what the Council wanted to do. Mr. Chang thought that account should be taken of the fact that the situation was continually developing: no one knew what would be the position of the Economic and Social Council and of the United Nations in two or three years and consequently those who were deeply devoted to the mission and work of the Council should adopt not a fixed but, on the contrary, a dynamic attitude towards the substance of the problem.

He thought that the members of the Council should be frank with themselves. The text which would finally be adopted for rule 1 of the rules of procedure should not be too rigid; that was one reason why Mr. Chang would oppose the substitution of the word "normally" for the words "in principle". The current situation could hardly be considered to be normal.

He thought that there was a fundamental difference between an organ like the Economic and Social Council, which was of a permanent nature, and an international conference. The sessions of the General Assembly, in contrast to those of the Council, could be considered as international conferences. The representatives of the Member States at the sessions of the General Assembly were persons responsible in their respective countries for the formulation and execution of a policy. The Economic and Social Council had an entirely different character and that was one aspect of the problem which it would be wise to consider realistically.

In view of the organization of its work, the Council functioned as a conference during about half of its sessions and as a council, in the strict sense of the word, during the other half. The second part of its work comprised questions which called for careful preparation and attentive and prolonged examination; the application of decisions taken in their respect should be closely observed. Most of the latter type of work, i.e. from eighty to ninety per cent, could be done by the permanent representatives of the States members of the Council; the remaining ten per cent, which represented the political aspect of that work, could be the subject of communications between the permanent delegations to the United Nations and the national Governments. Furthermore, he thought that, in any case, it might be possible for the commissions to meet at the same time as the Council. Generally speaking, that type of work could be carried on by the permanent delegation officials of diplomatic rank.

图片 8.18　张彭春在经社理事会第八届第 268 次会议发言纪要(1)

On the other hand, the relative importance of the type of work accomplished by a conference could vary according to the direction taken by the various international policies. The Council dealt with such a great number of topics that its work could not be given the importance it deserved if only one person with ministerial rank was sent. Mr. Chang thought that if they wished to give their full support to the work of the Council, the Governments should send to the Council two or three ministers in succession who would each represent their country for a week or two.

The result of such a method, if it were adopted, would be that the Council would sit almost permanently and would spend most of its time on slow and detailed work, which would be interrupted every year by a few brief periods during which the Council would function as an international conference, the Governments members of the Council being represented by responsible ministers.

He thought that the moment had not yet come to make a formal proposal to that effect but he requested the members of the Council to advise their respective Governments to remember the fundamental difference between the work of a council and that of a conference. If they were confused, both would be fruitless: for example, for the work of a council properly speaking, it would certainly not be necessary to work at the current pace of two meetings a day; only one or two meetings a week could be held, between which the members would have time to study carefully the questions on the agenda.

If that difference were taken into account the decisions of the Council would have much more weight; decisions on questions within the competence of a council strictly speaking would be more fully considered (for example the examination of the revision of the Council's rules of procedure would take about a month): working groups, for example, could be set up to study a particular question. The "conference" periods would be settled in advance and the agenda of those conferences would include only certain items appearing on the agenda of the Council. There again the representative of China would abstain from making a formal proposal which would not be realistic in existing circumstances.

Mr. Chang thought that, for the time being, the members of the Council should concentrate on clarifying their thoughts and not on laying down definitive rules of procedure for the Council. He thought that rule 1 of the rules of procedure could be considered as a temporarily satisfactory solution in a changing situation; he would not oppose the retention of that rule.

图片 8.19　张彭春在经社理事会第八届第 268 次会议发言纪要(2)

All the proposals which had been made with regard to rule 1 corresponded to one aspect of the problem. The first question to be decided was whether the Council should hold a definite number of sessions of limited duration each year or whether it should sit in almost permanent session. Once that decision had been made, a study should be undertaken of the work to be carried out by the Council and of the best method of doing it. About seventy per cent of the examination of reports submitted by specialized agencies should therefore consist of a detailed study of each paragraph of those reports and of the problems which they raised and only thirty per cent of general decisions which should be taken by responsible political persons.

It might be an advantage for at least some of the Council's commissions to meet at the same time as the Council so as to be able to submit interim reports, which would avoid delays in the examination of reports and the adoption of decisions.

He wondered whether, putting aside all question of prestige, it was really necessary for all the Council's commissions to meet invariably once or twice a year. A much more flexible system might be devised whereby the commissions would meet only when they had to consider a question falling within their competence. They would then sit as long as it was necessary in order to study the question thoroughly.

In conclusion, he stated that the most important thing was that an effort should be made to see clearly what was needed. The United Nations was still at an experimental stage and it was difficult to say exactly where its development would end. The members of the Council should show proof of great mental flexibility and should above all avoid having fixed ideas. It should be remembered that methods were meant to serve man and that men were not meant to be slaves of method.

图片 8.20　张彭春在经社理事会第八届第 268 次会议发言纪要(3)

【纪要译文】

张先生(中国)感谢黎巴嫩代表为辩论作出了如此有益的贡献。黎巴嫩代表团提交的文件(E/1227)载有许多内容,这些内容在讨论过程中极为有用。

他意识到这是一个极其重要的问题,但最好还是以某种怀疑的态度来看待它。关键是要知道理事会有志做什么。有志者事竟成。因此,第一个问题是确定理事会想要做什么。张先生认为,应该考虑到情况不断发展的事实:没有人知道联合国经济及社会理事会在两三年内的立场会是什么,因此,那些深深致力于理事会使命和工作的人,对问题的实质不应该采取固定的、反而应该采取动态立场。

他认为理事会成员应该坦诚相见。最后将通过的议事规则第1条的案文不应过于刻板;这就是张先生反对将“通常”一词替代“原则上”一词的一个原因。目前的情况很难被认为是正常的。

他认为,像经济及社会理事会这样具有常设性质的机构与国际会议之间有着根本的区别。与理事会的届会不同,大会的届会可被视为国际会议。出席大会届会的会员国代表是各自国家负责制定和执行政策的人员。经济和社会理事会有一个完全不同的特点,这是问题的一个方面,从现实角度考虑是明智的。

鉴于其工作组织,严格意义上说,理事会在其大约一半的届会期间发挥会议的作用,在另一半届会期间发挥理事会的作用。其工作的第二部分包括需要认真准备和专注和长期审查的问题;应严格遵守就其作出的决定的实施情况。后一类工作的大部分,即80%至90%,可由理事会成员国常驻代表完成;其余的10%代表这项工作的政治方面,可以作为常驻联合国代表团与各国政府之间交流的主题。此外,他认为,无论如何,各委员会都有可能与理事会同时开会。一般来说,这类工作可以由外交级别的常驻代表团官员进行。

另一方面,会议完成的工作类型的相对重要性可能因各种国际政策所采取的方向而有所不同。理事会处理的议题如此之多,以至于如果只派出一名部长级人员,其工作就无法得到应有的重视。张先生认为,如果各国政府希望全力支持理事会的工作,就应该向理事会连续派遣两三名部长,每人代表本国工作一两周。

如果采用这种方法,其结果将是,理事会将几乎永久性地开会,并将大部分时间花在缓慢而详细的工作上,而这项工作每年都会因理事会作为一个国际会议运作的几个短暂时期而中断,理事会成员国政府由负责的部长代表。

他认为,现在还没有提出这方面的正式提案,但他请理事会成员建议各自政府记住理事会工作与会议工作之间的根本区别。如果他们弄混,两者都将是徒劳的。例如,就一个理事会的工作而言,以目前每天两次会议的速度工作肯定是没有必要的;每周只能举行一两次会议,其间成员们将有时间仔细研究议程上的问题。

如果考虑到这一差异,理事会的决定将具有更大的分量;严格来说,关于理事会职权范围内的问题的作出决定将得到更充分的考虑(例如,审查理事会议事规则的修订将需要大约一个月的时间)。例如,可以设立工作组来研究某一特定问题。"会议"时间段将提前确定,这些会议的议程将只包括理事会议程上的某些项目。中国代表将再次放弃提出正式提案,这提案在目前情况下是不现实的。

张先生认为,理事会成员目前应集中精力澄清他们的想法,而不是为理事会制定明确的议事规则。他认为,议事规则第1条可被视为在不断变化的情况下暂时令人满意的解决办法;他不会反对保留这条规则。

就第1条规则提出的所有建议都符合问题的一个方面。第一个有待决定的问题是,理事会是否应每年举行一定数量的有限期届会,还是应举行几乎永久性的届会。一旦作出这一决定,就应该对理事会将要开展的工作以及开展工作的最佳方法进行研究。因此,在对专门机构提交的报告进行审查时,大约70%应由对这些报告的每一段及其提出的问题进行的详细研究组成,只有30%为应由负责的政治人士作出的一般性决定的。

至少理事会的一些委员会与理事会同时开会,以便能够提交临时报告,这可能是一个好处,这将避免在审查报告和采纳决定方面出现拖延。

他想知道,抛开所有的声望问题,理事会的所有委员会是否真的有必要每年都开一两次会。可以设计一种更加灵活的制度,根据这种制度,各委员会只有在必须审议属于其职权范围内的问题时才开会。为了彻底研究这个问题，他们可以能开多久就开多久。

最后，他说，最重要的是，应努力明确需要什么。联合国仍处于试验阶段，很难说其发展将归于何处。理事会成员应表现出极大的精神灵活性，首先应避免有固定的想法。应该记住，方法是为人服务的，人不是方法的奴隶。

16. 张彭春在经社理事会第八届第 269 次会议上的发言

1949 年 3 月 10 日上午 11 时，联合国经社理事会第八届第 269 次会议，在纽约成功湖召开。本次会议讨论亚洲和远东经济委员会的临时报告。中国代表张彭春率团参加了本次会议，并在会议上发言①，另外，查先生在本次会议上也做了两次发言②。张彭春先生发言内容纪要及其译文等如下：

【会议纪要】

Mr. CHANG (China) stated that his delegation was favourably disposed towards guaranteeing that sufficient funds should be made available for the activities of the Economic Commission for Asia and Far East. He asked for clarification whether there had been any proposal by representatives regarding that matter, and secondly whether the work of the Commission would be retarded if additional funds were not made available. He felt, however, that he would be obliged to support the Secretariat request for authorization of additional funds.

---

① UN Document: E/SR. 269, p. 535

② UN Document: E/SR. 269, p. 530, pp. 530-531.

【纪要影像】

Mr. CHANG (China) stated that his delegation was favourably disposed towards guaranteeing that sufficient funds should be made available for the activities of the Economic Commission for Asia and the Far East. He asked for clarification whether there had been any proposal by representatives regarding that matter, and secondly whether the work of the Commission would be retarded if additional funds were not made available. He felt, however, that he would be obliged to support the Secretariat request for authorization of additional funds.

图片 8.21　张彭春在经社理事会第八届第 269 次会议发言纪要

【纪要译文】

张先生(中国)说,中国代表团倾向于对保证为亚洲和远东经济委员会的活动提供足够的资金表示支持。他要求澄清代表们是否就这一事项提出了任何提议,其次,如果不提供额外资金,委员会的工作是否会受到阻碍。然而,他认为,他有义务支持秘书处关于核准追加资金的请求。

17. 张彭春在经社理事会第八届第 270 次会议上的发言

1949 年 3 月 10 日下午 3 时，联合国经社理事会第八届第 270 次会议，在纽约成功湖召开。本次会议讨论亚洲和远东经济委员会的临时报告、讨论建立中东经济委员会的有关因素的报告。中国代表张彭春率团参加了本次会议，并在会议上先后多次发言①，其发言内容纪要及其译文等如下：

【会议纪要】

Mr. CHANG (China) said it was no longer necessary to maintain the reservations he had previously made. The fact that the Economic Committee had noted the interim report of the Economic Commission for Asia and the Far East, without any objections being made, implied that the Economic Committee had approved the programme of work proposed by the Commission. The Council, therefore, had only to decide on a mere question of procedure.

As to the Australian amendment, he thought in view of the nature of the work contemplated on the one hand, and of the amount of funds granted to the other regional economic commissions, on the the other, that the funds visualized in the amendment were relatively small. The Australian amendment should therefore be adopted.

Mr. CHANG (China) thought that the question before the Council was not whether the latter should or should not admit the Government of the Korean Re-

① UN Document: E/SR. 270, p. 536, p. 539, p. 541, p. 543.

public to membership on the Economic Commission for Asia and the Far East, but whether the terms of reference of that Commission should be amended in order to allow the Government of the Republic of Korea to lay its candidature before it.

Mr. CHANG (China) thanked the Polish representative for having raised that question. The Economic and Social Council had defined the terms of reference of the regional economic commissions and it should therefore decide over which areas the competence of any particular commission extended. Moreover, if all the requests for admission had had first to be considered by the commissions concerned there was reason to wonder how the commissions themselves would have come into existence, since there would have been no commission to consider the admission of new members. If the Council thought that the situation had developed in such a way that, in its opinion, Korea could become an associate member of the Economic Commission for Asia and the Far East, then it could adopt a favourable decision on that subject.

Mr. CHANG (China) thought the USSR representative had made a slight mistake in apparently thinking that the proposal before the Council had been submitted by the United States and China; that was not so.

【纪要影像】

Mr. CHANG (China) said it was no longer necessary to maintain the reservations he had previously made. The fact that the Economic Committee had noted the interim report of the Economic Commission for Asia and the Far East, without any objections being made, implied that the Economic Committee had approved the programme of work proposed by the Commission. The Council, therefore, had only to decide on a mere question of procedure.

As to the Australian amendment, he thought in view of the nature of the work contemplated on the one hand, and of the amount of funds granted to the other regional economic commissions, on the other, that the funds visualized in the amendment were relatively small. The Australian amendment should therefore be adopted.

Mr. CHANG (China) thought that the question before the Council was not whether the latter should or should not admit the Government of the Korean Republic to membership on the Economic Commission for Asia and the Far East, but whether the terms of reference of that Commission should be amended in order to allow the Government of the Republic of Korea to lay its candidature before it.

Mr. CHANG (China) thanked the Polish representative for having raised that question. The Economic and Social Council had defined the terms of reference of the regional economic commissions and it should therefore decide over which areas the competence of any particular commission extended. Moreover, if all the requests for admission had had first to be considered by the commissions concerned there was reason to wonder how the commissions themselves would have come into existence, since there would have been no commission to consider the admission of new members. If the Council thought that the situation had developed in such a way that, in its opinion, Korea could become an associate member of the Economic Commission for Asia and the Far East, then it could adopt a favourable decision on that subject.

Mr. CHANG (China) thought the USSR representative had made a slight mistake in apparently thinking that the proposal before the Council had been submitted by the United States and China; that was not so.

图片 8.22 张彭春在经社理事会第八届第 270 次会议发言纪要

【纪要译文】

张先生(中国)说,没有必要再坚持他先前提出的保留意见。经济事务委员会注意到亚洲和远东经济委员会的临时报告没有提出任何反对意见,这意味着经济事务委员会已经批准了(亚洲和远东经济)委员会提出的工作方案。因此,理事会只需就一个程序问题作出决定。

关于澳大利亚的修正案,他认为,一方面考虑到所设想的工作的性质,另一方面考虑到向其他区域经济委员会提供的资金数额,修正案中设想的资金相对较少。因此,应采纳澳大利亚的修正案。

张先生(中国)认为,摆在理事会面前的问题不是后者是否应接纳大韩民国政府为亚洲和远东经济委员会成员,而是该委员会的职权范围是否应该修改,以便使大韩民国政府获得委员会成员候选资格。

张先生(中国)感谢波兰代表提出这一问题。经济及社会理事会确定了各区域经济委员会的职权范围,故应决定将任何特定委员会的职权范围扩大到哪些领域。此外,如果所有有关加入的要求都必须首先由有关委员会审议,那么有理由怀疑这些委员会本身是如何成立的,因为没有任何委员会考虑接纳新成员的问题。如果理事会认为情况发展到它认为韩国可以成为亚洲和远东经济委员会准成员的程度,那么它就可以就此问题作出有利的决定。

张先生(中国)认为苏联代表显然犯了一个小错误,认为理事会面前的提案是美国和中国提交的;事实并非如此。

18. 张彭春在经社理事会第八届第272次会议上的发言

1949年3月11日下午3时,联合国经社理事会第八届第272次会议,在纽约成功湖召开。本次会议讨论英国提交的有关区域经济委员会决议草案、讨论1949年区域经济委员会会议届数、讨论理事会工作的组织。中国代表张彭春率代表团参加了本次会议,并在会议上先后多次发言①,其发言内容纪要及其译文等如下:

【会议纪要】

Mr. CHANG (China) was glad to note that there was no question in the United Kingdom resolution of altering the terms of reference of the regional economic commissions in any way. He emphasized that under those terms of reference, in 1951 at the latest, the Council would have to undertake an overall examination of the work carried out by the regional economic commissions. The Council would doubtless carry out that examination during its eleventh or twelfth session. He concluded that if the United Kingdom resolution were adopted, it would be applied only during a period embracing three sessions of the Council. He therefore requested the United Kingdom representative to withdraw his proposal, while reserving his right to submit it again during the ninth session.

Mr. CHANG (China) thought that the New Zealand representative was quite right. He suggested that the Secretariat should be asked to contact the Ex-

① UN Document: E/SR. 272, p. 563, p. 564, p. 566, pp. 570–571.

ecutive Secretary of the Economic Commission for Asia and the Far East, with a view to arranging that the Committee of the Whole of the Commission, which was to meet in the near future, should consider the matter.

Mr. CHANG (China) felt that, although any excessively rigid rule was to be avoided, a rule was needed and that one of the Council's rules of procedure should fix the number of sessions to be held each year. He did not think that one session a year would be enough; he would therefore vote against both the Belgian and French proposals, and would support that of the United States. If the latter was rejected, he would vote for maintaining the existing rule of procedure.

Mr. CHANG (China) pointed out that, so far, the Belgian and French proposals had been defended by the contention that competent persons from the different countries could only be present at a relatively limited number of sessions of the Council. The Belgian representative had stressed that the Secretariat should have all the time necessary to carry out its work.

He thought that if the Council held only one session a year its duration should in no case be limited to two months. The spirit in which the Council had been established should be recalled. One of its founders had emphasized that he hoped to see the importance of the Economic and Social Council increasing gradually as that of the Security Council declined. The dynamic character of the Council's work should be stressed. For those reasons he was in favour of the United States proposal.

【纪要影像】

Mr. CHANG (China) was glad to note that there was no question in the United Kingdom resolution of altering the terms of reference of the regional economic commissions in any way. He emphasized that under those terms of reference, in 1951 at the latest, the Council would have to undertake an overall examination of the work carried out by the regional economic commissions. The Council would doubtless carry out that examination during its eleventh or twelfth session. He concluded that if the United Kingdom resolution were adopted, it would be applied only during a period embracing three sessions of the Council. He therefore requested the United Kingdom representative to withdraw his proposal, while reserving his right to submit it again during the ninth session.

Mr. CHANG (China) thought that the New Zealand representative was quite right. He suggested that the Secretariat should be asked to contact the Executive Secretary of the Economic Commission for Asia and the Far East, with a view to arranging that the Committee of the Whole of the Commission, which was to meet in the near future, should consider the matter.

Mr. CHANG (China) felt that, although any excessively rigid rule was to be avoided, a rule was needed and that one of the Council's rules of procedure should fix the number of sessions to be held each year. He did not think that one session a year would be enough; he would therefore vote against both the Belgian and French proposals, and would support that of the United States. If the latter was rejected, he would vote for maintaining the existing rule of procedure.

Mr. CHANG (China) pointed out that, so far, the Belgian and French proposals had been defended by the contention that competent persons from the different countries could only be present at a relatively limited number of sessions of the Council. The Belgian representative had stressed that the Secretariat should have all the time necessary to carry out its work.

He thought that if the Council held only one session a year its duration should in no case be limited to two months. The spirit in which the Council had been established should be recalled. One of its founders had emphasized that he hoped to see the importance of the Economic and Social Council increasing gradually as that of the Security Council declined. The dynamic character of the Council's work should be stressed. For those reasons he was in favour of the United States proposal.

图片 8.23　张彭春在经社理事会第八届第 272 次会议发言纪要

【纪要译文】

张先生(中国)高兴地注意到,英国的决议中没有以任何方式改变各区域经济委员会的职权范围的问题。他强调,根据这些职权范围,理事会最迟必须在 1951 年全面审查各区域经济委员会所开展的工作。毫无疑问,理事会将在其第十一届或第十二届会议期间进行这项审查。他总结说,如果英国的决议获得通过,它将只在包括理事会三届会议在内的一段时间内适用。因此,他请英国代表撤回其提案,同时保留在第九届会议期间再次提交提案的权利。

张先生(中国)认为新西兰代表说得很对。他建议秘书处应联系亚洲和远东经济委员会执行秘书,以安排在不久的将来召开的全体委员会审议此事。

张先生(中国)认为,尽管应避免任何过于严格的规则,但需要一项规则,理事会的议事规则之一应确定每年举行届会的次数。他认为一年一次会议是不够的;因此,他将投票反对比利时和法国的提案,并支持美国的提案。如果后者被否决,他将投票支持维持现行议事规则。

张先生(中国)指出,到目前为止,比利时和法国的提案一直受到这样一种论点辩护,即来自不同国家的主管人员只能出席理事会相对有限的几届会议。比利时代表强调,秘书处应该有开展工作所需的所有时间。

他认为,如果理事会每年只举行一届会议,其会期无论如何都不应限于两个月。应当回顾成立经社理事会的精神,其创始人之一曾强调,他希望看到经济及社会理事会的重要性逐渐增加,而安全理事会的重要性则逐渐下降。应该强调理事会工作的动态特征。出于这些原因,他赞成美国的提案。

19. 张彭春在经社理事会第八届第 273 次会议上的发言

1949 年 3 月 14 日上午 11 时,联合国经社理事会第八届第 273 次会议,在纽约成功湖召开。本次会议讨论经济与社会建议的实施,并选举理事会第九届日程委员会成员。中国代表张彭春率代表团参加了本次会议,并在会议上发言①,其发言内容纪要及其译文等如下:

【会议纪要】

Mr. CHANG (China) had been under the impression that the debate on rule 1 of the rules of procedure had been closed during the 272nd meeting of the Council and that, consequently, no new amendment would be presented. If the President declared the French amendment admissible, there was a risk that the debate might be re-opened.

Furthermore, the United States amendment was already an improvement on the old rule 1 which had provided for at least three sessions.

Mr. Chang did not think that the members of the Council should give the impression to the public at large that they were seeking to reduce the amount of work accomplished, and consequently, the efficiency of the Council.

Mr. CHANG (China) thought it unlikely that the rule would be misused and was consequently in favour of the United States proposal.

Mr. CHANG (China) agreed with the United States representative.

---

① UN Document: E/SR. 273, p. 576, p. 577.

【纪要影像】

Mr. CHANG (China) had been under the impression that the debate on rule 1 of the rules of procedure had been closed during the 272nd meeting of the Council and that, consequently, no new amendment would be presented. If the President declared the French amendment admissible, there was a risk that the debate might be reopened.

Furthermore, the United States amendment was already an improvement on the old rule 1 which had provided for at least three sessions. Mr. Chang did not think that the members of the Council should give the impression to the public at large that they were seeking to reduce the amount of work accomplished, and consequently, the efficiency of the Council.

Mr. CHANG (China) thought it unlikely that the rule would be misused and was consequently in favour of the United States proposal.

Mr. CHANG (China) agreed with the United States representative.

图片 8.24　张彭春在经社理事会第八届第 273 次会议发言纪要

【纪要译文】

张先生(中国)记得,关于议事规则第 1 条的辩论已在理事会第 272 次会议期间结束,因此不会提出新的修正案。如果主席宣布法国修正案可以接受,就有重新开始辩论的风险。

此外,美国的修正案对规定至少举行三届会议的旧规则 1 已经是一种改进。

张先生认为,理事会成员不应给公众留下这样的印象,即他们正在设法减少已完成的工作量,从而降低理事会的效率。

张先生(中国)认为该规则不太可能被滥用,因此赞成美国的提议。

张先生(中国)同意美国代表的意见。

20. 张彭春在经社理事会第八届第282次会议上的发言

1949年3月18日下午2时30分,联合国经社理事会第八届第282次会议,在纽约成功湖召开。本次会议讨论经济与社会建议的实施,并选举理事会第九届日程委员会成员。中国代表张彭春率代表团参加了本次会议,并在会议上先后多次发言①,其发言内容纪要及其译文等如下:

【会议纪要】

Mr. CHANG (China) emphasized the importance of the question, which had a direct bearing upon the effectiveness of the United Nations. It was not a question which could be dealt with entirely by such bureaucratic measures as the submission of reports. Some countries had large staffs skilled in writing reports, while others were not so advanced in that respect. Hence reports could not always be relied upon for an accurate picture of the facts. The Council was not a legislative body and, even if it carried out investigations into implementation, it had no means at its disposal to punish Governments which might have failed to put its resolutions into practice.

When the Council passed a resolution, it should do so with a real desire for its recommendations to be carried out and, at the same time, it should be prepared to give some tangible encouragement to Member Governments. It should not simply keep a check on their activities; it also had amoral responsi-

① UN Document:E/SR. 282, pp. 658-659, p. 661, p. 663, p. 664.

bility to assist them to put its recommendations into practice and to encourage wider co-operation in the social field.

The joint United Kingdom-Australian draft resolution required some drafting changes, which could be made at the next session. For example, there was not a great deal of time allowed for drawing up reports between the dates 1 October and 1 March. It was not urgent to adopt the draft resolution during the current session as it would not in any case be put into effect until 1 October.

He could not agree to the Belgian draft resolution since it merely proposed postponement of discussion on the United Kingdom-Australian draft resolution which dealt with only one aspect of the problem.

Mr. Chang hoped that the final discussion would cover all the aspects of the problem and he therefore submitted a draft resolution (E/1303) proposing the deferment of item 15 to the ninth session and requesting the Secretary-General to prepare a report on methods of implementation, taking into account the discussion at the eighth session, the resolutions and amendments submitted and any further comments which might be received from Member Governments. The following words should be added as a first paragraph to the text of the Chinese draft resolution as set forth in document E/1303.

> "Defers further consideration of item 15, implementation of recommendations on economic and social matters, to the ninth session."

Mr. CHANG (China) disagreed with the United States representative's opinion that deferment of item 15 to the ninth session would mean that the Council would not be in a position to submit a report on the question of implementation to the fourth session of the General Assembly. Sufficient material for that report was already at hand; the fact that the material was not yet complete was not essential.

Mr. CHANG (China) reiterated the views he had expressed during the consideration of item 15 and hoped that the question would be discussed more comprehensively at the ninth session of the Council. He wished it to be put on record that he hoped that comments on the lines he had suggested might be prepared by the Secretary-General despite the rejection of the Chinese draft resolution.

Mr. CHANG (China) nominated INDIA to serve on the Agenda Committee.

【纪要影像】

Mr. CHANG (China) emphasized the importance of the question, which had a direct bearing upon the effectiveness of the United Nations. It was not a question which could be dealt with entirely by such bureaucratic measures as the submission of reports. Some countries had large staffs skilled in writing reports, while others were not so advanced in that respect. Hence reports could not always be relied upon for an accurate picture of the facts. The Council was not a legislative body and, even if it carried out investigations into implementation, it had no means at its

disposal to punish Governments which might have failed to put its resolutions into practice.

When the Council passed a resolution, it should do so with a real desire for its recommendations to be carried out and, at the same time, it should be prepared to give some tangible encouragement to Member Governments. It should not simply keep a check on their activities; it also had a moral responsibility to assist them to put its recommendations into practice and to encourage wider co-operation in the social field.

The joint United Kingdom-Australian draft resolution required some drafting changes, which could be made at the next session. For example, there was not a great deal of time allowed for drawing up reports between the dates 1 October and 1 March. It was not urgent to adopt the draft resolution during the current session as it would not in any case be put into effect until 1 October.

图片 8.25　张彭春在经社理事会第八届第 282 次会议发言纪要(1)

He could not agree to the Belgian draft resolution since it merely proposed postponement of discussion on the United Kingdom-Australian draft resolution which dealt with only one aspect of the problem.

Mr. Chang hoped that the final discussion would cover all the aspects of the problem and he therefore submitted a draft resolution (E/1303) proposing the deferment of item 15 to the ninth session and requesting the Secretary-General to prepare a report on methods of implementation, taking into account the discussion at the eighth session, the resolutions and amendments submitted and any further comments which might be received from Member Governments. The following words should be added as a first paragraph to the text of the Chinese draft resolution as set forth in document E/1303:

"*Defers* further consideration of item 15, implementation of recommendations on economic and social matters, to the ninth session."

Mr. CHANG (China) disagreed with the United States representative's opinion that deferment of item 15 to the ninth session would mean that the Council would not be in a position to submit a report on the question of implementation to the fourth session of the General Assembly. Sufficient material for that report was already at hand; the fact that the material was not yet complete was not essential.

Mr. CHANG (China) reiterated the views he had expressed during the consideration of item 15 and hoped that the question would be discussed more comprehensively at the ninth session of the Council. He wished it to be put on record that he hoped that comments on the lines he had suggested might be prepared by the Secretary-General despite the rejection of the Chinese draft resolution.

Mr. CHANG (China) nominated INDIA to serve on the Agenda Committee.

图片 8.26 张彭春在经社理事会第八届第 282 次会议发言纪要(2)

【纪要译文】

张先生(中国)强调了这个问题的重要性,它直接关系到联合国的效率。这不是一个完全可以通过提交报告等官僚措施来解决的问题。一些国家拥有大量擅长撰写报告的工作人员,而另一些国家在这方面并不那么先进。因此,不能总是依靠报告来准确了解事实。理事会不是一个立法机构,即使它对执行情况进行调查,它也没有办法惩罚那些可能没有将其决议付诸实施的政府。

当理事会通过一项决议时,它应该真正希望其建议得到执行,同时,它应该准备给会员国政府一些切实的鼓励。它不应该简单地检查他们的活动;它还负有与道德无关的责任,协助他们将其建议付诸实施,并鼓励在社会领域开展更广泛的合作。

英国和澳大利亚联合提出的决议草案需要对措词作一些修改,这些修改可在下届会议上提出。例如,在 10 月 1 日至 3 月 1 日期间,没有足够的时间起草报告。在本届会议期间通过该决议草案并不紧迫,因为它无论如何要到 10 月 1 日才能生效。

他不能同意比利时的决议草案,因为它只是提议推迟讨论英国和澳大利亚的联合决议草案,该决议草案只涉及问题的一个方面。

张先生希望最后讨论将涵盖该问题的所有方面,因此他提交了一份决议草案(E/1303),提议将项目 15 推迟到第九届会议,并请秘书长考虑到第八届会议的讨论情况、提交的决议和修正案以及可能从成员国政府收到的任何进一步评论,编写一份关于执行方法的报告。以下文字应作为第一段在 E/1303 号文件所载的中国决议草案案文中。

> “将项目 15(经济和社会事项建议的执行情况)的进一步审议推迟到第九届会议。”

张先生(中国)不同意美国代表的意见,即将项目 15 推迟到第九届会议将意味着理事会无法向大会第四届会议提交关于执行问题的报告。已掌握该报告的足够材料;材料尚未完成这一事实并不重要。

张先生(中国)重申了他在审议项目 15 期间表达的观点,并希望在理事会第九届会议上更全面地讨论这个问题。他希望记录在案的是,尽管中国的决议草案被否决,他还是希望秘书长能够按照他建议的思路撰写评论。

张先生(中国)提名印度担任议程委员会成员。

第九章　联合国经社理事会第九届会议

（纪要）

1949年7月5日上午11时，联合国经社理事会第九届会议在日内瓦万国宫开幕，从1949年7月5日至8月15日，本届共召开了61次会议，分别从第283次会议至第343次会议。本届会议讨论了一系列有关经济社会等问题，包括讨论会议日程安排、讨论麻醉药品委员会第四届会议报告、讨论国际劳工组织报告、讨论欧洲经济委员会的年度报告、讨论经济与社会事务建议的落实情况、讨论农业地区用于防治疟疾的滴滴涕杀虫剂的供应情况、讨论拉丁美洲经济委员会的年度报告、讨论关于奴隶制问题、讨论欠发达地区的经济发展问题、讨论非政府组织理事会委员会关于非政府组织手册的报告、讨论经济委员会第四届会议报告、讨论世界卫生组织的报告、讨论新闻和出版自由小组委员会第三届会议报告、讨论强迫劳动及其废除措施的调查、讨论人权委员会第五届会议决议草案A(国际人权公约)和决议草案C(申诉的权利)、讨论美洲大陆土著人口和其他欠发达社会群体的社会问题等。

中国代表张彭春率团参加了本届会议，并在本届会议中的17次会议上进行了大会发言，包括第283次会议、第284次会议、第285次会议、第286次会议、第294次会议、第295次会议、第296次会议、第297次会议、第298次会议、第300次会议、第301次会议、第304次会议、第305次会议、第306次会议、第311次会议、第312次会议、第320次会议。另外，代表团代表助理曹保颐先生和于焌吉(Yu Tsune-chi)先生(Mr. Yu)分别参

图片 9.1　中国代表张彭春和智利代表桑塔·克鲁兹于 1949 年 7 月 5 日在日内瓦万国宫参加联合国经社理事会第九届会议

与了本届会议,其中曹先生在第 299 次会议[①]、第 313 次会议[②]、第 314 次会议[③]、第 323 次会议[④]和第 343 次会议[⑤]上发言,于先生在第 337 次会议[⑥]上发言。其中,张彭春先生的发言内容如下:

① UN Document: E/SR. 299, p. 216.
② UN Document: E/SR. 313, pp. 455-456.
③ UN Document: E/SR. 314, p. 460.
④ UN Document: E/SR. 323, p. 577.
⑤ UN Document: E/SR. 343, p. 935.
⑥ UN Document: E/SR. 337, p. 809.

1. 张彭春在经社理事会第九届第283次会议上的发言

1949年7月5日上午11时,联合国经社理事会第九届第283次会议,在日内瓦万国宫开幕,本次会议主要是开幕式及讨论会议日程安排。中国代表张彭春率团参加了本次会议,并在会议上先后多次发言,具体发言内容[①]纪要及其译文等如下:

【会议纪要】

Mr. P. C. CHANG (China) expressed profound appreciation of the way in which the President of the Council had guided the Agenda Committee, and of the constructive work which that Committee had done. He supported the proposal of the representative of the Lebanon that discussion of items 2 and 3 be deferred, since the Council should not insist on discussing them when the representative of the only country of the Middle East area represented on the Council was himself opposed to such a course, and because, although the Middle East was a very important region, the terms of reference of all the regional commissions of the Council would be reconsidered the following year, when the Council would be in a position to consider whether the general system of dealing with economic problems at regional level was satisfactory.

Mr. P. C. CHANG (China) supported the Chilean representative's proposal.

---

① UN Document: E/SR. 283, p. 4, p. 10, p. 11.

The Council unanimously adopted the proposal of the Chilean representative.

Mr. P. C. CHANG (China) suggested that item 32 (Report of the Secretary-General on the United Nations Appeal for Children) should not be separated from item 31, and that both should be discussed initially in plenary.

Mr. P. C. CHANG (China) stated that, in view of the New Zealand representative's explanation, he would not insist on item 31 being examined first in plenary.

He suggested, however, that consideration in plenary of item 32 (Report of the Secretary-General on the United Nations Appeal for Children) should be deferred until the report of the Social Committee relating to its examination of item 31 had been received, so that the two items might be considered together by the Council.

【纪要影像】

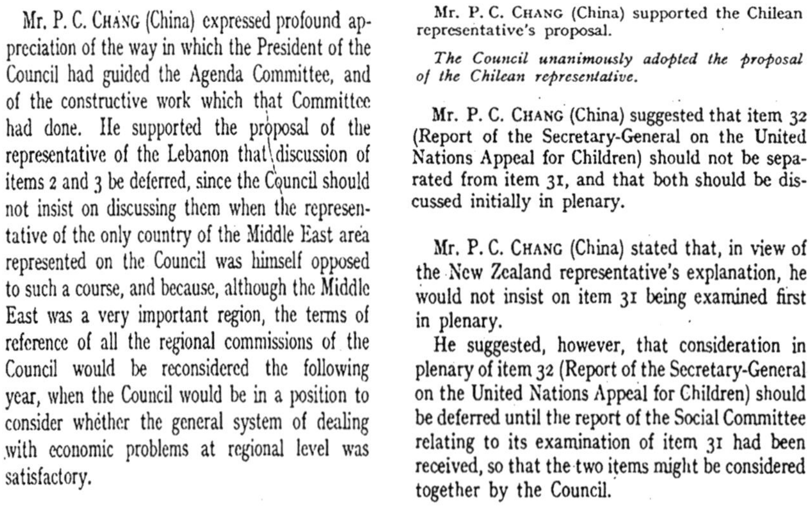

Mr. P. C. CHANG (China) expressed profound appreciation of the way in which the President of the Council had guided the Agenda Committee, and of the constructive work which that Committee had done. He supported the proposal of the representative of the Lebanon that discussion of items 2 and 3 be deferred, since the Council should not insist on discussing them when the representative of the only country of the Middle East area represented on the Council was himself opposed to such a course, and because, although the Middle East was a very important region, the terms of reference of all the regional commissions of the Council would be reconsidered the following year, when the Council would be in a position to consider whether the general system of dealing with economic problems at regional level was satisfactory.

Mr. P. C. CHANG (China) supported the Chilean representative's proposal.

The Council unanimously adopted the proposal of the Chilean representative.

Mr. P. C. CHANG (China) suggested that item 32 (Report of the Secretary-General on the United Nations Appeal for Children) should not be separated from item 31, and that both should be discussed initially in plenary.

Mr. P. C. CHANG (China) stated that, in view of the New Zealand representative's explanation, he would not insist on item 31 being examined first in plenary.

He suggested, however, that consideration in plenary of item 32 (Report of the Secretary-General on the United Nations Appeal for Children) should be deferred until the report of the Social Committee relating to its examination of item 31 had been received, so that the two items might be considered together by the Council.

图片 9.2　张彭春在经社理事会第九届第 283 次会议发言纪要

【纪要译文】

张彭春先生(中国)对理事会主席指导议程委员会的方式以及该委员会所做的建设性工作深表赞赏。他支持黎巴嫩代表关于推迟讨论项目2和项目3的提议,因为理事会不应在中东地区唯一一个在理事会有代表的国家的代表本人反对这样做时,仍坚持讨论这些项目,因为,虽然中东是一个非常重要的地区,但理事会的所有区域委员会的职权范围将在下一年重新审议,届时理事会将有权考虑在区域层面处理经济问题的一般制度是否令人满意。

张彭春先生(中国)支持智利代表的建议。

理事会一致通过了智利代表的提案。

张彭春先生(中国)建议,不应将项目32(秘书长关于联合国儿童申诉的报告)与项目31分开,而应首先在全体会议上讨论这两项内容。

张彭春先生(中国)说,鉴于新西兰代表的解释,他不会坚持在全体会议上首先审议项目31。

但是,他建议,全体会议对项目32(秘书长关于联合国儿童申诉的报告)的审议应推迟到收到社会事务委员会关于其审查项目31的报告后进行,以便理事会可以一并审议这两项内容。

2. 张彭春在经社理事会第九届第 284 次会议上的发言

1949 年 7 月 5 日下午 3 时，联合国经社理事会第九届第 284 次会议，在日内瓦万国宫召开，本次会议主要是讨论并通过会议日程安排。中国代表张彭春率团参加了本次会议，并在会议上发言，具体发言内容[①]纪要及其译文等如下：

【会议纪要】

Mr. P. C. CHANG (China) asked whether, in view of the decision to defer the consideration of item 9 to 21 July, item 12 might not be taken earlier.

【纪要影像】

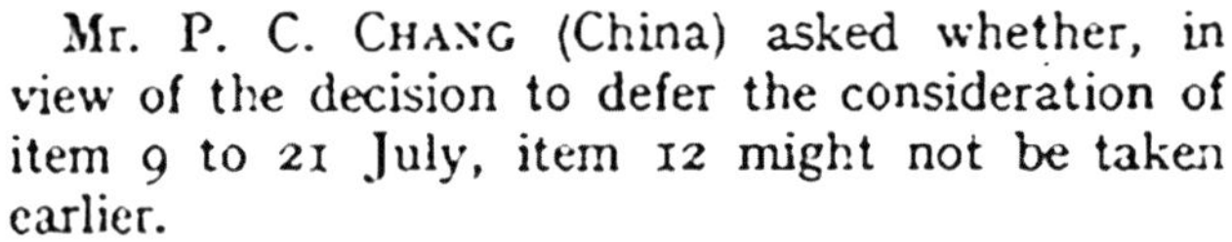
Mr. P. C. CHANG (China) asked whether, in view of the decision to defer the consideration of item 9 to 21 July, item 12 might not be taken earlier.

图片 9.3　张彭春在经社理事会第九届第 284 次会议发言纪要

① UN Document: E/SR. 284, p. 18.

【纪要译文】

张彭春先生(中国)问,鉴于将项目9推迟到7月21日审议的决定,项目12是否可能不提前审议。

3. 张彭春在经社理事会第九届第285次会议上的发言

1949年7月6日上午11时,联合国经社理事会第九届第285次会议,在日内瓦万国宫召开,本次会议主要是讨论麻醉药品委员会第四届会议报告。中国代表张彭春率团参加了本次会议,并在会议上进行了长篇发言,具体发言内容[①]纪要及其译文等如下:

【会议纪要】

Mr. P. C. CHANG (China) expressed his appreciation of the work of the Commission on Narcotic Drugs, and of the efficient secretariat which had assisted the Commission.

He wished to draw attention to the section in the Commission's report dealing with the unification of existing international instruments on narcotic drugs, which was the most important question that had been considered by the Commission at its fourth session.

He recalled that, as was stated on page 26 of the report, the Economic and Social Council had, at its seventh session, requested the Secretary-General to initiate studies and inquiries on the desirability of convening a conference of the opium-producing countries and of countries using opium in the manufacture of drugs for medical and scientific needs, with a view to reaching an interim agreement limiting the production and export of opium to those needs, pending

① UN Document: E/SR. 285, pp. 20-21, pp. 22-23.

the adoption of a single international convention containing provisions for the limitation of raw materials used in the manufacture of all narcotic drugs. ①

In the Commission's discussions, the Chinese representative, while acknowledging the difficulty of finding a practical solution to the age-old problem of opium production, had made a suggestion, finally adopted in 1949 by an overwhelming majority of the Commission, as to how the Commission could decide the question posed by the Director of the Division on Narcotic Drugs in the terms set out on page 28 of the Commission's report: namely, whether the interim agreement could be adopted within a short time, or whether it would have to wait until the single convention had entered into force, which could not be for at least six or seven years.

Although the Council had decided that a conference should be convened, the Chinese representative had agreed not to press for an immediate conference. The Commission had finally decided to establish a sub-committee to consider the desirability of convening a conference to conclude an interim agreement for limiting the production of raw opium to medical and scientific needs. The sub-committee had met and, as was stated on page 31 of the Commission's report, had reported back to the Commission that it was unanimously of the opinion that an interim agreement was necessary, and had proposed the setting up of an *ad hoc* committee.

By an overwhelming vote of 12 votes to 1 with 2 abstentions, the Commission had adopted the report of the sub-committee and had expressed its appreciation of the invitation extended by the Government of Turkey to the *ad hoc* committee to hold its meeting in Istanbul or Ankara. That near-unanimity was undoubtedly the result of the Chinese representative's willingness to compromise and not to press for an immediate conference, but to agree to the much more

① See *Economic and Social Council Resolutions*, seventh session, resolution 159 (VII), II, E.

modest approach represented by a small meeting of the principal opium-producing countries.

The results thus obtained had been most gratifying. Unfortunately, the question of the interim agreement had been lost sight of in the hurried preparation of the highly technical report for presentation to the Council. He drew attention to the draft resolution on the simplification of existing international instruments on narcotic drugs reproduced on pages 64 and 65 of the Commission's report, a resolution which he hoped would be unanimously adopted by the Council. By its terms, however, the Council would approve the decisions taken by the Commission on Narcotic Drugs only with a view to the elaboration of a new single convention, and request the Secretary-General to take all measures necessary to give effect to those decisions as expeditiously as possible. He therefore proposed the addition of the following penultimate paragraph :

> "Approves the decision of the Commission to convene a meeting of an ad hoc committee composed of the principal opium-producing countries to consider the possibility of reaching an interim agreement for limiting the production of raw opium to medical and scientific needs."

He finally pointed out that the references to a "special sub-committee" in the heading of section 2, and to "the sub-committee" in the fourth line of page 2, of document E/1361/Add. 1, were in fact references to the *ad hoc* committee, the setting up of which had been recommended by the sub-committee.

Mr. P. C. CHANG (China) felt that it was to the eternal credit of the opium-producing countries that they had unanimously supported the establishment of the *ad hoc* committee. The implications of such action had to be borne in mind to appreciate fully both it and the Turkish Government's most generous offer.

The Soviet Union representative had stated that an interim agreement was unnecessary. It had been indeed, the Soviet Union representative on the Commission who had been the only opponent of the proposal to convene the *ad hoc* committee. He would point out to the Soviet Union representative that, as was stated in the Commission's report, the French representative on the Commission had agreed with the Chinese representative that the interim agreement would be of great value as a proving ground for the feasibility of limiting the production of raw materials under the proposed single convention. The Council had just heard the French representative indicate some of the difficulties involved in concluding a single convention, and the Director of the Division of Narcotic Drugs had stated before the Commission that, as he (Mr. Chang) had pointed out earlier, it would be impossible for the single convention to enter into force for six or seven years. The problem could, however, best be approached by the method which had been almost unanimously recommended by the Commission: that of setting up a small committee of the principal producing countries to consider the possibility of reaching an agreement on the limitation of the production of opium to medical and scientific needs.

He stressed the absorbing interest in this problem felt by the Chinese people, on whom the use of opium had been forced by war. It was against the historical background of one hundred years, during which period China had been almost entirely at the receiving end of the opium trade, that the Chinese willingness to agree to an experimental approach should be viewed. The experimental approach now under consideration was, however, the very least that could be accepted.

【纪要影像】

Mr. P. C. Chang (China) expressed his appreciation of the work of the Commission on Narcotic Drugs, and of the efficient secretariat which had assisted the Commission.

He wished to draw attention to the section in the Commission's report dealing with the unification of existing international instruments on narcotic drugs, which was the most important question that had been considered by the Commission at its fourth session.

He recalled that, as was stated on page 26 of the report, the Economic and Social Council had, at its seventh session, requested the Secretary-General to initiate studies and inquiries on the desirability of convening a conference of the opium-producing countries and of countries using opium in the manufacture of drugs for medical and scientific needs, with a view to reaching an interim agreement limiting the production and export of opium to those needs, pending the adoption of a single international convention containing provisions for the limitation of raw materials used in the manufacture of all narcotic drugs.[1]

[1] See *Economic and Social Council Resolutions*, seventh session, resolution 159 (VII), II, *E*.

In the Commission's discussions, the Chinese representative, while acknowledging the difficulty of finding a practical solution to the age-old problem of opium production, had made a suggestion, finally adopted in 1949 by an overwhelming majority of the Commission, as to how the Commission could decide the question posed by the Director of the Division on Narcotic Drugs in the terms set out on page 28 of the Commission's report: namely, whether the interim agreement could be adopted within a short time, or whether it would have to wait until the single convention had entered into force, which could not be for at least six or seven years.

图片 9.4　张彭春在经社理事会第九届第 285 次会议发言纪要(1)

Although the Council had decided that a conference should be convened, the Chinese representative had agreed not to press for an immediate conference. The Commission had finally decided to establish a sub-committee to consider the desirability of convening a conference to conclude an interim agreement for limiting the production of raw opium to medical and scientific needs. The sub-committee had met and, as was stated on page 31 of the Commission's report, had reported back to the Commission that it was unanimously of the opinion that an interim agreement was necessary, and had proposed the setting up of an *ad hoc* committee.

By an overwhelming vote of 12 votes to 1 with 2 abstentions, the Commission had adopted the report of the sub-committee and had expressed its appreciation of the invitation extended by the Government of Turkey to the *ad hoc* committee to hold its meeting in Istanbul or Ankara. That near-unanimity was undoubtedly the result of the Chinese representative's willingness to compromise and not to press for an immediate conference, but to agree to the much more modest approach represented by a small meeting of the principal opium-producing countries.

The results thus obtained had been most gratifying. Unfortunately, the question of the interim agreement had been lost sight of in the hurried preparation of the highly technical report for presentation to the Council. He drew attention to the draft resolution on the simplification of existing international instruments on narcotic drugs reproduced on pages 64 and 65 of the Commission's report, a resolution which he hoped would be unanimously adopted by the Council. By its terms, however, the Council would approve the decisions taken by the Commission on Narcotic Drugs only with a view to the elaboration of a new single convention, and request the Secretary-General to take all measures necessary to give effect to those decisions as expeditiously as possible. He therefore proposed the addition of the following penultimate paragraph:

> "*Approves* the decision of the Commission to convene a meeting of an *ad hoc* committee composed of the principal opium-producing countries to consider the possibility of reaching an interim agreement for limiting the production of raw opium to medical and scientific needs."

He finally pointed out that the references to a "special sub-committee" in the heading of section 2, and to "the sub-committee" in the fourth line of page 2, of document E/1361/Add.1, were in fact references to the *ad hoc* committee, the setting up of which had been recommended by the sub-committee.

图片 9.5　张彭春在经社理事会第九届第 285 次会议发言纪要(2)

Mr. P.C. CHANG (China) felt that it was to the eternal credit of the opium-producing countries that they had unanimously supported the establishment of the *ad hoc* committee. The implications of such action had to be borne in mind to appreciate fully both it and the Turkish Government's most generous offer.

The Soviet Union representative had stated that an interim agreement was unnecessary. It had been indeed, the Soviet Union representative on the Commission who had been the only opponent of the proposal to convene the *ad hoc* committee. He would point out to the Soviet Union representative that, as was stated in the Commission's report, the French representative on the Commission had agreed with the Chinese representative that the interim agreement would be of great value as a proving ground for the feasibility of limiting the production of raw materials under the proposed single convention. The Council had just heard the French representative indicate some of the difficulties involved in concluding a single convention, and the Director of the Division of Narcotic Drugs had stated before the Commission that, as he (Mr. Chang) had pointed out earlier, it would be impossible for the single convention to enter into force for six or seven years. The problem could, however, best be approached by the method which had been almost unanimously recommended by the Commission : that of setting up a small committee of the principal producing countries to consider the possibility of reaching an agreement on the limitation of the production of opium to medical and scientific needs.

He stressed the absorbing interest in this problem felt by the Chinese people, on whom the use of opium had been forced by war. It was against the historical background of one hundred years, during which period China had been almost entirely at the receiving end of the opium trade, that the Chinese willingness to agree to an experimental approach should be viewed. The experimental approach now under consideration was, however, the very least that could be accepted.

图片 9.6　张彭春在经社理事会第九届第 285 次会议发言纪要(3)

【纪要译文】

张彭春先生(中国)感谢麻醉药品委员会的工作以及秘书处对委员会高效的协助工作。

他希望提请注意委员会报告中关于统一现有麻醉药品国际文书的部分,这是委员会第四届会议审议的最重要问题。

他回顾,如报告第 26 页所述,经济及社会理事会第七届会议,请秘书长展开研究和调查,是否适宜让鸦片生产国和使用鸦片生产医药和科研用药物的国家召开一次会议,以期达成一项临时协议,在通过一项载有限制用于制造所有麻醉药品的原材料规定的单一国际公约之前,将鸦片的生产和出口限制在满足这些需要的范围内。[1]

在委员会的讨论中,中国代表承认很难找到一个切实可行的办法来解决由来已久的鸦片生产问题,但提出了一项建议,该建议最终于 1949 年获得委员会压倒性多数成员的通过,关于麻醉药品委会如何才能决定麻醉药品司司长在委会报告第 28 页所提出的问题:即临时协议是否可以在短时间内通过,还是必须等到单一公约生效,至少要等六七年。

① 见《经济及社会理事会第七届会议决议》,第 159(VII)号决议,第二部分,E。

尽管理事会决定召开一次会议，中国代表同意不要求立即召开会议。委员会最终决定成立一个小组委员会，审议是否有必要召开一次会议，以便达成一项临时协议，将生鸦片生产限制于满足医疗和科学的需要。正如委员会报告第31页所述，小组委员会举行了会议，并向委员会报告，小组委员会一致认为有必要达成一项临时协议，并提议设立一个特设委员会。

委员会以12票对1票、2票弃权的压倒性表决通过了小组委员会的报告，并对土耳其政府邀请特设委员会在伊斯坦布尔或安卡拉举行会议表示感谢。这种近乎一致的意见无疑是中国代表愿意妥协的结果，他不要求立即召开会议，而是同意主要鸦片生产国举行小型会议所代表的更为温和的做法。

这样取得的结果非常令人满意。不幸的是，在匆忙编写向理事会提交的技术性很强的报告时，临时协议的问题被忽略了。他提请注意委员会报告第64和65页转载的关于简化现有麻醉药品国际文书的决议草案，他希望该决议能获得理事会一致通过。然而，按照其规定，理事会将核准麻醉药品委员会作出的决定，只是为了拟订一项新的单一公约，并请秘书长采取一切必要措施，尽快落实这些决定。因此，他建议增加以下倒数第二段：

> "批准委员会决定召开由主要鸦片生产国组成的特设委员会会议，审议是否有可能达成限制生鸦片生产于满足医疗和科学需要的临时协议。"

他最后指出，E/1361/Add. 1号文件第2部分标题中提到"特别小组委员会"，第2页第4行提到"小组委员会"。事实上，这是指小组委员会建议成立的特设委员会。

张彭春先生(中国)认为，鸦片生产国一致支持设立特设委员会，这是它们永远的功劳。这一行动的影响必须牢记，以充分理解这一行动和土耳其政府最慷慨的提议。

苏联代表说，临时协议是不必要的。事实上，委员会中的苏联代表是唯一反对召开特设委员会的提案的人。他将向苏联代表指出，正如委员会报告中所述，委员会的法国代表同意中国代表的意见，即临时协议将具有重大价值，可以作为根据拟议的单一公约限制原材料生产的可行性的试验场。理事会刚刚听到法国代表指出了缔结一项单一公约所涉及的一些困难，麻醉药品司司长在委员会面前表示，正如他（张先生）早些时候指出的，单一公约不可能在六七年内生效。然而，这个问题最好由委员会几乎一致建议的方法来解决：即设立一个主要生产国的小组委员会，审议是否有可能达成将鸦片生产限制于医疗和科学需求的协议。

他强调了中国人民对这个问题的浓厚兴趣，因为战争迫使他们使用鸦片。在这一百年中，中国几乎完全处于鸦片贸易的接受方，正是在一百年的历史背景下，中国同意试验性做法的意愿才应被正视。然而，目前正在审议的实验方法是可以接受的最起码的方法。

4. 张彭春在经社理事会第九届第 286 次会议上的发言

1949 年 7 月 6 日下午 3 时,联合国经社理事会第九届第 286 次会议,在日内瓦万国宫召开,本次会议主要是继续讨论麻醉药品委员会第四届会议报告。中国代表张彭春率团参加了本次会议,并在会议上发言,具体发言内容[①]纪要及其译文等如下:

【会议纪要】

Mr. P. C. CHANG (China) accepted the proposed amendment.

Replying to Mr. P. C. CHANG (China), who asked whether existing conventions adequately covered the production of all raw materials, Mr. STEINIG, Director of the Division of Narcotic Drugs, said that though some provisions had been included regarding opium production, there were none to prevent the production of coca leaves.

Mr. P. C. CHANG (China) replied that, in that case, the United States draft resolution would give added force to the existing conventions.

---

① UN Document: E/SR. 286, p. 32, p. 35.

【纪要影像】

Mr. P. C. Chang (China) accepted the proposed amendment.

Replying to Mr. P. C. Chang (China), who asked whether existing conventions adequately covered the production of all raw materials, Mr. Steinig, Director of the Division of Narcotic Drugs, said that though some provisions had been included regarding opium production, there were none to prevent the production of coca leaves.

Mr. P. C. Chang (China) replied that, in that case, the United States draft resolution would give added force to the existing conventions.

图片 9.7　张彭春在经社理事会第九届第 286 次会议发言纪要

【纪要译文】

张彭春先生(中国)接受了所提议的修改。

麻醉药品司司长斯特尼格先生在回答张彭春先生(中国)询问现有公约是否充分涵盖所有原料的生产时说,虽然列入了一些关于鸦片生产的规定,但没有任何规定可以阻止古柯叶的生产。

张彭春先生(中国)回答说,在这种情况下,美国的决议草案将使现有公约具有更大的效力。

5. 张彭春在经社理事会第九届第294次会议上的发言

1949年7月14日上午10时30分,联合国经社理事会第九届第294次会议,在日内瓦万国宫召开,本次会议主要是继续讨论经济与社会事务建议的落实。中国代表张彭春率团参加了本次会议,并在会议上发言,具体发言内容[①]纪要及其译文等如下:

【会议纪要】

Mr. P. C. CHANG (China) appreciated the effort made by the Australian representative, in submitting his draft resolution, to secure concrete action on what was an extremely important matter. That matter concerned the very purpose of the Council itself, since it was essential to ensure that its resolutions and recommendations were translated into action; otherwise there was a danger of world public opinion taking a cynical view when it found that the Council's work amounted to what he had once described in the Human Rights Commission as "nothing but verbal vanity and documentary deluge". Much energy and money had been spent by the United Nations in the last three years, and it was vitally important to ensure that the work had not been wasted and was yielding fruitful results. He himself was hopeful that their efforts had not been in vain, and he therefore supported the Australian draft resolution, which represented a step forward in securing information from Governments on the progress of imple-

① UN Document: E/SR. 294, pp. 136-137.

mentation.

However, he was anxious that the working group should not place too much emphasis on what might be described as checking and detecting, by which he meant that it should not direct all its attention to analysing in great statistical detail the replies of Governments, or to attempting to secure a greater and greater number of reports.

In his opinion that approach would be mistaken. Concrete results would be obtained if the emphasis were placed on encouraging Governments to put the Council's resolutions into effect, and not on chastising them for failing to render account of measures taken. The United Nations was, after all, not yet an international legislative body with powers to force Governments to implement its decisions. Perhaps some would regard him as an idealistic dreamer, but he was convinced that, if effort was not too much concentrated on blaming, shaming or taming Governments, the Council would achieve much by promoting concrete action and constructive co-operation—an educational task in the widest sense of the word.

With regard to the Australian draft resolution, he agreed that the working group should sit between the ninth and tenth sessions, but was opposed to the provision that it should report before the end of 1949. He would prefer that point to be left open, since if the working group were to be obliged to report before the end of the year, it would have to meet either two or three weeks before or after the General Assembly, a period of particularly strenuous activity for most permanent delegations, which would not be in a position to release high ranking members to serve on the working group. A decision as to the date might be left to the working group itself, in consultation with the Secretariat.

【纪要影像】

Mr. P. C. CHANG (China) appreciated the effort made by the Australian representative, in submitting his draft resolution, to secure concrete action on what was an extremely important matter. That matter concerned the very purpose of the Council itself, since it was essential to ensure that its resolutions and recommendations were translated into action; otherwise there was a danger of world public opinion taking a cynical view when it found that the Council's work amounted to what he had once described in the Human Rights Commission as "nothing but verbal vanity and documentary deluge". Much energy and money had been spent by the United Nations in the last three years, and it was vitally important to ensure that the work had not been wasted and was yielding fruitful results. He himself was hopeful that their efforts had not been in vain, and he therefore supported the Australian draft resolution, which represented a step forward in securing information from Governments on the progress of implementation.

However, he was anxious that the working group should not place too much emphasis on what might be described as checking and detecting, by which he meant that it should not direct all its attention to analysing in great statistical detail the replies of Governments, or to attempting to secure a greater and greater number of reports. In his opinion that approach would be mistaken. Concrete results would be obtained if the emphasis were placed on encouraging Governments to put the Council's resolutions into effect, and not on chastising them for failing to render account of measures taken. The United Nations was, after all, not yet an international legislative body with powers to force Governments to implement its decisions. Perhaps some would regard him as an idealistic dreamer, but he was convinced that, if effort was not too much concentrated on blaming, shaming or taming Governments, the Council would achieve much by promoting concrete action and constructive co-operation — an educational task in the widest sense of the word.

图片 9.8　张彭春在经社理事会第九届第 294 次会议发言纪要(1)

With regard to the Australian draft resolution, he agreed that the working group should sit between the ninth and tenth sessions, but was opposed to the provision that it should report before the end of 1949. He would prefer that point to be left open, since if the working group were to be obliged to report before the end of the year, it would have to meet either two or three weeks before or after the General Assembly, a period of particularly strenuous activity for most permanent delegations, which would not be in a position to release high ranking members to serve on the working group. A decision as to the date might be left to the working group itself, in consultation with the Secretariat.

图片 9.9　张彭春在经社理事会第九届第 294 次会议发言纪要(2)

【纪要译文】

张彭春先生(中国)赞赏澳大利亚代表在提交其决议草案时为确保就这一极其重要的问题采取具体行动所作的努力。这一事项关系到理事会本身的宗旨,因为必须确保理事会的决议和建议转化为行动;否则,当世界舆论发现理事会的工作相当于他曾经在人权委员会描述的“除了空话和大量文件之外,什么也没有”时,就会有持怀疑态度的危险。在过去三年中,联合国花费了大量精力和金钱,确保这项工作不被浪费并取得丰硕成果至关重要。他本人希望他们的努力没有白费,因此他支持澳大利亚的决议草案,该决议草案是在确保各国政府提供执行进展信息方面向前迈出的一步。

然而,他担心工作组不应过分强调可能被称为检查和检测的内容,这意味着工作组不应将全部注意力集中在对各国政府的答复进行详细的统计分析上,或集中在试图获得越来越多的报告上。

在他看来,这种做法是错误的。如果把重点放在鼓励各国政府执行理事会的决议上,而不是惩罚它们没有考虑到所采取的措施,就会取得具体成果。毕竟,联合国还不是一个有权迫使各国政府执行其决定的国际立法机构。也许有些人会认为他是一个理想主义的梦想家,但他相信,如果努力不过度集中于指责、羞辱或驯服政府,理事会将通过促进具体行动和建设性合作取得很大成就——这是一项最广泛意义上的教育任务。

关于澳大利亚的决议草案,他同意工作组应在第九届和第十届会议之间开会,但反对工作组应在 1949 年底之前提出报告的规定。他倾向于对这一点暂不作决定,因为如果工作组必须在年底之前提交报告,它将不得不在大会之前或之后的两三周举行会议,这对于大多数常驻代表团来说是一个特别紧张的活动时期,它们将无法腾出高级成员参加工作组的工作。关于日期的决定可由工作组自己与秘书处协商后作出。

6. 张彭春在经社理事会第九届第 295 次会议上的发言

1949 年 7 月 14 日下午 3 时，联合国经社理事会第九届第 295 次会议，在日内瓦万国宫召开，本次会议主要是继续讨论经济与社会事务建议的落实、讨论农业地区用于防治疟疾的滴滴涕杀虫剂的供应情况。中国代表张彭春率团参加了本次会议，并在会议上发言，具体发言内容[①]纪要及其译文等如下：

【会议纪要】

Mr. P. C. CHANG (China) proposed that, since it was not only to secure economic benefits that efforts were made to control malaria, the words "and social" should be inserted after the word "economic" in sub-paragraph (a) of the preamble to the draft resolution.

【纪要影像】

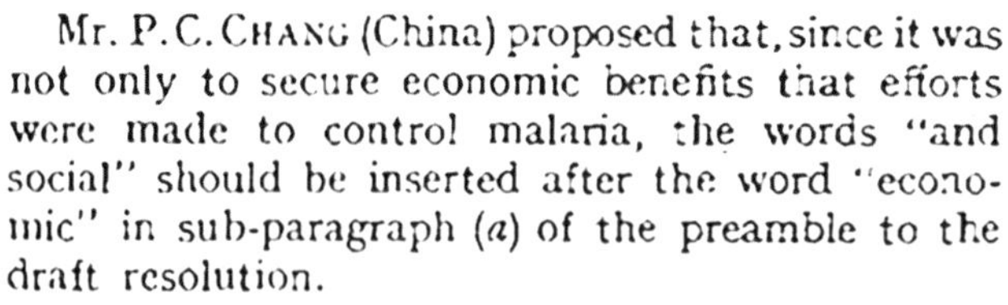
Mr. P.C. CHANG (China) proposed that, since it was not only to secure economic benefits that efforts were made to control malaria, the words "and social" should be inserted after the word "economic" in sub-paragraph (*a*) of the preamble to the draft resolution.

图片 9.10　张彭春在经社理事会第九届第 295 次会议发言纪要

① UN Document: E/SR. 295, p. 150.

【纪要译文】

张彭春先生(中国)提议,由于努力控制疟疾不仅是为了确保经济利益,因此应在决议草案序言部分(a)分段“经济”一词之后插入“和社会的”一词。

7. 张彭春在经社理事会第九届第 296 次会议上的发言

1949 年 7 月 15 日上午 10 时 30 分,联合国经社理事会第九届第 296 次会议,在日内瓦万国宫召开,本次会议主要是继续讨论拉丁美洲经济委员会的年度报告。中国代表张彭春率团参加了本次会议,并在会议上发言,具体发言内容[①]纪要及其译文等如下:

【会议纪要】

Mr. P. C. CHANG (China) said that his delegation had been extremely gratified at the work of the Economic Commission for Latin America, and congratulated it on its achievements. The Council had been wise in deciding that that Commission should deal chiefly with problems arising from the Second World War, and in particular problems of economic development. [②]Congratulations were also due to the representative of Chile for the leading part he had played in the Commission, as well as to the secretariat, which had given invaluable assistance in preparing the excellent reports. Those reports, while not perhaps covering all the points that could be desired, were nevertheless a useful beginning.

Two points should be stressed with relation to the report. First, in part II, section D 1 (a) it was stated that "the need for a larger number of trained

① UN Document: E/SR. 296, pp. 175-176.

② See *Economic and Social Council Resolutions*, resolution 106 (VI).

economists to serve Governments, central banks, etc., in Latin America was pointed out by several delegations". Although this matter had been discussed, there seemed to have been a lack of emphasis on the need for real technicians. By those, he meant people who used their hands, and were skilled in technical, scientific and mechanical leadership, rather than what he would call "literary" leadership.

The relationship between Latin America and Europe had been stressed by several speakers. That was natural, since most of the inhabitants of Latin America, apart from the indigenous population, had come originally from Europe and enjoyed close cultural and economic ties with that continent. However, some consideration should be given to Latin-American problems in the widest sense of the term. Those problems were generally linked with those of the so-called "under-developed" countries throughout the world. Exchanges of experience between such countries would be invaluable and could help solve the problem of technological training already mentioned. Latin America and the countries of the Far East, for example, could exchange invaluable information on such questions as road building and the manufacture of steel from low-grade ores.

Secondly, trade exchanges between Latin America, on the one hand, and Asia and the Far East, on the other, might also be intensified. For example, China might import more wines from Chile in exchange for greater quantities of tea and hand-made goods. Nor should the cultural bond which linked the Far East with Latin America be under-estimated.

Finally, he wholeheartedly supported the Resolution submitted to the Council in part II, section D 3, of the report.

【纪要影像】

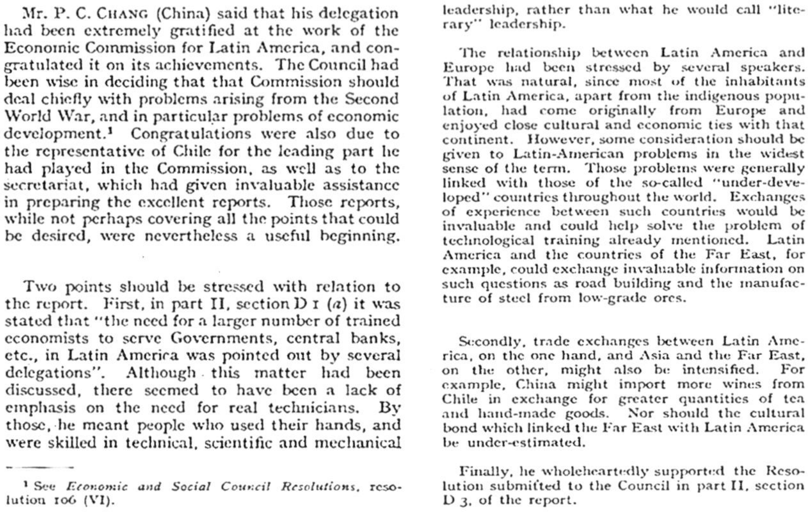

Mr. P. C. CHANG (China) said that his delegation had been extremely gratified at the work of the Economic Commission for Latin America, and congratulated it on its achievements. The Council had been wise in deciding that that Commission should deal chiefly with problems arising from the Second World War, and in particular problems of economic development.[1] Congratulations were also due to the representative of Chile for the leading part he had played in the Commission, as well as to the secretariat, which had given invaluable assistance in preparing the excellent reports. Those reports, while not perhaps covering all the points that could be desired, were nevertheless a useful beginning.

Two points should be stressed with relation to the report. First, in part II, section D I (*a*) it was stated that "the need for a larger number of trained economists to serve Governments, central banks, etc., in Latin America was pointed out by several delegations". Although this matter had been discussed, there seemed to have been a lack of emphasis on the need for real technicians. By those, he meant people who used their hands, and were skilled in technical, scientific and mechanical leadership, rather than what he would call "literary" leadership.

The relationship between Latin America and Europe had been stressed by several speakers. That was natural, since most of the inhabitants of Latin America, apart from the indigenous population, had come originally from Europe and enjoyed close cultural and economic ties with that continent. However, some consideration should be given to Latin-American problems in the widest sense of the term. Those problems were generally linked with those of the so-called "under-developed" countries throughout the world. Exchanges of experience between such countries would be invaluable and could help solve the problem of technological training already mentioned. Latin America and the countries of the Far East, for example, could exchange invaluable information on such questions as road building and the manufacture of steel from low-grade ores.

Secondly, trade exchanges between Latin America, on the one hand, and Asia and the Far East, on the other, might also be intensified. For example, China might import more wines from Chile in exchange for greater quantities of tea and hand-made goods. Nor should the cultural bond which linked the Far East with Latin America be under-estimated.

Finally, he wholeheartedly supported the Resolution submitted to the Council in part II, section D 3, of the report.

[1] See *Economic and Social Council Resolutions*, resolution 106 (VI).

图片 9.11　张彭春在经社理事会第九届第 296 次会议发言纪要

【纪要译文】

张彭春先生(中国)说,中国代表团对拉丁美洲经济委员会的工作极为满意,并祝贺其取得的成就。理事会明智地决定,该委员会应主要处理第二次世界大战引起的问题,特别是经济发展问题。① 还应祝贺智利代表在委员会中发挥的主导作用,并祝贺秘书处为编写出色的报告提供了宝贵的协助。这些报告虽然可能没有涵盖需要的所有要点,但仍然是一个有益的开端。

关于这份报告,应该强调两点。首先,在第二部分 D 1(a) 节中表示"有几个代表团指出,拉丁美洲需要更多训练有素的经济学家为政府、中央银行等服务"。虽然这个问题已经讨论过,但似乎没有强调真正的技术人员的需求。他所说的这些人是指那些实干的人,他们擅长技术、科学和机械的领导,而不是他所谓的"文人"领导。

① 见《经济及社会理事会决议》,第 106(VI) 号决议。

几位发言者强调了拉丁美洲和欧洲之间的关系。这是自然的,因为除了土著居民之外,拉丁美洲的大多数居民最初来自欧洲,并与该大陆有着密切的文化和经济联系。然而,应该从最广义上考虑拉丁美洲的问题。这些问题通常与全世界所谓的“不发达”国家的问题联系在一起。这些国家之间的经验交流是非常宝贵的,有助于解决已经提到的技术培训问题。例如,拉丁美洲和远东国家可以就道路建设和用低品位矿石炼钢等问题交流宝贵的信息。

第二,拉丁美洲与亚洲和远东之间的贸易交流也可以得到加强。例如,中国可能会从智利进口更多的葡萄酒,以更多的茶叶和手工制品相交换。也不应该低估连接远东和拉丁美洲的文化纽带。

最后,他完全支持报告第二部分 D 3 节中提交理事会的决议。

8. 张彭春在经社理事会第九届第297次会议上的发言

1949年7月15日下午3时,联合国经社理事会第九届第297次会议,在日内瓦万国宫召开,本次会议主要是继续讨论拉丁美洲经济委员会的年度报告。中国代表张彭春率团参加了本次会议,并在会议上发言,具体发言内容①纪要及其译文等如下:

【会议纪要】

Mr. P. C. CHANG (China), referring to the draft resolution submitted by the Commission for consideration by the Council (part Ⅳ, section C of the report), proposed that the words "and of the accompanying progress report of the Bureau of Flood Control on its programme of work" be inserted at the end of the first paragraph. As indicated in paragraph 25 of the Commission's annual report (E/1329), the Executive Secretary had undertaken to present the progress report (E/1404) at the ninth session of the Council; it should be regarded as part of the Commission's annual report.

Although there had been some delay before the Bureau of Flood Control had started work, its activities during the two or three months of its existence had covered much territory. The staff of the Bureau had worked hard, and the progress report, particularly the summary of the programme of work for 1949 (pages 11 and 12), well illustrated the businesslike and practical manner in

① UN Document: E/SR. 297, pp. 179-180, p. 191, p. 192.

which the Bureau had set to work.

As noted on page 14 of the progress report, "Governments of the countries visited by the staff of the Bureau welcomed the establishment of the Bureau of Flood Control". The Bureau intended to edit and publish certain studies relating to flood control methods, paying due attention to local traditions. On page 10 of the progress report, it was expressly stated that "flood control work in many countries of the region has been in existence for centuries. Hard lessons learned through experience, local ingenuity and trial and error have all contributed to the evolving of flood control methods and techniques which have answered local needs". That was another example of the practical and laudable way in which the Bureau was working.

The authors of the *Economic Survey of Asia and the Far East, 1948* deserved wholehearted congratulation. The *Survey* was, of course, far from perfect; but the authors had been able to produce a very useful report in circumstances of great complexity and confusion.

In the introduction to the *Survey* there appeared the frightening word "poverty". Poverty was the keynote of the economic situation in the region covered by the Commission. Millions and millions of people in that region lived in direst poverty. As he had said a year ago, the United Nations bodies concerned must be patient and endeavor to keep in its proper perspective the problem of raising the standards of living of those millions of people suffering from poverty. He was sure that the Council would do so.

No Member of the Council or the Commission was likely to offer opposition to the activities of the Bureau of Flood Control, since its purpose was to spread much-needed technical knowledge.

He was very glad that the Commission was paying close attention to the need for technical training. In the words of resolution 12, on technical training (part IV, section A of the Commission's annual report) he wished to recall "the urgency and importance with which the question of technical training is regarded by the Commission". He hoped that the Commission would pay even greater attention to the need for technical training. There should be included in the next annual *Survey* a chapter on technical training and technological emphasis in fundamental and general education.

The Commission should not limit its technical training activities to training of the kind given in more highly developed countries. There was no firm foundation in Asia and the Far East on which to base technical training activities suitable in highly developed countries, where the emphasis on technical training had been applied gradually over a long period.

He had used the term "fundamental education" to cover the need to spread knowledge, not only among the younger generation but also among adults, so many of whom in Asia had not enjoyed the advantage of compulsory education. He hoped that the Commission would get in touch with the United Nations Educational, Scientific and Cultural Organization, and state that technical training without a basis of fundamental education would be of little use in Asia and the Far East. Because of the lack of adequate information, and the fluid situation in Asia and the Far East, the Commission should, for the time being, place special emphasis on its work of spreading knowledge and technical training.

The Commission should also pay attention to need for an exchange of technological experience, as well as commodities, between the countries of Asia and the Far East, and other under-developed countries.

The Executive Secretary of the Commission and his staff deserved to be warmly congratulated on the excellent work they had done.

【纪要影像】

Mr. P. C. CHANG (China), referring to the draft resolution submitted by the Commission for consideration by the Council (part IV, section C of the report), proposed that the words "and of the accompanying progress report of the Bureau of Flood Control on its programme of work" be inserted at the end of the first paragraph.

As indicated in paragraph 25 of the Commission's annual report (E/1329), the Executive Secretary had undertaken to present the progress report (E/1404) at the ninth session of the Council; it should be regarded as part of the Commission's annual report.

Although there had been some delay before the Bureau of Flood Control had started work, its activities during the two or three months of its existence had covered much territory. The staff of the Bureau had worked hard, and the progress report, particularly the summary of the programme of work for 1949 (pages 11 and 12), well illustrated the businesslike and practical manner in which the Bureau had set to work.

As noted on page 14 of the progress report, "Governments of the countries visited [by the staff of the Bureau] welcomed the establishment of the Bureau of Flood Control". The Bureau intended to edit and publish certain studies relating to flood control methods, paying due attention to local traditions. On page 10 of the progress report, it was expressly stated that "flood control work in many countries of the region has been in existence for centuries. Hard lessons learned through experience, local ingenuity and trial and error have all contributed to the evolving of flood control methods and techniques which have answered local needs". That was another example of the practical and laudable way in which the Bureau was working.

The authors of the *Economic Survey of Asia and the Far East, 1948* deserved wholehearted congratulation. The *Survey* was, of course, far from perfect; but the authors had been able to produce a very useful report in circumstances of great complexity and confusion.

图片 9.12　张彭春在经社理事会第九届第 297 次会议发言纪要(1)

In the introduction to the *Survey* there appeared the frightening word "poverty". Poverty was the keynote of the economic situation in the region covered by the Commission. Millions and millions of people in that region lived in direst poverty. As he had said a year ago, the United Nations bodies concerned must be patient and endeavour to keep in its proper perspective the problem of raising the standards of living of those millions of people suffering from poverty. He was sure that the Council would do so.

No Member of the Council or the Commission was likely to offer opposition to the activities of the Bureau of Flood Control, since its purpose was to spread much-needed technical knowledge.

He was very glad that the Commission was paying close attention to the need for technical training. In the words of resolution 12, on technical training (part IV, section A of the Commission's annual report) he wished to recall "the urgency and importance with which the question of technical training is regarded by the Commission". He hoped that the Commission would pay even greater attention to the need for technical training. There should be included in the next annual *Survey* a chapter on technical training and technological emphasis in fundamental and general education.

The Commission should not limit its technical training activities to training of the kind given in more highly developed countries. There was no firm foundation in Asia and the Far East on which to base technical training activities suitable in highly developed countries, where the emphasis on technical training had been applied gradually over a long period.

He had used the term "fundamental education" to cover the need to spread knowledge, not only among the younger generation but also among adults, so many of whom in Asia had not enjoyed the advantage of compulsory education. He hoped that the Commission would get in touch with the United Nations Educational, Scientific and Cultural Organization, and state that technical training without a basis of fundamental education would be of little use in Asia and the Far East. Because of the lack of adequate information, and the fluid situation in Asia and the Far East, the Commission should, for the time being, place special emphasis on its work of spreading knowledge and technical training.

The Commission should also pay attention to need for an exchange of technological experience, as well as commodities, between the countries of Asia and the Far East, and other under-developed countries.

The Executive Secretary of the Commission and his staff deserved to be warmly congratulated on the excellent work they had done.

图片 9.13　张彭春在经社理事会第九届第 297 次会议发言纪要(2)

【纪要译文】

张彭春先生(中国)提到委员会提交理事会审议的决议草案(报告第四部分C节),建议在第一段末尾插入“以及所附的防洪局关于工作方案的进度报告”。如委员会年度报告(E/1329)第25段所述,执行秘书已承诺向理事会第九届会议提交进度报告(E/1404);它应被视为委员会年度报告的一部分。

虽然在防洪局开始工作之前有一些延误,但它在成立后的两三个月内的活动覆盖了很大一部分地区。防洪局的工作人员努力工作,进度报告,特别是1949年工作方案摘要(第11页和第12页),很好地说明了防洪局开展工作的高效与务实态度。

如进度报告第14页所述,“该局工作人员访问过的国家政府欢迎防洪局的成立”。该局打算编辑和出版与防洪方法有关的研究报告,同时适当注意当地的传统。进度报告第10页明确指出,“该区域许多国家的防洪工作已经存在了几个世纪。通过经验、当地的独创性和反复试验所获得的惨痛教训,都有助于发展满足当地需要的防洪方法和技术。”这是该局务实和值得称赞的工作方式的又一例证。

《1948年亚洲和远东经济调查报告》的作者值得衷心祝贺。当然,这项《调查报告》远非完美;但是,作者们能够在极为复杂和混乱的情况下写出一份非常有用的报告。

在《调查报告》的导言中出现了一个可怕的词“贫困”。贫困是委员会所涉区域经济状况的基调。该地区千百万人生活在极度贫困之中。正如他一年前所说的那样,联合国有关机构必须有耐心,努力正确看待提高数百万贫困人口生活水平的问题。他确信理事会会这样做。

理事会或委员会的任何成员都不可能反对防洪局的活动,因为其目的是传播急需的技术知识。

他很高兴委员会密切关注技术培训的需求。用关于技术培训的第12号决议(委员会年度报告第四部分A节)的话来说,他希望回顾“委员会认为技术培训问题的紧迫性和重要性”。他希望委员会更加重视技术培训的需求。在下一次年度《调查报告》中,应包括关于基础教育和普通教育中的技术培训和技术重点的章节。

委员会不应将其技术培训活动局限于较发达国家提供的那种培训。亚洲和远东没有坚实的基础来开展适合高度发达国家的技术培训活动,这些发达国家已经在很长一段时间里逐渐强调技术培训。

他用“基础教育”一词来涵盖不仅在年轻一代中,而且在成年人中传播知识的需要,亚洲的许多成年人没有享受到义务教育的好处。他希望委员会与联合国教科文组织取得联系,并指出,缺乏基础教育的技术培训在亚洲和远东就不好发挥作用。由于缺乏足够的信息,加之亚洲和远东地区局势多变,委员会目前应特别重视其传播知识和技术培训的工作。

委员会还应注意亚洲和远东国家与其他欠发达国家之间技术经验交流和商品流通的需要。

委员会执行秘书及其工作人员所做的出色工作值得热烈祝贺。

9. 张彭春在经社理事会第九届第 298 次会议上的发言

1949 年 7 月 16 日上午 10 时 30 分，联合国经社理事会第九届第 298 次会议，在日内瓦万国宫召开，本次会议主要是关于奴隶制问题。中国代表张彭春率团参加了本次会议，并在会议上发言，具体发言内容[①]纪要及其译文等如下：

【会议纪要】

Mr. P. C. CHANG (China) said the importance of the subject was beyond dispute. As a practical solution he would favour the last possibility suggested by the Belgian representative—namely, that the Secretariat should be instructed to make a preliminary study of the problem and that the Commission on Human Rights should then give it further consideration. Such a procedure might be provided for by the following draft resolution:

"*The Economic and Social Council*,

"*Taking note of* the resolution of the General Assembly 278 (III) of 13 May 1949,

"*Requests* the Secretary-General to gather and examine all information on the present situation with regard to slavery in its various forms in all countries where it is considered that slavery still exists, and to submit a report to the Commission on Human Rights for consideration in connexion

① UN Document: E/SR. 298, p. 196, pp. 202-203.

with the drafting of the Covenant on Human Rights and Measures of Implementation."

The words "to gather ... still exists" were taken from the original Belgian draft resolution submitted to the Assembly. The other alternatives suggested by the Belgian representative might lead to duplication of work, and it seemed that the best procedure would be to entrust the Commission on Human Rights with the problem of slavery. It was already mentioned in the Universal Declaration of Human Rights and in the draft Covenant on which the Commission was working.

Mr. P. C. CHANG (China) stated that there was no question as to the seriousness of the problem, which was a relic of the economic and social traditions of the past. He was anxious, however, that the Council should not become absorbed in detail. At that stage, the problem should be approached on general lines. The United Kingdom representative himself had not appeared to be very well versed in the different forms of slavery, but he would not join issue with him on technical points or on the alleged meaning of any existing institution. The Council should be mindful of the fact that the whole question should be related to the work of the Commission on Human Rights, since it formed a part of that body's duties in connexion with the implementation of the International Covenant on Human Rights.

He felt that a sufficient measure of agreement had been reached to enable the Council to adopt a compromise draft resolution, and would be in favour of the representatives who had made formal proposals being asked to serve as a small drafting committee.

As far as the United Kingdom draft resolution was concerned, he had certain doubts as to the constitutional implications of the first paragraph. Could the Council in fact instruct the Secretary-General to appoint a small *ad hoc* committee?

He personally would be against that procedure, as he felt that such a committee could function under instructions from the Council itself but not under the instructions of the Secretary-General alone. He would submit an alternative text, based largely on the considerations propounded by the Belgian representative, and reading as follows:

"*The Economic and Social Council*,

"*Taking note of* the resolution of the General Assembly of 13 May 1949 (278 (III)),

"*Requests* the Secretary-General, with the assistance of properly qualified experts, to gather and examine all information on the present situation with regard to slavery in its various forms in all countries where it is considered that slavery still exists, to submit a report to the Commission on Human Rights for consideration in connexion with the drafting of the Covenant on Human Rights and of Measures for Implementation, and to report to the Economic and Social Council within twelve months."

【纪要影像】

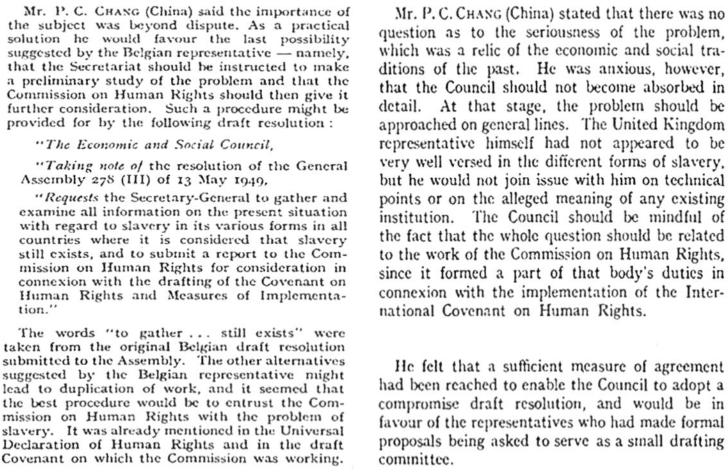

Mr. P. C. CHANG (China) said the importance of the subject was beyond dispute. As a practical solution he would favour the last possibility suggested by the Belgian representative — namely, that the Secretariat should be instructed to make a preliminary study of the problem and that the Commission on Human Rights should then give it further consideration. Such a procedure might be provided for by the following draft resolution:

"*The Economic and Social Council,*

"*Taking note of* the resolution of the General Assembly 278 (III) of 13 May 1949,

"*Requests* the Secretary-General to gather and examine all information on the present situation with regard to slavery in its various forms in all countries where it is considered that slavery still exists, and to submit a report to the Commission on Human Rights for consideration in connexion with the drafting of the Covenant on Human Rights and Measures of Implementation."

The words "to gather ... still exists" were taken from the original Belgian draft resolution submitted to the Assembly. The other alternatives suggested by the Belgian representative might lead to duplication of work, and it seemed that the best procedure would be to entrust the Commission on Human Rights with the problem of slavery. It was already mentioned in the Universal Declaration of Human Rights and in the draft Covenant on which the Commission was working.

Mr. P. C. CHANG (China) stated that there was no question as to the seriousness of the problem, which was a relic of the economic and social traditions of the past. He was anxious, however, that the Council should not become absorbed in detail. At that stage, the problem should be approached on general lines. The United Kingdom representative himself had not appeared to be very well versed in the different forms of slavery, but he would not join issue with him on technical points or on the alleged meaning of any existing institution. The Council should be mindful of the fact that the whole question should be related to the work of the Commission on Human Rights, since it formed a part of that body's duties in connexion with the implementation of the International Covenant on Human Rights.

He felt that a sufficient measure of agreement had been reached to enable the Council to adopt a compromise draft resolution, and would be in favour of the representatives who had made formal proposals being asked to serve as a small drafting committee.

图片 9.14　张彭春在经社理事会第九届第 298 次会议发言纪要(1)

As far as the United Kingdom draft resolution was concerned, he had certain doubts as to the constitutional implications of the first paragraph. Could the Council in fact instruct the Secretary-General to appoint a small *ad hoc* committee? He personally would be against that procedure, as he felt that such a committee could function under instructions from the Council itself but not under the instructions of the Secretary-General alone. He would submit an alternative text, based largely on the considerations propounded by the Belgian representative, and reading as follows :

"*The Economic and Social Council,*

"*Taking note* of the resolution of the General Assembly of 13 May 1949 (278 (III)),

"*Requests* the Secretary-General, with the assistance of properly qualified experts, to gather and examine all information on the present situation with regard to slavery in its various forms in all countries where it is considered that slavery still exists, to submit a report to the Commission on Human Rights for consideration in connexion with the drafting of the Covenant on Human Rights and of Measures for Implementation, and to report to the Economic and Social Council within twelve months."

图片 9.15　张彭春在经社理事会第九届第 298 次会议发言纪要(2)

【纪要译文】

张彭春先生(中国)说,这个问题的重要性是无可争议的。作为一种切实可行的解决办法,他赞成比利时代表提出的最后一种可能性,即应指示秘书处对这一问题进行初步研究,然后人权委员会应对这一问题进一步审议。以下决议草案可规定这种程序:

“经济及社会理事会,

“注意到大会 1949 年 5 月 13 日第 278(III)号决议,

“请秘书长收集和审查所有被认为仍然存在奴隶制的国家各种形式奴隶制现状的所有信息,并向人权委员会提交一份报告,供其在起草《人权公约》和《执行措施》时审议。”

“收集……仍然存在”这句话取自比利时提交大会的原始决议草案。比利时代表建议的其他备选办法可能导致工作重复,看来最好的程序是委托人权委员会处理奴隶制问题。《世界人权宣言》和委员会正在审议的公约草案中已经提到了这一点。

张彭春先生(中国)说,这个问题的严重性是毫无疑问的,这是过去经济和社会传统的遗留问题。然而,他迫切主张理事会不要陷于细节。在这一阶段,应该从总体上处理这个问题。英国代表本人似乎并不十分熟悉不同形式的奴隶制,但他不会就技术问题或任何现有机构的所谓含义与其争论。理事会应铭记,整个问题应与人权委员会的工作有关,因为它构成该机构在执行《国际人权公约》方面职责的一部分。

他认为,充分的一致意见已经达成,使理事会能够通过一项折衷决议草案,他赞成请提出正式提案的代表们以一个小型起草委员会形式履职。

就英国的决议草案而言,他对第一段的章程含义有一些疑问。理事会是否可以指示秘书长任命一个小型特设委员会?

他本人将反对这一程序,因为他认为这样一个委员会可以根据理事会本身的指示而运作,但不能仅根据秘书长的指示而运作。他将主要根据比利时代表提出的考虑因素提交一份备选案文,内容如下:

"经济及社会理事会,

"注意到大会1949年5月13日第278(III)号决议,

"请秘书长在具有适当资格的专家协助下,收集和审查所有被认为仍然存在奴隶制的国家各种形式奴隶制现状的所有资料,并向人权委员会提交一份报告,供其在起草《人权公约》和执行措施时审议,并在十二个月内向经济及社会理事会提交报告。"

10. 张彭春在经社理事会第九届第300次会议上的发言

1949年7月20日上午10时30分,联合国经社理事会第九届第300次会议,在日内瓦万国宫召开,本次会议主要是继续讨论关于奴隶制问题。中国代表张彭春率团参加了本次会议,并在会议上发言,具体发言内容[①]纪要及其译文等如下:

【会议纪要】

Mr. P. C. CHANG (China) stated that his remarks at that stage would refer only to the procedure to be followed; he reserved the right to speak later on the substance of the question.

He suggested that the Council was a little inclined to neglect the historical background it had already created for itself. He had therefore been very interested when the Council's attention had been drawn to the resolution on the terms of reference of the Commission on Human Rights[②] adopted three years previously at the second session. By the terms of that resolution, the Commission was "authorized to call in *ad hoc* working groups of non-governmental experts in specialized fields or individual experts, without further reference to the Council, but with the approval of the President of the Council and the Secretary-

① UN Document: E/SR. 300, pp. 224–226.

② See *Official Records of the Economic and Social Council*, first year, second session, page 400.

General". No use had yet been made of the businesslike procedure thus authorized. Yet the Council was now envisaging recourse to another method, which would involve additional staff and expenditure.

He recalled that the Chinese delegation had often suggested to the Council that, whereas the Security Council's main problem was to resolve conflict, the Economic and Social Council's constant preoccupation should be to avoid confusion. Recourse to new methods for dealing with each new problem had led to a multiplicity of organs and methods of work. He urged an orderly and objective approach, influenced neither by rigid adherence to precedents, nor by a tendency to adopt a new procedure for each new task.

A number of representatives had referred to the way in which the problem had been approached by the League of Nations. The League had had no economic and social council and no commission on human rights. It had been suggested that reference of the question to the Commission on Human Rights would delay completion of the study in view of that body's overloaded agenda. Was not the Council's agenda equally overloaded, and could not all problems be viewed as urgent from one angle or another? The provision to which he had referred, in the resolution laying down the Commission's terms of reference, had been designed specifically to expedite its work. Moreover, the Commission on Human Rights had completed its work in connexion with the Universal Declaration and was then working on the International Convention and the positive implementation of all the principles contained in those two documents. One of those principles was that slavery must be abolished. The view appeared to be held that the Commission on Human Rights was ineffective. He submitted that its record could bear comparison with that of the other functional commissions. Apart from the question of fairness, however, he felt that the Council would not be showing administrative efficiency if it by-passed an organ of its own creation. He therefore welcomed the statements of the representatives of Denmark, Venezuela, and France that the Commission on Human Rights should in some way or another be associated with the work on the problem of slavery, and he agreed in particular with the French representative that it should be associated with the work at both stages, that of study and that of implementation.

Like the Venezuelan representative, he would support the first French amendment, although he suggested that it was too much to ask for a "full" report on the question of slavery by the tenth session, and that the word "full" might in consequence be deleted. The substance of the first French amendment did not, he pointed out, differ from that of the unrevised Chinese amendment (E/1420).

With regard to the second phase of action envisaged, there were a number of alternative steps that might be taken by the Council there and then. He suggested, however, that it would be unwise to endeavour to bind the next session of the Council too rigidly. It was unnecessary, at that stage, to take any decision on the course of action which should be followed when the Secretary-General's report was submitted. The wisest course would be merely to invite the Secretary-General to place before the Council for guidance, at its tenth session, the various suggestions for the second phase of action made at the ninth session.

【纪要影像】

Mr. P. C. CHANG (China) stated that his remarks at that stage would refer only to the procedure to be followed; he reserved the right to speak later on the substance of the question.

He suggested that the Council was a little inclined to neglect the historical background it had already created for itself. He had therefore been very interested when the Council's attention had been drawn to the resolution on the terms of reference of the Commission on Human Rights[1] adopted three years previously at the second session. By the terms of that resolution, the Commission was "authorized to call in *ad hoc* working groups of non-governmental experts in specialized fields or individual experts, without further reference to the Council, but with the approval of the President of the Council and the Secretary-General". No use had yet been made of the businesslike procedure thus authorized. Yet the Council was now envisaging recourse to another method, which would involve additional staff and expenditure.

[1] See *Official Records of the Economic and Social Council*, first year, second session, page 400.

He recalled that the Chinese delegation had often suggested to the Council that, whereas the Security Council's main problem was to resolve conflict, the Economic and Social Council's constant preoccupation should be to avoid confusion. Recourse to new methods for dealing with each new problem had led to a multiplicity of organs and methods of work. He urged an orderly and objective approach, influenced neither by rigid adherence to precedents, nor by a tendency to adopt a new procedure for each new task.

图片 9.16　张彭春在经社理事会第九届第 300 次会议发言纪要(1)

A number of representatives had referred to the way in which the problem had been approached by the League of Nations. The League had had no economic and social council and no commission on human rights. It had been suggested that reference of the question to the Commission on Human Rights would delay completion of the study in view of that body's overloaded agenda. Was not the Council's agenda equally overloaded, and could not all problems be viewed as urgent from one angle or another? The provision to which he had referred, in the resolution laying down the Commission's terms of reference, had been designed specifically to expedite its work. Moreover, the Commission on Human Rights had completed its work in connexion with the Universal Declaration and was then working on the International Convention and the positive implementation of all the principles contained in those two documents. One of those principles was that slavery must be abolished. The view appeared to be held that the Commission on Human Rights was ineffective. He submitted that its record could bear comparison with that of the other functional commissions. Apart from the question of fairness, however, he felt that the Council would not be showing administrative efficiency if it by-passed an organ of its own creation. He therefore welcomed the statements of the representatives of Denmark, Venezuela, and France that the Commission on Human Rights should in some way or another be associated with the work on the problem of slavery, and he agreed in particular with the French representative that it should be associated with the work at both stages, that of study and that of implementation.

Like the Venezuelan representative, he would support the first French amendment, although he suggested that it was too much to ask for a "full" report on the question of slavery by the tenth session, and that the word "full" might in consequence be deleted. The substance of the first French amendment did not, he pointed out, differ from that of the unrevised Chinese amendment (E/1420).

With regard to the second phase of action envisaged, there were a number of alternative steps that might be taken by the Council there and then. He suggested, however, that it would be unwise to endeavour to bind the next session of the Council too rigidly. It was unnecessary, at that stage, to take any decision on the course of action which should be followed when the Secretary-General's report was submitted. The wisest course would be merely to invite the Secretary-General to place before the Council for guidance, at its tenth session, the various suggestions for the second phase of action made at the ninth session.

图片 9.17　张彭春在经社理事会第九届第 300 次会议发言纪要(2)

【纪要译文】

张彭春先生(中国)说,他在该阶段的发言将只提及应遵循的程序;他保留稍后就问题实质发言的权利。

他表示,理事会有点倾向于忽视它已经为自己创立的历史背景。因此,当理事会被提请注意三年前在第二届会议上通过的关于人权委员会[1]职权范围的决议时,他非常感兴趣。根据该决议的规定,委员会"有权召集专门领域的非政府专家或个人专家组成特设工作组,无须进一步提交理事会,但须经理事会主席和秘书长批准"。如此授权的公事公办的程序还没有使用,然而,理事会现在正在设想采用另一种方法,这将涉及增加工作人员和支出。

他回顾说,中国代表团经常向理事会建议,尽管安全理事会的主要问题是解决冲突,而经济及社会理事会的持续关注应该是避免混乱。采用新方法处理每一个新问题导致了机构和工作方法的多样性。他敦促采取有序和客观的做法,既不受恪守先例的影响,也不受为每项新任务采用新程序的趋势的影响。

一些代表提到了国际联盟处理这一问题的方式。该联盟没有经济及社会理事会,也没有人权委员会。有人建议,鉴于人权委员会议程超载,将这一问题提交人权委员会将推迟这项研究报告的完成。难道理事会的议程不是同样超载了吗?难道不能从这样或那样的角度将所有问题都视为紧迫问题吗?他在规定委员会职权范围的决议中提到的规定是专门为加快委员会的工作而设计的。此外,人权委员会已经完成了与《世界人权宣言》有关的工作,正在制定国际公约和积极实施这两份文件所载的所有原则。这些原则之一是必须废除奴隶制。似乎有人认为人权委员会效率低下。他认为,委员会的记录可以与其他职司委员会的记录进行比较。但是,除了公平问题外,他认为,如果理事会绕过自己设立的一个机构,就不会表现出行政效率。因此,他欢迎丹麦、委内瑞拉和法国代表的发言,即人

① 见《经济及社会理事会正式记录》,第一年,第二届会议,第400页。

权委员会应以某种方式参与有关奴隶制问题的工作,他特别同意法国代表的意见,即人权委员会应将这两个阶段的研究与实施工作结合起来。

与委内瑞拉代表一样,他将支持法国第一修正案,尽管他表示,要求在第十届会议之前就奴隶制问题提交一份"全面"报告强人所难,因此"全面"一词可能会被删除。他指出,法国第一项修正案的实质内容与未经修订的中国修正案(E/1420)并无不同。

关于所设想的第二阶段行动,理事会当时可以采取一些替代步骤。然而,他建议,试图对理事会下届会议过于严格的约束是不明智的。在该阶段,没有必要就秘书长提交报告时应遵循的行动方针作出任何决定。最明智的做法只能是请秘书长向理事会第十届会议达成第九届会议上提出的关于第二阶段行动的各种建议,以供指导。

11. 张彭春在经社理事会第九届第301次会议上的发言

1949年7月20日下午3时，联合国经社理事会第九届第301次会议，在日内瓦万国宫召开，本次会议主要是继续讨论关于奴隶制问题。中国代表张彭春率团参加了本次会议，并在会议上发言，具体发言内容①纪要及其译文等如下：

【会议纪要】

Mr. P. C. CHANG (China) pointed out that the adoption of the French amendments would allow immediate action to be taken on the problem, while postponing a decision on the terms of reference of the proposed *ad hoc* committee until the next session, after the Council had had an opportunity of studying the Secretary-General's report. He would therefore accept the French amendments, but would propose that points 2, 3 and 4 be replaced by the following paragraph:

> "*Requests* the Secretary-General to provide, in the budget for 1950, for the appointment of a small ad hoc working party of not more than five experts to survey the field of slavery within the framework of the definition adopted by the Council." (E/1436.)

① UN Document: E/SR. 301, pp. 241-242, p. 243.

The Council would note that he had used the term "working party" in order to differentiate between groups consisting of members of the Council, which should properly be described as "committees", and groups consisting of experts, which should be called "working parties".

【纪要影像】

Mr. P. C. CHANG (China) pointed out that the adoption of the French amendments would allow immediate action to be taken on the problem, while postponing a decision on the terms of reference of the proposed *ad hoc* committee until the next session, after the Council had had an opportunity of studying the Secretary-General's report. He would therefore accept the French amendments, but would propose that points 2, 3 and 4 be replaced by the following paragraph:

"*Requests* the Secretary-General to provide, in the budget for 1950, for the appointment of a small *ad hoc* working party of not more than five experts to survey the field of slavery within the framework of the definition adopted by the Council." (E/1436.)

The Council would note that he had used the term "working party" in order to differentiate between groups consisting of members of the Council, which should properly be described as "committees", and groups consisting of experts, which should be called "working parties".

图片 9.18　张彭春在经社理事会第九届第 301 次会议发言纪要

【纪要译文】

张彭春先生(中国)指出,法国修正案的通过将允许立即就这一问题采取行动,同时将关于拟议特设委员会职权范围的决定推迟到理事会有机会研究秘书长报告后的下届会议。因此,他将接受法国的修正案,但提议将第 2、3 和 4 点改为以下段落:

“请秘书长在1950年预算中为任命一个不超过五名专家的小型特设工作组提供经费，以便在理事会通过的定义框架内调查奴隶制问题。”(E/1436。)

理事会将注意到，他使用“工作组”一词是为了区分由理事会成员组成的小组（应适当称为“委员会”）和由专家组成的小组（应称为“工作组”）。

12. 张彭春在经社理事会第九届第304次会议上的发言

1949年7月22日上午10时30分,联合国经社理事会第九届第304次会议,在日内瓦万国宫召开,本次会议主要是讨论增加食品可及性措施、讨论非政府组织理事会委员会关于非政府组织手册的报告。中国代表张彭春率团参加了本次会议,并在会议上发言,具体发言内容①纪要及其译文等如下:

【会议纪要】

Mr. P. C. CHANG (China) shared the views of the representatives of the United States of America, Belgium and France. He proposed the deletion of the words "postpone publication of the Handbook and" from the second paragraph of the draft resolution. Those words were unnecessary, since the Secretary-General had not been requested by the Council to produce the Handbook, and, if included, would render the resolution liable to misinterpretation. The purpose of the resolution was not to postpone publication of the Handbook but to enable the Council Committee on Non-Governmental Organizations to do further work, which was necessary before it could be published. The Committee had not yet had the opportunity to review the material for the Handbook. If the draft resolution was adopted by the Council with the amendment he proposed, it would be clear that the Council wished the work on the Handbook to be carried out care-

① UN Document: E/SR. 304, p. 295, pp. 296-297.

fully, and wished its Committee on Non-Governmental Organizations to have an opportunity of reviewing that work.

Mr. P. C. CHANG (China) said that the fact that the Council Committee on Non-Governmental Organizations had recommended the adoption of the draft resolution contained in document E/1422 was evidence that it wished to discuss the Handbook at its meetings to be held in connexion with the tenth session of the Council, when the data it required should be available. If it adopted the proposal of the United Kingdom representative that the Committee should not be permitted to review the question of the Handbook even though it had made known a desire to do so, the Council would be guilty of improper administration.

【纪要影像】

Mr. P. C. CHANG (China) shared the views of the representatives of the United States of America, Belgium and France. He proposed the deletion of the words "postpone publication of the *Handbook* and" from the second paragraph of the draft resolution. Those words were unnecessary, since the Secretary-General had not been requested by the Council to produce the *Handbook*, and, if included, would render the resolution liable to misinterpretation. The purpose of the resolution was not to postpone publication of the *Handbook* but to enable the Council Committee on Non-Governmental Organizations to do further work, which was necessary before it could be published. The Committee had not yet had the opportunity to review the material for the *Handbook*. If the draft resolution was adopted by the Council with the amendment he proposed, it would be clear that the Council wished the work on the *Handbook* to be carried out carefully, and wished its Committee on Non-Governmental Organizations to have an opportunity of reviewing that work.

Mr. P. C. CHANG (China) said that the fact that the Council Committee on Non-Governmental Organizations had recommended the adoption of the draft resolution contained in document E/1422

was evidence that it wished to discuss the *Handbook* at its meetings to be held in connexion with the tenth session of the Council, when the data it required should be available. If it adopted the proposal of the United Kingdom representative that the Committee should not be permitted to review the question of the *Handbook* even though it had made known a desire to do so, the Council would be guilty of improper administration.

图片 9.19　张彭春在经社理事会第九届第 304 次会议发言纪要

【纪要译文】

张彭春先生(中国)赞同美国、比利时和法国代表的观点。他建议删除决议草案第二段中的“推迟手册的出版和”等字。这些文字是没有必要的,因为理事会没有要求秘书长编写手册,如果将这些文字包括在内,将容易导致决议被误解。该决议的目的不是推迟手册的出版,而是使理事会非政府组织委员会能够在手册出版之前开展必要的进一步工作。委员会还没有机会审查手册的材料。如果理事会通过了由他提出了修正案的决议草案,那么理事会显然希望认真开展关于该手册的工作,并希望其非政府组织委员会有机会审查这项工作。

张彭春先生(中国)说,理事会非政府组织委员会建议通过 E/1422 号文件所载的决议草案这一事实证明,它希望在理事会第十届会议期间举行的会议上讨论该手册,届时应可获取它所要求的数据。如果理事会通过了英国代表的建议,即尽管委员会已表示愿意审查手册的问题,也不应允许委员会审查手册的问题,否则,理事会将有管理不当的罪责。

13. 张彭春在经社理事会第九届第305次会议上的发言

1949年7月22日下午3时，联合国经社理事会第九届第305会议，在日内瓦万国宫召开，本次会议主要是继续讨论新闻自由：联合国新闻自由会议最后案文的决议。中国代表张彭春率团参加了本次会议，并在会议上发言，具体发言内容[①]纪要及其译文等如下：

【会议纪要】

Mr. P. C. CHANG (China) said he had voted in favour of resolution I recommended by the Social Committee, but that in doing so he had not meant to cast doubts on the merits of resolution 26 of the Conference on Freedom of Information. Inclusion in resolution I of the words "at this time" would not preclude future action by the Council.

【纪要影像】

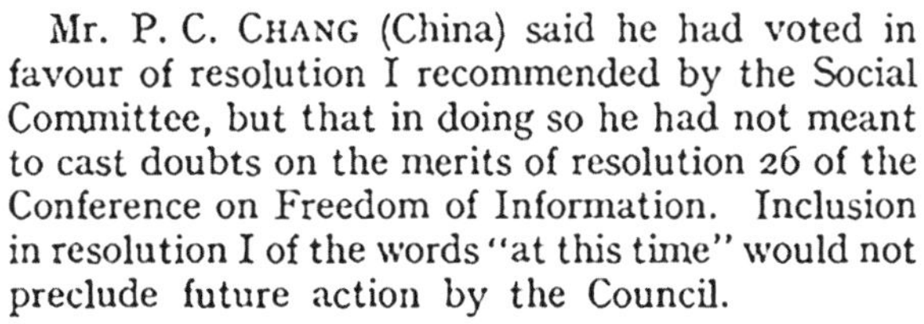
Mr. P. C. CHANG (China) said he had voted in favour of resolution I recommended by the Social Committee, but that in doing so he had not meant to cast doubts on the merits of resolution 26 of the Conference on Freedom of Information. Inclusion in resolution I of the words "at this time" would not preclude future action by the Council.

图片9.20　张彭春在经社理事会第九届第305次会议发言纪要

① UN Document: E/SR. 305, p. 309.

【纪要译文】

张彭春先生(中国)说,他对社会事务委员会建议的1号决议投了赞成票,但他这样做并不是要对新闻自由会议26号决议的优点提出质疑。在1号决议中加入“此时”一词并不妨碍理事会今后采取行动。

14. 张彭春在经社理事会第九届第306次会议上的发言

1949年7月23日上午10时30分,联合国经社理事会第九届第306次会议,在日内瓦万国宫召开,本次会议主要是继续讨论麻醉药品委员会第四届会议报告、讨论关于经济委员会第四届会议报告。中国代表张彭春率团参加了本次会议,并在会议上先后多次发言,具体发言内容①纪要及其译文等如下:

【会议纪要】

Mr. P. C. CHANG (China) said that he supported the proposal of the representative of New Zealand, since the draft resolution suggested by the Acting Secretary-General was an extended version of that contained in the Social Committee's report. For example, the former contained the words "to request the General Assembly to appropriate before 30 September 1949 the additional funds necessary to enable the Commission of Enquiry...", whereas the latter merely requested the Secretary-General "to take such administrative and financial measures as may be necessary to enable the Commission of Enquiry...". The Social Committee had no doubt limited its draft resolution in that way because it had been unaware that the Secretary-General had no power to increase the appropriation for the Commission of Enquiry specifically allocated by the General Assembly.

① UN Document: E/SR. 306, p. 312, p. 319, p. 320. pp. 321-322.

Mr. P. C. CHANG (China) wished to place on record for the future guidance of the Secretariat the suggestion which he had made in the Social Committee and which he thought had proved generally acceptable there—namely, that it would be more in accord with the lines along which the Council wished the programme to develop to refer to the countries benefiting by it as "participating" rather than as "recipient" countries.

Mr. P. C. CHANG (China) agreed with the principle stated by the United Kingdom representative, but felt that, in view of the Social Commission's exceptionally heavy programme of work, an exception should be made in its favour in 1949. He pointed out, moreover, that the programme for the remainder of the year had been carefully worked out so as to leave two and a half weeks free for meetings of the Commission.

Mr. P. C. CHANG (China) supported the views of the United Kingdom representative and pointed out that, if functional commissions were to meet only once a year, not only would economies be effected, but the Secretariat would be given the time it needed to deal satisfactorily with the preparatory work required. The Commission on Human Rights had already held one session of more than usual length, with satisfactory results.

【纪要影像】

Mr. P. C. CHANG (China) said that he supported the proposal of the representative of New Zealand, since the draft resolution suggested by the Acting Secretary-General was an extended version of that contained in the Social Committee's report. For example, the former contained the words "to request the General Assembly to appropriate before 30 September 1949 the additional funds necessary to enable the Commission of Enquiry...", whereas the latter merely requested the Secretary-General "to take such administrative and financial measures as may be necessary to enable the Commission of Enquiry...". The Social Committee had no doubt limited its draft resolution in that way because it had been unaware that the Secretary-General had no power to increase the appropriation for the Commission of Enquiry specifically allocated by the General Assembly.

Mr. P. C. CHANG (China) wished to place on record for the future guidance of the Secretariat the suggestion which he had made in the Social Committee and which he thought had proved generally acceptable there — namely, that it would be more in accord with the lines along which the Council wished the programme to develop to refer to the countries benefiting by it as "participating" rather than as "recipient" countries.

Mr. P. C. CHANG (China) agreed with the principle stated by the United Kingdom representative, but felt that, in view of the Social Commission's exceptionally heavy programme of work, an exception should be made in its favour in 1949. He pointed out, moreover, that the programme for the remainder of the year had been carefully worked out so as to leave two and a half weeks free for meetings of the Commission.

Mr. P. C. CHANG (China) supported the views of the United Kingdom representative and pointed out that, if functional commissions were to meet only once a year, not only would economies be effected, but the Secretariat would be given the time it needed to deal satisfactorily with the preparatory work required. The Commission on Human

Rights had already held one session of more than usual length, with satisfactory results.

图片 9.21　张彭春在经社理事会第九届第306次会议发言纪要

【纪要译文】

张彭春先生（中国）说，他支持新西兰代表的提议，因为代理秘书长建议的决议草案是社会事务委员会报告中所载决议草案的扩展版。例如，前者载有“请大会在1949年9月30日之前拨出必要的额外经费，使调查委员会能够……”等字，鉴于后者仅请秘书长“采取必要的行政和财政措施，使咨询委员会能够……”。毫无疑问，社会事务委员会以这种方式限制了其决议草案，因为它不知道秘书长无权增加大会专门分配给咨询委员会的拨款。

张彭春先生（中国）希望将他在社会事务委员会提出的建议记录在案，以供秘书处今后的指导，他认为该建议在社会事务委员会已被普遍接受，即：将受益于该方案的国家称为“参与”国家，而不是“受援”国，这将更符合理事会希望该方案发展的思路。

张彭春先生（中国）同意英国代表所述的原则，但认为，鉴于社会委员会的工作方案特别繁重，应在1949年对其作出例外处理。此外，他指出，今年剩余时间的方案是精心制定的,以便留出两周半的时间供委员会开会。

张彭春先生(中国)支持英国代表的意见,并指出,如果各职司委员会每年只举行一次会议,不仅会节省开支,而且秘书处将有足够的时间圆满完成所需的筹备工作。人权委员会已经举行了一届比平时更长的会议,取得了令人满意的结果。

15. 张彭春在经社理事会第九届第311次会议上的发言

1949年7月27日上午10时30分，联合国经社理事会第九届第311次会议，在日内瓦万国宫召开，本次会议主要是继续讨论欠发达国家的经济发展。中国代表张彭春率团参加了本次会议，并在会议上进行了长篇发言，具体发言内容①纪要及其译文等如下：

【会议纪要】

Mr. P. C. CHANG (China) said that three years had passed since the Council had first discussed the problem of the so-called under-developed areas. He himself, on 4 June 1946, had addressed the Council on the world significance of "economically low-pressure" areas.[1] At that time, after a long period of travel and residence in the Middle East and Latin America, he had been in a good position to speak of certain characteristics common to what were termed "under-industrialized" countries. That, however, was a term which required some clarification.

He would first express his appreciation of the report on technical assistance for economic development (E/1327/Add. 1). The Administrative Committee

1 See *Official Records of the Economic and Social Council*, first year, second session, 7th meeting.

① UN Document: E/SR. 311, pp. 413-416.

on Co-ordination had done a sound job, for which the Council should be grateful. In particular, chapter 2, entitled "Nature of the programme", provided an extremely lucid analysis of the problem. That report would obviously have to be referred to a committee, and though he had no strong feelings on the subject, he thought that, in the circumstances, it would perhaps be best for the Economic Committee to deal with it. Whatever body was chosen, however, it should be a committee of the whole, which could appoint small working groups to consider specific problems whenever necessary.

In an attempt to throw new light on the problem before the Council, and to put forward arguments that were "unrehashed", he would first stress some particular aspects of the question and then proceed to certain general observations. His specific comments concerned the "action mechanism" of the Council and were three fold. First, he would be in favour of what might better be termed a "central clearing-house of resources" than a fund, since the latter term was somewhat restrictive, in that it applied only to currencies. On the other hand, resources would cover human and material resources, and also services and supplies, in addition to financial assets. Closely related with that "central clearing-house of resources there should be a "central clearing-house of ideas" to channel and co-ordinate all the various programmes and projects. If such a clearing-house were not established, duplication, waste and confusion would ensue. It should be set up under the direct control of the Secretary-General, and should closely follow the directives of the Council. A highly qualified director should be appointed to control and develop it, who should also be chairman of the proposed technical assistance committee.

The second specific point to be stressed was, as the New Zealand representative had already pointed out, that all Member States should make some contribution towards the total cost of technical assistance. In other words, the scheme had to be what he would call "self-reliant"; that would give it a firm moral basis. As to the form of contributions, he thought the suggestions made by the New Zealand representative would prove useful. Contributions could be partly "distributive" (rather than compulsory) and partly voluntary.

The third specific point concerned the initiative, diagnosis and planning necessary for effective technical assistance. It should be remembered that the so-called under-developed countries themselves possessed men with initiative who could make diagnoses and draw up plans just as well as experts from the under-developed countries themselves, who not only knew their own country better than outside specialists, but also, in some cases, had gained considerable experience in the more advanced countries. Hitherto, the general problem of under-developed areas had been considered too often from the point of view of the more developed countries. That situation should be corrected. Moreover, the Economic Commissions for Asia and the Far East and for Latin America should be consulted in the matter.

To follow up those three specific comments with a more general analysis of the problem, he would attempt to clarify the term "industrialization", which had often been misused. In his speech to the Council on 4 June 1946, in which he had pointed out the world significance of "economically low-pressure areas", he had mentioned the hunger of certain countries for industrialization, and had stressed that the so-called under-industrialized areas of the world were no longer so subdued and overawed as they had been before the First World War. Those areas were no longer inclined to describe, in a docile manner, the orbits prescribed for them by the powerful industrial countries. That applied particularly to countries such as China, which had reached a stage of considerable development in manufacture (in the strict sense of the term) before the impact of modern industrialism. The fact was that 150 years ago China had been more advanced in certain branches of manufacture than had many Western European countries. She had, for example, exported to Western Europe large quantities of goods such as silk, china, paper, tea and lacquer, which had been manufactured mostly by hand. Owing to the unfavourable balance of trade, European countries had first sent Mexican silver to China and later forced her to accept opium in exchange for it.

What had happened during the last 150 years to reverse the situation and allow Western Europe to gain its present superiority in the field of production? It was merely that modern industrialization, by using non-human sources of power and labour-saving devices, had increased production to an unparalleled extent, and at the same time considerably raised standards of living. The steam engine (with its initial application to textiles), the electric motor, the gas turbine, the internal combustion engine and, to look into the future, the atomic prime mover, were examples of non-human sources of power which were inherent in the concept of industrialization. The first problem, which the Council had to face, therefore, was how to bring assistance to those countries which did not possess sufficient mechanical sources of power and the labour-saving devices which were their necessary corollary.

The second problem was that of that he would call the "early industrialized areas", which had experienced industrial development early in their evolution and whose machine equipment was now obsolete or obsolescent. That problem was urgent and would become more so.

The third problem involved the process of what he would call "catching up". If a given under-developed country could achieve the necessary unity to harness its natural resources and the skill of its people, then it could "catch up" and keep pace with the more highly developed countries. The Council would have to assist not only areas which almost completely lacked mechanical sources of power, but also those which lacked the necessary unity and capacity for "catching up".

In conclusion, as he had stated at the very first meeting of the Economic and Social Council,[1] on 23 January 1946, the United Nations had to win and nourish a "new loyalty" from the peoples of the world. That could be done only if those peoples were convinced that they would derive positive benefits from the organization.

---

1 See *Official Records of the Economic and Social Council*, first year, first session, 1st meeting.

【纪要影像】

Mr. P. C. CHANG (China) said that three years had passed since the Council had first discussed the problem of the so-called under-developed areas. He himself, on 4 June 1946, had addressed the Council on the world significance of "economically low-pressure" areas.[1] At that time, after a long period of travel and residence in the Middle East and Latin America, he had been in a good position to speak of certain characteristics common to what were termed "under-industrialized" countries. That, however, was a term which required some clarification.

---

[1] See *Official Records of the Economic and Social Council*, first year, second session, 7th meeting.

He would first express his appreciation of the report on technical assistance for economic development (E/1327/Add.1). The Administrative Committee on Co-ordination had done a sound job, for which the Council should be grateful. In particular, chapter 2, entitled "Nature of the programme", provided an extremely lucid analysis of the problem. That report would obviously have to be referred to a committee, and though he had no strong feelings on the subject, he thought that, in the circumstances, it would perhaps be best for the Economic Committee to deal with it. Whatever body was chosen, however, it should be a committee of the whole, which could appoint small working groups to consider specific problems whenever necessary.

In an attempt to throw new light on the problem before the Council, and to put forward arguments that were "unrehashed", he would first stress some particular aspects of the question and then proceed to certain general observations. His specific comments concerned the "action mechanism" of the Council and were threefold. First, he would be in favour of what might better be termed a "central clearing-house of resources" than a fund, since the latter term was somewhat restrictive, in that it applied only to currencies. On the other hand, resources would cover human and material resources, and also services and supplies, in addition to financial assets. Closely related with that "central clearing-house of resources" there should be a "central clearing-house of ideas" to channel and co-ordinate all the various programmes and projects. If such a clearing-house were not established, duplication, waste and confusion would ensue. It should be set up under the direct control of the Secretary-General, and should closely follow the directives of the Council. A highly qualified director should be appointed to control and develop it, who should also be chairman of the proposed technical assistance committee.

图片 9.22　张彭春在经社理事会第九届第 311 次会议发言纪要(1)

The second specific point to be stressed was, as the New Zealand representative had already pointed out, that all Member States should make some contribution towards the total cost of technical assistance. In other words, the scheme had to be what he would call "self-reliant"; that would give it a firm moral basis. As to the form of contributions, he thought the suggestions made by the New Zealand representative would prove useful. Contributions could be partly "distributive" (rather than compulsory) and partly voluntary.

The third specific point concerned the initiative, diagnosis and planning necessary for effective technical assistance. It should be remembered that the so-called under-developed countries themselves possessed men with initiative who could make diagnoses and draw up plans just as well as experts from the so-called developed countries. Adequate attention should therefore be given to experts from the under-developed countries themselves, who not only knew their own country better than outside specialists, but also, in some cases, had gained considerable experience in the more advanced countries. Hitherto, the general problem of under-developed areas had been considered too often from the point of view of the more developed countries. That situation should be corrected. Moreover, the Economic Commissions for Asia and the Far East and for Latin America should be consulted in the matter.

To follow up those three specific comments with a more general analysis of the problem, he would attempt to clarify the term "industrialization", which had often been misused. In his speech to the Council on 4 June 1946, in which he had pointed out the world significance of "economically low-pressure areas", he had mentioned the hunger of certain countries for industrialization, and had stressed that the so-called under-industrialized areas of the world were no longer so subdued and overawed as they had been before the first World War. Those areas were no longer inclined to describe, in a docile manner, the orbits prescribed for them by the powerful industrial countries. That applied particularly to countries such as China, which had reached a stage of considerable development in manufacture (in the strict sense of the term) before the impact of modern industrialism. The fact was that 150 years ago China had been more advanced in certain branches of manufacture than had many Western European countries. She had, for example, exported to Western Europe large quantities of goods such as silk, china, paper, tea and lacquer, which had been manufactured mostly by hand. Owing to the unfavourable balance of trade, European countries had first sent Mexican silver to China and later forced her to accept opium in exchange for it.

图片 9.23 张彭春在经社理事会第九届第 311 次会议发言纪要(2)

What had happened during the last 150 years to reverse the situation and allow Western Europe to gain its present superiority in the field of production? It was merely that modern industrialization, by using non-human sources of power and labour-saving devices, had increased production to an unparalleled extent, and at the same time considerably raised standards of living. The steam engine (with its initial application to textiles), the electric motor, the gas turbine, the internal combustion engine and, to look into the future, the atomic prime mover, were examples of non-human sources of power which were inherent in the concept of industrialization. The first problem, which the Council had to face, therefore, was how to bring assistance to those countries which did not possess sufficient mechanical sources of power and the labour-saving devices which were their necessary corollary.

The second problem was that of that he would call the "early industrialized areas", which had experienced industrial development early in their evolution and whose machine equipment was now obsolete or obsolescent. That problem was urgent and would become more so.

The third problem involved the process of what he would call "catching up". If a given under-developed country could achieve the necessary unity to harness its natural resources and the skill of its people, then it could "catch up" and keep pace with the more highly developed countries. The Council would have to assist not only areas which almost completely lacked mechanical sources of power, but also those which lacked the necessary unity and capacity for "catching up".

In conclusion, as he had stated at the very first meeting of the Economic and Social Council,[1] on 23 January 1946, the United Nations had to win and nourish a "new loyalty" from the peoples of the world. That could be done only if those peoples were convinced that they would derive positive benefits from the organization.

[1] See *Official Records of the Economic and Social Council*, first year, first session, 1st meeting.

图片 9.24 张彭春在经社理事会第九届第 311 次会议发言纪要(3)

【纪要译文】

张彭春先生(中国)说,理事会首次讨论所谓欠发达地区的问题已经过去了三年。1946年6月4日,他本人就"经济低压"地区的世界意义向理事会发表了讲话。[1] 当时,在中东和拉丁美洲的长时间的旅行和居住之后,他有了充分的发言权,可以谈论一些被称为"欠工业化"国家的共同特征。然而,这是一个需要澄清的术语。

他首先对关于经济发展技术援助的报告(E/1327/Add. 1)表示赞赏。行政协调委员会的工作做得很好,本理事会对此应表示感谢。特别是,题为"方案的性质"的第2章对这一问题作了极其清楚的分析。该报告显然必须提交给一个委员会,尽管他对这个问题没有强烈的感觉,但他认为,在这种情况下,也许最好由经济事务委员会来处理。不管选择什么样的机构,它都应该是一个全体委员会,可以在必要时任命小型工作组来审议具体问题。

为了更加明确理事会面前的问题,并提出"未经讨论"的论点,他将首先强调问题的某些特定方面,然后产生某些一般性意见。他的具体评论涉及理事会的"行动机制",包括三个方面。首先,他赞成称之为"中央资源交易所"比称之为基金更好,因为后者有点限制性,因为它只适用于货币。另一方面,资源将涵盖人力和物力资源,以及服务和供给,此外还有金融资产。与这个"中央资源交易所"密切相关的是,应该有一个"中央理念交易所",以引导和协调所有各种方案和项目。如果不建立这样一个信息交换所,就会出现重复、浪费和混乱。它应在秘书长的直接控制下设立,并应密切遵循理事会的指示。应任命一名高素质的管理者来控制和开发该系统,该管理者还应担任拟议的技术援助委员会主席。

第二个需要强调的具体问题是,正如新西兰代表已经指出的那样,所有会员国都应该对技术援助的总费用做出一些贡献。换句话说,这个计划

1 见《经济及社会理事会正式记录》,第一年,第二届,第7次会议。

必须是他所说的“自力更生”;这将为它提供坚实的道德基础。关于捐款形式,他认为新西兰代表提出的建议将证明是有益的。捐款可以部分是“分配性的”(而不是强制性的),一定程度上是自愿的。

第三个具体问题涉及有效技术援助所需的倡议、诊断和规划。应该记住,所谓的欠发达国家本身也有一些主动积极的人,他们可以像来自欠发达国家的专家一样作出诊断和制定计划,这些专家不仅比外部专家更了解自己的国家,而且在某些情况下,还在更先进的国家获得了相当多的经验。迄今为止,欠发达地区的普遍问题往往是从较发达国家的角度来考虑的。这种情况应该得到纠正。此外,在这个问题上,应该咨询亚洲和远东经济委员会和拉丁美洲经济委员会。

为了对这三个具体意见采取后续行动,对这个问题进行更全面的分析,他将试图澄清经常被误用的“工业化”一词。他在 1946 年 6 月 4 日向理事会发表的讲话中指出了“经济低压区”的世界意义,他提到了某些国家对工业化的渴望,并强调,世界上所谓的欠工业化地区不再像第一次世界大战前那样被压制和吓倒。这些地区不再倾向于以温顺的方式描述强大的工业国家为它们规定的轨道。这尤其适用于中国这样的国家,在现代工业主义的影响之前,中国的制造业(严格意义上)已经达到了相当高的发展阶段。事实是,150 年前,中国在某些制造业分支上比许多西欧国家更为先进。例如,她向西欧出口了大量货物,如丝绸、瓷器、纸张、茶叶和漆器,这些货物大多是手工制造的。由于贸易逆差,欧洲国家先将墨西哥银币运到中国,然后迫使中国接受鸦片作为交换。

在过去的 150 年中,发生了什么事情来扭转这种局面,使西欧在生产领域获得目前的优势?这仅仅是现代工业化通过使用非人力能源和节省劳力的设备,将生产提高到了前所未有的程度,同时也大大提高了生活水平。蒸汽机(最初应用于纺织品)、电动机、燃气轮机、内燃机,以及展望未来的原子原动机,都是工业化概念中固有的非人类动力源的例子。因此,理事会必须面对的第一个问题是,如何向那些没有足够的机械动力源和必要的节省劳力设备的国家提供援助。

第二个问题是,他称之为“早期工业化地区”,这些地区在其发展早期就经历了工业发展,其机器设备现在已经过时或已经淘汰。这个问题是紧迫的,而且会变得更加紧迫。

第三个问题涉及他所谓的“追赶”过程。如果一个特定的欠发达国家能够实现必要的团结,以利用其自然资源和人民的技能,那么它就可以“赶上”并跟上更发达国家的步伐。理事会不仅必须援助几乎完全缺乏机械动力源的地区,而且还必须援助那些缺乏必要的团结和“追赶”能力的地区。

最后,正如他在 1946 年 1 月 23 日在经济及社会理事会第一次会议[①]上所说,联合国必须赢得并培养世界各国人民的“新的忠诚”。只有当这些人民确信他们将从本组织获得积极收益时,才能做到这一点。

① 见《经济及社会理事会正式记录》,第一年,第一届会议,第 1 次会议。

16. 张彭春在经社理事会第九届第312次会议上的发言

1949年7月27日下午3时，联合国经社理事会第九届第312次会议，在日内瓦万国宫召开，本次会议主要是继续讨论欠发达国家的经济发展。中国代表张彭春率团参加了本次会议，并在会议上发言，具体发言内容①纪要及其译文等如下：

【会议纪要】

Mr. P. C. CHANG (China) recalled that at the previous meeting, in the course of certain general remarks, he had tried to clarify the terms "under-industrialized countries" and "under-developed countries". He had referred to the fact that European countries had forced opium on China, merely in order to support his statement that 150 years ago the manufacturing ability of the Chinese people was as great as that of any other people. He had not commented on the United States Government's proposals; everything he had said at the previous meeting had been in accordance with his speech before the Council on 4 June 1946,[1] and he had quoted excerpts from that speech. He had also commented on the Secretary-General's report on technical assistance for economic

1 See *Official Records of the Economic and Social Council*, first year, second session, 7th meeting.

① UN Document: E/SR. 312, pp. 431-432.

development (E/1327/Add. 1), and had made suggestions about the future "action mechanism" of the Council.

【纪要影像】

Mr. P. C. CHANG (China) recalled that at the previous meeting, in the course of certain general remarks, he had tried to clarify the terms "under-industrialized countries" and "under-developed countries". He had referred to the fact that European countries had forced opium on China, merely in order to support his statement that 150 years ago the manufacturing ability of the Chinese people was as great as that of any other people. He had not commented on the United States Government's proposals; everything he had said at the previous meeting had been in accordance with his speech before the Council on 4 June 1946,[1] and he had quoted excerpts from that speech. He had also commented on the Secretary-General's report on technical assistance for economic development (E/1327/Add.1), and had made suggestions about the future "action mechanism" of the Council.

[1] See *Official Records of the Economic and Social Council*, first year, second session, 7th meeting.

图片 9.25　张彭春在经社理事会第九届第 312 次会议发言纪要

【纪要译文】

张彭春先生(中国)回顾说,在上次会议上,在某些一般性发言中,他试图澄清"欠工业化国家"和"欠发达国家"这两个词。他提到欧洲国家将鸦片强加于中国的事实,仅仅是为了支持他的说法,即 150 年前中华民族的制造能力与其他任何民族一样强大。他没有对美国政府的建议发表评论;他在上次会议上所说的一切都与他 1946 年 6 月 4 日在理事会上的发言一致,[1] 他引述了该发言的摘录。他还对秘书长关于经济发展技术援助的报告(E/1327/Add. 1)发表了评论,并就理事会未来的"行动机制"提出了建议。

1 见《经济及社会理事会正式记录》,第一年,第二届,第 7 次会议。

17. 张彭春在经社理事会第九届第 320 次会议上的发言

1949 年 8 月 3 日下午 3 时，联合国经社理事会第九届第 320 次会议，在日内瓦万国宫召开，本次会议主要是继续讨论人权委员会第五届会议报告决议草案 A 和决议草案 C、讨论美洲大陆土族人口和其他欠发达社会群体的社会问题。中国代表张彭春率团参加了本次会议，并在会议上先后多次发言，具体发言内容[①]纪要及其译文等如下：

【会议纪要】

Mr. P. C. CHANG (China) stated that he was in favour of the Council taking no action whatsoever on draft resolution A, so as to avoid discussion of points which might arise even in connexion with the operative paragraph, such, for example, as whether articles 22-27 of the Universal Declaration of Human Rights were the only appropriate ones.

In any case, it was unnecessary to request the Secretary-General to carry out what was only a part of his normal duties — namely, to assist the functional commissions by carrying out the studies requested by them, although it might subsequently be necessary to endorse the results of those studies.

Mr. P. C. CHANG (China) pointed out the danger of recommending action on paragraph (a) since it might encourage other functional commissions to transmit requests to the Secretary-General through the Council. He also doubted

① UN Document: E/SR. 320, p. 526, p. 530, p. 533, p. 534, p. 538.

whether it would be proper for the Secretary-General to examine petitions as proposed in paragraph (b). He therefore formally moved that the Council should take no action on draft resolution C.

Mr. P. C. CHANG (China) stated that, as he understood it, the Secretariat would not undertake anything outside its normal duties involving a substantive decision, without the sanction of the Commission on Human Rights or of the Council.

The Chinese proposal that no action be taken on draft resolution C was adopted by 13 *votes to* 2, *with* 2 *abstentions.*

Mr. P. C. CHANG (China) then moved the adoption of the Chinese draft resolution (E/1473) recommending that the General Assembly take no further action on the problem of petitions at its fourth session. He was unable to understand the Soviet Union representative's contention that it involved a question of substance.

Mr. P. C. CHANG (China) considered the matter to be important and supported the joint draft resolution. The fact that Governments were being asked for their comments might encourage them to approach the United Nations for assistance.

【纪要影像】

Mr. P. C. CHANG (China) stated that he was in favour of the Council taking no action whatsoever on draft resolution A, so as to avoid discussion of points which might arise even in connexion with the operative paragraph, such, for example, as whether articles 22-27 of the Universal Declaration of Human Rights were the only appropriate ones.

In any case, it was unnecessary to request the Secretary-General to carry out what was only a part of his normal duties — namely, to assist the functional commissions by carrying out the studies requested by them, although it might subsequently be necessary to endorse the results of those studies.

Mr. P. C. CHANG (China) pointed out the danger of recommending action on paragraph (*a*) since it might encourage other functional commissions to transmit requests to the Secretary-General through the Council. He also doubted whether it would be proper for the Secretary-General to examine petitions as proposed in paragraph (*b*). He therefore formally moved that the Council should take no action on draft resolution C.

Mr. P. C. CHANG (China) stated that, as he understood it, the Secretariat would not undertake anything outside its normal duties involving a substantive decision, without the sanction of the Commission on Human Rights or of the Council.

The Chinese proposal that no action be taken on draft resolution C was adopted by 13 votes to 2, with 2 abstentions.

Mr. P. C. CHANG (China) then moved the adoption of the Chinese draft resolution (E/1473) recommending that the General Assembly take no further action on the problem of petitions at its fourth session. He was unable to understand the Soviet Union representative's contention that it involved a question of substance.

Mr. P. C. CHANG (China) considered the matter to be important and supported the joint draft resolution. The fact that Governments were being asked for their comments might encourage them to approach the United Nations for assistance.

图片 9.26　张彭春在经社理事会第九届第 320 次会议发言纪要

【纪要译文】

张彭春先生(中国)说,他赞成理事会对决议草案 A 不采取任何行动,以避免讨论可能提出的甚至与执行段落有关的问题,例如《世界人权宣言》第 22-27 条是否是唯一适当的问题。

无论如何,没有必要要求秘书长履行其正常职责的一部分——即协助各职司委员会进行它们要求的研究,尽管随后可能需要认可这些研究的结果。

张彭春先生(中国)指出就(a)段提出行动建议的危险,因为这可能会鼓励其他职司委员会通过理事会向秘书长提出请求。他还怀疑秘书长是否应该按照(b)段的建议审查请愿书。因此,他正式向理事会提出动议,不应对决议草案 C 采取行动。

张彭春先生(中国)说,按照他的理解,秘书处不会在未经人权委员会或理事会批准的情况下从事任何超出其正常职责范围的涉及实质性决定的活动。

中国关于不对决议草案C采取行动的建议以13票对2票、2票弃权获得通过。

张彭春先生(中国)随后提议通过中国的决议草案(E/1473),建议大会第四届会议不对请愿问题采取进一步行动。他不能理解苏联代表的论点,即这涉及实质问题。

张彭春先生(中国)认为这一事项很重要,并支持联合决议草案。要求各国政府发表意见这一事实可能会鼓励它们向联合国寻求援助。

第十章　联合国经社理事会第十届会议

（纪要）

1950年2月7日上午11时,联合国经社理事会第十届会议在美国纽约成功湖开幕,从1950年2月7日至3月6日,本届共召开了31次会议,分别从第344次会议至第374次会议。本届会议讨论了一系列有关经济社会等问题,包括讨论会议日程安排、讨论经济与社会事务建议的落实情况、讨论政府间组织、讨论新闻自由公约草案、讨论联合国秘书长关于资源保护与使用的联合国科学大会报告、讨论联合国与特别机构之间的协调问题、讨论理事会职司委员会程序规则的修改、讨论国际货币基金组织的报告、讨论社会委员会(第五届)报告、讨论人权委员会(第五届)报告、讨论1950年会议日程安排、讨论经济和就业委员会(第五届)报告、讨论世界经济形势、讨论非政府组织、讨论强迫劳动及其废除措施的调查、讨论欠发达地区的经济发展、讨论公共管理国际培训中心、讨论非洲经济研究与相关数据、讨论奴隶制特别委员会的临时报告等。

中国代表张彭春率团参加了本届会议,并在本届会议中的16次会议上进行了大会发言,包括第344次会议、第346次会议、第347次会议、第348次会议、第349次会议、第350次会议、第351次会议、第354次会议、第355次会议、第356次会议、第358次会议、第362次会议、第367次会议、第370次会议、第371次会议和第374次会议。另外,代表团代表助理曹保颐先生参与了本届会议,并在第347次会议[①]、第363次会议[②]和第365次会议[③]上发言。其中,张彭春先生的发言内容如下:

---

① UN Document: E/SR. 347, p. 19.

② UN Document: E/SR. 363, p. 141.

③ UN Document: E/SR. 365, p. 150.

1. 张彭春在经社理事会第十届第344次会议上的发言

1950年2月7日上午11时,联合国经社理事会第十届第344次会议,在纽约成功湖开幕,本次会议一开始,苏联代表就提出建议从理事会中剔除国民政府代表资格,得到了捷克斯洛伐克和波兰代表的支持,但由于美国等多数国家的反对,苏联的动议以10票反对、3票赞成、5票弃权,被否决。在这种情况下,苏联、捷克斯洛伐克和波兰代表愤然离开了本届会议。会议接着选举出了本届会议主席和副主席。张彭春率团参加了本次会议,并在会议上发言,具体发言内容①纪要及其译文等如下:

【会议纪要】

16. Mr. CHANG (China) observed that the point raised by the representative of the USSR had not come as a surprise; nevertheless, words which had lost all meaning through constant repetition must not be allowed to prevent the Council from seeing the situation as it actually existed.

17. The members of the Economic and Social Council were elected by the General Assembly. The Council was merely an advisory body responsible to the General Assembly, its sole duty being to study the conditions necessary to ensure the welfare of all countries, and particularly of the States Members of the United Nations. It was therefore not qualified to consider the problem of diplomatic recognition.

---

① UN Document: E/SR. 344, p. 2.

18. Certain speakers had asserted that the Chinese delegation represented only the "Kuomintang group". That was not true, for the delegation concerned represented the Chinese National Government. Despite the current conflict in China, that Government was the sole legal government of China. Its representatives in the United Nations had never failed to defend the interests of the Chinese people and to voice their aspirations.

19. It was true that China was going through a difficult period of adjustment to modern world conditions, yet its people would never give up their independence, the territorial integrity of China, justice, equal rights and security. They would never submit to foreign domination, Russian or any other, whatever its source.

20. Mr. Chang quoted a passage from the statement he had made on 23 January 1946 at the opening of the first session of the Economic and Social Council[1] when he had stressed that it was the duty of the United Nations to promote a new spirit of loyalty among nations. The Chinese delegation to the Economic and Social Council had always remained faithful to that principle, but the same could not be said of some of the other delegations.

21. The Economic and Social Council was faced with a problem for which its rules of procedure failed to provide a solution: the question of the recognition or non-recognition of the government of a Member State of the United Nations. The situation, however, in no way justified the refusal of some delegations to participate in the work of the Council. That refusal, far from contributing to a solution of the problem, would merely testify to a complete lack of respect for the sovereign rights of States with regard to the question of diplomatic recognition.

1 See *Official Records of the Economic and Social Council*, first year, first session, 1st meeting.

【纪要影像】

16. Mr. CHANG (China) observed that the point raised by the representative of the USSR had not come as a surprise; nevertheless, words which had lost all meaning through constant repetition must not be allowed to prevent the Council from seeing the situation as it actually existed.

17. The members of the Economic and Social Council were elected by the General Assembly. The Council was merely an advisory body responsible to the General Assembly, its sole duty being to study the conditions necessary to ensure the welfare of all countries, and particularly of the States Members of the United Nations. It was therefore not qualified to consider the problem of diplomatic recognition.

18. Certain speakers had asserted that the Chinese delegation represented only the "Kuomintang group". That was not true, for the delegation concerned represented the Chinese National Government. Despite the current conflict in China, that Government was the sole legal government of China. Its representatives in the United Nations had never failed to defend the interests of the Chinese people and to voice their aspirations.

19. It was true that China was going through a difficult period of adjustment to modern world conditions, yet its people would never give up their independence, the territorial integrity of China, justice, equal rights and security. They would never submit to foreign domination, Russian or any other, whatever its source.

20. Mr. Chang quoted a passage from the statement he had made on 23 January 1946 at the opening of the first session of the Economic and Social Council[1] when he had stressed that it was the duty of the United Nations to promote a new spirit of loyalty among nations. The Chinese delegation to the Economic and Social Council had always remained faithful to that principle, but the same could not be said of some of the other delegations.

21. The Economic and Social Council was faced with a problem for which its rules of procedure failed to provide a solution: the question of the recognition or non-recognition of the government of a Member State of the United Nations. The situation, however, in no way justified the refusal of some delegations to participate in the work of the Council. That refusal, far from contributing to a solution of the problem, would merely testify to a complete lack of respect for the sovereign rights of States with regard to the question of diplomatic recognition.

[1] See *Official Records of the Economic and Social Council, First year: First session, 1st meeting.*

图片 10.1　张彭春在经社理事会第十届第 344 次会议发言纪要

【纪要译文】

16. 张先生(中国)说,苏联代表提出的要点并不令人惊讶。这些话不断重复,已经失去意义,一定不能阻止理事会看到实际存在的局面。

17. 经济及社会理事会成员由大会选出。理事会只是一个对大会负责的咨询机构,其唯一职责是研究确保所有国家,特别是联合国会员国福利的必要条件。因此,它没有资格审议外交承认问题。

18. 某些发言者声称,中国代表团只代表"国民党集团"。事实并非如此,因为有关代表团代表中国国民政府①……它在联合国的代表从来就没有不捍卫中国人民的利益、表达他们的愿望。

19. 诚然,中国正在经历适应现代世界条件的困难时期,但中国人民永远不会放弃他们的独立、中国的领土完整、正义、平等权利和安全。他们决

① 中国是 1945 年成立的联合国的创始会员国,根据国际原则,中华人民共和国成立后,应由中国新政府指派代表参加联合国大会及其有关机构的工作,把已经不能代表中国人民所谓"中华民国"代表驱逐出联合国。但中国在联合国的席位一直被台湾国民党当局占据,直至 1971 年中国恢复联合国的合法权利。

不会屈服于外国统治，不管是俄罗斯还是任何其他国家，无论其来源如何。

20. 张先生引述了他在 1946 年 1 月 23 日经济及社会理事会第一届会议开幕式上所作的发言中的一段话[1]，当时他强调联合国有责任在各国之间促进新的忠诚。出席经济及社会理事会的中国代表团始终忠实于这一原则，但其他一些代表团却并非如此。

21. 经济及社会理事会面临一个其议事规则未能提供解决办法的问题：承认或不承认联合国会员国政府的问题。然而，这种情况决不能成为一些代表团拒绝参加理事会工作的理由。这种拒绝无助于问题的解决，只会证明在外交承认问题上完全缺乏对国家主权的尊重。

---

1 见《经济及社会理事会正式记录》，第一年，第一届，第 1 次会议。

2. 张彭春在经社理事会第十届第346次会议上的发言

1950年2月8日上午11时，联合国经社理事会第十届第346次会议，在纽约成功湖举行，本次会议讨论经济与社会事务建议的执行情况。张彭春率团参加了本次会议，并在会议上发言，具体发言内容[①]纪要及其译文等如下：

【会议纪要】

49. Mr. CHANG (China) stated that the report of the *Ad Hoc* Committee was of very great importance, in that it dealt with the possible results of the decisions taken by the Economic and Social Council. He expressed full support for the report and the resolutions annexed thereto.

50. He stressed the importance of securing the co-operation of governments. The Council's purpose would not be achieved if governments refused to furnish reports on the implementation of recommendations or if they confined themselves to forwarding statements of a purely bureaucratic nature. Hence, it should be made clear that those reports should be followed by deeds and should describe effective action that had been taken. The nature of the relationship between the government and the individual was of great importance. Indeed, it might so happen that, prompted by a certain political doctrine, some government would refuse to account for its policy to an international organization or to

① UN Document: E/SR. 346, p. 14.

the people it governed. It might also happen that it would be opposed to the establishment of closer contact between its people and the United Nations. Those were the difficulties with which the Council might be confronted in the discharge of its duty.

51. The future success of the Council would be gauged by the degree of loyalty shown by the peoples of the world to the United Nations. That loyalty, however, could not be won by the mere adoption of endless resolutions. Those resolutions had also to be effectively implemented. Each government had a part to play in that field.

52. The implementation of resolutions was obviously an impossible task without a certain level of education. In that connexion, the technical assistance programme which the Council had undertaken was of far-reaching importance. There would be no need for reports from any administration to gauge its success: the best proof of its success would be found in the feelings of the people who benefited from that programme.

67. Mr. CHANG (China) agreed with the three preceding speakers. All inquiries of a general nature should be undertaken by the Council itself, since a regional commission could ask governments for information on specific measures only.

80. Mr. CHANG (China) suggested that decision on the creation of the proposed *ad hoc* committee should be deferred to a later session of the Council.

It was so decided.

【纪要影像】

49. Mr. CHANG (China) stated that the report of the *Ad Hoc* Committee was of very great importance, in that it dealt with the possible results of the decisions taken by the Economic and Social Council. He expressed full support for the report and the resolutions annexed thereto.

50. He stressed the importance of securing the co-operation of governments. The Council's purpose would not be achieved if governments refused to furnish reports on the implementation of recommendations or if they confined themselves to forwarding statements of a purely bureaucratic nature. Hence, it should be made clear that those reports should be followed by deeds and should describe effective action that had been taken. The nature of the relationship between the government and the individual was of great importance. Indeed, it might so happen that, prompted by a certain political doctrine, some government would refuse to account for its policy to an international organization or to the people it governed. It might also happen that it would be opposed to the establishment of closer contact between its people and the United Nations. Those were the difficulties with which the Council might be confronted in the discharge of its duty.

51. The future success of the Council would be gauged by the degree of loyalty shown by the peoples of the world to the United Nations. That loyalty, however, could not be won by the mere adoption of endless resolutions. Those resolutions had also to be effectively implemented. Each government had a part to play in that field.

52. The implementation of resolutions was obviously an impossible task without a certain level of education. In that connexion, the technical assistance programme which the Council had undertaken was of far-reaching importance. There would be no need for reports from any administration to gauge its success: the best proof of its success would be found in the feelings of the people who benefited from that programme.

67. Mr. CHANG (China) agreed with the three preceding speakers. All inquiries of a general nature should be undertaken by the Council itself, since a regional commission could ask governments for information on specific measures only.

80. Mr. CHANG (China) suggested that decision on the creation of the proposed *ad hoc* committee should be deferred to a later session of the Council.

It was so decided.

图片 10.2　张彭春在经社理事会第十届第 346 次会议发言纪要

【纪要译文】

49. 张先生(中国)说,特设委员会的报告非常重要,因为它处理经济及社会理事会所作决定可能产生的结果。他表示完全支持该报告及其所附决议。

50. 他强调确保各国政府合作的重要性。如果各国政府拒绝提供关于建议执行情况的报告,或者如果它们仅限于提交纯粹官僚性质的声明,理事会的目的就无法实现。因此,应明确指出,这些报告之后应采取行动,并应说明已采取的有效行动。政府与个人之间关系的性质非常重要。事实上,在某种政治教条的推动下,某些政府可能会拒绝向一个国际组织或其所管理的人民解释其政策。它还可能反对在其人民与联合国之间建立更密切的联系。这些是理事会在履行职责时可能面临的困难。

51. 理事会今后的成功将由世界各国人民对联合国的忠诚程度来衡量。然而,仅仅通过无休止的决议是无法赢得这种忠诚的。这些决议也必须得到有效执行。每个政府都可以在这一领域发挥作用。

52. 如果没有一定的教育水平,执行决议显然是不可能的任务。在这方面,理事会开展的技术援助方案具有深远的重要性。没有必要用任何政府的报告来衡量它的成功:它成功的最好证明将在受益于该方案的人民的感受中找到。

67. 张先生(中国)同意三位发言者的意见。所有一般性的调查都应由理事会本身进行,因为区域委员会只能要求各国政府提供关于具体措施的信息。

80. 张先生(中国)建议,关于设立拟议的特设委员会的决定应推迟到理事会下一届会议。

就这样决定了下来。

3. 张彭春在经社理事会第十届第 347 次会议上的发言

1950 年 2 月 8 日下午 3 时，联合国经社理事会第十届第 347 次会议，在纽约成功湖举行，本次会议讨论印度尼西亚共和国申请加入教科文组织、讨论政府间组织等。张彭春率团参加了本次会议，并在会议上发言，具体发言内容①纪要及其译文等如下：

【会议纪要】

19. Mr. CHANG (China) said that his delegation had long held the view that the number of inter-governmental organizations should be limited to those which served a useful purpose. He therefore supported the draft resolution submitted by Brazil and Chile.

【纪要影像】

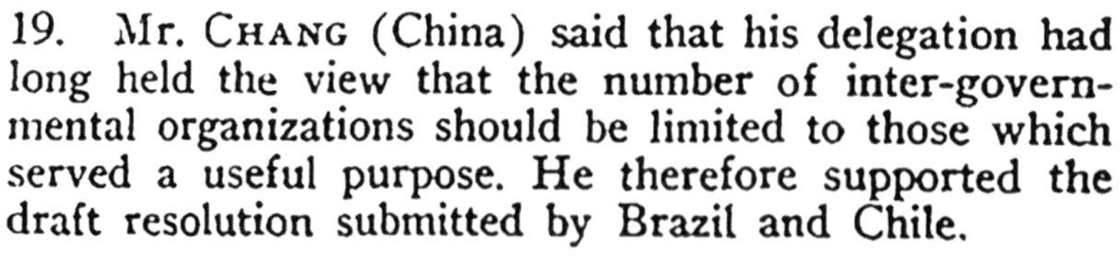
19. Mr. CHANG (China) said that his delegation had long held the view that the number of inter-governmental organizations should be limited to those which served a useful purpose. He therefore supported the draft resolution submitted by Brazil and Chile.

图片 10.3　张彭春在经社理事会第十届第 347 次会议发言纪要

① UN Document: E/SR. 347, p. 18.

【纪要译文】

19. 张先生(中国)说,他的代表团长期以来一直认为,政府间组织的数量应仅限于那些服务于有益目标的组织。因此,他支持巴西和智利提交的决议草案。

4. 张彭春在经社理事会第十届第348次会议上的发言

1950年2月13日上午11时，联合国经社理事会第十届第348次会议，在纽约成功湖举行，本次会议讨论新闻自由公约草案(E/1560，E/L.4，E/L.6)等。张彭春率团参加了本次会议，并在会议上发言，具体发言内容[1]纪要及其译文等如下：

【会议纪要】

14. Mr. CHANG (China) thought that the fourth paragraph of the French-Indian draft resolution might be misinterpreted and should be deleted. It seemed to imply that the Commission on Human Rights had to be instructed concerning the form to give to the "adequate provisions" on freedom of information mentioned in General Assembly resolution 313 (IV) which it was to incorporate in the draft International Covenant on Human Rights. The Commission had, in fact, never intended to embody in the Covenant all the important provisions of the draft Convention on Freedom of Information. It had a very clear understanding of the scope of the Covenant and fully realized that it would be neither wise nor feasible to attempt to incorporate in a single covenant definitive provisions on all the human rights proclaimed in the Declaration.

15. For that reason, it had been suggested at the fifth session of the Commission on Human Rights—and that suggestion had not been entirely ruled

① UN Document: E/SR. 348, p. 22, p. 23, p. 25.

out—that instead of a single covenant, there might be a series, perhaps, of three or four covenants drawn up in the space of two or three years. Moreover, the Commission had never contemplated any measures with regard to freedom of information which would preclude Assembly action on the draft convention. It had never considered that the inclusion in the Covenant of one of two articles on the subject would make a separate convention unnecessary.

34. Mr. CHANG (China) considered that it would be unwise for the Council to embark on a substantive discussion on the precise instructions to be given to the Commission on Human Rights. Obviously the draft resolution of India and France instructing the Commission "to consider inclusion of basic principles only" involved a matter of substance. In view of past discussions and particularly in view of the terms of General Assembly resolution 313 (IV) requesting the Economic and Social Council to transmit the matter to the Commission on Human Rights for action, the Council should restrict itself to procedural action and avoid duplication of discussions which had taken place in the General Assembly and the Commission on Human Rights.

53. Mr. CHANG (China) agreed with the Indian representative that the work of the United Nations Conference on Freedom of Information should not be forgotten. Since then, however, a number of other bodies had dealt with the draft conventions, two of which had been combined and adopted by the General Assembly. Their work and the changes it had brought, should also be taken into account.

54. He doubted, moreover, whether the Covenant should contain only basic principles. Those principles had already been proclaimed in the Universal Declaration of Human Rights, which might prove to be a document of greater historical value. The Covenant would, in all probability, contain not general principles but detailed legal provisions.

【纪要影像】

14. Mr. CHANG (China) thought that the fourth paragraph of the French-Indian draft resolution might be misinterpreted and should be deleted. It seemed to imply that the Commission on Human Rights had to be instructed concerning the form to give to the "adequate provisions" on freedom of information mentioned in General Assembly resolution 313 (IV) which it was to incorporate in the draft International Covenant on Human Rights. The Commission had, in fact, never intended to embody in the Covenant all the important provisions of the draft Convention on Freedom of Information. It had a very clear understanding of the scope of the Covenant and fully realized that it would be neither wise nor feasible to attempt to incorporate in a single covenant definitive provisions on all the human rights proclaimed in the Declaration.

15. For that reason, it had been suggested at the fifth session of the Commission on Human Rights — and that suggestion had not been entirely ruled out — that instead of a single covenant, there might be a series, perhaps, of three or four covenants drawn up in the space of two or three years. Moreover, the Commission had never contemplated any measures with regard to freedom of information which would preclude Assembly action on the draft convention. It had never considered that the inclusion in the Covenant of one of two articles on the subject would make a separate convention unnecessary.

34. Mr. CHANG (China) considered that it would be unwise for the Council to embark on a substantive discussion on the precise instructions to be given to the Commission on Human Rights. Obviously the draft resolution of India and France instructing the Commission "to consider inclusion of basic principles only" involved a matter of substance. In view of past discussions and particularly in view of the terms of General Assembly resolution 313 (IV) requesting the Economic and Social Council to transmit the matter to the Commission on Human Rights for action, the Council should restrict itself to procedural action and avoid duplication of discussions which had taken place in the General Assembly and the Commission on Human Rights.

53. Mr. CHANG (China) agreed with the Indian representative that the work of the United Nations Conference on Freedom of Information should not be forgotten. Since then, however, a number of other bodies had dealt with the draft conventions, two of which had been combined and adopted by the General Assembly. Their work and the changes it had brought, should also be taken into account.

54. He doubted, moreover, whether the Covenant should contain only basic principles. Those principles had already been proclaimed in the Universal Declaration of Human Rights, which might prove to be a document of greater historical value. The Covenant would, in all probability, contain not general principles but detailed legal provisions.

图片 10.4　张彭春在经社理事会第十届第 348 次会议发言纪要

【纪要译文】

14. 张先生(中国)认为法国—印度决议草案第四段可能被误解,应当删除。这似乎意味着,必须指示人权委员会以何种形式对大会第 313(IV)号决议中提到的新闻自由作出“适当规定”,并将其纳入《国际人权公约》草案。事实上,委员会从未打算在《公约》中体现关于新闻自由的公约草案的所有重要条款。它非常清楚地了解《公约》的范围,并充分认识到,试图在一个单一的《公约》中纳入关于《宣言》中宣布的所有人权的明确规定既不明智也不可行。

15. 因此,有人在人权委员会第五届会议上建议——这一建议并没有被完全排除——在两三年的时间里,可能会起草一系列,也许是三四个公约,而不是一个单一的公约。此外,委员会从未审议过任何有关新闻自由的措施,这些措施将妨碍大会对公约草案采取行动。它从未考虑在《公约》中列入关于这一主题的两条款中的一条会使单独的公约变得没有必要。

34. 张先生(中国)认为,理事会就给予人权委员会的确切指示展开实质性讨论是不明智的。显然,印度和法国的决议草案指示委员会“仅考虑纳入基本原则”涉及实质问题。鉴于过去的讨论,特别是鉴于大会第313(IV)号决议要求经济及社会理事会将此事转交人权委员会采取行动,理事会应仅限于程序性行动,避免重复大会和人权委员会的讨论。

53. 张先生(中国)同意印度代表的意见,即不应忘记联合国新闻自由会议的工作。然而,自那时以来,其他一些机构处理了公约草案,其中两项公约草案已合并并由大会通过。他们的工作及其带来的变化也应予以考虑。

54. 此外,他怀疑《公约》是否应该只包含基本原则。这些原则已经在《世界人权宣言》中宣布,这一宣言可能证明是一份更具历史价值的文件。《公约》很可能不包含一般原则,而是包含详细的法律条款。

5. 张彭春在经社理事会第十届第 349 次会议上的发言

1950 年 2 月 13 日下午 3 时,联合国经社理事会第十届第 349 次会议,在纽约成功湖举行,本次会议讨论联合国秘书长关于联合国资源保护与利用科学大会的报告等。张彭春率团参加了本次会议,并在会议上发言,具体发言内容①纪要及其译文等如下:

【会议纪要】

46. Mr. CHANG (China) felt that the fundamental problem which emerged from the Conference was that of the practical utilization of the eight volumes of records, which contained a considerable amount of theoretical and practical knowledge.

47. The Secretary-General should therefore endeavour primarily to determine what material among the wealth of information warranted world-wide dissemination, and he should then arrange for that dissemination.

48. Mr. Chang also thought that the final results obtained during the Conference should be disseminated in particular in the language which had undergone the fewest changes in the course of the centuries, namely Chinese.

① UN Document: E/SR. 349, p. 30.

【纪要影像】

46. Mr. CHANG (China) felt that the fundamental problem which emerged from the Conference was that of the practical utilization of the eight volumes of records, which contained a considerable amount of theoretical and practical knowledge.

47. The Secretary-General should therefore endeavour primarily to determine what material among the wealth of information warranted world-wide dissemination, and he should then arrange for that dissemination.

48. Mr. Chang also thought that the final results obtained during the Conference should be disseminated in particular in the language which had undergone the fewest changes in the course of the centuries, namely Chinese.

图片 10.5　张彭春在经社理事会第十届第 349 次会议发言纪要

【纪要译文】

46. 张先生(中国)认为,会议出现的根本问题是八卷记录的实际利用,这些记录中载有大量的理论和实践知识。

47. 因此,秘书长应主要努力确定在丰富的信息中哪些材料值得在全世界传播,且他应安排这种传播。

48. 张先生还认为,会议期间取得的最后成果应特别以几个世纪以来变化最少的语言传播,即中文。

6. 张彭春在经社理事会第十届第350次会议上的发言

1950年2月14日上午,联合国经社理事会第十届第350次会议,在纽约成功湖举行,本次会议讨论联合国与特别机构之间的协调问题等。张彭春率团参加了本次会议,并在会议上发言,具体发言内容[①]纪要及其译文等如下:

【会议纪要】

46. Mr. CHANG (China) stated that the discussion on co-ordination had so far centered only on the machinery to be used. It was important, however, to remember that machinery alone was inadequate to the task and that real co-ordination was based upon beneficial and imaginative common objectives which nations worked cooperatively to achieve. An example of such a common objective was the technical assistance programme.

47. Since all bureaucracies, whether national or international, tended to create more and more intricate machinery, organs such as the General Assembly and the Economic and Social Council were essential for inspiring co-operative efforts to attain common objectives. Without co-operation, bureaucracies would increase even further and untold duplication would result.

---

① UN Document: E/SR. 350, p. 37.

【纪要影像】

46. Mr. CHANG (China) stated that the discussion on co-ordination had so far centered only on the machinery to be used. It was important, however, to remember that machinery alone was inadequate to the task and that real co-ordination was based upon beneficial and imaginative common objectives which nations worked co-operatively to achieve. An example of such a common objective was the technical assistance programme.

47. Since all bureaucracies, whether national or international, tended to create more and more intricate machinery, organs such as the General Assembly and the Economic and Social Council were essential for inspiring co-operative efforts to attain common objectives. Without co-operation, bureaucracies would increase even further and untold duplication would result.

图片 10.6　张彭春在经社理事会第十届第 350 次会议发言纪要

【纪要译文】

46. 张先生(中国)说,到目前为止,关于协调的讨论只集中在拟使用的机制上。然而,重要的是要记住,仅仅依靠机制不足以完成这项任务,而真正的协调是基于各国合作实现的有益和富有想象力的共同目标。这种共同目标的一个例子就是技术援助方案。

47. 由于所有的官僚机构,无论是国家的还是国际的,都倾向于建立越来越复杂的机制,因此像大会和经济及社会理事会这样的机构对于激励合作努力以实现共同目标是必不可少的。没有合作,官僚机构会进一步增加,并会导致无数的重复。

7. 张彭春在经社理事会第十届第351次会议上的发言

1950年2月14日下午2时45分,联合国经社理事会第十届第351次会议,在纽约成功湖举行,本次会议讨论理事会职司委员会程序规则的修改等。张彭春率团参加了本次会议,并在会议上发言,具体发言内容[①]纪要及其译文等如下:

【会议纪要】

47. Mr. CHANG (China) thought that after four years of experience, the system of organization of the functional commissions revealed serious shortcomings. There was too much manoeuvring at the time of the election of commission members. Furthermore, he wondered whether it was really necessary for the Council's functional commissions to be established permanently. He regarded that matter as the crux of the question. Under the present system, functional commissions continued to meet even if the items on their agenda were of little significance.

48. In his opinion, the functional commissions of the Council should be convened only in order to assist the Council to solve a specific technical problem. It mattered little whether that work took them two weeks or two years. What did matter was that some of the commissions, particularly the Social Commission, had a tendency to transform themselves into Council committees and

① UN Document: E/SR. 351, p. 42.

that their members became more and more representatives of Governments. Such commissions should be called "committees" and the term "commission" should be reserved exclusively for organs composed entirely of experts convened by the Council in order to solve a specific technical problem.

49. If that were done, the problem of alternates would not arise, for the commission members would be chosen specifically on the basis of their competence with regard to the problem to be solved by the body on which they served.

50. Some functional commissions of the Council had scarcely any reason for continuing to exist and they were holding meetings simply as a matter of habit. According to the Charter, the Council was to concern itself with the economic and social welfare of all Member States. It was quite natural that when faced with a difficult technical problem it should have recourse to a functional commission; but it was equally natural that once the functional commission had completed the study requested by the Council, it should be dissolved.

51. The Council should therefore reconsider the entire question of the functional commissions, rather than adopt new rules of procedure, which, like the ones they were to replace, would only constitute an unsatisfactory compromise.

【纪要影像】

47. Mr. CHANG (China) thought that after four years of experience, the system of organization of the functional commissions revealed serious shortcomings. There was too much manoeuvring at the time of the election of commission members. Furthermore, he wondered whether it was really necessary for the Council's functional commissions to be established permanently. He regarded that matter as the crux of the question. Under the present system, functional commissions continued to meet even if the items on their agenda were of little significance.

48. In his opinion, the functional commissions of the Council should be convened only in order to assist the Council to solve a specific technical problem. It mattered little whether that work took them two weeks or two years. What did matter was that some of the commissions, particularly the Social Commission, had a tendency to transform themselves into Council committees and that their members became more and more representatives of Governments. Such commissions should be called "committees" and the term "commission" should be reserved exclusively for organs composed entirely of experts convened by the Council in order to solve a specific technical problem.

49. If that were done, the problem of alternates would not arise, for the commission members would be chosen specifically on the basis of their competence with regard to the problem to be solved by the body on which they served.

50. Some functional commissions of the Council had scarcely any reason for continuing to exist and they were holding meetings simply as a matter of habit. According to the Charter, the Council was to concern itself with the economic and social welfare of all Member States. It was quite natural that when faced with a difficult technical problem it should have recourse to a functional commission; but it was equally natural that once the functional commission had completed the study requested by the Council, it should be dissolved.

51. The Council should therefore reconsider the entire question of the functional commissions, rather than adopt new rules of procedure, which, like the ones they were to replace, would only constitute an unsatisfactory compromise.

图片 10.7 张彭春在经社理事会第十届第 351 次会议发言纪要

【纪要译文】

47. 张先生(中国)认为,经过四年的实践,各职司委员会的组织制度暴露出严重的缺陷。选举委员会成员时存在着太多的操纵。此外,他想知道理事会的职司委员会是否真的有必要永久设立。他认为那是问题的关键。在目前的制度下,各职司委员会继续开会,即使其议程上的项目意义不大。

48. 他认为,理事会各职司委员会只应在协助理事会解决具体技术问题时召开会议。这项工作花了他们两周还是两年都没什么关系。重要的是,一些委员会,特别是社会委员会,倾向于将自己转变为理事会事务委员会,其成员越来越多地成为政府的代表。这种委员会应称为"事务委员会"(Commitlee),而"委员会"(Commission)一词应专门用于完全由理事会为解决具体技术问题召集的专家组成的机构。

49. 如果做到了这一点,就不会出现候补的问题,因为委员会成员将专门根据他们对他们所服务的机构要解决的问题的能力来挑选。

50. 理事会的一些职司委员会几乎没有任何理由继续存在,它们只是遵照习惯举行会议。根据《宪章》,理事会应关注所有会员国的经济和社会福利。当面临困难的技术问题时,它自然应该求助于一个职司委员会;但职司委员会一旦完成理事会要求的研究,就应该解散,这同样是自然而然的。

51. 因此,理事会应重新考虑各职司委员会的整个问题,而不是采纳新的议事规则,因为新的议事规则同它们将要取代的议事规则一样,只会构成令人不满意的妥协。

8. 张彭春在经社理事会第十届第354次会议上的发言

1950年2月17日上午11时，联合国经社理事会第十届第354次会议，在纽约成功湖举行，本次会议讨论社会委员会（第五届）报告、讨论人权委员会（第五届）报告等。张彭春率团参加了本次会议，并在会议上发言，具体发言内容[①]纪要及其译文等如下：

【会议纪要】

50. Mr. CHANG (China) noted that resolution B II contained not only a statement on method but also an explanation of purpose. Whether or not the Council agreed with the method involved, it could not fail to agree that the purpose expressed, "the preparation of measures to extend the full enjoyment of human rights and fundamental freedoms to non-self-governing populations", was one of the goals of the United Nations.

51. If all reference to the resolution of the Commission on Human Rights were deleted, the purpose would by implication be rejected. While the Council might appropriately reject the precise methods proposed by the Commission and substitute the Indian draft resolution, it would be most unfortunate to deny even by implication the principle of the extension of human rights to Non-Self-Governing Territories.

52. The Chinese delegation would abstain in the vote on the Indian draft

① UN Document: E/SR. 354, p. 64, p. 65.

resolution as a whole but would vote against the proposal for the deletion of the first paragraph.

60. Mr. CHANG (China) said that a clarification of terms was plainly called for. The Charter enjoined "respect for human rights and fundamental freedoms"; when the Commission on Human Rights referred to "the preparation of measures to extend the full enjoyment of human rights and fundamental freedoms to the non-self-governing territories", it took a step towards the implementation of the Charter, as was its duty. The passage quoted could therefore not be described as a mere repetition of the Charter.

【纪要影像】

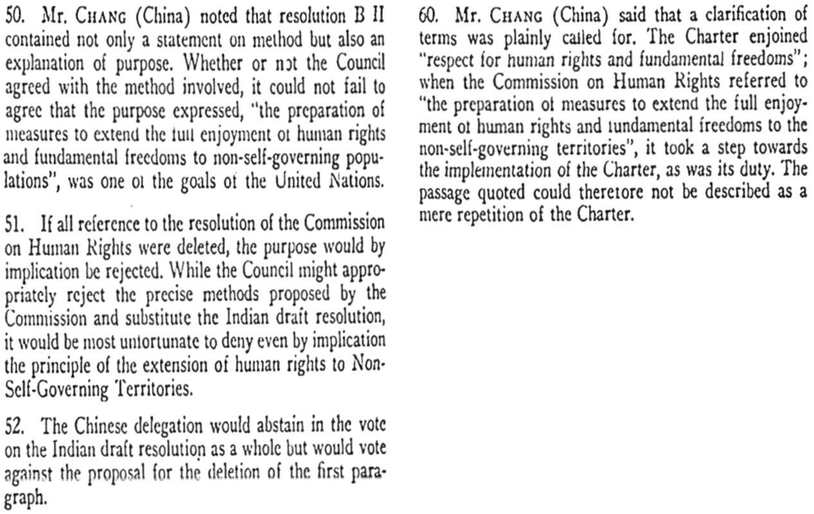

50. Mr. CHANG (China) noted that resolution B II contained not only a statement on method but also an explanation of purpose. Whether or not the Council agreed with the method involved, it could not fail to agree that the purpose expressed, "the preparation of measures to extend the full enjoyment of human rights and fundamental freedoms to non-self-governing populations", was one of the goals of the United Nations.

51. If all reference to the resolution of the Commission on Human Rights were deleted, the purpose would by implication be rejected. While the Council might appropriately reject the precise methods proposed by the Commission and substitute the Indian draft resolution, it would be most unfortunate to deny even by implication the principle of the extension of human rights to Non-Self-Governing Territories.

52. The Chinese delegation would abstain in the vote on the Indian draft resolution as a whole but would vote against the proposal for the deletion of the first paragraph.

60. Mr. CHANG (China) said that a clarification of terms was plainly called for. The Charter enjoined "respect for human rights and fundamental freedoms"; when the Commission on Human Rights referred to "the preparation of measures to extend the full enjoyment of human rights and fundamental freedoms to the non-self-governing territories", it took a step towards the implementation of the Charter, as was its duty. The passage quoted could therefore not be described as a mere repetition of the Charter.

图片 10.8　张彭春在经社理事会第十届第 354 次会议发言纪要

【纪要译文】

50. 张先生(中国)指出,决议 B II 不仅包括关于方法的说明,而且还包括对目的的解释。无论理事会是否同意所涉及的方法,它都不能不同意所表达的目的,"制定措施,使非自治人民充分享受人权和基本自由",是联合国的目标之一。

51. 如果删除所有提及人权委员会决议的内容,其目的将被含蓄地拒绝。虽然理事会可以适当地拒绝委员会提议的确切方法,并代之以印度的决议草案,但即使是含蓄地否认将人权扩大到非自治领土的原则,也是非常不幸的。

52. 我们将对印度决议草案全文投弃权票,但将对删除第一段的建议投反对票。

60. 张先生(中国)说,明确要求澄清用语。《宪章》规定"尊重人权和基本自由";当人权委员会提到"制定措施,使非自治领土充分享受人权和基本自由"时,它向《宪章》的实施迈出了一步,这是它的职责。因此,所引用的段落不能被描述为仅仅是对《宪章》的重复。

9. 张彭春在经社理事会第十届第355次会议上的发言

1950年2月17日下午3时，联合国经社理事会第十届第355次会议，在纽约成功湖举行，本次会议讨论1950年会议日程安排等。张彭春率团参加了本次会议，并在会议上发言，具体发言内容[①]纪要及其译文等如下：

【会议纪要】

15. Mr. CHANG (China) said that the Belgian representative had admirably explained the legal considerations which had moved him to support the President's decision. At the previous meeting, on the other hand, the representative of the United Kingdom had taken the opposite view. To hold a session at Geneva would, of course, entail additional expenditure which could be covered only by drawing on the Working Capital Fund.

16. He felt that a broader view should be taken of the question. He would confine his remarks to the general organization of the Council's work. The French representative had stressed that some of the activities of the United Nations should be carried on in different parts of the world, so that world public opinion might be kept informed of its work. That raised the question of what exactly was meant by the activities of the Economic and Social Council. Mr. Chang divided the work entrusted to the Council into two categories. On the one hand, it examined the various reports submitted to it, which covered an ever-

① UN Document: E/SR. 355, p. 68, p. 70.

growing field of activity. That might be described as the Council's routine work. In carrying out that type of work the presence of numerous Directors of Divisions in the Secretariat was required. To hold a session away from temporary headquarters, Secretariat officials had to be sent to the place of the Council meeting, which entailed considerable expenditure and loss of time. Moreover, the Directors concerned were unable to supervise the work of their respective Divisions.

17. On the other hand, the Council was called upon from time to time to consider a specific question, to study it in all its aspects and then to take a decision which might have far-reaching consequences. The successful results of the Council's ninth session, held at Geneva in 1949, could be attributed to the fact that it had spent nearly three weeks in an uninterrupted examination of the programme of technical assistance to under-developed countries. That was a very model for conference work.

18. Mr. Chang felt that the Council should meet at the temporary headquarters of the United Nations to do its ordinary routine work. For conference work, it could very well meet in different parts of the world. During its tenth session, the Council would be called upon to effect a preliminary examination of means to finance the development of under-developed countries. That was conference work which would not require the presence of many Secretariat officials. That type of work could be carried out away from temporary headquarters, preferably in an under-developed country.

19. In conclusion, he hoped that the Council would refrain from constantly discussing the respective merits of Geneva and Lake Success and would decide to meet at temporary headquarters to do its routine work and to hold a special session in another part of the world whenever conference work was undertaken.

43. Mr. CHANG (China) thought that the Agenda Committee might meet at Lake Success two or three weeks before the opening of the Council's eleventh

session at Geneva, and meet again at Geneva a few days before the opening of the Council's session.

50. Mr. CHANG (China) also supported the Australian proposal because it very clearly indicated that the moment was arriving for the Council to reconsider the whole question of its commissions and Sub-commissions. He wondered why the Sub-commission on Employment and Economic Stability should meet, when there was no item on its agenda.

【纪要影像】

15. Mr. CHANG (China) said that the Belgian representative had admirably explained the legal considerations which had moved him to support the President's decision. At the previous meeting, on the other hand, the representative of the United Kingdom had taken the opposite view. To hold a session at Geneva would, of course, entail additional expenditure which could be covered only by drawing on the Working Capital Fund.

16. He felt that a broader view should be taken of the question. He would confine his remarks to the general organization of the Council's work. The French representative had stressed that some of the activities of the United Nations should be carried on in different parts of the world, so that world public opinion might be kept informed of its work. That raised the question of what exactly was meant by the activities of the Economic and Social Council. Mr. Chang divided the work entrusted to the Council into two categories. On the one hand, it examined the various reports submitted to it, which covered an ever-growing field of activity. That might be described as the Council's routine work. In carrying out that type of work the presence of numerous Directors of Divisions in the Secretariat was required. To hold a session away from temporary headquarters, Secretariat officials had to be sent to the place of the Council meeting, which entailed considerable expenditure and loss of time. Moreover, the Directors concerned were unable to supervise the work of their respective Divisions.

43. Mr. CHANG (China) thought that the Agenda Committee might meet at Lake Success two or three weeks before the opening of the Council's eleventh session at Geneva, and meet again at Geneva a few days before the opening of the Council's session.

17. On the other hand, the Council was called upon from time to time to consider a specific question, to study it in all its aspects and then to take a decision which might have far-reaching consequences. The successful results of the Council's ninth session, held at Geneva in 1949, could be attributed to the fact that it had spent nearly three weeks in an uninterrupted examination of the programme of technical assistance to under-developed countries. That was a very model for conference work.

18. Mr. Chang felt that the Council should meet at the temporary headquarters of the United Nations to do its ordinary routine work. For conference work, it could very well meet in different parts of the world. During its tenth session, the Council would be called upon to effect a preliminary examination of means to finance the development of under-developed countries. That was conference work which would not require the presence of many Secretariat officials. That type of work could be carried out away from temporary headquarters, preferably in an under-developed country.

19. In conclusion, he hoped that the Council would refrain from constantly discussing the respective merits of Geneva and Lake Success and would decide to meet at temporary headquarters to do its routine work and to hold a special session in another part of the world whenever conference work was undertaken.

50. Mr. CHANG (China) also supported the Australian proposal because it very clearly indicated that the moment was arriving for the Council to reconsider the whole question of its commissions and sub-commissions. He wondered why the Sub-Commission on Employment and Economic Stability should meet, when there was no item on its agenda.

图片 10.9　张彭春在经社理事会第十届第 355 次会议发言纪要

【纪要译文】

15. 张先生(中国)说,比利时代表令人钦佩地解释了促使他支持主席决定的法律考虑。另一方面,在上次会议上,英国代表持相反的观点。当然,在日内瓦举行一届会议将需要额外支出,而这些支出只能通过动用周转基金来支付。

16. 他觉得应该从更广泛的角度看待这个问题。他将把发言限于理事会工作的总体组织。法国代表强调,联合国的一些活动应在世界不同地区进行,以便使世界舆论了解联合国的工作。这就提出了经济及社会理事会的活动究竟意味着什么的问题。张先生将委托给理事会的工作分为两类。一方面,它审查了提交给它的各种报告,这些报告涉及不断扩大的活动领域。这可以说是理事会的日常工作。在开展这类工作时,需要秘书处各司的司长在场。为了在临时总部之外举行会议,秘书处官员必须被派往理事会会议地点,这需要大量的开支和时间损失。此外,有关司长无法监督各自部门的工作。

17. 另一方面,理事会不时地呼吁考虑一个具体的问题,研究它的各个方面,然后作出一个可能产生深远影响的决定。1949 年在日内瓦举行的理事会第九届会议取得了成功的成果,这可归因于理事会花了近三个星期不间断地审查向欠发达国家提供技术援助的方案。这是会议工作的典范。

18. 张先生认为,理事会应在联合国临时总部开会,进行其日常工作。就会议工作而言,它很可能在世界不同地区举行会议。第十届会议期间,理事会将被要求对资助欠发达国家发展的方式进行初步审查。这是不需要许多秘书处官员出席的会议工作。这类工作可以在临时总部之外进行,最好是在欠发达国家。

19. 最后,他希望理事会不要老是讨论日内瓦和成功湖各自的优点,而是决定在临时总部开会做日常工作,并在会议工作进行期间在世界的另一个地方举行特别会议。

43. 张先生(中国)认为,议程委员会可能于理事会第十一届会议在日内瓦开幕前两三周在成功湖举行会议,并在理事会会议开幕前几天在日内瓦再次举行会议。

50. 张先生(中国)也支持澳大利亚的建议,因为它非常清楚地表明,理事会重新审议其委员会和小组委员会的整个问题的时机已经到来。他不知道就业和经济稳定小组委员会为什么要开会,因为其议程上没有任何项目。

10. 张彭春在经社理事会第十届第356次会议上的发言

1950年2月20日上午11时,联合国经社理事会第十届第356次会议,在纽约成功湖举行,本次会议讨论1950年会议日程安排、讨论经济和就业委员会(第五届)报告等。张彭春率团参加了本次会议,并在会议上发言,具体发言内容①纪要及其译文等如下:

【会议纪要】

13. Mr. CHANG (China) read paragraph 4 of the note by the Secretary-General (E/1616) and pointed out that the Secretary-General must have very good reasons for having reached such a definite conclusion. He did not, however, object to the United Kingdom representative's request.

【纪要影像】

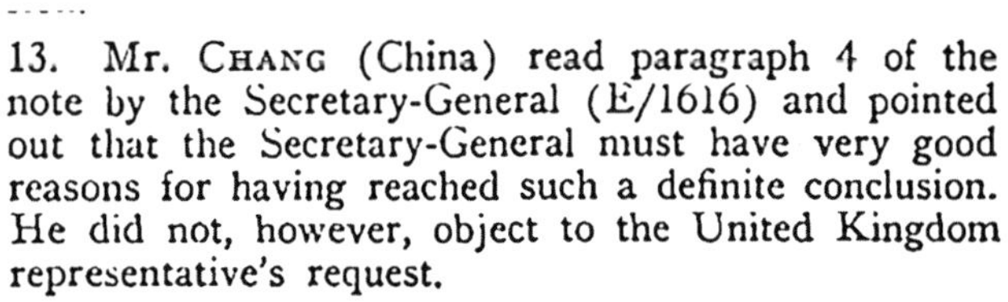
13. Mr. CHANG (China) read paragraph 4 of the note by the Secretary-General (E/1616) and pointed out that the Secretary-General must have very good reasons for having reached such a definite conclusion. He did not, however, object to the United Kingdom representative's request.

图片10.10 张彭春在经社理事会第十届第356次会议发言纪要

① UN Document: E/SR. 356, p. 75.

【纪要译文】

13. 张先生(中国)阅读了秘书长的说明(E/1616)第四段,并指出秘书长必须有充分的理由得出如此明确的结论。然而,他不反对英国代表的请求。

11. 张彭春在经社理事会第十届第358次会议上的发言

1950年2月21日上午11时，联合国经社理事会第十届第358次会议，在纽约成功湖举行，本次会议讨论经济和就业委员会（第五届）报告等。张彭春率团参加了本次会议，并在会议上发言，具体发言内容[①]纪要及其译文等如下：

【会议纪要】

67. Mr. CHANG (China) congratulated the members of the Group of Experts and of the Economic and Employment Commission on their remarkable study of the problem of full employment. That problem, which had been before the United Nations since the San Francisco Conference, was a fundamental problem, in that it linked institutions and economic phenomena with the well-being of mankind.

68. He noted that the Council was now stressing a different aspect of the problem; he approved of the Commission's recommendation, which made it clear that the question was so important that the report of the Group of Experts should be transmitted to all the Governments, specialized agencies and non-governmental organizations concerned. In that way everything that was said and written about the problem would be communicated to Governments and the members of the Council would be in a better position, at its eleventh session, to

---

① UN Document: E/SR. 358, p. 101.

criticize the substance of the report and to produce practical recommendations.

69. In conclusion, he remarked that consideration of the report of the Group of Experts was a typical case of a "conference" subject which the Council should examine at its following session.

【纪要影像】

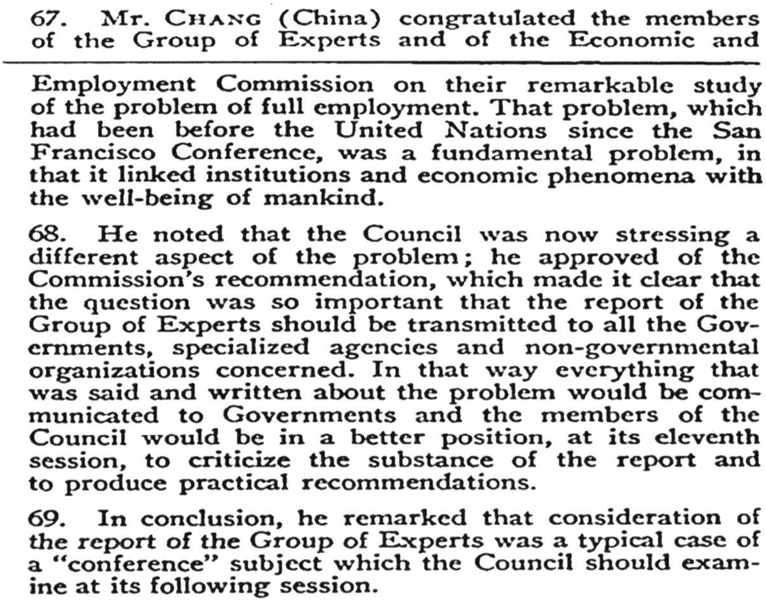

67. Mr. CHANG (China) congratulated the members of the Group of Experts and of the Economic and Employment Commission on their remarkable study of the problem of full employment. That problem, which had been before the United Nations since the San Francisco Conference, was a fundamental problem, in that it linked institutions and economic phenomena with the well-being of mankind.

68. He noted that the Council was now stressing a different aspect of the problem; he approved of the Commission's recommendation, which made it clear that the question was so important that the report of the Group of Experts should be transmitted to all the Governments, specialized agencies and non-governmental organizations concerned. In that way everything that was said and written about the problem would be communicated to Governments and the members of the Council would be in a better position, at its eleventh session, to criticize the substance of the report and to produce practical recommendations.

69. In conclusion, he remarked that consideration of the report of the Group of Experts was a typical case of a "conference" subject which the Council should examine at its following session.

图片 10.11 张彭春在经社理事会第十届第 358 次会议发言纪要

【纪要译文】

67. 张先生(中国)祝贺专家组成员和经济和就业委员会成员对充分就业问题进行了引人注目的研究。自从旧金山会议以来,这个问题一直是摆在联合国面前的一个根本问题,因为它把制度和经济现象与人类的福祉联系起来。

68. 他指出,理事会正在强调该问题的另一个方面;他赞同委员会的建议,该建议明确指出,这个问题非常重要,专家组的报告应转交所有有关政府、专门机构和非政府组织。这样,关于这一问题的所有言论和文字都将传达给各国政府，理事会成员将在其第十一届会议上更好地批评报告的实质内容并提出切实可行的建议。

69. 最后，他评价说，审议专家组的报告是一个典型的"会议"问题，理事会应在下届会议上审议这个问题。

12. 张彭春在经社理事会第十届第362次会议上的发言

1950年2月24日上午11时,联合国经社理事会第十届第362次会议,在纽约成功湖举行,本次会议的议题是讨论世界经济形势等。张彭春率团参加了本次会议,并在会议上发言,具体发言内容①纪要及其译文等如下:

【会议纪要】

13. Mr. CHANG (China) praised the Secretariat for the excellent work it had done in preparing the report "Major Economic Changes in 1949". But in view of the number of problems which it covered, a report of that sort, even if perfect, might well fail to be stimulating. As the Council made a detailed study of two or three special problems each year, it seemed desirable that the Secretariat should emphasize those problems.

14. In the report it would submit the following year, the Secretariat might, for example, pay particular attention to the consequences of the recent currency devaluations, thus enabling the Council to study that problem with full knowledge of the facts.

15. The Chinese representative agreed with members who had stressed the need for a study of the economic situation in Africa and who thought that the immediate creation of a regional economic commission for Africa would be

① UN Document: E/SR. 362, p. 130.

somewhat premature.

【纪要影像】

13. Mr. CHANG (China) praised the Secretariat for the excellent work it had done in preparing the report "Major Economic Changes in 1949". But in view of the number of problems which it covered, a report of that sort, even if perfect, might well fail to be stimulating. As the Council made a detailed study of two or three special problems each year, it seemed desirable that the Secretariat should emphasize those problems.

14. In the report it would submit the following year, the Secretariat might, for example, pay particular attention to the consequences of the recent currency devaluations, thus enabling the Council to study that problem with full knowledge of the facts.

15. The Chinese representative agreed with members who had stressed the need for a study of the economic situation in Africa and who thought that the immediate creation of a regional economic commission for Africa would be somewhat premature.

图片 10.12　张彭春在经社理事会第十届第 362 次会议发言纪要

【纪要译文】

13. 张先生(中国)赞扬秘书处在编写“1949 年重大经济变化”报告方面所做的出色工作。但鉴于它所涵盖的问题的数量,这样一份报告,即使是完美的,也很可能不会令人振奋。由于理事会每年对两三个特殊问题进行详细研究,秘书处强调这些问题似乎是可取的。

14. 例如,秘书处在下一年提交的报告中可以特别注意最近货币贬值的后果,从而使理事会能够在充分了解事实的情况下研究这一问题。

15. 我们同意一些成员的意见,他们强调有必要研究非洲的经济形势,并认为立即成立非洲区域经济委员会有些为时过早。

13. 张彭春在经社理事会第十届第367次会议上的发言

1950年2月28日下午3时,联合国经社理事会第十届第367次会议,在纽约成功湖举行,本次会议的议题是讨论世界经济形势等。张彭春率团参加了本次会议,并在会议上发言,具体发言内容[①]纪要及其译文等如下:

【会议纪要】

32. Mr. CHANG (China) stated that in the course of a fight during the last war he had been able to see for himself what resources, as yet unexploited, the African continent possessed.

33. He wondered whether the Governments responsible for the administration of those territories would want others to become aware of their tremendous possibilities. The fact was that it was not easy to visit some of the territories.

34. The Assistant Secretary-General had spoken of the work that had preceded the establishment of the regional Economic Commissions for Asia and the Far East and for Latin America. That work had been accomplished by the representatives of the countries concerned, who in every instance had prescribed the directives to be followed. Such would not be the case for Africa, where the Secretariat would have to work out the directives. The Secretariat was, however, in a very difficult position, for it did not know whether it was to carry out work of a general nature or whether it was to concentrate on certain specific

① UN Document: E/SR. 367, p. 169.

problems. The group that had carried out the preparatory work leading to the establishment of the Economic Commission for Asia and the Far East had concentrated its attention on the transformation of a pre-industrial economy into an industrial one. The group responsible for the study of Latin-American problems had limited its work to a consideration of the economic repercussions of the war upon the Latin-American countries. In the circumstances it might well be asked what was to be the main subject of a study on the African economy.

35. He did not think that the Council should adopt the Indian draft resolution or the United Kingdom amendment. It would be better advised to give more explicit reasons for asking the Secretariat to study the economic situation of Africa. Such a study might, perhaps, be included in the United Nations programmes of technical assistance.

36. He therefore suggested that a study of the economic situation of Africa should be considered as a preliminary step towards the adoption of measures which would be taken in conjunction with the work done by the Economic and Social Council in the matter of assistance to be granted for the economic development of under-developed areas.

37. In conclusion, he proposed that further consideration of item 31 of the agenda should be deferred to a later meeting, so that the objective of the draft resolution which the Council would adopt could be defined more clearly.

【纪要影像】

32. Mr. CHANG (China) stated that in the course of a flight during the last war he had been able to see for himself what resources, as yet unexploited, the African continent possessed.

33. He wondered whether the Governments responsible for the administration of those territories would want others to become aware of their tremendous possibilities. The fact was that it was not easy to visit some of the territories.

34. The Assistant Secretary-General had spoken of the work that had preceded the establishment of the regional Economic Commissions for Asia and the Far East and for Latin America. That work had been accomplished by the representatives of the countries concerned, who in every instance had prescribed the directives to be followed. Such would not be the case for Africa, where the Secretariat would have to work out the directives. The Secretariat was, however, in a very difficult position, for it did not know whether it was to carry out work of a general nature or whether it was to concentrate on certain specific problems. The group that had carried out the preparatory work leading to the establishment of the Economic Commission for Asia and the Far East had concentrated its attention on the transformation of a pre-industrial economy into an industrial one. The group responsible for the study of Latin-American problems had limited its work to a consideration of the economic repercussions of the war upon the Latin-American countries. In the circumstances it might well be asked what was to be the main subject of a study on the African economy.

35. He did not think that the Council should adopt the Indian draft resolution or the United Kingdom amendment. It would be better advised to give more explicit reasons for asking the Secretariat to study the economic situation of Africa. Such a study might, perhaps, be included in the United Nations programmes of technical assistance.

36. He therefore suggested that a study of the economic situation of Africa should be considered as a preliminary step towards the adoption of measures which would be taken in conjunction with the work done by the Economic and Social Council in the matter of assistance to be granted for the economic development of under-developed areas.

37. In conclusion, he proposed that further consideration of item 31 of the agenda should be deferred to a later meeting, so that the objective of the draft resolution which the Council would adopt could be defined more clearly.

图片 10.13　张彭春在经社理事会第十届第 367 次会议发言纪要

【纪要译文】

32. 张先生(中国)说,在上次战争期间,他亲眼看到非洲大陆拥有哪些尚未开发的资源。

33. 他想知道负责管理这些领土的政府是否希望其他人了解它们的巨大可能性。事实是,访问其中一些领土并不容易。

34. 助理秘书长谈到亚洲和远东以及拉丁美洲区域经济委员会成立之前的工作。这项工作是由有关国家的代表完成的,他们在任何情况下都规定了要遵守的指示。非洲的情况并非如此,秘书处必须制定指示。然而,秘书处的处境非常困难,因为它不知道是开展一般性工作,还是集中处理某些具体问题。为成立亚洲和远东经济委员会进行筹备工作的工作组把注意力集中在将前工业化经济转为工业化经济上。负责研究拉丁美洲问题的小组将其工作限于审议战争对拉丁美洲国家的经济影响。在这种情况下,人们很可能会问,非洲经济研究的主题是什么。

35. 他认为理事会不应通过印度的决议草案或英国的修正案。最好给出更明确的理由来要求秘书处研究非洲的经济状况。这种研究也许可以列入联合国技术援助方案。

36. 因此，他建议，对非洲经济状况的研究应被视为采取措施的一个初步步骤，这些措施将与经济及社会理事会在援助欠发达地区经济发展方面所做的工作相结合。

37. 最后，他提议将对议程项目 31 的进一步审议推迟到以后的一次会议，以便更清楚地定义理事会将通过的决议草案的目标。

14. 张彭春在经社理事会第十届第 370 次会议上的发言

1950 年 3 月 2 日上午 11 时，联合国经社理事会第十届第 370 次会议，在纽约成功湖举行，本次会议的议题是讨论欠发达地区的经济发展等。张彭春率团参加了本次会议，并在会议上发言，具体发言内容①纪要及其译文等如下：

【会议纪要】

1. Mr. CHANG (China) emphasized that no practical solutions to the problem of the economic development of under-developed countries had been proposed during the current session of the Economic and Social Council. The two draft resolutions before the Council, namely the Chilean draft resolution (E/L. 30) and the joint draft resolution submitted by Brazil, China, India and Peru (E/L. 29/Rev. 2), were concerned with only the methods for achieving practical results.

2. Before dealing with those suggested methods, members of the Council should clearly realize the need for a new approach to the problem. It would be impossible to reach any satisfactory solution if the attitude of mind which had characterized the previous hundred and fifty years were to continue. The former Western mentality had been characterized by over-confidence in modern science and technology. The mere fact, however, that areas formerly described as "un-

① UN Document: E/SR. 370, p. 199, p. 201.

civilized" were now referred to as "under-developed" indicated a much more positive approach to the problem. The task was to develop other parts of the world in terms of that same modern science and technology, and not merely condemn them for their so-called backward state.

3. Turning to the larger social and political implications of the question, Mr. Chang emphasized the need to effect a change in the attitude of mind of the peoples of the under-developed countries themselves. Indeed, it was essential that the benefits of modernization and industrialization should be equally shared by all. That was mainly a problem of education — the masses had to be made conscious of the need both to demand and obtain a fair distribution of all the benefits of technological advancement.

4. In his opinion, the Chilean draft resolution reflected a certain amount of dissatisfaction with the existing machinery of the United Nations for dealing with that particular problem. In the light of the experience of the previous four years, it could be argued that the United Nations had not used commissions and Sub-commissions as expert bodies for the study of specific technical subjects. That was the reason for the Chilean suggestion to create an *ad hoc* committee to prepare recommendations concerning the financing of economic development of under-developed countries. He sincerely hoped that in the future the United Nations would tend to use commissions as special bodies, composed of experts, and set up for definite periods so as to examine specific subjects. Under the existing arrangements the Social Commission, for instance, was concerned with so many subjects that its members could not possibly have an expert knowledge of all of them.

5. Turning to the joint draft resolution submitted by Brazil, China, India and Peru, he had submitted an amendment to paragraph 7 (E/L. 36) providing for the appointment of three specially qualified consultants to assist the Sub-commission on Economic Development during its forthcoming session. The ad-

vantage of having consultants rather than members of official bodies was that several of them could be appointed from the same country if their qualifications warranted it. He wished to emphasize that both the members of the Sub-commission on Economic Development and the consultants should work as experts in their personal capacity.

6. Paragraph 8 of the joint draft resolution, which was identical to paragraph 12 of the Chilean draft resolution, might be so amended as to make it perfectly clear that the Council did not expect all specialized agencies without exception, including even the Universal Postal Union or the International Civil Aviation Organization to give the highest priority in their programmes of work to the problem of economic development of under-developed areas. That aim could be achieved by the insertion of the words "especially concerned" after the words "Urges the specialized agencies".

26. Mr. CHANG (China) strongly supported that suggestion.

27. In reply to the United States representative, he said that the Chinese amendment would not create a new pattern in United Nations machinery. It had been prompted precisely by the desire to avoid innovations and confusion. Consultants had been used on previous occasions. If the Chinese amendment were adopted, the Sub-commission would continue to function as usual, but in dealing with the highly specialized problem before it, it would be able to call on the assistance of experts from capital-exporting countries. He was unable to accept the Chilean representative's addition to his amendment, because to endow consultants with the same powers as members of the Sub-commission would indeed confuse the situation.

28. He had originally intended to propose that the Secretary-General should be given the power to appoint, at his own discretion, one to three consultants to assist the Sub-commission; he was still prepared to accept such a solution.

【纪要影像】

1. Mr. CHANG (China) emphasized that no practical solutions to the problem of the economic development of under-developed countries had been proposed during the current session of the Economic and Social Council. The two draft resolutions before the Council, namely the Chilean draft resolution (E/L.30) and the joint draft resolution submitted by Brazil, China, India and Peru (E/L.29/Rev.2), were concerned with only the methods for achieving practical results.

2. Before dealing with those suggested methods, members of the Council should clearly realize the need for a new approach to the problem. It would be impossible to reach any satisfactory solution if the attitude of mind which had characterized the previous hundred and fifty years were to continue. The former Western mentality had been characterized by over-confidence in modern science and technology. The mere fact, however, that areas formerly described as "uncivilized" were now referred to as "under-developed" indicated a much more positive approach to the problem. The task was to develop other parts of the world in terms of that same modern science and technology, and not merely condemn them for their so-called backward state.

3. Turning to the larger social and political implications of the question, Mr. Chang emphasized the need to effect a change in the attitude of mind of the peoples of the under-developed countries themselves. Indeed, it was essential that the benefits of modernization and industrialization should be equally shared by all. That was mainly a problem of education — the masses had to be made conscious of the need both to demand and obtain a fair distribution of all the benefits of technological advancement.

4. In his opinion, the Chilean draft resolution reflected a certain amount of dissatisfaction with the existing machinery of the United Nations for dealing with that particular problem. In the light of the experience of the previous four years, it could be argued that the United Nations had not used commissions and sub-commissions as expert bodies for the study of specific technical subjects. That was the reason for the Chilean suggestion to create an *ad hoc* committee to prepare recommendations concerning the financing of economic development of under-developed countries. He sincerely hoped that in the future the United Nations would tend to use commissions as special bodies, composed of experts, and set up for definite periods so as to examine specific subjects. Under the existing arrangements the Social Commission, for instance, was concerned with so many subjects that its members could not possibly have an expert knowledge of all of them.

5. Turning to the joint draft resolution submitted by Brazil, China, India and Peru, he had submitted an amendment to paragraph 7 (E/L.36) providing for the appointment of three specially qualified consultants to assist the Sub-Commission on Economic Development during its forthcoming session. The advantage of having consultants rather than members of official bodies was that several of them could be appointed from the same country if their qualifications warranted it. He wished to emphasize that both the members of the Sub-Commission on Economic Development and the consultants should work as experts in their personal capacity.

图片 10.14　张彭春在经社理事会第十届第 370 次会议发言纪要(1)

6. Paragraph 8 of the joint draft resolution, which was identical to paragraph 12 of the Chilean draft resolution, might be so amended as to make it perfectly clear that the Council did not expect all specialized agencies without exception, including even the Universal Postal Union or the International Civil Aviation Organization, to give the highest priority in their programmes of work to the problem of economic development of under-developed areas. That aim could be achieved by the insertion of the words "especially concerned" after the words "*Urges* the specialized agencies".

26. Mr. CHANG (China) strongly supported that suggestion.

27. In reply to the United States representative, he said that the Chinese amendment would not create a new pattern in United Nations machinery. It had been prompted precisely by the desire to avoid innovations and confusion. Consultants had been used on previous occasions. If the Chinese amendment were adopted, the Sub-Commission would continue to function as usual, but in dealing with the highly specialized problem before it, it would be able to call on the assistance of experts from capital-exporting countries. He was unable to accept the Chilean representative's addition to his amendment, because to endow consultants with the same powers as members of the Sub-Commission would indeed confuse the situation.

28. He had originally intended to propose that the Secretary-General should be given the power to appoint, at his own discretion, one to three consultants to assist the Sub-Commission; he was still prepared to accept such a solution.

图片 10.15　张彭春在经社理事会第十届第 370 次会议发言纪要(2)

【纪要译文】

1. 张先生(中国)强调,在经济及社会理事会本届会议期间,没有提出任何切实可行的办法来解决欠发达国家的经济发展问题。理事会面前的两项决议草案，即智利决议草案（E/L. 30）和巴西、中国、印度和秘鲁提交的联合决议草案（E/L. 29/Rev. 2），只涉及取得实际成果的方法。

2. 在处理这些建议的方法之前，理事会成员应清楚地认识到需要对这个问题采取新的办法。如果延续过去 150 年的心态，就不可能达成任何令人满意的解决办法。之前西方思维的特点是对现代科学技术过于自信。然而，仅仅是以前被称为“未开化”的地区现在被称为“欠发达”这一事实就表明对这个问题采取了更加积极的办法。我们的任务是用同样的现代科学技术发展世界其他地区，而不仅仅是谴责他们所谓的落后状态。

3. 关于这个问题的更大的社会和政治影响，张先生强调需要改变欠发达国家人民本身的思想态度。事实上，现代化和工业化的好处应该由所有人平等分享，这一点至关重要。这主要是一个教育问题——必须让大众意识到既需要要求也需要获得公平分配技术进步的所有好处。

4. 他认为，智利的决议草案反映了对联合国处理这一具体问题的现有机制的某种程度的不满。根据过去四年的经验，可以说，联合国没有利用委员会和小组委员会作为研究具体技术主题的专家机构。这就是智利建议设立一个特设委员会来拟订关于欠发达国家经济发展筹资问题的建议的原因。他真诚地希望，联合国今后将倾向于将各委员会作为特别机构，由专家组成，并在一定时期内设立，以便审查具体问题。例如，根据现有的安排，社会委员会涉及的问题太多，其成员不可能对所有这些问题都掌握专业知识。

5. 关于巴西、中国、印度和秘鲁提交的联合决议草案，他提交了对第 7 段的修正案（E/L. 36），其中规定任命三名特别合格的顾问，在经济发展小组委员会即将举行的会议期间协助小组委员会。拥有顾问而不是官方机构成员的好处是，如果他们的资历允许，其中一些人可以从同一个国家任命。他希望强调，经济发展小组委员会成员和顾问都应以个人能力担任专家工作。

6. 联合决议草案第 8 段与智利决议草案第 12 段相同，可加以修正，以便完全清楚地表明，理事会并不期望甚至包括万国邮政联盟或国际民用航空组织的所有专门机构,无一例外在其工作方案中最优先重视欠发达地区的经济发展问题。这一目标可通过在“敦促各专门机构”之后插入“特别关注”等字来实现。

26. 张先生(中国)强烈支持这项建议。

27. 在回答美国代表的问题时,他说,中国的修正案不会在联合国机制中创造一种新的模式。这正是出于避免创新和混乱的愿望。以前曾使用过顾问。如果中国的修正案获得通过,小组委员会将继续照常运作,但在处理摆在它面前的高度专业化的问题时,它将能够要求资本输出国的专家提供援助。他不能接受智利代表对其修正案的补充,因为赋予顾问与小组委员会成员同等的权力确实会造成混乱。

28. 他本来打算提议,秘书长应被授权自行决定任命一至三名顾问协助小组委员会;他仍然准备接受这样的解决办法。

15. 张彭春在经社理事会第十届第 371 次会议上的发言

1950 年 3 月 2 日下午 3 时，联合国经社理事会第十届第 371 次会议，在纽约成功湖举行，本次会议的议题是讨论欠发达地区的经济发展、讨论公共管理国际培训中心、讨论非洲经济研究与相关数据等。张彭春率团参加了本次会议，并在会议上先后多次发言，具体发言内容①纪要及其译文等如下：

【会议纪要】

3. Mr. CHANG (China) complimented the authors of the joint draft resolution on the outcome of their work. He regretted that he had been unable to attend the group's meeting. Had he been present, he would have opposed the inclusion of alternative A as it was directly based on the Chinese amendment (E/L. 36), the purpose of which was to reconcile the various draft resolutions.

4. Alternative A was useless, as it had always been understood that, when necessary, the Secretary-General was entitled to call in consultants for specific tasks. There was no need whatsoever for the Council to adopt any proposal expressly inviting the Secretary-General to follow that procedure.

58. Mr. CHANG (China) considered the Indian draft resolution very useful. He would support it because in his opinion the point at issue in the case of Africa was not to extend the scope of the report on world economy but to solve a

① UN Document: E/SR. 371, p. 203, p. 206, p. 207, p. 208.

specific problem.

59. He suggested that the world "preliminary" should be inserted before the word "survey" in the second paragraph of the Indian draft resolution.

75. Mr. CHANG (China) said that by "preliminary survey" he meant a survey made with the idea that a fuller study would be prepared later, if that should later be thought desirable.

76. He further considered that the United States amendment did not depend on acceptance of the United Kingdom amendment, but was equally compatible with the Indian text.

84. Mr. CHANG (China) noted that the Assistant Secretary-General seemed to prefer the solution proposed in the United Kingdom amendment. Mr. Chang was in favour of the study called for in the Indian proposal but realized that it might be more expensive.

88. Mr. CHANG (China) thanked the Assistant Secretary-General for having informed the Council of the financial implications of the proposals before it.

89. He would vote for the Indian draft on the clear understanding that its adoption would not entail any additional expense. The Indian proposal requested the Secretary-General to prepare a survey relating to economic conditions in Africa "using material readily available". Thus, it was not a question of undertaking a special study or of hiring experts to undertake original work. Moreover, the insertion of the word "preliminary" would still further reduce the difficulty of such a task for the Secretariat.

90. In fact, the work would not be much more difficult than that envisaged in the United Kingdom amendment.

93. Mr. CHANG (China) stated that he would vote for the Indian proposal on the clear understanding that its adoption would not entail additional expenses.

【纪要影像】

3. Mr. CHANG (China) complimented the authors of the joint draft resolution on the outcome of their work. He regretted that he had been unable to attend the group's meeting. Had he been present, he would have opposed the inclusion of alternative A as it was directly based on the Chinese amendment (E/L.36), the purpose of which was to reconcile the various draft resolutions.

4. Alternative A was useless, as it had always been understood that, when necessary, the Secretary-General was entitled to call in consultants for specific tasks. There was no need whatsoever for the Council to adopt any proposal expressly inviting the Secretary-General to follow that procedure.

58. Mr. CHANG (China) considered the Indian draft resolution very useful. He would support it because in his opinion the point at issue in the case of Africa was not to extend the scope of the report on world economy but to solve a specific problem.

59. He suggested that the world "preliminary" should be inserted before the word "survey" in the second paragraph of the Indian draft resolution.

75. Mr. CHANG (China) said that by "preliminary survey" he meant a survey made with the idea that a fuller study would be prepared later, if that should later be thought desirable.

76. He further considered that the United States amendment did not depend on acceptance of the United Kingdom amendment, but was equally compatible with the Indian text.

84. Mr. CHANG (China) noted that the Assistant Secretary-General seemed to prefer the solution proposed in the United Kingdom amendment. Mr. Chang was in favour of the study called for in the Indian proposal but realized that it might be more expensive.

88. Mr. CHANG (China) thanked the Assistant Secretary-General for having informed the Council of the financial implications of the proposals before it.

89. He would vote for the Indian draft on the clear understanding that its adoption would not entail any additional expense. The Indian proposal requested the Secretary-General to prepare a survey relating to economic conditions in Africa "using material readily available". Thus, it was not a question of undertaking a special study or of hiring experts to undertake original work. Moreover, the insertion of the word "preliminary" would still further reduce the difficulty of such a task for the Secretariat.

90. In fact, the work would not be much more difficult than that envisaged in the United Kingdom amendment.

93. Mr. CHANG (China) stated that he would vote for the Indian proposal on the clear understanding that its adoption would not entail additional expenses.

图片 10.16　张彭春在经社理事会第十届第 371 次会议发言纪要

【纪要译文】

3. 张先生(中国)对联合决议草案的起草者的工作成果表示赞赏。他感到遗憾的是,他未能出席该小组的会议。如果他在场,他会反对列入备选案文 A,因为它直接基于中国的修正案(E/L. 36),其目的是协调各项决议草案。

4. 备选案文 A 是无用的,因为人们一直认为,必要时,秘书长有权为具体任务召集顾问。理事会完全没有必要通过任何明确邀请秘书长遵循这一程序的提案。

58. 张先生(中国)认为印度的决议草案非常有用。他将支持这项建议,因为他认为,非洲问题的关键不是扩大世界经济报告的范围,而是解决一个具体问题。

59. 他建议在印度决议草案第二段"调查"一词前插入"初步"一词。

75. 张先生(中国)说,他所说的"初步调查"是以如下理念实施的,即如果日后认为可取,则稍后准备更全面的研究报告。

76. 他进一步认为,美国的修正案并不取决于是否接受英国的修正案,而是与印度的案文是否完全相符。

84. 张先生(中国)指出,助理秘书长似乎更喜欢英国修正案中提出的解决办法。张先生赞成印度提案中要求进行的研究,但意识到研究费用可能更高。

88. 张先生(中国)感谢助理秘书长向理事会通报了理事会面前各项提案所涉经费问题。

89. 他将投票赞成印度的草案,是基于明确认识到通过该草案不会产生任何额外费用。印度的提案请秘书长"利用现有材料"编写一份关于非洲经济状况的调查报告。因此,这不是进行专门研究或雇用专家从事原创工作的问题。此外,插入"初步"一词将进一步降低秘书处执行这项任务的难度。

90. 事实上,这项工作不会比英国修正案所设想的困难多少。

93. 张先生(中国)说,他将对印度的提案投赞成票,是基于明确认识到通过该提案不会产生额外费用。

16. 张彭春在经社理事会第十届第374次会议上的发言

1950年3月6日下午3时，联合国经社理事会第十届第374次会议，在纽约成功湖举行，本次会议的议题是讨论奴隶制特别委员会的临时报告、讨论经社理事会职司委员会程序规则修订、列出对第十一届经社理事会规定日程的初步问题等。张彭春率团参加了本次会议，并在会议上发言，具体发言内容[①]纪要及其译文等如下：

【会议纪要】

2. Mr. CHANG (China) complimented the Committee on the work it had thus far accomplished. Referring to its terms of reference, he recalled that there had been some difference of opinion on the subject at the Council's previous session and that a counter proposal to the one actually adopted had been rejected only as a result of an equal vote.

3. The members of the *Ad Hoc* Committee had worked faithfully and enthusiastically, but he felt that they should have tried to achieve greater exactitude in terminology. For example, the report mentioned "institutions and customs analogous to slavery", an expression which might lead to confusion, since there was no indication how far the analogy would be carried. The use of the word "analogous" was unwise and rather dangerous, for, if the Committee were to deal with customs analogous to slavery as well as with slavery proper, that might

① UN Document: E/SR. 374, p. 219, p. 211, p. 225.

lead to abuses. The Committee would then be in danger of becoming a forum where complaints were brought simply for the purpose of blaming another country and bringing it to shame, in a spirit of mutual recrimination.

4. He fully sympathized with the Committee in its difficult task, but felt that it should have limited its discussions to the question of slavery proper, without embarking into the dangerous and undefined area of customs analogous to slavery. In his opinion, the Committee should concentrate on eradicating any survivals of practices which had been current one hundred and fifty years earlier involving the enforced seizure of persons and the claim to ownership of such persons. Such practices, like all old customs, usually survived longest in the outlying districts. He emphasized that the snobbishness nurtured and encouraged by the slave trade, including the rationalized righteousness which had become manifest after the abolition of slavery, were quite as harmful to the human soul as the depredation induced by poverty.

5. The institutions and customs described as analogous to slavery could be dealt with by the Social Commission, the International Labour Organisation and, in particular, the Commission on Human Rights. The *Ad Hoc* Committee on Slavery could therefore confine its activities to the question of slavery in the strict sense of the word.

6. He expressed general approval of the United States draft resolution (E/L. 43), although it was perhaps unnecessary to include the penultimate paragraph. In view of the discussions in the Council, he felt sure that the Committee would hold its hearings in closed meetings even if that was not actually specified in the draft resolution. He did not see any real reason to amend the final paragraph. His delegation had always held the view that the subsidiary organs of the Council should meet at Headquarters and he did not think that the fact that the documents were in Geneva was a sufficient reason in itself for the Committee to meet there. It should surely be possible to send the necessary docu-

ments to Headquarters. He pointed out, furthermore, that if the Committee could not finish its work in one session, the Council would still be free to decide the dates of any further sessions in February 1951.

24. Mr. CHANG (China) expressed his belief that the entire system of commissions and committees required thorough revision. The functional commissions were not working as small groups of experts, as they should. Their members were being elected on the basis of geographical distribution and appointed by various Governments.

25. In his opinion, the Council should be assisted in its task by two kinds of bodies: first, commissions of experts set up for a definite period of time and for a specific purpose, and, secondly, by committees whose task it was to stimulate the interest of Members of the United Nations and enlist their co-operation. The existing system was most confusing, because members of technical commissions were in fact representatives of Governments. Consequently, he found it somewhat difficult to vote on the Indian amendment. If the commissions were really expert bodies, their chairmen should be allowed to participate in the debates. If, on the other hand, they were large bodies composed of representatives of Governments, their chairmen might find it more convenient to make use of the services of alternates for taking part in the debates.

49. Mr. CHANG (China) observed that the fifty-one items of the provisional agenda could be divided into three categories: those dealing with reports of the regional and functional commissions; those dealing with reports of the specialized agencies; and those dealing with problems of major importance requiring special attention. The first two groups were routine matters, which could best be considered at Headquarters; the questions in the last category should be given special emphasis at the sessions held outside Headquarters. That division would assist Governments in planning the composition of their delegations to the various Council sessions.

50. Accordingly, in arranging the work programme for the eleventh session, the Secretariat and the Agenda Committee should make every effort to arrange for items in the first two categories to be discussed during the early weeks, if necessary, and for special topics such as full employment and economic development to be left for the final period.

【纪要影像】

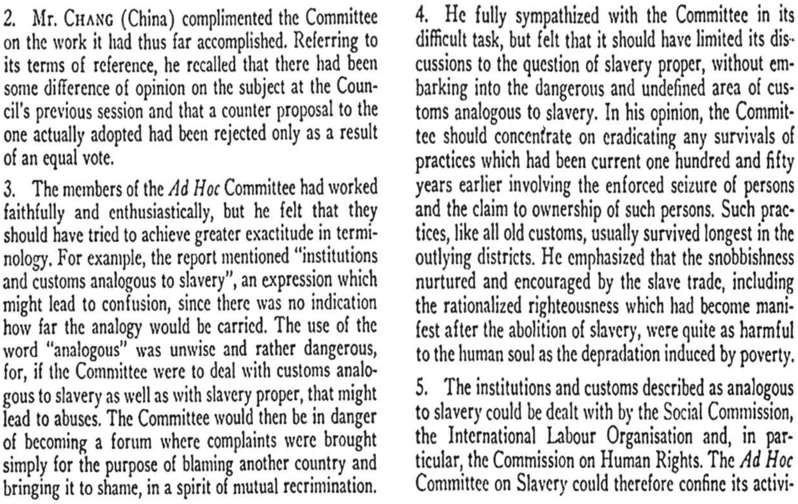

2. Mr. Chang (China) complimented the Committee on the work it had thus far accomplished. Referring to its terms of reference, he recalled that there had been some difference of opinion on the subject at the Council's previous session and that a counter proposal to the one actually adopted had been rejected only as a result of an equal vote.

3. The members of the *Ad Hoc* Committee had worked faithfully and enthusiastically, but he felt that they should have tried to achieve greater exactitude in terminology. For example, the report mentioned "institutions and customs analogous to slavery", an expression which might lead to confusion, since there was no indication how far the analogy would be carried. The use of the word "analogous" was unwise and rather dangerous, for, if the Committee were to deal with customs analogous to slavery as well as with slavery proper, that might lead to abuses. The Committee would then be in danger of becoming a forum where complaints were brought simply for the purpose of blaming another country and bringing it to shame, in a spirit of mutual recrimination.

4. He fully sympathized with the Committee in its difficult task, but felt that it should have limited its discussions to the question of slavery proper, without embarking into the dangerous and undefined area of customs analogous to slavery. In his opinion, the Committee should concentrate on eradicating any survivals of practices which had been current one hundred and fifty years earlier involving the enforced seizure of persons and the claim to ownership of such persons. Such practices, like all old customs, usually survived longest in the outlying districts. He emphasized that the snobbishness nurtured and encouraged by the slave trade, including the rationalized righteousness which had become manifest after the abolition of slavery, were quite as harmful to the human soul as the depradation induced by poverty.

5. The institutions and customs described as analogous to slavery could be dealt with by the Social Commission, the International Labour Organisation and, in particular, the Commission on Human Rights. The *Ad Hoc* Committee on Slavery could therefore confine its activi-

图片 10.17　张彭春在经社理事会第十届第 374 次会议发言纪要(1)

ties to the question of slavery in the strict sense of the word.

6. He expressed general approval of the United States draft resolution (E/L.43), although it was perhaps unnecessary to include the penultimate paragraph. In view of the discussions in the Council, he felt sure that the Committee would hold its hearings in closed meetings even if that was not actually specified in the draft resolution. He did not see any real reason to amend the final paragraph. His delegation had always held the view that the subsidiary organs of the Council should meet at Headquarters and he did not think that the fact that the documents were in Geneva was a sufficient reason in itself for the Committee to meet there. It should surely be possible to send the necessary documents to Headquarters. He pointed out, furthermore, that if the Committee could not finish its work in one session, the Council would still be free to decide the dates of any further sessions in February 1951.

24. Mr. CHANG (China) expressed his belief that the entire system of commissions and committees required thorough revision. The functional commissions were not working as small groups of experts, as they should. Their members were being elected on the basis of geographical distribution and appointed by various Governments.

25. In his opinion, the Council should be assisted in its task by two kinds of bodies: first, commissions of experts set up for a definite period of time and for a specific purpose, and, secondly, by committees whose task it was to stimulate the interest of Members of the United Nations and enlist their co-operation. The existing system was most confusing, because members of technical commissions were in fact representatives of Governments. Consequently, he found it somewhat difficult to vote on the Indian amendment. If the commissions were really expert bodies, their chairmen should be allowed to participate in the debates. If, on the other hand, they were large bodies composed of representatives of Governments, their chairmen might find it more convenient to make use of the services of alternates for taking part in the debates.

图片 10.18　张彭春在经社理事会第十届第 374 次会议发言纪要(2)

49. Mr. CHANG (China) observed that the fifty-one items of the provisional agenda could be divided into three categories: those dealing with reports of the regional and functional commissions; those dealing with reports of the specialized agencies; and those dealing with problems of major importance requiring special attention. The first two groups were routine matters, which could best be considered at Headquarters; the questions in the last category should be given special emphasis at the sessions held outside Headquarters. That division would assist Governments in planning the composition of their delegations to the various Council sessions.

50. Accordingly, in arranging the work programme for the eleventh session, the Secretariat and the Agenda Committee should make every effort to arrange for items in the first two categories to be discussed during the early weeks, if necessary, and for special topics such as full employment and economic development to be left for the final period.

图片 10.19　张彭春在经社理事会第十届第 374 次会议发言纪要(3)

【纪要译文】

2. 张先生(中国)对委员会迄今完成的工作表示赞赏。关于其职权范围,他回顾说,理事会上一届会议对这个问题存在一些意见分歧,一项与实际通过的提案相反的提案只是由于票数相等才被否决。

3. 特设委员会的成员忠实而热情地工作，但他认为他们应该努力在术语上做到更精确。例如，报告提到了"类似于奴隶制的制度和习俗"，这一表述可能会导致混乱，因为没有迹象表明这种类比会延伸到什么程度。使用"类似的"一词是不明智的，而且相当危险，因为如果委员会既要妥善处理奴隶制本身，又要处理类似奴隶制的习俗，这可能会导致滥用。这样，委员会就有可能成为一个论坛，在这里，人们提出投诉的目的只是为了本着相互指责的精神责怪另一个国家并使其蒙羞。

4. 他完全同情委员会的艰巨任务，但认为委员会应将其讨论限于奴隶制本身的问题，而不要涉及类似奴隶制的危险且未定义的习俗领域。他认为，委员会应集中精力消除 150 年前流行的强迫扣押人员和要求对这些人员掌握所有权的做法的任何残余。像所有的旧习俗一样，这种习俗通常在边远地区持续时间最长。他强调，奴隶贸易滋生和鼓励的势利感，包括废除奴隶制后表现出来的合理化的正义，对人类灵魂的伤害不亚于贫穷引起的破坏。

5. 被描述为类似奴隶制的制度和习俗可以由社会委员会、国际劳工组织，特别是人权委员会来处理。因此，奴隶制问题特设委员会可以将其活动局限于严格意义上的奴隶制问题。

6. 他表示大体赞同美国的决议草案（E/L. 43），尽管也许没有必要列入倒数第二段。鉴于理事会的讨论，他确信委员会将在非公开会议上举行听证会，即使决议草案中没有具体规定。他认为没有任何真正的理由修改最后一段。他的代表团始终认为，理事会附属机构应在总部举行会议，他认为文件在日内瓦这一事实本身并不足以成为委员会在日内瓦开会的理由。向总部发送必要的文件当然是可以的。此外，他指出，如果委员会不能在一届会议上完成其工作，理事会仍可以自由决定 1951 年 2 月任何其他届会的日期。

24. 张先生（中国）表示，他认为各委员会的整个制度需要彻底修改。各职司委员会并没有像它们应该的那样，以专家小组的形式开展工作。其成员是根据地域分配原则选举产生的,并由各国政府任命。

25. 他认为,理事会的任务应得到两类机构的协助:第一类是为一定时期和特定目的设立的专家委员会,第二类是以激发联合国会员国的兴趣和争取它们的合作为任务的委员会。现行制度最令人困惑,因为技术委员会的成员实际上是政府的代表。因此,他觉得就印度修正案进行表决有些困难。如果委员会是真正的专家机构,其主席应被允许参加辩论。另一方面,如果它们是由政府代表组成的大型机构,它们的主席可能会发现利用候补代表的服务参加辩论更为方便。

49. 张先生(中国)说,临时议程的 51 个项目可分为三类:处理区域委员会和职司委员会报告的项目;处理专门机构报告的项目;以及那些处理需要特别注意的重大问题的项目。前两组是日常事务,最好在总部审议;最后一类问题应在总部以外举行的会议上特别强调。这种划分将协助各国政府规划其出席理事会各届会议的代表团的组成。

50. 相应的,在安排第十一届会议的工作方案时,秘书处和议程委员会应尽一切努力安排在最初几周内讨论前两类项目,如果必要将充分就业和经济发展等专题留待最后一段时间讨论。

第十一章　联合国经社理事会第十一届会议

（未参加）

1950年7月3日上午11时,联合国经社理事会第十一届会议在日内瓦万国宫开幕,从1950年7月3日至8月16日,召开了本届第一部分会议,1950年10月12日至12月13日,召开了本届第二部分会议。两部分从第375次会议至第436次会议,本届共召开了62次会议。从联合国档案记录可以看出,张彭春没有参加本届会议,参加本届会议的是候补代表于(焌吉)先生、还有代表助理曹(保颐)先生和查(修)先生。其中,于焌吉先生在本届共20次会议上发言,包括第376次会议[①]、第377次会议[②]、第378次会议[③]、第379次会议[④]、第384次会议[⑤]、第387次会议[⑥]、第397次会议[⑦]、第402次会议[⑧]、第404次会议[⑨]、第405次会议[⑩]、第414次会

---

① UN Document: E/SR. 376, pp. 6-7, p. 7.

② UN Document: E/SR. 377, p. 17.

③ UN Document: E/SR. 378, p. 22, p. 24.

④ UN Document: E/SR. 379, p. 25, p. 27.

⑤ UN Document: E/SR. 384, pp. 68-72.

⑥ UN Document: E/SR. 387, p. 93.

⑦ UN Document: E/SR. 397, pp. 196-197, p. 197.

⑧ UN Document: E/SR. 402, pp. 243-244.

⑨ UN Document: E/SR. 404, p. 260, pp. 261-262, p. 263, p. 264.

⑩ UN Document: E/SR. 405, p. 269.

议[1]、第 415 次会议[2]、第 416 次会议[3]、第 418 次会议[4]、第 419 次会议[5]、第 428 次会议[6]、第 429 次会议[7]、第 430 次会议[8]、第 432 次会议[9]、第 433 次会议[10]和第 434 次会议[11]。代表助理曹保颐先生在第 403 次会议[12]和第 406 次会议[13]上发言，而查修先生在第 379 次会议[14]、第 399 次会议[15]、第 422 次会议[16]和第 427 次会议[17]上发言。

---

① UN Document：E/SR. 414，p. 350.
② UN Document：E/SR. 415，p. 356，p. 357，pp. 362–363.
③ UN Document：E/SR. 416，p. 366，pp. 367–368，pp. 368–369.
④ UN Document：E/SR. 418，p. 376，p. 377.
⑤ UN Document：E/SR. 419，p. 380.
⑥ UN Document：E/SR. 428，p. 425，p. 427.
⑦ UN Document：E/SR. 429，p. 430，p. 431.
⑧ UN Document：E/SR. 430，p. 436，p. 438.
⑨ UN Document：E/SR. 432，p. 447.
⑩ UN Document：E/SR. 433，p. 453.
⑪ UN Document：E/SR. 434，pp. 458–459.
⑫ UN Document：E/SR. 403，p. 253.
⑬ UN Document：E/SR. 406，p. 272，p. 281.
⑭ UN Document：E/SR. 379，p. 31.
⑮ UN Document：E/SR. 399，p. 216.
⑯ UN Document：E/SR. 422，p. 395.
⑰ UN Document：E/SR. 427，p. 419.

第十二章　联合国经社理事会第十二届会议

（纪要）

1951 年 2 月 20 日上午 11 时，联合国经社理事会第十二届会议在智利圣地亚哥召开，从 1951 年 2 月 20 日至 3 月 21 日，本届理事会共召开了 44 次会议，分别从第 437 次会议至第 480 次会议。本届会议讨论了一系列有关经济与社会等问题，包括讨论会议日程安排、讨论国际人权公约及其执行措施、听取理事会非政府组织报告、讨论麻醉药品委员会（第五届会议）报告、讨论联合国秘书长报告：联合国技术援助项目、讨论国际货币基金组织的报告、讨论国际重建和发展银行的报告、确认理事会职司委员会成员、讨论欠发达地区的经济发展、讨论世界经济形势、讨论强迫劳动及其废除措施、讨论申请联合国教科文组织成员资格、讨论 1951 年会议日程安排等。

CHINA

Representative

H.E. Dr. P. C. Chang, Ambassador

Alternate

H.E. Dr. Pao-yu Yin, Minister

Advisers

Mr. P. Y. Tsao
Dr. Hsiu Cha

Executive Secretary

Mr. Senba P. W. Seng

Secretary

Mr. Sen Ho Kao

图 12.1　联合国经社理事会第十二届会议中国代表团名单

中国代表张彭春先生率团参加了本届会议，并在本届会议中的9次会议上进行了大会发言，包括第437次会议、第439次会议、第456次会议、第460次会议、第463次会议、第474次会议、第477次会议、第479次会议和第480次会议。其具体发言仍以“会议纪要”“纪要影像”和“纪要译文”的形式来呈现。

1. 张彭春在经社理事会第十二届第437次会议上的发言

联合国经社理事会第十二届第437次会议,于1951年2月20日下午3时,在智利圣地亚哥举行。本次会议苏联代表首先提出中国代表权的问题,并提出决议草案,菲律宾代表接着提出推迟讨论的议案,该议案以12票赞成6票反对而得以通过。接着,选举了本届会议主席和副主席,印度代表提议智利代表桑塔·克鲁兹担任理事会主席,张彭春表示支持印度代表的提议①。另外,会议还通过了会议日程。张彭春在本次会议上发言,其具体发言内容②纪要及其译文等如下:

【会议纪要】

26. Mr. CHANG (China) regretted the impression which the discussion of his country's representation might have given to the people of Chile. The arguments used by a number of speakers seemed to him to be unworthy of an organ of the United Nations and to be more appropriate to soap-box oratory.

27. He found it difficult to believe that the references which had been made to the Kuomintang group related to himself. He had represented the only legally constituted government of China, not the Kuomintang group, in the Economic and Social Council ever since its establishment and still represented that government. Despite the vicissitudes of fortune, that government remained the

① UN Document: E/SR. 437-480, p. 3.

② UN Document: E/SR. 437-480, p. 3, p. 4.

only legally constituted government of China. While the Chinese people were passing through a difficult period of adjustment to the modern world, they would surmount their difficulties with typical Chinese patience and ability. No regime promoted by Soviet expansionism could truly represent them.

28. Unlike those delegations which had engaged in attacks upon the Kuomintang group, his delegation had always striven to make a practical and constructive contribution to the work of the Economic and Social Council. He had himself introduced the question of economic development in June 1946① and had participated in the drafting of the Universal Declaration of Human Rights.

29. He had voted for the Philippine proposal because he considered that compliance with General Assembly resolution 396 (V) was the proper course for the Council to take at that time. It seemed to him that the recommendations contained in resolution 396 (V) were at least morally binding on the Council; he had therefore been surprised to see that a number of delegations had not seen fit to comply with them.

46. Mr. CHANG (China) said that while there was no need for a secret ballot, he would not take part in the election of the Second Vice-President, and the Council's decision therefore could not be considered as unanimous.

① *See Official Records of the Economic and Social Council, Second Session, 7th meeting.*

【纪要影像】

26. Mr. CHANG (China) regretted the impression which the discussion of his country's representation might have given to the people of Chile. The arguments used by a number of speakers seemed to him to be unworthy of an organ of the United Nations and to be more appropriate to soap-box oratory.

27. He found it difficult to believe that the references which had been made to the Kuomintang group related to himself. He had represented the only legally constituted government of China, not the Kuomintang group, in the Economic and Social Council ever since its establishment and still represented that government. Despite the vicissitudes of fortune, that government remained the only legally constituted government of China. While the Chinese people were passing through a difficult period of adjustment to the modern world, they would surmount their difficulties with typical Chinese patience and ability. No regime promoted by Soviet expansionism could truly represent them.

28. Unlike those delegations which had engaged in attacks upon the Kuomintang group, his delegation had always striven to make a practical and constructive contribution to the work of the Economic and Social Council. He had himself introduced the question of economic development in June 1946[2] and had participated in the drafting of the Universal Declaration of Human Rights.

29. He had voted for the Philippine proposal because he considered that compliance with General Assembly resolution 396 (V) was the proper course for the Council to take at that time. It seemed to him that the recommendations contained in resolution 396 (V) were at least morally binding on the Council; he had therefore been surprised to see that a number of delegations had not seen fit to comply with them.

[2] See *Official Records of the Economic and Social Council, Second Session*, 7th meeting.

46. Mr. CHANG (China) said that while there was no need for a secret ballot, he would not take part in the election of the Second Vice-President, and the Council's decision therefore could not be considered as unanimous.

图 12.2　张彭春在经社理事会第十二届第 437 次会议发言纪要

【纪要译文】

26. 张先生(中国)对中国代表权的讨论可能给智利人民留下的印象表示遗憾。在他看来,一些发言者所使用的论点不配为联合国的一个机构发言,更适合于街头临时演说。

……

28. ……他的代表团一直努力为经济及社会理事会的工作做出实际和建设性的贡献。他本人于 1946 年 6 月[①]提出了经济发展问题,并参与了《世界人权宣言》的起草工作。

29. 他投票赞成菲律宾的提案,因为他认为遵守大会第 396(V)号决议是理事会当时应采取的正确作法。在他看来,第 396(V)号决议所载的建议至少在道义上对理事会具有约束力;因此,看到一些代表团认为不适合遵守这些规定,他感到惊讶。

46. 张先生(中国)说,虽然不需要无记名投票,但他不会参加第二副主席的选举,因此理事会的决定不能被认为是一致通过。

① 见《经济及社会理事会正式记录》第二届,第 7 次会议。

2. 张彭春在经社理事会第十二届第 439 次会议上的发言

联合国经社理事会第十二届第 439 次会议，于 1951 年 2 月 21 日下午 3 时，在智利圣地亚哥举行。本次会议的主要议题是讨论国际人权公约及其执行措施，张彭春参加了本次会议，并在本次会议上发言，其具体发言内容[1]纪要及其译文等如下：

【会议纪要】

32. Mr. CHANG (China) saw no need for the question to be referred to the Social Committee for detailed discussion as the Council would have to examine the draft covenant again when it was referred back to it from the Commission on Human Rights.

【纪要影像】

32. Mr. CHANG (China) saw no need for the question to be referred to the Social Committee for detailed discussion as the Council would have to examine the draft covenant again when it was referred back to it from the Commission on Human Rights.

图 12.3　张彭春在经社理事会第十二届第 439 次会议发言纪要

① UN Document: E/SR. 437-480, p. 18.

【纪要译文】

32. 张先生(中国)认为没有必要将这个问题提交社会事务委员会进行详细讨论,因为人权委员会将公约草案发回理事会时,理事会将不得不再次审查公约草案。

3. 张彭春在经社理事会第十二届第456次会议上的发言

联合国经社理事会第十二届第456次会议,于1951年3月6日上午10时15分,在智利圣地亚哥举行,本次会议的议题主要是讨论世界经济形势。张彭春参加了本次会议,并在会议上进行了长篇发言,这次发言也是他在本届会议上发言内容最长的一次,其具体发言内容①纪要及其译文等如下:

【会议纪要】

World economic situation (E/1907, E/1910, E/1910/Add. 1 and 2, E/1912, E/1912/Add. 1 to 3 and E/C. 2/280) (Continued)

[Agenda item 3]

19. Mr. CHANG (China) said that all the peoples of the world were waiting with bated breath to see what new reasons for hope or despair the future might bring. His delegation appreciated all sincere efforts at conscientious analysis of a very complex situation; but certain assertions and assumptions were intentionally misleading.

20. As a title for the first section of his observations he wished to quote words that would be found at the close of the Introduction of the *World Economic Report* 1949–1950. After describing the outlook as threatening, the report offered a somewhat more hopeful conclusion. It stated: "The economic develop-

---

① UN Document: E/SR. 437–480, pp. 156–159.

ment of the under developed countries remains the most important single long-run economic problem confronting the world. Its solution calls for a rapid expansion of the world economy. Such an expansion could, if appropriately oriented, provide the goods and services needed to raise the living standards of two-thirds of the world population, as well as the possibility of achieving without undue strain the economic adjustments that will be required in all parts of the world."

21. He would use the words "if appropriately oriented" as the title for the first section of his observations. Though seemingly innocent, those words represented for the thoughtful a most challenging qualification. The Council had begun its deliberations on the problem of the under-developed areas at its second session in 1946. On 4 June 1946 (7th meeting), his delegation had made a statement on the world significance of economically low-pressure areas. He quoted the following passage from that statement:

> "We are too much drawn to the temporary existing contentions and conflicts. We must learn to envisage the world as a whole, giving due consideration to the economically less developed areas not only because of the huge populations and potential resources, not only because they supply the raw materials and furnish the markets for the manufactured goods of the industrialized countries, but also because they serve as the meeting-places for conflicts and contentions of the industrialized Powers. It is in these economically 'low-pressure' areas that we can detect and delineate the shape of things to come in international struggles, actual and potential."

22. The under-industrialized areas, then, were the scene of conflicts between the industrialized Powers. That led him to section I, part 1, of his observations, entitled: "The centre and the periphery." There had been periods of

expansion in history. The modern period of European expansion had been going on for approximately four hundred years. The centre of that expansion had been Europe, but after 1917 new areas of power had emerged on the periphery.

23. The under-developed areas were of course found on the outer fringe of that periphery, and it had always been difficult to decide what relative degrees of attention should be devoted to the centre and the periphery. When areas of development had appeared on the outer periphery, they had been apt to give more attention to the affairs of the former centre than to the under-developed areas on the outer periphery. In the history of China there had been a period called "the Warring States". That period had lasted roughly for from 400 to 500 years and had ended in the third century B. C. That had also been a period of expansion, the expansion taking place in all directions from a centre located in the middle part of the Yellow River Basin. It was very odd that towards the end of that period of expansion in China, two focal areas on the inner periphery had emerged predominant. Had the final unification been effected under the influence of the area that paid more attention to the under-developed outer periphery or to the one that paid less? He would leave the answer to be supplied by those who cared to study the facts. Surely it must be clear that the under-developed outer periphery should not be neglected.

24. Section I, part 2, would be called "sympathetic understanding". He quoted the following from his statement of 4 June 1946:

> "under-industrialized areas of today are no longer as subdued and overawed as they were before the First World War. I think you understand what I mean. They no longer follow without protest the docile orbits prescribed for them by the powerful industrial nations. This applies especially to those countries which have experienced advanced degrees of cultural development at various times and in different aspects before the impact of modern industrialism."

25. Hunger for industrialization deserved sympathetic understanding. Mere material assistance was not enough. The under-developed peoples must receive imaginative, sympathetic understanding. In the world conflict, the side that would treat the peoples of the under-industrialized areas with sympathetic understanding would be likely to increase its influence. That remark he would also leave to those who studied the facts.

26. The third part of section I was called "truth and freedom". Truths somehow always sounded more poignant and more convincing when expressed in a minor key. But those who were eager for power asserted what might be called their "monistic intolerance". They were ruthless in their oppression of those who held different opinions. In that respect, however, the long history of China could show that the gentler philosophy of pluralistic exploration had always managed to be closer to the hearts and minds of the people, and consequently to last longer. Assertive repetition only exposed an inner lack of confidence. In Chinese history there had been two periods of ruthless monistic intolerance: the period of the first emperor of the Chin dynasty and the period of the Mongol invaders. However, neither period had lasted long. The use of slave labour in the building of the Great Wall of China under the first emperor had left among the Chinese people a hatred of tyranny; and the garrisoning of police in people's houses under the Mongols had caused revolt and resentment and shortened the period of thc invaders' power. He had so far commented on the section entitled "if appropriately oriented". Three points should not be lost sight of, namely, "the centre and the periphery", "sympathetic understanding" and "truth and freedom".

27. He next came to section II, which he called "the big bite". More than one speaker had openly described China as a kind of protectorate of the USSR. Would that not be a case of biting off more than one could chew? Those speakers had often claimed for the USSR and the People's Democracies a total

population of 750 million, of which, according to their estimate, 475 million were Chinese. Would not such a big piece stick in the throat? Even though some of it could be swallowed, would it not cause gnawing indigestion and even more painful disturbances? The situation might be compared to the case of Jonah and the whale, but with a very much bigger Jonah. Sooner than people realized, time would reveal the painful results of that terribly ambitious bite.

28. With regard to the inclusion of the material relating to China in the Secretariat's report, he would like to ask a question: was the Secretariat conscious of the danger of misinterpretation that might result from the inclusion of material on China under the communist regime? Had the communist regime thus been admitted into the United Nations by a side door? Would that not be taken advantage of by those who were only too ready to gain such admission? After all, a report of the United Nations was not a purely academic affair. It was official. He therefore expected the Secretariat to give some explanation of that delicate and important question.

29. With regard to the Secretariat's claim to objectivity, he was afraid all liberals of nineteenth century vintage were extremely naive, too easily misled and manipulated by the doctrinaires who justified all means by their ends. Furthermore, there was no way of conveying the amount of human suffering underlying the cold figures.

30. He would call section III of his observations "the perspective." In praising some of the reforms introduced by the communist regime, one representative had claimed that the situation was better now in China than it had been for thousands of years. Had China been backward for so long? Before answering that question, he would briefly advert to a number of facts and figures illustrating the reconstruction effort in Taiwan.

31. The economy of Taiwan had been almost completely destroyed by Allied bombings during the war with Japan. When the Chinese Government had

taken over, Taiwan's population of six million was left within sufficient means of production to maintain a normal standard of living. The government had had to pour into the island money, machinery and skilled workers to fill the vacuum created by the withdrawal from the island of all Japanese workers, who, in accordance with Japanese colonial policy, had formed the backbone of the island's economy. The progress made on the island during the five years after V-J Day, was one of the most encouraging signs of the vitality and efficacy of Chinese efforts. He would refer only to some of the items, and that briefly.

32. The first aspect of reconstruction with which he would deal was that of financial stabilization. That programme had been embarked upon in earnest in the summer of 1949, when inflation had been general on the mainland owing to the impact of military exigencies. A new Taiwan currency had been introduced in place of the old one and put into circulation at an exchange rate of 40,000 to one. The new Taiwan dollar, as it was called, had been pegged to a definite international unit. The rate of exchange had been maintained, with practically no black market rate to speak of, for over one year, until the outbreak of the Korean War. In view of the alarming proportions assumed by inflation, which at that time engulfed the entire country, the monetary reform had undoubtedly been an important achievement, and had had a decidedly healthy effect on other economic developments on the island. Even during the critical period from the time of the beginning of the Korean War to the end of 1950, when the stability of the new Taiwan dollar, like that of many other things in East Asia, had been challenged, the new Taiwan dollar had managed to maintain its own, fluctuating at times, but not reaching a rate of more than twice its original value.

33. From the point of view of the economics of everyday life, the all-important matter in that connexion was price stabilization. It was true that prices had fluctuated during that period, but the fluctuations had never at any time approached the magnitude of those then experienced by the rest of the country. As

most of those fluctuations had been in the categories of luxury articles and imported goods, they had not seriously affected the daily needs of the common people, the prices of which had been among the few things controlled by the government. Thanks to the success of the currency stabilization programme, price control had not proved too difficult.

34. Next came land reforms, which were perhaps the most outstanding achievement of Chinese social economy, and not only in Taiwan, where, during 50 years of Japanese colonialism, the landlords had had all the say and the farmers practically none. The farmers had been at the mercy of the landlords, who, as the owners of the land, had been able practically to dictate the terms of rentals. That problem had always figured prominently in Chinese social policy, but that policy had never been successfully carried out in full owing to the intervening vicissitudes of politics and war. Real attempts to put the policy into practice had been made in 1926. Then, in 1930, it had been formally included in the land laws promulgated by the Central Government. The difficulties of applying it, however, had been increased, first by internal military disturbances and then by Japanese aggression.

35. In 1949, the Government in Taiwan had revived those efforts. It had re-enacted in Taiwan a law promulgated by the government in 1930 providing that land rental should not exceed 37.5 per cent of the total yield of the land. That was now widely known as the "375 land-rental reduction" programme. Formerly the farmer had had to surrender as much as 50 per cent or even 70 per cent of his yield to the landlord as rent, now he had to pay no more than 37.5 per cent. In the year and a half during which that new programme, sternly enforced by the government, had been in operation, amazing successes had already been achieved. In 1949, rice lands in Taiwan had yielded 1,740 kilogrammes of rice per "chia", whereas the same area of land before had yielded only 1,175 kilogrammes. That represented an increase of 560 kilogrammes of

rice per "chia", or between 30 per cent and 50 per cent.

36. He next dealt with production increases in Taiwan, and first with the increase in agricultural production. As agricultural products constituted 50 percent of the total value of Taiwan's annual output, and rice accounted for about 70 per cent of the total agricultural produce, it was clear that the land reform programme resulting in the increased yield of the land briefly described above had a general economic significance almost as great as its social significance. Other important agricultural products, such as sugar-cane, tea, camphor, sweet potatoes, fruits, etc., had all shown substantial increases in output during the years 1949-1950.

37. Next to be considered was the increased output of minerals, of which Taiwan produced about eighty. They included gold, silver, copper, coal, aluminium and petroleum. Big strides had been made in 1949-1950. The position with regard to the production of coal had a direct bearing both on daily life and on general industrial production. At the time of the Japanese surrender, the total annual output of coal in Taiwan was 800,000 tons. Since the Chinese Government had taken over, production of coal had been gradually stepped up: it had risen to 1,050,000 metric tons in 1946; 1,300,000 tons in 1947; 1,600,000 tons in 1948; 1,800,000 tons in 1949; and approximately 2 million tons in 1950. Negotiations had been in progress in 1950 for the export of Taiwan coal to Korea, Thailand and some other East Asian countries, where there was a coal shortage.

38. He next referred to increases in Taiwan's industrial output, and first to the increase in the output of electric power. As modern industries were mostly based on electric power, the increase in Taiwan's electric power supply was perhaps a good gauge of other industrial tendencies. Electric power had been in abundant supply in Taiwan before the Second World War. The highest capacity in those days had been quoted at one thousand million kilowatts for the peak

year 1933. Owing to the destruction caused by war, that had been cut down to 350 million kw. at the time of the Japanese surrender. Through repeated improvements, the supply had been brought back to 560 million kw. in 1947, and to 830 million kw. in 1948. In 1949–1950, efforts had been redoubled; and the pre-war level had almost been reached as a result of the construction of two new power plants, the Tien-Fin hydraulic plant and the Li-Wu electricity plant.

39. Next to be considered were fertilizers, the supply of which was of paramount importance as they were an indispensable item in Taiwan's main economic pursuit, agriculture. Although Taiwan had its own chemical fertilizer plants before the Second World War, its annual output had never exceeded a meagre 20,000 tons. On taking over the island, the Chinese Government had at once made a serious effort to improve the situation. Production was at present approximately 5,000 tons a month, or 60,000 tons a year. Thus, the pre-war output had been tripled.

40. Another important commodity was textiles. As textile products were a necessity in the daily life of the people, the increased output was also noteworthy. During the fifty years of Japanese occupation, the textile industry in Taiwan had never gone beyond the capacity of 20,000 spindles. It had been even less than that when the Chinese Government had taken the island over. Now, after five years of improvement and labour, the Chinese Government had brought the total number of spindles in Taiwan up to about 50,000. That figure did not include spindles not yet in operation.

41. Approximately one-fifth of the total area of land under cultivation was being used for the production of sugar-cane. The sugar-refining industry therefore occupied a paramount position in the industry of Taiwan. In terms of sales value, refined sugar accounted for about 50 per cent of the whole industrial output of the province.

42. Owing to the vast destruction of refineries caused by the Second World

War, the total annual output of refined sugar at the time of the Japanese surrender had been only 30,880 metric tons. After the Chinese Government had taken over and repaired the damaged plants, the annual output had been steadily stepped up from year to year. In 1949, Taiwan's sugar output had amounted to over 631,000 metric tons. That meant an approximately twenty-fold increase in production, or an increase of 2,000 per cent. In 1950, that figure had been slightly reduced as a result of the government's programme to increase the production of rice. The annual output had been about 612,000 metric tons. Nevertheless, Taiwan was still one of the important suppliers of the world's sugar, as would be apparent from a study of Taiwan's international trade.

43. The principal exports were sugar, tea, coal, citronella oil, camphor, lumber and fruits. Sugar and tea accounted for by far the major part of the export trade. Sugar exports in the first six months of 1950 had been valued at more than 40 million US dollars, and had been distributed over areas in Asia, Europe and North America.

44. Tea was a traditional Chinese export. Since the discontinuance of exports of tea from the rest of China owing to disturbed conditions, Taiwan tea had been in great demand on the international market. In September 1950, Taiwan's exports of tea had amounted to 720,876 kilogrammes, and in October of the same year to 916,978 kilogrammes. Those exports had been distributed over areas in Asia, Europe, Asia Minor, Africa, and North and South America.

45. Coal was mostly needed for the use of the growing industries, but there had been such an increase in output that exports had been reported for the year 1949-1950.

46. The improvement of labour conditions was an important factor in increasing production. There was nothing to compare in importance with the new overall social insurance policy for labour, which had been instituted by the Pro-

vincial Government of Taiwan. That kind of labour insurance was a new thing in China. It was a group insurance system, covering health, accidents at work, welfare and death — all kinds of insurance in one policy. The payment of premiums for such a policy was apportioned as follows: the policy-holder contributed 20 per cent, the employer 60 per cent, and the government the remaining 20 percent. The amount of insurance and the premiums for each policy were based on a computation of the policy-holder's earning power. That system had been inaugurated in March 1950. Between the months of March and December 1950, a total of 559 industrial plants had joined the scheme. A total of 128,867 policies had been issued. During those first ten months of operation, a total of 5,886 cases had been settled, with the beneficiaries receiving the benefits due to them under their policies.

47. He then wanted to reply to the question: "Has China always been backward?"

48. Until the end of the eighteenth century, more books had been published in China than in the rest of the world put together. Furthermore, up to the end of the eighteenth century, China had been an industrial and commercial Power with a favourable balance of trade. European thinkers, from Voltaire, Diderot, Leibnitz and Goethe in the eighteenth century to Tolstoy at the beginning of the twentieth century, had shown a very sincere appreciation of the character of Chinese civilization. Tolstoy had written: "The Chinese are the oldest people in the world. The Chinese are the most populous people in the world. The Chinese are the most peaceful people in the world. They say: 'If a man claims that he is skilled in warfare, know that this man is a great criminal'." In one of Tolstoy's letters to Gandhi, he had particularly revealed his appreciation of the philosophy of Lao-Tze. Tolstoy had shown particular appreciation for example, of the two following sayings: "Return good for evil" and "The good I treat as good but the bad I also treat as if they were good".

49. In conclusion, he would like to say that whoever attempted to fish in the troubled waters of the turbulent sufferings of the Chinese people would receive his due reward in the inevitable and invincible awakening of that people. In the consciousness of the Chinese people there was a very powerful force which might be described as "resilient humanism". Like the bamboo, it might be bent by the storm but it would never break. When the storm passed, as all storms did, it would once again continue its growth in straight height.

【纪要影像】

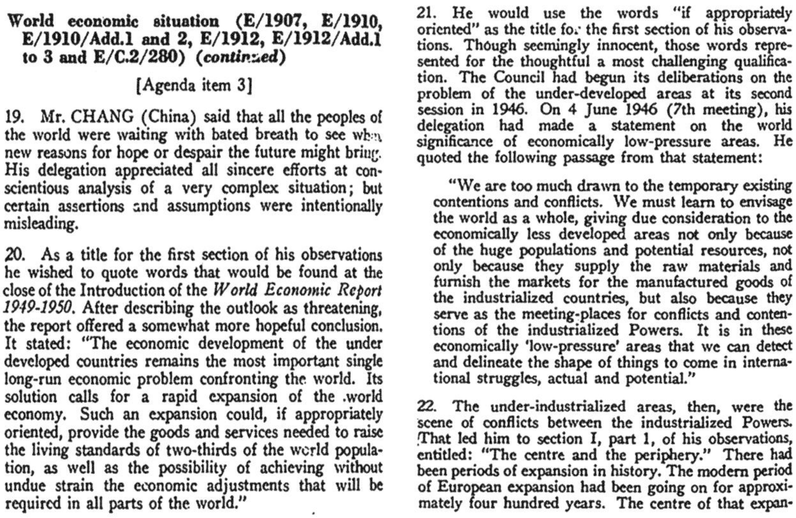

World economic situation (E/1907, E/1910, E/1910/Add.1 and 2, E/1912, E/1912/Add.1 to 3 and E/C.2/280) (*continued*)

[Agenda item 3]

19. Mr. CHANG (China) said that all the peoples of the world were waiting with bated breath to see what new reasons for hope or despair the future might bring. His delegation appreciated all sincere efforts at conscientious analysis of a very complex situation; but certain assertions and assumptions were intentionally misleading.

20. As a title for the first section of his observations he wished to quote words that would be found at the close of the Introduction of the *World Economic Report 1949-1950*. After describing the outlook as threatening, the report offered a somewhat more hopeful conclusion. It stated: "The economic development of the under developed countries remains the most important single long-run economic problem confronting the world. Its solution calls for a rapid expansion of the world economy. Such an expansion could, if appropriately oriented, provide the goods and services needed to raise the living standards of two-thirds of the world population, as well as the possibility of achieving without undue strain the economic adjustments that will be required in all parts of the world."

21. He would use the words "if appropriately oriented" as the title for the first section of his observations. Though seemingly innocent, those words represented for the thoughtful a most challenging qualification. The Council had begun its deliberations on the problem of the under-developed areas at its second session in 1946. On 4 June 1946 (7th meeting), his delegation had made a statement on the world significance of economically low-pressure areas. He quoted the following passage from that statement:

"We are too much drawn to the temporary existing contentions and conflicts. We must learn to envisage the world as a whole, giving due consideration to the economically less developed areas not only because of the huge populations and potential resources, not only because they supply the raw materials and furnish the markets for the manufactured goods of the industrialized countries, but also because they serve as the meeting-places for conflicts and contentions of the industrialized Powers. It is in these economically 'low-pressure' areas that we can detect and delineate the shape of things to come in international struggles, actual and potential."

22. The under-industrialized areas, then, were the scene of conflicts between the industrialized Powers. That led him to section I, part 1, of his observations, entitled: "The centre and the periphery." There had been periods of expansion in history. The modern period of European expansion had been going on for approximately four hundred years. The centre of that expan-

图 12.4　张彭春在经社理事会第十二届第 456 次会议发言纪要(1)

sion had been Europe, but after 1917 new areas of power had emerged on the periphery.

23. The under-developed areas were of course found on the outer fringe of that periphery, and it had always been difficult to decide what relative degrees of attention should be devoted to the centre and the periphery. When areas of development had appeared on the outer periphery, they had been apt to give more attention to the affairs of the former centre than to the under-developed areas on the outer periphery. In the history of China there had been a period called "the warring States". That period had lasted roughly for from 400 to 500 years and had ended in the third century B.C. That had also been a period of expansion, the expansion taking place in all directions from a centre located in the middle part of the Yellow River Basin. It was very odd that towards the end of that period of expansion in China, two focal areas on the inner periphery had emerged predominant. Had the final unification been effected under the influence of the area that paid more attention to the under-developed outer periphery or to the one that paid less? He would leave the answer to be supplied by those who cared to study the facts. Surely it must be clear that the under-developed outer periphery should not be neglected.

24. Section I, part 2, would be called "sympathetic understanding". He quoted the following from his statement of 4 June 1946:

> "Under-industrialized areas of today are no longer as subdued and overawed as they were before the First World War. I think you understand what I mean. They no longer follow without protest the docile orbits prescribed for them by the powerful industrial nations. This applies especially to those countries which have experienced advanced degrees of cultural development at various times and in different aspects before the impact of modern industrialism."

25. Hunger for industrialization deserved sympathetic understanding. Mere material assistance was not enough. The under-developed peoples must receive imaginative, sympathetic understanding. In the world conflict, the side that would treat the peoples of the under-industrialized areas with sympathetic understanding would be likely to increase its influence. That remark he would also leave to those who studied the facts.

26. The third part of section I was called "truth and freedom". Truths somehow always sounded more poignant and more convincing when expressed in a minor key. But those who were eager for power asserted what might be called their "monistic intolerance". They were ruthless in their oppression of those who held different opinions. In that respect, however, the long history of China could show that the gentler philosophy of pluralistic exploration had always managed to be closer to the hearts and minds of the people, and consequently to last longer. Assertive repetition only exposed an inner lack of confidence. In Chinese history there had been two periods of ruthless monistic intolerance: the period of the first emperor of the Chin dynasty and the period of the Mongol invaders. However, neither period had lasted long. The use of slave labour in the building of the Great Wall of China under the first emperor had left among the Chinese people a hatred of tyranny; and the garrisoning of police in people's houses under the Mongols had caused revolt and resentment and shortened the period of the invaders' power. He had so far commented on the section entitled "if appropriately oriented". Three points should not be lost sight of, namely, "the centre and the periphery", "sympathetic understanding" and "truth and freedom".

27. He next came to section II, which he called "the big bite". More than one speaker had openly described China as a kind of protectorate of the USSR. Would that not be a case of biting off more than one could chew? Those speakers had often claimed for the USSR and the People's Democracies a total population of 750 million, of which, according to their estimate, 475 million were Chinese. Would not such a big piece stick in the throat? Even though some of it could be swallowed, would it not cause gnawing indigestion and even more painful disturbances? The situation might be compared to the case of Jonah and the whale, but with a very much bigger Jonah. Sooner than people realized, time would reveal the painful results of that terribly ambitious bite.

28. With regard to the inclusion of the material relating to China in the Secretariat's report, he would like to ask a question: was the Secretariat conscious of the danger of misinterpretation that might result from the inclusion of material on China under the communist régime? Had the communist régime thus been admitted into the United Nations by a side door? Would that not be taken advantage of by those who were only too ready to gain such admission? After all, a report of the United Nations was not a purely academic affair. It was official. He therefore expected the Secretariat to give some explanation of that delicate and important question.

29. With regard to the Secretariat's claim to objectivity, he was afraid all liberals of nineteenth century vintage were extremely naive, too easily misled and manipulated by the doctrinaires who justified all means by their ends. Furthermore, there was no way of conveying the amount of human suffering underlying the cold figures.

30. He would call section III of his observations "the perspective." In praising some of the reforms introduced by the communist régime, one representative had claimed that the situation was better now in China than it had been for thousands of years. Had China been backward for so long? Before answering that question, he would briefly advert to a number of facts and figures illustrating the reconstruction effort in Taiwan

31. The economy of Taiwan had been almost completely destroyed by Allied bombings during the war with Japan. When the Chinese Government had taken over, Taiwan's population of six million was left with insufficient means of production to maintain a normal standard of living. The government had had to pour

图 12.5 张彭春在经社理事会第十二届第 456 次会议发言纪要(2)

into the island money, machinery and skilled workers to fill the vacuum created by the withdrawal from the island of all Japanese workers, who, in accordance with Japanese colonial policy, had formed the backbone of the island's economy. The progress made on the island during the five years after V-J Day, was one of the most encouraging signs of the vitality and efficacy of Chinese efforts. He would refer only to some of the items, and that briefly.

32. The first aspect of reconstruction with which he would deal was that of financial stabilization. That programme had been embarked upon in earnest in the summer of 1949, when inflation had been general on the mainland owing to the impact of military exigencies. A new Taiwan currency had been introduced in place of the old one and put into circulation at an exchange rate of 40,000 to one. The new Taiwan dollar, as it was called, had been pegged to a definite international unit. The rate of exchange had been maintained, with practically no black market rate to speak of, for over one year, until the outbreak of the Korean War. In view of the alarming proportions assumed by inflation, which at that time engulfed the entire country, the monetary reform had undoubtedly been an important achievement, and had had a decidedly healthy effect on other economic developments on the island. Even during the critical period from the time of the beginning of the Korean War to the end of 1950, when the stability of the new Taiwan dollar, like that of many other things in East Asia, had been challenged, the new Taiwan dollar had managed to maintain its own, fluctuating at times, but not reaching a rate of more than twice its original value.

33. From the point of view of the economics of everyday life, the all-important matter in that connexion was price stabilization. It was true that prices had fluctuated during that period, but the fluctuations had never at any time approached the magnitude of those then experienced by the rest of the country. As most of those fluctuations had been in the categories of luxury articles and imported goods, they had not seriously affected the daily needs of the common people, the prices of which had been among the few things controlled by the government. Thanks to the success of the currency stabilization programme, price control had not proved too difficult.

34. Next came land reforms, which were perhaps the most outstanding achievement of Chinese social economy, and not only in Taiwan, where, during 50 years of Japanese colonialism, the landlords had had all the say and the farmers practically none. The farmers had been at the mercy of the landlords, who, as the owners of the land, had been able practically to dictate the terms of rentals. That problem had always figured prominently in Chinese social policy, but that policy had never been successfully carried out in full owing to the intervening vicissitudes of politics and war. Real attempts to put the policy into practice had been made in 1926. Then, in 1930, it had been formally included in the land laws promulgated by the Central Government. The difficulties of applying it, however, had been increased, first by internal military disturbances and then by Japanese aggression.

35. In 1949, the Government in Taiwan had revived those efforts. It had re-enacted in Taiwan a law promulgated by the government in 1930 providing that land rental should not exceed 37.5 per cent of the total yield of the land. That was now widely known as the "375 land-rental reduction" programme. Formerly the farmer had had to surrender as much as 50 per cent or even 70 per cent of his yield to the landlord as rent, now he had to pay no more than 37.5 per cent. In the year and a half during which that new programme, sternly enforced by the government, had been in operation, amazing successes had already been achieved. In 1949, rice lands in Taiwan had yielded 1,740 kilogrammes of rice per "chia", whereas the same area of land before had yielded only 1,175 kilogrammes. That represented an increase of 560 kilogrammes of rice per "chia", or between 30 per cent and 50 per cent.

36. He next dealt with production increases in Taiwan, and first with the increase in agricutural production. As agricultural products constituted 50 per cent of the total value of Taiwan's annual output, and rice accounted for about 70 per cent of the total agricultural produce, it was clear that the land reform programme resulting in the increased yield of the land briefly described above had a general economic significance almost as great as its social significance. Other important agricultural products, such as sugar-cane, tea, camphor, sweet potatoes, fruits, etc., had all shown substantial increases in output during the years 1949-1950.

37. Next to be considered was the increased output of minerals, of which Taiwan produced about eighty. They included gold, silver, copper, coal, aluminium and petroleum. Big strides had been made in 1949-1950. The position with regard to the production of coal had a direct bearing both on daily life and on general industrial production. At the time of the Japanese surrender, the total annual output of coal in Taiwan was 800,000 tons. Since the Chinese Government had taken over, production of coal had been gradually stepped up: it had risen to 1,050,000 metric tons in 1946; 1,300,000 tons in 1947; 1,600,000 tons in 1948; 1,800,000 tons in 1949; and approximately 2 million tons in 1950. Negotiations had been in progress in 1950 for the export of Taiwan coal to Korea, Thailand and some other East Asian countries, where there was a coal shortage.

38. He next referred to increases in Taiwan's industrial output, and first to the increase in the output of electric power. As modern industries were mostly based on electric power, the increase in Taiwan's electric power supply was perhaps a good gauge of other industrial tendencies. Electric power had been in abundant supply in Taiwan before the Second World War. The highest capacity in those days had been quoted at one thousand million kilowatts for the peak year 1933. Owing to the destruction caused by war, that had been cut down to 350 million kw. at the time of the Japanese surrender. Through repeated improvements, the supply had been brought back to 560 million kw. in 1947, and to 830 million kw. in 1948. In 1949-1950, efforts had been redoubled; and the pre-war level had almost been reached as a result of the construction of two new power

图 12.6 张彭春在经社理事会第十二届第456次会议发言纪要(3)

plants, the Tien-Fin hydraulic plant and the Li-Wu electricity plant.

39. Next to be considered were fertilizers, the supply of which was of paramount importance as they were an indispensable item in Taiwan's main economic pursuit, agriculture. Although Taiwan had its own chemical fertilizer plants before the Second World War, its annual output had never exceeded a meagre 20,000 tons. On taking over the island, the Chinese Government had at once made a serious effort to improve the situation. Production was at present approximately 5,000 tons a month, or 60,000 tons a year. Thus, the pre-war output had been tripled.

40. Another important commodity was textiles. As textile products were a necessity in the daily life of the people, the increased output was also noteworthy. During the fifty years of Japanese occupation, the textile industry in Taiwan had never gone beyond the capacity of 20,000 spindles. It had been even less than that when the Chinese Government had taken the island over. Now, after five years of improvement and labour, the Chinese Government had brought the total number of spindles in Taiwan up to about 50,000. That figure did not include spindles not yet in operation.

41. Approximately one-fifth of the total area of land under cultivation was being used for the production of sugar-cane. The sugar-refining industry therefore occupied a paramount position in the industry of Taiwan. In terms of sales value, refined sugar accounted for about 50 per cent of the whole industrial output of the province.

42. Owing to the vast destruction of refineries caused by the Second World War, the total annual output of refined sugar at the time of the Japanese surrender had been only 30,880 metric tons. After the Chinese Government had taken over and repaired the damaged plants, the annual output had been steadily stepped up from year to year. In 1949, Taiwan's sugar output had amounted to over 631,000 metric tons. That meant an approximately twenty-fold increase in production, or an increase of 2,000 per cent. In 1950, that figure had been slightly reduced as a result of the government's programme to increase the production of rice. The annual output had been about 612,000 metric tons. Nevertheless, Taiwan was still one of the important suppliers of the world's sugar, as would be apparent from a study of Taiwan's international trade.

43. The principal exports were sugar, tea, coal, citronella oil, camphor, lumber and fruits. Sugar and tea accounted for by far the major part of the export trade. Sugar exports in the first six months of 1950 had been valued at more than 40 million US dollars, and had been distributed over areas in Asia, Europe and North America.

44. Tea was a traditional Chinese export. Since the discontinuance of exports of tea from the rest of China owing to disturbed conditions, Taiwan tea had been in great demand on the international market. In September 1950, Taiwan's exports of tea had amounted to 720,876 kilogrammes, and in October of the same year to 916,978 kilogrammes. Those exports had been distributed over areas in Asia, Europe, Asia Minor, Africa, and North and South America.

45. Coal was mostly needed for the use of the growing industries, but there had been such an increase in output that exports had been reported for the year 1949-1950.

46. The improvement of labour conditions was an important factor in increasing production. There was nothing to compare in importance with the new overall social insurance policy for labour, which had been instituted by the Provincial Government of Taiwan. That kind of labour insurance was a new thing in China. It was a group insurance system, covering health, accidents at work, welfare and death — all kinds of insurance in one policy. The payment of premiums for such a policy was apportioned as follows: the policy-holder contributed 20 per cent, the employer 60 per cent, and the government the remaining 20 per cent. The amount of insurance and the premiums for each policy were based on a computation of the policy-holder's earning power. That system had been inaugurated in March 1950. Between the months of March and December 1950, a total of 559 industrial plants had joined the scheme. A total of 128,867 policies had been issued. During those first ten months of operation, a total of 5,886 cases had been settled, with the beneficiaries receiving the benefits due to them under their policies.

47. He then wanted to reply to the question: "Has China always been backward?"

48. Until the end of the eighteenth century, more books had been published in China than in the rest of the world put together. Furthermore, up to the end of the eighteenth century, China had been an industrial and commercial Power with a favourable balance of trade. European thinkers, from Voltaire, Diderot, Leibnitz and Goethe in the eighteenth century to Tolstoy at the beginning of the twentieth century, had shown a very sincere appreciation of the character of Chinese civilization. Tolstoy had written: "The Chinese are the oldest people in the world. The Chinese are the most populous people in the world. The Chinese are the most peaceful people in the world. They say: 'If a man claims that he is skilled in warfare, know that this man is a great criminal'." In one of Tolstoy's letters to Gandhi, he had particularly revealed his appreciation of the philosophy of Lao-Tze. Tolstoy had shown particular appreciation for example, of the two following sayings: "Return good for evil" and "The good I treat as good but the bad I also treat as if they were good".

49. In conclusion, he would like to say that whoever attempted to fish in the troubled waters of the turbulent sufferings of the Chinese people would receive his due reward in the inevitable and invincible awakening of that people. In the consciousness of the Chinese people there was a very powerful force which might be described as "resilient humanism". Like the bamboo, it might be bent by the storm but it would never break. When the storm passed, as all storms did, it would once again continue its growth in straight height.

图 12.7　张彭春在经社理事会第十二届第 456 次会议发言纪要(4)

【纪要译文】

世界经济形势

(E/1907、E/1910、E/1910/Add. 1 和 2、E/1912、E/1912/Add. 1 至 3 和 E/C. 2/280)(续)

[议程项目 3]

19. 张先生(中国)说,世界各国人民都屏息以待,看看未来可能带来什么新的希望或绝望的理由。他的代表团赞赏为认真分析一个非常复杂的局势所作的一切真诚努力;但某些断言和假设是故意误导的。

20. 他想引用《1949—1950 年世界经济报告》导言结尾的话作为他意见第一节的标题。在将前景描述为威胁之后,报告给出了一个更有希望的结论:“不发达国家的经济发展仍然是世界面临的最重要的单一长期经济问题。其解决办法要求世界经济迅速扩张。这种扩张如果方向适当,可以提供提高世界三分之二人口生活水平所需的货物和服务,以及在不造成过度紧张的情况下实现世界各地所需的经济调整的可能性。”

21. 他将用“如果方向适当”作为其意见第一节的标题。虽然这些话看起来很天真,但对有思想的人来说,这些话代表了一种最具挑战性的资格。理事会在 1946 年第二届会议上开始审议欠发达地区问题。1946 年 6 月 4 日(第 7 次会议),他的代表团就经济低压地区的世界意义发表了声明。他引用了该声明中的以下段落:

> 我们过多地关注临时的争斗和冲突。我们必须学会把世界看成一个整体,给予经济欠发达地区应有的关注,这不仅仅由于它们拥有众多的人口和潜在的资源,也不仅仅由于它们为工业发达国家的产品提供原材料和市场,还因为它们成为工业化大国冲突与争斗的场所。正是在这些经济“低压”地区,我们能够看到实际的和潜在的国际间的争斗。

22. 当时,欠工业化地区是工业化大国之间冲突的场所。这使他进入了他的观察报告的第一节第一部分,题为“中心和外围”。历史上曾有过扩张时期。欧洲扩张的现代时期已经持续了大约四百年。扩张的中心是欧洲,但在 1917 年之后,外围出现了新的权力区域。

23. 欠发达地区当然位于该外围的外围,而且一直很难决定对中心和外围应给予的相对关注程度。当发展区出现在外围时,他们往往更关注前中心的事务,而不是外围欠发达的地区。在中国历史上有一个时期叫"战国"。这一时期大致持续了400到500年,在公元前三世纪结束,这也是一个扩张时期,从黄河盆地中部的一个中心向四面八方扩张。非常奇怪的是,在中国那段扩张期的末期,内部边缘的两个焦点区域开始占据主导地位。最终的统一是在更重视或不重视欠发达外围地区的影响下实现的?他将把答案留给那些愿意研究事实的人去回答。显然,不应该忽视欠发达的外围地区。

24. 第一节第二部分将称为"同情的理解"。他从1946年6月4日的声明中引述如下:

> 今天的欠工业化地区不再像第一次世界大战前那样被压制和被吓倒。我想你明白我的意思。它们对工业强国的指令不再唯命是从。特别是那些在现代工业化影响之前,在各个时期和不同方面都曾经历过较高程度的文化发展的国家。

25. 对工业化的渴望值得同情和理解。仅仅物质援助是不够的。欠发达国家的人民必须得到富有想象力、富有同情心的理解。在世界冲突中,以同情和理解对待欠工业化地区人民的一方可能会增加其影响力。他还将把这句话留给那些研究事实的人。

26. 第一节第三部分称为"真理与自由"。不知何故,当真理以小调表达时,听起来总是更尖锐,更令人信服。但是那些渴望权力的人宣称他们的"一元论不容忍"。他们无情地压迫持不同意见的人。然而,在这方面,中国悠久的历史可以表明,多元探索的温和哲学始终能够更贴近人民的心灵,因此能够持续更长的时间。自信的重复只会暴露出内心缺乏自信。中国历史上有两个残酷的一元论不宽容时期:秦始皇时期和蒙古侵略者时期。然而,这两个时期都没有持续很久。在第一位皇帝的统治下,在修建中国长城时使用奴隶劳动,在中国人民心目中留下了对暴政的仇恨;在蒙古人统治下，官差驻扎在人民的家园中，引起了反抗和不满，缩短了侵略者的权力周期。迄今为止，他对题为“如果方向适当”的第一节发表了评论。不应忽视三点，即“中心与外围”、“同情的理解”和“真理与自由”。

27. 他接着谈到第二节，他称之为“大咬一口”（the big bite）。不止一位发言者公开将中国描述为一种苏联的保护国。这难道不是贪多嚼不烂吗？这些发言者经常声称苏联及人民民主国家的总人口为7.5亿，据他们估计，其中有4.75亿是中国人。这么大的一块不会卡在喉咙里吗？即使有一部分可以吞下，它会不会引起消化不良和更痛苦的困扰？这种情况可以与约拿和鲸鱼的例子相比较，但约拿要大得多。人们很快就会意识到，时间会揭示这一可怕的野心之咬的痛苦结果。

28. 关于在秘书处的报告中列入与中国有关的材料，他想问一个问题：秘书处是否意识到列入有关共产主义体制下中国的材料可能导致误解的危险？……毕竟，联合国的报告并非纯粹的学术事务。这是官方的。因此，他希望秘书处对这一微妙而重要的问题作出一些解释。

29. 关于秘书处声称的客观性，他担心所有19世纪的自由主义者都极其幼稚，太容易受到教条主义者的误导和操纵，这些教条主义者以其目的为一切手段辩护。此外，这些冷酷数字下人类痛苦的程度无法表达。

30. 他将其意见的第三节称为“展望”。一位代表在赞扬共产党政权所推行的一些改革时声称，中国现在的情况比几千年来要好。中国落后了这么久吗？在回答这个问题之前，他将简要介绍一些事实和数字，说明台湾地区的重建工作。

31. 在对日战争期间，台湾地区的经济几乎被盟军的轰炸彻底摧毁。国民政府接管时，台湾地区600万人口留有的生产资料足以维持正常的生活水平。政府不得不向该岛投入资金、机械和技术工人，以填补所有日本工人撤离该岛所造成的真空。根据日本的殖民政策，日本工人是该岛经济的支柱。在“抗日战争胜利纪念日”之后的五年里，该岛所取得的进展是中国努力的活力和效力的最令人鼓舞的迹象之一。他只会而且是简短地提到其中一些项目。

32. 他将处理重建的第一个方面是金融稳定。该方案是在 1949 年夏天开始的,当时由于军事紧急情况的影响,普遍出现通货膨胀。新台币取代旧台币,以 4 万比 1 的汇率开始流通。新台币,顾名思义,与一个明确的国际单位挂钩。在朝鲜战争前的一年多里,汇率一直保持不变,几乎没有黑市汇率可言。鉴于当时通货膨胀的惊人程度,货币改革无疑是一项重要成就,并对该岛的其他经济健康发展产生了决定性的影响。即使在从朝鲜战争开始到 1950 年底的关键时期,新台币的稳定性像东亚其他许多东西一样受到挑战,新台币也成功地保持了自己的稳定,时而波动,但未达到其原始值两倍以上。

33. 从日常生活经济学的角度来看,这方面最重要的事情是稳定价格。在此期间,价格确实有所波动,但这种波动从未达到该国其他地区当时所经历的严重程度。由于这些波动大部分是在奢侈品和进口商品类别中,它们没有严重影响普通人的日常需求,这些商品的价格是政府控制的少数商品之一。由于货币稳定方案的成功,价格控制并不太困难。

34. 接下来是土地改革,这不仅是在台湾,而且也许是中国社会经济最杰出的成就。在日本殖民统治的 50 年里,地主拥有一切发言权,农民几乎没有发言权。农民一直受地主的支配,而地主作为土地的所有者,实际上可以决定租金的条件。这个问题在中国的社会政策中一直很突出,但由于其间政治和战争的变迁,这一政策从未得到全面成功的执行。将该政策付诸实践的真正尝试是在 1926 年。随后,在 1930 年,它被正式列入中央政府颁布的土地法中。然而,先是由于国内军事动乱,随后由于日本的侵略,适用这一原则的困难增加了。

35. 1949 年,台湾当局恢复了这些努力。台湾重新颁布了政府于 1930 年颁布的一项法律,规定土地租金不得超过土地总产量的 37.5%。这就是现在广为人知的“375 减租”计划。以前,农民必须向地主交出多达 50%甚至 70%的产量作为租金,现在他只需支付不超过 37.5%的产量。在政府严格执行的新方案实施的一年半时间里,已经取得了惊人的成就。1949 年,台湾的稻田产量为每“甲”1740 公斤,而以前的同一面积只有

1175 公斤。这意味着每“甲”增加 560 公斤大米,相当于增加 30%至 50%。

36. 他接着谈到台湾的生产增长,首先谈到农业生产的增长。由于农产品占台湾年产值的 50%,大米占农产品的 70%左右,显然,导致上述土地产量增加的土地改革方案具有普遍的经济意义,几乎与其社会意义同等重要。1949—1950 年间,甘蔗、茶叶、樟脑、红薯、水果等其他重要农产品的产量都有了大幅增长。

37. 接下来要考虑的是矿物产量的增加,其中台湾生产了大约 80 种。它们包括金、银、铜、煤、铝和石油。1949—1950 年取得了巨大的进步。煤炭生产的地位直接关系到日常生活和一般工业生产。日本投降时,台湾的煤炭年总产量为 80 万吨。自政府接管以来,煤炭生产逐步加快:1946 年,煤炭产量增至 105 万公吨;1947 年为 130 万吨;1948 年为 160 万吨;1949 年为 180 万吨;1950 年大约有 200 万吨。1950 年,台湾向朝鲜、泰国和其他一些缺煤的东亚国家出口煤炭的谈判正在进行。

38. 他接着提到台湾工业产量的增加,首先是电力产量的增加。由于现代工业大多以电力为基础,台湾电力供应的增加或许是衡量其他工业趋势的一个好的指标。第二次世界大战前,台湾电力供应充足。在 1933 年的高峰年,当时的最高发电量为 10 亿千瓦。由于战争造成的破坏,日本投降时,电力产能已减少到 3.5 亿千瓦。经过反复改进,1947 年电力供应已恢复到 5.6 亿千瓦。1948 年达到 8.3 亿千瓦。1949—1950 年,经加倍努力,且由于建造了两座新的发电厂,即天送埤水力发电厂(the Tien-Fin hydraulic plant)及立雾发电厂(the Li-Wu electricity plant),电力供应几乎达到了战前的水平。

39. 下一个要考虑的是化肥,化肥的供应应至关重要,因为化肥对台湾主要经济支柱农业不可或缺。虽然台湾在第二次世界大战前就有自己的化肥厂,但其年产量从未超过两万吨。中国政府接管该岛后,立即做出改善局势的努力。目前,产量约为每月 5 千吨,或每年 6 万吨。因此,比战前的产量增加了两倍。

40. 另一种重要商品是纺织品。由于纺织品是人们日常生活中的必需品,产量的增加也值得注意。在日本占据的50年间,台湾的纺织工业从未超过两万锭的产能。政府接管该岛时,这个数字甚至更低。现在,经过五年的改进和努力,政府已使台湾的纱锭总数达到约5万锭。这一数字不包括尚未运转的锭子。

41. 大约五分之一的耕地被用于生产甘蔗。因此,制糖业在台湾的工业中占有极其重要的地位。就销售价值而言,精制糖约占该省工业总产值的50%。

42. 由于第二次世界大战对精炼厂造成的巨大破坏,日本投降时精炼糖的年产量只有30,880吨。在政府接管并修复受损工厂后,年产量逐年稳步上升。1949年,台湾的糖产量超过63.1万吨。这意味着产量增加约20倍,即增加2000%。1950年,由于政府实施了增加水稻产量的计划,这一数字略有下降。年产量约为61.2万吨。然而,台湾仍然是世界糖的重要供应地之一,这一点从对台湾对外贸易的研究中可以明显看出。

43. 主要出口品是糖、茶、煤、香茅油、樟脑、木材和水果。糖和茶目前占出口贸易的主要部分。1950年前六个月的糖出口价值超过4000万美元,分布在亚洲、欧洲和北美地区。

44. 茶叶是中国的传统出口商品。自中国其他地区因局势动荡而停止出口茶叶以来,台湾茶叶在国际市场上的需求量一直很大。1950年9月,台湾茶叶出口量为720,876公斤,同年10月为916,978公斤。这些出口产品分布在亚洲、欧洲、小亚细亚、非洲以及北美和南美地区。

45. 日益增长的工业需要大量的煤,但是由于产量的增加,1949—1950年的出口量被报有所增加。

46. 劳动条件的改善是生产增加的一个重要因素。在重要性上,没有什么可以与台湾省政府制定的新的全面劳动社会保险政策相比。这种劳动保险在中国是新生事物。这是一个集团保险体系,涵盖健康、工伤事故、福利和死亡——所有种类的保险都在一份保单中。此类保单的保费分配如下:投保人缴纳20%,雇主缴纳60%,政府缴纳剩余的20%。每份保单的保险金额和保费是基于对投保人收入能力的计算。该系统于1950年3

月启用。在1950年3月至12月期间,共有559家工厂参加了该计划。共签发了128,867份保单。在开始运作的前10个月内,共解决了5,886个案例,受益人收到了他们根据保单应得的福利。

47. 然后他想回答这个问题:“中国一直落后吗?”

48. 18世纪结束之前,中国出版的书比世界其他地方的书加起来还多。此外,直到18世纪末,中国一直是一个贸易顺差的工商大国。欧洲思想家,从18世纪的伏尔泰、狄德罗、莱布尼茨和歌德到20世纪初的托尔斯泰,都对中国文明的特征表现出非常真诚的欣赏。托尔斯泰曾写道:“中国人是世界上最古老的民族。中国人是世界上人口最多的民族。中国人是世界上最和平的民族。他们说:‘如果一个人声称他擅长战争,就要知道这个人是个大罪犯。’”在托尔斯泰写给甘地的一封信中,他特别透露了他对老子哲学的欣赏。例如,托尔斯泰特别欣赏以下两句谚语:“以德报怨”和“我视善为善,视恶为善”。

49. 最后,他想说,无论谁试图在中国人民动荡的苦难中浑水摸鱼,都将在中国人民不可避免和不可战胜的觉醒中得到应有的报应。在中国人的意识中,有一种非常强大的力量,可以称之为“坚韧的人道主义”。就像竹子一样,它可能会被暴风雨压弯,但永远不会折断。当暴风雨(就像所有的暴风雨一样)过去时,它将再次继续挺拔向上生长。

4. 张彭春在经社理事会第十二届第460次会议上的发言

联合国经社理事会第十二届第460次会议,于1951年3月7日下午3时,在智利圣地亚哥举行。本次会议主要议题是讨论国际重建和发展银行报告、确认理事会职司委员会成员等。张彭春参加了本次会议,并在会议上发言①,其发言内容纪要及其译文等如下:

【会议纪要】

35. Mr. CHANG (China) said that the Government he represented was the National Government of China. To call it the "Kuomintang group" was an utter untruth. In any event it was completely out of order to raise the question of the representation of China at that stage in the Council's discussions. The question had been raised at the beginning of the session (437th meeting) and the Council had decided not to discuss it since it was under consideration by the General Assembly. Consequently, he represented the only legal Government of China recognized by the Council, and his was the only Government entitled to nominate members to represent China on the functional commissions. If any delegation questioned that right, it would in fact be questioning the right of a State member of the Council to nominate members of the functional commissions.

37. Mr. CHANG (China) requested a separate vote on the nomination of

① UN Document: E/SR. 437-480, p. 194.

Mr. Chernyshev as the USSR representative on the Economic, Employment and Development Commission and on the nomination of Mr. Suyazov as the USSR representative on the Transport and Communications Commission.

【纪要影像】

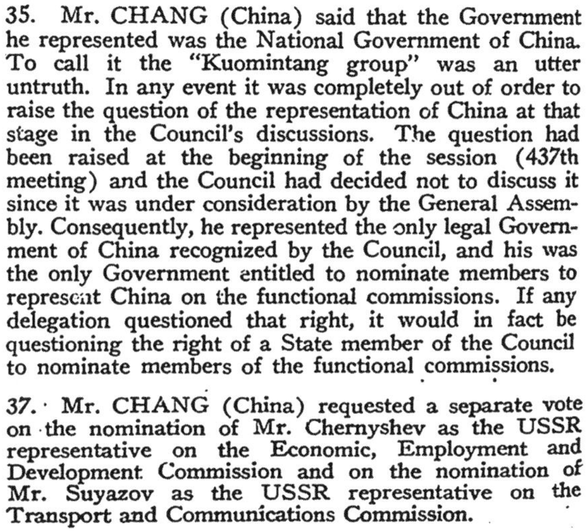

35. Mr. CHANG (China) said that the Government he represented was the National Government of China. To call it the "Kuomintang group" was an utter untruth. In any event it was completely out of order to raise the question of the representation of China at that stage in the Council's discussions. The question had been raised at the beginning of the session (437th meeting) and the Council had decided not to discuss it since it was under consideration by the General Assembly. Consequently, he represented the only legal Government of China recognized by the Council, and his was the only Government entitled to nominate members to represent China on the functional commissions. If any delegation questioned that right, it would in fact be questioning the right of a State member of the Council to nominate members of the functional commissions.

37. Mr. CHANG (China) requested a separate vote on the nomination of Mr. Chernyshev as the USSR representative on the Economic, Employment and Development Commission and on the nomination of Mr. Suyazov as the USSR representative on the Transport and Communications Commission.

图 12.8　张彭春在经社理事会第十二届第 460 次会议发言纪要

【纪要译文】

35. 张先生(中国)说,……该问题是在本届会议开始时(第 437 次会议)提出的,理事会决定不讨论该问题,因为大会正在审议该问题。……。

37. 张先生(中国)要求就提名车尔尼雪夫(Chernyshev)先生为经济、就业和发展委员会苏联代表和提名苏亚佐夫(Suyazov)先生为运输和通信委员会苏联代表进行单独表决。

5. 张彭春在经社理事会第十二届第463次会议上的发言

联合国经社理事会第十二届第463次会议，于1951年3月9日上午10时15分，在智利圣地亚哥举行。本次会议主要议题是讨论欠发达地区的经济发展、讨论国际重建和发展银行的报告等。张彭春参加了本次会议，并在会议上发言[①]，其发言内容纪要及其译文等如下：

【会议纪要】

43. Mr. CHANG (China) recalled that the problem of the under-industrialized areas had been envisaged as early as the second session of the Council and had been before the Council and the Assembly ever since that time. Attention had frequently been called to the problem of capital investment and financing for economic development. Money, machines and materials were indispensable for economic development, but one should never lose sight of the motive force behind them, namely men. Especially at the initial stages, the kind of technical assistance which was needed most was scientific knowledge and technical skill. Men must readapt themselves so that they might better master their environment, material and social, and improve their situation.

44. In that connexion, he emphasized the need for adequate preparation of visiting technicians. As pointed out in the second report of the Technical Assistance Committee (E/1920/Add. 1):

① UN Document: E/SR. 463, p. 220.

"The Committee also agreed to the recommendation of a representative that the report should contain information on the preparation and training of experts, with special reference to paragraphs 2, 3 and 5 under the heading 'Standards of Work and Personnel' in Annex I of resolution 222 (IX) of the Economic and Social Council."

45. He could scarcely stress that aspect of the problem too strongly, and he regretted that it had not been brought up before. Through the acquisition of modern science and technology, peoples in the under-industrialized countries were hoping to improve their living conditions, to augment their sense of independence and dignity, and to rid themselves of an inferiority complex. However, it was imperative to study the matter closely and to approach the problem of education for industrialization in a different manner than in the conventional way. It was not enough to set up a few professional or industrial schools where scientific and technical subjects only were taught. All education, at all levels and in all spheres, must be transformed. The prevalent distinction between those who worked with their minds and those who worked with their hands was at the core of the problem of educational readaptation. It had been said that the study of that aspect of the problem should perhaps be left to UNESCO, but obviously that aspect of education affected all realms of assistance, because the primary objective of that assistance was to ensure the independence of the local populations. Thus, when men were assisted in their various practical projects their readaptation should never be overlooked.

46. Returning to the problem of formation of experts, he referred to paragraph 6 of the part of Annex I to document A/983 on "Co-ordination of Effort". It was there stated that training programmes should be the subject of co-operative action among participating organizations. He stressed the crucial im-

portance of that part of the Council's work, and suggested several topics which might be considered for the training of experts:

(a) International significance of the under-industrialized areas in the world. (b) Common characteristics of the under-industrialized areas. (c) Cultural contacts before the Industrial Revolution. (d) Conditioning circumstances of industrialization. (e) Patterns of industrialization. (f) Cultural changes and educational re-orientation. (g) Creative approach to industrial education. (h) New educational tools. (i) Spread of industrialization and international economic ex-changes. (j) Standards of living and art of living.

47. He thought that courses under those topics would increase the experts, sympathetic understanding of the cultural backgrounds and specific needs of the countries to be assisted.

【纪要影像】

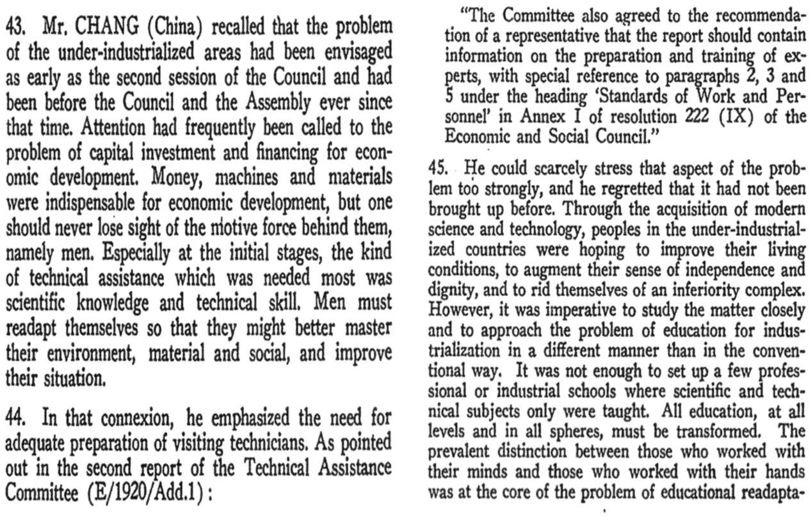

43. Mr. CHANG (China) recalled that the problem of the under-industrialized areas had been envisaged as early as the second session of the Council and had been before the Council and the Assembly ever since that time. Attention had frequently been called to the problem of capital investment and financing for economic development. Money, machines and materials were indispensable for economic development, but one should never lose sight of the motive force behind them, namely men. Especially at the initial stages, the kind of technical assistance which was needed most was scientific knowledge and technical skill. Men must readapt themselves so that they might better master their environment, material and social, and improve their situation.

44. In that connexion, he emphasized the need for adequate preparation of visiting technicians. As pointed out in the second report of the Technical Assistance Committee (E/1920/Add.1):

"The Committee also agreed to the recommendation of a representative that the report should contain information on the preparation and training of experts, with special reference to paragraphs 2, 3 and 5 under the heading 'Standards of Work and Personnel' in Annex I of resolution 222 (IX) of the Economic and Social Council."

45. He could scarcely stress that aspect of the problem too strongly, and he regretted that it had not been brought up before. Through the acquisition of modern science and technology, peoples in the under-industrialized countries were hoping to improve their living conditions, to augment their sense of independence and dignity, and to rid themselves of an inferiority complex. However, it was imperative to study the matter closely and to approach the problem of education for industrialization in a different manner than in the conventional way. It was not enough to set up a few professional or industrial schools where scientific and technical subjects only were taught. All education, at all levels and in all spheres, must be transformed. The prevalent distinction between those who worked with their minds and those who worked with their hands was at the core of the problem of educational readapta-

图 12.9 张彭春在经社理事会第十二届第 463 次会议发言纪要(1)

tion. It had been said that the study of that aspect of the problem should perhaps be left to UNESCO, but obviously that aspect of education affected all realms of assistance, because the primary objective of that assistance was to ensure the independence of the local populations. Thus, when men were assisted in their various practical projects their readaptation should never be overlooked.

46. Returning to the problem of formation of experts, he referred to paragraph 6 of the part of Annex I to document A/983 on "Co-ordination of Effort". It was there stated that training programmes should be the subject of co-operative action among participating organizations. He stressed the crucial importance of that part of the Council's work, and suggested several topics which might be considered for the training of experts:

(*a*) International significance of the under-industrialized areas in the world. (*b*) Common characteristics of the under-industrialized areas. (*c*) Cultural contacts before the Industrial Revolution. (*d*) Conditioning circumstances of industrialization. (*e*) Patterns of industrialization. (*f*) Cultural changes and educational re-orientation. (*g*) Creative approach to industrial education. (*h*) New educational tools. (*i*) Spread of industrialization and international economic exchanges. (*j*) Standards of living and art of living.

47. He thought that courses under those topics would increase the experts, sympathetic understanding of the cultural backgrounds and specific needs of the countries to be assisted.

图 12.10　张彭春在经社理事会第十二届第 463 次会议发言纪要(2)

【纪要译文】

43. 张先生(中国)回顾说,早在理事会第二届会议上就提出了欠工业化地区的问题,自那时以来,这个问题一直摆在理事会和大会面前。人们经常提请注意经济发展的资本投资和融资问题。金钱、机器和材料对于经济发展是不可或缺的,但人们决不能忽视它们背后的动力,即人。特别是在最初阶段,最需要的技术援助是科学知识和技术技能。人们必须重新调整自己,以便更好地掌握自己的环境、物质和社会,并改善自己的处境。

44. 在这方面,他强调需要为来访的技术人员作好充分准备。正如技术援助委员会第二次报告(E/1920/Add. 1)所指出的那样:

> "委员会还同意一位代表的建议,即报告应载有关于专家准备和培训的资料,特别是经济及社会理事会第 222(IX)号决议附件一"工作和人事标准"标题下的第 2、3 和 5 段。"

45. 他再怎么强调这方面的问题也不为过,并且他感到遗憾的是以前没有提出过这一问题。通过获得现代科学和技术,欠工业化国家的人民希望改善他们的生活条件,增强他们的独立和尊严感,并摆脱自卑情结。然而,必须仔细研究这一问题,并以不同于传统方式的方式处理工业化教育问题。仅仅建立一些只教授科学和技术科目的专业或工业学校是不够的。所有各级和各领域的所有教育都必须改革。脑力劳动者和体力劳动者之间的普遍区别是教育再适应问题的核心。有人说,对这一问题的研究或许应该留给教科文组织,但显然,教育这方面影响到所有援助领域,因为援助的主要目标是确保当地居民的独立性。因此,当人们在各种实际项目中得到帮助时,他们的重新适应决不能被忽视。

46. 关于专家的组成问题,他提到 A/983 号文件附件一关于“协调努力”部分的第六段。该段载明,培训方案应成为各参与组织之间合作行动的主题。他强调了理事会这一部分工作的极端重要性,并提出了可考虑用于培训专家的若干专题:

(a)世界欠工业化地区的国际意义。(b)欠工业化地区的共同特点。(c)工业革命前的文化接触。(d)工业化条件环境。(e)工业化模式。(f)文化变迁与教育重新定位。(g)创造性工业教育的方法。(h)新的教育工具。(i)工业化的传播和国际经济交流。(j)生活水平和生活艺术。

47. 他认为,这些专题下的课程将增加专家对接受援助国家的文化背景和具体需求的理解。

6. 张彭春在经社理事会第十二届第474次会议上的发言

联合国经社理事会第十二届第474次会议,于1951年3月17日上午10时,在智利圣地亚哥举行。本次会议主要议题是特别机构的关系及其协调等。张彭春参加了本次会议,并在会议上发言①,其发言内容纪要及其译文等如下:

【会议纪要】

79. Mr. CHANG (China) said that he felt a keen sense of loss at the imminent departure of Mr. Laugier, with whom it had been his privilege to be associated for the past five years. Mr. Laugier's scientific achievements were too well-known to call for comment. He had known Mr. Laugier personally as an international civil servant, who had given his very best to that service. It was a consolation to known that his services would not be lost to international endeavour. The United Nations often tended to become swamped with documents and to lose sight of reality but Mr. Laugier's foresight and his warm and sympathetic personality had been one of his most valuable contributions to the United Nations.

① UN Document: E/SR. 474, p. 301.

【纪要影像】

79. Mr. CHANG (China) said that he felt a keen sense of loss at the imminent departure of Mr. Laugier, with whom it had been his privilege to be associated for the past five years. Mr. Laugier's scientific achievements were too well-known to call for comment. He had known Mr. Laugier personally as an international civil servant, who had given his very best to that service. It was a consolation to known that his services would not be lost to international endeavour. The United Nations often tended to become swamped with documents and to lose sight of reality but Mr. Laugier's foresight and his warm and sympathetic personality had been one of his most valuable contributions to the United Nations.

图 12.11 张彭春在经社理事会第十二届第 474 次会议发言纪要

【纪要译文】

79. 张先生(中国)说,劳吉尔先生即将离任,他深感失落,过去五年来,他有幸与劳吉尔先生共事。劳吉尔先生的科学成就众所周知,无需评论。他本人知道劳吉尔先生是一名国际公务员,他为这项服务尽了最大努力。令人欣慰的是,国际社会不会忘记他的贡献。联合国往往会被文件淹没,看不到现实,但劳吉尔先生的远见以及热情和富有同情心的个性是他对联合国最宝贵的贡献之一。

7. 张彭春在经社理事会第十二届第 477 次会议上的发言

联合国经社理事会第十二届第 477 次会议，于 1951 年 3 月 20 日上午 10 时 15 分，在智利圣地亚哥举行。本次会议主题议题是讨论世界经济形势。张彭春参加了本次会议，并在会议上先后多次简短发言①，其具体发言内容纪要及其译文等如下：

【会议纪要】

26. Mr. CHANG (China) stated that his delegation would vote in favour of the joint draft resolution. He pointed out, however, that the wording of the second operative paragraph should be changed slightly so as to make the meaning clearer.

31. Mr. CHANG (China), on a point of order, explained that it was completely false to identify his government with the Kuomintang group. Such an allusion was in contempt of the decision taken by a majority of Council members. He requested that the expression should be deleted from official records each time it appeared; otherwise, he reserved the right to raise a point of order each time the expression was used by a representative.

35. Mr. CHANG (China) vigorously protested against the allusion just made by the USSR representative and deeply regretted such a lack of respect for the members of the Council as a whole.

---

① UN Document: E/SR. 477, p. 321, p. 322, 323.

49. Mr. CHANG (China) accepted the proposal of the United Kingdom representative.

【纪要影像】

26. Mr. CHANG (China) stated that his delegation would vote in favour of the joint draft resolution. He pointed out, however, that the wording of the second operative paragraph should be changed slightly so as to make the meaning clearer.

31. Mr. CHANG (China), on a point of order, explained that it was completely false to identify his government with the Kuomintang group. Such an allusion was in contempt of the decision taken by a majority of Council members. He requested that the expression should be deleted from official records each time it appeared; otherwise, he reserved the right to raise a point of order each time the expression was used by a representative.

35. Mr. CHANG (China) vigorously protested against the allusion just made by the USSR representative and deeply regretted such a lack of respect for the members of the Council as a whole.

49. Mr. CHANG (China) accepted the proposal of the United Kingdom representative.

图 12.12　张彭春在经社理事会第十二届第 477 次会议发言纪要

【纪要译文】

26. 张先生(中国)说,中国代表团将对联合决议草案投赞成票。然而,他指出,执行部分第二段的措词应稍作修改,以便使含义更明确。

……

35. 张先生(中国)强烈抗议苏联代表刚才的暗示,并对这种整体上不尊重理事会成员的行为深感遗憾。

49. 张先生(中国)接受英国代表的提议。

8. 张彭春在经社理事会第十二届第479次会议上的发言

联合国经社理事会第十二届第479次会议，于1951年3月21日上午9时，在智利圣地亚哥举行，这也是本届会议的闭幕会议。张彭春参加了本次会议，并在会议上发言①，其具体发言内容纪要及其译文等如下：

【会议纪要】

128. Mr. CHANG (China) congratulated and thanked the President of the Council for the invaluable contribution he had made to the work of the twelfth session. He thought the Secretariat could not be praised highly enough, particularly the two Assistant Secretary-Generals, whose indefatigable efforts had enabled all problems to be settled with ease.

129. Speaking in Chinese and himself translating his words into Spanish, he then referred to Chile's proverbial hospitality and paid tribute to all the Chileans for everything they had done during the stay — unfortunately rather short — of the members of the Council in Santiago.

① UN Document: E/SR. 479, p. 348.

【纪要影像】

128. Mr. CHANG (China) congratulated and thanked the President of the Council for the invaluable contribution he had made to the work of the twelfth session. He thought the Secretariat could not be praised highly enough, particularly the two Assistant Secretary-Generals, whose indefatigable efforts had enabled all problems to be settled with ease.

129. Speaking in Chinese and himself translating his words into Spanish, he then referred to Chile's proverbial hospitality and paid tribute to all the Chileans for everything they had done during the stay — unfortunately rather short — of the members of the Council in Santiago.

图 12.13　张彭春在经社理事会第十二届第 479 次会议发言纪要

【纪要译文】

128. 张先生(中国)祝贺并感谢理事会主席为第十二届会议的工作所作的宝贵贡献。他认为,对秘书处,特别是两位助理秘书长的赞扬再高也不为过,他们的不懈努力使所有问题得以轻松解决。

129. 他用中文发言,并将他的话翻译成西班牙语,然后提到智利众所周知的热情好客,并赞扬所有智利人为理事会成员在圣地亚哥逗留期间所做的一切,可惜的是,逗留时间相当短暂。

9. 张彭春在经社理事会第十二届第 480 次会议上的发言

联合国经社理事会第十二届第 480 次会议（特别会议），于 1951 年 4 月 13 日下午 3 时，在纽约成功湖举行。张彭春参加了本次会议，并在会议上发言[①]，这也是他在理事会最后一次发言，其具体发言内容纪要及其译文等如下：

【会议纪要】

31. Mr. CHANG (China) observed that the preliminary list of matters to be included in the provisional agenda of the thirteenth session included several items dealing with the consideration of reports. In several cases such consideration would have to be very rapid; furthermore, it ought to be possible to defer the consideration of the least urgent matters to the 1952 session; he was convinced that it would be better to consider a few really important problems in detail rather than dissipate attention among a heavy agenda. He asked the Peruvian representative to explain his reasons for estimating that the session would have to last seven weeks.

① UN Document: E/SR. 480, pp. 353-354.

【纪要影像】

31. Mr. CHANG (China) observed that the preliminary list of matters to be included in the provisional agenda of the thirteenth session included several items dealing with the consideration of reports. In several cases such consideration would have to be very rapid; furthermore, it ought to be possible to defer the consideration of the least urgent matters to the 1952 session; he was convinced that it would be better to consider a few really important problems in detail rather than dissipate attention among a heavy agenda. He asked the Peruvian representative to explain his reasons for estimating that the session would have to last seven weeks.

图 12.14　张彭春在经社理事会第十二届第 480 次会议发言纪要

【纪要译文】

31. 张先生(中国)说,拟列入第十三届会议临时议程的事项初步清单包括若干关于审议报告的项目。在一些情况下,这种审议必须非常迅速;此外,应该可以将最不紧急事项的审议推迟到 1952 年的会议;他深信,最好仔细审议一些真正重要的问题,而不是把注意力分散在一个繁重的议程中。他请秘鲁代表解释他估计会议必须持续七周的理由。